301
Ob6r

70176

ROBERT W. O'BRIEN
WHITTIER COLLEGE

CLARENCE C. SCHRAG
UNIVERSITY OF WASHINGTON

WALTER T. MARTIN
UNIVERSITY OF OREGON

Readings in General Sociology

FOURTH EDITION

HOUGHTON MIFFLIN COMPANY • BOSTON
NEW YORK • ATLANTA • GENEVA, ILL. • DALLAS • PALO ALTO

PREFACE

This book, like the three previous editions, is dedicated to the idea that the best way for students to learn sociology is by examining the methods, concepts, and theories employed in sociological research. The tools and methods of sociology are continuously changing, of course. They contribute to, and reflect the influence of, new knowledge about human organizations and social action. Thus, the feedback relationship between research and knowledge is a matter of increasing concern.

Sociological knowledge can be no more reliable than the information produced by our scientific investigations. Accordingly, the serious student does not simply memorize the content of sociology today. Instead, he learns how to evaluate knowledge in the light of the often elusive and sometimes flimsy evidence on which it is founded, to differentiate areas in which knowledge is relatively certain from those in which beliefs are subject to major revisions, and to anticipate the main trends and developments within the discipline. All of this requires that the student learn something about the problems involved in the collection of evidence and in its conceptual and empirical analysis. To assist in these tasks, the present work brings together a series of studies that illustrate the chief objectives, procedures, and findings of contemporary sociology, and that also give some clues as to where the field may be heading.

The editors feel that sociology has made more progress in the last five years than at any time since the first edition of this work was published in 1951. Sociologists are no longer restricted to methods of inquiry developed in other disciplines; they are designing procedures distinctive to the field of sociology and appropriate to the investigation of its special problems. They no longer depend primarily on static theories and models, but are almost universally interested in societal dynamics and in the analysis of social change. Moreover, the increasing popularity of comparative studies encourages theories that are relevant to underdeveloped societies and to other systems outside the American scene. Perhaps the most important advances, however, are found in general theories of social systems that promise to integrate many disparate facts about social life and to consolidate some of the information developed in various social disciplines. This book attempts to illustrate these advancements in sociological knowledge.

Many of our colleagues assisted in surveying the relevant literature and in evaluating the readings presented in this edition. We also acknowledge the advice, encouragement, and assistance of Robert C. Rooney in all phases of the preparation of this volume. In addition, we owe a special debt of gratitude to Professor Frank Miles for preparing the instructor's manual.

Each of the editors wrote the headnotes for the articles in the areas of his interest, and Clarence Schrag was responsible for the chapter introductions. They incorporate much of the material from two of his recent articles: "Science and the Helping Professions," *Journal of Nursing Research,* November-December, 1968, and "The Prison System: Problems and Prospects," *Annals of the American Academy of Political and Social Science,* January, 1969.

ROBERT W. O'BRIEN, *Whittier, California*

CLARENCE C. SCHRAG, *Seattle, Washington*

WALTER T. MARTIN, *Nairobi, Kenya*

CONTENTS

SCIENCE AND SOCIETY

Readings in General Sociology

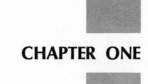

CHAPTER ONE

Man's Changing Social Milieu

Change is the fundamental fact of life. Without reproduction, metabolism, and other biochemical processes, for example, life would cease to exist. Social life, too, survives and progresses by means of change. If people did not learn from experience, or if they were unable to influence one another, their schedule of activities would be fixed at birth, and there would be no accumulation of knowledge and technology.

Change begets change. The greater the amassment of knowledge and technology, the greater a society's potential for change; and the temptation to prove its potentialities is a compelling one in modern societies. Even though change may be necessary and inevitable, however, its outcome is not always advantageous. It may sometimes mean decay or destruction instead of growth and production. Yet the absence of change precludes even the possibility of progress. These are some of the reasons why the management of change is perhaps the greatest social challenge of our time.

Sociology's basic concepts, ranging from socialization and organization to alienation and disorganization, deal primarily with processes of change; their origins and causes, their costs and consequences, and their patterns, sequences, and interconnections. But the changes that occur in man's social systems are not the only focus of sociological investigation. The environment surrounding these systems is also changing, and man's adaptations to this environment, to its climatic conditions, its natural resources, and its famines, floods, earthquakes, and the like, are of equal concern. The biological and social environments, of course, provide an even greater impetus to change.

In addition, there are important changes occurring within the discipline of sociology itself. Both the methods of inquiry and the resulting knowledge are undergoing constant revision due to the gradual maturation of this embryo science. To understand sociology, then, we need to learn about the principles that guide developments within the discipline as well as those that regulate activities in the broader society.

Sociology, like other sciences, may be described in terms of its methods and its substantive content. The content of sociology — the knowledge communicated by its theories, models, and other representations of reality — is the product of its methods, the questions raised, the assumptions made, and the evidence employed in testing the assumptions. No body of knowledge can be superior to the methods

1

by which it is attained. A consideration of methods is therefore essential to any realistic appraisal of contemporary sociology.

The methods of sociology, in general, are those of all the sciences. Science is an organized enterprise, a style of inquiry, which begins with the realization that our present knowledge is inadequate for handling many problems. It deals with these problems by developing better knowledge through the conceptual and empirical investigation of current information, the collection of new data, and the continuous reassessment of our theories, beliefs, and practices. Although the exact methods are always adapted to the particular question at issue, the basic procedures of science may be outlined as follows:

1. The scientist asks penetrating, precisely formulated, and (he hopes) answerable questions about a designated problem. Sometimes the problem concerns the adequacy of a certain theory or a research method, but it may also involve social issues, community policies, the management of a business concern, and the like. As our knowledge of a topic grows, the questions and problems tend to become more specific and manageable.

Inquiries about a problem such as the population "explosion," for example, may begin with the vague, unanswerable query, why is the number of people increasing so rapidly after remaining fairly constant for many centuries? Our initial investigations lead almost inevitably to more meaningful questions, such as, what are the personal, social, or environmental factors that are most closely associated with changes in death rates, birth rates, and rates of migration? We shift the focus from "why" to "how," and begin to identify classes of variables that are relevant to regional variations in population growth. The rephrasing of the question reflects, and contributes to, the redefinition of the problem, so that further research continues to produce further refinements in both methods and information.

2. The scientist tries to find plausible solutions to his questions by devising preliminary hunches and conjectures that are later replaced by specific hypotheses or more complex theories. These hunches, hypotheses, and theories are grounded on factual evidence and are, in principle, testable by empirical observations. The essential features of the proposed solutions are the assumptions made concerning the ways events are related in the world of experience.

In our study of population trends, for instance, we might assume a set of causal relationships for each of the variables — mortality, fertility, and migration — that jointly determine the amount of population growth or decrease. Thus, a community's death rate may be regarded as an indicator of conditions such as the age distribution of its population (the very young and the very old have the highest mortality), its relative numbers of males and females, its emphasis on warfare and other "high risk" occupations, its vulnerability to earthquakes, floods, or other natural calamities, and the state of its technology, especially its methods of food production (inadequate diet contributes mightily to the high mortality of the economically underdeveloped societies), its safety and sanitation practices, and its control of infectious diseases.

The birth rate also responds to many of the variables mentioned, particularly the demographic ones. But reproduction is always subject to additional cultural restraints, including the regulation of sexual relationships, celibacy, marriage and remarriage, abortion, birth control, and related practices. Without such restrictions, healthy women who live through their childbearing years might have, on the average, as many as twenty-five children, a number attained only by the exceptional individuals in any of the societies investigated.

As to the third factor, migration, we may assume that its magnitude depends upon the relative economic, political, social, or religious opportunities that are available in one community as compared with another, and that the perception of opportunity, whether valid or not, is a greater stimulus to mass migration than are the objective conditions at the points of destination and departure. Migratory excursions of masses of people may occur suddenly, at irregular intervals, for a variety of reasons. Sometimes they may take on the contagious character of a panic or a social epidemic, and in this respect they are less predictable than are the changes that ordinarily occur in mortality or fertility.

The preceding assumptions, of course, do not exhaust the list of relevant variables and relationships. Still, they may serve as guidelines in the search for at least a partial answer to our questions on population growth.

3. After stating his assumptions, the scientist spells out some of their practical implications and tests them against evidence collected in such a manner that the observed facts have a fair chance of disconfirming the assumptions.

Returning to our previous illustration, we might predict that physically or socially advantaged areas will be characterized by an excess of immigrants over emigrants, while the reverse should hold true for disadvantaged areas. Death rates, if we take into account variations in age and sex distributions, should be low in industrial societies and high in traditional ones, low in wealthy communities with abundant health facilities and high in the poorer communities with meager facilities, or low in middle class families that utilize the best medical services and high in the lower class families which may have limited access to these services. Birth rates, according to our assumptions, should be high where the social norms favor early marriage, or where they discourage the practice of birth control and abortion; these rates should be low where customs reward the voluntary restriction of family size.

These predictions, and numerous others that could be drawn from our illustration, may be tested by comparative studies of population trends in selected societies, communities, groups, and classes. To the extent that the research evidence corroborates the predictions, our confidence in the assumptions is justified.

4. However, if disconfirmation occurs, the scientist considers redefining the problem, rephrasing the questions, or revising the assumptions, hypotheses, and theories until an acceptable degree of agreement is attained between theoretical predictions and empirical observations. When such modifications are made, they must be tested against newly collected evidence, since it is nearly always possible to construct a plausible theoretical explanation for findings that are already familiar. It is therefore the prediction of future events that counts most; and the test of these predictions leads to new findings which suggest new theories that call for still further findings. Or, to state the sequence a little differently, the solution to one problem creates another, the solution to which creates still another, and so on.

The feedback between theories and evidence is crucial to the advancement of knowledge. Without it, science would be deprived of its capacity for self-correction. But the ability to correct itself means that the pursuit of scientific knowledge is an endless quest, and that current theories are always maintained tentatively, with the expectation that they will become obsolete as new findings and better theories are developed.

5. When a certain theory has gained sufficient corroboration for practical use, an attempt is made to consolidate it with the existing body of knowledge by proposing appropriate revisions of current beliefs and practices. These proposals are also stated tentatively, for the improvement of knowledge is chiefly a matter of successive approximations in which self-correcting research leads gradually to more reliable, but still approximate or partial, conceptions of reality.

Knowledge often results in the ability to control certain phenomena, and the recognition of the ability to control sometimes produces an almost irresistible demand for social action. Already many nations are attempting to curb their population growth by distributing intra-uterine devices, or other contraceptives, and disseminating information on their proper use. If such methods are at all successful, eventually we may expect to learn how to control, within limits, the size of the human population or to regulate its intelligence, physique, sex ratio, diversity, and other traits.

The basic technology for population control may be near at hand. Reproductive cells can be stored in a frozen state, a method long used in improving some breeds of cattle and other animals. Some geneticists maintain that it soon may be possible for a young married couple to store their most viable cells and use them years later if they decide to have a family, or for a man and a woman to have an offspring though they belong to separate generations and never see each other. Perhaps it will also be possible to produce the human embryo in a laboratory and implant it in the body of a woman who desires to have a child. Recent progress in organ transplants, although directed toward survival rather than quality control, affords another striking indication of the potentialities of our biological revolution.

Thus, the more we learn about the population problem, the more clearly do we see the many social, political, economic, military, and moral questions involved in what was once regarded as a simple problem in biology. And we are only beginning to recognize the subtle ways in which the population problem contributes to many other social issues.

The above procedures of science are illustrated graphically in Figure 1. The figure shows how knowledge is improved by conceptual and empirical analysis. Theories and other kinds of logical arguments are the instruments of conceptual analysis. But they have no virtue unless they are stated in contestable terms, so that their claims can conceivably be disconfirmed by the facts of observation. Observed facts are the building blocks of science, the instruments of corroboration. Without facts, there are no scientific theories; without theories, no scientific facts.

Science, then, operates under a model of *contest* and *corroboration*. In employing this model, the motto is: Audacity in theory construction, prudence in testing and corroboration. The scientist is encouraged to use his imagination in making theoretical assumptions, but in testing these assumptions he is discouraged from taking anything for granted. Accordingly, no theory is refused consideration so long as it is logically coherent and empirically contestable, and no theory is accepted because of its plausibility or public appeal unless it also meets the test of factual evidence. Knowledge, to be accepted in science, must survive the tests of both conceptual and empirical inquiry.

Systems and Environments

We have seen that science seeks to find orderly relationships among events in the world of experience. An easy way of expressing order is by the use of concepts such as system and subsystem. The term "system," in its broadest sense, refers

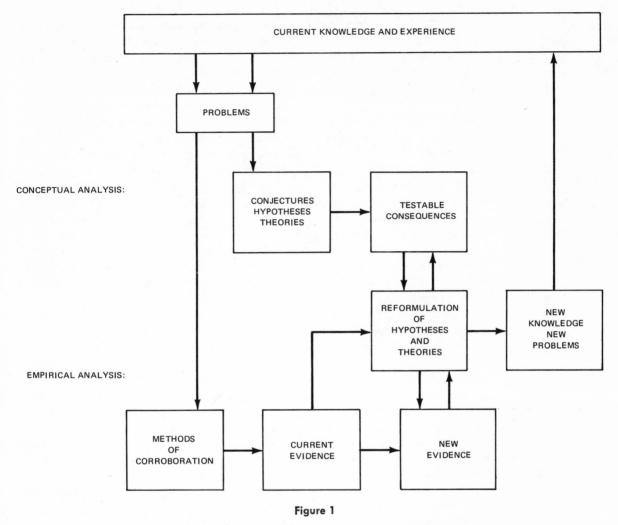

Figure 1

Paradigm of conceptual and empirical procedures in science. Research is evaluated by the changes it produces in the body of knowledge and by the new problems it poses.

to any set of interrelated variables, which are called elements. To illustrate, the heart is a system whose elements are living cells. Each cell is a system of molecules, and each molecule a system of atoms. In turn the heart is a subsystem within the circulatory system, which is a subsystem within a biological organism (another living system), which is a subsystem within the ecological system, and so on. A vast amount of physical, biological, and social information can be integrated with these concepts.

A system's elements may have various kinds of interrelations. Perhaps the simplest of these is the causal relationship, in which one element has a determining influence on another without itself being affected. The light reflected from a landscape upon the film in a camera is an example, since the effects flow in only one direction and the reflection in no way influences the landscape or the light source. We exploit such relationships in photographing galaxies, harnessing energy, eliminating certain diseases, and doing a lot of other things that are possible because we can sometimes manipulate the causal elements in relatively simple systems.

However, the elements of many systems have complex relationships that cannot be reduced to cause-effect sequences. An example is the free economy and the feedback relationships among its elements. Any change in the supply of a commodity has an indirect influence, through price adjustments, upon demand for that commodity, and the resulting change in demand has a feedback effect upon the available supply. In this hypothetical system, price varies inversely with supply and directly with demand. The influences counteract one another, resulting in a tendency toward equilibrium in the system. But if price were to vary directly with supply as well as demand, the influences would be cumulative. The system would expand without limit and perhaps tend to disintegrate. Indeed, some economists contend that the system does tend to move toward an uncontrolled expansion.

Accordingly, feedback systems are sometimes designed to avoid mishap by providing for the control of one or more of their elements. Some illustrations of such control efforts are the "checks and balances" and the "separation of powers" that were built into the federal constitution. Another example is the heating system found in many houses. A thermostat senses the temperature of a room, selects the on or off position of a switch, and activates or shuts off the furnace to maintain the temperature within a fixed range of variation. Also, the thermostat can be set for high or low temperatures, depending upon the preference of the operator.

Control implies that the system has certain goals or objectives and special strategies for achieving them. Implementation of a strategy calls for the system to perform several distinctive functions, such as *detection, selection,* and *reaction.* Detection means that the system is sensitive to the condition of the elements to be controlled; selection requires different responses, depending upon the condition of the elements and the set of the selection mechanism; reaction implies that the selected response produces an appropriate change in the condition of the controlled elements. All these functions are illustrated in the operation of an ordinary thermostat or, with varying degrees of success, the numerous social agencies that try to regulate the activities of people in modern societies.

The main distinguishing feature of a controlled system is the ability to modify its preferred states. For example, in a heating system, the thermostat can be set for almost any desired level. Ordinarily, a free economy is regarded as an uncontrolled equilibrium. Yet there is increasing evidence of at least partial control through the manipulation of credit, interest, taxes, public expenditures, dollar values, and other devices. Should these variables demonstrate an ability to eliminate our economic booms and depressions in favor of an adjustable level of activity, we will then be able to establish a controlled economy. But such ability is not tantamount to the exercise of control. Disagreements over objectives or strategies involved are often as difficult to resolve as are the technical problems of control.

Therefore, complete control is not often achieved. However, some degree of control seems essential to all living systems. In order to survive, these systems must find the energy to maintain their internal operations and to make appropriate adaptations to their external environment. Members of the animal kingdom, for example, must obtain energy sources from the environment through respiration and food ingestion. These sources are transformed metabolically in the digestive process and are distributed among the organs by the alimentary canal and the blood stream. The energy is consumed in maintaining the organism, promoting growth, and making body repairs. In time, the death of the organism returns its substance to the environment.

Human communities may also be viewed as systems engaged in the production, distribution, and utilization of energy. In the earliest societies, nearly all man's energies were devoted to attaining a marginal existence. Here the main source of energy was the food man consumed, and the chief method of energy utilization was the muscle power man expended in his pursuit of food. This style of life is found even today among isolated tribes of hunters and food-gatherers which have escaped the influence of the agricultural revolution.

The agricultural revolution called for a more complex system of energy production and utilization. Man's physical powers were greatly augmented, first by the domestication of animals as beasts of burden, and later by the use of internal combustion engines. Hand tools were replaced by heavier and more efficient farm implements. Plants were cultivated and harvested in a seasonal pattern that resulted in periodic food surpluses, which were stored and distributed as needed. These and many other agricultural improvements enabled a few families to furnish the necessities for an entire community, thus allowing more persons to engage in other kinds of activities. Out of such adaptive behaviors evolved the more elaborate social systems observed in modern societies.

Large cities existed in some places during prehistoric times. But urban societies are of recent origin. Major social and economic developments occur primarily in urban centers, increasing their share of the labor force to as high as 90 per cent of all the workers in some societies. This shift in the labor force is possible because urbanization requires more manpower in the cities and less in rural areas; agriculture becomes more efficient, while city life creates a demand for new services and facilities.

Urban societies can exist only so long as certain minimum requirements are met through the collective actions of their inhabitants. The focal point of action is the central city, the area most accessible to the greatest number of persons. Goods and services are centralized in this area where space is at a premium and land values are high. Only the most renumerative enterprises can survive. Less profitable services and activities tend to be moved out to secondary centers near the edges of the city or in the suburbs. Some industries, food stores, drug centers, and theaters have recently been relocated in this manner. These processes of spatial distribution are called *centralization* and *decentralization,* respectively.

There are many advantages in locating similar businesses and services near one another. "Automobile row" and the "bright lights area" illustrate this. That the same advantages accrue to semi-legitimate enterprises, perhaps for different reasons, is suggested by the kinds of recreational facilities that occasionally flourish in "twilight" zones and areas of transition adjacent to the downtown business district or near the city limits. The tendency for similar activities or population types to locate adjacent to one another is called *segregation.* Not all segregation is based on utilitarian motives; traditions of prejudice and discrimination frequently support the process, as evidenced by the residential segregation of social classes, ethnic groups, religious sects, races, and nationality groups.

It is often possible to delineate certain types of comparatively homogeneous areas within a community. There are residential areas, such as the "Gold Coast," the slum, Chinatown, the flop-house area, and the tract developments in the suburbs. Commercial areas include the centers of wholesale meats and groceries, centers of banking and finance, and honky-tonk, hippy, or other recreational areas. Areas may also be organized around industry, transportation, government, or other essential functions.

The functional links between different types of businesses and services are also important influences in the spatial patterning of urban communities. *Nucleation* refers to the tendency for enterprises with numerous linkages, whether similar or dissimilar in nature, to locate in clusters. A familiar example of the nucleation of dissimilar enterprises is the neighborhood shopping center. Such centers characteristically include a grocery store, a drug store, a meat market, a dry cleaning establishment, a beauty parlor, and possibly a shoe repair shop. There has been some tendency in recent years to bring many of these functions under one roof in a supermarket.

An area characterized by a certain kind of land use or by a particular type of inhabitants may sometimes undergo rapid and radical changes. One ethnic group moves out, another moves in. Old buildings are torn down and new ones put in their place. Large houses near the city center are made into crowded apartments. Streets are widened and freeways constructed. Small businesses grow into residential sections. The intrusion of a new population or a new service is called *invasion,* while the replacement of the old by the new is called *succession.* Such sequences of land use are prominent features of any urban community.

However, the spatial patterning of a community, as described above, is no more distinctive than its social or cultural patterning. A community, like the larger society of which it is a part, is a social system. It consists of many interrelated elements, each performing functions that vitally affect the whole. If it is to survive, a community must have sufficient stability to organize its elements, and it must be flexible enough to adapt to changing conditions, both internal and external. The state of a community is ordinarily that of a dynamic equilibrium, partly controlled by the deliberate efforts of its inhabitants, but also under strong pressures from hoary traditions and other forces over which the members have little control.

The Pilot Variables

The above discussion suggests that we should not overestimate the rationality of social systems or assume that their main sources of change are events that occur within the systems themselves. No doubt the greatest impetus to change comes from external phenomena of global significance, such as the population explosion, urbanization, instantaneous communication, automation, and the advancement of science. Except, perhaps, for science and automation, these great upheavals cannot be interpreted as products of rational planning. Yet they exert a crucial influence upon all systems and societies, increasing the interdependence of men, reducing their autonomy, and creating radical changes in the environment with which they must cope. The barriers of space, time, and tradition are being weakened, so that it is beginning to make sense for us to think in terms of a global society, a system of social systems, or an ecosystem. The time is at hand when any drastic change in a given social system is likely to set off a series of adaptations in other systems and in this way to permeate all of human society.

To analyze the pervasive changes that are occurring in human society, we need to identify the variables that have the greatest general relevance. These are called the PILOT variables and are described briefly on the next page:

P — The human *population;* its size, density, and its age and sex distributions; its occupational, educational, and social class structures; its abilities, interests, and other social traits.

I — The *information* that is accessible to the population, including the accumulation, storage, and communication of opinion, knowledge, and belief.

L — The *location* of the population, with special reference to the physical and biological environments of human communities, and their actual and potential resources.

O — The *organization* of the population into groups and communities, including their goals, strategies, activities, and achievements, and the relationships among these.

T — *Technology.* The tools, implements, machines, equipment, and other instruments that are used by people, and the knowledge and skills that make their use possible.

All the studies reported in this book deal in one way or another with these variables and their interrelations. No description of a social system can be complete without some reference to each of these PILOT variables, and no theory of sociology can afford to neglect any of these aspects of man's changing social milieu.

POPULATION TRENDS

1 World Population Growth: An International Dilemma*

Harold F. Dorn

In the following discussion of population trends around the world, attention is given to both the determinants and consequences of population growth. By placing different emphases on the control of fertility and the control of mortality in various parts of the world, man has created a situation

* From *Science*, Vol. 135 (January 22, 1962), pp. 283–90. Copyright © 1962 by the American Association for the Advancement of Science. Reprinted by permission.

in which the rate of population growth varies greatly in time and place. How is population growth related to changes in man's beliefs and values? What is the role of value conflicts in the growth of population? How does culture influence fertility and mortality? Can changes in role prescriptions and patterns of social relations have an effect on population growth? What do you propose as possible solutions to the population dilemma?

Only fragmentary data are available to indicate the past rate of growth of the population of the world. Even today, the number of inhabitants is known only approximately. Regular censuses of populations did not exist prior to 1800, although registers were maintained for small population groups prior to that time. As late as a century ago, around 1860, only about one-fifth of the estimated population of the world was covered by a census enumeration once in a 10-year period. The commonly accepted estimates of the population of the world prior to 1800 are only informed guesses. Nevertheless, it is possible to piece together a consistent series of estimates of the world's population during the past two centuries, supplemented by a few rough guesses of the num-

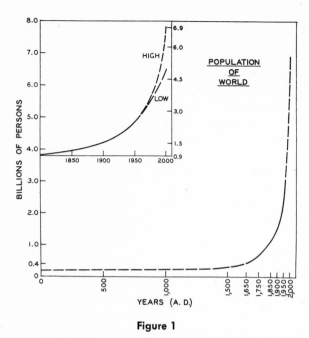

Figure 1

Estimated population of the world, A.D. *1 to* A.D. *2000.*

ber of persons alive at selected earlier periods. The most generally accepted estimates are presented in Fig. 1.

These reveal a spectacular spurt during recent decades in the increase of the world's population that must be unparalleled during the preceding millennia of human existence. Furthermore, the rate of increase shows no sign of diminishing (Table 1). The period of time required for the population of the world to double has sharply

TABLE 1 *The Number of Years Required to Double the Population of the World. [From United Nations Data.]*

Year (A.D.)	Population (Billions)	Number of Years to Double
1	0.25 (?)	1650 (?)
1650	0.50	200
1850	1.1	80
1930	2.0	45
1975	4.0	35
2010	8.0*	?

* A projection of United Nations estimates.

decreased during the past three centuries and now is about 35 years.

Only a very rough approximation can be made of the length of time required for the population of the world to reach one-quarter of a billion persons, the estimated number at the beginning of the Christian era. The present subgroups of Homo sapiens may have existed for as long as 100,000 years. The exact date is not necessary, since for present purposes the evidence is sufficient to indicate that probably 50,000 to 100,000 years were required for Homo sapiens to increase in number until he reached a global total of one-quarter of a billion persons. This number was reached approximately 2000 years ago.

By 1620, the year the Pilgrims landed on Plymouth Rock, the population of the world had doubled in number. Two hundred years later, shortly before the Civil War, another 500 million persons had been added. Since that time, additional half billions of persons have been added during increasingly shorter intervals of time. The sixth half billion, just added, required slightly less than 11 years, as compared to 200 years for the second half billion. The present rate of growth implies that only 6 to 7 years will be required to add the eighth half billion to the world's population. The change in rate of growth just described has taken place since the first settlers came to New England.

IMPLICATIONS

The accelerating rate of increase in the growth of the population of the world has come about so unobtrusively that most persons are unaware of its implications. There is a small group who are so aroused by this indifference that, like modern Paul Reveres, they attempt to awaken the public with cries of "the population bomb!" or "the population explosion!"

These persons are called alarmists by those who counter with the assertion that similar warnings, such as "standing-room only" and "mankind at the crossroads," have been issued periodically since Malthus wrote his essay on population, about 200 years ago. Nevertheless, says this group, the level of living and the health of the average person has continued to improve, and there is no reason to believe that advances in technology will not be able to make possible a slowly rising level of living for an increasing world population for the indefinite future. Furthermore, the rate of population increase almost certainly will slow down as the standard of education and living rises and as urbanization increases.

A third group of persons has attempted to estimate the maximum population that could be supported by the world's physical resources provided existing technological knowledge is fully utilized. Many of these calculations have been based on estimates of the quantity of food that could be produced and a hypothetical average daily calorie consumption per person.

As might be expected, the range of the various estimates of the maximum world population that could be supported without a lowering of the present level of living is very wide. One of the lowest, 2.8 billion, made by Pearson and Harper in 1945 on the assumption of an Asiatic standard of consumption, already has been surpassed. Several others, ranging from 5 to 7 billion, almost certainly will be exceeded by the end of this century. Perhaps the most carefully prepared estimate as well as the largest — that of 50 billions, prepared by Harrison Brown — would be reached in about 150 years if the present rate of growth should continue.

I believe it is worth while to prepare estimates of the maximum population that can be supported and to revise these as new information becomes available, even though most of the estimates made in the past already have been, or soon will be, demonstrated to be incorrect (in most instances too small), since this constitutes a rational effort to comprehend the implications of the increase in population. At the same time it should be recognized that estimates of the world's carrying capacity made in this manner are rather unrealistic and are primarily useful only as very general guidelines.

In the first place, these calculations have assumed that the earth's resources and skills are a single reservoir available to all. In reality this is untrue. The U.S. government attempts to restrict production of certain agricultural crops by paying farmers not to grow them. Simultaneously, in Asia and Africa, large numbers of persons are inadequately fed and poorly clothed. Except in a very general sense there is no world population problem; there are population problems varying in nature and degree among the several nations of the world. No single solution is applicable to all.

Since the world is not a single political unity, the increases in production actually achieved during any period of time tend to be considerably less than those theoretically possible. Knowledge, technical skill, and capital are concentrated in areas with the highest level of living, whereas the most rapid increase in population is taking place in areas where such skills and capital are relatively scarce or practically nonexistent.

Just as the world is not a single unit from the point of view of needs and the availability of resources, skills, and knowledge to meet these needs, so it also is not a single unit with respect to population increase. Due to political barriers that now exist throughout the entire world, overpopulation, however defined, will become a serious problem in specific countries long before it would be a world problem if there were no barriers to population redistribution. I shall return to this point later, after discussing briefly existing forecasts or projections of the total population of the world.

Most demographers believe that, under present conditions, the future population of areas such as countries or continents, or even of the entire world, cannot be predicted for more than a few decades with even a moderate degree of certainty. This represents a marked change from the view held by many only 30 years ago.

In 1930 a prominent demographer wrote, "The population of the United States ten, twenty, even fifty years hence, can be predicted with a greater degree of assurance than any other economic or social fact, provided the immigration laws are unchanged." Nineteen years later, a well-known economist replied that "it is disheartening to have to assert that the best population forecasts deserve little credence even for 5 years ahead, and none at all for 20–50 years ahead."

Although both of these statements represent rather extreme views, they do indicate the change that has taken place during the past two decades in the attitude toward the reliability of population forecasts. Some of the reasons for this have been discussed in detail elsewhere and will not be repeated here.

It will be sufficient to point out that knowledge of methods of voluntarily controlling fertility now is so widespread, especially among persons of European ancestry, that sharp changes in the spacing, as well as in the number, of children born during the reproductive period may occur in a relatively short period of time. Furthermore, the birth rate may increase as well as decrease.

FORECASTING POPULATION GROWTH

The method of projecting or forecasting population growth most frequently used by demographers, whenever the necessary data are available, is the "component" or "analytical" method. Separate estimates are prepared of the future trend of fertility, mortality, and migration. From the total population as distributed by age and sex on a specified date, the future population that would result from the hypothetical combination of fertility, mortality, and migration is computed. Usually, several estimates of the future population are prepared in order to include what the authors believe to be the most likely range of values.

Such estimates generally are claimed by their authors to be not forecasts of the most probable future population but merely indications of the population that would result from the hypothetical

assumptions concerning the future trend in fertility, mortality, and migration. However, the projections of fertility, mortality, and migration usually are chosen to include what the authors believe will be the range of likely possibilities. This objective is achieved by making "high," "medium," and "low" assumptions concerning the future trend in population growth. Following the practice of most of the authors of such estimates, I shall refer to these numbers as population projections.

The most authoritative projections of the population of the world are those made by the United Nations (Table 2). Even though the most recent of these projections were published in 1958, it now seems likely that the population of the world will exceed the high projection before the year 2000. By the end of 1961 the world's population at least equaled the high projection for that date.

Although the United Nations' projections appear to be too conservative in that even the highest will be an underestimate of the population only 40 years from now, some of the numerical increases in population implied by these may be beyond the ability of the nations involved to solve. For example, the estimated increase in the population of Asia from A.D. 1950 to 2000 will be roughly equal to the population of the entire world in 1958! The population of Latin America 40 years hence may very likely be four times that in 1950. The absolute increase in population in

TABLE 2 *Estimated Population of the World for A.D. 1900, 1950, 1975, and 2000. [From United Nations Data, Rounded to Three Significant Digits.]*

| Area | Estimated Population (Millions) | | Projected Future Population (Millions) | | | |
| | | | Low Assumptions | | High Assumptions | |
	1900	1950	1975	2000	1975	2000
World	1550	2500	3590	4380	3860	6900
Africa	120	199	295	420	331	663
North America	81	168	232	274	240	326
Latin America	63	163	282	445	304	651
Asia	857	1380	2040	2890	2210	4250
Europe including U.S.S.R.	423	574	724	824	751	967
Oceania	6	13	20	27	21	30

Latin America during the last half of the century may equal the total increase in the population of Homo sapiens during all the millennia from his origin until about 1650, when the first colonists were settling New England.

Increases in population of this magnitude stagger the imagination. Present trends indicate that they may be succeeded by even larger increases during comparable periods of time. The increase in the rate of growth of the world's population, shown by the data in Table 1, is still continuing. This rate is now estimated to be about 2 percent per year, sufficient to double the world's population every 35 years. It requires only very simple arithmetic to show that a continuation of this rate of growth for even 10 or 15 decades would result in an increase in population that would make the globe resemble an anthill.

But as was pointed out above, the world is not a single unit economically, politically, or demographically. Long before the population of the entire world reaches a size that could not be supported at current levels of living, the increase in population in specific nations and regions will give rise to problems that will affect the health and welfare of the rest of the world. The events of the past few years have graphically demonstrated the rapidity with which the political and economic problems of even a small and weak nation can directly affect the welfare of the largest and most powerful nations. Rather than speculate about the maximum population the world can support and the length of time before this number will be reached, it will be more instructive to examine the demographic changes that are taking place in different regions of the world and to comment briefly on their implications.

DECLINE IN MORTALITY

The major cause of the recent spurt in population increase is a world-wide decline in mortality. Although the birth rate increased in some countries — for example, the United States — during and after World War II, such increases have not been sufficiently widespread to account for more than a small part of the increase in the total population of the world. Moreover, the increase in population prior to World War II occurred in spite of a widespread decline in the birth rate among persons of European origin.

Accurate statistics do not exist, but the best available estimates suggest that the expectation of life at birth in Greece, Rome, Egypt, and the Eastern Mediterranean region probably did not exceed 30 years at the beginning of the Christian era. By 1900 it had increased to about 40 to 50 years in North America and in most countries of northwestern Europe. At present, it has reached 68 to 70 years in many of these countries.

By 1940, only a small minority of the world's population had achieved an expectation of life at birth comparable to that of the population of North America and northwest Europe. Most of the population of the world had an expectation of life no greater than that which prevailed in western Europe during the Middle Ages. Within the past two decades, the possibility of achieving a 20th-century death rate has been opened to these masses of the world's population. An indication of the result can be seen from the data in Fig. 2.

In 1940, the death rate in Mexico was similar to that in England and Wales nearly 100 years earlier. It decreased as much during the following decade as did the death rate in England and Wales during the 50-year period from 1850 to 1900.

In 1946–47 the death rate of the Moslem population of Algeria was higher than that of the population of Sweden in the period 1771–80, the earliest date for which reliable mortality statistics are available for an entire nation. During the following 8 years, the drop in the death rate in Algeria considerably exceeded that in Sweden during the century from 1771 to 1871.

The precipitous decline in mortality in Mexico and in the Moslem population of Algeria is illustrative of what has taken place during the past 15 years in Latin America, Africa, and Asia, where nearly three out of every four persons in the world now live. Throughout most of this area the birth rate has changed very little, remaining near a level of 40 per 1000 per year, as can be seen from Fig. 3, which shows the birth rate, death rate, and rate of natural increase for selected countries.

Even in countries such as Puerto Rico and

Japan where the birth rate has declined substantially, the rate of natural increase has changed very little, owing to the sharp decrease in mortality. A more typical situation is represented by Singapore, Ceylon, Guatemala, and Chile, where the crude rate of natural increase has risen. There has been a general tendency for death rates to decline universally and for high birth rates to remain high, with the result that those countries with the highest rates of increase are experiencing an acceleration in their rates of growth.

REGIONAL LEVELS

The absolute level of fertility and mortality and the effect of changes in them upon the increase of population in different regions of the world can be only approximately indicated. The United Nations estimates that only about 33 percent of the deaths and 42 percent of the births that occur in the world are registered. The percentage registered ranges from about 8 to 10 percent in tropical and southern Africa and Eastern Asia to 98

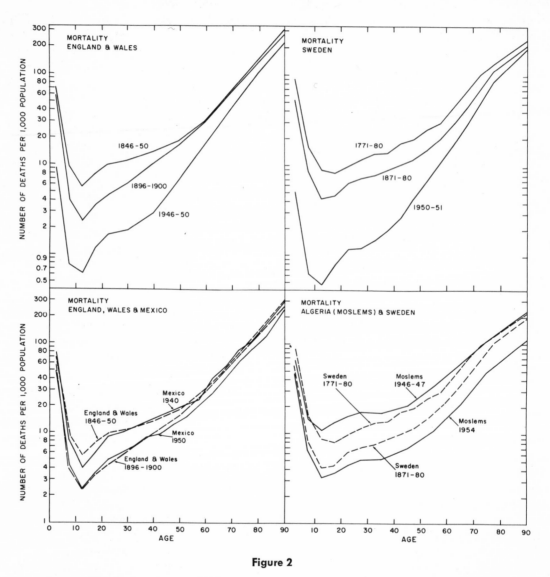

Figure 2

Age-specific death rates per 1000 per year for Sweden, England and Wales, Mexico, and the Moslem population of Algeria for various time periods from 1771 to 1954.

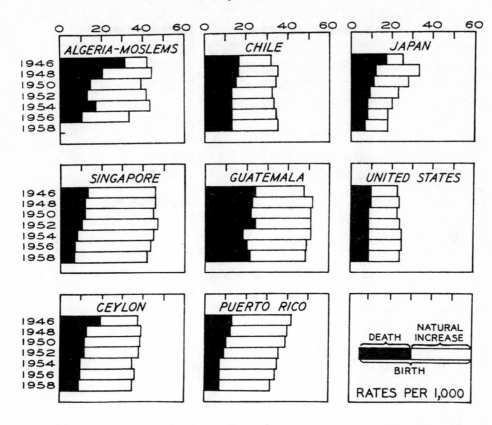

Figure 3

Birth rate, death rate, and rate of natural increase per 1000 for selected countries for the period 1946–1958.

to 100 percent in North America and Europe. Nevertheless, the statistical staff of the United Nations, by a judicious combination of the available fragmentary data, has been able to prepare estimates of fertility and mortality for different regions of the world that are generally accepted as a reasonably correct estimation of the actual but unknown figures. The estimated birth rate, death rate, and crude rate of natural increase (the birth rate minus the death rate) for eight regions of the world for the period 1954–58 are shown in Fig. 4.

The birth rates of the countries of Africa, Asia, Middle America, and South America average nearly 40 per 1000 and probably are as high as they were 500 to 1000 years ago. In the rest of the world — Europe, North America, Oceania, and the Soviet Union — the birth rate is slightly more than half as high, or about 20 to 25 per 1000. The death rate for the former regions, although still definitely higher, is rapidly approaching that for people of European origin, with the result that the highest rates of natural increase are found in the regions with the highest birth rates. The most rapid rate of population growth at present is taking place in Middle and South America, where the population will double about every 26 years if the present rate continues.

These regional differences in fertility and mortality are intensifying the existing imbalance of population with land area and natural resources. No matter how this imbalance is measured, that it exists is readily apparent. Two rather crude measures are presented in Figs. 4 and 5, which show the percentage distribution of the world's population living in each region and the number of persons per square kilometer.

An important effect of the decline in mortality

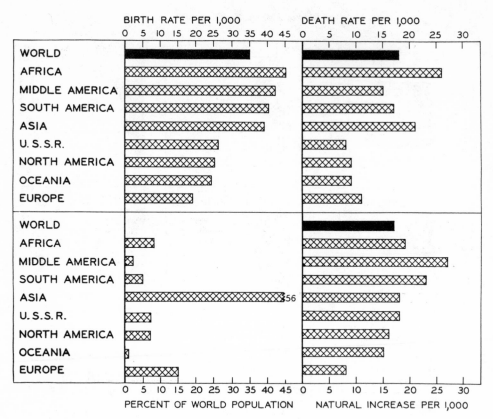

Figure 4

Percentage of the 1958 world population, birth rate, death rate, and rate of natural increase, per 1000, for the period 1954–1958 for various regions of the world.

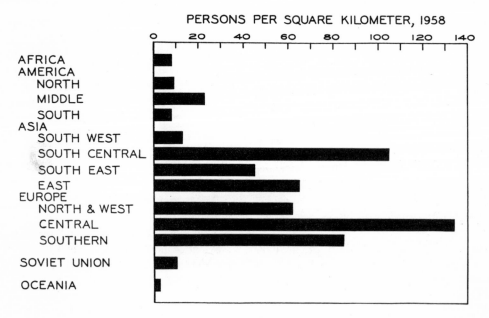

Figure 5

Number of persons per square kilometer in various regions of the world in 1958.

16

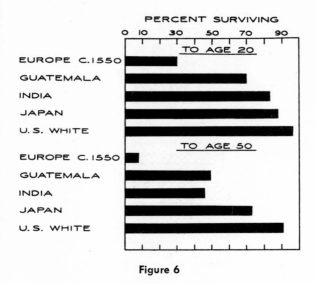

Figure 6

Percentage of newborn females who would survive to the end of the reproductive period according to mortality rates in Europe around A.D. 1500 and in selected countries around 1950.

rates often is overlooked — namely, the increase in effective fertility. An estimated 97 out of every 100 newborn white females subject to the mortality rates prevailing in the United States during 1950 would survive to age 20, slightly past the beginning of the usual childbearing age, and 91 would survive to the end of the childbearing period (Fig. 6). These estimates are more than 3 and 11 times, respectively, the corresponding estimated proportions for white females that survived to these ages about four centuries ago.

In contrast, about 70 percent of the newborn females in Guatemala would survive to age 20, and only half would live to the end of the childbearing period if subject to the death rates prevailing in that country in 1950. If the death rate in Guatemala should fall to the level of that in the United States in 1950 — a realistic possibility — the number of newborn females who would survive to the beginning of the childbearing period would increase by 36 percent; the number surviving to the end of the childbearing period would increase by 85 percent. A corresponding decrease in the birth rate would be required to prevent this increase in survivorship from resulting in a rapid acceleration in the existing rate of population growth, which already is excessive. In

other words, this decrease in the death rate would require a decrease in the birth rate of more than 40 percent merely to maintain the status quo.

As can be seen from Fig. 3, the birth rate in countries with high fertility has shown little or no tendency to decrease in recent years. Japan is the exception. There, the birth rate dropped by 46 percent from 1948 to 1958 — an amount more than enough to counterbalance the decrease in the death rate, with the result that there was a decrease in the absolute number of births. As yet there is very little evidence that other countries with a correspondingly high birth rate are likely to duplicate this in the near future.

Another effect of a rapid rate of natural increase is demonstrated by Fig. 7. About 43 percent of the Moslem population of Algeria is under 15 years of age; the corresponding percentage in Sweden is 24, or slightly more than half this number. Percentages in the neighborhood of 40 percent are characteristic of the populations of the countries of Africa, Latin America, and Asia.

This high proportion of young people constitutes a huge fertility potential for 30 years into the future that can be counterbalanced only by a sharp decline in the birth rate, gives rise to serious educational problems, and causes a heavy drain on the capital formation that is necessary to improve the level of living of the entire population. A graphic illustration of this may be found in the recently published 5-year plan for India for 1961–66, which estimates that it will be necessary to provide educational facilities and teachers for 20 million additional children during this 5-year period.

HISTORICAL PATTERN IN WESTERN EUROPE

Some persons, although agreeing that the current rate of increase of the majority of the world's population cannot continue indefinitely without giving rise to grave political, social, and economic problems, point out that a similar situation existed in northwestern and central Europe during the 18th and 19th centuries. Increasing industrialization and urbanization, coupled with a rising standard of living, led to a decline in the birth rate, with a consequent drop in the rate of increase of

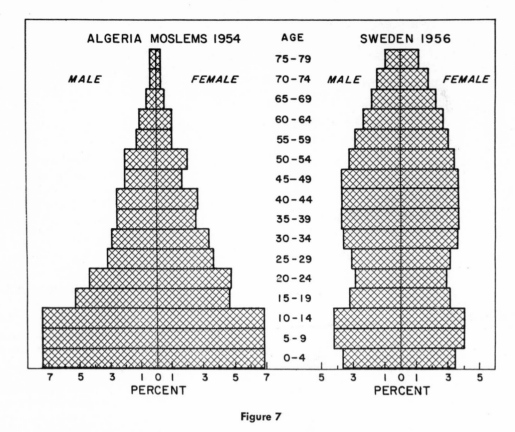

Figure 7

Percentage distribution by age of the population of Sweden in 1956 and the Moslem population of Algeria in 1954.

the population. Why should not the rest of the world follow this pattern?

There is small likelihood that the two-thirds of the world's population which has not yet passed through the demographic revolution from high fertility and mortality rates to low fertility and mortality rates can repeat the history of western European peoples prior to the development of serious political and economic problems. A brief review of the circumstances that led to the virtual domination of the world at the end of the 19th century by persons of European origin will indicate some of the reasons for this opinion.

Around A.D. 1500 the population of Europe probably did not exceed 100 million persons (perhaps 15 to 20 percent of the population of the world) and occupied about 2 percent of the land area of the earth. Four hundred years later, around 1900, the descendants of this population numbered nearly 550 million, constituted about

one-third of the world's population, and occupied or controlled five-sixths of the land area of the world. They had seized and peopled two great continents, North and South America, and one smaller continent, Australia, with its adjacent islands; had partially peopled and entirely controlled a third great continent, Africa; and dominated southern Asia and the neighboring islands.

The English-, French-, and Spanish-speaking peoples were the leaders in this expansion, with lesser roles being played by the Dutch and Portuguese. The Belgians and Germans participated only toward the end of this period of expansion. Among these, the English-speaking people held the dominant position at the end of the era, around 1900.

The number of English-speaking persons around 1500, at the start of this period of expansion, is not known, but it probably did not exceed 4 or 5 million. By 1900 these people numbered about

129 million and occupied and controlled one-third of the land area of the earth and, with the non-English-speaking inhabitants of this territory, made up some 30 percent of the population of the world.

This period was characterized by an unprecedented increase in population, a several-fold expansion of the land base for this population, and a hitherto undreamed of multiplication of capital in the form of precious metals, goods, and commodities. Most important of all, the augmentation in capital and usable land took place more rapidly than the growth in population.

A situation equally favorable for a rapid improvement in the level of living associated with a sharp increase in population does not appear likely to arise for the people who now inhabit Latin America, Africa, and Asia. The last great frontier of the world has been closed. Although there are many thinly populated areas in the world, their existence is testimony to the fact that, until now, these have been regarded as undesirable living places. The expansion of population to the remaining open areas would require large expenditures of capital for irrigation, drainage, transportation facilities, control of insects and parasites, and other purposes — capital that the rapidly increasing populations which will need these areas do not possess.

In addition, this land is not freely available for settlement. The entire land surface of the world is crisscrossed by national boundaries. International migration now is controlled by political considerations; for the majority of the population of the world, migration, both in and out of a country, is restricted.

The horn of plenty, formerly filled with free natural resources, has been emptied. No rapid accumulation of capital in the form of precious metals, goods, and commodities, such as characterized the great 400-year boom enjoyed by the peoples of western-European origin, is possible for the people of Africa, Asia, and Latin America.

Last, but not least, is the sheer arithmetic of the current increase in population. The number of persons in the world is so large that even a small rate of natural increase will result in an almost astronomical increment over a period of time of infinitesimal duration compared to the duration of the past history of the human race. As was pointed out above, continuation of the present rate of increase would result in a population of 50 billion persons in another 150 years. A population of this magnitude is so foreign to our experience that it is difficult to comprehend its implications.

Just as Thomas Malthus, at the end of the 18th century, could not foresee the effect upon the peoples of western Europe of the exploration of the last great frontier of this earth, so we today cannot clearly foresee the final effect of an unprecedented rapid increase of population within closed frontiers. What seems to be least uncertain in a future full of uncertainty is that the demographic history of the next 400 years will not be like that of the past 400 years.

WORLD PROBLEMS

The results of human reproduction are no longer solely the concern of the two individuals involved, or of the larger family, or even of the nation of which they are citizens. A stage has been reached in the demographic development of the world when the rate of human reproduction in any part of the globe may directly or indirectly affect the health and welfare of the rest of the human race. It is in this sense that there is a world population problem.

One or two illustrations may make this point more clear. During the past decade, six out of every ten persons added to the population of the world live in Asia; another two out of every ten live in Latin America and Africa. It seems inevitable that the breaking up of the world domination by northwest Europeans and their descendants, which already is well advanced, will continue, and that the center of power and influence will shift toward the demographic center of the world.

The present distribution of population increase enhances the existing imbalance between the distribution of the world's population and the distribution of wealth, available and utilized resources, and the use of nonhuman energy. Probably for the first time in human history there is a universal aspiration for a rapid improvement in the standard of living and a growing impatience with conditions that appear to stand in the way of its attainment. Millions of persons in Asia, Africa, and Latin America now are aware of the standard of living enjoyed by Europeans and North Americans. They are demanding the opportunity to attain the same standard, and they resist the idea that they must be permanently content with less.

A continuation of the present high rate of human multiplication will act as a brake on the already painfully slow improvement in the level of living, thus increasing political unrest and possibly bringing about eventual changes in government. As recent events have graphically demonstrated, such political changes may greatly affect the welfare of even the wealthier nations.

The capital and technological skills that many of the nations of Africa, Asia, and Latin America require to produce enough food for a rapidly growing population and simultaneously to perceptibly raise per capita income exceed their existing national resources and ability. An immediate supply of capital in the amounts required is available only from the wealthier nations. The principle of public support for social welfare plans is now widely accepted in national affairs. The desirability of extending this principle to the international level for the primary purpose of supporting the economic development of the less advanced nations has not yet been generally accepted by the wealthier and more advanced countries. Even if this principle should be accepted, it is not as yet clear how long the wealthier nations would be willing to support the uncontrolled breeding of the populations receiving this assistance. The general acceptance of a foreign-aid program of the extent required by the countries with a rapidly growing population will only postpone for a few decades the inevitable reckoning with the results of uncontrolled human multiplication.

The future may witness a dramatic increase in man's ability to control his environment, provided he rapidly develops cultural substitutes for those harsh but effective governors of his high reproductive potential — disease and famine — that he has so recently learned to control. Man has been able to modify or control many natural phenomena, but he has not yet discovered how to evade the consequences of biological laws. No species has ever been able to multiply without limit. There are two biological checks upon a rapid increase in number — a high mortality and a low fertility. Unlike other biological organisms, man can choose which of these checks shall be applied, but one of them must be. Whether man can use his scientific knowledge to guide his future evolution more wisely than the blind forces of nature, only the future can reveal. The answer will not be long postponed.

2   Population Growth and the American Way of Life*

Lincoln H. Day · Alice Taylor Day

Many Americans are aware that rapidly increasing population can threaten the welfare of societies, but they are almost unanimous in identifying problems of population growth with the newly developing or nonindustrialized countries. Few of us realize

* Excerpted from Lincoln H. Day and Alice Taylor Day, *Too Many Americans.* Boston: Houghton Mifflin Co., 1964. Reproduced by permission.

the threats that rapid population increase poses for the most advanced and wealthy nations. In the poorest countries, the rapid growth of population may threaten the health or even survival of large segments of the population. In a highly industrialized country, the dangers may be less dramatic, but they are serious enough to require informed action. The authors of this selection are able to link many of America's pressing problems and obnoxious nuisances to the rapid increase in population. They show clearly that population increase greatly aggravates the problems of urbanization and industrialization, and that even now the quality of American life is being corroded.

How a people experiences population growth will be mediated very largely through its cultural practices and standards. Population increase does not lead to crowded schools in a country of low educational levels. But when the median length of schooling approaches 12 years, as it does today in the United States, rapid growth means teacher shortages, split sessions, and a decreasing adequacy of school facilities. A 20 percent increase over a decade brings with it no corresponding increase in traffic jams, no overcrowding of vacation spots, no loss of land to roads and municipal facilities if only a few own cars, or live in suburbs, or have vacations. But with more than 340 automobiles per 1000 population, a housing ratio of less than one person to a room and the single family dwelling unit the national norm, with a probable majority of the work force enjoying an annual paid vacation, and with a third of the population required by the distribution of employment opportunities (if nothing else) to live in urban concentrations of more than a million people, rapid population growth makes ever more difficult the task of maintaining those levels already achieved and, when continued, must eventually lead to their very deterioration. Of course, urbanization, industrialization, or rising material levels of living (a per capita increase in the number of automobiles, for example) can have corrosive effects on the quality of life even when a population is small or remains stable. The traffic congestion now spreading over many parts of Europe is certainly the legacy of a postwar rise in affluence. But when the size of a population is rising simultaneously with its material standards and expectations, the difficulties are compounded and the blight spread over a wider area.

Declines in quality are ultimately to be defined in terms of values. Data on the increasing difficulty of coping with the problems occasioned by population growth can simply offer clues to the existence and magnitude of these declines, and a foretaste of what is in store should population growth continue.

Some profess to see in our numerical increase a source of aberrant forms of behavior: crime, juvenile delinquency, mental illness, racial antagonisms. But the evidence for this seems tenuous, at most. Any growth in numbers might be expected to produce a higher incidence of deviant behavior, if only because there will be more people to commit crimes (and to have crimes committed against them), more to become mentally ill, and so on. But this does not mean that population growth is necessarily causally related to these conditions; that it increases their *rate* or heightens their *severity*. Because of the difficulty of isolating it as a variable, the effect of density on individual and social well-being has been the subject of little more than claims and counterclaims. Some recent experiments have shown high density to result in profoundly pathological behavior among rats. But whether this is analogous to the human situation, is as yet little more than a hypothesis.

The case for arresting American population growth need not depend on such tenuous claims, however. There are numerous examples of the deleterious effects of rapid growth on our conditions of life which are at once more concrete and more obviously related in a causal fashion to our growth in numbers. It is to examples of such cases that we now turn. These we discuss under separate headings only to facilitate description. Actually, considerable overlap exists between them. Rising economic costs and an increase in external controls, for example, are germane in some measure to each.

SPACE AND RECREATION

We Americans have a strong tradition of love of natural beauty, open space, and outdoor recreation. This is attested to by the establishment of our national parks and forests and the rapidly expanding recreational use being made of them (from 61 million visits in 1950 to 151 million less than a decade later); the popularity of vacations — or just picnics — in scenic areas (more than 259 million visits to state parks in 1960); the growth of the pleasure boat and skiing business; the more than 20 million fishing and 15 million hunting licenses sold annually.

To be sure, the outdoors has no monopoly over the sources of recreation and aesthetic satisfaction. But would any deny its importance? The availability of *both* indoor and outdoor satisfactions would seem an essential element of the "good life" for a majority of Americans. But preservation of the latter, because of its very nature, will require far more effort and imaginative planning than has up to now been expended on it. It will also be immeasurably advanced by an early cessation of population growth.

Our need as a people for parks, wilderness areas, beaches, and other recreational and restorative areas has never been greater. The combination of population increase, higher incomes, shorter working hours, and ever greater concentration in ever larger metropolitan centers has resulted in a demand for these kinds of facilities far exceeding that which existed when we were a less numerous, less materially affluent, less urban people. Recreational use of public lands has more than trebled since the end of World War II, and it is still increasing. More of these facilities, if not absolutely essential from the standpoint of physical survival, are certainly essential from the standpoint of the quality of life. Population growth, with its attendant increase in population density, makes the ready accessibility of space and recreation facilities ever more necessary while at the same time making it ever more difficult to attain.

In sheer acreage the United States is plentifully endowed with the land and the water area to meet current needs. But little of it is very accessible. The South and North Central regions of the country, each with about 30 percent of the population, have but 12 percent of the recreational acreage of the forty-eight contiguous states. The Northeast, with one-quarter of it, has only 4 percent. And it is in the Northeast that open lands like farming and grazing areas are also in shortest supply.

Estimates of future increases in population, coupled with predictions on travel, leisure time, and income, forecast an increase in visits to our National Parks from 63 million in 1959 to 240 million by 1980, and well over 400 million by the year 2000. Yet, facilities in most of them are already overburdened. Crowding and overuse have in some instances jeopardized and, in others, made it difficult to enjoy, the scenic and natural wonders which the establishment of these parks was to preserve and make forever available to the people of this country. This arises in part, of course, from higher levels of living — particularly the extension of paid vacations. But population increase *alone* would have brought the probable number of visitors up to the capacity of these parks

by 1955, had the level of living risen no higher than it was in 1940. That material levels of living have increased at the same time as population merely adds to the problem.

Young sequoia trees in California's Sequoia and Yosemite National Parks, seeded from the oldest living things on earth, are becoming sick "because the great number of visitors is trampling the earth down so hard during visits that rain water is running off and not getting down to the roots." Everglades National Park, Florida's best recreational area and a "world-famous wonderland of nature," has suffered the inroads of real estate speculators and is in considerable danger of suffering irreparable damage as "expanding Miami makes it desirable to drain more of the area adjacent to the park, and expanding markets for winter crops create an irrigation demand for the water which might otherwise be drained to the park."

But these are the famous places, the places of national importance established by a national government for a nation's people. As long as they have vacations and money, Americans will flock to Yosemite, Yellowstone, the Great Smokies, and the Everglades. A visit to one of these parks occurs once a decade, or once a lifetime. What of the areas closer to home — the areas for weekend and daily living? The increasing shortage of space is probably for the majority of Americans the most obvious consequence of population growth. Witness the traffic jams that beset all our major cities and most of our smaller ones as well. In some places this blight has afflicted us so long that it is now an accepted part of urban life. But the traffic jam is spreading to places where no one could have expected it ten or fifteen years ago: Yellowstone National Park and the mountains west of Denver, for example. While the increased mobility that has come with the spread of the automobile has to some extent enlarged our recreational opportunities,

the blessing is a mixed one, for the very apparatus that has made the outdoors more accessible has changed the nature of much of it. As people push outward, they push the countryside before them. "Non-residents not allowed" signs go up on county beaches, and what yesterday was a pleasant hour's drive to a picnic spot is now only a gruelling preliminary.[1]

And all too often the situation is little better on arrival. To quote Lewis Mumford: Do we "increase the opportunities for recreation when we turn a woodland into a parking lot, or an ocean beach into a fishing net filled with squirming human bodies?" State park facilities in California were already 31 percent short of requirements four years ago. In Colorado, hand signals have been devised to prevent collisions between skiers on certain of the state's once-spacious ski slopes, and there has been talk of installing traffic lights at various locations in the ski area at Winter Park. Michigan, which calls itself the "Water Wonderland," had to turn away 28,000 campers — one in every five — for lack of space in 1958. And this is but a minimum figure, for we have no way of knowing how many would-be campers the crowded facilities discouraged from even trying.

And then there are the cities and towns that run together, connected by a gum of suburbia and "highway culture": a picnic or walk in the open country within easy motoring distance of home has become a virtual impossibility for a near-majority of our citizens. Once-green countryside is being bulldozed under at the rate of 1.1 million acres a year — three thousand acres a day; and, as William H. Whyte, Jr. has noted, "It is not merely that the countryside is ever receding; in the great expansion of the metropolitan areas the subdivisions of one city are beginning to meet up with the subdivisions of another."

ECONOMIC COSTS

The explosive combination of multiplying possessions and multiplying people is causing an ever larger portion of our high level of living to be used to escape from the consequences of congestion.[2]

[1] Outdoor Recreation Resources Review Commission, *Outdoor Recreation for America,* Washington: U.S. Government Printing Office, 1962, p. 22.

[2] Kingsley Davis, "Population and Welfare in Industrial Societies," Fourth Annual Dorothy Nyswander Lecture, Berkeley, California, April 16, 1960, printed in *Health Education Monographs,* Number 9 (no date), p. 15.

An accompaniment of our growing population and its increasing density, cases of higher real costs for the maintenance of the standards Americans regard as minimal can be multiplied over and over. Air and water purification, traffic control, urban renewal, the acquisition and processing of natural resources, provision of social services, upkeep and preservation of parks and recreational areas, protection and conservation of wildlife all offer numerous examples. It costs us more simply to hold onto the standards of life we have already attained, let alone to achieve any improvement. That so many of these standards, outward signs of our quality of life, have already had to be lowered as a consequence of population pressure is evidence that the cost is more than merely monetary.

As our population grows and becomes more urbanized we must spend more on nearly every kind of public service — partly because of the increased demand these added numbers represent, and partly because of the increased competition they produce for scarce land and materials.

Housing, schools, roads, industries all compete with one another and with parks and recreational areas for an increasingly limited supply of land in areas of high population density. Industry competes with community for water and drainage facilities. Airlines compete with airlines, and with community interests, for space around airports. Some localities, becoming conscious of the health hazards in air pollution, are even moving to restrict industrial use of the atmosphere as an avenue for the elimination of wastes.

The economic costs of transportation and communication have also risen in response to our population growth. Sunday afternoon traffic jams are seldom costly, at least in economic terms. But those in the middle of the week are. In all our larger urban areas road and air traffic seems already to be running into increasing costs from traffic density. Motor trucks average less than six miles an hour in New York traffic today, as against eleven for horse-drawn trucks in 1910. The cost of traffic jams, according to estimates by business and automotive groups, is $5 billion yearly. And as only the most recent in a long series of appropriations to this end, our Federal government has allocated some $41 billion for the construction of an additional 41,000 miles of highway (and note how much that is per mile), an extension of roads which, upon completion, will cover as much area as there is in the whole state of Rhode Island.

But it is probably with recreation that the economic effects of competing demands arising from population and urbanization are at their most obvious. The Department of the Interior estimates that its proposed acquisition of a badly needed 4.6 million acres for national parks and forests will run as high as $250 million a year for a period of ten years. The Outdoor Recreation Resources Review Commission, noting that "all levels of government must provide continuing and adequate funds for outdoor recreation," warns that "in most cases, this will require a substantial increase over present levels."

But if these higher economic costs come in the main from the spread of urbanization that accompanies our population growth, there are others that originate in the fact of numerical increase itself. Population growth may once have been essential for economic prosperity in the United States, but it can hardly be considered so any longer. When a man's strength was an important source of energy, and per capita consumption was at a low level, a growing population in a sparsely settled land was indeed an important factor in creating a high level of material living. The more people, the more energy, the greater the possible division of labor, the greater the potential market for goods.

It is different today. The combination of an increasing population and a generally rising level of consumption has revealed limitations in the supply of raw materials and increased the costs of developing them. All minerals and most of the sources of energy in current use are *non-renewable*. It took millions of years to create them. They represent capital. As we use them up we are using capital, not income. Though the outlook is not altogether bleak, rising demand has, even in the case of certain *renewable* resources, produced some serious and costly shortages. One of these is in water. Despite extensive efforts at development and conservation of this resource, our continued growth in numbers, combined with our

rising level of living, has placed steadily mounting demands upon it. As the Rienows have noted:

More than a thousand cities and towns [in the United States] already have been forced to curtail their water service. Near Chicago, where artesian wells flowed under their own pressure a hundred years ago, new wells must go down 2000 feet to reach the water table. Dallas is already pumping the salt-tainted Red River into its main, and New York faces the likelihood that eventually it will have to purify the polluted Hudson to slake its growing thirst. In Mississippi, wells are now 400 feet deeper, on the average, than they were only ten years ago. Denver, eager for new industry, has been turning away manufacturers whose production processes involve a heavy use of water.[3]

Even if our population ceased to grow, we could expect rising costs for many of the raw materials essential to our way of life, first, because of higher production costs attending depletion of the more readily accessible supplies and, second, because of greater competition for these materials from other countries as a result of their own population increases and efforts to raise their levels of living. Since our population is not stable, but is, instead, growing rapidly, there is added to these two sources of higher costs a third — an annual addition of some three million people to that population with the world's highest rate of material consumption.

In a private or mixed economy one can expect higher prices to spur development of new techniques for reclaiming scrap, encourage more extensive exploration, and bring into production marginal, low-yield deposits. A mining geologist and businessman has assured us that these approaches will postpone "beyond the foreseeable historic future . . . the evil date of drastic scarcities," but not even he would claim it can be done without substantial increases in real costs.

POLLUTION

And what of our rivers? Most are not fit to swim in. Pollution has destroyed them as habitats of fish and in most instances of water fowl, as well;

[3] Robert and Leona Rienow, "The Day the Taps Run Dry," *Harper's*, October, 1958, p. 72.

and the majority are pretty ugly and evil smelling. They are also something of a health hazard. In recent years outbreaks of infectious hepatitis have been traced to pollution of streams in Oregon and Utah; outbreaks of paralytic polio in New Jersey have been found by public health experts to be correlated with the prevalence of open sewers; polluted water has caused a typhoid epidemic in Keene, New Hampshire, and infection in clams dug off New York and New Jersey. On the opening day of the 1961 swimming season, the New York City Department of Health listed four of the city's beaches as safe for bathing, six as marginal where bathing is permissible in dry weather but dangerous in wet, and four (the largest) as so polluted that the Department does not even bother to test them.

Our water supply contains an ever increasing "dividend" of insecticides, herbicides, detergents, solvents, dyes, petroleum wastes, synthetic compounds, radioactive wastes, waste materials from canneries, hospitals, and slaughter houses, human wastes, myriads of germs and viruses, corrosive chemicals. The rate at which we pollute our water rises with every increase in our material level of living. Yet, increasing urbanization makes us ever more dependent on these same sources of water for satisfaction of both recreational and utilitarian needs. As our population increases, the effect of these forces is intensified.

The same three factors that in combination pollute our water lead also in combination to pollution of the air: population growth, greater concentration, higher material levels of living. The heaviest contributors to air pollution in the United States are automobiles (in pulverized rubber and asphalt, as well as gases), industrial plants, households, and municipal installations, in that order. If our population becomes still larger and more concentrated, minimum health standards will necessitate resort to costly control devices and far more stringent restrictions on both public and private use of the atmosphere.

But just as the battle against water pollution has so far met with few successes, so also has the battle against air pollution.

"We pledge . . . Federal authority," the Republicans cautiously and laconically wrote in their 1960 national platform, "to identify, after appro-

priate hearings, air pollution problems and to recommend proposed solutions." That was all. Candidate Kennedy's Conference on Urban Affairs showed a certain awareness of the problem and its origins in noting, "The air we breathe is fouled by exhaust fumes, industrial smoke and furnaces, creating a menace to public health. The problem grows more critical as our population increases." But its conclusion hardly outdistanced that of the Republicans: "We must act to conquer these hazards and purify our air and water, our two most precious natural resources."

The haze of polluted air that surrounds our cities is readily visible to anyone flying near them. On occasion it is also visible to those less airborne. Nor is this true only of the larger cities. A new York State report on air pollution in 1958 found that only one of the state's forty communities with a population of 25,000 or more had air pollution so slight that it could be termed "negligible." Among the smaller cities, either major or minor air pollution affected approximately 60 percent of those of 5000 to 25,000 population, and one-third of those with fewer than 5000. Whether or not they see it, those on the ground most certainly sense it — in smarting eyes, burning throats, headaches, dirty eyeglasses, shirts that require laundering after but a few hours' wear. But the problem is more than one of mere discomfort and dirt. There is growing evidence that contaminated air may actually initiate disease.

As long as the volume of wastes is related to the combination of material levels of living and population size, an increase in either of these will be accompanied by increases in costs, and in the need for controls. To the extent that future Americans will be able to live at levels as high as those current today, the already serious problem of pollution can hardly help becoming at once more hazardous to health and more burdensome to control.

SOCIAL SERVICES

Continuous, rapid population growth threatens the quality of life from yet another direction: the provision of social services. Many an American community already faces difficulties in providing such services as schooling, public transportation, roads, courts, housing, prisons, libraries, and nursing homes as a consequence of its rapidly expanding population. Inevitably, it seems, the supply and quality of social services must fall behind the greater demand generated by numerical increase.

There are three reasons for this. First is the difficulty of estimating future needs and appropriating for them. Though present requirements can often be determined with a fair measure of accuracy, the calculation of future demand is necessarily a much less certain undertaking. For one thing, fashions and attitudes change. So also do the size and distribution of the incomes with which a society's members can act on their beliefs or pursue the dictates of fashion. Twenty years ago, who could have reasonably predicted the present vogue in outdoor recreation, the extensive participation in costly sports like skiing and boating? Professor Charles Westoff predicts an increase in the mental hospital population over the next 20 years, not only because, as he says, "in its simplest terms, more people mean more patients," but because "people will become more educated about mental health and more sensitized to its importance." Given a general prediction like this, the problem is then to translate it into concrete estimates of the additional facilities and personnel that will be required — a difficult task even under conditions of population stability, but one made all the more difficult by population increase. Faced with such uncertainty on the one hand, and with appropriations that often involve thousands or even millions of dollars on the other, the easiest course is to play it "safe" with the public's money and appropriate with a view primarily to meeting present demand — with a fraction occasionally added to cover marginal increases in the future.

A second source of lag between need and provision of service (once a decision has been reached about the character of the need and an appropriation been made for it) lies in the time it takes to train the necessary personnel and to construct the necessary facilities.

There is now a shortage of physicians. There has been no increase in the last ten years in numbers of graduating doctors. We have been able to hold the line only by the importation of foreign doctors. Seventeen per cent of physicians entering practice in the United States last year received their training abroad.

In 1959 there were 5,000 vacancies in hospital staff residencies.

The situation is worsening. By 1970 there will be 33,000,000 more of us . . .[4]

Here we see clearly illustrated the consequences of a lack of population stability. For the demographic determinants of this shortage of physicians arise not only in the rapid increase in population since World War II, but also in the sharp decline in the birth rate during the depression of the 1930's. Had the birth rate either not risen in the postwar period, or else not fallen during the 1930's, there would have been no doctor shortage (other things being equal). But, as it was, the two worst things that could happen so far as the provision of physicians is concerned did, in fact, take place: a rapid and sustained *increase* in the birth rate followed upon a rapid and temporary *decline* in such a way as to maximize the demand for physicians at precisely the time when their number had been depleted through changes in age structure brought about by the earlier decline in fertility. Those nonexistent physicians of the 1950's and today were simply not born. Thus, we see the need not only for a ceiling on our numbers, but also for a minimal fluctuation in the number of births around that figure necessary to maintain the population: in short, population *stability* in the fullest sense.

Were we willing to mobilize our energies and resources to that purpose, a year or two might suffice to end *for the present* the shortage of hospital facilities arising from our growth in numbers. But under current professional standards it takes some ten years of college and postgraduate training to produce a physician. Thus, the number of new entrants to the medical profession in 1973 will have started training this year; the number of new entrants in 1972, last year; the number of new entrants in 1971, two years ago, and so forth. Thus, even if our population ceased growing to-

[4] Dr. Lindsley Fiske Kimball, treasurer and trustee of the Rockefeller Institute, quoted in *New York Times*, October 3, 1961, p. 24.

morrow, we would have a decreasing ratio of physicians to patients for at least another decade. The training of other health personnel — nurses and technicians, for example — takes less time, but recruitment into these fields has also lagged far behind our growth in population.

What has been said of health personnel can also be said in varying degrees of other skilled service personnel: teachers, social workers, parole and probation officers, for example.

Finally, population growth in the United States produces a deterioration in our social services because of the fact that a certain amount of overuse must precede any enlargement of facilities or staff. We do not add, say, 124 cubic feet to the local schoolhouse and one-fifteenth of a teacher to its faculty for every additional pupil. Relying on the private automobile to provide mass transportation may appear at first to be an exception — one more commuter: one more automobile. And unquestionably, the automobile does allow for an immediate adjustment of carrying capacity to the number of people to be moved. But to be an effective means of transportation it requires other goods and services — roads and traffic control, for instance — the expansion of which is subject to the same kinds of difficulties that we have observed to be the case with other social services and to which, moreover, there are definite geographical limitations.

Depreciation may be quite considerable before a community's efforts can be mustered to expand an overloaded service. How much pressure has to be generated before something is done will depend on a number of things: the nature of the service involved (roads seem to fare better than most other community services — certainly better than schools or parks), the financial position and predominant values of the community, its political leadership, etc. But there will always be a delay of some extent between the decline in quality of service that arises from its overuse and the awareness of the need to expand it.

The provision of social services for a growing population must of necessity be a never-ending race against the threat of declining standards. A constant upwards adjustment must be made to avoid falling behind. Facilities conceived to meet future needs may well be rendered obsolete by population increases between the blueprint stage and the time they are ready for use. Moreover, because of the difficulties of assessing future needs and of incorporating them into concrete programs, there is an understandable reluctance to undertake any long-range plans — the only kind that could be expected to measure up to the task. Thus the present administration in Washington is looking only a decade or two ahead in its plans for coping with the needs of Americans for additional housing, schooling, mass transport, recreational facilities. About what is to happen then, the planners are conspicuously reticent. Yet, the most optimistic assessment is that even if executed, these programs could succeed in little more than keeping pace with our growth in numbers. Without a concomitant cessation of this growth, any long-range improvement can hardly even be hoped for.

FREEDOM

If freedom for the individual can be defined as the "opportunity to achieve his goals without external restraints," the average American is at once more free and less free today than formerly. His freedom has been increased by the general improvement in his economic position, by his greater amount of education and training, his higher productivity, his gain in power through the extension of collective bargaining. It has been decreased by his country's involvement in a "cold war," and by the increasing size and urbanization of the American population.

Under present conditions the Cold War is probably the greatest single threat to those freedoms that distinguish a democratic from a non-democratic society: freedom of speech, thought, assembly; the right to oppose; the right to a fair trial; the right to privacy; the right to travel freely. What is threatened by the growth and concentration of population, however, are those more mundane freedoms which, for all their lack of dramatic content and emotional appeal, still figure prominently in our daily lives.

With growing numbers, life becomes more complex. There develops a wider range and frequency of interpersonal contact, and a greater competition for scarce resources like space, raw materials, air, water, and social services. At the same time, the need is intensified for fire and police protection, sanitation, traffic and pollution control, zoning, building codes, custodial care for the mentally and physically dependent — services that are far less essential to the functioning of smaller or less densely settled populations, and which, though capable of being handled by more individual means when a population is small, require increasingly collective action when it is large and growing. In combination, these social changes lead to an ever greater need for external control over the individual, for a narrowing of the range of his unregulated behavior. For as the complexity of life increases, there must be a corresponding increase in the organization of human activities to assure, first, the necessary minimum predictability in social relations and, second, the required efficiency in the use and distribution of scarce resources.

Were our numbers to double, many of what are today but trifling restrictions would necessarily be hardened into onerous constraints. This would be part of the price we would have to pay to achieve the efficiency in the use of land area and other resources, and in the provision of social services, that these numbers would make necessary.

Some of the means to this control over the individual are already in use. Others are being strongly urged. Though speed laws, traffic signals, stop signs are not especially burdensome, pollution ordinances, building codes, and zoning restrictions often are; and we can expect them to become even more so as further population growth brings about a necessary extension of their range. In urban areas, zoning is now so commonplace as to be generally tolerated — if not invariably welcomed. But opposition to zoning in rural areas, a form of control likely to become increasingly necessary with continued growth, will undoubtedly be more strenuous. Proposals made at a zoning symposium at the 1960 meeting of the American Association for the Advancement of Science suggest the possible shape of such controls in the near future: establishment of public corporations to buy land and hold it until conditions warrant its resale for the most desirable use; extension of the size of present government landholdings to include the most important areas for agriculture, watersheds, greenbelts, and recreation; a requirement that suburban developers exhaust the acreage unsuited to agriculture before being allowed to loose their power shovels on farm land.

In the longer run, of course, even more stringent controls would have to be imposed. To the extent that land could be allowed to remain privately owned in a United States with double or triple its present numbers, its use would have to be further and further circumscribed. Eventually, there could be no such thing as a "family farm" or a "place in the country" — or, under still greater pressure of numbers, even a backyard — whose owner could be allowed the luxury of determining for himself how he wanted to use it, whether to use if for growing flowers instead of for the production of food or minerals. In these more extreme conditions, the right of eminent domain would become little more than a museum piece; the idea that a man's home was his castle, something of a wry joke.

Continual population growth will require ever greater efficiency in our use of recreational areas, too. Ultimately, of course, a growing population would force the transfer of all such areas to the production of food and minerals, or to the provision of sites for housing or transportation facilities. But even in the very near future there is a strong possibility that pressure on these facilities will become so great that access to them will have to be considerably limited.

And when it comes to mass transportation the need for extensive controls is already blatantly obvious in most of our metropolitan areas, even with population no larger than it is now. The question presents itself with growing urgency: how much longer can the individual be allowed to exercise freedom of choice in the mode of transportation he will take to work or shopping? A source of pleasure and freedom on the open road, the private automobile was never suited to mass commutation. No matter how well organized the car pools, automobiles can move people at a rate one-seventh that for buses, and only one-twentieth that for rail facilities. In view of relationships like these, it seems certain that as cities strive to adjust to their growing populations, the freedom of movement afforded the individual by the private automobile will eventually have to give way to more efficient means of mass transport.

At the same time that population growth forces

a decline in the degree of flexibility allowed the individual it widens the gulf between him and his government. To be sure, such a gulf has no necessary bearing on either the efficiency of government agencies or the quality of their personnel. Nevertheless, the individual under these circumstances will have increasingly less influence both on decision-making and on administration. In 1900, the average Congressman represented 190,000 people. By 1960 this number had risen to 410,000. Letters received by Congressmen concerning any particular issue are now so voluminous that if they have any influence at all it is — to judge from the statements of politicians themselves — to be reckoned in terms of quantity rather than content: "My mail is running four to one in favor." In Australia, with one-eighteenth as many people as the United States, an ordinary citizen (not just an officer of the American Medical Association or an oil millionaire) can submit a question to his representative and actually have it brought up and discussed in Parliamentary session.

No wonder, then, that in the United States those who perceive their interests particularly at stake must resort to lobbying to receive a hearing. On his own, the individual citizen has hardly a chance. Yet with lobbying, because of its very nature, some groups will have far greater access to and influence over legislators and executives than will others. It is the well-financed, well-organized lobbyists for business, veterans, doctors, the military, farmers, and labor unions whose efforts meet most frequently with success. Compared with these powerhouses, the civil libertarians, conservationists, consumers' representatives, or peace groups are but 90-pound weaklings.

If the ordinary citizen must speak with a group voice to be heard, there is still no assurance that the group to which he attaches himself will actually represent *him*. In fact, the larger and more durable the group, the more certain is it that the sounds it makes will be representative of the interests of its leaders — men who, as the Swiss sociologist, Robert Michels, pointed out two generations ago, are, by their very positions in the organizational structure of the group, increasingly removed from the way of life and thought of its members.

So, with a large and increasing population, the individual finds his day-to-day existence ever more circumscribed: he must do certain things that he would not otherwise do and limit or refrain altogether from doing certain things that he would otherwise do. At the same time, again partly as a consequence of population growth, his chances of having a say at either the decision-making or administrative stages of his control are necessarily reduced. Yet, should he seek to gain a voice by joining with others who supposedly share his views, he is more than likely to find himself blocked, first, by the differences in the distribution of power as between petitioning groups and, second, by the system of leadership within the group itself.

The deleterious effects of population growth are all alike in one important respect: they do not arrive suddenly. With no dramatic warning of their onset, they creep upon their victims so slowly it is hard to tell when the attack began. Because these costs — monetary, social, and personal — do not come all at once, it is possible that man, with his nearly infinite powers of adjustment, may for a time grow used to them in much the same way that one grows used to a chronic ailment.

Yet, why (when it can be avoided) should we allow ourselves to become victims of the chronic ailment — the lack of elbow room, the air and water pollution, the destruction of wild life, the ever greater restrictions on our freedom of action — just because we might "grow used to it"? As John Stuart Mill wrote more than a century ago:

A population may be too crowded, though all be amply supplied with food and raiment. It is not good for man to be kept perforce at all times in the presence of his species. A world from which solitude is extirpated is a very poor ideal. Solitude, in the sense of being often alone, is essential to any depth of meditation or of character; and solitude in the presence of natural beauty and grandeur, is the cradle of thoughts and aspirations which are not only good for the individual, but which society could ill do without. Nor is there much satisfaction in contemplating the world with nothing left to the spontaneous activity of nature; with every rood of land brought into cultivation, which is capable of growing food for human beings; every flowery waste or natural pasture ploughed up, all quadrupeds or birds which are not domesticated for man's use exterminated as his rivals for food, every hedgerow or superfluous tree rooted out, and scarcely a place left where a wild shrub or flower could grow without being eradicated as a weed in the name of improved agriculture.

URBANIZATION

3 Urban Social Differentiation*

Raymond W. Mack · Dennis C. McElrath

As the world's population grows it is increasingly becoming concentrated in urban places. This urbanization of the human population brings about important changes in the existing way of life. Urban living calls for different patterns of social relations than those of the farm or small village. The number of potential interpersonal contacts increases rapidly as population grows larger and more densely settled. New and more complex forms of organization become possible in the urban situation. Specialization flourishes. Traditional and informal means of social control are weakened and deviation from traditional norms is tolerated. Urbanization transforms the nature of human society.

A high proportion of human ills and of social problems are clearly evident in the urban situation, and much has been written about the noise, the dirt, the frenzied pace, the congestion, and the degradation of the city. Man has yet to learn how to provide a gracious and pleasant way of life for all segments of the metropolitan population. At the same time large cities are found on all continents and urbanization is occurring at a rapid rate in the newly industrialized countries. How do you explain continuing urbanization in view of the well known liabilities of urban living? What does the city offer that attracts and holds new residents? What role might urban belief and value systems play in this attraction? How does the development of more efficient technology facilitate city growth?

Urbanization is the development of a social and spatial organization within which both the valued and the deplored products of a complex and elaborate society are allocated. The urban mode of distribution has been built upon a folk, peasant, feudal, and industrializing past. These backgrounds influence the present state of urbanization in contemporary societies throughout the world. They are the foundation upon which this process of urbanization has developed.

URBANIZATION

Is it possible to look at this process in broad enough terms to specify its impact on the distribution of choice and constraint; of ideas and products wherever it occurs? We believe so: to do this we shall first sketch the process of urbanization and then link it to its corresponding mode of distribution.

Scale

Urbanization involves the transformation of a total society. Only in the past century and a half has the world approached truly urban *societies*, in which a high proportion of the total population lives in cities. As recently as 1800, only 2.4 per cent of the world's population lived in cities of 20,000 or more; today over one-fifth of the people live in such cities. Furthermore, the proportion of people living in large cities has risen even more dramatically. By 1950 the proportion of people in the world living in cities was higher than that in even the most urbanized country before modern times.

* From Raymond W. Mack and Dennis C. McElrath, "Urban Social Differentiation and Allocation of Resources," *The Annals of the American Academy of Political and Social Science*, Vol. 352, March 1964, pp. 26–32. Reproduced by permission.

Between 1800 and 1850, the total population of the world increased only 29 per cent, but the population living in cities of 5,000 or more grew by 175 per cent, that in cities of 20,000 or more by 132 per cent, and the population in cities of 100,000 or more increased by 76 per cent. Then, from 1850 to 1900, the impact of scientific technology began to be felt in rapid industrialization. During this period, the total population of the world increased by 37 per cent. But, in this span of time, cities of 5,000 or more increased by 192 per cent, those of 20,000 or more by 194 per cent, and those of 100,000 or more by 222 per cent. During the next half century, from 1900 to 1950, cities expanded at an even more accelerated rate. While the population of the world increased by 49 per cent, the three size categories of urban population grew, respectively, 228, 240, and 254 per cent.

If this trend continues at its present rate, more than a fourth of the world's people will be living in cities of 100,000 or more by the year 2000, and more than half by 2050. If the present rate of urbanization continues to the year 2050, over 90 per cent of the world's people will live in cities of 20,000 or more.

Today, we have whole societies which can be called "urbanized." Over four-fifths of the people in England live in urban places; nearly 40 per cent of them live in cities of over 100,000. In societies such as our own, with radio, television, rapid transportation, and an industrial distribution system, what is a fad on Manhattan Island today is a fad in Manhattan, Kansas tomorrow.

Even if the present rate of urbanization should slow, the prospect is that the future will see an ever-increasing proportion of the world's people living in urbanized societies.

The most obvious change associated with urbanization is the development of a far-reaching network of interdependent activities. This network usually proceeds from the loose linking of peasant villagers to the city through tangential interdependence with urban commercial, religious, political, or military centers to the almost complete interdependence of an urbanized world. This change in the scale of society obviously affects the ways in which the products of civilization are allocated. For example, most of the world's pop-ulation lives in little communities on the fringes of urban society where interdependence with distant urban centers is slight and limited in scope. Redfield has noted the special place of "hinge people" in these communities. These representatives of limited areas of interdependence — the schoolteacher, the village priest, the merchant-traders, or the representatives of distant political and military authority — have special access to the benefits of urban civilization. They act as filters or transmitters in the system of allocation centered in the city. Their power derives from limited interdependence between village and city. Their role is important today and likely to become increasingly so as interdependence increases.

This description of the process of urbanization leans heavily on the aggregation of people in cities. This aggregation is one important sociological change which defines the process of urbanization. But, in addition to this increase in scale, urbanization is characterized by the accretion of control and co-ordination activities in cities and by the development of a network of urban centers.

Co-ordination and Control

Urbanization involves locating co-ordination and control functions in cities. Wide-ranging activities are originated in, funneled through, or transformed by the urban posts of command and co-ordination. This centralizing function is evidenced by the presence in all modern cities of a substantial tertiary labor force. It is a truism that the city is the home of workers whose major functions involve co-ordinating and controlling wide-ranging economic, political, military, and religious activities.

The urban mode of distribution, thus, always places the city dweller at the hub of the distribution system. Through his hands and mind pass the products of an urban society. His access to these products is built into a society where cities are the accumulators and distributors of the products of civilization.

Network of Urban Sites

Finally, the process of urbanization involves the development of a system of urban sites, a network of cities which jointly house a myriad of urban activities. This system varies widely in contemporary societies. Students have attempted to describe it in such terms as: primacy and a hierarchy of cities; functional specialization of cities; regional networks of dominant and subdominant centers; sheer relative aggregation of the population; cities vis-à-vis their hinterlands or vis-à-vis a peasant foreland. Clearly, this variety is crucial to the way in which the products of civilization are distributed. If, for example, a society contains a single, multifunctioned primary city with all other centers being much smaller, one would expect the flow of products and access to this flow to be quite different from those in societies with a lower level of primacy or a flattened hierarchy of cities. In the high primacy situation, the flow of ideas, beliefs, and products of civilization would be highly centralized in every institutional area. Control personnel and initiators of action within the major institutional arenas might well overlap. How different this is from the society where religious centers are separate from the economic and these from the political seats of power! Here, in a society with several large and specialized cities, one is likely to find centralization within each institutional area, but little overlapping and substantial insulation.

Increasing scale, centralizing control and co-ordination, and developing a network of urban sites — these describe the process of urbanization. Any society may be situated at a given scale, with a certain degree of co-ordination and control, and characterized by a particular system of urban locations. Each of these facets of the urbanization of that society influences the way in which products are, or could be, allocated.

DIFFERENTIATION AND ALLOCATION

The pattern of distribution which emerges in societies with relatively advanced levels of urbanization is characterized by three broad systems of distribution and deprivation: (1) occupational differentiation, (2) ethnic and migrant differentiation, and (3) life style or familial differentiation.

Occupational Differentiation and Class Access

Until the past couple of centuries, there has been relatively little differentiation of the labor force beyond that based on age and sex. Only within the last 200 years, with the technological applications of the discoveries of scientists, have societies existed in which a large proportion of the population learned occupational roles differentiated from one another on other grounds.

Other consequences of the growth of science and technology are elaborate occupational specialization and an increase in the content of culture. Bushmen do not have much more to transmit than one Bushman can know. Americans have so much more shared, learned behavior to transmit than one American could know that the task of organizing a program of general education becomes staggering.

A complex division of labor through a whole society leads to what some sociologists have called "situses" — sets of related occupational specialties arranged hierarchically parallel to and separate from other sets of related roles, which also are arranged in hierarchies. Each situs, or family of related occupations, builds up a set of norms peculiar to it. These occupational subcultures insulate their participants from the members of another situs. Doctors and nurses hold values not shared by railroaders and truck drivers; the occupational norms of the longshoreman are not those of the laboratory worker.

Occupational specialization contributes a good share to what we call the impersonality of urban life. People in urban-industrial societies have segmentalized roles. One may be an assembly-line worker, a Methodist, a Grand Vizier at the lodge, a father, a member of the bowling team. No one of these bears the same necessary relationship to another that the roles filled by a tribesman in an unspecialized society do. In a society which has not felt the impact of technology, one need only know a man's clan membership to predict his occupation, his religion, his educational attainment. Among the segmentalized roles which a man plays in an urban-industrial society, occupation is crucial. It is more specialized than most of his roles; he has an enormous investment in it. An adult male in our labor force spends more of his waking hours at work than at home; his work is likely to be a powerful factor in shaping his view of the world.

Societies with elaborate occupational differentiation, therefore, while bound together by a common culture, are at the same time fragmented by occupational subcultures. People who share an occupational history develop norms, enforce an in-group ideology, and come to serve as a reference group for each other. We see this at its extreme when physicists from the Soviet Union and from the United States have more to talk about with each other than either group has with the farmers from its own country.

But let us remember that role segmentalization is not synonymous with a fragmented social structure. The stuff of occupational subcultures can serve as the specialized urban-industrial worker's social substitute for community. Occupational codes can contribute to what Durkheim called organic solidarity; they can help replace the mechanical solidarity of the rural village. Occupational groups, with their shared values, can contribute to the sense of purpose which formerly was a function of the small community.

Various occupations, incomes, and amounts of education lead people to share different norms and to behave differently. In other words, the existence of a class structure leads to the development of class subcultures. And, in time, the subcultures themselves become criteria of placement in the class structure. Not just one's income but the way he spends it, not just his occupational status but his attitude toward it — these become factors partially determining his class status.

The evidence of differences in access to and enjoyment of the products of civilization includes variations by class in family pattern, religious participation, and many other culture patterns. People in the lowest income strata spend nearly three-fourths of their total income for food, while those in the higher strata spend less than one-fourth of their income for food. Obviously, this leaves lower-class families with not only less money but a lower proportion of their total incomes available for education and other expenditures which might improve their class position. The smaller amount of money available for purposes other than groceries is reflected in the fact that a sample of lower-class people exceeded those in wealthier classes both in symptoms of illness and in the proportion of those symptoms which were not being treated by a physician. Lack of money is likely to be only one of the factors accounting for this situation; lower education levels would make it less likely that the lower-income classes would be aware of the need for treatment of some symptoms.

The basic variables of class structure reinforce each other through the medium of life chances. People who have high incomes and college educations are more likely than those wo do not to be able to afford to send their children to college.

A person's occupation, with its concomitant income, education, and class status, affects greatly the likelihood that certain things will happen to him. An individual's position in the class structure alters everything from the chance to stay alive during the first year after birth to the chance to view fine art, the chance to remain healthy and grow tall, and, if sick, to get well again quickly, the chance to avoid becoming a juvenile delinquent — and, very crucially, the chance to complete an intermediary or higher educational grade. It is easy to dismiss many factors which are really life chances with the notion that the individual controls his own destiny: the statement, for instance, that class status influences one's chances to view fine art can be brushed aside with the retort that museums are free and that, if a person does not take advantage of them, it is his own fault. Such an attitude fails to take into account the power of subculture. A child reared in a slum area who does not even know about the existence of museums or who has been socialized to believe that painting is for "sissies" has different chances for art experience than one brought up in a wealthy home and taught that all respectable people know something about art.

The significance of class consciousness for social mobility lies in the fact that attitudes and values have consequences in behavior patterns. If one believes he can be mobile, he will try to be. One's level of aspiration depends on what he has been taught to believe about his present status and the chances and desirability of altering it. Research has shown that manual workers are aware that most of them are not going to rise to managerial positions and that, reconciled to the status in which they find themselves, they do not plan upward mobility for themselves but project their ambitions onto their children. But we also know that the ones most likely to be upwardly mobile are those who actively seek to achieve upward mobility. This being so, there is an element of the self-fulfilling prophecy in vertical mobility.

Thus, just as race can become an ascribed status through the social definition imposed by the culture, so can class subcultures make education and occupation, and hence income, tend to be ascribed.

Access to the products of civilization in an urban society is structured, then, largely by class position, and, for many, this position is likely to persist for generations. Underlying this system is occupational differentiation built upon the requirements of large-scale enterprise which has become the dominant pattern in each institutional area. Big government, big military, big business, big church, big medicine and welfare are the *leit motif* of a society characterized by wide-ranging inter-dependence and centralized co-ordination and control housed in a web of urban locations. As other societies move toward this kind of social organization and as peripheral societies become enmeshed in it, they, too, may be expected to generate similar patterns of occupational differentiation and a corresponding way of distributing the social products.

Ethnic and Migrant Differentiations

Building an urban society requires a massive movement of peoples; the process of urbanization involves a redistribution of the population in space. Since urban fertility rates are never as high as those in the hinterland, a growing *proportion* of the total population can be settled in cities only by a net migration balance from rural to urban areas. Further, as the scale of society increases, the concentration of population as well as other resources brings people into cities from an ever-widening geographic base. This means that the cities of large-scale societies not only are composed of a substantial proportion of migrants but of migrants from widely dispersed origins. Thus, both the *rate* and *level* of urbanization are reflected in the ethnic composition of city populations. Rates of urbanization affect the relative volume of migration, and levels are reflected in the dispersion of origins of migrants.

At a given rate and level of urbanization, cities are composed of a proportion of migrants from a particular web of recruitment bases. This compositional change, when compounded with the selective character of migration, provides a basis for ethnic and migrant differentiation in every urban society: the establishment of a socially defined ethnic and migrant pecking order.

Excellent studies of the "newcomers" have been carried out in New York, Yankee City, London, and from Durban to Dallas. They all point to differential allocation patterned along the dimensions of ethnicity and migrancy.

The fastest *rates* of urbanization now are occurring in societies with relatively low *levels* of urbanization. Under this condition, the cities of these developing nations will be composed of a high proportion of migrants, but these migrants are likely to be recruited from a fairly narrow hinterland. *Migrant* differentiation is important in these areas today. As they increase in scale and widen their recruitment base, *ethnic* differentiation is likely to become more important to the distribution of life chances. More advanced societies, on the other hand, with existing high levels of urbanization, are now experiencing declining rates of urbanization. Here, ethnic differences are likely to persist for some time while migrancy declines as a basis for differentiation and allocation.

Life-Style Differentiation

A third dimension along which variation in access to facilities and rewards occurs is emergent in the urban sectors of advanced societies. This dimension appeared first among fairly wealthy city dwellers. It is a variation in style of life which we often associate with suburban growth and the development of familistic orientation. Recent urban developments, including advances in transportation technology, decentralized production location, opportunities for women to work outside the household, and a widening array of housing opportunities, permit variations in life style. By now, in most American cities, all except the central-city ethnics and recent migrants have generally become distributed along a life-style continuum. At one end of this continuum lie the fertile, familistic plains of suburbia. At the other are the more centrally located, small family or aged apartment dwellers oriented to career or consumption.

Access to the benefits of advanced societies are distributed along this continuum as well. Benefits available to the familistic consumer are in some instances constrained and in other cases widened by the demands of his orientation and location. Opportunities for neighboring, local acquaintances and local area participation may be high. He may find a limited but intense local community. He has access to the patio or rumpus-room culture and the creative pursuits of a garage or basement workshop. For him, the benefits of civilization are likely to revolve around family, school, and the local area.

Much of this is not available to the career- and consumption-oriented urbanite, but just beyond his elevator lie all the resources of the old central city. All the variety, liveliness, and sophistication of modern society are stored at his stoop, and much of it available in a stroll or a short commute. These products are available not only because of location but also as a consequence of the way in which he may allocate his scarce time, resources, and social capital. He has neither the choices nor the constraints of familism.

Increasing concern has been expressed about the durability of this variation. In recent years, thoughtful critics have suggested that rampant familism and the apparent popular association of it with suburban location may lead to the destruction of the advantages of central-city urban life style. Jane Jacobs, for example, has deplored the systematic destruction of urban liveliness. Others have questioned the ability of the institutions in the core city to survive in the midst of growing sprawl.

The evidence seems to support the optimists, however. Variation in life style can and does persist even in the most sprawling metropolitan areas. Marked variations in orientation and consumption have been observed even within the white middle class in Los Angeles.

A close look at these newer cities and the fringes of the old preautomobile cities suggests that several changes are likely to occur in the near future. The first is that life style will become less bound to a locality. Familism can and probably will return to the central area, and urbanism may spread to the suburbs and exurbs. At the same time, many of the advantages of the old

urban core will be made more available to a diffused populace. This view does not deny the fact that the central city is likely to contain self-imposed ghettos of lively urbanites for some time nor deny that the suburbs will generally hold the familistically oriented community. Rather, we suggest that the differences will be less dramatic and that a much finer gradation will occur along the life-style continuum.

CONCLUSION

Our thesis has been that the process of urbanization arrays a populace along three major dimensions. Most of the cultural resources of an urban society are allocated via occupational, ethnic and migrant, and life-style differentiation. These three dimensions of differentiation develop and become effective at different points in the urbanization process. The occurrence of and persistence of ethnic and migrant differentiation apparently are contingent upon the rate and level of urbanization. Life-style differentiation appears to develop fairly late in this process of urbanization, while occupational differentiation arises quite early in the process and persists to relatively advanced levels.

Urbanization thus initiates a variety of systems of allocation. Ever since David Riesman added "inner-directed" and "other-directed" to the American lexicon, we have been asking one another whether there is too much conformity in American life. We worry that there is not enough encouragement of individualism, that we are too much a herd. We have, of course, a tradition of concern for fear we are too much bounded by social expectations; it has found expression from Henry David Thoreau to Sinclair Lewis. Still each new analysis of "the Organization Man" or of "mass culture" brings a fresh rash of sermons, seminars, and soul-searching.

It is, perhaps, a healthy sign that so many Americans worry about whether there is too much conformity in our society, but there is something wryly amusing about it, too. The people of the United States tolerate a range of behavior in their fellow citizens which the people of most societies throughout human history would have found simply incredible. Our society defines as acceptable a wide range of behavior and will tolerate an enormous amount of deviance in familial roles, educational policy, economic behavior, political participation, and religious beliefs.

Urbanization gives rise to a great heterogeneity in the population. Urban life leads to ethnic and migrant differentiation and allows people with a different skin color or language or religion to pass relatively unnoticed in a way that could never be possible in the primary organization of a folk community. In addition, the occupational specialties associated with the complex division of labor create differences in the population: variations in training, values, work hours, recreation patterns, and, ultimately, differentiation in style of life.

TECHNOLOGY

4   The Intellectual Foundations of Automation*

J. F. Reintjes

Some of the most important changes taking place in man's social environment are those involving the shift from human muscle to simple machines to highly sophisticated computer systems. These advances in technology have revolutionized man's ability to accumulate, store, retrieve, and disseminate information. The knowledge "explosion" of recent years would have been impossible without modern technology, and would soon be swamped in a sea of unorganized data without recent developments in data storage and retrieval. These same technological developments are radically altering the occupational structure of modern society by eliminating certain tasks, or at least greatly reducing the need for human labor, while at the same time they increase the need for new types of technically skilled personnel. This selection sketches the history of these developments.

* Excerpted from *The Annals of the American Academy of Political and Social Science,* Vol. 342, March 1962, pp. 1–9. Reproduced by permission.

What are some specific benefits that these technological developments should provide in years to come? What threats do they pose to personal privacy and individual freedom? Would it be desirable or possible to call a moratorium on further developments until we learn to cope with the present array of sophisticated machines?

Primitive man has left behind many examples of the implements he devised to sustain his livelihood. Clumsily fashioned first from stone and later from metals, these artifacts were principally tools and weapons which he used to procure sustenance and shelter. As civilizations progressed, these implements were repeatedly refined and made more elaborate in order that they would be more effective for their purpose. The crude stone ax gradually evolved into a well-polished and sharpened knife; the hand-thrown arrow was superseded by the spring-action bow and arrow. Collectively, these and all the devices which characterize early civilizations had certain features in common: They depended for their effectiveness upon the personal energy of the user, and they were designed so that the personal energy imparted to them was strategically concentrated in a manner which enabled them to accomplish their purpose. Thus, designs took the form of a sharp cutting edge, as in the ax and knife blade, or the shape of a needle-like spear, as in the arrow.

As man became more advanced, he became interested in devices which would conserve his personal energy and thus enable him to control its release at a rate more in keeping with his physical ability to regenerate personal energy. This interest led to the development of simple machines — such as the lever, inclined plane, wheel and axle, and the pulley — devices which enabled him to trade time for the opportunity to expend his energy at a lower rate. Through these devices he was now able to achieve a mechanical advantage, a capability which allowed him to put forth for long periods a sustained effort on tasks which would otherwise overtax his strength.

For thousands of years, man exploited his past and devised many ingenious and increasingly complex methods of harnessing, controlling, and releasing personal energy. As the occasion demanded, he found ways to combine his mental powers with muscular energy to yield manual dexterity and skills. To gain mobility at sea, for example, oar-propelled ships were built — first with a few sets, later with many sets arranged in double banks — and crews were taught to operate these in unison to give remarkable propulsion power. Writing, as a means of preserving and communicating information, was invented, and mechanisms for performing it were continually improved. In the realm of manual skills, pottery making, hand weaving, glassmaking, and building techniques were developed and refined to a high degree by succeeding generations.

Inevitably, the demands for goods to satisfy the trade and commerce which these advancements brought about created need for new methods of manufacturing and new ways of organizing people who produced the goods. An essential requirement was a new source of energy which could augment or supplant personal energy. Although use of domesticated draft animals and the harnessing of water power supplied this need in a crude way for centuries, it was not until the seventeenth and early eighteenth centuries, when certain key inventions and technological advancements came along, that it became possible to exploit the latent energy found in nature in a major way. In fact, the substitution of fossil fuels as an energy source for personal energy represented a major break with the past and brought about a series of interrelated events which, taken together, set the stage for the eighteenth-century Industrial Revolution

INFLUENCE OF POWER MACHINERY

Power machinery driven by the energy from fossil fuels characterizes the industrial scene of the eighteenth century. Introduction of this machinery interposed a revolutionary device between the worker and his workpiece and, in consequence, brought about drastic changes not only in his work habits but in his whole mode of living. For the first time he was concerned not so much with the control and release of his own energy as with the manipulation of mechanical devices which governed the release of energy by machines whose power was derived from outside sources. His productivity became more directly a function of his physical dexterity in controlling machines than of his physical endurance. His effectiveness as a worker passed beyond the stage of being personal-energy limited and entered the stage of being personal-skill limited.

The factory system of grouping workers together evolved from this new technology. Although workshops existed in ancient and medieval times, they consisted mostly of informal groups of people working independently, with occasional sharing of hand tools. The need for appreciable capital to defray power-machine costs resulted in a new approach to manufacturing, with factory owners providing the machines and workers providing the operating skills.

The prime inventions and discoveries which contributed to the eighteenth-century upsurge in the use of machines were those which made possible the exploitation of fossil fuels as an energy source. Noteworthy are the invention of the steam engine and several important refinements in metallurgical processes which yielded metals with the physical properties required in the fabrication of high-power machinery and machine tools. With power sources and structural metal thus assured, machinery of all kinds made its appearance in factories. Although power-driven tools for metal removal came into being at this time, it was largely upon textile manufacturing that machines made their greatest impact, first during the eighteenth century in Europe and later during the nineteenth century in this country. Quite interestingly, this industry seems to be relatively uninfluenced by the twentieth-century technological progress which has served to inspire modern automation.

Forerunners of present-day automatic-control and data-processing devices came into being during the eighteenth century. Included on a steam engine of James Watt was an automatic-control device for maintaining constant engine speed. The flyball governor was a mechanical device which rotated at a speed proportioned to that of the engine. It was attached to the steam throttle. Whenever the engine speed increased, centrifugal force caused revolving balls to move outward and, in so doing, to throttle the engine, thus reducing speed. A decrease in speed caused the opposite effect — additional steam would be injected and the engine would speed up. Continuous speed control was thus obtained automatically.

During this period, also, the French mechanical engineer, Jacquard, introduced a completely automatic loom for weaving patterns in cloth. In this loom, weaving instructions were supplied on a series of punched cards, and the various motions of the machine were carried out automatically in accordance with the previously prepared instructions.

Base of Modern Technology

Whereas eighteenth- and nineteenth-century technological progress had its roots mainly in mechanical innovation, modern technology is built upon a much broader base and stems from widespread advancements in the physical, mathematical, chemical, and electrical sciences, as well as from the exploitation of these advancements by the various engineering disciplines. The prelude to modern technology was the discovery of electricity. The enormity of this new-found force of nature became recognizable once it was realized that electricity is inherent in the structure of all matter and that matter and energy are, in fact, related. In rapid succession, there followed a myriad of events which served to expand many times over our store of scientific knowledge and engineering skills. Techniques for generating and distributing electric power in large blocks were developed, and ways were found to convert it back and forth among electrical, mechanical, and chemical forms. Ability to communicate with many people at remote distances was made possible first through the telegraph and later through the telephone, a device that figures importantly in every discussion of automation. The invention of the

vacuum tube not only helped to put communication on a global basis but also created a component which is common to many types of devices used in automation. With the advent of the automobile, the mobility of people on land was no longer limited by the extent of their physical endurance nor that of their domesticated animals. The invention of heavier-than-air craft further increased the speed of mobility nearly tenfold. A new kind of fuel was demanded for autos and aircraft, however, and, thus, impetus was given to the development of petrochemical refining processes.

But, if the scientific progress of the past several decades has made automation technically feasible, the economic and social patterns and pressures which this progress has brought about have largely created the need for it. As in all other stages of man's cultural and social development, the availability of modern devices, goods, and services which add to his personal well-being has generated intense demand for these things, and they in turn have motivated him to search for new ways to fulfill the demand. Automation is one manifestation of this search.

Originally coined to describe the production lines in the automobile industry, the term automation has gradually assumed broader significance and is now applied to almost any device which reduces the amount of human effort — physical and mental — required to do a job. One aspect of automation is aimed at continuous automatic or semiautomatic production and makes use of an integrated set of machines which permits a product to proceed through various stages of manufacture with a minimum amount of assistance and handling from human operators. An example of this form of automation is the set of machines which perform the various broaching, drilling, boring, and milling operations on automobile engine blocks, transport the blocks automatically from machine to machine in proper sequence, check tolerances, and stop the entire process if faulty operation is detected. Another example is an automatic-assembly machine which places the various electrical components of a radio or television receiver in their proper place on a printed-wire board and then solders the components in place.

APPLICABILITY OF AUTOMATIC-PRODUCTION MACHINERY

Mechanization of this kind is particularly suited to manufacturing operations which are repetitive and not subject to modification over large production runs. Since continuous automatic-production equipment necessitates an appreciable outlay of capital, it is most frequently employed in the manufacture of products for which there is a strong replacement market and in those industries which stand a good chance of profiting from their investment before product obsolescence or market saturation sets in. Bread making, electric-lamp fabrication, and cigarette manufacturing are illustrative of processes which meet these criteria almost to the letter. It is noteworthy that, in the case of cigarette manufacturing, the applicability of continuous automatic manufacturing equipment was recognized years ago, and cigarette manufacturers employed automation long before the word was invented. Each day, millions of cigarettes are manufactured, about the same number are consumed, and, in the past half century, really only two product-design changes have been made — one in length, the other through addition of a filter tip. Specific kinds of service which have to be performed repetitively in accordance with established rules are also appropriate for mechanization. As an illustration, the telephone companies make extensive use of mechanization in order to provide the quality, speed, and scope of service which are expected by their customers.

Feedback Control

Technologically, automation draws upon a broad spectrum of tools and techniques in our present store of engineering skills, but concepts which evolved from the great scientific effort put forth during World War II are contributing to the more spectacular aspects of the subject. One of these concepts is feedback control. This type of control is accomplished by feeding back either continuously or intermittently part of the output, or response, signal of a system so that a comparison of it can be made with the input, or command, signal. Should an error exist, a signal is generated automatically which tends to reduce the error to zero. Prior to 1940, feedback control was of a

relatively elementary kind, and usually a human being was included in the feedback system. In the control of chemical and metallurgical processes, for example, it was common practice, and in some instances it still is, to have human operators read instruments — pressure gauges, thermometers, pyrometers, and so forth — and to make adjustments manually in order to correct observed errors. In this arrangement the operator's eyes serve as an error detector, his brain is used first to compare observed readings with the correct ones stored in his mind and then to give a signal to his muscles which enable him to turn controls so as to minimize the error. Feedback-control technology enables this error-checking procedure, and many others of a similar nature, to be carried out continually and automatically through use of machines.

Feedback constitutes the heart of a class of automatic-control devices called servomechanisms. The distinguishing features of a servomechanism are the various circuits which enable signals to be fed back from one part of the device to another for comparison and error-correcting purposes and the ability of the device to amplify power. Command signals are supplied to a servomechanism at a low power level, and these commands cause a high power mechanism, such as an electric, hydraulic, or pneumatic motor, to respond automatically in accordance with the commands. The ratio of the power controlled to the power in the controlling signal may often be a million to one. Thus, by supplying low-power command signals to servomechanisms attached to the bedplate and cross slides of a power machine tool, a milling machine for example, it is possible to control the motions of the machine without human intervention.

IMPACT OF FEEDBACK CONTROL

Feedback-control technology has added a new dimension to automation in that it permits design of control mechanisms which are electromechanical analogues of the human neuromuscular system. In fact, servomechanisms might well be thought of as mechanical muscles which are under control of sensing instruments and uniquely arranged circuitry that perform essentially the same functions as the human nerve system. Because the manipulative ability of the human is sluggish, servomechanisms are excellent replacements in control operations which call for precision and fast reaction time. Also, because the human is limited in the number of devices he can control simultaneously, servomechanisms can readily accomplish control in situations where the number of elements to be controlled are too numerous for a human operator to cope with. More specifically, in a manual-tracking operation which requires a person to manipulate a handle in order to keep a pointer aligned with another which is moving in a random manner, it has been determined that the human can follow random motions satisfactorily provided the highest frequency involved is no greater than one or two cycles per second. Servomechanisms can easily be built to increase this speed of response at least fiftyfold.

Equal in importance to feedback control as a contributor to automation has been the evolution of the electronic computer. Extensive development work on computers was conducted during World War II. Their purpose was mainly to assist in pointing guns and bringing fire power to bear against targets. Data about the range, bearing, and elevation of a target in space were fed to the computer, together with information concerning target velocity, projectile ballistics, wind behavior, and so on. From manipulation of these data, signals were derived which could be used for the proper training of guns.

DIGITAL COMPUTERS

Just prior to and during World War II, mathematicians, engineers, and scientists also investigated the possibility of devising electronic computing machines whose central computational mechanism is based directly on numbers. From their efforts, there evolved the electronic digital computer, a machine which has greatly expanded the horizon for automatic data processing and computation. The characteristic features of digital computers are these: they have a memory in which large quantities of data can be stored in electrical form; they permit rapid access to stored data; they are able to manipulate data and to carry out mathematical computations at a high speed.

In performing their computational operations, digital computers make use of short bursts of electrical signals, called pulses. Each pulse persists for only a fraction of a microsecond (a microsecond is one millionth of a second), and number representations are formed by establishing patterns of pulses, coded in accordance with the principles of a number system. Because electronic circuits with two stable states (an "on" state and an "off" state) are easy to build and simple, digital computers operate in the base 2, or binary number system, rather than in the decimal system. Mathematical operations are carried out by manipulating the pulses of the number system.

Although the capabilities of these machines are being expanded almost monthly, it is possible to illustrate the general order of magnitude of the storage, access time, and computational speeds of representative machines now in operation. If it is assumed that this volume of THE ANNALS contains a total of 65,000 words and that the average length of the word is six characters (five letters plus a space), machines now in industrial use can store at least one half of this volume. With machines under development, storage of the entire volume is possible, and the trend in storage capacity is steadily upward. Present machines are also able to gain access to any stored word in about ten microseconds and can perform of the order of 100,000 additions per second. In the near future, the arithmetic-addition capability of machines will be more nearly a million per second.

Digital computers are quickening the tempo of research through their ability to provide quantitative solutions to highly complicated and complex mathematical problems. Thus, they are serving as a major contributor to our scientific growth and expansion. In addition, their memory, fast access to stored data, and computational features are making possible the automation of a host of routine, repetitive-type industrial and office procedures such as payroll computation, inventory and production control, accounting, and sales forecasting. These machines are obvious candidates for continued or future employment in banks for the processing of checks and accounts; in insurance companies for premium billing, accounting, and actuarial forecasting; in airline offices for quick ticketing and answers to queries on availability of seating space; in libraries for the automatic retrieval of information; in government service for making patent searches, the processing and checking of income-tax returns, statistical analyses, and processing social security data; and in practically any endeavor that processes, analyzes, or otherwise operates on large masses of data repetitively in accordance with a fixed pattern — and that can justify the capital outlay.

TAPE-CONTROLLED MACHINES

With the availability of feedback-control systems which simulate the human neuromuscular system and electronic computers to carry out decision-making and data processing, it is only natural that engineers have merged computers and control into the equivalent of a psychoneuromuscular system. These machines are known as digitally, or numerically, controlled machines, or. simply as tape-controlled machines. The latter term is an appropriate description, since commands that govern machine behavior are supplied in the form of coded numbers which appear as patterns of holes on paper tape or as patterns of magnetic-field intensities on magnetic tape. The taped information is fed to a digital data-processing machine which translates the code into electrical signals suitable for controlling servomechanisms. These servomechanisms in turn cause the machines to which they are connected to execute the motions or operations called for on the input tape. Thus, machines of this kind function automatically under direction of instructions prepared in advance by an operator who is not necessarily at the machine location.

MAN-MACHINE INTEGRATION

It should be evident, therefore, that modern technology has contributed heavily to the evolutionary progress of machinery. Not only can machines now serve as replacements for man's muscular energy, but they can also simulate in small measure his nerve system and imitate, however crudely, some of his mental powers. In certain situations, chemical-process control being one, where highly agile manipulative dexterity must be combined with mathematical operations,

machines can outperform humans. But the challenge resides not in machines as replacements for humans but in determining how men and machines can work together to yield an over-all system more effective than either when acting alone. Man-machine integration ignores full use of machines to the exclusion of human beings and seeks, rather, to make critical appraisals of the capabilities of each in order to derive maximum effectiveness from their combination.

Man-machine integration offers interesting opportunities for the future, and progress in specific situations is already being made. As an illustration, in the tape-controlled machine-tool field, the time-consuming job is the programing of the machines; that is, in the preparation of the great many coded instructions which are needed to complete the entire workpiece. These instructions define, in effect, the road map for the cutting tool. But many calculations enter into the determination of this road map, including allowance for cutter speed, cutter size, the type of cutting tool, the hardness of the metal being machined and, of course, precise statements about the various motions which take place along each axis of the machine. In the early stages of development of tape control, programing was carried out manually with the aid of desk calculators. More recently, methods have been devised so that large general-purpose computers can take over many of the calculations, thereby assisting the programmer in reducing the amount of time consumed in programing.

The next logical step for the future in tape-controlled machine manufacturing is at the design stage itself. Here a computer offers an interesting possibility to the designer as a partner in his job of creating a mechanical part to perform a specified function. Within our present primitive understanding of digital machines, it is conceivable that even now the tasks of making routine calculations such as stress analyses on trial shapes and of selecting materials capable of meeting various specifications on weight, kinds of materials, and expansion tolerances can be delegated to computers. But the more interesting challenge lies in the possibility of using computers to assist in the creative-design process itself. Much remains to be understood about the technology of computers, their use, and their relationship to the human operator before this will come to pass.

During the next few decades the work of researchers in machine technology will be motivated by the exciting possibilities for machines which can learn, possess the power of judgment, and assume properties of artificial intelligence. In their search for ways to build these machines, researchers will naturally turn to the human psychoneuromuscular system for clues. Succeeding levels of sophistication in machines will likely depend, in large measure, upon our ability to understand how the human accepts data, stores, processes, and releases it, and how he recognizes and manipulates patterns of information in order to develop powers of thought and expression.

CHAPTER TWO

Culture and the Normative Order

The term "culture" refers to the norms of judgment, belief, and conduct that prescribe the behavior expected of the members of groups, communities, societies, and other social systems. Usually, the symbolic and material products of behavior — books, buildings, machines, equipment, and other aspects of technology — are also included within the meaning of the term. Social norms and products have an existence independent of a group's members. They tend to survive even though the group's members may be constantly changing. Indeed, membership depends largely upon a person's conforming to his group's norms. Deviant individuals may be excluded, and if too many members violate their assignments, the group becomes disorganized, loses its identity, and eventually disappears as a social system.

Consider, for example, the chaos and bedlam that would occur in an ordinary classroom if the students and the teacher were suddenly deprived of social norms. Language would disappear. Symbols and other social objects would lose their conventional meaning. Communication would be reduced to physical contacts, unregulated expressions of emotion, and perhaps coarse gestures, such as beckoning, frowning, and so on. The pursuit of knowledge, or any other kind of organized activity, could not occur with any efficiency. Thus, social norms are essential to any kind of sustained and organized interaction between two or more persons.

There are several kinds of norms. Formal *prescriptions* are preserved in writings, paintings, monuments, drawings, charts, and other symbolic devices that have the official endorsement of an organized group. Illustrations include the legislation of governmental or administrative agencies, the Constitution of the United States, the Ten Commandments, the Magna Charta, the personnel chart of a factory or a business concern, the rule-book of baseball, and similar rules and regulations that are maintained by various groups and organizations. Formal prescriptions are usually sanctioned by authorized agents who follow official procedures in rewarding conformity and punishing deviant behavior.

Prescriptions are legitimated by official decisions and are usually communicated by indirect methods. A person can read the Bible in privacy, and an insurance company can handle its official business by impersonal means. Prescriptions are preserved in various kinds of documents and are not completely dependent upon face-to-face communication. They therefore have a high survival value.

Informal *expectations,* by contrast, are legitimated by personal experience and are generally communicated through direct interpersonal contacts. They are usually sanctioned by unofficial methods involving social stigma or ostracism for norm

The Normative
Basis of Social
Action

violations and social approval or prestige for conspicuous conformity. A familiar illustration is the set of unwritten expectations assigned to a given person by members of the different groups to which he belongs. The father is expected to be faithful, loyal, and attentive to other members of his family. The salesman is expected to display his wares and demonstrate their desirable features. Hardly any social situation can be imagined in which expectations are nonexistent. Even riotous mobs conform to certain normative conventions, and dissentient groups soon acquire codes of ethics which, although different from the codes of the broader society, may demand complete conformity among their adherents. Accordingly, the outstanding features of informal expectations are their ubiquity and their relevance to everyday affairs.

Informal expectations are primarily concerned with the details of human behavior, while formal prescriptions are more often related to general objectives or principles of action. In the classroom, for instance, activities are governed by a whole array of prescriptions and expectations. Formal statutes spell out the age and attendance requirements of students, the criteria for granting degrees and diplomas, and the minimum qualifications of teachers. Informal expectations cover matters of speech, dress, and conduct, except for extreme departures from the conventions. Mutual expressions of courtesy and an attitude of dignity are supposed to prevail in school. The teacher is expected to learn his subject well, to organize his materials, and to present his information in an impartial and objective fashion. Students are expected to study their assignments before class meetings, to attend regularly and punctually, and to participate with appropriate interest and attention. These social norms may survive to govern succeeding generations of students. They comprise an essential part of the classroom culture.

Social Change: The Normative Endorsement of Behavioral Modifications

Every social system maintains some sort of feedback relationship between stability and change. The persistence of interaction patterns is a basic characteristic of social systems, for without order there is only chaos. However, chaos may also result from unrelenting resistance against change. Changes in the external environment may demand changes within the system. Exhaustion of food supplies, for example, may force primitive food-gatherers to migrate, and the same effect may result from floods, fires, diseases, and other natural disasters. But changes may also be produced by forces intrinsic to social systems — changes in goals and objectives, in normative prescriptions and expectations, and in group structure. Therefore the changes we observed in human conduct may often reflect significant modifications in the normative systems that regulate man's activities.

Institutions, communities, and other organizations are often described as stable, repetitive social systems. They usually outlast the careers of their individual members. It therefore may seem to an observer that the social order does not change perceptibly, even though changes may occur in the behavior of individuals. This illusion is exaggerated in preliterate societies, where there is no information about the past except in memories transmitted from one generation to another. In sharp contrast are modern societies where it sometimes appears that rapid and incessant changes in laws and other norms transform the world in a matter of decades. Differences in the rate of change are only relative, however. Whether it proceeds by almost imperceptible increments or by dramatic upheavals, normative change is an essential feature of every social system.

The invention of language, especially writing and printing, makes deliberative change possible. Values, beliefs, and rules of conduct can be recorded and objectively examined. That which can be recorded can conceivably be modified. The notion that organizations can be modified gives man the capacity to think of alternative courses of action and to choose among the conceivable alternatives. How one alternative is chosen over another is the basic problem in the analysis of social change and planning.

The press of circumstance is such that nearly everyone, on occasion, takes liberties with the prescribed ways of doing things. These deviant acts, whether accidental or carefully planned, are *inventions*. If an invention is observed by other persons, if it meets their felt needs, and if it does not interfere too violently with the established order, it may grow in popularity and eventually become a part of the social norms.

Inventions rarely are sudden, cataclysmic events produced by geniuses. Ordinarily, two things are required for an invention to occur. First is the identification of a problem, and perhaps the belief that something can be done about it. In many cases, necessity is indeed the mother of invention. But the recognition of a problem does not insure a successful solution, unless the inventor has sufficient know-how and other resources to get the job done. Thus, the second requirement for invention is a background of sufficient skill and knowledge to give trial and error a good chance for success.

Invention consists largely of a new synthesis of existing information. For example, the automobile combined the four-wheel carriage and the internal combustion engine, both of which were developed earlier. Similarly, the vaccines for poliomyelitis, the atom bomb, and spacecraft were developed after tremendous amounts of time and money were spent on laboratory equipment, trained personnel, and trial-and-error experimentation based upon the best scientific knowledge. With an increase in knowledge and research facilities, accident tends to give way to planned experimentation as a basis for invention. The management of change thereby becomes a large and well-organized business.

Billions of dollars are spent annually by government and industry to increase the efficiency with which discovery and invention operate in many fields of endeavor. Perhaps the most apparent results are technological, with emphasis on the perfection of tools and devices that are necessary for waging wars or defending the country against attack. The ramifications of these developments are extremely pervasive, however. Already the modifications in social structure that are necessary to support them have had important effects on the daily behavior of people in all societies.

Once an invention or discovery has been made, it tends to spread from person to person and community to community around the world. This spread of a trait within a society or from one society to another is called cultural *diffusion*. People imitate one another. Artifacts survive and are improved long after their inventors are gone. Devices for the instantaneous analysis and transmission of information facilitate the speed and ease with which cultural changes can be made. The inevitable result is an increased interest in invention, along with the development of trained technologists whose specific task is the utilization of science in alleviating the world's ills.

Of course, people and communities differ in their willingness to accept cultural changes. Industrialization and urbanization tend to speed up the processes of invention, discovery, and diffusion. In addition, changes occur more easily in the fields of technology than in normative areas. For example, the manufacturers of automobiles, household appliances, and clothing make minor changes in design on a regular schedule to stimulate sales. At the same time, any deviation from traditional views about the nature of man, his basic beliefs and morals, or the nature of his social organizations is met with fear and suspicion. Accordingly, the laws and other norms dealing with society and human relations tend to lag behind the more rapid changes produced in the physical environment. This tendency for changes to occur at unequal rates in different parts of a culture is called *cultural lag*.

Cultural lag may be more apparent in modern societies than in earlier times. For instance, a peasant from ancient Egypt would have felt quite at home on a farm in the United States during our frontier era. Yet many Americans are alive today who remember that in their youth our society was without automobiles, airplanes, or electricity. In one generation, these people had seen the end of the horse-and-buggy era and the dawning of the atomic age. While modern technology has eased many of man's burdens, it has also created many new problems by its unanticipated consequences. Who could have foretold the size, complexity, and economic dominance of the automobile industry, the rise of freeways and service stations, air pollution, the political power of oil companies, and the growth of the commuter culture? And these are only the most obvious effects of the automobile.

Furthermore, the impact of cultural lag may be greater in the future than it is today. The automobile's influence is primarily a local phenomenon, by comparison with the supersonic transport, the spaceship, the communications satellite, and the electronic computer, which does calculations in a few minutes that would take a mathematician a lifetime. This new technology may have alarming national and international consequences. No doubt we will fly from New York to London in three hours. But will this make New York or London a safer or a more rewarding place in which to live? Many observers do not think so. As a result, there appears to be a growing demand for a reexamination of our cultural priorities, our basic goals and objectives.

Never before have the issues of war, crime, discrimination, riot, and other signs of social conflict had such wide impact and visibility. Nor has there previously been such an urgent demand for the involvement of scientists in public programs and policies. For these reasons authorities in all branches and levels of government have recently attempted to establish a responsible role for scientists, including social scientists, in the formulation of programs dealing with a staggering and always expanding array of social problems. Should a new rapprochement between science and government occur, there is little doubt that one result will be a reorganization of the normative aspects of many of our social systems.

Rational
Systems: Some
Problems and
Prospects

Demand for the reorganization of society receives an added impetus from some model systems that operate in fields of activity ranging from scientific research to organized athletics, and from small cooperatives for consumers to vast international alliances in health and finance. Urban industrial societies encourage the formation of rational systems designed to achieve certain objectives by the coordination of human effort, and to profit from the collection, analysis, and utilization of scientific information about their operation and experience.

Of course, no system is completely rational in its operation, because traditional influences and personal considerations always affect the activities of its members. But the concept of rationality prescribes an ideal to which an organization or a community may aspire. Rationality implies that the system's elements are interrelated in a logically consistent manner, that the assumptions used in operating the system are founded upon reliable information and knowledge, that the members' assignments are feasible and mutually compatible, and that the activities of the members are coordinated in such a way as to produce a cumulative movement toward their chosen objectives.

Rational systems may be described in terms of their elements and their major subsystems. The basic elements of a system are:

Goals specifying the system's main objectives and purposes.

Strategies spelling out the methods by which the goals are to be achieved and clarifying the assumptions that are made in the choice of methods.

Structures indicating the division of labor among the system's members, the social positions to which members are assigned, the channels of communication and authority, the patterns of access to information and other resources, and the like.

Roles detailing the behavioral requirements of the members assigned to any given position, including duties and responsibilities as well as rights and privileges.

Sanctions encouraging the members' conformity to their role requirements by the appropriate allocation of rewards and penalties.

These elements have feedback relationships which encourage changes that facilitate the attainment of the system's goals and discourage changes that may have harmful effects. Figure 1 portrays the relationships within the system as well as those that connect the system with the pilot variables in its environment.

In the analysis of social systems, whether they are rational or not, it is helpful to think of the elements as comprising three distinct but interconnected subsystems. The *normative* subsystem, consisting of cultural elements, involves the system's plans and prescriptions. It is a formula, or blueprint, for a desired state of affairs. The *action* subsystem refers to the actual behavior of the members, the way the system's plans and prescriptions are carried out in practice. The *reaction* subsystem includes the mechanisms by which a system profits from experience and corrects or adapts its plans and practices. The subsystems, in general, correspond to the regulative, active, and evaluative modes of behavior, respectively.

If science is to assist in the formation of a rational system, the first requirement is a comprehensive plan that prescribes the behavior expected of the system's members. Equally important, of course, are the enactment of the plan and the assessment of its effectiveness. The main problems of implementation and evaluation will be examined in the next chapter. Here we are concerned primarily with the normative subsystem, involving all the elements, as indicated below.

Prescribed goals and objectives. A rational system has clearly defined goals and objective criteria with which to measure the degree of their attainment. Although the major goals are to be achieved by the joint efforts of the system's members, there are often special subgoals for the people who occupy different positions. For example, social workers and psychiatrists are assigned the task of rehabilitating their clients, but their individual goals of wealth, prestige, and status may be dominant in certain cases. So long as the individual's goals do not interfere with those of the group, the system may operate with efficiency.

Goals are sometimes arranged in a hierarchy according to their relative value, and the system's members may choose among them in terms of personal interest and ability. Some students may prefer a rich social life over scholarship, although

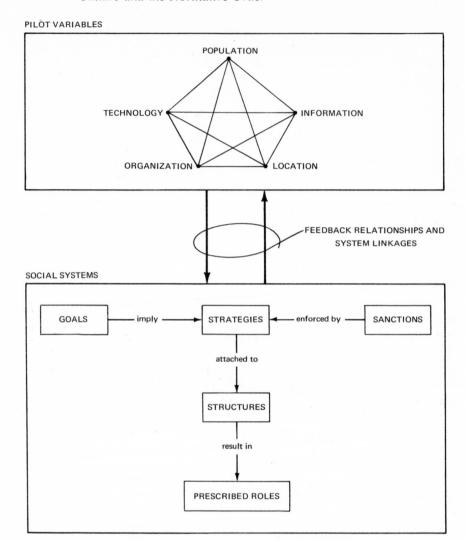

PILOT VARIABLES

SOCIAL SYSTEMS

Figure 1

Social systems, at any given place and time, reflect the state of the pilot variables, the degree of their development, and their interrelations. By means of feedback relationships, the systems produce changes in the pilot variables and their interrelations.

the latter presumably has a higher priority in the educational system. Again, goals may be arranged in a sequential pattern so that one must be achieved before another can be pursued. Thus, a high school diploma is usually required for entrance into a university, and a bachelor's degree precedes the award of a doctorate in law, medicine, or science.

Such goal specializations and sequences are illustrated in the operation of our correctional system. Crime must be defined before the criminal can be identified, and identification must precede corrective treatment. The definition of crime occurs by legislative action, while the identification of offenders is a function of the police and the courts. Treatment, in turn, is provided by prisons and other institutions, probation and parole agencies, and a variety of related organizations. But if the goals of legislators, police, courts, and treatment officials conflict, the correctional system is disorganized and irrational.

Of course, science has no special qualifications for telling us what our goals ought to be. But it can help in clarifying them, identifying their uncertainties and inconsistencies, assessing their feasibility, and estimating the kinds of knowledge and other resources necessary for their attainment. Certainly, the selection of goals cannot be separated from judgments on their practicality, coherence, costs, or consequences, and here science can often provide information of crucial significance.

Prescribed strategies for goal achievement. In rational systems, the strategies for achieving goals are based on tested knowledge and reliable information. They prescribe roles that are clear, feasible, and consistent. Role conflicts must be at a minimum. Conflict implies that one role contradicts another which is equally permissible within the system. Thus, a criminal court judge, in sentencing a convicted offender, may be required by law to employ the death penalty even though he may feel that capital punishment is immoral or ineffective. In the judicial system the law must prevail, but in the broader culture, both judgments are permitted. Such conflicts and strains are especially prominent in complex systems which require that people choose among alternatives that are of approximately equal merit, based on untested or mutually exclusive assumptions, or have unpredictable consequences.

Accordingly, a central concern of any system is the establishment of decision-making procedures which result in the most appropriate choices when alternatives are available. One of our most pressing problems is the lack of empirically validated theories dealing with politics, education, welfare, and the like. This is not to say that we lack theories of popular appeal or widespread usage. Rather, it asserts that, in the operation of social systems, choices among alternative prescriptions cannot often be made on the basis of evidence demonstrating the greater effectiveness of one over another. It is science's function to provide such evidence when commonsense views are inconclusive. However, the major focus of science has been on technological issues instead of on studies of the merit of social objectives or the adequacy of achievement strategies.

Prescribed sanctions. Rational systems provide for the administering of sanctions designed to encourage desired behavior and to inhibit inadequate performance. These sanctions may take the form of positive rewards or negative penalties, and they may consist of physical, symbolic, or social variables administered by formal or informal procedures.

Again, the main problem is that our assumptions about the consequences of alternative sanctions are based largely on unverified conjecture. Are rewards more effective than penalties? Does punishment for deviant behavior serve to deter other persons from violating the norms? Is punishment inimical to therapy? How do norms acquire their legitimacy? Answers to such questions are usually stated in moralistic or legalistic language that discourages research and tends to perpetuate our current state of ignorance; and in the absence of reliable knowledge, a chaotic conglomeration of practices seems justified. There is no aspect of social systems that is more in need of scientific investigation.

Prescribed structures. The structure of a rational system is comprised of a minimum set of social positions which clearly indicates the division of labor among its members, the flow of power and authority, the channels of information and communication, the relative accessibility of resources, and other work tasks. Generally, the fewer the positions, the easier it is for people to produce an agreement between precepts and practices. However, large and complex structures may be necessary, especially in social institutions and other systems that cover a wide range of activities, or in those characterized by an intricate division of labor, many specialized skills, numerous and widely scattered members, and feedback devices designed to help the system correct itself on the basis of its experience.

The nuclear family affords an example of a simple structure. There are three main positions: father, mother, and child. The system has a great deal of autonomy, an elementary division of labor, and usually its power is concentrated in one or the other parent. By contrast, a society's economy is ordinarily characterized by a complex division of labor, numerous focal points of power and authority, indirect and often concealed channels of communication, and various kinds of linkages with other agencies and institutions. Each type of structure has advantages for certain purposes, the family serving as the cradle of personality and a focus for the development of self-identity and a sense of personal worth, while the economy is designed to coordinate the varied activities of numerous individuals in the production of goods and the procurement of profit.

Some systems, especially the traditional ones that are noted for their stability and simplicity, ascribe positions on the basis of sex, age, and other characteristics over which the members have little control. Others open their positions to competition and achievement, and these may need objective indicators of special skills and abilities in order to make appropriate allocations of their personnel. Sometimes career pathways or position sequences may be prescribed for members who demonstrate superior talents, or for those who fail at their assigned tasks and need relief from certain duties and responsibilities. Such articulation of positions over time, a feature of many modern systems, implies a great deal of flexibility in the assignments of members, depending upon their interests and performances. In all this, an important influence is exerted by motivation and by the various kinds of linkages that may occur between personal systems and social systems.

Role requirements. The elements that finally coordinate the efforts of individuals are the diverse roles prescribed for the occupants of different social positions. Because the role prescriptions are attached to positions rather than to individuals, the system can maintain its identity even though its membership may be constantly changing. The system can be described and investigated independently of the behavior of any given individual or group. Such investigation may reveal contradictions, inconsistencies, or ambiguities in the role requirements, and these are indicators of disorganization within the normative subsystem.

However, a system's viability is assessed by its empirical consequences as well as by its logical structure. What happens when people actually perform their prescribed roles is an essential consideration. And what happens depends upon the adequacy of the system's assumptions as much as it does upon the fidelity with which the roles are performed. If the assumptions are faulty, the system is inadequate and irrational, regardless of the faithful performance or the attitudinal support of its members. This is why scientific research is indispensable to the formation of rational systems.

The above review of system elements and their interrelations makes it clear that rational organization is not frequently observed, even in modern societies. Still more important, however, is the extent to which rational organization is discouraged by groups and individuals having a vested interest in the *status quo*. Rationality requires that we clarify and test our assumptions, and this is perceived by many as a threat to the established order.

Thus, many people, especially in traditional societies, are taught that social assessment and planning are immoral or disloyal activities. This kind of argument makes senses as an instrument of social control. The dictator who can convince his subjects that democracy is not a feasible form of government, the religious sect which can convince its followers that obedience is the only road to salvation, or the parent who can convince his child that the ways of the world are inferior to those of his family, are all engaged in a strategy aimed at preserving their power and authority. Indeed, if we grant the legitimacy of their objectives, we may have to concede the rationality of their strategies. But faith in traditional authority is difficult to maintain in a pluralistic culture, and the current reassessment of basic goals and values, apparent in nearly all societies around the world, is evidence of a search for a higher degree of normative integration. Perhaps the concept of social systems, if elaborated and corroborated, can facilitate that search.

CULTURAL UNIFORMITY AND VARIATION

5 Uniformities in Culture*

George Peter Murdock

George P. Murdock here describes the early development of one of the most important research projects in the social sciences. This is the Cross-Cultural Survey, a central repository for the recording, filing, and indexing of all available information on many of the important cultures of the world. Duplicate copies of these files are available in a number of large universities. In order to file the voluminous materials on the different cultures included in the Survey, a detailed plan for the system-

atic classification of cultural data was needed. The construction of this classification system required that certain assumptions be made regarding the nature of culture. Murdock lists the following assumptions: (1) that culture is learned and transmitted from one generation to the next through interaction among people; (2) that culture is supported by verbal justifications or ideas; (3) that it satisfies man's basic needs; (4) that its change is adaptive; and (5) that in any given society it tends to form a consistent and integrated whole.

For a number of years, the Institute of Human Relations at Yale University has been conducting a general program of research in the social sciences, with particular reference to the areas common to, and marginal between, the special sciences of sociology, anthropology, and psychiatry. In 1937, as one of the specific research projects on the anthropological and sociological side of this program, the Cross-Cultural Survey was organized.

A year of previous experience in collaborating with other social scientists in research and discussion had made it clear to the anthropologists associated with the Institute that the rich resources of ethnography, potentially of inestimable value to workers in adjacent fields, were practically inaccessible to them. Working in the laboratory, the clinic, or the community, the psychologists, soci-

* Excerpted from the *American Sociological Review*, Vol. 5 (June 1940), pp. 361–369, by permission. Copyright © 1940 by the American Sociological Association.

ologists, and others made frequent requests of the cultural anthropologists for comparative data on various aspects of behavior among primitive peoples. Sometimes they wanted perspective, sometimes suggestions, sometimes a check on their own scientific formulations. In trying to assist them, the anthropologists found that they could usually cite a limited number of cases from their own knowledge and give an impressionistic judgment as to the general status of ethnography on the question. For scientists, however, this was often not enough. What guarantee was there that the remembered cases were representative, or the impressions valid? What was needed was access to a dependable and objective sample of the ethnographic evidence. Only rarely was it possible to refer the seeker to an adequate summary of the evidence; in the majority of instances, he could satisfy his scientific curiosity only by resorting to the vast descriptive literature itself and embarking on a research task of discouraging magnitude.

An actual example will illustrate the difficulty. Several years ago, a group of physiologists, working in the laboratory, had come to a series of conclusions with respect to the relationship between periodicity of eating and bodily health as reflected in measurements of weight, stature, etc. It occurred to them that the literature of anthropology should contain data by which their conclusions might be independently tested, and they referred to the author for advice. He was able to tell them that ethnographers customarily report the relevant data on eating habits — the number of meals per day, their temporal spacing, the degree of regularity or irregularity in eating, etc. — that physical anthropologists present the pertinent somatological information. Since the material had been gathered, it could be assembled and the crucial correlations drawn. To have done so, however, would have required several months of research, since the data had nowhere been summarized and it would have been necessary to ransack an immense amount of descriptive literature to assemble it. Understandably enough, the physiologists were discouraged from undertaking this promising but formidable task.

Other sciences have systems of abstracts, bibliographical aids, and quantities of secondary collections, by means of which the researcher can quickly track down the pertinent data and acquaint himself with previous research on any subject. With a few notable exceptions, anthropology lacks such aids. Its materials are widely scattered in descriptive reports, an immense number of which must be scanned if adequate information is desired on any particular topic. The factual data of sociology are in a similarly chaotic condition. It became apparent, therefore, that if these sciences were to be brought to bear effectively in the cooperative research program of the Institute, a representative sample of the cultural materials on the various societies of the world needed to be organized for ready accessibility on any subject. The Cross-Cultural Survey was developed, in part to fill this need, in part to facilitate a distinctive type of scientific research which will be described below.

The first problem was to devise a standard system of classification for the arrangement and use of the collected materials. After six months of preliminary research, with the aid of helpful suggestions from about a hundred anthropologists, sociologists, and other specialists, the author and five collaborators published the *Outline of Cultural Materials*. Although the manual has proved of some incidental utility in field research, it was in no sense designed for such a purpose. It was written solely as a guide for organizing and filing our abstracted cultural materials, and for facilitating reference to the data already classified and filed.

Since the publication of the manual, in 1938, the staff of the Cross-Cultural Survey has been engaged in the actual assembling of materials. To date, the descriptive data on nearly a hundred cultures have been abstracted, classified, and filed.[1] It is hoped ultimately to assemble and organize all the available cultural information on several hundred peoples, who will be adequately distributed with regard to geography and fairly representative of all major types and levels of culture. Although primitive cultures will preponderate numerically, because they reveal the widest range of human

[1] EDITOR'S NOTE. This article was written in 1940. The Cross-Cultural Survey was reorganized after World War II on an inter-university basis as the Human Relations Area Files. As of September, 1963, the number of cultures classified in the combined Area Files and Cross-Cultural Survey totaled 298.

behavioral variations, there will be a fair representation of the historical civilizations of the past, of modern folk cultures, and of the communities studied by contemporary sociologists.

For each of the cultures analyzed, the entire literature is covered, including manuscript materials when available. In some instances, more than a hundred books and articles have been combed for a single tribe or historical period. All material in foreign languages has been translated into English. The information, if of any conceivable cultural relevance, is transcribed in full — in verbatim quotations or exact translations. The object has been to record the data so completely that, save in rare instances, it will be entirely unnecessary for a researcher using the files to consult the original sources. Mere abstracts are deemed unsatisfactory and are resorted to only in exceptional cases, when the information is excessively detailed or technical. The *Outline of Cultural Materials* is not a "trait list," nor are the files confined to data on the items listed on it. These items are merely suggestions as to the kinds of material to be filed — or sought — under a particular heading, and they make no pretense of being exhaustive. Special pains are taken to preserve intact the functional relationships of the data. Wherever division according to the categories of the manual would be arbitrary, or would destroy the context, the original account is preserved intact and is filed in one place, with a carbon copy or a cross-reference slip under each category to which the information is pertinent. Each file, moreover, contains a short synopsis of the total culture to which any note can be referred for context.

The collection of organized and classified materials in the files of the Cross-Cultural Survey should prove useful in nearly every type of research which anthropologists and other social scientists have hitherto pursued. If an investigator wishes to study a particular culture, he will find all the data, from whatever source, organized conveniently for his use. If he is interested in a topic, he can run through the material under one or more headings for as many cultures as he likes, and secure his information in a mere fraction of the time required to comb the sources for himself. If he desires to test an hypothesis, he can similarly examine the material under two or more cate-

gories and obtain a quantitative check in the form of a correlation. A cross-cultural test of the physiologists' hypothesis on the periodicity of eating, alluded to above, could, for example, probably now be made with not more than two days of research. Even regional or distributional studies are possible for areas, like the Gran Chaco of South America, on which the files approach completeness. The Cross-Cultural Survey, in short, should prove useful in a wide variety of scientific researches for which ready access to a body of organized cultural data is needed. It is intended, of course, to make the material generally available on a cooperative basis. Recent users of the files include — to cite but a few examples — a sociologist analyzing social classes, a psychologist interested in adolescent problems, and a psychiatrist seeking cultural definitions of insanity.

In addition to its practical objective of facilitating diverse forms of social science research, the Cross-Cultural Survey has a special theoretical objective. It is organized so as to make possible the formulation and verification, on a large scale and by quantitative methods, of scientific generalizations of a universally human or cross-cultural character. Sociologists and most other social scientists regard the establishment of generalizations or "laws," i.e., verified statements of correlations between phenomena, as their primary aim, but anthropologists tend to shy away from theory, as Kluckhohn has pointed out, and to confine themselves to historical rather than scientific interpretations of their subject matter. Nevertheless, it seems premature to conclude that anthropology cannot be made a science until, using all known safeguards, we have made at least one serious and systematic attempt to formulate scientific generalizations about man and culture which will withstand a quantitative test. Anthropology has many objectives. That envisaged by the Cross-Cultural Survey is not intended to supplant the others, nor does it lay claim to greater importance. It is simply regarded as legitimate, promising, and opposed by no insuperable theoretical obstacles.

The plan rests, at bottom, on the conviction that all human cultures, despite their diversity, have fundamentally a great deal in common, and that these common aspects are susceptible to scientific analysis. Its theoretical orientation may be expressed in a series of seven basic assumptions.

These are not claimed to be original, since many of them are shared by all social scientists, and all of them by many.

1. *Culture Is Learned*. Culture is not instinctive, or innate, or transmitted biologically, but is composed of habits, i.e., learned tendencies to react, acquired by each individual through his own life experience after birth. The principles of learning are known to be essentially the same, not only for all mankind but also for most species. Hence, we should expect all cultures, being learned, to reveal certain uniformities reflecting this universal common factor.

2. *Culture Is Inculcated*. All animals are capable of learning, but man alone seems able, in any considerable measure, to pass on his acquired habits to his offspring. The factor of language presumably accounts for man's preeminence in this respect.

3. *Culture Is Social*. Habits of the cultural order are not only inculcated and thus transmitted over time; they are also social, that is, shared by human beings living in organized aggregates or societies and kept relatively uniform by social pressure. They are, in short, group habits. The habits which the members of a social group share with one another constitute the culture of that group.

4. *Culture Is Ideational*. To a considerable extent, the group habits of which culture consists are conceptualized (or verbalized) as ideal norms or patterns of behavior. Most people show in marked degree an awareness of their own cultural norms, an ability to differentiate them from purely individual habits, and a facility in conceptualizing and reporting them in detail, including the circumstances where each is considered appropriate and the sanctions to be expected for nonconformity.

5. *Culture Is Gratifying*. Culture always, and necessarily, satisfies basic biological needs and secondary needs derived therefrom. Its elements are tested habitual techniques for gratifying human impulses in man's interaction with the external world of nature and fellow man. This assumption is an inescapable conclusion from modern stimulus-response psychology.

6. *Culture Is Adaptive*. Culture changes; and the process of change appears to be an adaptive one, comparable to evolution in the organic realm but of a different order.

7. *Culture Is Integrative*. As one product of the adaptive process, the elements of a given culture tend to form a consistent and integrated whole.

If the seven fundamental assumptions enumerated above, or even any considerable proportion of them, are valid, then it must necessarily follow that human cultures in general, despite their historical diversity, will exhibit certain regularities or recurrences which are susceptible to scientific analysis, and which, under such analysis, should yield a body of scientific generalizations. A primary objective of the Cross-Cultural Survey is to formulate and test generalizations of this sort.

6   The Diversity of Cultures*

Ruth Benedict

In the following selection the universality of behavior patterns in different societies is discussed. Most of us tend to regard our society and our ways

* Excerpt from Ruth Benedict, *Patterns of Culture.* Boston: Houghton Mifflin Company, 1934, pp. 22–37. Used by permission of the publisher. Copyright © 1962 by Ruth Valentine.

of doing things as normal and correct. This tendency is called *ethnocentrism*. The social scientist learns to avoid enthnocentric interpretations of behavior and broadens his perspective by studying cultures that are very different from his own. The naïve student might think that the transition from puberty to adulthood, and the resulting changes in behavior, are simply a biological matter that occurs uniformly in all societies. This, of course, is not the whole truth by any means. The behavior of a person is more significantly influenced by his culture and the expectations of his elders and peers than by biological factors. The plasticity of human nature is verified by the many varied and conflicting activities that are regarded as normal in different societies.

Before reading this selection, try to answer these questions: Is war inevitable because of man's natural pugnacity? Is capitalism more consistent with human nature than other types of economy? Is puberty always characterized by self-consciousness and feelings of guilt?

The course of life and the pressure of environment, not to speak of the fertility of human imagination, provide an incredible number of possible leads, all of which, it appears, may serve a society to live by. There are the schemes of ownership, with the social hierarchy that may be associated with possessions; there are material things and their elaborate technology; there are all the facets of sex life, parenthood and post-parenthood; there are the guilds or cults which may give structure to the society; there is economic exchange; there are the gods of supernatural sanctions. Each one of these and many more may be followed out with a cultural and ceremonial elaboration which monopolizes the cultural energy and leaves small surplus for the building of other traits. Aspects of life that seem to us most important have been passed over with small regard by peoples whose culture, oriented in another direction, has been far from poor. Or the same trait may be so greatly elaborated that we reckon it as fantastic.

It is in cultural life as it is in speech; selection is the prime necessity. The numbers of sounds that can be produced by our vocal cords and our oral and nasal cavities are practically unlimited. The three or four dozen of the English language are a selection which coincides not even with those of such closely related dialects as German and French. The total that are used in different languages of the world no one has ever dared to estimate. But each language must make its selection and abide by it on pain of not being intelligible at all. A language that used even a few hundred of the possible — and actually recorded — phonetic elements could not be used for communication. On the other hand a great deal of our misunderstanding of languages unrelated to our own has arisen from our attempts to refer alien phonetic systems back to ours as a point of reference. We recognize only one *k*. If other people have five *k* sounds placed in different positions in the throat and mouth, distinctions of vocabulary and of syntax that depend on these differences are impossible to us until we master them. We have a *d* and an *n*. They may have an intermediate sound which, if we fail to identify it, we write now *d* and now *n*, introducing distinctions which do not exist. The elementary prerequisite of linguistic analysis is a consciousness of these incredibly numerous available sounds from which each language makes its own selections.

In culture too we must imagine a great arc on which are ranged the possible interests provided either by the human age-cycle or by the environment or by man's various activities. A culture that capitalized even a considerable proportion of these would be as unintelligible as a language that used all the clicks, all the glottal stops, all the labials, dentals, sibilants, and gutturals from voiceless to voiced and from oral to nasal. Its identity as a culture depends upon the selection of some segments of this arc. Every human society everywhere has made such selection in its cultural institutions. Each from the point of view of another ignores fundamentals and exploits irrelevancies. One culture hardly recognizes monetary values; another has made them fundamental in every field of behavior. In one society technology is unbelievably slighted even in those aspects of life which seem necessary to ensure survival; in another, equally simple, technological achievements are complex and fitted with admirable nicety to the situation. One builds an enormous cultural superstructure upon adolescence, one upon death, one upon after-life.

The case of adolescence is particularly interesting, because it is in the limelight in our own civilization and because we have plentiful information from other cultures. In our own civilization a whole library of psychological studies has emphasized the inevitable unrest of the period of puberty. It is in our tradition a physiological state as definitely characterized by domestic explosions and rebellion as typhoid is marked by fever. There is no question of the facts. They are common in America. The question is rather of their inevitability.

The most casual survey of the ways in which

different societies have handled adolescence makes one fact inescapable: even in those cultures which have made most of the trait, the age upon which they focus their attention varies over a great range of years. At the outset, therefore, it is clear that the so-called puberty institutions are a misnomer if we continue to think of biological puberty. The puberty they recognize is social, and the ceremonies are a recognition in some fashion or other of the child's new status of adulthood. This investiture with new occupations and obligations is in consequence as various and as culturally conditioned as the occupations and obligations themselves. If the sole honourable duty of manhood is conceived to be deeds of war, the investiture of the warrior is later and of a different sort from that in a society where adulthood gives chiefly the privilege of dancing in a representation of masked gods. In order to understand puberty institutions, we do not most need analyses of the necessary nature of *rites de passage;* we need rather to know what is identified in different cultures with the beginning of adulthood and their methods of admitting to the new status. Not biological puberty, but what adulthood means in that culture conditions the puberty ceremony.

Adulthood in central North America means warfare. Honor in it is the great goal of all men. The constantly recurring theme of the youth's coming-of-age, as also of preparation for the war-path at any age, is a magic ritual for success in war. They torture not one another, but themselves: they cut strips of skin from their arms and legs, they strike off their fingers, they drag heavy weights pinned to their chest or leg muscles. Their reward is enhanced prowess in deeds of warfare.

In Australia, on the other hand, adulthood means participation in an exclusively male cult whose fundamental trait is the exclusion of women. Any woman is put to death if she so much as hears the sound of the bull-roarer at the ceremonies, and she must never know of the rites. Puberty ceremonies are elaborate and symbolic repudiations of the bonds with the female sex; the men are symbolically made self-sufficient and the wholly responsible element of the community. To attain this end they use drastic sexual rites and bestow supernatural guarantees.

The clear physiological facts of adolescence,

therefore, are first socially interpreted even where they are stressed. But a survey of puberty institutions makes clear a further fact: puberty is physiologically a different matter in the life-cycle of the male and the female. If cultural emphasis followed the physiological emphasis, girls' ceremonies would be more marked than boys'; but it is not so. The ceremonies emphasize a social fact: the adult prerogatives of man are more far-reaching in every culture than women's, and consequently, as in the above instances, it is more common for societies to take note of this period in boys than in girls.

Girls and boys' puberty, however, may be socially celebrated in the same tribe in identical ways. Where, as in the interior of British Columbia, adolescent rites are a magical training for all occupations, girls are included on the same terms as boys. Boys roll stones down mountains and beat them to the bottom to be swift of foot, or throw gambling-sticks to be lucky in gambling; girls carry water from distant springs, or drop stones down inside their dresses that their children may be born as easily as the pebble drops to the ground.

In such a tribe as the Nandi of the lake region of East Africa, also, girls and boys share an even-handed puberty rite, though, because of the man's dominant role in the culture, his boyhood training period is more stressed than the woman's. Here adolescent rites are an ordeal inflicted by those already admitted to adult status upon those they are now forced to admit. They require of them the most complete stoicism in the face of ingenious tortures associated with circumcision. The rites for the two sexes are separate, but they follow the same pattern. In both the novices wear for the ceremony the clothing of their sweethearts. During the operation their faces are watched for any twinge of pain, and the reward of bravery is given with great rejoicing by the lover, who runs forward to receive back some of his adornments. For both the girl and the boy the rites mark their *entrée* into a new sex status; the boy is now a warrior and may take a sweetheart, the girl is marriageable. The adolescent tests are for both a premarital ordeal in which the palm is awarded by their lovers.

Puberty rites may also be built upon the facts of girls' puberty and admit of no extension to boys. One of the most naïve of these is the institution of the fatting-house for girls in Central Africa. In the region where feminine beauty is all but identified with obesity, the girl at puberty is segregated, sometimes for years, fed with sweet and fatty foods, allowed no activity, and her body rubbed assiduously with oils. She is taught during this time her future duties, and her seclusion ends with a parade of her corpulence that is followed by her marriage to her proud bridegroom. It is not regarded as necessary for the man to achieve pulchritude before marriage in a similar fashion.

Do not all cultures have to cope with the natural turbulence of this period, even though it may not be given institutional expression? Dr. Mead has studied this question in Samoa. There the girl's life passes through well-marked periods. Her first years out of babyhood are passed in small neighborhood gangs of age mates from which the little boys are strictly excluded. The corner of the village to which she belongs is all-important, and the little boys are traditional enemies. She has one duty, that of baby-tending, but she takes the baby with her rather than stay home to mind it, and her play is not seriously hampered. A couple of years before puberty, when she grows strong enough to have more difficult tasks required of her and old enough to learn more skilled techniques, the little girls' play group in which she grew up ceases to exist. She assumes woman's dress and must contribute to the work of the household. It is an uninteresting period of life to her and quite without turmoil. Puberty brings no change at all.

A few years after she has come of age, she will begin the pleasant years of casual and irresponsible love affairs that she will prolong as far as possible into the period when marriage is already considered fitting. Puberty itself is marked by no social recognition, no change of attitude or of expectancy. Her pre-adolescent shyness is supposed to remain unchanged for a couple of years. The girl's life in Samoa is blocked out by other considerations than those of physiological sex maturity, and puberty falls in a particularly unstressed and peaceful period during which no adolescent conflicts manifest themselves. Adolescence, therefore, may not only be culturally passed over without ceremonial; it may also be without importance in the emotional life of the child and in the attitude of the village toward her.

Warfare is another social theme that may or may not be used in any culture. Where war is made much of, it may be with contrasting objectives, with contrasting organization in relation to the state, and with contrasting sanctions. War may be, as it was among the Aztecs, a way of getting captives for the religious sacrifices. Since the Spaniards fought to kill, according to Aztec standards they broke the rules of the game. The Aztecs fell back in dismay and Cortez walked as victor into the capital.

There are even quainter notions, from our standpoint, associated with warfare in different parts of the world. For our purposes it is sufficient to notice those regions where organized resort to mutual slaughter never occurs between social groups. Only our familiarity with war makes it intelligible that a state of warfare should alternate with a state of peace in one tribe's dealings with another. The idea is quite common over the world, of course. But on the one hand it is impossible for certain peoples to conceive the possibility of a state of peace, which in their notion would be equivalent to admitting enemy tribes to the category of human beings, which by definition they are not, even though the excluded tribe may be of their own race and culture.

On the other hand, it may be just as impossible for a people to conceive of the possibility of a state of war. Rasmussen tells of the blankness with which the Eskimo met his exposition of our custom. Eskimos very well understand the act of killing a man. If he is in your way, you cast up your estimate of your own strength, and if you are ready to take it upon yourself, you kill him. If you are strong, there is no social retribution. But the idea of an Eskimo village going out against another Eskimo village in battle array or a tribe against tribe, or even of another village being fair game in ambush warfare, is alien to them. All killing comes under one head, and is not separated, as ours is, into categories, the one meritorious, the other a capital offense.

I myself tried to talk of warfare to the Mission Indians of California, but it was impossible. Their misunderstanding of warfare was abysmal. They did not have the basis in their own culture upon which the idea could exist, and their attempts to reason it out reduced the great wars to which we are able to dedicate ourselves with moral fervor to the level of alley brawls. They did not happen to have a cultural pattern that distinguished between them.

War is, we have been forced to admit even in the face of its huge place in our own civilization, an asocial trait. In the chaos following the World War all the wartime arguments that expounded its fostering of courage, of altruism, of spiritual values, gave out a false and offensive ring. War in our own civilization is as good an illustration as one can take of the destructive lengths to which the development of a culturally selected trait may go. If we justify war, it is because all peoples always justify the traits of which they find themselves possessed, not because war will bear an objective examination of its merits.

Warfare is not an isolated case. From every part of the world and from all levels of cultural complexity it is possible to illustrate the overweening and finally often the asocial elaboration of a cultural trait. Those cases are clearest where, as in dietary or mating regulations, for example, traditional usage runs counter to biological drives. Social organization, in anthropology, has a quite specialized meaning owing to the unanimity of all human societies in stressing relationship groups within which marriage is forbidden. No known people regard all women as possible mates. This is not an effort, as is so often supposed, to prevent inbreeding in our sense, for over great parts of the world it is an own cousin, often the daughter of one's mother's brother, who is the predestined spouse. The relatives to whom the prohibition refers differ utterly among different peoples, but all human societies are alike in placing a restriction. No human idea has received more constant and complex elaboration in culture than this of incest. The incest groups are often the most important functioning units of the tribe, and the duties of every individual in relation to any other are defined by their relative positions in these groups. These groups function as units in religious ceremonials and in cycles of economic exchange, and it is impossible to exaggerate the importance of the role they have played in social history.

Some areas handle the incest tabu with moderation. In spite of the restrictions there may be a considerable number of women available for a man to marry. In others the group that is tabu has been extended by a social fiction to include vast numbers of individuals who have no traceable ancestors in common, and choice of a mate is in consequence excessively limited. This social fiction receives unequivocal expression in the terms of relationship which are used. Instead of distinguishing lineal from collateral kin as we do in the distinction between father and uncle, brother and cousin, one term means literally "man of my father's group (relationship, locality, etc.) of his generation," not distinguishing between direct and collateral lines, but making other distinctions that are foreign to us. Certain tribes of eastern Australia use an extreme form of this so-called classificatory kinship system. Those whom they call brothers and sisters are all those of their generation with whom they recognize any relationship. There is no cousin category or anything that corresponds to it; all relatives of one's own generation are one's brothers and sisters.

This manner of reckoning relationship is not uncommon in the world, but Australia has in addition an unparalleled horror of sister marriage and an unparalleled development of exogamous restrictions. So the Kurnai, with their extreme classificatory relationship system, feel the Australian horror of sex relationship with all their "sisters," that is, women of their own generation who are in any way related to them. Besides this the Kurnai have strict locality rules in the choice of a mate. Sometimes two localities, out of the fifteen or sixteen of which the tribe is composed, must exchange women, and can have no mates in any other group. Sometimes there is a group of two or three others. Still further, as in all Australia, the old men are a privileged group, and their prerogatives extend to marrying the young and attractive girls. The consequences of these rules is, of course, that in all the local group which must by absolute prescription furnish a young man with his wife, there is no girl who is not touched by one of these tabus. Either she is one of those who through relationship with his mother is his "sister," or she is already bargained for by an old man, or for some lesser reason she is forbidden to him.

That does not bring the Kurnai to reformulate their exogamous rules. They insist upon them with every show of violence. Therefore, the only way they are usually able to marry is by flying violently in the face of regulations. They elope. As soon as the village knows that an elopement has occurred, it sets out in pursuit, and if the couple are caught the two are killed. It does not matter that possibly all the pursuers were married by elopement in the same fashion. Moral indignation runs high. There is, however, an island traditionally recognized as a safe haven, and if the couple can reach it and remain away till the birth of a child, they are received again, with blows, it is true, but they may defend themselves. After they have run the gauntlet and been given their drubbing, they take up the status of married people in the tribe.

The Kurnai meet their cultural dilemma typically enough. They have extended and complicated a particular aspect of behavior until it is a social liability. They must either modify it, or get by with a subterfuge. And they use the subterfuge. They avoid extinction, and they maintain their ethics without acknowledged revision. This manner of dealing with the mores has lost nothing in the progress of civilization. The older generation of our own civilization similarly maintained monogamy and supported prostitution, and the panegyrics of monogamy were never so fervent as in the days of the red-light districts. Societies have always justified favorite traditional forms. When these traits get out of hand and some form of supplementary behavior is called in, lip service is given as readily to the traditional form as if the supplementary behavior did not exist.

Such a bird's-eye survey of human cultural forms makes clear several common misconceptions. In the first place, the institutions that human cultures build up upon the hints presented by the environment or by man's physical necessities do not keep as close to the original impulse as we easily imagine. These hints are, in reality, mere rough sketches, a list of bare facts. They are pin-point potentialities, and the elaboration that takes place around them is dictated by many alien considerations. Warfare is not the expression of the instinct of pugnacity. Man's pugnacity is so small a hint in the human equipment that it may not be given any expression in inter-tribal relations. When it is institutionalized, the form it takes follows other grooves of thought than those im-

plied in the original impulse. Pugnacity is no more than the touch to the ball of custom, a touch also that may be withheld.

Such a view of cultural processes calls for a recasting of many of our current arguments upholding our traditional institutions. These arguments are usually based on the impossibility of man's functioning without these particular traditional forms. Even very special traits come in for this kind of validation, such as the particular form of economic drive that arises under our particular system of property ownership. This is a remarkably special motivation and there are evidences that even in our generation it is being strongly modified. At any rate, we do not have to confuse the issue by discussing it as if it were a matter of biological survival values. Self-support is a motive our civilization has capitalized. If our economic structure changes so that this motive is no longer so potent a drive as it was in the era of the great frontier and expanding industrialism, there are many other motives that would be appropriate to a changed economic organization. Every culture, every era, exploits some few out of a great number of possibilities. Changes may be very disquieting, and involve great losses, but this is due to the difficulty of change itself, not to the fact that our age and country has hit upon the one possible motivation under which human life can be conducted. Change, we must remember, with all its difficulties, is inescapable. Our fears over even very minor shifts in custom are usually quite beside the point. Civilizations might change far more radically than any human authority has ever had the will or the imagination to change them, and still be completely workable. The minor changes that occasion so much denunciation today, such as the increase of divorce, the growing secularization in our cities, the prevalence of the petting party, and many more, could be taken up quite readily into a slightly different pattern of culture. Becoming traditional, they would be given the same richness of content, the same importance and value, that the older patterns had in other generations.

The truth of the matter is rather that the possible human institutions and motives are legion, on every plane of cultural simplicity or complexity, and that wisdom consists in a greatly increased tolerance toward their divergencies. No man can thoroughly participate in any culture unless he has been brought up and has lived according to its forms, but he can grant to other cultures the same significance to their participants which he recognizes in his own.

7   The Silent Language*

Edward T. Hall

Sociologists have repeatedly called attention to the problem of "A Certain Blindness in Human Beings," namely, the difficulty of putting ourselves imaginatively in another person's shoes. At the time of the generation gap, it is in some cases difficult for persons in the same cultural milieu to communicate. For those in vastly different cultures it may seem impossible. The author, a social anthropologist, suggests some of the "hangups" in understanding found among peoples of the Americas. Often the problem lies in hidden psychological patterns, specifically in the areas of time concepts, space concepts, and friendship patterns. To what extent are these "Silent Language" aspects critical in grasping the internal relations between Negroes and Whites or between Anglos and Mexicans?

There is a great reservoir of mutual good will among the peoples of the Americas. Much of it is needlessly dissipated in the desert sands of misunderstanding because in today's troubled world good will alone is not enough. Between the people of the United States and their southern neighbors there are deep and subtle differences. What is needed is an understanding and an appreciation of each other's psychology that will help to bridge political and economic gaps when these exist. Surface differences can be seen and dealt with. What defeats all of us are the hidden elements in man's psychological make-up whose presence is all too often not even suspected.

I will use the Spanish word *ocultos* — "not seen" — in a new sense to stand for these hidden

* Reprinted from *Américas,* monthly magazine published by the Pan American Union in English, Spanish, and Portuguese. Vol. 14. (Feb., 1962).

psychological patterns that stand between peoples. Like germs that can't be seen, there are many ocultos that cause psychological difficulty. All one sees are the symptoms, the outward manifestation of the oculto.

One can never hope to uncover all these unsuspected patterns that influence the communication between people. Even reviewing the principal elements at work here is virtually impossible, because each country in the Americas is unique and has a unique relationship with its fellow states.

DEFINING THE OCULTO

I will particularize about three specific topics to demonstrate a principle. These are Time, Space, and Friendship. Ocultos between the U.S. citizen and his neighbors differ in all three. One must keep in mind, however, that times are changing very fast: therefore, some of my examples no longer apply to regions where there has been a great influx of North Americans.

I first became aware of space as a patterned aspect of human behavior when I noted that people raised in other cultures handled it differently. In the Middle East I felt crowded and was often made to feel anxious. Fellow U.S. citizens, also, found it hard to adapt themselves to houses and offices arranged so differently, and often commented on how there was too little or too much space, and how much space was wasted. These spatial differences are not limited to offices and homes: towns, subway systems, and road networks usually follow patterns that appear curious to one not accustomed to the culture.

The "natural" way to describe space may be different in two cultures. For instance, I discovered in Japan that intersections of streets were named and the streets were not. Similarly, Europeans find it almost impossible to follow directions given by Arabs until a whole new system of visualizing space is learned. One reason for this is that the Arab takes so completely for granted the details of a familiar route that he thinks that if he identifies the desired destination as being near a well-known landmark, he has given adequate directions. He visualizes each area as a fixed unit, instead of focusing on the positional relationship between units.

These differing ideas of space — like the ideas of time and place — contain traps for the uninformed. A person raised in the United States is often likely to give an unintentional snub, without realizing it, to a Latin American because of the way he handles space relationships, particularly the physical distance between individuals during conversations. A Colombian or Mexican often feels that the *Norteamericano* he is talking to is cold and withdrawn.

A conversation I once observed between a Latin and a North American began at one end of a forty-foot hall. I watched the two conversationalists until they had finally reached the other end of the hall. This maneuver had been effected by a continual series of small backward steps on the part of the North American as he unconsciously retreated, searching for a comfortable talking distance. Each time, there was an accompanying closing of the gap, as his Latin friend attempted to reestablish his own accustomed conversation distance.

In formal business conversations in North America, the "proper" distance to stand when talking to another adult male who is simply a business acquaintance you don't know well, is usually about two feet. This distance diminishes, of course, at social functions like the cocktail party, but anything under eight to ten inches is likely to irritate. An easy way to test where the hidden line is, is to watch for the first point in closeness that causes the other person to back up, or move. To the Latin, with his own ocultos, a distance of two feet seems remote and cold, sometimes even unfriendly. One of the things that gives the South American or Central American the feeling that the North American is *simpático* is when he starts to use space in a sympathetic way and is no longer made uncomfortable by closeness or being touched.

North Americans, working in offices in Latin America, may keep their local acquaintances at a distance — not the Latin American distance — by remaining behind a desk or typewriter. Even North Americans who have lived in Latin America for years have been known to use the "barricade approach" to communication, and to remain completely unaware of its cultural significance. They are aware only that *they* "feel comfortable" when not crowded, without realizing that the distance and the desk often create an oculto that distorts or gives a cold tone to virtually everything that takes place. The hold of the oculto is so strong, however, that the Latin is sometimes observed trying to "climb over" the intervening obstacles — leaning over the desk, for instance — in order to achieve a distance at which he can communicate comfortably.

The Spanish colonial house is usually built around a patio that is adjacent to the sidewalks, but hidden from outsiders behind a wall. Small architectural differences like these sometimes affect outsiders to a degree that seems out of proportion to the actual facts. North American Point Four technicians residing in Latin America often said that they felt "shut off" and "left out" of things. Many kept wondering "what went on behind those walls." When North Americans live next door to people in Latin America, they soon find that sharing of adjacent space does not always conform to their own pattern. In the United States, propinquity is the sole basis of many relationships. In the North, being a neighbor gives one certain privileges and rights as well as responsibilities. The North American is accustomed to borrowing things, including food and drink, from his neighbor, but also assumes the responsibility of taking his neighbor to the hospital in an emergency, even if they are not well acquainted or particularly congenial. In the United States, except perhaps in a big city apartment house, your neighbor has as much claim on you as a cousin, and what's more you are supposed to get along with him, and hide any unkind thoughts.

Because of this oculto, the North American usually picks his neighborhood carefully and appears to segregate himself in a golden ghetto because he knows he is going to be thrown into intimate contact with the people who live near him, and share his living space. He knows that his children will go to the same schools and that the men will belong to the same clubs, and that the wives will visit: that his life will be an open book to his neighbors.

TIME — PATTERNS OF PUNCTUALITY

As with space, there are many time ocultos that characterize each people. The North American has developed a language of time that involves much more than being prompt. He can usually tell you when his own ocultos have been violated, but not how they work. His blood pressure rises and he loses his temper when he is kept waiting; this is because time and the ego have been linked. As a rule, the longer a North American is kept waiting *in his own setting,* the greater the discrepancy between the status of the two parties. Because of their high status, important people can keep less important people waiting. Also, very important business takes precedence over less important business. Five minutes brings a mild apology; thirty minutes a very long explanation; forty-five minutes is a slap in the face. In addition, the North American has developed a pattern for seeing one person at a time.

Individual appointments aren't usually scheduled by the Latin American to the exclusion of other appointments. The Latin often enjoys seeing several people at once even if he has to talk on different matters at the same time. In this setting, the North American may feel he is not being properly treated, that his dignity is under attack, even though this simply is not true. The Latin American clock on the wall may look the same, but it tells a different sort of time.

By the U.S. clock, a consistently tardy man is considered undependable. To judge a Latin American by the same time values is to risk a major error.

This cultural error may be compounded by a further miscalculation. Suppose the *Norteamericano* has waited forty-five minutes or an hour and finally gets to see the Latin American with whom he has an appointment, only to be told, with many apologies, that "there is only five minutes — maybe a meeting can be arranged for tomorrow or next week?" At this point, the North American's schedule has been "shot." If it is important, he

will have to *make the time*. What he may not understand is an oculto common in Mexico, for example, and that is that one is very likely to take one's time before doing business, in order to provide time for "getting acquainted." First meetings leave the North American with the feeling he isn't getting anywhere. If not forewarned by a friendly advisor, or by experience, he keeps trying to get down to business and stop "wasting time." This, too, turns out to be a mistake. In the United States, *discussion* is used as a means to an end: the deal. One tries to make his point with neatness and dispatch — quickly and efficiently. The North American begins by taking up major issues, leaving details for later, perhaps for technicians to work out.

Discussion, however, is to the Latin American an important part of life. It serves a different function and operates according to rules of form; it has to be done right. For the Latin American, the emphasis is on courtesy, not speed. Close friends who see each other frequently, shake hands when they meet and when they part. It is the invisible social distance that is maintained, not the physical distance. Forming a new friendship, or a business acquaintance, must be done properly. The Latin American wants to know the human values of a new acquaintance — his cultural interests, his philosophy of life — not his efficiency, before he can establish confidence. And this is all accompanied by elaborate and graceful formal verbal expressions, which people in the United States have long felt too busy to take time for. They tend to assume familiarity very quickly, to invite new acquaintances to their homes after one or two meetings. But the Latin American entertains only friends of very long standing in his home — and never for business reasons.

Of course, times are changing, and the North American can be fooled, too, because there is an increasing number of Latin businessmen who now demand punctuality even greater than in the North. However, there are still a great many times when the old patterns prevail and are not understood. The hidden differences seem to center around the fact that in the North, the ego of the man is more on the surface, whereas in the South preserving institutional forms is important.

THE LANGUAGE OF FRIENDSHIP

It has been observed that in the United States, friendships may not be long lasting. People are apt to take up friends quickly and drop them just as quickly. Friendships formed during school days persist when neither party moves away, but this is unusual. A feature influencing North American friendship patterns is that people move constantly (in the twelve-year period from 1946–1958, according to U.S. census data, two thirds of those owning homes had moved, while virtually all those renting property had moved). The North American, as a rule, looks for and finds his friends next door and among those with whom he works. There are for him few well-defined, hard and fast rules governing the obligations of friendship. At just what point our friendships give way to business opportunism or pressure from above is difficult to say. In this, the United States seems to differ from many other countries in the world.

In Latin America, on the other hand, while friendships are not formed as quickly or as easily as in the United States, they often go much deeper and last longer. They almost always involve real obligations. For example, it is important to stress that in Latin America your "friends" will not let you down. The fact that they, personally, are having difficulties is never an excuse for failing friends. You, in turn, are obligated to look out for their interests.

Thus, friends and family around the world — and especially in Latin America — represent a kind of social insurance that is hard to find in the United States, where friends are often a means of getting ahead — or at least, getting the job done. Frequently, friendship in the U.S. system involves a series of carefully, though silently, tabulated favors and obligations, doled out where they will do the most good. The least that North Americans expect in exchange for a favor is gratitude.

The weight of tradition presses the Latin American to do business within a circle of friends and relatives. If a product or service he needs is not available within his circle, he hesitates to go outside; if he does so, he looks for a new friend who can supply the want. Apart from the cultural need to "feel right" about a new relationship, there is the logic of the business system. One of the realities of life is that it is dangerous to enter into business with someone over whom you have no "control." The difference between the two systems lies in the controls. One is formal, personal, and depends upon family and friends. The other is technical-legal, impersonal, and depends upon courts and contracts.

SPEAKING ONE'S MIND

Europeans often comment on how candid the North American is. Being candid, he seeks this in others. What fools him is that the Latin American does not readily reciprocate. One has to be known and trusted — admitted into the circle of friendship — before this happens. Even then, what is not said may be just as important, and just as much noticed, as what is said. Much of the miscuing that takes place can be traced to the reciprocity oculto in the North American friendship pattern. North Americans tend to believe much too much of what they hear, and then are shocked when things turn out differently. The Latin American, in particular, will not speak his mind to someone involved in his own operation unless there is complete confidence.

UNCOVERING THE OCULTO CAN HELP

Latin Americans are tired of trying to find North Americans who will understand and who are *simpático*. Some have given up trying. They value the whole man, not just his skill or knowledge in one or two fields. They feel that North Americans are so engrossed in getting things done that they never take time to live. This observation is corroborated by the statistics that show how quickly U.S. men whose whole energy has been devoted to their jobs, to the exclusion of other interests and hobbies, die when forced to retire while still vigorous. These have much to learn from their southern neighbors. But there are today many people in the United States who, tired of the trapped feeling of being caught in their inflexible daily rounds, find these Latin American values deeply congenial.

Nevertheless, until we face up to the reality of

the ocultos, and make them explicit, difficulties in communication are going to continue. Ocultos drain the great reservoir of good will that the people of the Americas feel in their hearts for each other.

The Latin American must help the North American to understand. And the North American must do everything in his power to reach his friends in Latin America. He must continue to inform himself about the tremendously rich heritage, and the vitality and subtlety, of Hispano-American culture.

CONFLICTS AND
SUBCULTURES

8 Cultural Contradictions and Sex Roles*

Mirra Komarovsky

Women are women and men are men, but cultural expectations may have more influence on their behavior than biological differences. A changing culture confronts the individual with conflicting sets of expectations. The college women studied 20 years ago by Komarovsky reflect the impact of cross-pressures to be "feminine" and at the same time to be "modern" — assertive, self-reliant, and competitive for status with men. The study also shows regional and class differences in the roles of college women.

Do today's college women experience the same conflicting pressures?

This article sets forth in detail the nature of certain incompatible sex roles imposed by our society upon the college woman. It is based on data collected in 1942 and 1943. Members of an

undergraduate course on the family were asked for two successive years to submit autobiographical documents on the topic; 73 were collected. In addition, 80 interviews, lasting about an hour each, were conducted with every member of a course in social psychology of the same institution — making a total of 153 documents ranging from a minimum of five to a maximum of thirty typewritten pages.

The generalization emerging from these documents is the existence of serious contradictions between two roles present in the social environment of the college woman. The goals set by each role are mutually exclusive, and the fundamental personality traits each evokes are at points diametrically opposed, so that what are assets for one become liabilities for the other, and the full realization of one role threatens defeat in the other.

One of these roles may be termed the "feminine" role. While there are a number of permissive variants of the feminine role for women of college age (the "good sport," the "glamour girl," the "young lady," the domestic "home girl," etc.), they have a common core of attributes defining the proper attitudes to men, family, work, love, etc., and a set of personality traits often described with reference to the male sex role as "not as dominant, or aggressive as men," or "more emotional, sympathetic."

The other and more recent role is, in a sense, no *sex* role at all, because it partly obliterates the differentiation in sex. It demands of the woman much the same virtues, patterns of behavior, and attitude that it does of the men of a corresponding age. We shall refer to this as the "modern" role.

Both roles are present in the social environment of these women throughout their lives, though, as the precise content of each sex role varies with age, so does the nature of their clashes change

* Excerpts reprinted from the *American Journal of Sociology,* Vol. 52 (November 1946), pp. 184–189, by permission of The University of Chicago Press. Copyright © 1946 by The University of Chicago.

from one stage to another. In the period under discussion the conflict between the two roles apparently centers about academic work, social life, vocational plans, excellence in specific fields of endeavor, and a number of personality traits.

One manifestation of the problem is the inconsistency of the goals set for the girl by her family.

Forty, or 26 per cent, of the respondents expressed some grievance against their families for failure to confront them with clear-cut and consistent goals. The majority, 74 per cent, denied having had such experiences. One student writes:

How am I to pursue any course singlemindedly when some way along the line a person I respect is sure to say, "You are on the wrong track and are wasting your time." Uncle John telephones every Sunday morning. His first question is: "Did you go out last night?" He would think me a "grind" if I were to stay home Saturday night to finish a term paper. My father expects me to get an "A" in every subject and is disappointed by a "B". He says I have plenty of time for social life. Mother says, "That 'A' in philosophy is very nice dear. But please don't become so deep that no man will be good enough for you." And, finally, Aunt Mary's line is careers for women. "Prepare yourself for some profession. This is the only way to insure yourself independence and an interesting life. You have plenty of time to marry."

A Senior writes:

I get a letter from my mother at least three times a week. One week her letter will say, "Remember that this is your last year at college. Subordinate everything to your studies. You must have a good record to secure a job." The next week her letters are full of wedding news. This friend of mine got married; that one is engaged; my young cousin's wedding is only a week off. When, my mother wonders, will I make up my mind? Surely, I wouldn't want to be the only unmarried one in my group. It is high time, she feels, that I give some thought to it.

A student reminisces:

All through my high school my family urged me to work hard because they wished me to enter a first-rate college. At the same time they were always raving about a girl schoolmate who lived next door

to us. How pretty and sweet she was, how popular and what taste in clothes! Couldn't I also pay more attention to my appearance and to social life? They were overlooking the fact that this carefree friend of mine had little time left for school work and had expected me to become Eve Curie and Hedy Lamarr wrapped in one.

Another comments:

My mother thinks that it is very nice to be smart in college but only if it doesn't take too much effort. She always tells me not to be too intellectual on dates, to be clever in a light sort of way. My father, on the other hand, wants me to study law. He thinks that if I applied myself I could make an excellent lawyer and keeps telling me that I am better fitted for this profession than my brother.

Another writes:

One of my two brothers writes: "Cover up that high forehead and act a little dumb once in a while"; while the other always urges upon me the importance of rigorous scholarship.

The students testified to a certain bewilderment and confusion caused by the failure on the part of the family to smooth the passage from one role to another, especially when the roles involved were contradictory. It seemed to some of them that they had awakened one morning to find their world upside down: what had hitherto evoked praise and rewards from relatives, now suddenly aroused censure. A student recollects:

I could match my older brother in skating, sledding, riflery, ball, and many of the other games we played. He enjoyed teaching me and took great pride in my accomplishments. Then one day it all changed. He must have suddenly become conscious of the fact that girls ought to be feminine. I was walking with him, proud to be able to make long strides and keep up with his long-legged steps when he turned to me in annoyance, "Can't you walk like a lady?" I still remember feeling hurt and bewildered by his scorn, when I had been led to expect approval.

Once during her freshman year in college, after a delightful date, a student wrote her brother with great elation:

"What a wonderful evening at ———— fraternity house! You would be proud of me, Johnny! I won all ping-pong games but one!"

"For heaven's sake," came the reply, "when will you grow up? Don't you know that a boy likes to think he is better than a girl? Give him a little competition, sure, but miss a few serves in the end. Should you join the Debate Club? By all means, but don't practice too much on the boys." Believe me I was stunned by this letter, but then I saw that he was right. To be a success in the dorms one must date, to date one must not win too many ping-pong games. At first I resented this bitterly. But now I am more or less used to it and live in hope of one day meeting a man who is my superior so that I may be my natural self.

It is the parents and not the older sibling who reversed their expectations in the following excerpt:

All through grammar school and high school my parents led me to feel that to do well in school was my chief responsibility. A good report card, an election to student office, these were the news Mother bragged about in telephone conversations with her friends. But recently they suddenly got worried about me: I don't pay enough attention to social life, a woman needs *some* education but not that much. They are disturbed by my determination to go to the School of Social Work. Why my ambitions should surprise them after they have exposed me for four years to some of the most inspired and stimulating social scientists in the country, I can't imagine. They have some mighty strong arguments on their side. What is the use, they say, of investing years in training for a profession, only to drop it in a few years? Chances of meeting men are slim in this profession. Besides, I may become so preoccupied with it as to sacrifice social life. The next few years are, after all, the proper time to find a mate. But the urge to apply what I have learned and the challenge of this profession is so strong that I shall go on despite the family opposition.

The final excerpt illustrates both the sudden transition of roles and the ambiguity of standards:

I major in English composition. This is not a completely "approved" field for girls so I usually just say "English". An English Literature major is quite liked and approved by boys. Somehow it is lumped with all the other arts and even has a little glamour. But a composition major is a girl to beware of because she supposedly will notice all your grammar mistakes, look at your letters too critically, and consider your ordinary speech and conversation as too crude.

I also work for a big metropolitan daily as a correspondent in the city room. I am well liked there and may possibly stay as a reporter after graduation in February. I have had several spreads (stories running to more than eight or ten inches of space), and this is considered pretty good for a college correspondent. Naturally, I was elated and pleased at such breaks, and as far as the city room is concerned I'm off to a very good start on a career that is hard for a man to achieve and even harder for a woman. General reporting is still a man's work in the opinion of most people. I have a lot of acclaim but also criticism, and I find it confusing and difficult to be praised for being clever and working hard and then, when my efforts promise to be successful, to be condemned and criticized for being unfeminine and ambitious.

Here are a few of these reactions:

My father: "I don't like this newspaper set-up at all. The people you meet are making you less interested in marriage than ever. You're getting too educated and intellectual to be attractive to men."

My mother: "I don't like your attitude toward people. The paper is making you too analytical and calculating. Above all, you shouldn't sacrifice your education and career for marriage."

A lieutenant with two years of college: "It pleased me greatly to hear about your news assignment — good girl."

A Navy pilot with one year of college: "Undoubtedly, I'm old-fashioned, but I never expect or feel right about a girl giving up a very promising future to hang around waiting for me to finish college. Nevertheless, congratulations on your job on the paper. Where in the world do you get that wonderful energy? Anyway I know you were thrilled at getting it and feel very glad for you. I've an idea that it means the same to you as that letter saying 'report for active duty' meant to me."

A graduate metallurgist now a private in the Army: "It was good to hear that you got that break with the paper. I am sure that talent will prove itself and that you will go far. But not too far, as I don't think you should become a career woman. You'll get repressed and not be interested enough in having fun if you keep after that career."

A lieutenant with a year and a half of college: "All this career business is nonsense. A woman belongs in the home and absolutely no place else. My wife will have to stay home. That should keep her happy. Men are just superior in everything, and women have no right to expect to compete with them. They should do just what will keep their husbands happy."

A graduate engineer — my fiance: "Go right ahead and get as far as you can in your field. I am glad you are ambitious and clever, and I'm as anxious to see you happily successful as I am myself. It is a shame to let all those brains go to waste over just dusting and washing dishes. I think the usual home life and children are small sacrifices to make if a career will keep you happy. But I'd rather see you in radio because I am a bit wary of the effect upon our marriage of the way of life you will have around the newspaper."

Sixty-one, or 40 per cent, of the students indicated that they have occasionally "played dumb" on dates, that is, concealed some academic honor, pretended ignorance of some subject, or allowed the man the last word in an intellectual discussion. Among these were women who "threw games" and in general played down certain skills in obedience to the unwritten law that men must possess these skills to a superior degree. At the same time, in other areas of life, social pressures were being exerted upon these women to "play to win," to compete to the utmost of their abilities for intellectual distinction and academic honors. One student writes:

I was glad to transfer to a women's college. The two years at the co-ed university produced a constant strain. I am a good student; my family expects me to get good marks. At the same time I am normal enough to want to be invited to the Saturday night dance. Well, everyone knew that on that campus a reputation of a "brain" killed a girl socially. I was always fearful lest I say too much in class or answer a question which the boys I dated couldn't answer.

Here are some significant remarks made from the interviews:

When a girl asks me what marks I got last semester I answer, "Not so good — only one 'A'." When a boy asks the same question, I say very brightly with a note of surprise, "Imagine, I got an 'A'!"

I am engaged to a southern boy who doesn't think too much of the woman's intellect. In spite of myself, I play up to his theories because the less one knows and does, the more he does for you and thinks you "cute" into the bargain. . . . I allow him to explain things to me in great detail and to treat me as a child in financial matters.

One of the nicest techniques is to spell long words incorrectly once in a while. My boyfriend seems to get a great kick out of it and writes back, "Honey, you certainly don't know how to spell."

When my date said that he considers Ravel's *Bolero* the greatest piece of music ever written, I changed the subject because I knew I would talk down to him.

A boy advised me not to tell of my proficiency in math and not to talk of my plans to study medicine unless I knew my date well.

My fiance didn't go to college. I intend to finish college and work hard at it, but in talking to him I make college appear a kind of a game.

Once I went sailing with a man who so obviously enjoyed the role of a protector that I told him I didn't know how to sail. As it turned out he didn't either. We got into a tough spot, and I was torn between a desire to get a hold of the boat and a fear to reveal that I had lied to him.

It embarrassed me that my "steady" in high school got worse marks than I. A boy should naturally do better in school. I would never tell him my marks and would often ask him to help me with my homework.

I am better in math than my fiance. But while I let him explain politics to me, we never talk about math even though, being a math major, I could tell him some interesting things.

Mother used to tell me to lay off the brains on dates because glasses make me look too intellectual anyhow.

I was once at a work camp. The girls did the same work as the boys. If some girls worked better, the boys resented it fiercely. The director told one capable girl to slow down to keep peace in the group.

How to do the job and remain popular was a tough task. If you worked your best, the boys resented the competition; if you acted feminine, they complained that you were clumsy.

On dates I always go through the "I-don't-care-anything-you-want-to-do" routine. It gets montonous but boys fear girls who make decisions. They think such girls would make nagging wives.

I am a natural leader and, when in the company of girls, usually take the lead. That is why I am so active in college activities. But I know that men fear bossy women, and I always have to watch myself on dates not to assume the "executive" role. Once a boy walking to the theater with me took the wrong street. I knew a short cut but kept quiet.

I let my fiance make most of the decisions when we are out. It annoys me but he prefers it.

I sometimes "play dumb" on dates, but it leaves a bad taste. The emotions are complicated. Part of me enjoys "putting something over" on the unsuspecting male. But this sense of superiority over him is mixed with feeling of guilt for my hypocrisy. Toward the "date" I feel some contempt because he is "taken in" by my technique, or if I like the boy, a kind of a maternal condescension. At times I resent him! Why isn't he my superior in all ways in which a man should excel so that I could be my natural self? What am I doing here with him, anyhow? Slumming?

And the funny part of it is that the man, I think, is not always so unsuspecting. He may sense the truth and become uneasy in the relation. "Where do I stand? Is she laughing up her sleeve or did she mean this praise? Was she really impressed with that little speech of mine or did she only pretend to know nothing about politics?" And once or twice I felt that the joke was on me: the boy saw through my wiles and felt contempt for me for stooping to such tricks.

Another aspect of the problem is the conflict between the psychogenetic personality of the girl and the cultural role foisted upon her by the milieu. At times it is the girl with "masculine" interests and personality traits who chafes under the pressure to conform to the "feminine" pattern. At other times it is the family and the college who thrusts upon the reluctant girl the "modern" role.

While, historically, the "modern" role is the most recent one, ontogenetically it is the one emphasized earlier in the education of the college girl, if these 153 documents are representative. Society confronts the girl with powerful challenges and strong pressure to excel in certain competitive lines of endeavor and to develop certain techniques of adaptations very similar to those expected of her brothers. But then, quite suddenly as it appears to these girls, the very success in meeting these challenges begins to cause anxiety. It is precisely those most successful in the earlier role who are now penalized.

It is not only the passage from age to age but the moving to another region or type of campus which may create for the girl similar problems. The precise content of sex roles, or, to put it another way, the degree of their differentiation, varies with regional, class, nativity, and other subcultures.

9 Women's Roles and Politics: India and The United States*

Gerald D. Berreman

In most complex cultures we find contradictory and inconsistent assumptions and values. The article on rank order of discrimination illustrated this in the area of race relations and cultural expectations. What of the role of women in the Western world?

* Part of this paper appeared originally in two Letters to the Editor, "On the Role of Women," *Bulletin of Atomic Scientists,* Vol. 22, No. 9 (Nov. 1966), pp. 26–28, and Vol. 23 (March 1967), pp. 28–29.

Robert S. Lynd once pointed out that many Americans acted as if "Women are the finest of God's creatures, but are usually inferior to men in reasoning power and in general ability." Americans and Canadians often assume that the position of women in Asian countries is always inferior to that of women in the West. Why is it that in countries where the status of women is traditionally inferior they hold high positions in the government of that country?

In January, 1966, for the second time in two years, India was forced by death to choose a new Prime Minister. Mrs. Indira Gandhi assumed this role with stated determination to strengthen the cause of peace in India and abroad.

There was special interest in the West that the second most populous of the world's nations, beset by almost unimaginably severe social, economic, and political problems, selected a woman as its leader. Only one other woman has been a head of state in this century, Mrs. Sirimavo Bandaranaike, Prime Minister of nearby and culturally related Ceylon, from 1960 to 1965. The *San Francisco Chronicle,* on January 20, put the question which must have entered the minds of many, when it noted editorially: "It is curious that the only women chosen to head governments are products of a society where the status of women is inferior, where the male is lord and master. . . ." We in the West are likely to find this hopeful as well as curious, for here women are associated with peaceful intent as well as political inffectiveness.

Why indeed have Western nations, with pride in their high regard for women, given them little place in government, while nations with seemingly quite opposite traditions have given them the highest of such positions? The answers lie in a more sophisticated understanding of the roles of women in each society. It is fitting that Americans think on these facts and their implications, for this is a time of soul-searching about the functions of representative government in America; about respect for the individual in society, about individual and collective rights, and about the relationship between the United States, its leaders, and its populace to governments and peoples in other parts of the world.

The woman of traditional India is a subordinate individual. She defers to her father, her brother, and most importantly, her husband. Throughout her life she remains in the home carrying out the household duties of daughter, wife, and mother. She acquires no education beyond that of her household; she seeks no honor or influence beyond that inherent in her role and reflected upon her by her male kinsmen. She marries young and only once. She serves her husband, she honors him, she obeys him. In modern India there is no legal enforcement of this status; people are equal before the law regardless of sex. Education and other means to realization of individual aspirations are officially open to all. But tradition is strong, conditions are hard, and opportunities are limited.

In America women are "emancipated." They are educated, independent, and mobile in and out of the family. Their opportunities for employment, public recognition, and participation in al-

most every institution of our society are widely advertised.

This is the contrast we all know. But there is another contrast which must be recognized if we are to understand women's political participation in the two societies.

For many of their qualities American women are admired, even idealized, and often pampered. Considerably more than lip service is given to their rights. *But in very crucial ways women are not taken seriously as individuals and as human beings.* A woman is admired if she is pretty, stylish, affectionate, clever, sophisticated, pleasant, mannerly, housewifely, motherly, or if she does well in appropriate occupations such as teacher, nurse, secretary, entertainer — in short, if she knows her place as a woman. But let her be serious in other spheres, or let her undertake to participate in the important concerns of public life, and no matter how capable, how expert, or how dedicated she may be, a woman is likely to be ignored, patronized, or ridiculed. These are among the severest and most effective sanctions known to man. They force her back toward behavior consistent with the limited horizons of her feminine role. Girls learn early from others that they are illogical, emotional, impractical, and unpredictable just because they are females. This has some of the attributes of a self-fulfilling prophecy, for people often define themselves in response to the ways in which others respond to them. Women become parties to their own disparagement and there results more than a grain of truth in the stereotypes. Thus it becomes truly a man's world in which women are a suppressed "minority." The attitudes run so deep that even the identification of this fact is greeted by amusement in masculine circles — amusement tinged, perhaps, like much amusement, with anxiety.

Examples of the failure to take American women's activities seriously are legion. The suffragettes were cruelly ridiculed, their idealism denigrated, their intelligence impugned, their accomplishments belittled. In the 1930's Eleanor Roosevelt was ridiculed for her self-sacrifice and social consciousness, often by men incapable of understanding her activities and consequently unworthy to comment, much less to criticize. Today the Women for Peace suffer from the failure of public officials and the press to take seriously their efforts no matter how significant they may be, and this very fact reduces their effectiveness. Women's serious undertakings are not evaluated on the merits of the issues or facts, but are prejudged on the basis of negative stereotypes. This is true when a woman applies for graduate school, professional employment, or when she runs for office, as it is when she supports a cause or appeals to reason. She consistently confronts the stereotype of the Helen E. Hokinson clubwoman, the woman driver, the dizzy dame, the little old lady in tennis shoes. She is continuously responded to in terms of this rather heterogeneous but consistently limiting — because patronizing — set of female role models. This is not a situation conductive to selection for high political office.

In India, by contrast, women's roles are no doubt more sharply defined and are defined as more explicitly subsidiary to those of men in family and neighborhood life than is true in America. There is a difference, however, between high social status and being taken seriously as individuals. The two seem capable of independent variation. This is revealed by a crucial difference between India and America, for *in India women are taken seriously as human beings*. They and their undertakings are not regarded as trivial. They are traditionally circumscribed by the explicit rules of their society, but they are not hampered by lack of respect for their motives, emotions, capabilities, and intellect as in the case of America.

The reasons for this difference would have to be sought in a comparative study of cultural values and social structure with special reference to family organization and child rearing. Also relevant would be an investigation of the nature of contemporary social and cultural change in the two societies. With reference to the last, Ralph Linton noted thirty years ago that "societies living under new and changing conditions are usually characterized by a wealth of achievable statuses and by very broad delimitation of the competition for them." Pauline Kolenda, a sociologist who has done research on the family in India, suggests that perhaps because there is a relative scarcity of trained talent in rapidly changing contemporary India, qualified women are accorded important roles which might be denied them under more

stable conditions. This is doubtless a factor which, in addition to Indian values, family organization, and child training, contributes to the nature of women's political participation there as contrasted to that in America. But to seek and assess such reasons in detail is beyond the scope of this dis-discussion.

The fact is that when, through education and other advantages, an Indian woman moves to a position outside of the traditional family and neighborhood context, she is evaluated by men and women alike as a person — and as an administrator, lawyer, student, social reformer — rather than being regarded as a woman masquerading in some other role. Being a woman does not automatically ascribe to the woman in India, as it does in the West, a syndrome of characteristics which obscure or devalue her personal attributes and attainments. And she does not define herself as so limited. Thus, when she escapes the environment and the attributes which bestow low status upon her, she retains and accrues the benefits of the human dignity which the society accords, and the self-esteem which it engenders. In America and the West women have largely escaped their low status, but they suffer the pervasive lack of public and even self-esteem which would enable them to participate fully in the serious affairs of their society.

Mrs. Gandhi was chosen as Prime Minister of India because she was considered by her people to be the most able individual available for that post. Mrs. Bandaranaike was chosen in Ceylon for the same reason. It is true, of course, that these two women were close relatives of former heads of the states they themselves headed — daughter and wife, respectively. Like all holders of high office in democracies, perhaps, they were also compromise choices for office. But these facts say nothing about why *women* attained that high office there and have never done so here — have here never even received consideration as candidates. They only suggest reasons why these *particular* women, rather than others, did so. Western leaders have relatives too, male and female, and in the West, too, reflected or "inherited" prestige can lead to office, but the significant fact is that here it leads to office for *men* — almost never for women and never to the highest office.

Mrs. Gandhi and Mrs. Bandaranaike are not

isolated instances of women in public office in their countries, they are only the best-known and most conspicuous examples. They are symbolic of a pervasive pattern of political participation by women in those countries, for there women hold political office in far greater numbers and proportions than is the case in the United States. In India, for example, women abound in public office at every level, national, state and local. Their numbers are likely to astound westerners. An impressive list could be easily gathered. It would have to include Mrs. Sucheta Kripalani, elected Chief Minister of Uttar Pradesh, India's largest state with a population of over 80 million, and one of the most difficult political climates in the world's democracies in which to reach the top and survive there. Others which come readily to mind include: Padmaja Naidu (Governor of West Bengal and daughter of a prominent Indian nationalist who was also a woman, Sarojini Naidu); Dr. Sushila Nayar (Minister of Health); Laxmi Menon (Deputy Minister for External Affairs); the late Rajkumari Amrit Kaur (Minister for Health in successive Nehru cabinets); Dr. T. S. Soundaram (Deputy Minister for Education); Durgabai Deshmukh (Member of the first Planning Commission and one of the architects of the first 5-year plan); Achamma Matthai (Chairman of the Central Social Welfare Board). Among women who are members of parliament in addition to the Ministers listed above, mention should be made of M. Chandrasekhar, the first "Harijan lady" elected to the House of the People, in 1952 (others followed), and Deputy Health Minister in the first Nehru administration. Nehru's sister, Vijayalaxmi Pandit was a prominent political figure in her own right. Most recently, on December 6, 1966, Mrs. Shanno Devi was unanimously elected Speaker of the legislative assembly of India's newest state — the Haryana Vidhan Sabha.

A policy which would be shocking in the United States was adopted by India's predominant Congress Party: to include in the selection of candidates for public office a significant percentage of women (the figure has been 15 per cent in recent years). This is an indication both of the seriousness with which women are taken in political life in India, and of the magnitude of traditional barriers to be overcome before they will be in a position to participate fully. Perhaps most important, it is an indication of the realism with which Indians face the problem of full political participation — realism which is also indicated in the reservation by law of political representation for members of disadvantaged ethnic minorities.

The elevation to high office of Mrs. Gandhi and Mrs. Bandaranaike was possible because, in the cultural tradition of those nations, women are significant individuals who are taken seriously. Americans, like people of most other Western nations, would not choose a woman as head of state because we do not yet take women that seriously. This is a limiting factor in our realization of a democratic society administered by representative government, where full rights are accorded to all. This is not a problem for men alone; neither is it a problem for women alone. It is a problem for our society. Americans value conformity and feel threatened and offended by diversity. India has manifold social problems and is faced with tremendous obstacles to full realization of political democracy, but one she is spared is intolerance of diversity. India takes seriously her minorities, including women.

Achievement of true humanity in a society as well as true democracy in a nation depends upon serious regard for the aspirations, commitments, capabilities, and intellect of all who comprise it. In their serious regard for women — for their dignity as persons — India and Ceylon are ahead of the United States, as their choice of political leadership has demonstrated.

10 An Overview of Teen-Age Culture*

Jessie Bernard

The following selection describes teen-age culture as a product of American affluence involving extended education, certain kinds of clothing, automobiles, and the paraphernalia of sports and recreation. The culture of the younger adolescents is characteristically lower-class, while that of the older teenagers is middle-class. The author suggests that at the college level the old "rah-rah" culture is giving way to more serious vocational and academic norms and activities. If the trend continues, teen-age culture may soon end with high school graduation.

A PRODUCT OF AFFLUENCE

Our teen-age culture — in contradistinction to the teen-age culture of the past or of other societies — is a product of affluence. It is possible because our society can afford a large leisure class of youngsters not in the labor force but yet consumers on a vast scale, or, if in the labor force, free to spend their earnings on themselves. And they spend it primarily on clothes, cosmetics, recreational paraphernalia, records, cars, travel, and other leisure class goods and services.

Material Aspects

Clothes are an important part of teen-age culture. Industry first discovered the profitable teen-age consuming market in this area. Clothes were once sized and styled very simply — little-girl dresses, for example, until about age thirteen or fourteen and misses' and women's thereafter. The common lament of mothers and their teen-age daughters was that there was nothing suitable for the in-between age — once called the awkward age — when the girl was no longer a child but not yet a woman. Once industry discovered this mar-

ket, the teen-age girl became one of the most catered-to segments of the buying public. Deb, sub-deb, sub-teen, and scores of other categories were developed, sized, and styled — by the most talented designers — for her. Her figure, not that of the mature woman, became the norm of fashion. An analogous development occurred for boys, who once jumped from knickers to long trousers in one dramatic leap. "Ivy league" is now as important in clothes for teen-age boys as Jonathan Logan is for girls. Leather jackets and chinos are equally standard for the younger or lower socio-economic class boys.

The importance of clothes in teen-age culture in the case of girls is illustrated by the following document:

A girl should dress as the other girls do but with just a touch of individuality. If she is considered a good dresser, she wears labels. Her dresses are Lanz or Jonathan Logan. She wears shoes by Capezio for people who dare to be different. Her skirts are Pendleton and the right length and the sweaters to match are Garland. Her coat is a Lassie, and no good dresser uses any make-up but the current fad which usually alternates between Revlon and Coty. All of these labels show (1) that she has money, (2) that she is allowed to spend it on her choices, and (3) that those choices are ones of quality.

The automobile is another basic trait in the material culture of teen-agers. It is taken for granted that every teen-ager will learn to drive and that, if he does not have a car of his own, individually or as member of a group, he will certainly have access to one. In one community, a car dealer takes it for granted that when a boy reaches the age of sixteen he will be in the market for a used car. There were some 1½ million cars owned by teen-agers in 1960. The number of licensed drivers was, of course, much greater — some 5.9 million in 1958, or 7.2 per cent of all drivers — and they did 5 per cent of all driving done. The psychological and social problem aspects of the automobile are important but do not concern us here; the cultural aspect, however, is interesting and relevant.[1]

---

* From Jessie Bernard, "Teen-Age Culture: An Overview," *Annals of the American Academy of Political and Social Science,* Vol. 338 (November 1961), pp. 1–12. Copyright © 1961 by the American Academy of Political and Social Science. Reproduced by permission.

[1] Ross A. McFarland and Roland C. Moore, 'Youth and the Automobile," in *Values and Ideals of American Youth,* Eli Ginzberg, ed. (Columbia University Press, 1961), pp. 173, 176.

. . . automobiles have become a factor of great importance in adolescent culture. For example, in many cities it is an accepted pattern that in order to date a girl, a boy must be able to provide a car for transportation; she may not go in a cab or allow herself and her date to be driven by parents. To many boys the car itself becomes a dominant motivating force. Having acquired a car for transportation, socialization, and dating, a boy becomes so involved in its care and upkeep he has little time or interest left for other activities. . . . "For many, the clubhouse on wheels is a medium for holding a party. . . ."

Popular records — $75,000,000 worth annually — constitute another important trait in teen-age culture; the contents will be analyzed below. Bongo drums, athletic equipment, high fidelity phonographs, travel, camping are other elements which loom large in the material aspect of teen-age culture.

To get these clothes, cars, bongo drums, record players, and cosmetics to the teen-agers, an enormous market has developed. It amounted to an estimated $10 billion in 1959 and was expected to reach twice that amount by 1970. The girls in this market have been called the "teen tycoons."

". . . A POWER TO RECKON WITH"

The existence of this great leisure class with so much buying power at its disposal has had profound repercussions on the relationships between teen-agers and the adult world. They have had to be catered to. The values of teen-age culture become a matter of concern to the advertising industry. What teen-agers like and want, what they think is important. As contrasted with the traditional agencies charged with socializing youngsters, the advertisers and the mass media flatter and cajole. They seek to create desires in order to satisfy, rather than, as the parent, teacher, or minister must often do, to discipline, restrict, or deny them. The advertiser is, thus, on the side of the teen-ager. "The things bought are determined by what the child wants rather than by what the parents want for him." Coffee is encouraged, as is smoking, if not — as yet — drinking. In fact, the rebound of the cigarette industry after the first cancer scare in the 1960's has been attributed to a big increase in teen-age smokers. The teen-age press — to be commented on in greater detail below — reflects values and standards which teen-agers select for themselves, rather than those selected for them. They have the money to call the tune; they are "patrons" of the arts and must, therefore, be catered to.

The coalition of advertisers and teen-agers is, thus, buttressed not only by psychological props but also by economic ones. For, "if parents have any idea of organized revolt, it is already too late. Teen-age spending is so important that such action would send quivers through the entire national economy." Many parents feel that they are dealing with a piper who, though never pied, nevertheless draws children after him. The teen-ager's "relentless consumption" — to use Keynes' phrase — is essential to the economy, and it is they who direct it, not their parents.

NONMATERIAL TRAITS

The language of teen-agers serves to maintain barriers between them and the outside world. This language may vary from community to community and from class to class. The following expressions were current on one campus in 1961: "clod," a person who is socially unacceptable by real collegiates; "tweedy," fashionably dressed; "tweeded down," dressed up; "rough and tough," well-accepted individual; "whip," to transport one's self; "roomy," roommate; "wheels," a car; "zowies," happy surprises; "tough dresser," a stunning dresser; "mickey mouse," anything easy, as a college course.

The values and preoccupations of teen-age culture may be discovered by analyzing those aspects of the mass media beamed directly to them: teen-age periodicals and popular records. The "tribal customs" of teen-age culture can best be observed in the teen-age hangout.

Teen-agers constitute an important set of publics as well as of markets. Children who used to have a hard time coming by pennies now have quarters and half dollars to spend on a bewildering variety of periodicals beamed primarily at them. These range from highly technical magazines for hot rod and railroad buffs all the way to lonely-hearts-type magazines for shy little girls. Photography, sports, athletics, as well, of course, as pornography, have their publics also. The teen-type magazine, characterized usually by the term "teen" in its title, reveals the major positive — fun and popularity — and negative — overweight or underweight and adolescent acne — values of its readers. How to be attractive in order to be popular in order to have fun is the major burden of their contents. The teen-type magazine differs from its slick counterparts — *Seventeen* and *Mademoiselle,* for example — in a way analogous to the way true-story magazines for adult women differ from the service-type women's magazines. The class background of these differing publics is revealed in the relative sophistication of the contents as well as in the nature of the advertising. The values, however, are the same in both class levels — beauty, fun, popularity.

Popular songs, almost exclusively a teen-age cultural trait, have been subjected to content analysis by several researchers. One author finds that they fit neatly into what he calls the drama of courtship. There is a Prologue which emphasizes wishing and dreaming. Act I deals with courtship, and songs in this category constitute about a third of all popular songs. Five scenes deal respectively with: direct approach, sentimental appeal, desperation, questions and promises, impatience and surrender. Act II, contributing about 8 per cent of all lyrics, is on the honeymoon. The downward course of love, including about 14.5 per cent of the songs, is depicted in four scenes of Act III: temporary separation, hostile forces, threat of leaving, and final parting. Then, alas, Act IV concerns All Alone, about a fourth of the songs, in three scenes: pleading, hopeless love, and new beginnings. He found remarkable similarities wherever he turned for materials, the Hit Parade, lists of Song Hits, Country Song Roundup, or Rhythm and Blues. In all categories, courtship and downward course of love songs accounted for well over half of all songs.

The values of teen-age culture are also reflected in what is rewarded among high school students. Schools differ markedly, but there is great uniformity in one respect: athletic ability is far more rewarded and prized than intellectual ability. James Coleman believes one factor involved is that, when an athlete shows great achievement, the school and the community share the honor; when a bright student shows great achievement, he does it as an individual and he alone shares the honor; he may even be viewed as a rate-buster.

TRIBAL CUSTOMS

Contrary to the pattern of past generations, present-day teen-age boys and girls do not pass through a stage of withdrawal from one another. It has been found that as early as the fifth or sixth grades the sexes are already interested in one another; dating may begin as early as age ten or eleven. This teen-age culture already has a set of sex mores of its own. Kissing games — spin the bottle and post office — are very old; they antedate current teen-age culture by many years. What is new is parental acceptance by many, grudging in some cases, but resigned. Kissing games are supplemented by parking as soon as the boys acquire cars. Along with parking goes the custom of "bushwacking" or "hunting"; peers find the parked cars and flash their headlights on the petting couple.

Group norms may be observed in the hangout, as values can be noted in the mass media. In the early teens, the hangout may be a local malt shop or soda fountain. If the community provides a canteen, it may take the place of a hangout, but it is not the same thing, because it is supervised by adults.

The hangout can be usefully analyzed in terms of the framework of "the establishment," as suggested by Erving Goffman:[2]

A social establishment is any place surrounded by fixed barriers to perception in which a particular kind of activity regularly takes place. . . . Any social establishment may be studied profitably from the point of view of impression management. Within the walls of a social establishment we find a team of performers who cooperate to present to an audience a given definition of the situation. This will include the conception of own team and of audience and assumptions concerning the ethos that it is to be maintained by rules of politeness and decorum. . . .

[2] Erving Goffman, *The Presentation of Self in Everyday Life* (Garden City, N. Y.: Doubleday Anchorage, 1959), p. 238.

Among members of the team we find that familiarity prevails, solidarity is likely to develop, and that secrets that could give the show away are shared and kept. A tacit agreement is maintained between performers and audience to act as if a given degree of opposition and of accord existed between them.

In the teen-age hangout, the "teams" are likely to be the boys on one side and the girls on the other. One study found that going to hangouts — drugstore, fountain bar — almost equalled pleasure-driving in terms of numbers of participants involved.

WORK IN TEEN-AGE CULTURE

The teen-ager participates in the economy primarily as a consumer. It is true that teen-agers work very hard — customizing automobiles, for example, or organizing and soliciting members for fan clubs — and it is conceivable that such work might have a market. But it is usually not marketed and, therefore, not subjected to the discipline of the adult work world. When the teen-ager sells his labor in the market, he is participating in adult culture, not his own.

When he does participate in the labor market, it is likely to be as a marginal producer, usually in part-time jobs which articulate well with the other demands of teen-age culture and, therefore, do not remove him from it. Certain occupations are characteristically teen-age. The paper route, odd jobs such as cutting lawns and shoveling snow, and baby sitting are standard teen-age jobs. Between high school and college, summer jobs may be in the adult world and constitute a first introduction to its demands. Some kinds of jobs at supermarkets are sometimes reserved for teen-agers. But, for many teen-agers, the typical job is at a summer camp or resort; and most of these articulate well with the other demands of teen-age culture and, therefore, do not remove the worker from its impact.

THE POLITICAL VALUES

Teen-age culture provides for an absorbing way of life. It is fairly well insulated against outside forces except those beamed directly at it. One of the commonest characteristics of American teen-agers, in fact, has been that, in alleged contrast to those of some other societies, they are politically apathetic. Interest in politics is not an integral part of teen-age culture.

When pressed for opinions on political questions by adults, however, teen-agers reply in ways which reflect, as clearly as other aspects of their culture, a distinct class bias. Polls of high school students during the 1940's and 1950's with respect to political opinions and attitude corroborate with almost uncanny accuracy the conclusion which Seymour Lipset arrived at after analyzing adult voting behavior. With respect to government control, that is, lower class teen-agers are more likely than upper class teen-agers to be "liberal"; but, with respect to civil liberties and race relations, they are more likely to be reactionary (see Table 1).

CLASS AND TEEN-AGE CULTURE

Hollingshead reported more than a decade ago on the pervasiveness of class in high schools in the 1940's. Teen-age society is still stratified and class still pervades teen-age culture. By and large, the cleavage still divides high school students into the college preparatory or academic students and the vocational or commercial students. All aspects of teen-age culture — like political attitudes referred to above — differ for the different classes — taste in moving pictures and dress, hangouts, dancing, and dating practices. The ideal-typical girl is different. The following reports document these differences.

Class and moving pictures in teen-age culture

My town had three movies, two of which showed grade A movies while the third showed grade F — cowboy and horror movies. Two different classes of boys and girls attended these features. In the grade F theater one would find the "cats" of the town, mostly boys. Conduct in this movie could be characterized by whistling, throwing empty candy boxes, and placing feet on chairs. Loud conversations also could be heard.

In the grade A movie houses one usually saw the girls and boys of middle class families. Of course, while these individuals did not attend the horror shows in the other theater, once in a while the "other

TABLE 1 *Teen-Age Political Opinion Related to Socioeconomic Class*

Issue	Per Cent Upper Income Group Teen-Agers	Per Cent Lower Income Group Teen-Agers
Civil Liberties and Race Relations		
Democratic institutions depend on free business enterprise	64%	54%
Democratic institutions depend on freedom of the press	47	42
Unwarranted search and seizure is permissible	11	26
Third degree is permissible to gain criminal confessions	53	59
Taking the Fifth Amendment is acceptable	28	39
Wiretapping is not acceptable	37	29
School desegregation is approved	46	38
Disturbances and pupil strikes to prevent desegregation are disapproved	70	50
Government Control of Economy and Private Ownership		
Government should have control of railroads and airlines	11	26
Basic industries should be owned by government	14	21
Large unused estates should be divided among the poor for farming	48	63
Slum clearance should be privately controlled	18	16
Private ownership and/or control is advocated for:		
Peaceful uses of atomic energy	25	13
Electric power from rivers and dams	26	18
Electric power from steam plants	55	38
Oil resources	53	49
Nativism		
Immigration should be restricted	35	42
Foreign countries have little to contribute to American progress	10	19

Source: H. H. Remmers and D. H. Radler, *The American Teenager* (Indianapolis: Bobbs-Merrill, 1957), pp. 208 ff.

element" would attend the better movies. Personal conduct in the grade A movies was opposite to that in the grade F movies — no throwing boxes, placing of feet on chairs, engaging in loud conversations. Once in a while the boys might whistle, though.

Class and dress

From my experience, I've found that the clothes a boy wears definitely elevate or lower his social status. When a boy dresses in the current fashion, it shows that he knows what's going on and is not "out of it." On first impression, a boy is rated on his appearance — either tweedy or cloddy, as the case may be.

To rate well socially, a boy should look as tweedy as possible. This means wearing tan raincoats, crew-neck sweaters, button-down oxford cloth shirts, khaki, corduroy or flannel pants, and loafers or sneakers. Not only must he wear these clothes, but he must choose the correct style in each. Sweaters should be in neutral or dark shades, shirts are white, blue, or pin-striped, and the pants are continental or at least tapered and slim in the legs.

A boy may be considered a clod if he wears flannel or non-button-down shirts, baggy pants or deviates from the traditional crew-neck style sweaters. Shoes with laces (oxfords) worn with casual clothes are also in poor taste.

A girl may also be socially rated as to the clothes she wears. Girls dress to look tweedy or collegiate. Tweedy girls wear button-down blouses or round or pilgrim collar blouses, pleated, bandstand, or flared skirts, wool crew-neck or fur-blend sweaters, knee socks and loafers. . . . Girls should beware of rayon-type or felt skirts which are too long, wing collar blouses, banlon sweaters, and low socks. Sneakers are being replaced by loafers in the really "in" groups. The goal is to look simple, the characteristic of tweediness. Most of the kids I know feel that sharp clothes indicate a hip personality.

Class and hangouts

In my town of 20,000 people, there were two main hangouts for the teen-agers. The YMCA recreation room was a place where one could snack, watch TV, play ping pong, and dance to juke box music. But it was more of a canteen, I guess, than a real hangout. It was considered a nice place for the kids to go. Most of the girls and boys would usually drop in after school for an hour or two in evening. Since the canteen was a part of the Y, it was considered quite respectable.

Another gathering place for the students was a little drug store. The boys and girls who frequented this particular drug store were the smokers and drinking set of the school. They were considered to be off-limits by the more respectable students. Perhaps not strictly off-limits — one could talk to them, but, on the other hand, interdating would not occur. This element of our town, while they did attend the Y-teen dances, also had their own little restaurant dancing spot where they would go on weekdays and week ends. It was not considered such a good place to go. One needed transportation to get to this second hangout.

Class and the ideal-typical girl

The girls who are high school cheerleaders and those who are high school majorettes differ markedly in background, appearance, and personality. The cheerleader is typically an academic student preparing for college and representing the middle and upper class. . . . She is a clean-cut, all-American girl. . . . She is not made up nor does she wear her hair in anything but a simple, classic, schoolgirl hairdo. . . . She is a breathing replica of a *Seventeen* model. . . . She belongs to the right clubs and dates a football hero or the student body president. She is in the know but not conceited about her position. . . . As a rule she doesn't associate with the majorettes.

The majorettes, who lead the band, seldom lead the school. They are usually commercial students who are planning to be secretaries. Most of them are from lower middle or upper lower classes. Their attitude toward school is poor and, as a result, their grades are low. Or, if their grades are good, they are discounted by the fact that they are in a commercial curriculum.

The twirlers are opposite in appearance, also, to the cheerleaders. They are pretty but in a gaudy way. Their hairdos and make-up are overdone and in poor taste, and they wear tight and often suggestive clothing that suggests cheapness. As a rule, they are not the popular girls nor do they try to be. Often being a majorette is their only activity. . . .

Because the cheering squad was so selective and enviable, many very capable girls who qualified were disappointed each year because they failed to make it. A group of these girls, who wanted to be in on things at school knew that they couldn't make cheering yet wouldn't settle for being a majorette. They began to organize a marching squad which would be chosen on the same criteria as the cheering squad except that these girls would do precision drills with the band. At first their group was small and only performed at talent shows and the like. But it soon became a part of pep rallies. . . . These girls formed their own in-group and at last have status almost equal to the cheerleaders and far above the majorettes.

Related to these class distinctions is the existence of alienation among teen-agers. There are the clods, the outs. And they constitute a sizeable proportion of the high school population. One study, for example, found that there were 22 per cent who felt left out of things, 11 per cent who felt "different," 44 per cent who seldom had dates, 13 per cent who felt they were not wanted, 20 per cent who felt lonesome, and 25 per cent who felt ill at ease at social affairs. This alienation occurred in all classes, but it was more common in teen-agers with low income backgrounds than it was in those with high income backgrounds.

THE COLLEGE LEVEL

Up to now, the class selective factor has operated to weed out teen-agers with lower class backgrounds from the older teen-age culture, leaving the upper middle class teen-agers as bearers of teen-age culture at the college level. Typically, it took the form of the so-called "rah-rah" culture.

Today, however, many young people from lower socioeconomic class backgrounds also go to colleges and universities. Some are absorbed into the collegiate culture. But many others have a strong vocational orientation. They do not participate in the old collegiate culture; they are preparing for adult roles. And even students from upper class backgrounds now find that they must take higher education more seriously. The tendency is, therefore, for teen-age culture to end with high school for an increasing number of young people. The forces at work making for this result have been analyzed by Clark and Trow, whose findings we follow here.

They distinguish four models of student cultures, namely: collegiate, vocational, academic, and nonconformist.

The collegiate culture is the world of football, Greek letter societies, cars, and drinking. Courses and professors occupy a dim background position. This culture is not hostile to the college; it is only indifferent and resistant to serious demands and involvement in intellectual activities. "This culture is characteristically middle and upper middle class — it takes money and leisure to pursue the busy round of social activities — and flourishes on, though is by no means confined to, the resident campuses of big state universities."

The vocational culture tends to prevail in urban colleges and universities attended by the children of lower middle class families. Because many of these students are married and working hard, their culture is not teen-age in character. They are customers not in a luxury market but in a diploma market. "They buy their education somewhat as one buys groceries," to use an idea of Riesman and Jencks. "If the symbol of the collegiate culture is the football and fraternity weekend, the symbol of this vocationally oriented culture is the student placement office."

The academic culture has learning and knowledge and ideas as a central set of values. "The distinctive qualities of this group are (a) they are seriously involved in their course work beyond the minimum required for passing and graduation and (b) they identify themselves with their college and its faculty." No more than the vocational culture, therefore, is this one teen-age in its essential characteristics.

The nonconformist culture belongs to the intellectual, radical, alienated Bohemian. The authors who distinguish it concede that it is elusive, that it may be merely a residual category, difficult to distinguish from the academic culture. "The academic cultures we speak of include students with intellectual interests as well as grinds submissive to the demands of the faculty. When students' intellectual interests are not merely independent of but also at odds with the curriculum, they often form the nucleus of what we have called 'nonconformist' cultures, which however also include styles and interests that are by no means intellectual. In our typology, the members of the academic subcultures tend to link their interests to the curriculum; the nonconformists pursue theirs outside it."

It is the conclusion of Clark and Trow that, because of the career demands in large bureaucratic organizations whose hiring staffs scrutinize transcripts and evaluate grades, the characteristically teen-age or collegiate culture is now on the decline. As more and more children of lower middle class background go to college and as the demands of society call for greater training, the vocational and academic cultures wax. "Both the vocational and the academic orientation are 'adult' in a way that the collegiate culture is not."

ETHNICITY AND RACE

Our discussion so far has emphasized class and age differences in teen-age culture. Ethnicity and race are also significant factors, closely related to class. The child of the recent immigrant is pulled between the ethnic culture of his family, which is separatist in effect, and the teen-age culture of his peers. After two or three generations, the ethnic factor all but disappears. Not so the racial factor. The Negro teen-ager is in many ways an even newer phenomenon than the white teen-ager today. It is only very recently that a substantial middle class could afford to keep children in high school, let alone college. The upper level teen-age Negro finds himself caught in two intersecting cultures. The clash is between the traditional values professed by American society which he now studies in school and the discriminating culture he still sees in operation around him. In 1960 the Negro college student decided to do something about it.

CHANGE AND
MODERNIZATION

11 Death by Dieselization*

W. F. Cottrell

Perhaps the most obvious case of social change is the modification of the local community that results from major technological inventions. All of us are familiar with the revolution in American communities that followed the widespread use of the private automobile. But we may be less aware of the changes that resulted from the substitution of diesel oil for steam in railroad engines. Use of diesel led to the abandonment of "division points" along railroad lines and thus the economic base for many small towns. A similar phenomenon occurred in the closing of mining communities and lumber towns. When the economic base of a community is lost, what alternative courses of action are available to the inhabitants? What major changes in community social structure can be anticipated? The following study provides some answers.

In the following instance it is proposed that we examine a community confronted with radical change in its basic economic institution and trace the effects of this change throughout the social structure. From these facts it may be possible in some degree to anticipate the resultant changing attitudes and values of the people in the community, particularly as they reveal whether or not there is a demand for modification of the social structure or a shift in function from one institution

* Excerpt from W. F. Cottrell, "Death by Dieselization: A Case Study in the Reaction to Technological Change," *American Sociological Review*, Vol. 16 (June 1951), pp. 358–365. Copyright © 1951 by the American Sociological Association. Reproduced by permission.

to another. Some of the implications of the facts discovered may be valuable in anticipating future social change.

The community chosen for examination has been disrupted by the dieselization of the railroads. Since the railroad is among the oldest of those industries organized around steam, and since therefore the social structure of railroad communities is a product of long-continued processes of adaptation to the technology of steam, the sharp contrast between the technological requirements of the steam engine and those of the diesel should clearly reveal the changes in social structure required. Any one of a great many railroad towns might have been chosen for examination. However, many railroad towns are only partly dependent upon the railroad for their existence. In them many of the effects which take place are blurred and not easily distinguishable by the observer. Thus, the "normal" railroad town may not be the best place to see the consequences of dieselization. For this reason a one-industry town was chosen for examination.

In a sense it is an "ideal type" railroad town, and hence not complicated by other extraneous economic factors. It lies in the desert and is here given the name "Caliente" which is the Spanish adjective for "hot." Caliente was built in a break in an eighty-mile canyon traversing the desert. Its reason for existence was to service the steam locomotive. There are few resources in the area to support it on any other basis, and such as they are would contribute more to the growth and maintenance of other little settlements in the vicinity than to that of Caliente. So long as the steam locomotive was in use, Caliente was a necessity. With the adoption of the diesel it became obsolescent.

This stark fact was not, however, part of the expectations of the residents of Caliente. Based upon the "certainty" of the railroad's need for Caliente, men built their homes there, frequently of concrete and brick, at the cost, in many cases, of their life savings. The water system was laid in cast iron which will last for centuries. Business men erected substantial buildings which could be paid for only by profits gained through many years of business. Four churches evidence the faith of Caliente people in the future of their community.

A twenty-seven bed hospital serves the town. Those who built it thought that their investment was as well warranted as the fact of birth, sickness, accident and death. They believed in education. Their school buildings represent the investment of savings guaranteed by bonds and future taxes. There is a combined park and play field which, together with a recently modernized theatre, has been serving recreational needs. All these physical structures are material evidence of the expectations, morally and legally sanctioned and financially funded, of the people of Caliente. This is a normal and rational aspect of the culture of all "solid" and "sound" communities.

Similarly normal are the social organizations. These include Rotary, Chamber of Commerce, Masons, Odd Fellows, American Legion and the Veterans of Foreign Wars. There are the usual unions, churches, and myriad little clubs to which the women belong. In short, here is the average American community with normal social life, subscribing to normal American codes. Nothing its members had been taught would indicate that the whole pattern of this normal existence depended completely upon a few elements of technology which were themselves in flux. For them the continued use of the steam engine was as "natural" a phenomenon as any other element in their physical environment. Yet suddenly their life pattern was destroyed by the announcement that the railroad was moving its division point, and with it destroying the economic basis of Caliente's existence.

Turning from this specific community for a moment, let us examine the technical changes which took place and the reasons for the change. Division points on a railroad are established by the frequency with which the rolling stock must be serviced and the operating crews changed. At the turn of the century when this particular road was built, the engines produced wet steam at low temperatures. The steel in the boilers was of comparatively low tensile strength and could not withstand the high temperatures and pressures required for the efficient use of coal and water. At intervals of roughly a hundred miles the engine had to be disconnected from the train for service. At these points the cars also were inspected and if they were found to be defective they were either removed from the train or repaired while it was

standing and the new engine being coupled on. Thus the location of Caliente, as far as the railroad was concerned, was a function of boiler temperature and pressure and the resultant service requirements of the locomotive.

Following World War II, the high tensile steels developed to create superior artillery and armor were used for locomotives. As a consequence it was possible to utilize steam at higher temperatures and pressure. Speed, power, and efficiency were increased and the distance between service intervals was increased.

The "ideal distance" between freight divisions became approximately 150 to 200 miles whereas it had formerly been 100 to 150. Wherever possible, freight divisions were increased in length to that formerly used by passenger trains, and passenger divisions were lengthened from two old freight divisions to three. Thus towns located 100 miles from a terminal became obsolescent, those at 200 became freight points only, and those at three hundred miles became passenger division points.

The increase in speed permitted the train crews to make the greater distance in the time previously required for the lesser trip, and roughly a third of the train and engine crews, car inspectors, boilermakers and machinists and other service men were dropped. The towns thus abandoned were crossed off the social record of the nation in the adjustment to these technological changes in the use of the steam locomotive. Caliente, located midway between terminals about six hundred miles apart, survived. In fact it gained, since the less frequent stops caused an increase in the service required of the maintenance crews at those points where it took place. However, the introduction of the change to diesel engines projected a very different future.

In its demands for service the diesel engine differs almost completely from a steam locomotive. It requires infrequent, highly skilled service, carried on within very close limits, in contrast to the frequent, crude adjustments required by the steam locomotive. Diesels operate at about 35 per cent efficiency in contrast to the approximately 4 per cent efficiency of the steam locomotives in use after World War II in the United States. Hence diesels require much less frequent stops for fuel and water. These facts reduce their operating costs sufficiently to compensate for their much higher initial cost.

In spite of these reductions in operating costs the introduction of diesels ordinarily would have taken a good deal of time. The change-over would have been slowed by the high capital costs of retooling the locomotive works, the long period required to recapture the costs of existing steam locomotives, and the effective resistance of the workers. World War II altered each of these factors. The locomotive works were required to make the change in order to provide marine engines, and the costs of the change were assumed by the government. Steam engines were used up by the tremendous demand placed upon the railroads by war traffic. The costs were recaptured by shipping charges. Labor shortages were such that labor resistance was less formidable and much less acceptable to the public than it would have been in peace time. Hence the shift to diesels was greatly facilitated by the war. In consequence, every third and sometimes every second division point suddenly became technologically obsolescent.

Caliente, like all other towns in similar plight, is supposed to accept its fate in the name of "progress." The general public, as shippers and consumers of shipped goods, reaps the harvest in better, faster service and eventually perhaps in lower charges. A few of the workers in Caliente will also share the gains, as they move to other division points, through higher wages. They will share in the higher pay, though whether this will be adequate to compensate for the costs of moving no one can say. Certain it is that their pay will not be adjusted to compensate for their specific losses. They will gain only as their seniority gives them the opportunity to work. These are those who gain. What are the losses, and who bears them?

The railroad company can figure its losses at Caliente fairly accurately. It owns 39 private dwellings, a modern clubhouse with 116 single rooms, and a twelve-room hotel with dining-room and lunch-counter facilities. These now become useless, as does much of the fixed physical equipment used for servicing trains. Some of the machinery can be used elsewhere. Some part of the roundhouse can be used to store unused locomo-

tives and standby equipment. The rest will be torn down to save taxes. All of these costs can be entered as capital losses on the statement which the company draws up for its stockholders and for the government. Presumably they will be recovered by the use of the more efficient engines.

What are the losses that may not be entered on the company books? The total tax assessment in Caliente was $9,946.80 for the year 1948, of which $6,103.39 represented taxes assessed on the railroad. Thus the railroad valuation was about three-fifths that of the town. This does not take into account tax-free property belonging to the churches, the schools, the hospital, or the municipality itself which included all the public utilities. Some ideas of the losses sustained by the railroad in comparison with the losses of others can be surmised by reflecting on these figures for real estate alone. The story is an old one and often repeated in the economic history of America. It represents the "loss" side of a profit and loss system of adjusting to technological change. Perhaps for sociological purposes we need an answer to the question "just who pays?"

Probably the greatest losses are suffered by the older "non-operating" employees. Seniority among these men extends only within the local shop and craft. A man with twenty-five years' seniority at Caliente has no claim on the job of a similar craftsman at another point who has only twenty-five days' seniority. Moreover, some of the skills formerly valuable are no longer needed. The boilermaker, for example, knows that jobs for his kind are disappearing and he must enter the ranks of the unskilled. The protection and status offered by the union while he was employed have become meaningless now that he is no longer needed. The cost of this is high both in loss of income and in personal demoralization.

Operating employees also pay. Their seniority extends over a division, which in this case includes three division points. The older members can move from Caliente and claim another job at another point, but in many cases they move leaving a good portion of their life savings behind. The younger men must abandon their stake in railroad employment. The loss may mean a new apprenticeship in another occupation, at a time in life when apprenticeship wages are not adequate to meet the obligations of mature men with families. A steam engine hauled 2,000 tons up the hill out of Caliente with the aid of two helpers. The four-unit diesel in command of one crew handles a train of 5,000 tons alone. Thus, to handle the same amount of tonnage required only about a fourth the man-power it formerly took. Three out of four men must start out anew at something else.

The local merchants pay. The boarded windows, half-empty shelves, and abandoned store buildings bear mute evidence of these costs. The older merchants stay, and pay; the younger ones, and those with no stake in the community will move; but the value of their property will in both cases largely be gone.

The bondholders will pay. They can't foreclose on a dead town. If the town were wiped out altogether, that which would remain for salvage would be too little to satisfy their claims. Should the town continue there is little hope that taxes adequate to carry the overhead of bonds and day-to-day expenses could be secured by taxing the diminished number of property owners or employed persons.

The church will pay. The smaller congregations cannot support services as in the past. As the church men leave, the buildings will be abandoned.

Homeowners will pay. A hundred and thirty-five men owned homes in Caliente. They must accept the available means of support or rent to those who do. In either case the income available will be far less than that on which the houses were built. The least desirable homes will stand unoccupied, their value completely lost. The others must be revalued at a figure far below that at which they were formerly held.

In a word, those pay who are, by traditional American standards, *most moral*. Those who have raised children see friendships broken and neighborhoods disintegrated. The childless more freely shake the dust of Caliente from their feet. Those who built their personalities into the structure of the community watch their work destroyed. Those too wise or too selfish to have entangled themselves in community affairs suffer no such qualms. The chain store can pull down its sign, move its equipment and charge the costs off against more profitable and better located units, and against taxes. The local owner has no such alternatives.

In short, "good citizens" who assumed family and community responsibility are the greatest losers. Nomads suffer least.

The people of Caliente are asked to accept as "normal" this strange inversion of their expectations. It is assumed that they will, without protest or change in sentiment, accept the dictum of the "law of supply and demand." Certainly they must comply in part with this dictum. While their behavior in part reflects this compliance, there are also other changes perhaps equally important in their attitudes and values.

The first reaction took the form of an effort at community self-preservation. Caliente became visible to its inhabitants as a real entity, as meaningful as the individual personalities which they had hitherto been taught to see as atomistic or nomadic elements. Community survival was seen as prerequisite to many of the individual values that had been given precedence in the past. The organized community made a search for new industry, citing elements of community organization themselves as reasons why industry should move to Caliente. But the conditions that led the railroad to abandon the point made the place even less attractive to new industry than it had hitherto been. Yet the effort to keep the community a going concern persisted.

There was also a change in sentiment. In the past the glib assertion that progress spelled sacrifice could be offered when some distant group was a victim of technological change. There was no such reaction when the event struck home. The change can probably be as well revealed as in any other way by quoting from the Caliente *Herald:*

. . . (over the) years . . . (this) . . . railroad and its affiliates . . . became to this writer his ideal of a railroad empire. The (company) . . . appeared to take much more than the ordinary interest of big railroads in the development of areas adjacent to its lines, all the while doing a great deal for the communities large and small through which the lines passed.

Those were the days creative of (its) enviable reputation as one of the finest, most progressive — and most human — of American railroads, enjoying the confidence and respect of employees, investors, and communities alike!

One of the factors bringing about this confidence

and respect was the consideration shown communities which otherwise would have suffered serious blows when division and other changes were effected. A notable example was . . . (a town) . . . where the shock of division change was made almost unnoticed by installation of a rolling stock reclamation point, which gave (that town) an opportunity to hold its community intact until tourist traffic and other industries could get better established — with the result that . . . (it) . . . is now on a firm foundation. And through this display of consideration for a community, the railroad gained friends — not only among the people of . . . (that town) . . . who were perhaps more vocal than others, but also among thousands of others throughout the country on whom this action made an indelible impression.

But things seem to have changed materially during the last few years, the . . . (company) . . . seems to this writer to have gone all out for glamor and the dollars which glamorous people have to spend, sadly neglecting one of the principal factors which helped to make . . . (it) . . . great: that fine consideration of communities and individuals, as well as employees, who have been happy in cooperating steadfastly with the railroad in times of stress as well as prosperity. The loyalty of these people and communities seems to count for little with the . . . (company) . . . of this day, though other "Big Business" corporations do not hesitate to expend huge sums to encourage the loyalty of community and people which old friends of . . . (the company) . . . have been happy to give voluntarily.

Ever since the . . . railroad was constructed . . . Caliente has been a key town on the railroad. It is true, the town owed its inception to the railroad, but it has paid this back in becoming one of the most attractive communities on the system. With nice homes, streets and parks, good school . . . good city government . . . Caliente offers advantages that most big corporations would be gratified to have for their employees — a homey spot where they could live their lives of contentment, happiness and security.

Caliente's strategic location, midway of some of the toughest road on the entire system has been a lifesaver for the road several times when floods have wrecked havoc on the roadbed in the canyon above and below Caliente. This has been possible through storage in Caliente of large stocks of repair material and equipment — and not overlooking manpower — which has thus become available on short notice.

. . . But (the railroad) or at least one of its big officials appearing to be almost completely divorced from policies which made this railroad great, has ordered changes which are about as inconsiderate as anything of which "Big Business" has ever been accused! Employees who have given the best years of their lives to this railroad are cut off without anything to which they can turn, many of them with homes in which they have taken much pride; while others, similarly with nice homes, are told to move elsewhere and are given runs that only a few will be able to endure from a physical standpoint, according to common opinion.

Smart big corporations the country over encourage their employees to own their own homes — and loud are their boasts when the percentage of such employees is favorable! But in contrast, a high (company) official is reported to have said only recently that "a railroad man has no business owning a home!" Quite a departure from what has appeared to be (company) tradition.

It is difficult for the Herald to believe that this official however "big" he is, speaking for the . . . (company) . . . when he enunciates a policy that, carried to the letter, would make tramps of (company) employees and their families!

No thinking person wants to stand in the way of progress, but true progress is not made when it is overshadowed by cold-blooded disregard for the loyalty of employees, their families, and the communities which have developed in the good American way through the decades of loyal service and good citizenship.

This editorial, written by a member of all the service clubs, approved by Caliente business men, and quoted with approbation by the most conserative members of the community, is significant of changing sentiment.

The people of Caliente continually profess their belief in "The American Way," but like the editor of the *Herald* they criticize decisions made solely in pursuit of profit, even though these decisions grow out of a clear-cut case of technological "progress." They feel that the company should have based its decision upon consideration for loyalty, citizenship, and community morale. They assume that the company should regard the seniority rights of workers as important considerations, and that it should consider significant the effect of permanent unemployment upon old and faithful employees. They look upon the community integrity as an important community asset. Caught between the support of a "rational" system of "economic" forces and laws, and sentiments which they accept as significant values, they seek a solution to their dilemma which will at once permit them to retain their expected rewards

for continued adherence to past norms and to defend the social system which they have been taught to revere but which now offers them a stone instead of bread.

12 Religious Aspects of Modernization in Turkey and Japan*

Robert N. Bellah

We have seen that social change sometimes involves sharp conflict between traditional values and newly emerging values. Recognizing the dominant role of religion in traditional societies, we may anticipate that "modernization" in these societies is not likely to proceed far without involving the religious institutions. The following study reports similarities and differences in the role of religion in the attempts at modernization of Turkey and Japan. The evidence is that in Japan religion has played a leading part in legitimizing social change.

The process of modernization of the "backward" nations such as Turkey and Japan, which will be considered here, involves changes in the value system as well as economic, political, and social changes. In traditional societies the value system tends to be what Howard Becker calls "prescriptive." A prescriptive system is characterized by the comprehensiveness and specificity of its value commitments and by its consequent lack of flexibility. Motivation is frozen, so to speak, through commitment to a vast range of relatively specific norms governing almost every situation in life. Most of these specific norms, usually including those governing social institu-

* Excerpt reprinted from Robert N. Bellah, "Religious Aspects of Modernization in Turkey and Japan," *American Journal of Sociology*, 64, 1 (July 1958), pp. 1–5, by permission of The University of Chicago Press. Copyright © 1962 by The University of Chicago.

tions, are thoroughly integrated with a religious system which invokes ultimate sanctions for every infraction. Thus changes in economic or political institutions, not to speak of family and education, in traditional societies tend to have ultimate religious implications. Small changes will involve supernatural sanctions.

Yet such a society, when faced with grave dislocations consequent to Western contact, must make major changes in its institutional structure if it is to survive. What changes must be made in the organization of the value system so that these structural changes may go forward?

We may say that the value system of such a society must change from a prescriptive type to a "principial" type, to borrow again from Becker. Traditional societies, as we have said, tend to have a normative system, in which a comprehensive, but uncodified, set of relatively specific norms governs concrete behavior. But in a modern society an area of flexibility must be gained in economic, political, and social life in which specific norms may be determined in considerable part by short-term exigencies in the situation of action, or by functional requisites of the relevant social subsystems. Ultimate or religious values lay down the basic principles of social action; thus such a normative system is called "principial," but the religious system does not attempt to regulate economic, political, and social life in great detail, as in prescriptive societies. Looking at this process another way, we may say that there must be a differentiation between religion and ideology, between ultimate values and proposed ways in which these values may be put into effect. In traditional prescriptive societies there is no such discrimination. Difference of opinion on social policy is taken to imply difference as to religious commitment. The social innovator necessarily becomes a religious heretic. But in modern society there is a differentiation between the levels of religion and social ideology which makes possible greater flexibility at both levels.

How is the normative system in a traditional society to be changed from prescriptive to principial, and how is the differentiation of the religious and ideological levels to be effected, especially in the face of the concerted effort of the old system to avoid any changes at all? I would assert that only a new religious initiative, only a new movement which claims religious ultimacy for itself, can successfully challenge the old value system and its religious base. The new movement, which arises from the necessity to make drastic social changes in the light of new conditions, is essentially ideological and political in nature. But, arising as it does in a society in which the ideological level is not yet recognized as having independent legitimacy, the new movement must take on a religious coloration in order to meet the old system on its own terms. Even when such a movement is successful in effecting major structural changes in the society and in freeing motivation formerly frozen in traditional patterns so that considerable flexibility in economic and political life is attained, the problems posed by its own partly religious origin and its relation to the traditional religious system may still be serious indeed.

Let us turn to the example of Turkey.

Ottoman Turkey in the eighteenth century was a traditionalistic society with a prescriptive value system. Virtually all spheres of life were theoretically under the authority of the religious law, the Shari'ah. Indeed, the government was supposed to have an area of freedom within the law. But this freedom had become narrowly restricted. Precedents of governmental procedure were tacitly assimilated to the religious law.

Beginning with Selim III in the late eighteenth century, a series of reforming sultans and statesmen attempted to make major changes in Turkish society in an effort to cope with increasingly desperate internal and external conditions. While some changes were made, especially in areas remote from the central strongholds of the religious law, the reforming party was unable to attain any ultimate legitimacy in the eyes of the people, and, although Turkish society was shaken to its foundations, periods of reform alternated with periods of blind reaction in which reformers were executed or banished.

The last of these reactionary periods was that of the rule of the despotic Sultan Abdul Hamid II, who was overthrown in 1908 by a coup of young army officers whom we know as the "Young Turks." By this time it had become clear to leading intellectuals that more was needed than another interim of liberal reform. They saw that a basic change in the cultural foundation of Turkish society was demanded if the long-delayed changes in economic, political, and social structure were to be effected. Some felt that a modern purified Islam could provide the new cultural basis, but orthodox Islam was so deeply imbedded in the fabric of traditional society that the Islamic modernists found little response in the religious party. Others looked to Western liberal democracy as a satisfactory foundation. Those sensitive to the mind of the Turkish masses, however, pointed out that the Turkish people would never accept a value system so obviously "made abroad" and which could so easily be condemned by the conservatives with the stigma of unbelief.

It was Ziya Gökalp, a sociologist much influenced by Durkheim, who ardently championed Turkish nationalism as the only satisfactory cultural foundation for the new Turkey. Gökalp found the referent for all symbols of ultimate value in society itself. His answer to the religious conservatives was that the true Islam was that of the Turkish folk, not of the effete religious hierarchy which was largely educated in the Arabic and Persian languages rather than the Turkish language. Here at last was an ideology to which the people could respond with emotion and which could challenge religious conservatism on its own grounds.

But the course of world history did as much as Gökalp's eloquence to decide in favor of the nationalist alternative for Turkey. Not only did World War I shear Turkey of her empire, but the subsequent invasions of Anatolia threatened the very life of the nation itself. Mustafa Kemal, who led the ultimately successful effort of national resistance, partly chose and partly was impelled to make the nation the central symbol in his subsequent drive for modernization. As a result, the highest value and central symbol for the most articulate sections of the Turkish people became not Islam but Turkism, or nationalism, or Kemalism, or, simply, "the Revolution." Having a strong national and personal charismatic legitimacy, Mustafa Kemal, later known as "Ataturk," was able to create a far-reaching cultural revolution in which the place of religion in the society was fundamentally altered. We may note some of the landmarks in this revolution. In 1924 the office of caliph was abolished. In the same year all religious schools were closed or converted into secular schools. The most important change of all took place in 1926: the Muslim Civil Law was abandoned and the Swiss Civil Code adopted almost without change. Finally, in 1928, the phrase in the constitution stating that the religion of Turkey is Islam was deleted, and Turkey was declared a secular state.

That the Turks were deeply conscious of what they were doing is illustrated by the following quotation from Mahmud Essad, the minister of justice under whom the religious law was abandoned:

> The purpose of laws is not to maintain the old customs or beliefs which have their source in religion, but rather to assure the economic and social unity of the nation.
>
> When religion has sought to rule human societies, it has been the arbitrary instrument of sovereigns, despots, and strong men. In separating the temporal and the spiritual, modern civilization has saved the world from numerous calamities and has given to religion an imperishable throne in the consciences of believers.

This quotation illustrates well enough the transition from prescriptive to principial society and the differentiation of religion and ideology as two distinct levels. It is clear that the great advances of Turkish society in economic, political, and social life are based on this new cultural foundation. But implicit in Essad's words are some of the yet unsolved problems about that new cultural pattern.

For Essad and other Turkish reformers "the Revolution" was a criterion for everything, even for the place of religion in society, and thus, whether consciously or not, they gave the revolution an ultimate, a religious, significance. The six principles upon which the constitution is based — republicanism, nationalism, populism, étatism, secularism, and revolution — are taken as self-subsisting ultimates. Thus the religious implications of the political ideology remain relatively unchecked. These express themselves in party claims to ultimate legitimacy and in an inability on the part of the party in power to accept the validity of an opposition, which are not in accord with the flexibility appropriate in a modern principial society.

On the other hand, Islam in Turkey has not on the whole been able to redefine its own self-image and face the theological issues involved in becoming a religion primarily, in Essad's words, "enthroned in men's consciences." Nor has it been able to provide a deeper religious dimension of both legitimation and judgment of the six principles which are the basis of the new social life. It remains, on the whole, in a conservative frame of mind in which the ideological claims are considerable, thus still posing a threat, possibly a great one, to return the society to a less differentiated level of social organization. Considering the trend of the last forty years, however, we seem to be observing a differentiation in the process of becoming, but it is too soon to say that it has been entirely accomplished.

Japan, while illustrating the same general processes as Turkey, does so with marked differences in important details. Premodern Japan was a traditionalistic society with a prescriptive normative system closely integrated with a religious system composed of a peculiar Japanese amalgam of Shinto, Confucianism, and Buddhism. In the immediate premodern period, however, a conjuncture of the Confucian stress on loyalty and a revived interest in Shinto began to have explosive consequences. The actual rule at this time was in the hands of a military dictator, or Shogun, hereditary in the Tokugawa family. The emperor was relegated to purely ceremonial functions in the palace at Kyoto. But, as economic and social conditions deteriorated under Tokugawa rule, important elements in the population became alienated from the political status quo. They proved extremely receptive to the religious message of the revival Shintoists and legitimist Confucians, who insisted that the true sovereign was the emperor and that the Shogun was a usurper. According to their conception, the emperor is divine, descended from the sun-goddess, and his direct rule of the Japanese people could be expected to bring in a virtually messianic age.

This movement was already vigorous when Perry's ships moved into Tokyo Bay in 1853. The inability of the Tokugawa government to keep foreigners from desecrating the sacred soil of Japan added the last fuel to the flames of resentment, and, with the slogan "Revere the Emperor; expel the barbarians," a successful military coup overthrew the Tokugawa and restored the emperor to direct rule.

I would suggest that Japan was at this point, in 1868, virtually at the beginning of serious Western influence, in a position that Turkey reached only in the early 1920's under Mustafa Kemal. But she reached it in quite a different way. Unlike Turkey, one of the very foundations of the old traditional order in Japan, the divine emperor, provided the main leverage for the radical reorganization of that order. The young samurai who put through the Meiji Restoration used the central value of loyalty to the emperor to legitimize the immense changes they were making in all spheres of social life and to justify the abandoning of many apparently sacred prescriptions of the traditional order. No other sacredness could challenge the sacredness inherent in the emperor's person.

Here we see an ideological movement, essentially political in nature, whose aim was the strengthening and thus the modernizing of Japan, taking a much more openly religious coloration than was the case in Turkey. There was in the early Meiji period an attempt to make Shinto into the national religion and a determined effort to root out all rival religions. Christianity was sharply discouraged, but it was on Buddhism, the chief native religious tradition with little relation to the imperial claims to divinity, that the ax fell. The Buddhist church was disestablished, and all

syncretism with Shinto prohibited. In the words of D. C. Holtom:

> Members of the royal family were debarred from continuing in Buddhist orders; Buddhist ceremonials in the imperial palace were prohibited; Buddhist temples all over the land were attacked and destroyed. A blind fury of misplaced patriotic zeal committed precious Buddhist writings, fine sculptures, bronzes, wood-carvings, and paintings to the flames, broke them in pieces, cast them away, or sold them for a pittance to whosoever would buy. Buddhist priests were prohibited from participating in Shinto ceremonies. They were subjected to beatings and threatened with military force. Monks and nuns in large numbers were obliged to take up secular callings.

Grave foreign protests on the subject of Christianity plus serious unrest among the masses devoted to Buddhism forced the abandoning of the policy of religious persecution. Liberal elements within the country agitated for the complete separation of church and state, and the Meiji leaders were brought to understand that religious freedom was a principle of the modern society they were trying to establish. Consequently, the government included in the constitution of 1889 a clause guaranteeing freedom of religion. At the same time it continued its support of the state Shinto cult, whose main aim was the veneration of the emperor. It solved this seeming contradiction by declaring that state Shinto was not a religion but merely an expression of patriotism. Nevertheless, the existence of the national cult imposed a real limitation on the independence and effectiveness of the private religious bodies. Though in the 1920's there was a strong tendency to differentiate religion and ideology, in times of stress such as the late 1930's and early 1940's religion was completely subordinated to and fused with a monolithic ideology, an ideology which had demonic consequences both for Japan and for the rest of the world. The new, 1946, constitution, by disestablishing Shinto and deriving sovereignty from the people rather than from the sacred and inviolable emperor, theoretically completed the process of secularization.

But, in fact, serious religious problems remain. All religious groups with the exception of the

Christians were compromised by their connection with the nationalistic orgy. In the absence of any really vigorous religious life, except for the popular faith-healing cults and the small Christian community, the religious impulses of the Japanese people find expression for the more radical in the symbol of socialism, for the conservatives in a longing for a new and more innocent version of state Shinto. Here, as in Turkey, the differentiation between religion and ideology remains to be completed.

Other examples of the processes we have been discussing come readily to mind. Communism is an example of a secular political ideology which successfully came to power in the prescriptive, religiously based societies of Russia and China. But communism itself makes an ultimate religious claim, and here, as in the case of Japan, a secular ideology claiming religious ultimacy has embarked on courses of action which hinder, rather than further, the transition to modern principal society. It is perhaps safe to say that alongside the serious political and economic problems which communism faces today is the perhaps even more serious cultural problem, the problem of the differentiation of the religious and ideological levels.

In conclusion, it seems worthwhile to stress that the process of secularization, which is in part what the transition from prescriptive to principial society is, does not mean that religion disappears. The function of religion in a principal society is different from that in a prescriptive society, but it is not necessarily less important. Moreover, in the very process of transition religion may reappear in many new guises. Perhaps what makes the situation so unclear is its very fluidity. Even in highly differentiated societies, such as our own, traditional religion, so deeply associated with the prescriptive past, is still in the process of finding its place in modern principial society.

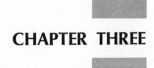

CHAPTER THREE

Social Structures:
The Forms of Organization

Systems are planned and designed in order to be enacted, and the result of their enactment is of primary interest. Therefore, every element in the normative subsystem has a counterpart in the action subsystem, which deals with the precise ways in which the prescriptions are carried out in practice. The enactment of norms requires the performance of several functions that cut across both elements and subsystems. Among the most important of these functions are:

Planning. The conceptual and physical operations involved in designing or redesigning a system.

Implementing. The performance of assignments and the utilization of resources in accordance with the system's prescriptions.

Monitoring. The detection of any discrepancies between a member's normative requirements and his performances, or between the overall blueprint and the patterns of action.

Sanctioning. The corrective efforts made in response to any discrepancies revealed by the monitoring process.

Evaluating. The collection and analysis of information needed to assess the system's adequacy in terms of its consequences as related to its objectives.

Legitimating. The official endorsement or rejection of proposed changes and innovations in the system.

Ideally, these functions have feedback relationships, so that any significant change in the system sets off a series of adaptations which maintain a controlled equilibrium or a progressive movement in a desired direction. This kind of control is sometimes exhibited by military establishments, sales agencies, factories, professional athletic teams, and other organizations with highly specialized objectives and efficient styles of management.

The action subsystem is the most visible and perhaps the best understood of a system's components. We live in a sensate culture in which action and its products are of almost universal interest. In fact, many sociologists tend to define norms in terms of actions rather than prescriptions. The most frequent act is regarded as the best indicator of a norm. However, there are several reasons why it is

Actions and
Reactions

advisable to treat norms and acts as distinctive elements that can be in conflict or harmony in any given case.

First, we usually judge a system by its potentials as they are revealed in its design, its blueprint, or its prescriptions. If we were to assess the system entirely by its consequences, we would have to assume that the members' performances are faithful representations of their prescriptions. Sometimes this assumption is warranted, sometimes not. Too often the discrepancies between precepts and practices are so great as to make evaluation of the blueprint difficult or impossible.

A good illustration of such discrepancies is found in the recent federal efforts in the field of delinquency control. Many of these efforts were allegedly based on theories of relative deprivation, role conflict, differential opportunity, and the like. But few of the government's programs were actually carried out consistently with the claims of these theories. There were numerous controversies over administrative procedure, community involvement, and client participation, resulting in frequent and sometimes drastic changes during the course of a program's career. Thus, the relationship between theory and practice was uncertain in many cases, and we have to conclude that the theories simply were not tested. Before we can test our prescriptions, we must learn how to implement them so as to maintain their integrity. And the consideration of integrity involves a clear distinction between normative prescriptions and people's performances.

A second reason for distinguishing between norms and acts is the inadequacy of our historical records. Longitudinal studies are difficult in sociology, especially if our interest is in man's earliest systems. About all that remains of these systems are the artifacts we can uncover. But the meanings of these artifacts in terms of man's plans, blueprints, and prescriptions are largely a matter of conjecture, lacking any conclusive evidence. To understand historical systems, we need records of prescriptions, actions, and reactions, in addition to the material objects that may happen to survive.

The information that is available on contemporary systems is not much better. Most systems have a much longer career than does the individual researcher. Learning something about their life cycle will therefore require the organized efforts of several generations of researchers. Accordingly, some scientists advocate the establishment of a network of social data stations, similar to the weather stations that provide a continuous record of atmospheric conditions. The records of social systems will certainly be more complex, involving a greater amount of variation in a larger number of variables. It may take several decades to establish the kind of information needed, but this task must be accomplished if we are to deal effectively with some of the concepts already employed in the social sciences without benefit of reliable observations and records.

A third factor is that we cannot change behavior directly. We attempt to modify man's conduct by changing his symbolic environment, including his laws, norms, values, beliefs, and knowledge. This linguistic environment serves as a guide to conduct by enabling man to profit from his experience and learning. The way this happens is illustrated by a game such as baseball. The game's goals and regulations are listed in an official rule-book. Regulations prescribe the number of players on each team, the methods of scoring, the roles of the players who occupy different positions, and the order of events on the field of play. They specify the behavior permitted by managers, coaches, and even spectators. Violations of these norms may result in penalties fixed by the game's sanction system, which is the responsibility of umpires who are not supposed to be interested in the game's outcome, only in maintaining its official character. Without these norms and sanctions there would be no recognizable game.

There are also informal expectations enforced by managers, coaches, and the players themselves. Players are expected to learn how to "slide," "steal bases," "bunt" the ball, throw to the proper position, and so on. Team members learn secret gestures with which to communicate among themselves without informing their opponents. A player who fails to perform as expected is removed from the team and a substitute is assigned to his position. Conversely, outstanding players are given bonuses, promoted to the major leagues, and honored in various other ways. Young boys imitate them. Spectators memorize their performance records. Commercial agencies pay them for endorsing products such as razors, tobacco, and deodorants. Obviously, the game is a group phenomenon that transcends the activities observed on a given field at a given time. But the only effective way to change the game is by modifying the rules that regulate its activities, whether formal or informal. And the best source of ideas for making such changes is a careful analysis of the game's experiences. This kind of analysis and feedback of the resulting information is the main function of the reaction subsystem.

Social group is one of many common-sense terms employed in sociology. In ordinary usage, it has a variety of meanings that are more or less taken for granted. Thus, most people distinguish between large and small groups, work and play groups, formal and informal groups, organized and unorganized groups, permanent and transitory groups, voluntary and caste-like groups, membership and reference groups, public and private groups, face-to-face and indirect contact groups, and homogeneous and heterogeneous groups. Other kinds of groups include gangs, cliques, associations, mobs, crowds, audiences, sects, publics, parties, collectives, and so on. The sociologist is less interested in listing a vast array of groups than in identifying and analyzing the essential features common to all.

The Nature of Groups and Collectives

To the sociologist, then, a group is any set of two or more persons who communicate with each other so as to establish among themselves certain distinctive social norms and patterns of interaction. Groups may be viewed as embryo social systems comprised of elements connected in a relatively cohesive structure. The structure of a group is somewhat independent of the particular persons who happen to be members at a given time. The role of the baseball pitcher, for example, is the same regardless of the person who happens to be playing at the moment. Group membership may change without any significant disruption of group structure.

The system of relationships among positions and roles gives a group its distinctive character. Were there no pitcher, catcher, batter, and so forth, the group involved in a baseball game would lose its identity. The social system of a factory or business organization would be changed if there were reversals or other modifications in the positions or roles of the foreman, laborer, accountant, personnel officer, or administrator. But if the positions and roles are stable, the variations in behavior that are caused by differences in personality are not likely to have any drastic influence on the group's functions or effectiveness.

College students are acquainted with small discussion groups that meet informally to review public issues and topics. The members have relatively equal status. Often the discussions are undirected and no leaders or other functionaries are appointed. Even under these conditions, some kind of group structure quickly emerges. For example, one person may take the lead in the discussion, perhaps

The Structure of Informal Groups

because he is especially interested or informed about the topic in question. Gradually a pattern develops in which some members are leaders and others, followers. Physical factors may also influence the performance of informal groups. The seating arrangement, for instance, has some effect. People like to see those with whom they are talking. If given their choice, they will ordinarily arrange their chairs in a crude circle. The temperature of the room, the noise level, the time of day, and the size of the group also have distinct effects on the group's activities.

But more important are the social constraints placed on the kinds and amounts of interaction among the group's members. *Leadership patterns* are one form of social constraint. They may develop informally as a result of the different abilities, interests, and habits of the members. Once developed, they exert control of the group's activities by regulating the members' expectations. Should a certain member violate these informal norms — by constantly changing the subject of the discussion, by monopolizing it, by disagreeing with everything said, or by failing to pay attention — he is likely to be ostracized or punished in some other way. This means that a *pattern of sanctions* operates in the group. Again, the *communication pattern* indicates who speaks to whom and how much. The *power pattern indicates* who can make decisions and who can give orders to whom. The *pattern of affect* depends upon the personal likes and dislikes among the members. Such attractions and rejections among a group's members are the special subject of sociometric research.

Other patterns of interaction in the structure of informal groups can often be identified. There is usually a division of labor among the group's members, for example. This *task pattern* reveals the specialized work assignments of individual members and shows how they are coordinated. Thus, one person may arrange a meeting-place for a discussion group, while another prepares announcements and advertisements, and still another mails the materials to the members. Too, there is ordinarily a *pattern of access* that indicates the various items of information, resources, and pieces of equipment, and so on which are made available to certain group members. Some members may be restricted from using certain resources available to others. The access pattern largely determines the distribution of relative opportunities for achievement among the group's members. Similarly, a *prestige pattern* may also be identified. The prestige pattern portrays the relative amounts of confidence and respect the members accord one another.

Clearly, social structure, even in small and informal groups, is not a simple unidimensional phenomenon. Comprehensive analysis of group structure would require detailed consideration of each of the patterns mentioned and the interrelations among them. Knowledge of social structure permits better understanding of a group's activities and facilitation of its performance.

Consideration of social structure also helps us understand why the size of a group is so important. The smallest group possible is a *dyad*. Agreement between the two members of a dyad means unanimity within the group; disagreement means isolation. This may be why the most intense and intimate social relationships are ordinarily restricted to dyads. As the size of the group increases, the number of interpersonal relations that must be maintained increases progressively. That is, two persons can be linked together by means of a single relationship, while three persons need three relationships, four persons need six relationships, five persons need ten relationships, six persons need fifteen relationships, and so on. Furthermore, if time is held constant, the amount of time available to each member for maintaining these relationships is correspondingly less. In addition, there is always the possibility that the group will split into subgroups or cliques. In the *triad,* for example, any two members can agree to exclude the third, who is then left without support. Four-person groups face the possibility of a deadlock between two pairs of members. Should a member of one of the pairs join the opposing pair, this will leave the single deviant isolated. Groups of five members do not face the deadlock issue, and being in the minority does not necessarily isolate an individual. Also, it is easier for a member to shift his role inconspicuously and withdraw from an awkward position. It is clear that size has important implications for the kinds of decisions a group is likely to make and for the level of performance.

The greater variety of skills, interests, and opinions available in large groups is often a temptation to increase the group's size. But the complex relations involved in large groups place greater demands on internal organization. Consequently, the time and energy spent in maintaining the group's organization may tend to encroach on the amount of effort that can be devoted to goal achievement. Goal-oriented groups may therefore run into the law of diminishing returns with respect to the effects of increased size. In playing the game of "Twenty Questions," for instance, small groups can solve the problem faster than single individuals. The groups need fewer questions and succeed more often. However, if the results are analyzed in terms of man-hours expended, the group's advantage tends to disappear. In general, then, the optimum size of the group depends upon the complexity of the assigned task, the number of different skills required, and the amount of work to be done.

Large and complex groups often find it advantageous to organize their activities by means of formal or official rules and regulations. When groups are formally organized, the behavior of an individual member may be influenced less by his interaction with other members than by his perception of the relevant social norms and the effectiveness with which these norms are enforced. Thus, *formal organization* refers to an interaction system in which the activities of members are regulated by official prescriptions. Formal rules spell out the task pattern which indicates the precise activities required of every member. Communication channels are officially prescribed. Similarly, the authority to make decisions is placed in the hands of designated persons. Rules govern access to information and other resources. There may even be official procedures designed to regulate leadership, prestige, and affect, but these patterns usually retain a strong informal aspect.

In formal organizations there is always the problem of regulating the informal groupings that tend to develop within the official structure. When formal and informal norms conflict, overt performance may or may not conform to the official prescriptions. As a consequence, training programs may be instituted in an attempt to make certain that all members have a complete and correct perception of their normative requirements. In addition, there is an official sanction system that provides rewards and penalties, depending upon the performance of any given member or of any given group. Such formal organizations can be combined in a vast complex such as the General Motors Corporation. The trend toward formation of such organizational complexes is one of the primary characteristics of modern bureaucratic society.

Bureaucratic organizations have a hierarchical arrangement of staff positions that provides clear and consistent lines of communication and authority. Generally, detailed information is passed from lower ranks of workers to the topmost positions.

Formal
Organizations
and the Decline
of Bureaucracy

Decisions are made in the higher ranks. Orders are passed from the top level to the lower ranks. A finely graded style of salaries and other benefits is based on assigned duties and responsibilities.

The blueprint of bureaucracy is that of a machine. The role played by any given member is geared to the roles of other members by the official rules and regulations. So long as all members perform according to their role requirements, the bureaucratic organization operates with clock-like precision.

However, a number of things tend to go wrong with the bureaucratic machine. For instance, the organization tends to lose sight of its avowed objectives. Once an organization is established, one of its primary functions is to perpetuate itself. Activities aimed at maintaining the organization — mostly integrative functions involving tension management — may overshadow the instrumental functions aimed at achieving the group's goals and objectives. In such cases, formal rules may acquire a sacred character, blind obedience among the members may gain recognition as a virtue, and loyalty to the organization may be interpreted as evidence of personal integrity. In today's changing world the defects of the bureaucratic style of management are producing some important changes in the nature of complex groups.

There is a notable shift from autonomy to interdependence in the management of many organizations. In traditional societies management was often entrusted to a single individual who formulated the policies, implemented them, assessed their adequacy, and rewarded the members according to criteria of his own making. The table of organization was exceedingly simple, involving a single focus upon the leader.

Early prisons, for example, had only three positions, those of warden, keeper, and inmate. Inmates were all treated alike, and reformation was regarded as entirely their own responsibility. Factual information about the inmates was gathered by the keepers and submitted to the warden, who collated the data, acted upon them and passed his judgments on to the keepers in the form of rules and orders. Inmates had very little interaction with either the keepers or one another.

In time, the idea evolved that criminals are incapable of reforming themselves because of inadequacies in their personal make-up. Prison programs were then redesigned to provide treatment aimed at correcting these inadequacies. Accordingly, professional workers were needed for diagnosis, vocational and academic training, and other forms of therapy. Diagnosis encouraged the classification of prisoners, and this called for diversified treatment, degrees of custody, special housing and work assignments, and similar specializations in all phases of the program. Such specialization demanded a larger number of social positions within the staff, resulting in a "tall" bureaucratic organization table, with the superintendent at the top of the status hierarchy and a number of assistants in charge of different operations. Under each assistant were several ranks of lesser officers. But in general, the bureaucratic organization preserved the upward flow of information and the downward flow of directives, as in the pre-bureaucratic era. This kind of organization is typical of many prisons even today.

Nevertheless, there is a good deal of evidence that the "tall" bureaucracy is losing is popularity. Bureaucratic policies tend to become overcentralized, compartmentalized, and solidified to such an extent that self-correction fails to occur within the organization. Prisons and many other institutions are therefore inclined to adopt a relatively "flat" and fluid organization which favors the decentralization of certain

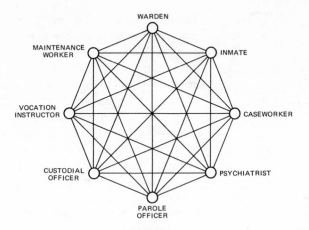

Figure 1

Illustration of a flat, fluid, "tilting wheel" table of organization. Dominance of any given individual depends upon the topic under discussion, so that status changes under changing conditions.

decisions, encourages the involvement of more workers (and even clients) in policy planning and evaluation, and facilitates adaptations to changing conditions or to new information and knowledge. This type of "tilting wheel" organization is illustrated in Figure 1. It places a premium on communication and complicates the flow of authority and decisions. But it more than compensates for this by utilizing manpower, regardless of rank or position, in a manner that helps workers and clients to understand the system better and to involve themselves more vigorously in its affairs.

NATURE OF
ORGANIZATION

13   Max Weber on Bureaucracy*

Reinhard Bendix

Max Weber, a German sociologist of the early twentieth century, was perhaps the foremost student of bureaucracy. He traced the development of bureaucratic organizations and analyzed their impact on the social order. In the following account, Reinhard Bendix discusses some of Weber's conclusions concerning bureaucracy.

Weber's discussions of bureaucracy[1] distinguish among several levels of analysis: (1) the historical and technical (administrative) reasons for the process of bureaucratization, especially in Western civilization; (2) the impact of the rule of law upon the functioning of bureaucratic organizations; (3) the occupational position and typical personal orientation of bureaucratic officials as a status group; (4) the most important attributes and consequences of bureaucracy in the modern world, especially of governmental bureaucracy.[2]

These topics are not strictly separate and this accounts for the partial redundancy and discrepancy in Weber's several enumerations. Some of the reasons for the development of bureaucracy necessarily refer to attributes that have consequences in the modern world, and the rule of law necessarily affects both the functioning of bureaucratic organizations and the occupational position of the incumbents. The brief account that follows separates these overlapping perspectives.[3]

Where the rule of law prevails, a bureaucratic organization is governed by the following principles:

(1) Official business is conducted on a continuous basis.

(2) It is conducted in accordance with stipulated rules in an administrative agency characterized by three interrelated attributes: (*a*) the duty of each official to do certain types of work is delimited in terms of impersonal criteria; (*b*) the official is given the authority necessary to carry out his assigned functions; (*c*) the means of compulsion at his disposal are strictly limited, and the conditions under which their employment is legitimate are clearly defined.

(3) Every official's responsibilities and authority are part of a hierarchy of authority. Higher offices are assigned the duty of supervision, lower offices, the right of appeal. However, the extent of supervision and the conditions of legitimate appeal may vary.

(4) Officials and other administrative employees do not own the resources necessary for the performance of their assigned functions but they are accountable for their use of these resources. Official business and private affairs, official revenue and private income are strictly separated.

(5) Offices cannot be appropriated by their incumbents in the sense of private property that

---

* Excerpt from Reinhard Bendix, *Max Weber: An Intellectual Portrait*, Doubleday and Company (1960), pp. 418–425. Used by permission. Copyright © 1960 by Reinhard Bendix.

[1] The analysis published in *Essays*, pp. 196–244, was written first (1911–13); the related discussion in *Theory*, pp. 329–41, contains Weber's subsequent effort at systematization. His political analysis of bureaucracy is not available in English.

[2] These several topics are considered in the following passages: (1) *Essays*, pp. 204–24, 235–39; (2) *Theory*, pp. 329–33, *Essays*, pp. 196–98, 216–221, *Law*, Chapters 8–10; (3) *Essays*, pp. 198–204, *Theory*, pp. 333–36; (4) *Essays*, pp. 224–35, 240–44, *Theory*, pp. 337–41.

This division can be only suggestive, for the reasons indicated in the text. There are many other passages in Weber's work where he dealt with the problem of bureaucratization. Cf. also pp. 432–49 for a further discussion of the fourth topic on the basis of Weber's political writings.

[3] The historical reasons for the process of bureaucratization were summarized at the end of Chapter XI; this topic is therefore omitted from the present discussion.

can be sold and inherited. (This does not preclude various rights such as pension claims, regulated conditions of discipline and dismissal, etc., but such rights serve, in principle at least, as incentives for the better performance of duties. They are not property rights.)

(6) Official business is conducted on the basis of written documents.[4]

Without (1) the continuity of official business; (2) the delimitation of authority through stipulated rules; (3) the supervision of its exercise; (4) and (5) the separation of office and incumbent; and (6) the documentary basis of official business, there cannot be a system of legal domination in which the exercise of authority consists in the implementation of enacted norms.

This specification of the "apparatus" under legal domination can be contrasted to the system of administration under patrimonial rule. First, whether or not the patrimonial ruler and his officials conduct administrative business is usually a matter of discretion; normally they do so only when they are paid for their troubles. Second, a patrimonial ruler resists the delimitation of his authority by the stipulation of rules. He may observe traditional or customary limitations, but these are unwritten; indeed, tradition endorses the principled arbitrariness of the ruler. Third, this combination of tradition and arbitrariness is reflected in the delegation and supervision of authority. Within the limits of sacred tradition the ruler decides whether or not to delegate authority, and his entirely personal recruitment of "officials" makes the supervision of their work a matter of personal preference and loyalty. Fourth and fifth, all administrative "offices" under patrimonial rule are a part of the ruler's personal household and private property; his "officials" are personal servants, and the costs of administration are met out of his treasury. Sixth, official business is transacted in personal encounter and by oral communication, not on the basis of impersonal documents.[5]

Under legal domination the occupational position and personal orientation of officials is bound to be affected by the contrasting administrative organization. Where the implementation of enacted rules is emphasized, the employment of the official is also governed by rules, and once hired, the official obeys impersonal rules, not the will of his lord and master. Obedience to rules and the conduct of official business by means of written documents require technical qualifications that are more or less absent from administrative work done as a personal service or an avocation. Under legal domination the implementation of rules must be regular as well as regulated, or else the rule of law would be applied only intermittently; also, to be continuous, administrative work must be a full-time occupation. Finally, where each office involves regulated duties and authorizations, these must be independent from the person of the incumbent. Consequently his compensation cannot be derived from the revenue of the office, nor can he be permitted to appropriate either the perquisites of office or the office itself. The typical bureaucratic alternative is to reward the official by monthly allowances in money or in kind, and to ensure the quality and continuity of his service by offering him the opportunity of a lifetime career, usually with pension provisions upon retirement.[6]

Under legal domination, therefore, the bureaucratic official's position is characterized by the following attributes:

(1) He is personally free and appointed to his position on the basis of contract.

(2) He exercises the authority delegated to him in accordance with impersonal rules, and his loyalty is enlisted on behalf of the faithful execution of his official duties.

(3) His appointment and job placement are dependent upon his technical qualifications.

(4) His administrative work is his full-time occupation.

---

[4] *Theory*, pp. 330–32.

[5] These conditions apply also under feudalism in a modified form, but there is no need to specify these modifications.

[6] Weber repeatedly discussed the differences between bureaucratic and patrimonial administration, which have been restated briefly in the preceding two paragraphs. However, he did not distinguish the administrative consequences that result from the type of supreme authority and the characteristics of the officialdom that emerge from these consequences. Cf. *Theory*, pp. 342–45, and *WuG*, Vol. II, pp. 679, 737–38, 752.

(5) His work is rewarded by a regular salary and by prospects of regular advancement in a lifetime career.

With the characteristics of administrative organization under legal domination before us, we may now turn to the most important attributes and consequences of bureaucracy in the modern world.

According to Weber, such an organization is technically superior to all other forms of administration, much as machine production is superior to nonmechanical methods. In precision, speed, lack of equivocation, knowledge of the documentary record, continuity, sense of discretion, uniformity of operation, system of subordination, and reduction of frictions, bureaucracy surpasses honorific and avocational forms of administration.[7] This is a long list of advantages, but they are relative. Weber emphasized that bureaucracy also produces obstacles when a decision must be adapted to an individual case. This reservation is noteworthy as a concomitant of the attribute that is central to his conception of bureaucracy: the idea of calculability. This is a logical consequence of the rule of law. In an administration governed by rules, decisions must be predictable if the rules are known. Weber expressed this notion by the exaggerated simile of the "modern judge [who] is a vending machine into which the pleadings are inserted together with the fee and which then disgorges the judgment together with its reasons mechanically derived from the Code." [8]

[The calculability of decision-making] and with it its appropriateness for capitalism . . . [is] the more fully realized the more bureaucracy "depersonalizes" itself, i.e., the more completely it succeeds in achieving the exclusion of love, hatred, and every purely personal, especially irrational and incalculable, feeling from the execution of official tasks. In the place of the old-type ruler who is moved by sympathy, favor, grace, and gratitude, modern culture requires for its sustaining external apparatus the emotionally detached, and hence rigorously "professional," expert.[9]

[7] The translation of this passage in *Essays*, p. 214, makes Weber's statement more absolute than it is. Cf. *Law*, p. 349, for a more accurate translation.

[8] *Ibid.*, p. 354.

[9] *Law*, p. 351.

Thus, contrary to many interpretations, Weber did not maintain that bureaucratic organizations operate as efficiently as "slot machines." He said rather that such organizations operate more efficiently than alternative systems of administration and that they increase their efficiency to the extent that they "depersonalize" the execution of official tasks.

A second attribute of modern bureaucracy is its "concentration of the means of administration." By using the same terminology as Marx, Weber wanted to emphasize that this process of concentration had occurred not only in the economy but also in government, the army, political parties, universities, and indeed in most large-scale organizations. As the size of such organizations increases, the resources necessary to run them are taken out of the hands of autonomous individuals and groups and placed under the control of a ruling minority, in part because such resources exceed the financial capacity of individuals.[10] Thus the craftsman was expropriated as merchant enterprises came to own the tools of production; the feudal vassal was expropriated as a public official when governments came to monopolize the administration of public affairs; the private scholar was expropriated as the universities built up their own laboratories and libraries upon which the scholar came to depend. The means of production, of administration, and of scholarship all were integral parts of the individual household at one time, but became separated as the process of concentration advanced. As a result, modern bureaucratic administration is distinguished by the separation of business from the family household, of public office from its incumbent, and of research facilities from the individual scholar.

A third attribute of modern bureaucracy is its leveling effect on social and economic differences. This effect is seen most easily if bureaucratic and

[10] This is, of course, related to the increasing complexity of functions performed by governments and other organizations as their size increases. Cf. the earlier reference to this process in Chapter XI, pp. 380–81. Weber's emphasis on the parallelism of this process in all types of large-scale organization is contained in his lecture on socialism. Cf. *GAzSuS*, pp. 498–99. See also *Essays*, pp. 221–24, and *GPS*, p. 140.

nonbureaucratic methods of administration are contrasted.

Every non-bureaucratic administration of a large social structure [such as patrimonial government] depends upon the fact that those who outrank others in social, economic, or honorific terms are associated in one way or another with the performance of administrative functions. This usually means that the incumbent is rewarded for his assumption of administrative duties by the economic exploitation of his position, which he may also use for purposes of social prestige.[11]

The development of bureaucracy does away with such plutocratic privileges, replacing unpaid, avocational administration by notables with paid, full-time administration by professionals, regardless of their social and economic position. Also, it rejects the "decision-making from case to case" that is typical of nonbureaucratic forms of administration. Authority is exercised in accordance with rules, and everyone subject to that authority is legally equal. Connected with these leveling tendencies is a major change in the system of education. Administration by notables usually is administration by amateurs; bureaucracy usually is administration by experts. Equal eligibility for administrative appointments means in fact equal eligibility of all who meet the stipulated educational requirements. Educational diplomas have replaced privilege as the basis of administrative recruitment, just as scientific education and technical expertise have replaced the cultivation of the mind through classical literature and the cultivation of manners through competitive games

among social equals. The expert, not the cultivated man, is the educational ideal of a bureaucratic age.[12]

Fourth and finally, a fully developed bureaucracy implements a system of authority relationships that is practically indestructible. Whereas the notable does administrative work on an avocational and honorific basis, the bureaucrat's economic sustenance and entire social existence are identified with the "apparatus." He shares the interests of his administrative colleagues in the continued functioning of the machine in which they are so many specialized cogs. The population ruled by a bureaucracy cannot, on the other hand, dispense with it or replace it with something else. Short of chaos, public affairs depend today upon the expert training, functional specialization, and coordination of a bureaucratic administration with its uninterrupted performance of the manifold tasks that are regularly assigned to the modern state. Weber emphasized that the bureaucratic form of administration is both permanent and indispensable, contrary to the arguments of anarchists and socialists who believe that administration can be done away with in an ideal society or that it can be used to implement a freer and more equitable social order. In Weber's view bureaucracy is here to stay, and any future social order promises only to be more oppressive than the capitalist society of today.

---

[11] *WuG,* Vol. II, p. 666. This same passage is translated more literally in *Essays,* p. 224.

[12] *Essays,* pp. 240–43. Note especially Weber's statement that the struggle between the ideal of the expert and the older ideal of the educated or cultivated man is at the basis of all present discussions of the educational system. This is as true in the age of man-made earth satellites as it was before World War I when Weber wrote. Cf. also the earlier discussion of feudal and patrimonial education, pp. 363–64, and the contrast between an autonomous and a university-trained legal profession, pp. 406–411.

14   The Social Structure of the Restaurant*

William Foote Whyte

Social scientists have done a great deal of research on the social organization of factories and other industrial and business structures. Although such organizations do not always possess all the characteristics of a bureaucracy, they frequently exhibit many such properties. The extent of bureaucratization varies with the size of the concern. The social organization of a small restaurant operated by the owner, his wife, and two employees might reveal all the informality and flexibility of a small group. On the other hand, a large restaurant exhibits the chain of command, the procedural rules, and the status hierarchy of the bureaucracy although in less extreme form perhaps than found in larger organizations.

In this article the writer analyzes the complexity of the social organization of the large restaurant. What conditions lead to a need for more elaborate rules of procedure in such concerns? In what ways are interpersonal relationships among employees influenced more by the customary ways of the larger society than by the regulations of the employer?

The restaurant is a combination production and service unit. It differs from the factory, which is solely a production unit, and also from the retail store, which is solely a service unit.

The restaurant operator produces a perishable product for immediate sale. Success requires a delicate adjustment of supply to demand and skilful coordination of production with service. The production and service tie-up not only makes for difficult human problems of coordinating action but adds a new dimension to the structure of the organization: the customer-employee relationship.

The problems of coordination and customer relations are relatively simple in the small restaurant, but they become much more difficult as the organi-

* Reprinted from the *American Journal of Sociology*, Vol. 54 (January 1949), pp. 302–308, by permission of The University of Chicago Press. Copyright 1949 by The University of Chicago.

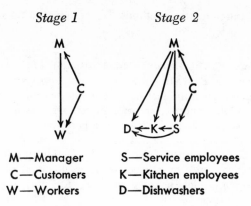

Stage 1   *Stage 2*

M—Manager	S—Service employees
C—Customers	K—Kitchen employees
W—Workers	D—Dishwashers

zation grows. This may be illustrated structurally in terms of five stages of growth.

In the first stage, we have a small restaurant where the owner and several other employees dispense short orders over the counter. There is little division of labor. The owner and employees serve together as cooks, countermen, and dishwashers.

In the second stage, the business is still characterized by the informality and flexibility of its relationships. The boss knows most customers and all his employees on a personal basis. There is no need for formal controls and elaborate paper work. Still, the organization has grown in complexity as it has grown in size. The volume of business is such that it becomes necessary to divide the work, and we have dishwashers and kitchen employees, as well as those who wait on the customers. Now the problems of coordination begin to grow also, but the organization is still small enough so that the owner-manager can observe directly a large part of its activities and step in to straighten out friction or inefficiency.

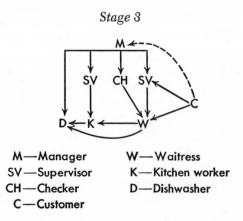

Stage 3

M—Manager	W—Waitress
SV—Supervisor	K—Kitchen worker
CH—Checker	D—Dishwasher
C—Customer	

Stage 4

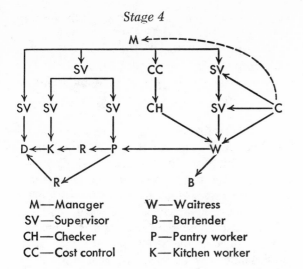

M—Manager
SV—Supervisor
CH—Checker
CC—Cost control

W—Waitress
B—Bartender
P—Pantry worker
K—Kitchen worker

As the business continues to expand, it requires a still more complex organization as well as larger quarters. No longer able to supervise all activities directly, the owner-manager hires a service supervisor, a food production supervisor, and places one of his employees in charge of the dishroom as a working supervisor. He also employs a checker to total checks for his waitresses and see that the food is served in correct portions and style.

In time, the owner-manager finds that he can accommodate a larger number of customers if he takes one more step in the division of labor. Up to now the cooks have been serving the food to the waitresses. When these functions are divided, both cooking and serving can proceed more efficiently.

Therefore, he sets up a service pantry apart from the kitchen. The cooks now concentrate on cooking, the runners carry food from kitchen to pantry and carry orders from pantry to kitchen, and the pantry girls serve the waitresses over the counter. This adds two more groups (pantry girls and runners) to be supervised, and, to cope with this and the larger scale of operation, the owner adds another level of supervision, so that there are two supervisors between himself and the workers. Somewhere along the line of development, perhaps he begins serving drinks and adds bartenders to his organization.

Stage 5 need not be diagrammed here, for it does not necessarily involve any structural changes in the individual unit. Here several units are tied together into a chain, and one or more levels of authority are set up in a main office above the individual unit structures.

This expansion process magnifies old problems and gives rise to new ones. They may be considered under three headings: administration, the customer relationship, and the flow of work. Whenever we lengthen the hierarchy, adding new levels of authority to separate top executive from workers, the problem of administration becomes more complex. However, this is true for any organization, and therefore these problems of hierarchy need not be given special attention in an article on restaurants.

The particular problem of the large restaurant is to tie together its line of authority with the relations that arise along the flow of work. In the first instance, this involves the customer relationship, for here is where the flow of work begins. The handling of the customer relationship is crucial for the adjustment of the restaurant personnel, and a large part of that problem can be stated in strictly quantitative interaction terms: Who originates action for whom and how often? In a large and busy restaurant a waitress may take orders from fifty to one hundred customers a day (and perhaps several times for each meal) in addition to the orders (much less frequent) she receives from her supervisor. When we add to this the problem of adjusting to service pantry workers, bartenders, and perhaps checkers, we can readily see the possibilities of emotional tension — and, in our study, we did see a number of girls break down and cry under the strain.

Our findings suggested that emotional tension could be related directly to this quantitative interaction picture. The skilful waitress, who maintained her emotional equilibrium, did not simply respond to the initiative of customers. In various obvious and subtle ways she took the play away from customers, got them responding to her, and fitted them into the pattern of her work. She was also more aggressive than the emotionally insecure in originating action for other waitresses, service pantry people, and supervisor.

While in the rush hours the waitress works under a good deal of tension at best, the supervisor can either add to or relieve it. Here again we can speak in quantitative terms. In one restaurant we observed a change in dining-room management when a supervisor who was skilful in originating action for customers (thus taking pressure off waitresses) and who responded frequently to the initiation of waitresses was replaced by a supervisor who had less skill in controlling customers and who originated for the girls much more frequently and seldom responded to them. (Of the new supervisor, the waitresses would say, "She's always finding something to criticize"; "She's never around when we need her"; "She's always telling you; she doesn't care what you have to say"; etc.) This change was followed by evidences of increased nervous tension, especially among the less experienced waitresses, and finally by a series of waitress resignations.

Here we see that the customer-waitress, waitress-supervisor, waitress-service-pantry-worker relationships are interdependent parts of a social system. Changes in one part of the system will necessarily lead to changes in other parts. Furthermore, if the people involved in the system are to maintain their emotional balance, there must be some sort of compensatory activity to meet large interactional changes. For example, when waitresses are subject to a large increase in the originations of customers (at the peak of rush hours), the supervisor allows them to originate action for her with increasing frequency and diminishes the frequency with which she gives them orders. This is, in fact, the sort of behavior we have observed among supervisors who enjoy the closest cooperation with waitresses, as reported by the waitresses.

The customer relationship is, of course, only one point along the flow of work which brings orders from dining-room to kitchen and food from kitchen to dining-room. In a large restaurant operating on several floors, this is a long chain which may break down at any point, thus leading to emotional explosions in all quarters. The orders may go from waitress to pantry girl and then, as the pantry girl runs low in supplies, from pantry girl to pantry supplyman, from pantry supplyman to kitchen supplyman, and from kitchen supplyman to cook. And the food comes back along the same route in the opposite direction. Where drinks are served, the bar must be tied in with this flow of work, but there the chain is short and the problem less complex.

We have here a social system whose parts are interdependent in a highly sensitive manner. Thus the emotional tension experienced by waitresses is readily transmitted, link by link, all the way to the kitchen.

I have already noted how a skilful dining-room supervisor may help to relieve the tension on the entire system at its point of origin. Here we may consider other factors which affect the relations among employees along the flow of work: status, sex relations, and layout and equipment.

I would propose the hypothesis that relations among individuals along the flow of work will run more smoothly when those of higher status are in a position to originate for those of lower status in the organization and, conversely, that frictions will be observed more often when lower-status individuals seek to originate for those of higher status. (This is, of course, by no means a complete explanation of the friction or adjustment we observe.)

While more data are needed on this point, we made certain observations which tend to bear out the hypothesis. For example, in one kitchen we observed supplymen seeking to originate action (in getting food supplies) for cooks who were older, of greater seniority, more highly skilled, and much higher paid. This relationship was one of the sore points of the organization. Still, we discovered that there had been one supplyman who got along well with the cooks. When we got his story, we found that he had related himself to the cooks quite differently from the other supplymen. He sought to avoid calling orders to the cooks and instead just asked them to call him when a certain item was ready. In this way, he allowed them to increase the frequency of their origination for him, and, according to all accounts, he got better cooperation and service from the cooks than any other supplyman.

Much the same point is involved in the relations between the sexes. In our society most men grow up to be comfortable in a relationship in which they originate for women and to be uneasy, if not more seriously disturbed, when the originations go in the other direction. It is therefore a matter of some consequence how the sexes are distributed along the flow of work. On this question we gave particular attention to the dining-room-service pantry and dining-room-bar relationships.

In the dining-room-pantry situation there are four possible types of relationship by sex: waiter-counterman, waiter-pantry-girl, waitresses-pantry girl, and waitress-counterman. We were not able to give much attention to the first two types, but we did make intensive studies of two restaurants illustrating the third and fourth types. Ideally, for scientific purposes, we would want to hold everything else constant except for these sex differences. We had no such laboratory, but the two restaurants were nevertheless closely comparable. They were both large, busy establishments, operating on several floors, and serving the same price range of food in the same section of the city.

Perhaps the chief differences were found in the dining-room-pantry relationship itself. In restaurant A, waitresses gave their orders orally to the pantry girls. On the main serving floor of restaurant B, waitresses wrote out slips which they placed on spindles on top of a warming compartment separating them from the countermen. The men picked off the order slips, filled them, and put the plates in the compartment where the waitresses picked them up. In most cases there was no direct face-to-face interaction between waitresses and countermen, and, indeed, the warming compartment was so high that only the taller waitresses could see over its top.

These differences were not unrelated to the problems of sex in the flow of work. One of the countermen in restaurant B told us that, in all his years' experience, he had never before worked in such a wonderful place. Most workers who express such sentiments talk about their relations with their superiors or with fellow-employees on the same job or perhaps about wages, but this man had nothing to say about any of those subjects. He would discuss only the barrier that protected him from the waitresses. He described earlier experiences in other restaurants where there had been no such barrier and let us know that to be left out in the open where all the girls could call their orders in was an ordeal to which no man

should be subjected. In such places, he said, there was constant wrangling.

This seems to check with experience in the industry. While we observed frictions arising between waitresses and pantry girls, such a relationship can at least be maintained with relative stability. On the other hand, it is difficult to prevent blowups between countermen and waitresses when the girls call their orders in. Most restaurants consciously or unconsciously interpose certain barriers to cut down waitress origination of action for countermen. It may be a warming compartment as in this case, or, as we observed in another restaurant, there was a man pantry supervisor who collected the order slips from the waitresses as they came and and passed them out to the countermen.

One bartender and one counterman not only enjoyed their work but were considered by waitresses to be highly efficient and pleasant to deal with. Both of them had independently worked out the same system of handling the job when the rush hour got under way. Instead of handling each order slip in turn as it was handed to them (thus responding to each individual waitress), they would collect several slips that came in at about the same time, lay them out on the counter before them, and fill the orders in whatever order seemed most efficient. For example, the bartender would go through the slips to see how many "Martinis," "Old Fashions," and so on were required. Then he would make up all the "Martinis" at once before he went on to the next drink.

When the work was done this way, the girl first in was not necessarily first out with her tray, but the system was so efficient that it speeded up the work on the average, and the girls were content to profit this way in the long run. The men described the system to us simply in terms of efficiency; but note that, in organizing their jobs, they had changed quantitatively the relations they had with the waitresses. Instead of responding to each waitress, they were originating action for the girls (filling their orders as the men saw fit and sending them out when the men were ready).

Along with our consideration of layout and equipment in the flow of work, we should give attention to the communication system. Where the restaurant operates on one floor, the relations at each step in the flow can be worked out on a face-to-face basis. There may be friction, but there is also the possibility of working out many problems on a friendly, informal basis.

When a restaurant operates on two or more floors, as many large ones do, face-to-face interaction must be supplemented by mechanical means of communication. We saw three such mechanical means substituted for direct interaction, and each one had its difficulties.

People can try to coordinate their activities through the house telephone. Without facial expressions and gestures, there is a real loss of understanding, for we do not generally respond solely to people's voices. Still, this might serve reasonably well, if the connection between kitchen and pantry could be kept constantly open.

The public address system has the advantage over the telephone that it can be used all the time, but it has the great disadvantage of being a very noisy instrument. Busy kitchens and service pantries are noisy places at best, so that the addition of a public address system might be most unwelcome. We do not yet know enough of the effect of noise upon the human nervous system to evaluate the instrument from this point of view, but we should recognize the obvious fact that surrounding noise affects the ability of people to communicate with each other and becomes therefore a problem in human relations.

The teleautograph makes no noise and can be used at all times, yet it has its own disadvantages. Here we have an instrument in the service pantry and one in the kitchen. As the pantry supplyman writes his order, it appears simultaneously on the kitchen teleautograph. The kitchen's replies are transmitted upstairs in the same way. The machine records faithfully, but it does not solve the problem of meaning in interaction. We may pass over the problem of illegibility of handwriting, although we have seen that cause serious difficulties. The more interesting problem is this: How urgent is an order?

When the rush hour comes along, with cus-tomers pushing waitresses, waitresses pushing pantry girls, and pantry girls pushing supplymen, the supplyman is on the end of the line so far as face-to-face interaction is concerned, and he is likely to get nervous and excited. He may then put in a larger order than he will actually use or write "Rush" above many of his orders. If he over-orders, the leftovers come back to the kitchen at the end of the meal, and the kitchen supplymen and cooks learn thus that the pantry supplyman did not really know how much he needed. They take this into account in interpreting his future orders. And, when everything is marked "Rush," the kitchen supplymen cannot tell the difference between the urgent and no so urgent ones. Thus the word becomes meaningless, and communication deteriorates. Stuck in this impasse, the pantry supplyman may abandon his machine and dash down to the kitchen to try to snatch the order himself. The kitchen people will block this move whenever they can, so, more often, the pantry supplyman appeals to his supervisor. In the heat of the rush hour, we have seen pantry supervisors running up and down stairs, trying to get orders, trying to find out what is holding up things in the kitchen. Since they have supervisor status, the kitchen workers do not resist them openly, but the invasion of an upstairs supervisor tends to disrupt relations in the kitchen. It adds to the pressures there, for it comes as an emergency that lets everybody know that the organization is not functioning smoothly.

It is not the function of this article to work out possible solutions to this problem of communication. I am concerned here with pointing out a significant new area for sociological investigation: the effects on human relations of various mechanical systems of communication. It is difficult enough to coordinate an organization in which the key people in the supervisory hierarchy are in direct face-to-face relations. It is a much more difficult problem (and one as yet little understood) when the coordination must be achieved in large measure through mechanical communication systems.

COMMUNITIES

15 The Correlation of Social Phenomena with Community Size*

Fenton Keyes

One of the major advantages of the city is that the concentration of population facilitates interaction and collective activity among a large number of people. Concentration not only permits individuals to specialize in their occupations but it actually requires a high degree of specialization of labor. It is only as individuals become specialized in their skills and in the exchange of goods and services that productivity is increased enough to maintain a dense urban population.

In a small community, such as a village or a hamlet, specialization is necessarily limited. At the general store one can buy gasoline, men's work socks or gloves, or select from a limited variety of groceries, meats, and sundry articles. Nowhere in the village can one find a women's dress shop that specializes in Size 10, a store that sells only men's ties, a dealer who handles rare and expensive art items, or a doctor who limits his practice to brain surgery. Such specialization does occur, however, as we move from small towns into large urban centers. Here labor is highly specialized, ranging from the worker who tightens certain nuts on an automobile chassis as it moves along an assembly line to the lawyer or doctor whose interests are so technical that he has difficulty finding people with whom he can discuss his work. Such specialization can be achieved only if people's day-to-day activities are effectively coordinated. Thus one characteristic of urban society is the functional interdependence

* Reprinted from *Social Forces*, Volume 36 (May 1958), pp. 311–315, by permission. Copyright © 1958, University of North Carolina Press.

that can be observed among workers and agencies.

The following article provides information on the relationship between community size and selected social phenomena. As expected, nearly all towns of around 2,000 persons have grocery stores, while none of these has sight-saving classes. Some sight-saving classes may be found in cities of 10,000–20,000 persons, but there are such classes in every city having a population of a million or more persons. The author limits his attention to certain types of business concerns and social agencies. Is it likely that certain less tangible social phenomena are also correlated with city size? What differences do you expect in religious and political attitudes? In family organization and relationships? In visiting patterns? In voluntary associations, their membership, and their activities? What is the probable impact of urbanization on social life in general?

Some recent monographs and textbooks have both criticized and utilized hitherto unpublished material, gathered in 1939–1941, which attempted to answer two questions: (1) Is there a correlation between community size and variety of social phenomena? (2) When a vast range of communities is considered, are differentiable groups discovered which are helpful in determining the location of the rural-urban dividing line, the points at which the community becomes unmistakably "urban" and attains city status? The study examined the 3,890 communities which had populations of 2,000 or more in 1930. Nice distinctions were necessary in deciding what social phenomena to select. Desired were those which might be expected to differentiate communities when the distribution community-wise was examined. This meant that phenomena which occurred in almost every American community were not germane, e.g., graveyards, or those which were primarily pervasive elements of our culture and therefore not specifically concomitants of size or urbanization, e.g., elementary schools. This was the first culling process. As much as possible, facilities were omitted, the absence of which might be explained by the presence of equivalent services or by historical accident, e.g., Negro newspapers. The group of phenomena that remained had to pass another test: only those could be utilized for which data were available in terms of distribution by communities.

The 94 social phenomena that survived fell, as it happened, into six main groups: Retail Establishments, Social Welfare, Education, Municipal Administration, Transportation and Communication, Recreation. After division of all communities into size-groups, the percentage of each group possessing a particular facility was determined as shown in the accompanying tabulation of communities of different size groups possessing various facilities (Table 1).

The table indicates the communities with 100 per cent incidence and those with less for the Retail Establishments considered. The most significant aspect of the picture thus revealed was a correlation between the variety of stores and their frequency of occurrence with size of community. The larger the community, the more specialty shops appeared, although with comparatively late emergence, as would be expected, of stores which cater to relatively small groups of the population. There is a rather significant quadrupling of the number of "complete coverages" when the 25,000 population point was reached and doubling at the 100,000 population point. In the 250,000–500,000 group of communities, the "city" appears to be virtually complete.

Considering the group of Social Welfare provisions as a whole, we find that there is a positive correlation with size of community. The larger places tend to have these facilities more often than the small places because much of the time relatively specialized groups exist in sizeable numbers in large communities. Catering to these groups is not only necessary, as is not always the case in the smaller communities, but their numbers are large enough to make such special care feasible and the community problems more apparent. The presumption is that much of the decided correlation with community size is explained by the larger municipalities having both the income and the increased demands to bring forth these services.

In the two categories of facilities thus far considered, i.e., Retail Establishments and Social Welfare, one discerns significant peaks or "jumps" at the population marks of 25,000, 100,000 and 500,000. These seem to indicate zones of transition reflected by the frequent marked changes in percentages at these points. These three peaks

divide the spectrum of urbanization into four groups of communities. As we examine the table by groups of facilities, we find corresponding significance in these population points. With considerable justification one can contend that the rural urban "break" comes at or around the 25,000 population point, that at the 100,000 population point the well-defined city makes its emergence, and that the 500,000 size gives birth to the metropolitan center. Keeping this in mind, let us proceed to an examination of the rest of the table.

Considering Education, it will be seen that the places with large populations have more facilities than those with small, some of this doubtless due to their greater wealth or to the fact that there are fewer persons with special interests and needs in the small community. In the large place provision for these special groups is not only more likely to be feasible but facilities for them may be absolutely necessary.

Turning to Municipal Administration, one wonders if perhaps the City Manager form of government might be considered a variant form of the Council-Manager type which has been especially adapted to small communities. This would suggest that to obtain a meaningful distribution in the spectrum these percentages should be combined for the groups of smaller communities. It is clear that there is a correlation between community size and the city-manager and council-manager forms of government but, unlike most of the other categories, it seems that the communities which are likely to possess this facility are not those of the largest population but rather communities between 50,000 and 250,000. The larger the community, up to the 100,000 population mark, the more likely it is that one will find a council-manager form of government. Beyond that point the likelihood decreases, and the phenomenon disappears altogether in communities of 1,000,000 or more. Comparisons may be made with certain items in the Retail Establishments category, e.g., General, Hardware and Farm Implement Stores. A preponderance of communities at the more rural end of the spectrum of urbanization boasts these establishments while they are found in only a relatively few communities at the metropolitan end. In the case of city planning, zoning, and Art Commissions, we see again

TABLE 1 *Percentages of Communities of Different Size Groups Possessing Various Facilities*

Population of the City in Thousands	2.0– 2.5	2.5– 5.0	5– 10	10– 25	25– 50	50– 100	100– 250	250– 500	500– 1000	1000 and Over
Number of Cities Studied	580	1440	880	614	135	98	56	24	8	5
Stores:										
Grocery	96	100	99	99	100	100	100	100	100	100
Drug	95	96	99	100	100	100	100	100	100	100
Filling Station	93	96	99	99	100	100	100	100	100	100
Restaurant	91	91	97	99	100	100	100	100	100	100
Combination	87	92	99	100	100	100	100	100	100	100
Automobile Agency	86	95	92	98	99	100	100	100	100	100
Garage	83	89	95	96	100	100	100	100	100	100
General	78	72	68	54	41	44	35	87	50	60
Furniture	74	80	87	93	94	99	100	100	100	100
Lumber Yard	73	80	87	90	94	99	100	100	100	100
Farmer's Supply	69	73	79	87	95	93	100	100	100	100
Jewelry	66	76	85	93	99	100	100	100	100	100
Candy	66	77	89	96	100	100	100	100	100	100
Dry Goods	66	73	85	91	88	95	100	100	100	100
Variety	63	70	81	93	95	96	100	100	100	100
General Merchandise	60	51	64	85	83	86	92	100	100	100
Meat	60	69	81	91	99	100	100	100	100	100
Men's Clothing	54	68	96	93	98	99	100	100	100	100
Hardware and Farm Tools	49	73	53	50	57	49	66	87	75	60
Family Clothing	49	53	55	73	87	95	100	100	100	100
Radio	48	58	79	94	100	100	100	100	100	100
Other Eating Establishments	46	53	74	89	94	96	100	100	100	100
Household Supplies	45	60	88	85	89	95	100	100	100	100
Heating & Plumbing Supplies	44	56	74	86	94	92	100	100	100	100
Coal Dealer	43	56	70	84	94	99	92	99	100	100
Other Automotive Supply	41	55	79	95	100	100	100	100	100	100
Shoe	39	53	80	99	100	100	100	100	100	100
Women's Dress	39	43	83	91	96	100	100	100	100	100
Women's Accessory	39	43	71	92	94	98	99	100	100	100
Cigar	39	45	65	34	97	100	100	100	100	100
Hardware	23	60	87	95	99	100	100	100	100	100
Other Apparel	18	24	48	87	89	96	98	100	100	100
Electrical Supply	15	27	45	64	63	66	93	100	100	100
Paint	15	26	47	79	90	96	100	100	100	100
Department	10	21	45	68	78	78	98	100	100	100
Book	7	25	25	37	61	75	96	100	100	100
Other Home Furnishing	6	18	21	45	75	88	99	100	100	100
Floor Covering	1	2	6	24	36	43	86	88	100	100

TABLE 1   *(Continued)*

Population of the City in Thousands	2.0–2.5	2.5–5.0	5–10	10–25	25–50	50–100	100–250	250–500	500–1000	1000 and Over
Number of Cities Studied	580	1440	880	614	135	98	56	24	8	5
Social Welfare Facilities:										
Hospital	23	37	61	74	86	94	100	100	100	100
Public Health Nurse	18	35	59	81	87	97	100	100	100	100
Juvenile Court	14	17	30	45	74	84	95	88	100	100
Probation Officer	14	16	30	46	76	84	95	92	100	100
Children's Home	4	7	15	29	61	79	89	92	100	100
Home for the Aged	3	4	10	18	47	62	82	96	100	100
Social Worker	2	3	17	19	49	79	96	96	100	100
Psychiatric Clinic	1	3	7	16	27	48	61	83	100	100
Tuberculosis Sanitarium	1	2	3	6	19	29	55	65	38	100
Day Nursery	1	1	4	11	32	63	88	96	100	100
Community Chest	0	1	4	15	51	65	84	92	100	100
Children's Corrective Institution	0	1	2	2	2	4	17	17	25	100
School for the Deaf	0	0	1	4	14	26	52	83	100	100
School for the Blind	0	0	0	1	7	8	11	42	50	100
Sight-saving Classes	0	0	0	1	6	14	45	58	88	100
Legal Aid Bureau	0	0	0	0	1	10	41	83	100	100
Educational Facilities:										
College	2	4	6	13	17	39	45	79	100	100
Teacher's College	2	2	5	6	6	16	25	42	100	100
Private School	1	3	7	16	35	64	79	100	100	100
Art School	1	2	3	8	10	26	45	92	100	100
Class for Exceptional Children	1	1	2	3	47	76	86	92	100	100
Professional School	0	2	2	7	10	22	34	79	100	100
University	0	1	1	4	6	11	32	63	100	100
Nursery School	0	1	1	2	3	11	11	50	63	100
Governmental Facilities:										
City Planning Board	3	7	15	16	54	74	88	58	100	100
Zoning Commission	5	9	19	20	58	67	86	100	100	100
Art Commission	0	0	0	0	0	1	2	13	63	100
City Manager	3	3	3	2	0	0	0	0	0	0
Council-Manager	3	5	11	17	17	23	20	21	13	0
Transportation & Communication Facilities:										
Railroad Connection	58	73	80	96	95	100	100	100	100	100
Airport	9	12	20	36	60	60	75	96	100	100
Radio Station	1	1	6	14	35	59	80	100	100	100
Daily Newspaper	3	10	47	69	85	85	88	100	100	100
Semi-weekly Newspaper	3	8	9	8	12	13	14	33	50	100

TABLE 1 *(Continued)*

Population of the City in Thousands	2.0– 2.5	2.5– 5.0	5– 10	10– 25	25– 50	50– 100	100– 250	250– 500	500– 1000	1000 and Over
Number of Cities Studied	580	1440	880	614	135	98	56	24	8	5
Transportation & Communication Facilities:										
Fortnightly Newspaper	1	2	9	4	12	13	34	67	100	100
Tri-weekly Newspaper	0	1	2	1	2	0	5	13	12	100
Recreational Facilities:										
B.P.O. Elks Club	1	11	45	54	85	94	100	100	100	100
Lions Club	23	21	28	35	71	82	91	96	100	100
Women's Club	6	16	22	37	66	80	95	92	100	100
Junior League Organization	0	0	0	0	8	21	61	83	100	100
Chapter of American Fed'n of Arts	0	1	3	4	19	38	68	83	100	100
Music Organization	1	3	5	0	25	43	77	96	100	100
Symphony Orchestra	0	0	0	0	4	15	21	46	75	100
Regular Opera Season	0	0	0	0	0	2	4	25	25	60
Scout Council	1	1	7	20	74	84	93	100	100	100
Y.M.C.A. Facilities	2	6	5	29	70	83	93	96	100	100
Y.W.C.A. Facilities	0	1	5	14	48	71	91	96	100	100
Boys' Club Affiliated with American Fed'n of Boys' Clubs	0	0	1	2	11	23	50	54	100	100
School-Center	2	7	10	11	22	36	55	58	75	100
Settlement House	0	0	0	0	2	6	23	50	100	100
Golf Course	24	33	46	49	76	76	93	88	100	100
Park Recreation Area	0	1	11	33	65	93	95	100	100	100
Playground	2	3	12	28	68	90	91	96	100	100
Municipal Tennis Courts	2	2	10	19	58	85	86	100	100	100
Municipal Swimming Pools	2	2	4	12	29	49	64	79	88	100
Zoos, etc.	0	0	0	1	7	14	55	83	100	100

that the 25,000 and 100,000 population points have particular significance for the absence and presence of urban phenomena.

Correlation with community size is also revealed by an examination of the occurrence of Transportation and Communication facilities. It not only supports the conclusions drawn above but suggests that the first marked difference in community traits correlated with community size appears at the 25,000–50,000 level. The rural-urban cutting point may therefore come at about this point rather than at 2,500, 5,000, or 10,000, as has been suggested by others in the past.

The items in the table which pertain to newspapers indicate their close relationship with community size, with specialties and comparative novelties confined to the larger communities. The statistics tend to support the thesis that the press replaces some of the feeling of loss accompanying the decline in primary group relationships in the city. Actually, of course, the papers of large cities are read, in addition, by many who live in smaller places.

Turning our attention to Recreation, we see that more of the larger communities by far had these organizations than small ones. This finding supports the familiar thesis that secondary groups prevail in larger communities where primary group relationships are limited or even lacking altogether. Large places are principally occupied with business; organizational membership is a business asset. In addition, in the impersonality of a large place, it is difficult for an individual, in many cases, to make his influence felt unless he is a member of such a group. The findings for recreational facilities resemble those for other categories of facilities.

Examining the table as a whole, one sees that the percentages of incidence of facilities for the various groups of communities bring out the relations between them. A continuous and fundamental common character is discernible. In addition, there is a progression, a spectrum of urbanization, with its beginnings in the very small, simple community and its terminus in the large complex metropolis. Question 1 can be answered, therefore, in the affirmative: There is a direct correlation between community size and the extent of social phenomena. In addition, the spectrum probably indicates the presence in this country of a condition of "rurbania" with cities and related hinterlands comprising a functional whole, the smaller places in the hinterland possessing, in turn, subregions of their own.

The spectrum must be examined more closely. Superficially the table does not point to a conclusion that any groups of communities are differentiable. Neither does the spectrum reflect a sharp break between "urban" and "rural." Inspection of the table reveals no difference between the groups of communities immediately above and below the 2,500 line. In general, the situation in the 2,000–2,500 group is about the same as in the 2,500–5,000, 5,000–10,000, and the 10,000–25,000 groups. If there is any rural-urban break at all, it comes at the 25,000 population mark, at which point in the table we have already discerned repeated shifts and jumps, and not, as some have supposed, at the 2,500 population point. A "city,"

therefore, is a community with, in general, more than 25,000 population. This would be the answer to the first part of our question 2. But examination of the whole range of the spectrum is necessary.

In the foregoing much mention was made of the role of the 25,000, the 100,000, and the 500,000 population points — their significance for the distribution of many of the facilities studied was noted repeatedly. The table proves that these population points are important although they are subordinated to the common cultural thread extending from the smallest community to the largest. Moreover, if we arbitrarily consider 50 percent and 75 percent as noteworthy in interpreting the averages, the 25,000 and the 100,000 population points again emerge as important. Furthermore, it is within the vicinity of a population of 500,000 that the averages begin to approach 100.

Another way in which the spectrum may be examined is to determine the number of cases of predominance for the population groups. "Predominance" is taken to mean percentages of 50 or over. Also of significance is the incidence of complete coverage. Again we see the importance of the 25,000, the 100,000, and the 500,000 population points for the spectrum. If we investigate the groups which exhibit the greatest number of increases of percentages over those of the preceding size group we find that the 25,000, as well as the 100,000 population points, assume significance here as well. The negative result for the 500,000 population point and for groups of communities of large population may derive from the fact that it is inevitable that "jumps" become less common as one approaches 100 percent, beyond which they are nonexistent.

The 25,000 and 100,000 and, to a lesser extent, the 500,000 population points divide the spectrum into four levels or plateaus. Are these sufficiently marked off from each other to suggest different ranges of phenomena which may be given separate designations?

In the rural-urban continuum from its beginnings in the small, essentially rural community to its end in the huge metropolis, actually a world city as much as a national center, there is discernible a more or less consistent development of the distinctive way of life typically associated with city residence. What is rural self-sufficiency at the beginning is supplanted at the other extreme by economic specialization and interdependence. The urban dweller can rely, indeed often insists, upon the availability of extremely specialized businesses, stores, and services. Informal procedures in the case of illness and other individual and familiar crises fail or are impossible in the larger community where medical care, social work, welfare institutions, and philosophies largely originated and have had their most marked development. In the city places are found the prestige, income, and facilities which attract the specialist. Along with the wealth to support it, here, too, is a premium on formal education and its newest developments.

With the complexity of community that accompanies size come attempts to develop the machinery of efficient government, often late and usually inadequate. Similarly, transportation, communication, and recreation reflect the shift away from family self-sufficiency toward dependency on outside facilities and organizations; a shift from family to individual participation; a tendency for one's residence to be separate from one's work place. Despite the complaints of many city dwellers about certain features of their communities and the lives they themselves lead, the fact that metropolitan residents give higher ratings to vocations more frequently found in the city than in the country (e.g., artist or musician) reflects a well-integrated subculture in the urban place with its own concepts of status, prestige, economic adjustment, and individual integrity. These findings of North and Hatt suggest that different degrees of urbanization may correlate not only with community institutions, as we have shown, but also with urban dwellers' beliefs and practices.

16 Sentiment and Symbolism as Ecological Variables*

Walter Firey

Man has the capacity to develop sentimental attachments toward almost any object, and sentiment frequently influences behavior to such an extent that questions of utility are disregarded. When we examine a community, we are first impressed by the complex interdependence of its parts and their subtle organization into a dynamic and efficiently operating unit. But on closer observation we begin to see many nonutilitarian features that are protected even if they seriously threaten survival.

The following study examines the role sentiment plays in the use made of land in an overcrowded city. If you were a city planner, would you demand the destruction of the Boston Common? Why, or why not?

In this paper it will be our purpose to describe certain ecological processes which apparently cannot be embraced in a strictly economic analysis. Our hypothesis is that the data to be presented, while in no way startling or unfamiliar to the research ecologist, do suggest an alteration of the basic premises of ecology. This alteration would consist, first, of ascribing to space not only an impeditive quality but also an additional property, viz., that of being at times a symbol for certain cultural values that have become associated with a certain spatial area. Second, it would involve a recognition that locational activities are not only economizing agents but may also bear sentiments which can significantly influence the locational process.[1]

A test case for this twofold hypothesis is afforded by certain features of land use in central

* Excerpts from the *American Sociological Review,* Vol. 10 (April 1945), pp. 140–146. Copyright © 1945 by The American Sociological Association. Reproduced by permission.

[1] Georg Simmel, "Der Raum und die raumlichen Ordnungen der Gesellschaft," *Soziologie* (Munich: 1923), pp. 518–522.

Boston. In common with many of the older American cities, Boston has inherited from the past certain spatial patterns and landmarks which have had a remarkable persistence and even recuperative power despite challenges from other more economic land uses. The persistence of these spatial patterns can only be understood in terms of the group values that they have come to symbolize. We shall describe three types of such patterns: first, an in-town upper-class residential neighborhood known as Beacon Hill; second, certain "sacred sites," notably the Boston Common and the colonial burying-grounds; and third, a lower-class Italian neighborhood known as the North End. In each of these land uses we shall find certain locational processes which seem to defy a strictly economic analysis.

The first of the areas, Beacon Hill, is located some five minutes' walking distance from the retail center of Boston. This neighborhood has for fully a century and a half maintained its character as a preferred upper-class residential district, despite its contiguity to a low rent tenement area, the West End. During its long history Beacon Hill has become the symbol for a number of sentimental associations which constitute a genuine attractive force to certain old families of Boston. Some idea of the nature of these sentiments may be had from statements in the innumerable pamphlets and articles written by residents of the Hill. References to "this sacred eminence," [2] "stately old-time appearance," [3] and "age-old quaintness and charm," [4] give an insight into the attitudes attaching to the area. One resident reveals rather clearly the spatial referability of these sentiments when she writes of the Hill:

It has a tradition all of its own, that begins in the hospitality of a book-lover, and has never lost that flavor. Yes, our streets are inconvenient, steep, and slippery. The corners are abrupt, the contours perverse. . . . It may well be that the gibes of our envious neighbors have a foundation and that these dear

crooked lanes of ours were indeed traced in ancestral mud by absent-minded kine. [5]

Thus a wide range of sentiments — aesthetic, historical, and familial — have acquired a spatial articulation in Beacon Hill. The bearing of these sentiments upon locational processes is a tangible one and assumes three forms: retentive, attractive, and resistive. Let us consider each of these in order. To measure the retentive influence that spatially referred sentiments may exert upon locational activities, we have tabulated by place of residence all the families listed in the *Boston Social Register* for the years 1894, 1905, 1914, 1929, and 1943. This should afford a reasonably accurate picture of the distribution of upper-class families by neighborhoods within Boston and in suburban towns. There has been the consistent increase of upper-class families in the suburban towns and the marked decrease (since 1905) in two of the in-town upper-class areas, Back Bay and Jamaica Plain. Although both of these neighborhoods remain fashionable residential districts, their prestige is waning rapidly. Back Bay in particular, though still surpassing in numbers any other single neighborhood, has undergone a steady invasion of apartment buildings, rooming houses, and business establishments which are destroying its prestige value. The trend of Beacon Hill has been different. Today it has a larger number of upper-class families than it had in 1894. Where it ranked second among fashionable neighborhoods in 1894, it ranks third today, being but slightly outranked in numbers by the suburban city of Brookline and by the Back Bay. Beacon Hill is the only in-town district that has consistently retained its preferred character and has held to itself a considerable proportion of Boston's old families.

There is, however, another aspect to the spatial dynamics of Beacon Hill, one that pertains to the "attractive" locational role of spatially referred sentiments. From 1894 to 1905 the district underwent a slight drop, subsequently experiencing a steady rise for twenty-four years, and most recently undergoing another slight decline. These

[2] John R. Shultz, *Beacon Hill and the Carol Singers,* Boston, 1923, p. 11.

[3] *Bulletin of the Society for the Preservation of New England Antiquities,* 4:3, August, 1913.

[4] Josephine Samson, *Celebrities of Louisburg Square,* Greenfield, Mass., 1924.

[5] Abbie Farwell Brown, *The Lights of Beacon Hill,* Boston, 1922, p. 4.

variations are significant, and they bring out rather clearly the dynamic ecological role of spatial symbolism. The initial drop is attributable to the development of the then new Back Bay. Hundreds of acres there had been reclaimed from marshland and had been built up with palatial dwellings. Fashion now pointed to this as the select area of the city, and in response to its dictates a number of families abandoned Beacon Hill to take up more pretentious Back Bay quarters. Property values on the Hill began to depreciate, old dwellings became rooming houses, and business began to invade some of the streets. But many of the old families remained on the Hill, and a few of them made efforts to halt the gradual deterioration of the district. Under the aegis of a realtor, an architect, and a few close friends, there was launched a program of purchasing old houses, modernizing the interiors and leaving the colonial exteriors intact, and then selling the dwellings to individual families for occupancy. Frequently, adjoining neighbors would collaborate in planning their improvements so as to achieve an architectural consonance. The results of this program may be seen in the drift of upper-class families back to the Hill. From 1905 to 1929 the number of Social Register families in the district increased by 120. Assessed valuations showed a corresponding increase: from 1919 to 1924 there was a rise of 24 per cent; from 1924 to 1929 the rise was 25 per cent.[6] The nature of the Hill's appeal, and the kind of persons attracted, may be gathered from the following popular write-up:

> To salvage the quaint charm of colonial architecture on Beacon Hill, Boston, is the object of a well-defined movement among writers and professional folk that promises the most delightful opportunities for the home-seeker of moderate means and conservative tastes. Because men of discernment were able to visualize the possibilities presented by these architectural landmarks and have undertaken the gracious task of restoring them to their former glory, this historic quarter of old Boston, once the center of literary culture, is coming into its own.[7]

The independent variable in this "attractive" locational process seems to have been the symbolic quality of the Hill, by which it constituted a referent for certain strong sentiments of upper-class Bostonians.

While this revival was progressing there remained a constant menace to the character of Beacon Hill, in the form of business encroachments and apartment-hotel developments. Recurrent threats from this source finally prompted residents of the Hill to organize themselves into the Beacon Hill Association. Formed in 1922, the declared object of this organization was "to keep undesirable business and living conditions from affecting the Hill district."[8] At the time the city was engaged in preparing a comprehensive zoning program and the occasion was propitious to secure for Beacon Hill suitable protective measures. A systematic set of recommendations was drawn up by the Association regarding a uniform 65-foot height limit for the entire Hill, the exclusion of business from all but two streets, and the restriction of apartment house bulk.[9] It succeeded in gaining only a partial recognition of this program in the 1929 zoning ordinance. But the Association continued its fight against inimical land uses year after year. In 1927 it successfully fought a petition brought before the Board of Zoning Adjustment to alter the height limits in one area so as to permit the construction of a four million dollar apartment-hotel 155 feet high. Residents of the Hill went to the hearing en masse. In spite of the prospect of an additional twenty million dollars worth of exclusive apartment hotels that were promised if the zoning restrictions were withheld, the petition was rejected, having been opposed by 214 of the 220 persons present at the hearing.[10] In 1930 the Association gained an actual reduction in height limits on most of Beacon Street and certain adjoining streets, though its leader was denounced by opponents as "a rank sentimentalist who desired to keep Boston a village."[11] One year later the Association defeated a petition to re-zone Beacon Street for business purposes.[12] In other campaigns the Association successfully

[6] *The Boston Transcript*, April 12, 1930.
[7] *Ibid.*, December 6, 1932.

[8] Harriet Sisson Gillespie, "Reclaiming Colonial Landmarks," *The House Beautiful*, 58:239–41, September, 1925.
[9] *The Boston Transcript*, March 18, 1933.
[10] *Ibid.*, January 29, 1927.
[11] *Ibid.*, April 12, 1930.
[12] *Ibid.*, January 10–29, 1931.

pressed for the re-zoning of a business street back to purely residential purposes, for the lowering of height limits on the remainder of Beacon Street, and for several lesser matters of local interest. Since 1929, owing partly to excess assessed valuations of Boston real estate and partly to the effects of the depression upon families living on securities, Beacon Hill has lost some of its older families, though its decline is nowhere near so precipitous as that of the Back Bay.

Thus for a span of one and a half centuries there have existed on Beacon Hill certain locational processes that largely escape economic analysis. It is the symbolic quality of the Hill, not its impeditive or cost-imposing character, that most tangibly correlates with the retentive, attractive, and resistive trends that we have observed. And it is the dynamic force of spatially referred sentiments, rather than considerations of rent, which explains why certain families have chosen to live on Beacon Hill in preference to other in-town districts having equally accessible location and even superior housing conditions. There is thus a non-economic aspect to land use on Beacon Hill, one which is in some respects actually dis-economic in its consequences. Certainly the large apartment-hotels and specialty shops that have sought in vain to locate on the Hill would have represented a fuller capitalization on potential property values than do residences. In all likelihood the attending increase in real estate prices would not only have benefited individual property holders but would have so enhanced the value of adjoining properties as to compensate for whatever depreciation other portions of the Hill might have experienced.

If we turn to another type of land use pattern in Boston, that comprised by the Boston Common and the old burying-grounds, we encounter another instance of spatial symbolism which has exerted a marked influence upon the ecological organization of the rest of the city. The Boston Common is a survival from colonial days when every New England town allotted a portion of its land to common use as a cow pasture and militia field. Over the course of three centuries Boston has grown entirely around the Common so that today we find a 48-acre tract of land wedged directly into the heart of the business district. On three of its five sides are women's apparel shops, department stores, theaters, and other high-rent locational activities. On the fourth side is Beacon Street, extending alongside Beacon Hill. Only the activities of Hill residents have prevented business from invading this side. The fifth side is occupied by the Public Garden. A value map portrays a strip of highest values pressing upon two sides of the Common, on Tremont and Boylston Streets, taking the form of a long, narrow band.

Before considering the ecological consequences of this configuration let us see what attitudes have come to be associated with the Common. There is an extensive local literature about the Common, and in it we find interesting sentiments expressed. One citizen speaks of

. . . the great principle exemplified in the preservation of the Common. Thank Heaven, the tide of money making must break and go around that.[13]

Elsewhere we read:

Here, in short, are all our accumulated memories, intimate, public, private.[14]

Boston Common was, is, and ever will be a source of tradition and inspiration from which the New Englanders may renew their faith, recover their moral force, and strengthen their ability to grow and achieve.[15] The Common has thus become a "sacred" object, articulating and symbolizing genuine historical sentiments of a certain portion of the community. Like all such objects its sacredness derives, not from any intrinsic spatial attributes, but rather from its representation in people's minds as a symbol for collective sentiments.[16]

Such has been the force of these sentiments that the Common has become buttressed up by a number of legal guarantees. The city charter forbids Boston in perpetuity to dispose of the Common or

---

[13] Speech of William Everett, quoted in *The Boston Transcript,* March 7, 1903.

[14] T. R. Sullivan, *Boston New and Old,* Boston, 1912, pp. 45–46.

[15] Joshua H. Jones, Jr., "Happening on Boston Common," *Our Boston,* 2:9–15, January, 1927.

[16] Cf. Emile Durkheim, *The Elementary Forms of the Religious Life,* London, 1915, p. 345.

any portion of it. The city is further prohibited by state legislation from building upon the Common, except within rigid limits, or from laying out roads or tracks across it.[17] By accepting the bequest of one George F. Parkman, in 1908, amounting to over five million dollars, the city is further bound to maintain the Common, and certain other parks, "for the benefit and enjoyment of its citizens." [18]

What all this has meant for the spatial development of Boston's retail center is clear from the present character of that district. Few cities of comparable size have so small a retail district in point of area. Unlike the spacious department stores in most cities, those in Boston are frequently compressed within narrow confines and have had to extend in devious patterns through rear and adjoining buildings. Traffic in downtown Boston has literally reached the saturation point, owing partly to the narrow one-way streets but mainly to the lack of adequate arterials leading into and out of the Hub. The American Road Builders Association has estimated that there is a loss of $81,000 per day in Boston as a result of traffic delay. Trucking in Boston is extremely expensive. These losses ramify out to merchants, manufacturers, commuters, and many other interests.[19] Many proposals have been made to extend a through arterial across the Common, thus relieving the extreme congestion on Tremont and Beacon Streets, the two arterials bordering the park.[20] Earlier suggestions, prior to the construction of the subway, called for street car tracks across the Common. But "the controlling sentiment of the citizens of Boston, and of large numbers throughout the state, is distinctly opposed to allowing any such use of the common." [21] Boston has long suffered from land shortage and unusually high real estate values as a result both of the narrow confines of the peninsula comprising the

city center and as a result of the exclusion from income-yielding uses of so large a tract as the Common.[22] A further difficulty has arisen from the rapid southwesterly extension of the business district in the past two decades. With the Common lying directly in the path of this extension the business district has had to stretch around it in an elongated fashion, with obvious inconvenience to shoppers and consequent loss to business.

The Common is not the only obstacle to the city's business expansion. No less than three colonial burying-grounds, two of them adjoined by ancient church buildings, occupy downtown Boston. The contrast that is presented by nine-story office buildings reared up beside quiet cemeteries affords visible evidence of the conflict between "sacred" and "profane" that operates in Boston's ecological pattern. The dis-economic consequences of commercially valuable land being thus devoted to non-utilitarian purposes goes even further than the removal from business uses of a given amount of space. For it is a standard principle of real estate that business property derives added value if adjoining properties are occupied by other businesses.[23] Just as a single vacancy will depreciate the value of a whole block of business frontage, so a break in the continuity of stores by a cemetery damages the commercial value of surrounding properties. But, even more than the Common, the colonial burying-grounds of Boston have become invested with a moral significance which renders them almost inviolable. Not only is there the usual sanctity which attaches to all cemeteries, but in those of Boston there is an added sacredness growing out of the age of the grounds and the fact that the forebears for many of New England's most distinguished families as well as a number of colonial and Revolutionary leaders lie buried in these cemeteries. There is thus a manifold symbolism to these old burying-grounds, pertaining to family lineage, early nationhood, civic origins, and the like, all of which have

[17] St. 1859, c. 210, paragraph 3; Pub. sts., c. 54, paragraph 13.

[18] M. A. De Wolfe Howe, *Boston Common,* Cambridge, 1910, p. 79.

[19] Elisabeth M. Herlihy, ed., *Fifty Years of Boston,* Boston, 1932, pp. 53–54.

[20] See, for example, letter to editor, *The Boston Herald,* November 16, 1930.

[21] *First Annual Report of the Boston Transit Commission,* Boston, 1895.

[22] John C. Kiley, "Changes in Realty Values in the Nineteenth and Twentieth Centuries," *Bulletin of the Business Historical Society,* 15, June, 1941, p. 36; Frank Chouteau Brown, "Boston: More Growing Pains," *Our Boston,* 3, February, 1927, p. 8.

[23] Richard M. Hurd, *Principles of City Land Values,* New York, 1903, pp. 93–94.

strong sentimental associations. What has been said of the old burying-grounds applies with equal force to a number of other venerable landmarks in central Boston. Such buildings as the Old South Meeting House, the Park Street Church, King's Chapel, and the Old State House — all foci of historical associations — occupy commercially valuable land and interrupt the continuity of business frontage on their streets. Nearly all of these landmarks have been challenged at various times by real estate and commercial interests which sought to have them replaced by more profitable uses. In every case community sentiments have resisted such threats.

In all these examples we find a symbol-senti-

ment relationship which has exerted a significant influence upon land use. Nor should it be thought that such phenomena are mere ecological "sports." Many other older American cities present similar locational characteristics. Delancey Street in Philadelphia represents a striking parallel to Beacon Hill, and certain in-town districts of Chicago, New York, and Detroit, recently revived as fashionable apartment areas, bear resemblances to the Beacon Hill revival. The role of traditionalism in rigidifying the ecological patterns of New Orleans has been demonstrated in a recent study. Further studies of this sort should clarify even further the true scope of sentiment and symbolism in urban spatial structure and dynamics.

17 Age and Sex Composition of Urban Subareas*

Calvin F. Schmid

As the neighborhoods and other subareas of a city become differentiated, they become differentially attractive and accessible to various elements of the population and to different commercial and industrial concerns. Occupational, political, racial, and religious characteristics are sifted out and located quite differently in urban areas, depending upon a variety of social, cultural, and financial factors. Differences in the composition of neighborhood populations are overshadowed by present concern over residential segregation by race, but this does not mean that these differences are inconsequential. For example, population pyramids for subareas of a large city — such as census tracts — make it clear that age and sex composition varies widely from one area to another. The "skid road," for instance, is inhabited chiefly by older unattached

* Reprinted with major adaptations and 1960 census data from Calvin F. Schmid, *Social Trends in Seattle.* Seattle: University of Washington Press, 1944, pp. 93–97, by permission. Copyright, 1944, by Calvin F. Schmid.

males, with very few females, and even fewer children. A rooming-house area within walking distance of office buildings has few children and a large proportion of young adult females. A suburban residential district has a large proportion of children. These age and sex patterns occur so frequently in various cities that it is often possible to judge the social and economic characteristics of an area from its population pyramid.

The following discussion of population pyramids is based on data obtained from the 1960 census in Seattle, Washington. How might these data be used by politicians, recreation workers, school administrators, businessmen, and police officials? What major social problems are suggested by each of the pyramids?

Sex and Age Composition of Certain Typical Census Tracts. In order to obtain a more detailed and comprehensive picture of the age and sex structure of the population in various parts of the city, certain tracts were selected for special analysis. These tracts represent typical ecological areas found in most large American cities. In this group of nine census tracts selected for special study are the central business district, a major apartment and rooming house area, Skid Road and two other transitional areas in the central segment of the city, a public housing project, a Negro family area, an outlying business and industrial

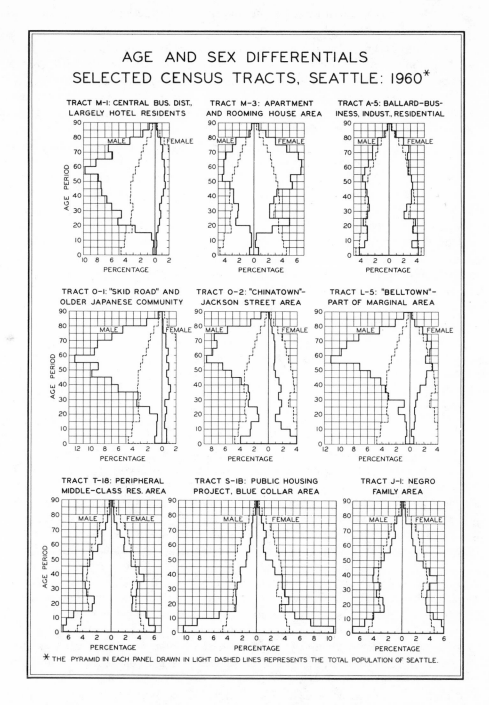

AGE AND SEX DIFFERENTIALS
SELECTED CENSUS TRACTS, SEATTLE: 1960*

TRACT M-1: CENTRAL BUS. DIST., LARGELY HOTEL RESIDENTS

TRACT M-3: APARTMENT AND ROOMING HOUSE AREA

TRACT A-5: BALLARD–BUSINESS, INDUST., RESIDENTIAL

TRACT O-1: "SKID ROAD" AND OLDER JAPANESE COMMUNITY

TRACT O-2: "CHINATOWN"–JACKSON STREET AREA

TRACT L-5: "BELLTOWN"–PART OF MARGINAL AREA

TRACT T-18: PERIPHERAL MIDDLE-CLASS RES. AREA

TRACT S-18: PUBLIC HOUSING PROJECT, BLUE COLLAR AREA

TRACT J-1: NEGRO FAMILY AREA

* THE PYRAMID IN EACH PANEL DRAWN IN LIGHT DASHED LINES REPRESENTS THE TOTAL POPULATION OF SEATTLE.

area, and a peripheral middle-class residential section.

In order to facilitate more reliable comparisons of the sex and age structure of the nine census tracts, the age and sex configuration for the city as a whole has been superimposed in dashed lines on each of the nine pyramids in the figure.

It will be observed that the pyramid for Tract M1, which embraces most of the central business district, is markedly asymmetrical, indicating a pronounced excess of males (85.3 per cent), and a very small proportion of children (0.4 per cent under 5 or 1.4 per cent under 15 years of age). The proportion of the population in the upper age groups is considerably higher in the central business district than in the city as a whole (22.0 per cent of the population in the central business district are 65 years and over, as compared to 12.0 for the entire city). In addition, the Negro (0.1 per cent as compared to 4.8 per cent for the entire city), as well as other non-white population (1.8 per cent for the central business district and 3.5 per cent for the city as a whole), is relatively small. The educational level of the population in the central business district is relatively low (median grade for the population 25 years old and over is 9.0, as compared to 12.2 for the entire city; 3.8 per cent are college graduates, in comparison to 12.4 for the city as a whole). In the central business district, the proportion of male laborers is high (20.2 per cent) as is the proportion of unemployed males (32.9 per cent).

Tract M3 is representative of a centrally located rooming-house and apartment-house area, characterized by a high proportion of females (59.3 per cent) and a small proportion of children (2.4 per cent of the population is under 15 years of age, as compared to 25.9 per cent for the city as a whole). Also, there is a pronounced excess of people in the older age brackets (26.7 per cent are 65 and over, in comparison to 12.0 per cent for the entire city). The socio-economic status of the population is relatively high in terms of educational level and occupation. Only 31.9 per cent of the population 14 years of age and over are married, as compared to 62.6 per cent for the city as a whole. The incidence of separation, divorce, and widowhood is very high.

Tract A5 represents the main business district of Ballard, one of the more important outlying industrial sections of Seattle. A relatively high proportion of both native and foreign-born Scandinavians live in this area. It will be observed from the figure that there is a marked coincidence between the age and sex structures of Tract A5 and of the entire city. In Tract A5, 49.2 per cent of the population is male, as compared to 48.9 per cent for the city as a whole. The age group under 15 years comprises 22.0 per cent of the population in A5 and 25.9 per cent for the entire city. The corresponding percentages for the population 65 years and over are 15.8 and 12.0.

Also included in the figure are three tracts — O1, O2, and L5 — which represent transitional areas contiguous to the central business district. O1 is mainly a "hobohemia" colloquially referred to as "Skid Road"; O2 includes Chinatown and smaller clusterings of Filipinos, Negroes, and Japanese; and L5 is inhabited largely by an unstable proletarian white population. In all three tracts there is a heavy preponderance of the male sex, with 88.8 per cent in O1, 75.6 per cent in O2, and 72.5 per cent in L5. The proportion of children under 15 years of age in these three tracts is small, with 4.3 per cent, 17.6 per cent, and 3.0 per cent, respectively; while on the other hand, the proportion of the population 65 years of age and over is comparatively large, with 25.4 per cent in O1, 26.6 per cent in O2, and 31.6 per cent in L5. It will be recalled that for the city as a whole, 25.9 per cent of the population is under 15 years of age, and 12.0 per cent 65 years and over. These three tracts are also characterized by a declining population, a high proportion of foreign-born, a high proportion of separated, divorced, and widowed, low educational level, low occupational status, and a large proportion of unemployed.

Tract T18 represents a relatively new, growing, middle-class residential area toward the northern periphery of the city. The great majority of the homes (84.7 per cent) are owner-occupied. There is a relatively high proportion of children (34.4 per cent under 15, as compared to 25.9 per cent for the city as a whole) and a low proportion of older people (5.9 per cent in comparison to 12.0 per cent for the entire city). There is only one Negro and 25 other non-white in this tract. The proportion of the population 14 years of age and over that is married is relatively high (77.5), the incidence of separation, divorce, and widowhood is low (3.9 per cent), and the proportion of foreign-born is small (5.8 per cent). The educational level of the population, as well as occupational status, conforms very closely to that for the city as a whole.

The most distinctive characteristic of the age and sex structure of the population in tract S1b is the extraordinarily large proportion of children; 47.5 per cent of those living in this tract are under 15 years of age. Also, the proportion of adults in the childbearing age group is high. The educational and occupational level of this group is noticeably below that of the city as a whole.

The most highly concentrated Negro population in Seattle is found in Tract J1; 84.3 per cent are Negro, 4.3 other non-white, and 11.4 white. The percentage of males (48.3) is very close to that for the city as a whole (48.9). The proportion of children in this tract is above the city average (32.3 per cent under 15 years of age, as compared to 25.9 per cent for the entire city) and the proportion of older people below the city average (7.1

per cent 65 years of age and over, in comparison to 12.0 for the city as a whole). Home-ownership, as indicated by the percentage of owner-occupied housing units (55.6 per cent), is slightly above the city average (53.3 per cent). The median value of owner-occupied housing units in Tract J1 is $9,800, as compared to $13,500 for the entire city. The educational and occupational level of the population in this tract is below the city average and the incidence of separation and divorce, above the city average.

18   The Changing Color of Our Big Cities*

Leo F. Schnore · Harry Sharp

The following discussion of the concentrations of America's black population in the largest central cities is profoundly relevant to an understanding of the contemporary urban crisis. The trends they describe for the 1950–1960 decade have continued since 1960, bringing about even greater color differences between the central cities and their suburbs. For example, between 1960 and 1966 about nine-tenths of the increase in the nonwhite population was in the central cities of the standard metropolitan statistical areas (SMSA's). By 1966 55 per cent of the nonwhite population lived in central cities. In contrast, the white population residing in central cities declined by almost one million between 1960 and 1966 (a decrease of 0.8 per cent), leaving 27 per cent of the white population in central cities in 1966. About seven-eighths of all gain in the white population occurred in the areas of the SMSA's lying outside the central cities. These general trends have continued up to the present time.

What are the implications for a nation to have two-thirds of its population concentrated in metropolitan areas, with the white and black populations within these areas separated out into the central

cities and suburban areas? How does this affect programs to provide integrated schools? What obstacles might it place in the path of central city and suburban residents who must work together to solve the larger problems faced by the entire metropolitan area?

It is no exaggeration to call the growth of nonwhite population in our major cities one of the truly outstanding social trends of the twentieth century. In 1900, when 43 per cent of the white population was living in urban communities, only 22.7 per cent of the nonwhite population lived in cities. At our most recent census in 1960, 69.5 per cent of all whites and 72.4 per cent of all nonwhites were urban dwellers, making the nonwhites more urbanized than the rest of the American population.

The concentration of nonwhites in very large cities is even more dramatic. The central cities of our twelve largest metropolitan areas contained 13.2 per cent of the United States population in 1960. At the same time, these cities held over 31 per cent of American Negroes. (These cities are New York, Los Angeles-Long Beach, Chicago, Philadelphia, Detroit, San Francisco-Oakland, Boston, Pittsburgh, St. Louis, Washington, Cleveland, and Baltimore. In the California cities there are substantial numbers of persons of Chinese and Japanese ancestry, who are also treated as "nonwhites" in census statistics; but the nonwhite population in most cities is almost entirely Negro.)

Actually the rapid influx of nonwhites is not confined to a handful of very large places. Every one of the fifty largest cities in the continental United States each containing at least 250,000 inhabitants in 1960 showed increases in their proportions of nonwhites between 1950 and 1960, our two most recent censuses. This trend was evident in all sections of the country, North and South, East and West. In some cases (e.g., Minneapolis, St. Paul, and El Paso), the increases are modest, with a difference of only one or two percentage points. In other instances, however, the changes are substantial; for example, Newark changed from 17.2 to 34.4 per cent nonwhite, and Washington's proportion of nonwhites rose from 35.4 to 54.8 in 1960.

There were regional differences, however, in the experience of metropolitan areas. Fully 70 per cent of the 212 Standard Metropolitan Statistical Areas currently recognized showed increasing proportions of nonwhites between 1950 and 1960, but this figure conceals an important difference between the South and the rest of the country. Outside the South, nine out of every ten metropolitan areas showed nonwhite increases over the decade. In the South itself, the trend was radically different, for only 35 per cent of the southern metropolitan areas (27 out of 77) experienced relative gains in numbers of nonwhite. *In other words, six out of every ten southern metropolitan areas had lower proportions of nonwhites in 1960 than in 1950.* In general, it was only the larger southern metropolitan areas that gained large numbers of nonwhites.

DARK CORE

The twelve largest metropolitan areas listed earlier now contain almost a third of the American Negro population. The proportion of whites in the United States who lived in the twelve central areas has fallen slightly but steadily since 1930, while the proportion of nonwhites has consistently increased, doubling in the thirty-year interval. Between 1950 and 1960 these central cities lost over two million whites while gaining 1.8 million nonwhites. In addition, although the white population has become progressively more concentrated in the suburban "rings" around these cities, the relative number of nonwhites in these rings (only 3 per

cent in 1930) has grown by just two percentage points in thirty years.

The collective pattern described above is generally reproduced in each of the twelve areas taken individually. *The total population increased rather slowly in the depression decade of 1930–1940, then grew faster over the last two decades, with the nonwhite populations growing at rates from two to four times greater than those of the white populations.*

In fact, the only central area of the twelve which did not experience an absolute loss in number of whites between 1950 and 1960 was Los Angeles-Long Beach; and in this case the rate of growth of whites fell off during the last decade while that for nonwhites continued to rise at an extremely rapid rate. As a result of these trends, eight of the twelve central cities have considerably fewer whites within their borders now than they did thirty years ago. New York, San Francisco-Oakland, and Washington have approximately the same number as in 1930. Only the Los Angeles-Long Beach area can show a noticeable *absolute* increase in the number of whites in 1960 as compared to 1930 and a substantial proportion of its central growth must be attributed to annexations.

WHITES LEAVE WASHINGTON

Thus the *relative* number of whites in every one of the twelve large central cities has decreased drastically over the last thirty years. This trend started slowly in the 'thirties, gained momentum in the 'forties, and became most pronounced during the 'fifties. The experience of one central city — Washington, D.C. — touches on the dramatic. In 1930 almost three-quarters of the inhabitants living in the city of Washington were white; currently, more than one-half of the residents of this city are nonwhite.

In contrast to the sharp drop in the proportion of whites in the central cities, the most common pattern in the suburban rings is one of near stability in racial composition. Thus despite the rapid absolute growth of the ring area, and despite the fact that the nonwhite *rate* of growth in the ring often is higher than that of the whites, the proportion of whites in eight of the twelve suburban rings changed by less than three percentage points between 1930 and 1960. In Washington, D.C., and in Baltimore, the relative number of whites in the ring actually *increased* substantially during these thirty years.

WHITE RINGS

Since 1930 the nonwhite population has expanded rapidly in every one of the large central cities; correspondingly, the central city white population has remained relatively stable or has substantially declined. This process of racial turnover reached a peak of intensity between 1950 and 1960. The population decline of our largest cities would have been much more pronounced if increased numbers of nonwhites had not partially compensated for the loss of the white population. As we have noted, the flow to the rings was even greater over the last ten years than it was earlier.

But this "decentralization" movement involves a distinct color line. While the cities are becoming more and more nonwhite, the rings maintain an amazingly high and constant proportion of white residents; without exception, from 93 to 99 per cent of the population in the rings of our twelve largest metropolitan communities are white and this situation is basically unchanged since 1930.

Continuation of the trends documented here would certainly have tremendous implications for the future of the metropolitan community in the United States.

What are the reasons for these massive shifts?

How far will the population redistribution by race continue?

Will our largest metropolitan areas eventually consist of white rings surrounding nonwhite cities?

WHY THE POPULATION SHIFTS

One reason why the central city is losing its white population is that whites in the city are older and have higher death rates. More importantly, under-developed city land for the building of new homes is in very short supply. Those dwellings that are available often are not as attractive to young white families as comparably priced homes in the suburbs. Finally, for a number of whites, fears of various kinds — threats of possible physical violence, hazards of declining property values, concern over the color composition of schools — begin to operate when nonwhites become neighbors.

The ring population is increasing at a tremendous rate not only because of movements into them but also because suburban areas have a high proportion of young couples who are producing children at a very rapid pace. They are "baby farms" in an almost literal sense. Additional factors which have contributed to the accumulation of population in the ring include the greater ability of American families to pay the higher costs of transportation; the decentralization of industrial and commercial enterprises; and the construction of vast suburban housing tracts and massive expressways which lead into the heart of the city.

Nonwhites are increasing in the larger cities because of the higher birth rates of central city nonwhites and because of the "pull" of a more favorable political-economic climate. The big cities have the jobs to which nonwhites can aspire, even though they may not pay well.

Why have nonwhites clustered near the center of the city and avoided the outer city and the ring? Part of the explanation is certainly the low economic status of the nonwhite and his inability to afford a new home in a more expensive neighborhood. *Most observers would agree, however, that the major factors in residential clustering by race are restrictive selling practices which ultimately create separate housing markets for whites and nonwhites.*

FORECAST FOR CHICAGO

In any case, the trend is one of long standing and is not likely to be reversed in the near future. A series of population projections by two University of Chicago sociologists, Donald J. Bogue and D. P. Dandekar, is instructive. The city of Chicago lost almost 400,000 white residents between 1950 and 1960 and gained 328,000 nonwhites in exchange. Part of this was due to "natural increase" on the part of nonwhites, for births exceeded deaths by almost 171,000. (The other

157,000 new nonwhites were migrants.) Non-white fertility was higher than that of the white population; in fact it increased 17 per cent between 1950 and 1960, while white fertility went up by only 9 per cent. The projections by Bogue and Dandekar assumed that the volume of Negro in-migration will remain about the same as in recent decades, but that Negro fertility will decline.

On this basis, the population of Chicago in 1990 would consist of 1,941,000 whites and 1,777,000 nonwhites, or a bare majority of whites. This compares with the 76.4 per cent white population counted in the 1960 census. If the exact trends of the 1950–60 decade were to be extrapolated into the future, however, Chicago nonwhites would achieve a majority as early as 1975.

We can anticipate that the rest of the twentieth century will be marked by a continuation of the established trend toward concentration of the American Negro in large cities and a continuation of the accompanying social upheavals that have captured the attention of the nation in recent years.

19   The Natural History of a Reluctant Suburb*

William M. Dobriner

An outstanding characteristic of population growth in the United States in recent decades had been the continuing concentration of population in the great standard metropolitan statistical areas (SMSA's). Half the counties in the United States actually lose population, while the already densely settled counties continue to accumulate residents both from migration and the excess of births over deaths. However, most of this increase takes place in the area of the SMSA lying outside the central city. For example, between 1950 and 1960 the following increases took place: SMSA's, 26.4 per cent (central cities 10.8 per cent; outlying areas, 48.5 per cent); area outside SMSA's, 7.1 per cent. These same general trends have continued since 1960 although at a slower rate because of the slackening rate of total population growth. Between 1960 and 1966 about seven-eighths of the total increase in the nation's white population took place in the outlying areas of the SMSA's. (In contrast, about nine-tenths of the increase in the nonwhite population was in the central cities of the SMSA's.) This continuing suburbanization of the white population, a spectacular and familiar phenomenon since World War

* From *The Yale Review*, XLIX (Spring 1960), pp. 399–412. Copyright Yale University Press. Reproduced by permission.

II, is best known for the mushrooming of new suburban housing developments and all new suburban communities. Less well known is the experience of the established and independent small town that found itself engulfed in the overflow of the metropolitan center. The type of fundamental social change described in the following essay about Old Harbor — the reluctant suburb — was experienced by many small towns and villages all over the nation if they happened to be located adjacent to a growing metropolis.

What aspects of new technology influenced the spread of Old Harbor's metropolitan neighbor? What conflicts occurred between the villagers and suburbanites? Why did this conflict in values not lead to complete separation or an outbreak of violence between the two groups?

THE FIRST 300 YEARS

What it means for a long-established village to be suburbanized can be seen from the recent history of a community here called "Old Harbor." It is a real place, in the New England area, on the Atlantic Coast. Over 300 years old, Old Harbor lies at the foot of a curving valley between two green necks of land stretching into the sea. Its history resembles that of many another New England village. In 1662, for example, a "morals committee" of six "respectable" citizens and the minister carefully scrutinized all new settlers who arrived in the community. A newcomer who failed to pass the committee's standards of morality and respectability was asked to leave. So Old Harbor's tradition of skepticism and caution as to the worth of recent arrivals is anchored in over 300 years of experience.

In its early years, Old Harbor served as the nexus of an agrarian and colonial society. Its grist mills ground local grain into flour through the power of the impounded waters of the tide ponds and mill dams. The natural harbor drew shipping from all over the East Coast. Whaling ships worked out of the port, and coastal shipping from ports as far away as the West Indies unloaded hides, rum, cattle, cordwood, charcoal, and other commodities, on Old Harbor's busy wharfs. Farmers worked the land on the gently rolling slopes leading down to the water. Wheelwrights turned out wheels, metal smiths pounded out pewterware, shipbuilders sent vessels splashing into the bay, and carpenters built saltbox cottages down near the harbor. The village prospered but remained comparatively changeless in some fundamental ways — it continued to be a Yankee village of industrious merchants, seamen, farmers, and craftsmen. Certain family names appear again and again in its records: Rodgers, Platt, Titus, Woods, Brush, Conklin, Wicks, Scudder, Soper, Skidmore. In time more land was cleared, more ships were built, and small but vigorously independent men set up industries and crafts, farms, and homes. Yet the essential ethos of the village remained constant — Yankee, Protestant, independent, cautious, shrewd, calculating, hard working, and conservative.

Old Harbor figured in the American Revolution. One of its churches (still standing and functioning) served as headquarters for the local British forces. George Washington came to Old Harbor and slept there. By the middle of the nineteenth century, in a society where so many persons, traditions, and things were new, Old Harbor had a heritage of 200 years to look back upon. But change was imminent. In 1867 the railroad came to the village and became a serious competitor of marine transportation, and thereafter the harbor declined as a vital force in the village's economy. Even more ominous was the fact that 36.6 miles from the village lay the borders of a city. By today's standards, it was an urban infant, but even then it was showing a capacity for incredible growth and its influence was extending beyond its borders. Though it was still an entity apart and a universe removed from Old Harbor, some of the more perceptive villagers looked to "the city" with something more than casual Yankee curiosity and superiority. In writing to a relative in 1872, one villager noted: "There has been a very curious thing this summer, I must have seen 15 or 20 strangers in town during July and August."

The first invaders of Old Harbor were members of the new industrial aristocracy that emerged in the decades after the Civil War. They were the first outsiders to discover the little coves and their verdant overcover, the unspoiled woodlands, the tiny village with so much history, and the green, gentle hills with the spectacular sweep of the sea. By the turn of the century, Old Harbor had become their carefully guarded preserve. They bought the old farms and cleared away acres for their summer playgrounds and gigantic estates. They fenced off two- and three-hundred acre parcels and created separate dukedoms populated by communities of servants and laborers.

On the surface, things had not changed much. The rolling hills, the snug harbor, the Yankee village with its saltbox cottages and local crafts, the busy farms — all remained the same. The estates were secluded behind acres of greenery and the new leisure class strove to protect "the colonial charm" of the village and its surroundings. The old inhabitants kept to themselves. They ran the village as they always had, but supplied the estates with provisions and such services as they were capable of providing. Though there was little basic understanding and compatibility between the "high society" of the nation and the "high society" of the village, the coming of the estates brought a new prosperity to Old Harbor and helped to take up the slack left by the decline of the fishing and whaling industries and the harbor in general. By the turn of the century, Old Harbor was passing into another stage of its life. By now the grist mills were great swaybacked structures rotting by the mill dams. The brickkilns, the tannery, and Ezra Prime's thimble factory were alive only in the memories of the very old. Children played sea games in the soft, pungent, peeling hulks of the whalers as they lay beached in the harbor marshes, their masts pointing like splayed fingers against the evening sky.

And in the meantime, to the east, the urban goliath was yawning and stretching and looking fitfully about.

By the early 1920's, the township in which Old Harbor is located was undergoing rather intensive immigration from the metropolitan area. The city was going through one of its growth spasms, and the population was spilling over the city limits into the adjacent counties. Old Harbor was one county removed, but this was the decade in which the automobile drastically changed the character of American society and culture. Mass production had made Henry Ford's dream of a low-priced car for every family almost a reality. And a few miles to the south of the village, in "Old Harbor Station," the railroad terminus, a new and rather singular figure stood on the platform waiting for the 8:05 to the city: the commuter, the classic suburbanite, with his freshly pressed tight trousers, starched white collar, and morning paper folded neatly under his arm.

The Coming of Suburbia

Now the automobile and the new concrete highways were bringing transient strangers to Old Harbor. The strangers were noisily evident on hot summer nights when a two-hour drive would carry them from the heat and congestion of the city to the beaches and cool valleys of Old Harbor. The character of Old Harbor weekends rudely changed as streams of cranky autos on spindly wheels rattled through the center of town and jammed up at traffic lights. Not only was Main Street becoming a thoroughfare for the beach traffic on weekends, but the city people intruded into the private bathing places along the waterfront. "Private Property" and "No Admittance" signs began to obliterate "the view." The number of both permanent residents and weekend transients, or, as the villagers called them, "shoe boxers," increased.

By the 1930's, the age of the palatial estates, begun seventy-five years earlier, was about over. The huge mansions in English Tudor, Renaissance, Baroque, Spanish, and various combinations of styles had served their purpose. They had proclaimed the grandeur of American industrial growth and had bestowed calculated and lavish honor on those who built them. Now they were in the hands of the third generation or had been sold to second and third buyers, and each time a portion of the land had been sliced off in the transaction. In addition, government action unfriendly to the rich in the New Deal decade was making it difficult to maintain huge houses; income and inheritance taxes were forcing the estate holders to sell their property or simply to let the places go to seed. A few were given to educational institutions and one or two more were turned over to Old Harbor Township as museums or public parks. But there is little contemporary use for a decaying 30-room castle with its entourage of outbuildings, so they waste away in their crabgrass kingdoms, the gargantuan headstones of an age of excess.

Suburbanites and Villagers

After World War II population that had been trapped in the city during the war years exploded into the county neighboring Old Harbor. In ten years, the number of people in this "rural" county passed a million and made it one of the most rapidly growing areas in the United States. Large numbers also spilled over into Old Harbor's county, whose sociological border by 1950 was well within the rural-urban fringe. In the ten years from 1945 to 1955, Old Harbor Township doubled its population, and the village itself has now absorbed between two and three times the number it had in 1940. In just ten years, a 300-year-old village, with many of the descendants of the original founders still living there, underwent a social shock that wrenched it from whatever remained of the patterns of the past.

As Old Harbor soaks up the steady stream of suburban migrants, it has taken on a physical pattern quite different from the community of twenty years ago. Toward the center of town is the "old village," the nucleus of the "oldtimer" community. There the streets are lined with aging oaks, elms, and maples. The houses are comparatively large and reflect the architectural trends of 150 years — authentic and carefully preserved saltboxes and Cape Cods, two-story clapboard or brick Colonials, straight and angular American Gothics, and prissy, frivolous Victorians. They stand fairly close to each other, but property lines are marked by mature hedges of privet, forsythia, and weigelia. Each house proclaims an identity of its own. In front of an occasional Colonial or cottage a small sign will read "1782" or "1712." In the old village, even on a sunny day, there is shade and the scent of many carefully tended flowers. The sunlight filters through the great branches overhead and throws delicately filigreed shafts of yellow-green light on the clipped lawns, on the small barns and garages tucked behind backyard shrubbery, and on the hulls of old sailboats that will never again put to sea. The sidewalk slates are rippled by the massive roots below. Two elderly ladies, straight and thin, walk by with their market bags. There are few children. There is little noise. You sense that whatever these neighborhoods are now, the best in them is gone.

Out along the periphery of the old village, up on what were farmlands five years ago, out along the land necks reaching toward the bay, down in the cove valleys, and up among the woody ridges, range the dwellings of suburbia. Here among the asbestos shingle or "hand-split shakes," the plastic and stainless steel, the picture window, the two-car garages and pint-sized dining areas, the weathered wagon wheel and ersatz strawberry barrel, live the suburbanites in their multi-level reconstructions of Colonial America. It is impossible to avoid them. The signs strung along the highways point the way. "Butternut Hill — Turn Right." "This Way to Strawberry Farm Homes." This is no proletarian Levittown. "Peppermill Village" starts with a "minimum" house of "just" seven rooms and two baths for $22,500 and goes on up. But the architectural themes of all of the developments are the same — antiquity, early American, "good taste." The Limited Dream finds a concretized expression of the past's myth in "Authentic Farmhouse Reconstructions" and the "Modernized New England Village."

Where the villagers live in comparative quiet against the steady but increasing hum of Main Street, the suburbanites live in sun and din. The Suburban Sound is a blend of children, dogs, doors, machines, and mothers. The bedlam of children at play is a universal sound, but the constant clatter of small machines and the ever-present yapping of frustrated dogs are uniquely suburban. In the summer months, the machines of suburbia are particularly vocal — the power lawn mowers (the grunt, click, and chug of the reel type serving as bass for the steady, high-powered whine of the rotary), the exhaust fans, the concrete mixers, the post-hole diggers, the tree cutters, the roto-tillers, the flooded-cellar pumpers, the hedge trimmers, and softly, in the distance, the growl and clink of the bulldozer steadily at work making more suburbs. Add to this the shouts of children, the cries of babies, the calls of mothers, and the muted tones of the dual tailpipes on the station wagon headed into the village, and the Suburban Sound is complete.

No longer is there enough space in Old Harbor. You can't park your car on Main Street any more; there may not be room in church if you arrive late on Sunday; classrooms are overcrowded; and you have to wait your turn for telephones to be installed in your new house. But these are simply the unsurprising results of sudden growth, and the Old Harborites are on their way to solving many of them. They have built schools and plan more. They are tearing down bits of the old village surrounding Main Street and are putting in parking lots. Some churches are adding wings or erecting entirely new buildings. They have added policemen and fire engines, and have widened the critical streets. The physical problems, in general, are understood and are being coped with realistically.

The fundamental schism between the world of the oldtimers and the world of the newcomers makes a problem that is less obvious but both more important and harder to cope with.

In their occupational characteristics, the old settlers range between the middle and upper-middle class. The majority are employed in Old Harbor as merchants, small manufacturers, and businessmen. They constitute the current rear guard of the entrepreneurs of the last century. The rest are mostly white collar people of various persuasions who are employed either in Old Harbor or the neighboring, highly suburbanized county. Less than 20 per cent commute into the central city.

The average villager is middle-aged, married, and probably has two children either finishing high school or going to college. As a group the oldtimer's formal education did not go beyond high school, but they want their children to go to college and they will generally pick one of the better ones. About half of the oldtimers are Protestant, a third are Catholic, and 7 per cent are Jewish. The Catholic and Jewish populations represent the changes in Old Harbor's ethnic or religious character that began at the turn of the century. The median family income for the oldtimers in 1955 was about $6700; roughly $2300 over the national median for that year. Obviously not all oldtimers in Old Harbor are high-school educated, regular church attendants, and securely anchored in the white collar occupations, but enough are to justify the image of the oldtimer as localistic, Protestant, economically comfortable, conservative, and middle class.

Some of the villagers trace their family lines back ten or twelve generations. Even those who arrived only fifteen or twenty years ago have spent enough time in Old Harbor to have become personally and deeply involved in the community. For them Old Harbor has become a way of life and an object of deep affection. When the oldtimer thinks of himself, of his identity as a person, he also thinks of Old Harbor. The community, the social system, the institutions, the organizations, the friendships have become a part of his character. Whatever is the fate of the village has also become each oldtimer's personal fate. An oldtimer merchant put the matter this way:

I have traveled a lot in this country and I've been to Europe a couple of times too. But the biggest thrill in my life was when I got back from Europe and drove over Potter's Hill and saw the spire of Old First Church down in the valley. It was the most beautiful sight in the world. I really love this town — Old Harbor is the finest community in the United States.

The suburbanites are another story. They are a high-income group ($9700 a year) of professional men and executives. Ninety-seven per cent arrived in Old Harbor married and almost 94 per cent bought houses there. They average two grade-school children per family. Only a fourth are Roman Catholics; the great majority are Protestants, although a few more Jews have entered the community in recent years. Nearly four out of every ten of the newcomers were born outside the

state. Two-thirds have been exposed to a college education. Close to half commute to the central city, and another third are employed in the county adjacent to the city.

Though the villagers are economically comfortable, they are nonetheless rather stationary on the income ladder. They are pretty well frozen into an occupation *cul de sac.* The suburbanites, on the other hand, are upward bound — their jobs pay better and carry more prestige than the villagers'. For them the primary world is the metropolitan area. They work there, play there, and their most intimate friends live there. They tend to see in Old Harbor the familiar culture of the apartment house now spread into one-acre "country estates." To the villager, Old Harbor represents continuity between the generations, stability instead of the city's chaos, and a place of permanence in a universe of bewildering change. The suburbanite sees in the village a weekend away from the advertising agency or the pilot's compartment. He experiences Old Harbor as a series of isolated, fragmented, unconnected social situations. Old Harbor is the family, a cocktail party, a bathing beach, a movie, a supermarket, a country club, a school, a church, a PTA meeting. It is a one-acre wooded retreat from all of the drive, bureaucracy, and anxiety of the city. But a weekend is enough for the necessary physical and psychological repairs; it's back to the city on Monday.

The temper of the suburbanite "community" may be summarized in the way the suburbanites talk about Old Harbor:

I came to Old Harbor because there is still some green around here and yet I can still get to the airport in 45 minutes. It's a nice place to live — the schools are good, and I like being near the water. It is hard to say how long we'll be here. I would like to be based further south, but as a place to live Old Harbor is fine.

I can't think of Old Harbor as my own town or anything like that. Most of my friends live closer to the city and I work there. I don't have any feeling of living in a small community or anything like that. I guess I sleep more of my time here than anything else, but it's a good place for the kids. I've got a lot of contacts and interests outside.

I have to go pretty much where the company sends me. I was transferred up to the office over a year ago so we bought a place out here in Old Harbor. Probably be here for three or four years then most likely I'll be sent to South America. We like Old Harbor although the way it's building up it will be like the city in no time. Well, it doesn't bother me much; we won't be around here forever.

But an oldtimer says:

They [the suburbanites] don't know what's going on around here. They don't care. But I do; this is my town. I used to fish down at the tide basin. Now they're talking of tearing it down. I went to school here. All my friends live around here. It's crazy what's happening. I can look out of my shop window and can't recognize 49 out of 50 faces I see. There was a time I knew everybody. It used to be our town. I don't know whose it is any more.

For the villagers, Old Harbor is their community and they have a fierce sense of possession about it. It is a property that they share. And like any valuable property it is cared for and cherished. It must not be profanely or rudely used. This is the real issue that splits the suburbanite and villager communities apart. For the suburbanites, Old Harbor is another commodity; it is a product that can be rationally consumed; it is a means by which they hope to achieve a complex series of personal goals. For the villagers, on the other hand, Old Harbor is not a means to anything; it is simply an end in itself.

The two communities inevitably brush against each other in the course of everyday life. They flow together on the central streets, in the movie houses, on the beaches, at graduation exercises, and in the stores and shops of Main Street. In their economic relationships, villager and suburbanite have struck a symbiotic truce. They need each other, the villager to sell and the suburbanite to buy. Suburbia has brought new prosperity to the villager. Traffic and congestion on Main Street mean crowds of buyers. Parking lots may be expensive, but they also mean customers. On the other hand, there are signs that increasing suburbanization will threaten the retailers of Main Street. The shiny super shopping centers to the south of the village, where a couple of thousand cars can park with ease, make the village shops

seem dingy and dull. The discount stores and mechanized supermarkets of the shopping centers out along the highway augur a bleaker future along Main Street.

Perhaps the greatest single issue separating villager from suburbanite has been the school problem. With the tripling of the school population, Old Harbor has been faced with an intensive building program. Since they are essentially realists in their village microcosm, the oldtimers have reluctantly admitted the need for more schools. Enough of them have been eventually worn down in public meetings to cast an approving vote for new construction. For many a villager, however, it has seemed to mean money out of his pocket to pay for the schooling of other people's children. But the basic and decisive issue has not been whether to build more schools or not, but what kind of schools to build and what kind of education the children should have.

In their approach to this question, the villagers are traditionalists and conservative. They see a good education as including the basic skills taught by a dedicated but maidenly teacher in a plain school building. The suburbanites, on the other hand, are educational radicals; they are irrepressible spenders and cult-like in their dedication to the cause of modern education. It is an axiom among the oldtimers that the more costly a pending proposition is the more the newcomers will take to it, and they are not entirely wrong. The newcomers appear willing to sacrifice all else to their children's education. At PTA gatherings and public meetings of the school board, an ecstatic speaker can bring tears to sophisticated suburbanite eyes and justify the most outlandish cause by reminding his audience that "no expense is too great when it comes to our children's welfare. It will just cost the price of a few cartons of cigarettes a year to give our children this new gymnasium. Isn't our children's education, and clean, wholesome recreational facilities worth a few cents more a year? Is there any parent here who can deny their children this? Is there anyone here who will deny their children what America can offer . . .?"

Everyone will be on his feet applauding, for the side of "the children" has won again, and every villager who voted against the plastic gymnasium or marble swimming pool will have to face the terrible question: "Do I really hate children?"

For the newcomers, anything that is educationally worthwhile must also be very expensive. "After all, you get what you pay for." The villagers, on the other hand, will battle the frills and extravagances and will turn down "excessive" curricular and building proposals. Eventually a compromise is worked out. But in the suburbias of the upper-middle class, education is the cohesive issue around which a consciousness of kind develops among the newcomers. For many, education seems to have taken the place of religion.

While the newcomers have taken over the PTA and infiltrated the school board, the villagers continue to control the churches. Suburbanites usually join the PTA before they become members of a church, though they swell the numbers of those attending religious services. But even in the ranks of the devout, there have been indications of a schism.

The villagers look upon their churches as something more than formal religious centers. Over the years they have served as rallying points for a good deal of cooperative community activity, and they tend to stand for a morality and a traditionalism highly compatible with villager perspectives. One villager remarked that one can hardly keep from feeling a little possessive about a church he has helped to build. The minister of one Protestant church, who rather reluctantly admitted that all was not harmony within his flock, pointed out that the older residents had finished paying off the church mortgage sometime around 1947, and a few years later the church had almost doubled its congregation. As the minister saw it, the villagers were indignant over the invasion of "their" church by "outsiders." They were especially smarting over the fact that, because of the devoted work of the oldtimers, the newcomers had inherited a church free and clear of any financial encumbrance. The villagers felt that the solvency of their church had made it more attractive, and that the enthusiasm the suburbanites showed for it was not without crass implications. As a consequence, the oldtimers began to champion those church causes that were particularly expensive. It has been the villagers who have stoutly called for

a new Sunday School building and a finer parish house. The villagers have been on the side of free and easy spending by the church ever since the suburban influx began.

This is not the whole story. A few years back, one of the most fashionable churches of Old Harbor made some sympathetic overtures to a purely newcomer religious group — Jews of the Reform group who were conducting their services in an empty store on Main Street. The minister of this old Protestant church, which traces its origins back to the American Revolution and whose membership consists of the elect of Old Harbor society, offered the facilities of his church to the Jewish newcomers. The Jews happily accepted the offer. This not only brought the two worlds together, but the Protestant and localistic villagers and the Jewish, cosmopolitan suburbanites even sponsored joint functions together. The differences between the villagers and suburbanites are not insurmountable, nor are the two separated by an impenetrable curtain of prejudice and ignorance.

The newcomers have largely ignored the formal political organizations of Old Harbor. Traditionally the community has been solidly Republican, and the upper-middle class suburbanites have not threatened the political balance. There are a few more egg-head Democrats in Old Harbor in recent years who write books or teach in college, but they are regarded as odd and harmless, and no one pays much attention to them. This does not mean that the suburbanites are not politically active; they are, but they act outside political parties to do political things. Their means is the civic association. Each development or combination of developments has organized its own. Through the Peppermill Village Civic Association they lobby for sidewalks or against sidewalks, for street lights and sewers, or to keep out the sand and gravel contractor who wants to use the adjacent property for commercial purposes. Through the civic associations, the suburbanites engage in running skirmishes with the villagers over local issues. Usually what they want costs more, so the villagers are against it.

The oldtimers fill almost all the political offices, where they serve to balance the limited and self-interested objectives of the civic associations against the broader needs of the village and the township. But in this capacity the oldtimers are more than oldtimers; they are also politicians. Having learned that the suburbanites are amazingly perceptive on the level of neighborhood self-interest, the politicians throw an occasional sop to the militant civic associations, with an eye to coming elections. Though the suburbanites are circumscribed in their interests, they are nonetheless organized, and can marshal massive political displeasure at the polls. As a consequence, the villager politicians must somehow walk a tightrope, balancing the political expediency of pleasing the newcomers against their own desire to keep the village what it was.

GROUPS AND ASSOCIATIONS

20   Corner Boys: A Study of Clique Behavior*

William Foote Whyte

The oldest and most universal form of human group is the informal or primary group. Setting aside the family, the informal gang or peer group is probably the most important primary group both in numbers and in influence. Although small in size, usually with fewer than thirty members, the gang or clique is not easy to study. Such a group does not have formally elected officers, dues, or a written constitution. Membership may be transient and many cliques themselves are short-lived. The nature of the clique makes participant observation the best means of observation.

The following study demonstrates several methods of observing and interpreting activities among the members of a social group. The author spent several years in close contact with a gang of men in the slum area of a large city. He observed the group and frequently participated in its activities. He also used sociometric procedures to illustrate processes of social influence and to identify the group's leaders and isolates.

Sociometric methods delineate lines of communication and influence within a social group. The members, for example, are asked to name their friends in the group. Their responses indicate that a few persons receive most of the friendship choices, while other persons receive few choices or none at all. When leaders and isolates have been identified in this way, they can be compared in terms of various other traits and characteristics.

Sociometric methods can easily be adapted to studies of interracial contacts, patterns of attraction and rejection among college students or inmates of various institutions, and communication networks in gangs, neighborhoods, and villages. They have also been applied to cities and large organizations by means of a sampling design.

How does Whyte define leadership? Is the definition explicitly stated? What are the distinguishing characteristics of leaders in this study? By what means do they maintain their status? What factors tend to hold the group together? Why?

This paper presents some of the results of a study of leadership in informal groupings or gangs of corner boys in "Cornerville," a slum area of a large eastern city. The aim of the research was to develop methods whereby the position (rank or status) of the individual in his clique might be empirically determined; to study the bases of group cohesion and of the subordination and superordination of its members; and, finally, to work out means for determining the position of corner gangs in the social structure of the community.

Throughout three and a half years of research, I lived in Cornerville, not in a settlement house, but in tenements such as are inhabited by Cornerville people.

* Excerpts adapted and reprinted from the *American Journal of Sociology*, Vol. 46 (March, 1941), pp. 647–664, by permission of The University of Chicago Press. Copyright © 1941 by The University of Chicago.

The population of the district is almost entirely of Italian extraction. Most of the corner boys belong to the second generation of immigrants. In general, they are men who have had little education beyond grammar school and who are unemployed, irregularly employed, or working steadily for small wages.

The existence of a hierarchy of personal relations in these cliques is seldom explicitly recognized by the corner boys. Asked if they have a leader or boss, they invariably reply, "No, we're all equal." It is only through the observation of actions that the group structure becomes apparent. My problem was to apply methods which would produce an objective and reasonably exact picture of such structures.

In any group containing more than two persons there are subdivisions to be observed. No member is equally friendly with all other members. In order to understand the behavior of the individual member it is necessary to place him not only in his group but also in his particular position in the subgroup.

My most complete study of groupings was made from observations in the rooms of the Cornerville Social and Athletic Club. This was a club of corner boys, which had a membership of about fifty and was divided primarily into two cliques which had been relatively independent of each other before the formation of the club. There were, of course, subdivisions in each clique.

I sought to make a record of the groupings in which I found the members whenever I went into the club. While the men were moving around, I would be unable to retain their movements for my record, but on most occasions they would settle down in certain spatial arrangements. In the accompanying example (Figure 1) two were at a table playing checkers with one watching, four at another table playing whist and three more watching the game, and six talking together toward the back of the room. As I looked around the room, I would count the number of men present so that I should know later how many I should have to account for.

In this case, I have the following notes on movements of the members:

Eleven walked over to One and pinched his cheek hard, went out of the club rooms, returned and pinched cheek again. One pretended to threaten Eleven with an ash tray. Eleven laughed and returned to seat on couch. I (the observer) asked Eleven about the purpose of the club meeting. He asked Ten, and Ten explained. Eleven laughed and shrugged his shoulders. Sixteen, the janitor, served beer for the card players.

On the basis of a number of maps such as this it is not difficult to place most of the men in the clique and grouping within the clique to which they belong. I did not attempt to place all the men, because the club had a fluctuating membership and some of the men were available for observation for only a short time. There were, throughout the ten months of my observation, some thirty-odd members who were active most of the time. Events in the club could be explained largely in terms of the actions of these men; and, therefore, when I had placed them in relation to one another, I did not need to press further in this direction.

Positional map-making is simply an extension of the techniques of observation and recording which have been used in the past by social anthropologists and sociologists. All these techniques require practice before they can be effectively applied.

While the data from such maps enable one to determine groupings, they do not reveal the position or rank of the men in the groupings. For this purpose other data are needed. In practice they may be gathered at the same time as the positional arrangements are observed.

It is observation of set events which reveals the hierarchical basis of informal group organization. As defined by Arensberg and Chapple,

a set is an aggregate of relations such that every individual related in the set is a member either (*a*) of a class of individuals who only originate action, or (*b*) of an intermediate class of individuals who at some time originate action and at another time terminate action, or (*c*) of a class of individuals who only terminate action.[1]

[1] *Measuring Human Relations: An Introduction to the Study of the Interaction of Individuals* (Provincetown, Mass.: Journal Press, 1940), p. 54. To terminate an action is to follow the initiative of another person.

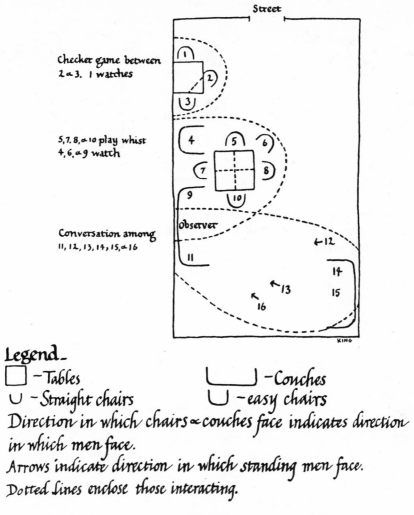

The Cornerville S. & A. Club
February 29, 1940   8–8:15 P.M.

Street

Checker game between
2 & 3. 1 watches

5, 7, 8, & 10 play whist
4, 6, & 9 watch

Conversation among
11, 12, 13, 14, 15, & 16

Observer

KING

Legend.
☐ –Tables   ⊔ –Couches
⊔ –Straight chairs   ⊔ –easy chairs
Direction in which chairs & couches face indicates direction
in which men face.
Arrows indicate direction in which standing men face.
Dotted lines enclose those interacting.

Figure 1

Spatial arrangements at the Cornerville S. and A. Club, February 29, 1940.

Study of corner-boy groups reveals that the members may, indeed, be divided and ranked upon this basis. Several examples will illustrate.

At the top of the Cornerville S. and A. Club (see Figure 2), we have Tony, Carlo, and Dom. They were the only ones who could originate action for the entire club. At the bottom were Dodo, Gus, Pop, Babe, Marco, and Bob, who never originated action in a set event involving anyone above their positions. Most of the members fell into the intermediate class. They terminated action on the part of the top men and originated action for the bottom men. Observations of the actions of the men of the intermediate class when neither top nor bottom men were present revealed that there were subdivisions or rankings within that

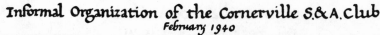

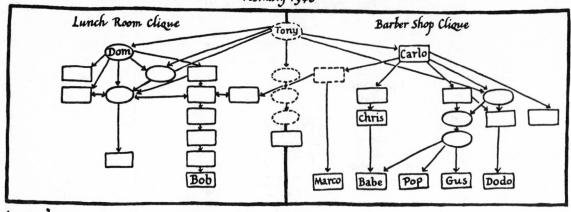

Legend-

◯ — *Members employed in the policy racket organization.*
▭ — *Members not employed in the policy racket organization.*
---- — *Those infrequently present.*
     Level of boxes indicates relative status.
     Arrows indicate chief lines of influence.
     For purposes of simplification, names of members not mentioned in text are omitted.

Figure 2

Informal organization of the Cornerville S. and A. Club, February, 1940.

class. This does not mean that the intermediate or bottom men never have any ideas as to what the club should do. It means that their ideas must go through the proper channels if they are to go into effect.

All my observations indicate that the idea for group action which is carried out must originate with the top man or be accepted by him so that he acts upon the group. A follower may originate action for a leader in a pair event, but he does not originate action for the leader and other followers at the same time — that is, he does not originate action in a set event which includes the leader.

One may also observe that, when the leader originates action for the group, he does not act as if his followers were all of equal rank. Implicitly he takes the structure of the group into account. An example taken from the corner gang known as the "Millers" will illustrate this point. The Millers were a group of twenty corner boys, who were divided into two subgroups. Members of both sub-

groups frequently acted together; but, when two activities occupied the men at the same time, the division generally fell between the subgroups. Sam was the leader of the Millers. Joe was directly below him in one subgroup. Chichi led the other subgroup. Joe, as well as Sam, was in a position to originate action for Chichi and his subgroup.

It was customary for the Millers to go bowling every Saturday night. On this particular Saturday night Sam had no money, so he set out to persuade the boys to do something else. They followed his suggestion. Later Sam explained to me how he had been able to change the established social routine of the group. He said:

I had to show the boys that it would be in their own interests to come with me — that each one of them would benefit. But I knew I only had to convince two of the fellows. If they start to do something, the other boys will say to themselves, "If Joe does it — or if Chichi does it — it must be a good thing for us too." I told Joe and Chichi what the idea was, and I got them to come with me. I didn't pay no attention to the others. When Joe and Chichi came, all the other boys came along too.

Under ordinary circumstances the leader implicitly recognizes and helps to maintain the position of the man or men immediately below him, and the group functions smoothly. In this respect the informal organization is similar to the formal organization. If the executive in a factory attempts to pass over his immediate subordinates and give orders directly to the men on the assembly line, he creates confusion. The customary channels must be used.

The social structures vary from group to group, but each one may be represented in some form of hierarchy. The members have clearly defined relations of subordination and superordination, and each group has a leader. Since we are concerned with informal organization, the Cornerville S. and A. members must be considered as two groups, with Carlo leading the barbershop boys, and Dom leading the lunchroom boys. Since Tony's position requires special consideration, he will be discussed later.

Observation not only serves to provide a description of the group structure, it also reveals information upon the bases of structure and the factors differentiating between the positions of members. The clique structure arises out of the habitual association of the members over a long period of time. The nuclei of most gangs can be traced back to early boyhood years when living close together provided the first opportunities for social contacts. School years modified the original pattern somewhat, but I know of no corner gangs which arose through classroom or school-playground association. The gangs grew up "on the corner" and have remained there with remarkable persistence. In the course of years some groups have been broken up by the movement of families away from Cornerville, and the remaining members have merged with gangs on near-by corners; but frequently movement out of the district does not take the corner boy away from his corner. On any evening in Cornerville, on almost any corner, one finds corner boys who have come in from other parts of the city or from the suburbs to be with their old friends. The residence of the corner boy may also

change within the district, but nearly always he retains his allegiance to his original corner.

The leader of one group spoke to me in this way about corner boys:

Fellows around here don't know what to do except within a radius of about 300 yards. That's the truth, Bill. . . . They come home from work, hang on the corner, go up to eat, back on the corner, up [to] a show, and they come back to hang on the corner. If they're not on the corner, it's likely the boys there will know where you can find them. . . . Most of them stick to one corner. It's only rarely that a fellow will change his corner.

The stable composition of the group over a long period and the lack of social assurance felt by most of the members contribute toward producing a very high rate of social interaction within the group. The structure to be observed is a product of past interactions.

Out of these interactions there arises a system of mutual obligations which is fundamental to group cohesion. If the men are to carry on their activities as a unit, there are many occasions when they must do favors for one another. Frequently, one member must spend money to help another who does not have the money to participate in some of the group activities. This creates an obligation. If the situation is later reversed, the recipient is expected to help the man who gave him aid. The code of the corner boy requires him to help his friends when he can and to refrain from doing anything to harm them. When two members of the group have a falling-out, their actions form a familiar pattern. One tells a story something like this: "What a heel Blank turned out to be. After all I've done for him, the first time I ask him to do something for me, he won't do it." The other may say: "What does he want from me? I've done plenty for him, but he wants you to do everything." In other words, the actions which were performed explicitly for the sake of friendship are now revealed as being part of a system of mutual obligations.

Not all the corner boys live up to their obligations equally well, and this factor partly accounts for the differentiation in status among the men. The man with a low status may violate his obligations without much change in his position. His fellows know that he has failed to discharge certain obligations in the past, and his position reflects his past performances. On the other hand, the leader is depended upon by all the members to meet his personal obligations.

Relations of rivalry or outright hostility with other groups are an important factor in promoting in-group solidarity, as has been well recognized in the literature. Present-day corner gangs grew up in an atmosphere of street fighting against gangs of Irish or of fellow-Italians. While actual fights are now infrequent, the spirit of gang loyalty is maintained in part through athletic contests and political rivalries.

As the structures indicate, members have higher rates of interaction with men close to their own positions in their subgroups than with men who rank much higher or much lower or belong to a different subgroup. That is a significant fact for the explanation of group cohesion.

A Cornerville friend, who was aware of the nature of my observations, commented in this manner:

On any corner, you would find not only a leader but probably a couple of lieutenants. They could be leaders themselves, but they let the man lead them. You would say, They let him lead because they like the way he does things. Sure, but he leans upon them for his authority. . . . Many times you find fellows on a corner that stay in the background until some situation comes up, and then they will take over and call the shots. Things like that can change fast sometimes.

Such changes are the result not of an uprising of the bottom men but of a shift in the relations between men at the top of the structure. When a gang breaks into two parts, the explanation is to be found in a conflict between the leader and one who ranked close to him in the structure of the original gang.

The distinctive functions of the top men in promoting social cohesion are readily observable in the field. Frequently, in the absence of their leader the members of a gang are divided into a number of small groups. There is no common activity or general conversation. When the leader appears, the situation changes strikingly. The small units form into one large group. The con-

versation becomes general, and unified action frequently follows. The leader becomes the focal point in discussion. One observes a follower start to say something, pause when he notices that the leader is not listening, and begin again when he has the leader's attention. When the leader leaves the group, unity gives way to the divisions that existed before his appearance. To a certain extent the lieutenants can perform this unifying function; but their scope is more limited because they are more closely identified with one particular subgroup than is the leader.

The same Cornerville friend summed up the point in this way:

If we leave the followers, they'll go find some other leader. They won't know what they're doing, but that's what they'll do, because by themselves they won't know what to do. They gather around the leader, and it is the leader that keeps them together.

The leader is the man who knows what to do. He is more resourceful than his followers. Past events have shown that his ideas were right. In this sense "right" simply means satisfactory to the members.

It is significant to note that the leader is better known and more respected outside of his group than is any of his followers. His social mobility is greater. One of the most important functions he performs is that of relating his group to other groups in the district. His reputation outside the group tends to support his standing within the group, and his position in the group supports his reputation among outsiders.

It should not be assumed from this discussion that the corner boys compete with one another for the purpose of gaining leadership. Leadership is a product of social interaction. The men who reach the top in informal groups are those who can perform skillfully the actions required by the situation. Most such skills are performed without long premeditation. What the leader is has been discussed in terms of what he does. I doubt whether an analysis in terms of personality traits will add anything to such an explanation of behavior.

For a community study, data upon five corner gangs are hardly more than a beginning. Two problems were involved in extending the research. First, I had to discover whether I could safely generalize my conclusions to apply them to all corner gangs in Cornerville. Second, I had to fit the corner gangs into the fabric of Cornerville society.

To accomplish the first end I solicited the aid of a number of corner-boy leaders, who made for me more or less systematic observations of their own groups and of groups about them. The generalizations, presented earlier, upon the functions of leaders, indicate why I found them the best sources of information upon their groups. This procedure could not be relied upon as a substitute for observation, for it is only through observation that the student can discover what his informants are talking about and understand their remarks in terms of group structure. Observation suggests a framework of significant behavior patterns and indicates subjects that are relevant for discussion with informants.

The student should realize that this procedure changes the attitude of the corner boy toward himself and his group. The quotations from Cornerville men presented here all show the effects of prior discussion with me. However, the effort of informants to make explicit statements upon unreflective behavior does not distort the factual picture as long as they are required to tell their stories in terms of observed interactions.

Accomplishment of the second purpose — fitting corner gangs into the fabric of society — required study of the relations which linked group to group and the group to persons who held superior positions in Cornerville — politicians and racketeers, for example.

The observation that the leader is the person to relate his group to other people provides the most important lead for such a study. We see that the social behavior of groups pivots around the actions of certain men who hold strategic positions in them. This does not mean that the leader can make his followers do anything he desires. It does mean that he customarily leads the group activity and that outsiders, in order to influence the members, must deal with the group through him. This is to be observed particularly at the time of a political campaign when politicians seek to mobilize group support. Similar observations may be made in order to explain the position and influence of the racketeer in relation to corner-boy groups.

Brief reference to the Cornerville S. and A.

study will indicate the nature of the results that may be obtained. Tony, the top man in the chart, was a prominent policy racketeer. The chart indicates that certain members were agents who turned their policy slips in to him. While Tony belonged to the club, his interests were so widespread that he had little time to spend with the members. It was recognized that he held a higher status, that he was not a corner boy.

At the time of the formation of the club, Tony knew Dom, his agent, and recognized Dom's position among the lunchroom boys. He knew Carlo only casually and was not aware of his position as leader of the barbershop clique. In the course of a political campaign (November, 1939) a conflict arose over the indorsement of a candidate for alderman. By playing off one clique against the other, Tony was able to secure the adoption of his policy, but Carlo opposed him vigorously and lost out in a close vote. Carlo's position was strengthened when his candidate defeated the man supported by Tony. Following the election, there was a marked change in Tony's actions. He began to attend every meeting and to spend more time with the members. For his purposes, Carlo was the most important man in the club, and he made every effort to cement his social relations with Carlo and to place Carlo under obligations to him. During this period a basis for cooperation between the two men was established. When Tony turned his attention to other activities, he was able to deal with the club through Carlo as well as through Dom.

This story illustrates a method of study, not a set of conclusions. Through observing the interactions between Tony and Dom, Tony and Carlo, Dom and the members of his clique, Tony and the members of his clique, one can establish the position and influence of the racketeer in relation to his particular organization of corner boys. Other observations establish Tony's position in the racket organization, which extends throughout the district and far beyond it. They also point out Tony's relations with certain politicians. Only in the study of such specific situations can one arrive at reliable generalizations upon the positions and influence of men in the community.

The methods I have used call for precise and detailed observation of spatial positions and of the origination of action in pair and set events between members of informal groups. Such observations provide data by means of which one may chart structures of social relations and determine the basis of the structures — a system of mutual obligations growing out of the interactions of the members over a long period of time. Observations also point out the distinctive functions of the leader, who serves as chief representative of his group and director and coordinator of group activity. A knowledge of the structure and of the social processes carried on through it serves to explain the behavior of individual members in a manner which could not be accomplished if one considered the men as an unstructured aggregation.

Such an understanding of clique behavior seems a necessary first step in the development of knowledge of the nature of the larger social organization into which the cliques fit. Instead of seeking a place for each clique member in relation to the total social organization, the investigator may concentrate his attention upon the actions of the leader, who relates his corner boys to other groups and to persons holding superior positions. By discovering these strategic points for social integration and by extending the network of social relations through them, the investigator can place a large number of the inhabitants of his community in their social positions.

This is a painstaking and time-consuming method. While it does not produce statistics which count all the inhabitants in terms of certain characteristics, it does provide the investigator with a close-up view of the social organization in action.

21 Primary Groups in the American Army*

Edward Shils

Small groups and associations should not be thought of as separate and unrelated types of social organization. A great deal of small-group interaction takes place before, after, or during club meetings, conferences of professional societies, and church services. Even in such impersonal and authoritarian bureaucracies as prisons and military establishments, small groups are numerous and often regarded as vitally important by their members. In prison an inmate's relationships with a small group of acquaintances may provide him with the fortitude to withstand the pressures and tensions of incarceration. So important does this group become, the prisoner may accept solitary confinement for a rule infraction he did not commit rather than violate the trust of his friends.

As any veteran will recall, small groups contribute much to the meaning of life in a military organization. Just how much these groups mean to the soldier is revealed by the following selection. The data analyzed are from *The American Soldier,* a monumental study of the American Army in World War II carried out by social scientists in the Research Branch of the Information and Education Division of the War Department. The findings reported are particularly impressive since the original study was not primarily an analysis of the inner workings of the small group and the data were apparently obtained largely for immediate practical purposes rather than for theoretical ones.

What are the implications of these findings for the efficient operation of the army? For the morale of the troops?

The first problem of primary group analysis in relation to corporate bodies is: how does the influence of membership in the group affect the operation of the corporate body, and particularly, the attainment of the goals of the corporate body? This problem is forthrightly faced in *The American Soldier.*

The re-discovery of the primary group (or the informal group as it is usually called in *The American Soldier*) has not blinded them — as it has blinded some of its other re-discoverers — to the

* Reprinted with permission of The Macmillan Company from *Continuities in Social Research* by Robert K. Merton and Paul S. Lazarsfeld. Copyright by The Free Press, a Corporation 1950.

fundamental fact that a large corporate body like an Army is more than an assembly of primary groups accidentally coordinated with one another by primary group relationships. They are well aware that the army is an organization in which formally constituted agencies exercise authority over persons with whom they have no primary group relations whatsoever. The fundamental significance of command and sanction never disappears from their field of vision. They understand that whole constellations of motives and sets of institutions broader than and prior to the Army and much narrower than the Army are intertwined with formal military authority (with its powers of command and coercion) in directing the conduct of the effective soldier. They are at pains to assign to each of these different factors their proper weight, but they are hampered by the paucity of their data and to some extent by the form in which they were gathered.

The crucial data bearing directly on the limited power of expectations of coercive sanctions are relatively scanty and not entirely free from self-contradiction at certain points. The appearance of contradiction is however diminished by the relative infrequency with which soldiers mention coercion and the fear of sanctions in explaining their *own* behavior in battle. It is also diminished by the insight of the Research Branch that moral considerations (i.e., conceptions of duty and legitimacy), primary group sanctions and formal military sanctions in most cases move in the same direction, reinforcing one another in ways which present research techniques and conceptual schemes do not allow us easily to disentangle from one another. "One important general function of the existence of formal sanctions was . . . that when imposed they called into automatic operation informal sanctions both social and internalized. The existence of these informal sanctions gave the formal sanction much of its force."

The formal coercive powers of the Army must moreover lose some of their directive force in the very situation towards which the entire military organization is directed: namely, the situation of battle. Here, as a result of the high probability of the unforeseen, the need for discretion is at a maximum and the dangers can be faced and contended with only if there is a positive self-impelled effort coming from within the general disposition of the individual soldier and reinforced by the most diverse kinds of gratifications and compensatory pressures. And it is in this very situation that formal authority changes some of its bases and formal sanctions become less effectively coercive. The actual role of expectations of coercion and of specific stipulated rewards in the instigation of effort on behalf of corporate goals and their place among the other influences on behavior in corporate bodies represents a central and still unsolved problem of social science. Among these alternative or complementary influences are loyalties to general impersonal standards, to large collectivities such as state, nation, army, or party and loyalty to primary groups.

One of the most significant contributions to the clarification and very tentative resolution of this problem and thereby to our knowledge of the importance of primary groups in the execution of the goals of large corporate organizations comes from certain inquiries made by the Research Branch into the soldier's own assessment of the factors which caused him "to keep going." Two major inquiries conducted on different occasions and somewhat differently phrased both indicated that the desire to avoid "letting the other fellow down" was one of the most important of all factors and was surpassed only by prayer when the "going was tough," or by the "desire to get the job over with" in the second inquiry. In reply to the query: "Generally in your combat experience, what was most important to you in making you want to keep going and to do as well as you could?" addressed to infantry combat veterans in Europe, 39 per cent mentioned "ending the task"; 14 per cent, solidarity with group, "cannot let the other fellows or the outfit down"; "sticking together," "buddies depending on me"; "my friends around me"; 9 per cent, "sense of duty and self-respect"; 10 per cent, "thoughts of home and loved ones." Five per cent mentioned "idealistic reasons," 2 per cent vindictiveness, only 3 per cent indicated absence of alternatives, leadership, and discipline. In another inquiry into the factors which helped when the "going was tough," Pacific and Mediterranean veterans answered as follows: "prayer helped a lot," was indicated by 70 per cent of the Pacific veterans and 83 per cent of the Mediterranean veterans; "couldn't let the other men down," by 61 per cent and 56 per cent, respectively; "had to finish the job in order to get home again," 42 per cent and 28 per cent; "thoughts of hatred for the enemy," 38 per cent and 28 per cent; "what we are fighting for," 34 per cent and 29 per cent.

It will be noted that in both inquiries and in both theaters, motives connected with primary group solidarity were estimated as very important and that none of the preponderant "motives" refers to the acceptance of a formal command from a formally appointed authority although obviously a good share of their importance consists in the extent to which they furthered the execution of commands or the exercise of initiative within the general framework of commands.

These data support the more complex hypothesis that primary group solidarity functions in the corporate body to strengthen the motivation for the fulfillment of substantive prescriptions and commands issued by the official agents of the corporate body, within the context of *a set of generalized moral predispositions* or *sense of obligation*. The latter need not be strongly present in consciousness but some measure of identification with the collectivity and some sense of generalized obligation and readiness to acknowledge the legitimacy of its demands in numerous particular situations must exist. Thus, for example, the soldiers who thought first of getting the job done must, in some way, have accepted the legitimacy of the "job" and felt some degree of obligation to carry it out. The general setting of their goal was given by their identification with the United States and this made for an acceptance of specific commands from their officers. But even the 39 per cent who mentioned "ending the task" as a motivating consideration might have been lax and reluctant if they had not been subject to the pressure of their comrades who, more or less hiding the same belief, added the autonomous weight of their approval and affection for those who conformed and disapproval for those who were deviant. In other words then, it cannot be said that goals are set by membership in the primary group but only that efforts to achieve the legitimate, formally prescribed goals may be strengthened by such membership.

However great the importance of broad communal loyalties as matrices which predispose the individual soldier to strive to achieve authoritatively commended goals, their effect in motivation does not emerge as directly as the pressure of primary group obligations. Patriotism, and hatred of the enemy which in combat might be considered as the obverse side of patriotism, were not accorded very high rating by the soldiers themselves. Feelings of vindictiveness toward the enemy did not show a very significant relationship with feelings of readiness for combat, which we may be permitted to interpret as readiness to strive to achieve corporate goals. The role of hatred of the enemy soldier or hatred of the enemy people thus seems to have been relatively insignificant in the determination of combat motivation.

It is moreover noteworthy that hatred of the enemy decreased as the soldiers came into combat. Soldiers still in training in the United States or in rear areas hated the enemy more than soldiers who had actually fought against the enemy in combat situations. The authors believe that "hatred of the enemy, personal and impersonal, was not a major element in combat motivation."

Similarly the evidence does not support the hypothesis that devotion to patriotic ideals directly played a great part in the motivation of the soldiers in the performance of the numerous specific actions which make up the military life in battle and behind the front. Most of the soldiers attributed a relatively low order of efficacy to patriotic or political ideals in their assessment of their own experience under fire. There was a strong taboo against extremely patriotic expression in soldiers' circles, especially in groups under combat conditions — just as there was a strong taboo on extremely disloyal remarks. "The broad picture . . . is one of a matter of fact adjustment, with a minimum of idealism or heroics in which the elements which come closest to the conventional stereotypes of soldier heroism enter through the close solidarity of the immediate combat group." When directly confronted with the question as to their own justification for the war most of the soldiers answered in ways which indicated a general acceptance of the war as legitimate and as a largely just basis for their risks and discomforts. Only a small fraction of the soldiers "very often" thought that the war was "not worth fighting" and although doubts were slightly more frequent among combat veterans than among soldiers in training, even at the extremes, doubt was relatively rare. "The issues behind the war were singularly unreal to [the soldier] in contrast to the issues and exigencies of his day to day existence." Yet it would be a mistake to say that the tacit patriotism of the soldiers played no significant part in disposing the men to acceptance, obedience and initiative. The widespread character of their acceptance of the legitimacy of the war although in itself not a strong combat motivation must still be viewed as flowing both directly and indirectly into combat motivation. First of all, as we have already indicated above, it makes for a general readiness to accept commands and to execute them. Also, through its provision of a very general common universe of discourse, it provided the rudiments of one of the most important pre-conditions for the formation of primary groups which have a more positive and immediate function in strengthening the soldier's will to exert himself under dangerous conditions.

The careful analysis of this problem in *The American Soldier,* the respect for the data and for common sense in its interpretation leaves us with the conclusion that in the main, identification with specific secondary symbols is not enough nor are clearly defined commands enough to make a military organization an effective mechanism for moving men to action. The authors of *The American Soldier* do not possess the information necessary to analyze the general moral matrix which underlay the desire to "get the job done." The primary group has been put into its proper context and by ingenious use of material which is often tangential in its connection, they have succeeded in adding to our knowledge of how primary groups in conjunction with other factors affect the achievement of collective goals.

22   Membership in Voluntary Associations*

Charles R. Wright · Herbert H. Hyman

Voluntary associations differ from most informal gangs in that they are usually organized for the attainment of fairly specific goals. It has been said that most Americans are "joiners" and "organization men." How apt are these designations? The following study may provide an answer by reporting on findings from several surveys of the associations to which people belong. Some of the findings are based on data obtained in 1953 and 1955 from large samples of the adult population of the United States. Other findings are drawn from smaller

* Charles R. Wright and Herbert H. Hyman, "Voluntary Association Memberships of American Adults: Evidence from National Sample Surveys," *American Sociological Review,* Vol. 23 (June 1958), pp. 284–294. Copyright © 1958 by the American Sociological Association. Reproduced by permission.

studies of residents in Denver, metropolitan New York, and several counties in Ohio.

The survey is a technique by which data from a variety of sources are collated and analyzed in order to shed light on a number of issues. Surveys are especially useful in the formulation of hypotheses to be tested later by more rigorous methods. Usually their results are regarded as suggestive rather than definitive and plausible rather than confirmed. This is why surveys are often an important first step in scientific inquiry.

What proportion of American adults belong to two or more associations? Does membership vary by age, race, religion, or economic status? What are some factors that do not seem importantly related to membership? How do members differ from non-members?

FINDINGS

Memberships of Americans

Data from the national surveys confirm the conclusions drawn by previous researchers based on local studies, which showed that a sizeable group of Americans are not members of any vol-

TABLE 1   *Membership in Voluntary Associations for Two National Cross-Sections of American Adults, 1953 and 1955*

Number of Voluntary Associations	Percentage of Families Whose Members Belong to Organizations as Indicated (1953)[a]	Percentage of Adults Who Were Themselves Members of the Organizations as Indicated (1955)[b]
None	47	64
One	31	20
Two	12	9
Three	5	4
Four or more	4	3
Unknown	1	0
	100%	100%
Total	(2,809)	(2,379)

[a] "Does anyone in the family belong to any sort of club, lodge, fraternal order, or union with ten or more members in it?" If *yes*, "What organization? Any other?" (Source: NORC Survey 335.)

[b] Union membership is *not* included in these data because the interviewing on organizational membership during this part of the survey concerned associations other than union. The question was, "Do you happen to belong to any groups or organizations in the community here?" If *yes*, "Which ones? Any other?" (Source: NORC Survey 367.)

untary associations and that only a minority belong to more than one such organization. Table 1 presents data from two surveys, one of which inquired about the voluntary association membership of *any* member of the family, the other survey pertained to activities of the respondent himself. Calculated either way, voluntary association membership is not a major characteristic of Americans. Nearly half of the families (47 per cent) and almost two-thirds of the respondents (64 per cent) belong to no voluntary associations. About a third of the families (31 per cent) and a fifth of the respondents belong to only one such organization. Only about a fifth of the families (21 per cent) and a sixth of the respondents (16 per cent) belong to two or more organizations. These findings hardly warrant the impression that Americans are a nation of joiners.[1]

[1] To some extent, the open-ended form of the questions in the national studies might have reduced the proportion of memberships reported insofar as respondent recall might be faulty. There is some indication,

Data on the types of organizations to which Americans belong are also revealing. In the 1953 survey, which contained an account of organizations to which any family member belonged, only two (unions and fraternal or secret societies) have relatively large memberships, 23 per cent and 19 per cent respectively. Next in order are neighborhood-ethnic-special interest groups (8 per cent), veterans' organizations (7 per cent), civic organizations (5 per cent), church sponsored organizations (3 per cent), youth organizations (2 per cent), and professional and learned societies (2 per cent). These findings provide national perspective on the data recorded by former studies of local populations, such as the Detroit Area Study, in which unions and fraternal organizations also accounted for more of the citizens' voluntary memberships than any other type of association.[2]

however, that the impact of question format was not great in this instance. In the Denver study a card listing several types of organizations was handed to the respondent before he reported memberships. Under these conditions, 36 per cent of the Denverites reported that they belonged to no organizations, including unions. In the 1953 national survey, which used an open-ended question, 39 per cent of the urbanites living in large cities (1,000,000 or more) and 42 per cent of those living in any sizeable city (50,000 or more) reported no organizational memberships, including unions, for anyone in their family.

Obviously, primary research on voluntary association membership would require more and different questioning in this area, including check lists of organizations, investigation of the meaning of "belonging" to the respondent, etc. The data used in the current secondary analysis, however, were obtained from studies in which information on membership was only incidental to the primary purposes of the surveys, for which the open-ended questions sufficed. Confidence in the interpretation of the findings as indicative of low membership among Americans is increased through the use of data from *several* national and local surveys, which support one another, in general, despite variations in the wording of questions.

Of course, this is not to dispute the fact that, from a *comparative* point of view, Americans may be more prone to such membership than other national groups. Such a mode of analysis is illustrated, for example, by Arnold Rose, *Theory and Method in the Social Sciences*, Minneapolis: The University of Minnesota Press, 1954, pp. 72–115.

[2] Morris Axelrod, "Urban Structure and Social Participation," *American Sociological Review*, 21 (February, 1956), pp. 13–18. Also see *A Social Profile of Detroit: 1952*. A report of the Detroit Area Study, Ann Arbor: The University of Michigan Press, 1952, pp. 13–19.

Racial and Religious Subgroups

Table 2 presents figures on the membership patterns for two types of subgroups within American society: racial and religious. Comparison of Negro and white respondents shows that voluntary association membership is somewhat more characteristic of whites than Negroes. Less than half (46 per cent) of the white families and 63 per cent of the white respondents belong to no associations in contrast to 60 per cent of the Negro families and 73 per cent of the Negro adults. And nearly a quarter (23 per cent) of the white families belong to two or more organizations in contrast to only 11 per cent of the Negro families.

Differences in rates of memberships also distinguish the major religious subgroups of the population. Whether measured on a family or individual basis, the highest rate of membership is found among the Jews. On a family basis, the next highest participants in voluntary associations are the Catholics (56 per cent), and the least active are the Protestants (51 per cent). Data on individual memberships, however, are different, with a higher percentage of Protestants than Catholics belonging to any organizations.

Interesting comparisons with national data on memberships of religious subgroups are available from the local studies of New York City and Denver. In both cities the ordering of memberships agrees with the national sample on individual memberships: the rate of membership is highest for Jews, next for Protestants and lowest for Catholics. In New York, 64 per cent of the Jewish respondents reported membership in at least one voluntary association, 54 per cent of the Protestants and 37 per cent of the Catholics. In Denver, the membership rates were 77 per cent for Jews, 65 per cent Protestants and 55 per cent for Catholics. Thus the Catholic membership rates in these urban settings appear lower than those of the Jews and Protestants, as in the 1955 national survey.[3]

TABLE 2   *Voluntary Association Memberships of Racial and Religious Subgroups Based on National Samples*

(A) Family Data (1953)	Per Cent of Families Whose Members Belong to:			
	No Organization	One	Two or More	N 100%
Race[a]				
Negro	60	29	11	279
White	46	31	23	2,472
Religion[b]				
Jewish	31	37	32	99
Catholic	44	34	22	579
Protestant	49	30	21	1,992

(Source: NORC Survey 335.)

(B) Respondent Data (1955)	Per Cent of Respondents Who Belong to:			
	No Organization	One	Two or More	N (100%)
Race[c]				
Negro	73	18	9	229
White	63	20	17	2,139
Religion[d]				
Jewish	45	25	30	71
Protestant	63	20	17	1,701
Catholic	69	17	14	519

[a] Figures exclude 58 cases of other races or of unknown race.

[b] Figures exclude 139 cases who report some other religion or none at all.

[c] Figures exclude 11 cases of other races.

[d] Figures exclude 88 cases who report some other religion or none at all.

(Source: NORC Survey 367.)

Social Stratification and Membership

On the local level, several studies have demonstrated a relationship between the social status of the respondent, as measured by a variety of indices, and membership in voluntary associations.[4]

[3] These findings are consistent with those reported by Wendell Bell and Maryanne T. Force, "Urban Neighborhood Types and Participations in Formal Associations," *American Sociological Review,* 21 (February, 1956), pp. 25–34, from their study in San Francisco during 1953. They not only found that Protestants were more likely than Catholics to belong to formal associations but also that the relationship persisted even when economic level was controlled.

[4] See, for example, Mirra Komarovsky, "The Voluntary Association of Urban Dwellers," *American Sociological Review,* 11 (December, 1946), pp. 686–698; Dotson, *op. cit.,* and Bell and Force, *op. cit.*

These studies generally agree that there is an increase in the percentage of memberships in formal associations the higher the status of the respondents. The magnitude of the difference in any membership between classes varies considerably, however, from study to study. For example, Komarovsky found that 60 per cent of working class men in her sample of New Yorkers belonged to no voluntary association in contrast to only 53 per cent of white collar workers. Similarly, Dotson's study of families in New Haven reported that 70 per cent of the working class adults in his sample belonged to no organizations. On the other hand, Bell and Force in a recent study of San Francisco report that even in low status neighborhoods about three-quarters of the men belong to at least one formal group.

Data from the national samples support the correlation between social status and membership. Table 3 presents data on the membership of the 1955 sample classified by five indices of social status: family income, education of respondent, interviewer's rating of family's level of living, occupation of head of household, and home ownership. Whichever index of status is used, an appreciably higher percentage of persons in higher status positions belong to voluntary associations than do persons of lower status. For example, fully 76 per cent of the respondents whose family income falls below 2,000 dollars do not belong to any organizations in contrast to only 48 per cent of those whose income is 7,500 dollars or more. Furthermore, there is an increase in the percentage of persons who belong to *several* organizations as social status increases. For example, only 7 per cent of the lowest income group belong to two or more associations in contrast to 30 per cent of the highest income group. Similar findings are obtained from inspection of the data on education, level of living, occupation, and home ownership, as examination of Table 3 reveals.[5]

One set of findings warrant special mention. The pattern of voluntary association membership among different occupational levels indicates even less participation among blue collar workers than had been noted in previous local studies. For example, from 68 to 87 per cent of the blue collar workers belong to no organizations (not counting union membership), in contrast to 59 per cent of the white collar workers and 47 per cent of the businessmen and professionals. The higher rate of voluntary association membership among businessmen and professionals is clearly documented by the national data, which show that 29 per cent of the members of these two occupational categories belong to two or more organizations, in contrast with only 5 to 13 per cent of the blue collar workers. These data extend to the national level a relationship noted by Komarovsky in her New York study, namely that it is only in the business and professional classes that the majority is formally organized.

Urbanization and Voluntary Association Membership

Voluntary associations customarily have been identified as characteristic of the urban way of life, and membership in such associations has been assumed to be more common for city residents than rural people. Recent observers, however, have noted that the spread of urbanization in America is reducing such differences between city and country. Williams,[6] for example, has noted that "Formally organized special-interest associations are most highly developed in urban areas, but have increasingly pervaded the open country as well." Nevertheless, we have lacked specific information on the differential rates of voluntary association membership of residents of various sized communities. A breakdown of national survey data provides considerable information on this question.

From the 1953 national survey it is possible to

---

[5] Data from the 1953 sample on family participation in voluntary associations generally corroborated the findings presented above and hence are not reproduced here. In addition, several of the local studies contain data in support of the relationships described. For example, home ownership data were available in Denver and provided an opportunity to examine the influence of this factor within an urban setting. Here, as on the national level, home owners were more likely to be members than

were renters, 67 per cent versus 59 per cent respectively. And in New York, families employing domestic help were more likely to be members than those without help, 73 per cent versus 45 per cent.

[6] Robin Williams, *American Society: A Sociological Interpretation,* New York: Alfred Knopf, 1951, pp. 467–468.

TABLE 3 *Indices of Stratification and Voluntary Association Membership, 1955*[a]

	Per Cent Who Belong to:			
	No Organization	One Organization	Two or More	No. of Cases (100%)
A. Income level				
Under $2,000	76	17	7	385
2,000–2,999	71	17	12	304
3,000–3,999	71	18	11	379
4,000–4,999	65	21	14	450
5,000–7,499	57	22	21	524
7,500 and over	48	22	30	328
B. Education				
0–6 years	83	12	5	348
7–8 years	73	17	10	522
9–11 years	67	20	13	495
12 years	57	23	20	610
1–3 yrs. of college	46	24	30	232
4 yrs. college or more	39	25	36	170
C. Level of living (Interviewer's rating)				
Very low	92	7	1	125
Below average	81	14	5	580
Average	61	22	17	1,318
Above average	43	25	32	288
Very high	18	18	64	44
D. Occupation				
Professional	47	24	29	259
Prop., mgrs., officials	47	24	29	294
Farm owners	58	28	14	265
Clerical and sales	59	21	20	240
Skilled labor	68	19	13	447
Semi-skilled labor	77	14	9	492
Service	73	18	9	142
Non-farm labor	79	16	5	155
Farm labor	87	13	0	54
Retired, unemployed	77	11	12	35
E. Home ownership				
Owns home	57	22	21	1,407
Rents	75	16	9	968

[a] Data exclude union membership. (Source: NORC Survey 367.)

determine the number of associational affiliations of family members living in counties of varying degrees of urbanization, taking the size of the largest city in the county as a crude index of its degree of urbanism. Three types of counties can be examined: (1) highly urbanized counties, those with at least one city of 50,000 population or more; (2) moderately urbanized, with at least one city of 10,000 to 50,000 population; and (3) least urbanized, having no city of 10,000 or more. Examination of the memberships of residents of these three types of counties reveals that only 57 per

TABLE 4   *Urbanism and Voluntary Association Membership, 1953*

| Per Cent of Families Whose Members Belong to: | Place of Residence | | | | | | | | |
| | Metropolitan Counties (with City of 50,000 or more) | | | Other Urbanized Counties (with City of 10–50,000) | | | Primarily Rural Counties (Have No Town of 10,000) | | |
	Urban Residence	Rural Non-farm	Rural Farm	Urban	RNF	RF	Urban	RNF	RF
No organization	42	40	67	46	46	53	54	52	70
One organization	33	37	21	36	34	28	27	24	21
Two or more organizations	25	23	12	18	20	19	19	24	9
Total	100%	100%	100%	100%	100%	100%	100%	100%	100%
Cases	1,394	193	48	294	115	134	110	264	252

(Source: NORC Survey 335.)

cent of the families who live in highly urbanized counties have members in at least one voluntary association, 53 per cent of those in moderately urbanized counties, and 41 per cent of those living in the least urbanized or predominantly rural counties. Thus some correlation appears between the degree of urbanization and voluntary association membership, although the difference between the most urban and least urban counties is not great.

But the type of county is only a crude index of the social atmosphere within which the citizen lives. Within each county, for example, there are areas of more *and* less urban nature. Therefore a finer breakdown is desirable in order to determine more precisely the relationship between urbanism and membership in voluntary associations. Table 4 presents data on membership according to urban, rural non-farm, and rural farm residences within each type of county.

Several interesting findings emerge. First, it appears that, with one exception (rural farm residents in moderately urbanized counties) the relationship between urbanization of county and membership in voluntary associations persists. That is, more of the residents of highly urbanized counties belong to organizations than do persons living in similar types of neighborhoods but in less urbanized counties. For example, only 42 per cent of the urbanites in highly urbanized counties

belong to no organization, in contrast with 46 per cent of the urbanites in moderately urbanized counties, and 54 per cent in the least urbanized.

Secondly, within each type of county, rural farm residence is more closely associated with non-membership than is either rural non-farm or urban residence. For example, within highly urbanized counties 67 per cent of the rural farm residents belong to no voluntary association, in contrast to only 40 per cent of the rural non-farm residents and 42 per cent of the urbanites.[7]

Third, there is *no* appreciable difference between the membership rates of urbanites and rural non-farm residents within any type of county. This finding, in connection with the second, suggests an interesting hypothesis about the spread of urbanism into American suburban and rural areas. If the countryside were becoming urbanized then one might expect that rural-urban differences

[7] The higher incidence of organizational membership among urban residents in contrast with their rural neighbors also was evident in the Hancock County, Ohio survey. In this survey a distinction was made between the residents of a small town (Findley, pop. approximately 24,000) and persons in the surrounding county. Fifty-six per cent of the Findley townspeople belonged to some voluntary association, in contrast to 49 per cent of the ruralites. For a recent summary of some surveys on rural memberships see Raymond Payne, "Some Comparisons of Participation in Rural Mississippi, Kentucky, Ohio, Illinois, and New York," *Rural Sociology,* 18 (June, 1953), pp. 171–172.

would be minimal in counties which contained large cities and maximal in counties still rural. Such is not the case, at least with respect to voluntary association membership. True, the urban pattern of membership prevails in rural non-farm areas but it does not extend to rural farms. Furthermore, an anomaly (requiring further substantiation) appears in that rural farm persons living in *moderately* urbanized counties resemble their urban and rural non-farm neighbors more than do ruralites in either highly urbanized or heavily rural counties. Perhaps this finding means that rural-urban differences in general are polarized — being greatest in both highly urban and highly rural counties and least in partially urbanized areas.

Some Situational Determinants of Membership

In this section some data from the Denver survey are examined to clarify certain situational factors which might be presumed to affect urban participation in voluntary associations. Specifically, data are presented on the effect of length of residence in the community, length of residence at the same address, type of residence (for example, single family dwelling versus apartment), travel time to work, and family status (for example, single, married with children or without children). The presumed influence of such factors is illustrated by the hypothesis that long-time residents in the community or in the neighborhood are more likely to be involved in formal organizations. Or, persons living in apartments might be expected to participate less in voluntary associations than those living in single family dwellings. Persons who spend less time commuting to work, it may be argued, should have more time to devote to organizations and therefore should show a higher incidence of membership. Similarly, single men and women, who are unencumbered by children, might have more spare time and hence be more apt to belong to voluntary groups. Table 5 presents data which fail to support several of these arguments.

None of the residential factors shows a systematic relationship with the incidence of affiliation with voluntary associations. For example, persons born in Denver are hardly more likely to belong to voluntary associations than those who

have arrived recently.[8] Apartment dwellers are slightly more likely to be voluntary association members than persons renting homes. Commuters who spend more than 45 minutes getting to work are about as likely to belong to organizations as are those people who have to travel only 25 minutes or less.

Only two of these situational factors — home ownership and family status — seem related to voluntary association membership. Home ownership as a determinant of membership, as brought out above, is related to social stratification. The data on family status show that married persons are more likely to be members of organizations than single persons; and that men and women with children are more likely to be members than childless couples. One might hypothesize that children — and perhaps the expectation of children — draw adults into participation in the voluntary associations in the urban community. This finding corroborates that of Janowitz in his study of Chicago residents in which he notes that neighborhood involvement often centers around activities connected with the rearing of children in a metropolis. As Janowitz remarks, on the neighborhood level, "children are not only the best neighbors in the community but they lead their parents to neighborhood community participation and orientation."[9]

[8] These data are consistent with those obtained in Hancock County, Ohio, where 51 per cent of the persons who had resided in the county for 20 years or more were members of voluntary associations, 57 per cent of the 10–19 year residents were members, 58 per cent of the 5–8 year residents, and 57 per cent of the persons living there less than five years. The survey was conducted in May 1952. On the other hand, Zimmer, in a study of married men in a mid-western community of 20,000, found that membership in formal organizations increased directly with length of time in the community. Zimmer's relationship persisted within age, occupational and educational control categories. See Basil Zimmer, "Participation of Migrants in Urban Structures," *American Sociological Review,* 20 (April, 1955), pp. 218–224. And a recent study in Spokane, Washington, indicates a relationship between mobility and voluntary association membership; see Howard Freeman, Edwin Novak and Leo Reeder, "Correlates of Membership in Voluntary Associations," *American Sociological Review,* 22 (October, 1957), pp. 528–533.

[9] Morris Janowitz, *The Community Press in an Urban Setting,* Glencoe, Ill.: The Free Press, 1952, p. 124.

TABLE 5   *Some Situational Determinants of Voluntary Association Membership: Evidence from Denver Survey*

	Percentage of Each Type Who Belong to Voluntary Associations	No. of Cases In Base
A. Residential history		
Born in Denver or lived there at least 20 years	65	504
Lived in Denver less than 20 years	62	404
Lived in Denver at present address over 20 years	63	200
Lived at present address for 5 to 20 years	67	346
Lived at present address less than 5 years	60	358
B. Residential mobility		
Moved to Denver from place of under 2,500 population	61	272
Moved from place of 2,500 to 25,000 population	60	205
Moved from place larger than 25,000	64	281
C. Type of residence		
Single family house rented	57	81
Multiple family dwelling, rented	59	165
Apartment building, rented	60	117
Owned, all types of dwelling	67	512
D. Travel time to work		
45 minutes or more daily	60	81
35–44 minutes	70	185
30–34 minutes	64	256
25–29 minutes	66	192
Less than 25 minutes	57	205
E. Family status		
Men: Not married	66	79
Married, no children under 18 years old	74	182
Married, with children under 18 years old	82	162
Women: Not married	51	149
Married, no children under 18 years old	53	174
Married, with children under 18 years old	56	174

(Source: Denver Community Survey, NORC–12B.)

Civic Involvement of Voluntary Association Membership

In this final section, data from the Denver Survey are presented which demonstrate psychological and behavioral differences between citizens who are members and those who are not members of formal organizations. Admittedly the data do not

indicate that such differences can be attributed solely to the respondents' patterns of associational membership. Clearly several factors already established as correlates of membership (for example, high socio-economic status, occupation, place of residence) may also account for differences in political interest, voting and charitable acts of members and non-members. The authors feel, however, that comparison of members and non-members without controlling these associated factors is proper insofar as the purpose is solely to *describe* the differences between persons who are

---

Janowitz's remark is made in connection with family structure as a determinant of readership of the community press, but its import extends to other forms of involvement in community activities.

or are not members of voluntary organizations, regardless of the ultimate causes of such differences.[10] Hence Table 6 presents simple comparisons between the formally organized and unorganized, concerning their interest in political topics, voting records, and contributions to charity.

Several measures of interest in public affairs (including presidential elections, unemployment, labor relations, minority problems, public schools, and city planning) indicate that persons belonging to voluntary associations are more concerned with such topics than are non-members. For example, fully 84 per cent of the Denverites who belonged to any voluntary association said they took a great deal of interest in presidential elections, in contrast with only 73 per cent of the non-members. And members were more likely than non-members to be interested in city planning, 50 per cent to 31 per cent respectively.

[10] For a discussion of the differential demands of descriptive vs. explanatory analysis see Herbert Hyman, *Survey Design and Analysis: Principles, Cases and Procedures,* Glencoe: The Free Press, 1955, especially pp. 121–124.

Political interest is backed by participation in the political process, insofar as participation is measured by voting. Data on behavior in four elections — the 1944 Presidential, 1946 Congressional, 1947 City Charter, and 1948 Primary — indicate in every instance a greater percentage of voting among Denverites who were members of voluntary associations than among non-members.

Finally, in the non-political sphere of community life, charity, 72 per cent of the persons belonging to associations reported having made a contribution to the Community Chest in Denver, in contrast to 56 per cent of the non-members.

Thus three separate measures — interest in social issues, voting, and support of community charities — show that voluntary association participants are more involved civically than the non-members. Further research might fruitfully be addressed to such questions as the following: (1) to what extent does the citizen's interest in public affairs lead him to join voluntary associations; (2) to what extent do the voluntary associations contribute to their members' interest in

TABLE 6 *Political Interests and Behavior Associated with Voluntary Association Membership: Evidence from Denver Survey, 1949*

	Persons Who Were Members of:	
	No Organizations	One or More Organizations
A. Per cent who said they take "a great deal of interest in:		
Presidential elections	73	84
Unemployment in the U. S.	53	57
The Denver public schools	33	50
City planning in Denver	31	50
Labor relations	31	45
The situation of Denver Negroes	23	35
B. Per cent who voted in each of the following elections:		
1944 Presidential	36	40
1946 Congressional	27	36
1947 City charter	15	24
1948 Primary	24	34
C. Per cent who report making a contribution to the		
Community Chest in Denver	56	72
Total cases	335	585

(Source: Denver Community Survey, NORC–12B.)

public affairs; (3) to what extent is membership in one or more voluntary associations functional for the citizen who has a great deal of interest in public affairs. Questions of this order, however, fall beyond the scope of this secondary analysis.[11]

SUMMARY

A secondary analysis of two national and several local surveys provides evidence on the topics: the pattern of membership in voluntary associations of Americans in general and of such specific subgroups as class and religion, some possible determinants of membership, for example, socioeconomic status; and certain correlates of membership which relate to civil participation, for example, interest in public issues and voting.

The major findings are listed below in abbreviated form. In each case, the major source of data, that is, national or local survey, is indicated in parentheses. Subject to the qualifications noted above, the major findings are:

[11] For examples of earlier theoretical and empirical work on the functions of voluntary association membership, see Rose, *op. cit.*; and Bernard Barber, "Participation and Mass Apathy in Associations," in Alvin Gouldner (ed.), *Studies in Leadership: Leadership and Democratic Action,* New York: Harper and Brothers, 1950, pp. 477–504.

(1) Voluntary association membership is not characteristic of the majority of Americans (National).

(2) A relatively small percentage of Americans belong to two or more voluntary associations (National).

(3) Membership is more characteristic of the white than Negro population (National).

(4) Membership is more characteristic of Jewish than Protestant persons, and of Protestant than Catholics (National).

(5) Membership is directly related to socioeconomic status, as measured by level of income, occupation, home ownership, interviewer's rating of level of living, and education (National).

(6) Membership is more characteristic of urban and rural non-farm residents than of rural farm residents (National).

(7) Membership does not appear to be related to a variety of situational factors, for example, length of residence in the community, length of residence at the same address, type of dwelling unit, commuting time to work (Denver).

(8) Membership is related to family status, being higher for couples with children than without (Denver).

(9) Membership is accompanied by a greater interest in such public affairs as unemployment problems, city planning, and public schools (Denver).

(10) Membership is associated with voting in Presidential, Congressional and local elections (Denver).

(11) Membership is associated with support for local charities (Denver).

23 Sociometric Patterns in Hysterical Contagion*

Alan C. Kerckhoff · Kurt W. Back

Norman Miller

Sociologists and social psychologists have long had a major interest in the influence of the group on the behavior of the individual member. Carefully controlled experiments demonstrate that the individual in his group will modify his behavior, radically alter his judgments, and participate in acts that fall outside his personal code of behavior — if the rest of the group indicate that this is the proper and expected thing to do. Thus we find that many juvenile delinquents commit their first offense in the presence of companions who are already delinquents, a college man smokes marijuana for the first time at a "pot party," and a law-abiding, respected citizen participates in a destructive riot.

One rather extreme example of this group influence is where several individuals report observations and experiences which are completely without basis in the judgment of competent and objective investigators. There are many authenticated instances of such "hysterical" behavior and this undoubtedly includes many persons who have reported seeing "flying saucers" in recent years.

If we exclude charlatans who deliberately falsify reports and limit our discussion to persons who actually experienced the reported sensations or observations, it becomes important to understand how such bizarre events could occur. Since this is a group phenomenon, it should be helpful to utilize

* Excerpted from *Sociometry*, Vol. 28 (March, 1965), pp. 2–15. Reprinted with revised footnotes by permission. Copyright © 1965 by The American Sociological Association.

our knowledge of group structure in any investigations that are made. The particular experiences investigated in the following selection were reported by sixty-two workers in a large manufacturing plant. How did these workers come to have the experiences they reported? Did the experiences occur at random throughout the plant or was there some pattern in time and space in the occurrences? Were those workers who reported the experience unknown to one another or were they usually members of some common network of social relations within the plant? In reading this selection, see if it has any implications for your own behavior in a group situation.

We propose to offer an analysis of hysterical contagion in which the basic problem is to define the degree to which there is a sociometric pattern related to the spread of the hysterical symptoms. The central question will be: What relevance does an individual's position in a network of social relations have for predicting whether he will or will not exhibit the hysterical symptoms in question?

To raise this question is not to deny that other factors may *also* be important in a complete analysis of a case of hysterical contagion. Most of the literature on contagion would, in fact, lead one to minimize the importance of lasting social relationships as a significant factor in the spread of hysterical symptoms. More emphasis is given in such literature to a degree of strain experienced by the population in which the symptoms become contagious and to the personal characteristics of the individuals affected. Smelser, for instance, indicates that: "Some form of strain must be present if an episode of collective behavior is to occur," and he includes the spread of hysterical symptoms under the general rubric of collective behavior. Similarly, the Langs note that it is necessary to find "areas of chronic stress which account for the failure of organized expectations to control a situation." Personal characteristics of participants are also seen as important by the Langs. Although acknowledging the importance of the *relationship* between the characteristics of the person and the characteristics of the situation, they note that much of the literature in this area of inquiry points to the differential susceptibility to suggestion and contagion by different kinds of personalities.

Our concern is not to dispute the importance of these situational and personality factors but to raise the further question of the relevance of social relations as channels of transmission of, or hindrance to, the hysterical pattern involved. It is undoubtedly true that, even in the situation we will investigate, these situational and personality factors played an important role. It will not be possible, however, within the limits of this report to take all such variables into account, and our attention will be directed solely to the question of whether or not patterns of social relations are relevant to an understanding of hysterical contagion.

The importance and complexity of this issue are enhanced by the fact that there is little literature that is directly relevant to the problem, and conflicting expectations may be derived from the several bodies of literature that are indirectly relevant. In order to simplify the discussion of these conflicting expectations, we will first describe the particular case of hysterical contagion analyzed in this study, and we will then indicate what basis there would be for each different expectation.

The incident under study occurred in a southern clothing manufacturing plant in which raw fibers are spun, dyed, and woven, and the finished cloth is cut, sewn, boxed and shipped to wholesale and retail outlets. Within about one week in the summer of 1962, sixty-two persons suffered what purported to be insect bites, and received some kind of medical attention. Although some of these persons exhibited only very minor symptoms, most of them either fainted or complained of severe pain, nausea or feelings of disorientation. Almost all of the victims were women; almost all were white; almost all worked on the first shift; and the great majority were physically located within one functional area of the plant. A physician and an entomologist from the Communicable Disease Center in Atlanta visited the plant but could find no toxic element capable of causing these symptoms, although they searched for both insects and other possible causes, such as chemical elements in the dyes and the air conditioning system. The only reasonable conclusion seemed to be that this was a phenomenon that was "almost exclusively psychogenic in nature."

Since this was evidently a case of hysterical

contagion, and given the fact that it occurred in a situation in which the members of the population had had an opportunity to develop patterns of social relations with each other, our basic question is whether these relations were in any way significant in the spread of the symptoms within the population.[1] There appear to be bases for three different expectations: that those who are linked together in a network of social relations should be more likely to be affected; that those who are outside the network of social relations should be more likely to be affected; and that the pattern of social relations should be irrelevant to the spread of the hysterical symptoms. We will refer to these under the following three headings: "Group Influence," "Social Isolation," and "Crowd Response." The basis for each of the expectations will be considered first, after which we will examine the data in hand in light of these three expectations.

Group Influence

There is a considerable body of literature which can be used to generate the prediction that the contagion should follow channels of interpersonal ties. This prediction undoubtedly has great appeal for sociologists, given the discipline's emphasis on social structure. The many studies of the adoption of innovations, especially those of farming innovations, indicate that social relations among adopters are often found, and that once informal leaders adopt a new practice, it is likely to be adopted by others. Even more closely analogous to the pres-

[1] We do not consider here the presumably prior question of why there should have been contagion with respect to insect bite fears at this time and in this place but no such contagion in other times and places. Briefly, our position on this question is that models of hysterical behavior occur frequently in any social situation, but they are generally either ignored or defined as the behavior of a deviant person and thus not worthy of concern. When they are attended to, we would expect that two other conditions are present: (1) There is a state of tension in the situation, and (2) the behavior is relevant to the situation being experienced by others as well as the person providing the model. There is evidence of a state of tension in the plant being studied. The women had worked a great deal of overtime, production pressures were great, the plant was not well-organized, and there was the prospect that a layoff would follow the peak season. Since insects of some kind or other are found in all such plants, the behavior was relevant to the situation in which the women experienced this tension.

ent case is the study by Coleman, Katz and Menzel of the diffusion of the use of a new drug among physicians. In that study it was found that the adoption of the drug followed sociometric channels, and that members of social cliques were likely to adopt the drug at about the same time. There is a body of experimental literature which might also lead to the expectation that sociometric channels would facilitate diffusion. The classical experiments of Sherif and Asch, and the numerous experimental variations and theoretical interpretations of them, all indicate that both perception and behavior can be made to conform to group definitions when the other members of the group define the situation consistently.

There is thus considerable basis for expecting that interpersonal relations will be highly relevant to dissemination for a new pattern of behavior in a population. However, one may well question whether the literature just cited is, in fact, germane to our interests. The studies of the adoption of innovations deal with the spread of a behavior pattern which is positively related to a central value in the population studied. Farmers certainly value abundant crops and high quality produce, and the studies of innovation in farming deal with the adoption of practices which are supposed to serve these ends. The doctors studied by Coleman, *et. al.,* value effective drugs as aids in their professional duties; and the drug whose adoption was studied was, in fact, an effective drug. On the other hand, it could hardly be argued that the behavior pattern whose spread we are studying was valuable in the same sense. However it was viewed, one must acknowledge that it was dysfunctional in the specific situation in which it was observed. Not only did the hysteria disrupt the operations of the plant and thus leads to losses for the company, it also led to lost work time for the affected persons and thus reduced their income for the period in question, not to mention the emotional costs involved. It may well be that the dissemination of *any* behavior pattern within a population follows the same channels, but the differences in the kinds of behavior studied in the earlier investigations and that found in the present situation makes such an assumption at least questionable.

The experimental studies noted above, although they often deal with bizarre and dysfunctional behavior (such as misperceiving the relative length of two lines), also provide some reason to doubt the "group influence" expectation in the present situation. These experiments indicate that *if* there is *consistent* behavior on the part of the members of the group, the naive subject will tend to adopt that behavior as his own, even though it might ordinarily be rejected by him. They also indicate that if there is *not* consistent behavior by the group members, the naive subject is much less likely to adopt the unusual behavior. In the plant we studied, the majority of the workers never exhibited the hysterical symptoms. Thus, there were always social reference points for those who might have tended to resist the contagion. Also, since the behavior in question was not only dysfunctional but also rather bizarre, it seems unlikely that we could assume that any social grouping had developed a facilitative "norm" regarding such behavior in advance of the initiation of the contagion. It is much more likely that most people in the plant would have defined the behavior as at least "unusual" and "undesirable." If a facilitative norm functioned at all, it must have evolved during the period of contagion, and this would certainly take time and would probably have had to occur in the face of some social resistance. Finally, and perhaps most importantly, the relevance of this body of experimental literature might also be questioned because it is based on *ad hoc* groups in which prior social relations had not been formed, whereas the central focus of our inquiry is the importance of such previously established social relations.

Social Isolation

Given the fact that only a minority exhibited the hysterical symptoms, it seems likely that the average worker in the factory would have some significant social contacts with persons who did not exhibit hysterical symptoms and who rejected the seriousness of the threat. This would not be true, however, for the person who was a social isolate. The isolate would not have access to such social reference points. Although isolates might vary in the degree to which they would be personally susceptible to the effects of contagion, as a category they would seem to be more likely to be susceptible than would those who are socially integrated.

The converse of this can also be argued. At least since the work of McDougall, it has been noted that the structure of groups tends to inhibit the spread of contagion among its members. If this is so, socially integrated women would be *less* likely to be susceptible. The same expectation would be reasonable if we interpret the hysterical behavior as an attention-getting device, isolates being seen as more in need of such social response than those with prior social ties. Finally, it has been noted by many students of collective behavior that the outcast, the person with little investment in the social system, is more likely to take part in all forms of collective behavior. This kind of person has been defined either in terms of his social position or his personal degree of "social adequacy," but in both cases the point is made that a lack of full integration into the network of social relations increases the tendency for a person to become a participant in collective behavior. For all these reasons, then, we might expect isolates to exhibit the hysterical symptoms more frequently than those who are socially integrated.

Crowd Response

A third expectation is also possible from the literature on collective behavior, namely, that social relationships would have no relevance to the spread of the contagion. There is a common belief with respect to crowd behavior, substantiated by participants' reports, that contagion is often effective for persons who are not at all related to others in the crowd and who are not particularly concerned with the issue central to the crowd action. The "magic" of contagion has been described and analyzed by many, but our knowledge remains less than adequate. Yet, it is very easy to find references to the unstructured nature of contagion, especially hysterical contagion, within a population. Perhaps this passage from the Langs' book says it as well as any:

The kind of identification that occurs in hysteria, Freud maintains, "may arise with every new perception of a common quality shared with some other person who is not an object of the sexual instinct. The more important this common quality is, the more successful may this partial identification become,

and it may thus represent the beginning of a new tie." *The identification does not presuppose any prior emotional or sympathetic relationship; it results directly from the definition of the situation of those exhibiting the behavior as analogous to one's own.*[2]

If this is the case, we might expect that the simple fact that all of those affected by the hysteria in the plant were fellow-workers, and the great majority of them were women, would be enough basis for the kind of identification just referred to. There would thus be no reason to expect that previously established social relations would be at all relevant to the spread of the symptoms.

We thus have three theoretical positions, each based on literature that is presumably relevant, and each calling for a different kind of relationship between sociometric position and the probability of being affected by the spread of hysterical contagion. Each is plausible in its own way, but seemingly all three cannot be correct. In fact, no two could seem to be correct. Yet it is our contention that all three *are* correct, within certain limits which we will attempt to define. We will make reference to the data of our study of the insect bite epidemic to help make our point; and though the data are not sufficient basis to demonstrate, its adequacy, they justify its serious consideration.

Sample and Method

Because of the apprehensions on the part of management about what effect a series of interviews in the plant might have, it was not possible for us to begin our formal research activities until two months after the incident. Throughout the investigation, however, we received cooperation from management, and we encountered little resistance from the employees.

In order to make the task feasible within the limits of our resources, we interviewed only women and only those who worked on the first shift. Within this population, we drew a systematic 25 per cent sample, and then added all those women who had been affected by "the bug" who had not

---

[2] Kurt Lang and Gladys Engel Lang, *Collective Dynamics,* New York: Thomas Y. Crowell Company, 1961, p. 227.

been drawn in the sample. We thus had both a sample of the first-shift women and the entire population of first-shift women who had been affected by "the bug." The total number of subjects was 185, of whom 58 were "affected" cases and 127 were "controls." All of these women were interviewed, the vast majority in the plant,[3] by two women interviewers who were employees of the National Opinion Research Center and who lived in the vicinity.

The present report is based largely on a question which asked the respondents to name her three best friends in the plant. In addition to the data from that question and our knowledge of which women were affected and which were controls, we also had a record of the date on which each affected case had been "bitten." We will thus be examining the relationship between sociometric position, the affected versus control distinction, and the date affected. Because the vast majority of the cases occurred on two successive days, we will simply divide the cases into those occurring on "Day One" (the first big day), "Day Two" (the second big day), and those which occurred "Before" and "After" those two days. The fifty-eight affected cases were distributed through time as follows: ten "Before," twenty-four on "Day One," twenty on "Day Two," and four "After."

We have noted that it is possible to generate three different hypotheses about the sociometric positions of the affected women. The first (based on a "group influence" argument) calls for a pattern of sociometric ties among the affected women which sets them off from the controls. The second (based on a "social isolation" argument) calls for a greater proportion of the affected women than the controls to be isolates. The third (based on a "crowd response" argument) calls for no relation between sociometric position and being affected by the contagion.

[3] Sixteen of the affected women were not interviewed in the plant. They had either terminated their employment there, or were on vacation or on leave or were ill at the time of the interviews. All of these were interviewed at their homes. Because of the expense involved, when a control subject was not available for interview in the plant, a substitution was made. The person interviewed in her place was the next one on the payroll list, this list having been used as the original definition of the population to be sampled.

If we simply ask which of the three predictions comes closest to the mark, and if we base our evaluation on the overall differences between affected cases and controls (without considering the date a woman was affected), the prediction based on the "group influence" argument seems to be the best. (See "Total Sample" columns of Table 1.) First, there are no more isolates within the affected category than among the controls. In fact, there is a slightly higher proportion of isolates among the controls. Also, the affected women are chosen as friends somewhat more often on the average than are the controls. Thus, there is certainly no general tendency for the affected women to be socially ostracized, and there may even be a limited positive relationship between sociometric position and being affected.

More important, we find that the links between affected women and *other* affected women are more common than between controls and affected women. A higher proportion of the choices *made* by affecteds go to other affecteds than do choices made by controls go to affecteds. A greater proportion of choices *received* by affecteds come from other affecteds than do the choices received by controls. Affecteds are twice as likely to be chosen solely by other affecteds, and controls are twice as likely to be chosen solely by other controls. Finally, of the mutual choices participated in by affecteds, three-fifths are with other affecteds. Similarly, of the mutual choices participated in by controls, two-thirds are with other controls. We find, therefore, that the affected women are not only generally integrated into a social network, but they are linked *together* much more closely than they are to women who were not affected. This is presumably evidence that the contagion followed sociometric channels.

There was one other matter that we thought should be taken into consideration before accepting this general picture, however. The vast majority of the women employed in the plant worked in one huge, open room in which the cutting, sewing, pressing, inspecting and packing operations were carried out. It was in this room that most of the affected cases had occurred. Our sample, however, also included women who were located elsewhere in the plant and who had less

TABLE 1   *Sociometric Status of Affected Cases and Controls*

Characteristic	Total Sample		Restricted Sample	
	Affected	Control	Affected	Control
Proportion of cases which are isolates	.28 (58)	.33 (127)	.23 (47)	.30 (88)
Average number of times chosen	1.43	1.12	1.43	1.16
Proportion of choices directed toward affecteds	.27 (167)	.09 (363)	.27 (140)	.10 (257)
Proportion of choices directed toward controls	.25 (167)	.28 (363)	.22 (140)	.27 (257)
Proportion of choices received from affecteds	.57 (83)	.26 (142)	.58 (67)	.27 (102)
Proportion of choices received from controls	.43 (83)	.74 (142)	.42 (67)	.73 (102)
Proportion chosen by affecteds only	.31 (58)	.13 (127)	.34 (47)	.15 (88)
Proportion chosen by controls only	.21 (58)	.43 (127)	.26 (47)	.44 (88)
Proportion of mutual choices with affecteds	.59 (46)	.30 (64)	.64 (39)	.28 (50)
Proportion of mutual choices with controls	.41 (46)	.70 (64)	.36 (39)	.72 (50)

NOTE: The "Restricted Sample" is made up of those women from our total sample who were located in the one large room in which most of the affected cases were located. This analysis was carried out to insure that the differences between affecteds and controls were not simply a function of the spatial distribution of the affected cases.

The N on which each proportion is based is noted in parentheses. The total number of cases in each major category was: Affected, 58; Control, 127; Restricted Sample Affected, 47; Restricted Sample Control, 88. The asterisk indicates proportions which do not total to 1.00 because choices could be made of nonaffected persons not in the sample.

contact with and were visually separated from the women in this large room. Since the affected cases were not evenly distributed spatially throughout the plant, there was some concern on our part that we not err in the direction of overestimating the differences between affected cases and controls due to the expected tendency of the women to choose as friends those who were spatially near them.

To test the relevance of such a spatial factor, we computed all of the indexes again by using only those subjects who worked in this one large room where most of the affected cases occurred. These data are presented in the "Restricted Sample" columns of Table 1. They provide little evidence that the results are biased by the spatial distribution of our cases. Some of the indexes for the restricted sample are even more clearly

in support of the "group influence" expectation than are those of the total sample. Thus, the use of the total sample and the conclusions based on it appears to be justified.

We can offer further insight, however, if we analyze the affected category according to the period in which the women were affected. It will be recalled that there are four periods: "Before" the two big days, "Day One," "Day Two," and "After" the two big days. Since there were only four cases in the "After" period, we will not refer to that period in most of what follows. Looking at the distribution of cases in the "Before" category, the first ones to exhibit the symptoms, we note that 50 per cent of them are isolates. (See Table 2.) By contrast, no more than one-fourth of the cases occurring in any of the other periods are isolates. Thus, although isolates are found during all periods, they are most heavily concentrated at the beginning of the epidemic. This fact is also reflected in the differences in the average number of times the women in the three periods were chosen as friends, this number being much lower in the "Before" period than in any of the others.

We also find that through the three major periods, the later a woman is affected, the more likely she is to be chosen by other affected women and to be chosen *exclusively* by other affected women. Correspondingly, there is a *decreasing* tendency for affected women to be chosen only by controls. That is, there is an increasing tendency for the affected cases to be sociometrically linked exclusively with other affected cases and a decreasing tendency for them to be linked exclusively with controls. We find the same pattern of increase of the proportion of mutual choices within the affected category. This would seem to indicate an increasing tendency for the contagion to localize within one social network (or series of networks) to the exclusion of other networks.

We have thus far, then, seen that there is a concentration of isolates during the initial phase of the epidemic followed by an increasing tendency for the later cases to be linked together sociometrically. Thus, the pattern in the early phase is in keeping with the "social isolation" expectation, and the pattern in the major portion of the epidemic is in keeping with the "group influence" expectation. These findings would seem to indicate that the "crowd response" expectation is without support in these data. We are not certain that such a negative conclusion should be reached, however.

Although there are only four cases in the "After" phase, they present a rather different picture than the data in the earlier phases. One of these cases is an isolate, which continues the one-fourth proportion of "Day Two." These four women are chosen 1.50 times each on the average, which is comparable to "Day One" and "Day Two" women. On the other hand, only eighteen per cent of their choices are directed toward other affecteds, and only half of their choices come from other affecteds. Only one is chosen solely by other affecteds, and two are chosen solely by controls. Of the mutual choices participated in by these women, two out of three are with controls. Thus, in every one of the indices considered, there is evidence of a spread of the epidemic to persons who have more links *outside* the affected category. If we assume that this is a meaningful rather than a chance ordering of a very small number of cases, two interpretations are possible. First, we might argue that what is occurring is simply the

TABLE 2 *Sociometric Status of Affected Cases by Time Affected*

Characteristic	"Before"	"Day One"	"Day Two"
Proportion of cases which are isolates	.50 (10)	.21 (24)	.25 (20)
Average number of times chosen	1.00	1.67	1.35
Proportion of choices directed toward affecteds	.27 (30)	.31 (70)	.25 (57)
Proportion of choices directed toward controls	.23 (30)	.29 (70)	.21 (57)
Proportion of choices received from affecteds	.40 (10)	.58 (40)	.63 (27)
Proportion of choices received from controls	.60 (10)	.43 (40)	.37 (27)
Proportion chosen by affecteds only	.10 (10)	.29 (24)	.45 (20)
Proportion chosen by controls only	.20 (10)	.21 (24)	.15 (20)
Proportion of mutual choices with affecteds	.50 (4)	.61 (23)	.63 (16)
Proportion of mutual choices with controls	.50 (4)	.39 (23)	.38 (16)

NOTE: The N on which each proportion is based is noted in parentheses. The total number of cases in each time period was: "Before," 10; "Day One," 24; "Day Two," 20.

The asterisk indicates proportions which do not total to 1.00 because choices may be made of non-affected persons not in the sample.

entry of the contagion into another sociometric network, and that since the spread is curtailed by the end of the entire epidemic, there are not enough cases to demonstrate this. On the other hand, it might be argued that what is happening is that a more random distribution of cases is occurring, that the spread of the epidemic has moved out of sociometric channels and is becoming more general. This would be another way of saying that it has become a "crowd response."

DISCUSSION

We interpret these findings as being at least consistent with the following theoretical position. An epidemic such as this begins when one or more persons, due to idiosyncratic characteristics outside our present area of concern, exhibit symptoms which serve as a model for at least a limited number of others in the same situation. Since the symptoms and their explanation are somewhat unusual, those most likely to follow this lead are persons less well integrated into a set of social relationships which, for most of those present, provide a referential base for defining the model as irrelevant or objectionable. As a number of other persons follow the lead, however, it is increasingly likely that some persons who are socially integrated will be affected. (Perhaps these will be persons of somewhat unusual psychological make-up, or ones who are in a particularly anxiety-producing situation.) Through some such channel, the contagion enters social networks and is disseminated with increasing rapidity in what can be termed a "chain reaction." The acceleration is undoubtedly in part a function of the fact that, as more cases appear, the behavior becomes increasingly legitimized — increasingly accepted according to an evolving generalized belief in the group involved. The rapidity of legitimation *within* such networks is greater than outside them, and "outsiders" are thus slower to respond. However, as larger and larger numbers of persons exhibit the behavior, the sheer size of the affected category makes the credibility of the phenomenon greater. We thus find that ultimately "everyone" believes in "the bug" (or whatever the belief is that justifies the behavior), and cases begin to occur throughout the population. It thus becomes a "crowd response."

We argue, then, that isolates are instrumental in providing the initial few cases and providing a credible model for one or more particularly vulnerable persons who are socially integrated. The behavior of such "insiders" is more influential vis-á-vis their friends and increases the likelihood of contagion within sociometric networks. Since such contagion accelerates due to increasingly greater legitimation within the group, it soon forms a phenomemon of such proportions that its credibility can no longer be easily denied by anyone in the population. Cases then begin to occur more frequently in scattered, unrelated segments of the population. The end of the epidemic comes when some additional factor enters the situation (in this case experts who denied the legitimacy of the behavior and exterminators whose sprays "killed the bugs") and/or when the behavior becomes seriously dysfunctional for the participants. We have thus attempted to bring about a synthesis of three different theoretical positions within the framework of the longitudinal analysis of an epidemic of hysterical symptoms and to indicate the contribution each makes to a fuller view of the phenomenon.[4]

In conclusion, it may be worthwhile to compare this study and our interpretation of the data with the study of doctor's adoption of a new drug referred to earlier. The similarity of the two is striking, but there are important differences. Both the present study and the drug study point up the importance of a network of social relations for the dissemination of a new behavioral pattern. However, our data more clearly indicate a lag in the rate of adoption of the behavior pattern by persons integrated in the social network. In both studies there is an "S-shaped" accelerated curve of adoptions in the case of the socially integrated subjects, indicating a kind of "snowball" effect. Perhaps more noteworthy, however, is the fact that in our study the original rate of adoption by isolates is higher than for those who are socially integrated,

[4] It may be noted that some of our other data are in keeping with this interpretation, although it is not possible to present a complete analysis here. For instance, although both affecteds and controls expressed a belief in the existence of a toxic insect, those controls who had sociometric links with affecteds (chose or were chosen by them) expressed this belief more often than those without such links. This adds support to the idea that the belief was disseminated through sociometric channels.

whereas in the drug study the integrated doctors adopt the drug at a higher rate throughout the period studied.

We interpret this difference as being due to the *kind* of behavior involved. The doctor, whether socially isolated or integrated, presumably is highly receptive to the adoption of new practices which promote medical values. However, if we accept the general proposition that the leaders in any group are better informed and more fully reflect the group's norms and values, the difference between the integrated and isolated doctor is seen as a difference in the rapidity with which they will act in accordance with those norms and values when the occasion arises. In the case of the hysterical behavior, however, there is no question about the normative preference for or legitimation of such behavior. There is no normatively based readiness to respond. Rather, we would argue, what occurs in such cases is the evolution of a generalized belief that is not previously held, in this case a belief that there *is* an insect, that it *is* dangerous, and that it *can* and *does* cause serious symptoms. Our data indicate that this belief, and the behavior based on it, develop among isolates at a steady rate, but among those who are socially integrated the rate is slow at first and accelerates rapidly in the later phases. In fact, the rate of acceleration and the ultimate level of acceptance is highest in the most fully integrated segment of the population.

Presumably, then, in our case the social network acted as both a resistor and a conductor, at different points during the epidemic. Thus, although there are important similarities between the present study and the earlier one, the content of the pattern being disseminated must also be taken into account. In this study, since the behavior involved was not normatively approved, the social network was both resistant and facilitative. The transition from resistance to facilitation was a function, we believe, of the evolution within the social network of a new definition of the situation, and the time required to develop this new definition is reflected in the lag of the rate of hysterical behavior among highly integrated women behind that of the isolates in the first phase of the epidemic.

Except in very special populations, behavior as unusual as that represented by the hysterical reaction found in the clothing plant would not originally be adopted by highly integrated persons. On the other hand, unless it were ultimately adopted by such persons, the contagion would not reach epidemic proportions. Thus, in cases of such unusual "innovations" as discussed here, we see isolates as crucial in the initial stages, and channels of interpersonal relations as important agencies of rapid dissemination in the pattern of behavior, until, finally, the number of cases is so great as to bring about a "crowd reaction" in which prior social relations are irrelevant.

24 Violence on the Fanatical Right and Left*

Arnold Forster

The following discussion makes it clear that ideological violence has been no stranger in American history. At all periods there have been individuals

* From *The Annals of the American Academy of Political and Social Science,* Vol. 364, March 1966, pp. 141–148. Reproduced by permission.

and organizations who have rejected the democratic and constitutional processes and have advocated or used violence in an effort to achieve their political objectives. A review of the history of violence in America may be useful in reaching an understanding of contemporary violence. Make a list of the individuals and organizations you know that advocate or participate in violence. How would you classify them in terms of socio-economic status? Political ideology? Now read the article by H. Edward Ransford which follows this selection. What additional insights does this give into violence?

If violence is the refuge of unreason, then we must never be greatly surprised to find violent tendencies far out on those political extremities of the Left and the Right which have exchanged reason for passion and mystical faith. Extremism of thinking and extremism of action are close to parallel. The "revolution" and the "holy war" are similar fanaticisms in which the impassioned ends necessarily justify any and all means. And history indicates that our Centrist constitutional democracy tends not so much to check as merely to frustrate political unreason, to drive it into the hills or into the dark of night, often increasing its desperation and virulence.

THE UNITED STATES

Tracing the history of violence in the United States — at least with respect to establishing responsibility — is no simple task, violence by its very nature being beyond any simple or reasonable laws of causation. It is, rather, a kind of contagious irresponsibility which allows its advocates to shrug off all blame for specific acts frequently resulting from the emotions they have generated. The leaders of the two main branches of today's Ku Klux Klan (KKK), for example, both have piously disavowed violence and denied using it. One of them, James Venable, leader of the National Knights of the KKK, nonetheless told an Atlanta audience a few years ago that schools should be burned to the ground if necessary to prevent them from being integrated. The other, Robert Shelton, head of the United Klans (the largest of the KKK groups today), has declared:

"We don't advocate violence. If someone steps on our toes we are going to knock their heads off their shoulders." [1]

Klan leaders denied any part of the bombing of a Baptist church in Birmingham, Alabama, in 1963, which took the lives of four little Negro girls, but a Klan speaker in St. Augustine, Florida, told an assembly of Klansmen:

If they can find those fellows, they ought to pin medals on them. It wasn't no shame they was killed. . . . Why? Because when I go out to kill rattlesnakes, I don't make no difference between little rattlesnakes

[1] *Long Island Newsday*, March 27, 1965.

and big rattlesnakes. . . . I say good for whoever planted the bomb. [2]

And so it goes. The Know-Nothings, the "Wobblies," and the Black Muslims have all disavowed violence at one time or another — it is always someone else stepping on their toes — and yet American history is littered with the heart-breaking reminders of their agitational words spoken on more fiery occasions.

It is, perhaps, an almost automatic reaction to the thought of violence as the weapon of ideological fanatics to think immediately of the Ku Klux Klan. Under various leaderships the hooded terror has been with us for a century now. It provides the classic patterns for our study — the hatred planted and nurtured, the cowardice behind a mask (the covering of cloth or of a crowd), the barbarism of murder, the distrust of this nation's democratic process, or the open contempt for its laws. The Klan is our showcase — but hardly our sole exhibit.

The Nineteenth Century

A fiercely emotional superpatriotism shaking America throughout the nineteenth century gave birth to a series of huge political movements whose national platforms — nativist bigotry — inevitably produced precinct-level violence on a wide scale.

The first of these, the Native American party, was an anti-Catholic, anti-immigrant political organization strong in the eastern cities and manufacturing areas in the 1830's and 1840's. Rooted in a long history of prejudices, this party quickly rose to power at the time of an increased Irish immigration, electing a mayor of New York in 1843 and sending several members to Congress. In Philadelphia, in 1844, a series of Native American party street meetings and parades (in which marchers were well armed) led to serious rioting over a period of three months. Two Catholic churches, two parochial schools, and at least a dozen homes owned by Catholics were burned to

[2] Eyewitness account, KKK meeting, St. Augustine, Florida, September 1963. Also, for this and all other references to the KKK: "The Ku Klux Klans — 1965," *Facts* (Anti-Defamation League), Vol. 16, No. 3 (May 1965).

the ground. Several persons were killed and many injured. The militia, and eventually United States Cavalry and Marine units, had to be called to quell the uprisings. At its national convention in 1845, the Native American party excused the violence as defensive, claiming that Philadephia mobs had put down the "foreign aggression" of Irish Catholics.

The Native American organization was followed in the 1850's by the Know-Nothings — technically, the Grand Council of the United States of North America — the initial purpose of which was to prevent foreigners and Catholics from holding political office.[3] But the devotees of the new nativism instigated anti-Catholic riots in dozens of American cities. In May 1854, a mob marched on New York's city hall, assaulting everyone who looked Irish. Three months later, St. Louis, Missouri, saw a 48-hour orgy of mob violence in which a dozen persons were killed and fifty or more homes belonging to Irish Catholics were wrecked and looted. In 1855, twenty persons were killed in a two-day riot instigated by Know-Nothings in Louisville.

This was no hate fringe; for when, in the election of 1854, the secret and violent order entered the open political arena (under the name of "the American party"), it elected governors in nine states and placed 104 of its members in the United States House of Representatives — then a body of 234. In 1856, former President Millard Fillmore, running as the Know-Nothing candidate, captured almost a million votes — about one-fifth of the total cast.

Nine years later, in the early months of the Reconstruction, the focus of terror's history moved south as the Negro, with the founding of the first Klan, became the victim. By 1871, the invisible empire had a membership of over half a million, and a Congressional investigation that year uncovered hangings, shootings, whippings, and mutilations in the thousands. In Louisiana alone, two thousand persons had been killed, wounded, or injured in a short few weeks before the election of 1868. The commanding general of federal forces in Texas reported: "Murders of Negroes are

so common as to render it impossible to keep accurate accounts of them." [4]

The Early Twentieth Century

Between the original KKK and the one that rides today lies the noteworthy history of the "second Klan." With its heyday in the 1920's, this one hit a peak membership of between four and five million and became a major factor on the national political scene, amassing substantial power in the North and West as well as in the South. Once again, it was political power on the barbaric mob level. The *New York World* reported these statistics on Klan activities within a single year (October 1920 to October 1921):

Four killings, one mutilation, one branding with acid, forty-two floggings, twenty-seven tar-and-feather parties, five kidnappings, forty-three persons warned to leave town or otherwise threatened, fourteen communities threatened.[5]

The period of the second Klan and the years immediately preceding World War I — with its war fever, its strikes and draft riots, and its Palmer Raids — constituted an era of heightened emotions and hatreds, one in which the extremist political tempers had short fuses. The enemy — the anarchist, the Red, the capitalist oppressor, the Hun, the Jew, the Papist — was carrying out his plots everywhere and had to be immediately and forcefully clubbed down (if one were viewing from the Right) or overthrown (in the view from the Left). By this time the KKK had added anti-Semitism and anti-Catholicism to its race hatred. And the Communist party had arrived.

It is hardly surprising, in view of the events in Russia in 1917, that the word "violence" became synonymous with the word "communism" in the public mind. According to the "conditions" imposed upon it by the Third International, the American Communist party had to reject democratic parliamentarianism openly in favor of violent revolution. But the Communists in America, even at their peak of influence, were far from realizing

---

[3] Gustavus Myers, *History of Bigotry in the United States* (New York: Capricorn Books, 1960), pp. 123 ff.

[4] *Ibid.*, p. 216.

[5] Samuel Tenenbaum, *Why Men Hate* (Philadelphia: Jewish Book Guild of America, 1947), p. 236 (quoting *New York World*).

their dreams as to size and power, and they were under a tight disciplinary control; as a result of these factors there had been less open violence under their direction, whatever may have been the designs of their foreign mentors.

The Industrial Workers of the World (IWW) — in the turbulent atmosphere of labor disputes — provided a different story. The IWW, the well-known Wobblies, were a union, controlled by hardcore syndicalists, revolutionary socialists who opposed political democracy, teaching that "a struggle must go on until the workers of the world organize as a class, take possession of the earth and the machinery of production and abolish the wage system" — a victory to be won by force. The Wobblies advocated sabotage as a matter of policy. IWW strikes saw violence against non-member workers as well as against public and private property. But as to our focus on "political" movements: these American syndicalists' contempt for the democratic process kept them, as they vainly awaited the Revolution, from achieving or even trying to achieve any degree of political power by the accepted processes of the nation.

Violence swirls about the history and deliberations of the Left. The American Communist party itself had emerged (ultimately, in 1919) from a 1912 debate within the Socialist party on the very question of violence as a social weapon — the Socialist convention voting overwhelmingly to expel anyone "who opposes political action or advocates crime, sabotage or other methods of violence as a weapon of the working class." [6]

Much of the violence involving the Left, however, has resulted from the agitation of its extremist enemies. Super-patriots have indulged in many an orgy of Red-hunting, and the end result has been, as in most such crusades, the justification of violent acts. During the World War I hysteria, a Tulsa newspaper went so far as to advise its readers:

If the IWW . . . gets busy in your neighborhood, kindly take the occasion to decrease the supply of hemp. . . . The first step in the whipping of Germany is to strangle the IWW's. Kill 'em just as you would any other kind of snake. Don't scotch 'em; kill 'em! And kill 'em dead! It is no time to waste money on trials. [7]

There is little doubt that the extreme Left has welcomed and capitalized on such cries from the other side, and may on occasions have encouraged them in order to foster the persecution image and rally naïve civil libertarians to their side.

The instances of organizational or mob violence in American history always seem, upon reflection, shocking — this, in all probability, because they are so alien to the theory and the usual operation of the American political system with its democratic superstructure, its dynamic usefulness, its protection of enumerated human rights, and its imperfect but nonetheless visible devotion to the values both of order and of change. The turbulence and repressions and the resulting fears that have characterized societies in so much of the world are out of place here.

It is logical, then, that our manifestations of political violence should accompany political doctrines which assail democracy, which deny rights, which despise order, or which resist enlightened change.

It is logical also that the forces of violence themselves seem alien, if not exotic — the Klan, for example, pursuing its nighttime quests in ghostly Inquisitional robes, or the Black Muslims founding their "Nation" in weird, science-fiction-alized distortions of Mohammedanism. The second Klan actually reached its climax, in 1940, in a burst of pagan pageantry in which it joined with the German-American Bund, at the Nazis' Camp Nordland in New Jersey, to sing Hitler's marching songs and burn a cross forty feet high.

But even in the most "nativist" of the camps of violence there is something that might be called "un-American" in the truest sense of that abused word: an inability to come to terms with the American system and to take advantage of the unique opportunities which our system offers for the free expression and propagation of dissent. The most

---

[6] Irving Howe, *The American Communist Party* (Boston: Beacon Press, 1957), p. 15.

[7] John P. Roche, *The Quest for the Dream* (New York: The Macmillan Company, 1963), p. 64 (quoting from the *Tulsa World,* November 9, 1917).

obvious reason for the links between the espousal of violence and a contempt for democracy lies in the common tendencies of crusaders and revolutionaries to value some impersonal abstraction above both the individual's rights and the majority's will. Thus, the industrial units of the syndicalists or the almost mystical "race" of the Klan, the Nazis, or the Muslims — or some such ineffable idealization as "God and Country" or "the Common Man" — is glorified to the denigration of the individual human person and of society's laws.

While violence ultimately fails — for the very reason that it will not come to terms with American principles — it is, nevertheless, real, and by its nature it stimulates fear and heartbreak and deep concern.

Mid-twentieth Century

Parallel to the rise of the new Radical Right since 1960, and that of the new Left subsequently, there has been a sharp increase in the interest shown in weaponry, military tactics, "self-defense," "riot control," and the like. Advertisements in gun journals across the country reflect a short supply of small arms. Much of this interest, certainly, has been stimulated by the growth of the KKK, by the rise of "guerrilla" bands such as the Minutemen, and by excited advertisements for weapons in the hate sheets — publications such as *The Thunderbolt,* distributed by the National States' Rights Party (NSRP), a Nazilike group with Klan connections and a passion for military pageantry.

The present era of racist violence in the South began in the late 1950's, when it was highlighted by the dynamiting of a number of synagogues.[8] Police arrested five suspects, all having connections with the National States' Rights Party, after a bomb tore apart the temple of a Reform Jewish congregation in Atlanta in October 1958. The police investigators had noted close similarities in this bombing to others in Jacksonville, Miami, Nashville, and Birmingham — patterns indicating a criminal conspiracy working in several Southern states. The suspects were never convicted, though the weighty evidence introduced at the trial of one

[8] Anti-Semitism in the South," *Facts* (Anti-Defamation League), Vol. 13, No. 4 (October-November 1958).

of the men provided a detailed picture of the religious hatred and the potential violence in the National States' Rights Party's activities. In the subsequent renaissance of the KKK, the NSRP has appeared to be a militant ally of the hooded order.

The current rise of the Klan was heralded by the race riots which rocked Jacksonville, Florida, on "Axe Handle Saturday" — August 27, 1960. Jacksonville was then the target of civil rights "sit-in" demonstrations. From a meeting of the Jacksonville klavern of the Florida Knights of the Ku Klux Klan held earlier that week, a call went out to all Klan units urging them to converge on the city the following Saturday. On that day, local stores reported brisk sales of baseball bats and axe handles. Violence erupted and continued sporadically for several days.

In the three or four years that followed, years of increased activity — and increasing progress — in civil rights, Ku Klux Klan membership climbed into the thousands for the first time in decades. And violence, as usual, has followed upon this growth, the memory of its headlines still fresh: eighteen bomb blasts in Negro churches and homes in McComb, Mississippi, alone during 1964 (Klansmen convicted in at least one case); the bombing of the Birmingham church in which four little Negro girls were killed (Klansmen arrested, freed); the 1964 murder of Negro educator Lemuel Penn (four Georgia Klan members arrested, two tried and acquitted by an all-white jury); the 1965 murder of Mrs. Viola Gregg Liuzzo (three Klan members convicted of violating her civil rights); the murder of three civil rights workers in Philadelphia, Mississippi (six Klansmen among those arrested); weeks of violent racial incidents in St. Augustine, Florida, in 1964, during desegregation efforts by Dr. Martin Luther King (the Klan staging open parades and street harangues on the scene).

And accompanying such recent history have been literally thousands of cross-burnings — the Klan's traditional ritual of terror. As always, however, the hooded "empire" has expressed shocked denials of its responsibility for such outrages. But even without the evidence of its active participation, stand the words of its leaders, the pitchmen whose emotional exhortations are essential for the marshaling of a mob or the poisoning of an individual mind. At about the time the Civil Rights Bill became law in 1964, Klan recruiting posters in Jackson, Mississippi, declared:

> If we don't win in the next eight months, we're all destined for Communist slavery and our wives and daughters will be chattels in Mongolian and African brothels. . . . Absolutely refuse to register or give up arms. . . . Stock up on rifles and shotguns and pistols, all of the standard make, and lots of ammunition. . . . Form an organization with next-door neighbors. . . . Be your own leader of your own household and make it an armed arsenal.

It is not among the white supremacists alone that racial tensions have led to violent talk or violent actions. The Black Muslims — advocates of Negro supremacy — first came to national attention thirty years ago when they rioted in a Chicago courtroom where one of their members was facing trial on a minor charge.[9] Before the riot squad was called, one police officer was killed and several injured, and the courtroom was wrecked. The Muslims today are urged to refrain from violence, but their seemingly cautious leaders still preach a crude and fantastic racism — that white men, the "blue-eyed devils," are base, inferior, and totally evil — the very hate from which violence springs. And to this race hatred the so-called "Nation of Islam" adds a measure of anti-Christian bigotry, and — like their hooded white counterparts — anti-Semitism.

On the extreme Left, the leader of the Harlem branch of the "Progressive Labor Movement" has been arrested and charged with attempting to use the 1964 riot in New York's ghetto for violent revolutionary purposes.[10] William Epton had stated (according to the testimony of a New York City detective who had infiltrated the movement under orders) that his organization planned to "fight and carry arms" against the police and the National Guard as the spearhead of a proposed Negro rebellion designed to overthrow the government by force and violence. Epton's plans, the

[9] Cf. C. Eric Lincoln, *The Black Muslims in America* (Boston: Beacon Press, 1961).
[10] *New York Times,* December 1, 1965, p. 34.

detective further testified, called for mobilization of Harlem residents "block by block" with terrorist bands being trained for guerrilla warfare against the police.

The Progressive Laborites are Marxist extremists who prefer the Peking "line" to that of Moscow — at least insofar as the Red China theorists hold to the necessity of war and violence to accomplish ultimate Communist aims. Testimony such as that of the New York police investigator is hardly surprising in view of such admitted leanings. The antidemocratic Left has advocated war and violence before.

The John Birch Society

As mentioned earlier, the recent period which has witnessed the resurgence of the Ku Klux Klan, the rise of the armed Minutemen in the hills, and all sorts of stirrings in the various ideological camps has also been the time of an unparalleled growth on the Radical Right. A natural question arises: Where do the organizations of this phenomenon stand — the John Birch Society, particularly — on the matters under consideration? Does the fear-ridden vision of Robert Welch arouse violent thought in his followers? We might ask the same with respect to the written invective of the Birchers' Revilo P. Oliver or the frightpeddling orations of Billy James Hargis.

First, it is important to remember that the Radical Right of the 1960's has been, predominantly, and in the areas of its greatest influence and noise, a middle-class movement — also, a movement with quasi-religious overtones and with a largely suburban membership. Many members of this movement are shocked by the activities of the Klan and feverishly disassociate themselves from such things — despite their own similar, almost hysterical view of current racial problems and their similar fears of an imminent Bolshevik takeover of America.

But, secondly, it is important to realize that many of the manifestations of the Radical Right over recent years display a degree of violence — even if only a small degree — that generally has been considered unthinkable among the "fine, upstanding citizens" which the Birch Society claims to have at its core. Opponents of the Extreme

Right have been threatened or harassed with anonymous telephone calls and poison-pen letters. Meetings that could not be controlled or swayed have been disrupted. Those who would not go along with this or that temporary Rightist fanaticism have been intimidated or blackballed. Character has been maligned, dedication insulted, opinions censored. The late Adlai Stevenson was spat upon in Dallas by a follower of the Birchers' General Edwin A. Walker.

Violence must be a state of mind before it can be translated into action. The "nice" suburbanite may never kill a civil rights worker — but the impact of his aroused fury may differ only by degree. What has been produced in the Radical Rightist ideologues is a state of mind *relatively* fevered. The Birch view of the Selma civil rights march ("a horde of termites from all over the country, led by half-crazed ministers . . . in a typical demonstration of Communist activism") would serve to arouse the frenzy of hooded rednecks as well as anything the Klan itself has whipped up. The actions of different persons in response to such propaganda would vary with differing personal factors, but the state of mind is already there.

The California Senate Fact-Finding Subcommittee on Un-American Activities, which always has been noticeably partial to conservative, "anti-Communist" causes, reported, after a 1965 investigation of the John Birch Society, that Robert Welch's organization "has attracted a lunatic fringe that is now assuming serious proportions," and that it has been "beset by an influx of emotionally unstable people, some of whom have been prosecuted in the courts for their hoodlum tactics." [11]

Extremism can and does attract such people, and it can instill similar attitudes in others who had not displayed them previously. At more than one far-right-wing meeting the Birch Society's cry of "Impeach Earl Warren" has been followed by the suggestion that the United States Chief Justice be hanged or shot rather than impeached — and this suggestion has been met on such occasions with tumultuous cheers.

It is hardly surprising that the members of the John Birch Society, like the KKK, like the IWW, and like all the revolutionaries and Rightist radicals of our history, have disdain for the processes of democracy. The Birchers, too, prefer to operate outside of politics, and their founder and chieftain, Robert Welch, wrote in his famous *Blue Book* that democracy is "a fraud," [12] and "the worst of all forms of government." [13] Such is the pattern of the state of mind from which violent action tends to arise.

Such action has produced tragic blots on the pages of the American record in all times, but the pages also indicate that when political democracy has been kept strong and dynamic, political violence has ultimately failed. It has ever been thus — and will be again in respect to the current crop of extremists on the Left and Right.

[11] "Un-American Activities in California: Thirteenth Report, 1965," California Senate Fact-Finding Subcommittee on Un-American Activities (June 1965), p. 174.

[12] Robert Welch, *Blue Book of the John Birch Society* (Fourth Printing), p. 159.

[13] *Ibid.,* p. xv.

25   Isolation, Powerlessness, and Violence: A Study of Attitudes and Participation in the Watts Riot*

H. Edward Ransford

As the previous selection by Forster makes clear, whites in America have carried out violent acts against Negroes ever since the earliest days of slavery. Where actual violence was not present, its threat permeated much of the relations between the two races. In the summer of 1965 the long smoldering resentment of the Negro in America burst into dramatic violence. Despite the efforts of many of their leaders it has been impossible to limit Negro protest to nonviolence since that time. There are continuing threats of "the long hot summer" to come.

Among blacks as among whites, the majority do not favor violence and only a small minority are active participants in the violent episodes. What are the characteristics of the Negroes who participated in the Watts riot in Los Angeles in 1965 or who responded favorably to this violence? Very few sociological studies are available but the following selection will provide some insights. Are the explanatory concepts used by Ransford of any value in understanding disciples of violence among students' groups or organizations of the Far Right?

A Theoretical Perspective

Studies dealing with political extremism and radical protest have often described the participants in such action as being isolated or weakly tied to the institutions of the community. Kerr and Siegel demonstrated this relationship with their finding that wildcat strikes are more common among isolated occupational groups, such as mining, maritime, and lumbering. These isolated groups

* Reprinted from *American Journal of Sociology*, 73 (March 1968), pp. 581–591, by permission of The University of Chicago Press. Copyright © 1968 by The University of Chicago.

are believed to have a weak commitment to public pressures and the democratic norms of the community. Thus, when grievances are felt intensely and the bonds to the institutions of the community are weak, there is likely to be an explosion of discontent (the strike) rather than use of negotiation or other normative channels of expression.

More recently, mass society theory has articulated this relationship between isolation and extremism. The mass society approach sees current structural processes — such as the decline in kinship, the increase in mobility, and the rise of huge bureaucracies — as detaching many individuals from sources of control, meaning, and personal satisfaction. Those who are most isolated from centers of power are believed to be more vulnerable to authoritarian outlooks and more available for volatile mass movements. Indeed, Kornhauser instructs us that the whole political stability of a society is somewhat dependent upon its citizens being tied meaningfully to the institutions of the community. He suggests that participation in secondary organizations — such as unions and business groups — serves to mediate between the individual and the nation, tying the individual to the democratic norms of the society.

The relationship between structural isolation and extremism is further accentuated by the personal alienation of the individual. Isolated people are far more likely than non-isolated people to feel cut off from the larger society and to feel an inability to control events in the society. This subjective alienation may heighten the individual's readiness to engage in extreme behavior. For example, Horton and Thompson find that perceived powerlessness is related to protest voting. Those with feelings of political powerlessness were more likely to be dissatisfied with their position in society and to hold resentful attitudes toward community leaders. The study suggests that the discontent of the powerless group was converted to action through the vote — a vote of "no" on a local bond issue being a form of negativism in which the individual strikes out at community powers. This interpretation of alienation as a force for protest is consistent with the orginal Marxian view of the concept in which alienation leads to a radical attack upon the existing social structure.

In summary, there are two related approaches commonly used to explain participation in extreme political behavior. The first deals with the degree to which the individual is structurally isolated or tied to community institutions. The second approach deals with the individual's awareness and evaluation of his isolated condition — for example, his feeling of a lack of control over critical matters or his feeling of discontent due to a marginal position in society. Following this orientation, this research employs the concepts of racial isolation, perceived powerlessness, and racial dissatisfaction as theoretical tools for explaining the participation of Negroes in violence.

Study Design and Hypotheses

In the following discussion, the three independent variables of this study (isolation, powerlessness, and dissatisfaction) are discussed separately and jointly, as predictors of violence participation.

Racial Isolation

Ralph Ellison has referred to the Negro in this country as the "invisible man." Although this is a descriptive characterization, sociological studies have attempted to conceptualize more precisely the isolation of the American Negro. For example, those studying attitudes of prejudice often view racial isolation as a lack of free and easy contact on an intimate and equal status basis. Though the interracial contact may be frequent, it often involves such wide status differentials that it does not facilitate candid communication, nor is it likely to give the minority person a feeling that he has some stake in the system. In this paper, intimate white contact is viewed as a mediating set of relationships that binds the ethnic individual to majority-group values — essentially conservative values that favor working through democratic channels rather than violently attacking the social system. Accordingly, it is reasoned that Negroes who are more racially isolated (by low degrees of intimate contact with whites) will have fewer channels of communication to air their grievances and will feel little commitment to the leaders and institutions of the community. This group, which is blocked from meaningful white communication, should be more willing to use violent protest than the groups with greater involvement in white society.

Powerlessness and Racial Dissatisfaction

In contrast to structural isolation, powerlessness and racial dissatisfaction are the subjective components of our theoretical scheme. A feeling of powerlessness is one form of alienation. It is defined in this research as a low expectancy of control over events. This attitude is seen as an appropriate variable for Negroes living in segregated ghettos; that is, groups which are blocked from full participation in the society are more likely to feel powerless in that society. Powerlessness is also a variable that seems to have a logical relationship to violent protest. Briefly, it is reasoned that Negroes who feel powerless to change their position or to control crucial decisions that affect them will be more willing to use violent means to get their rights than those who feel some control or efficacy within the social system. For the Negro facing extreme discrimination barriers, an attitude of powerlessness is simply a comment on the society, namely, a belief that all channels for social redress are closed.

Our second attitude measure, racial dissatisfaction, is defined as the degree to which the individual feels that he is being treated badly because of his race. It is a kind of racial alienation in the sense that the individual perceives his position in society to be illegitimate, due to racial discrimination. The Watts violence represented an extreme expression of frustration and discontent. We would expect those highly dissatisfied with their treatment as Negroes to be the participants in such violence. Thus, the "highs" in racial dissatisfaction should be more willing to use violence than the "lows" in this attitude. In comparing our two forms of subjective alienation (powerlessness and racial dissatisfaction), it is important to note that, although we expect some correlation between the two attitudes (a certain amount of resentment and dissatisfaction should accompany the feeling of powerlessness), we propose to show that they make an independent contribution to violence.

UNIFICATION OF PREDICTIVE VARIABLES

We believe that the fullest understanding of violence can be brought to bear by use of a social-psychological design in which the structural variable (racial isolation) is joined with the subjective attitudes of the individual (powerlessness and dissatisfaction).

In this design, we attempt to specify the conditions under which isolation has its strongest effect upon violence. It is reasoned that racial isolation should be most important for determining participation in violence (*a*) when individuals feel powerless to shape their destiny under existing conditions or (*b*) when individuals are highly dissatisfied with their racial treatment. Each of the attitudes is seen as a connecting bridge of logic between racial isolation and violence.

For the first case (that of powerlessness), we are stating that a weak attachment to the majority group and its norms should lead to a radical break from law and order when individuals perceive they cannot affect events important to them; that is, they cannot change their racial position through activity within institutional channels. Violence, in this instance, becomes an alternative pathway of expression and gain. Conversely, racial isolation should have much less effect upon violence when persons feel some control in the system.

For the second case (racial dissatisfaction), we believe isolation should have a far greater effect upon violence when dissatisfaction over racial treatment is intense. Isolation from the society then becomes critical to violence in the sense that the dissatisfied person feels little commitment to the legal order and is more likely to use extreme methods as an outlet for his grievances. Statistically speaking, we expect an interaction effect between isolation and powerlessness, and between isolation and dissatisfaction, in the prediction of violence.[1]

---

[1] In contrast to the mass society perspective, in which structural isolation is viewed as a cause of subjective alienation, we are viewing the two as imperfectly correlated. For example, many Negroes with contact (nonisolates) may still feel powerless due to racial discrimination barriers. We are thus stressing the partial independence of objective and subjective alienation and feel it necessary to consider both variables for the best prediction of violence.

METHODS

Our hypotheses call for measures of intimate white contact, perceived powerlessness, and perceived racial dissatisfaction as independent variables, and willingness to use violence as a dependent variable. The measurement of these variables, and also the sampling techniques, are discussed at this time.

SOCIAL CONTACT

The type of social contact to be measured had to be of an intimate and equal status nature, a kind of contact that would facilitate easy communication between the races. First, each Negro respondent was asked if he had current contact with white people in a series of situations: on the job, in his neighborhood, in organizations to which he belongs, and in other situations (such as shopping). After this general survey of white contacts, the respondent was asked, "Have you ever done anything social with these white people, like going to the movies together or visiting in each other's homes?" The responses formed a simple dichotomous variable: "high" contact scores for those who had done something social (61 per cent of the sample) and "low" contact scores for those who had had little or no social contact (39 per cent).[2]

POWERLESSNESS

Following the conceptualization of Melvin Seeman, powerlessness is defined as a low expectancy of control over events. Twelve forced-choice items were used to tap this attitude. The majority of items dealt with expectations of control over the political system. The following is an example:

———— The world is run by the few people in power, and there is not much the little guy can do about it.

---

[2] As a further indication that this measure was tapping a more intimate form of interracial contact, it can be noted that 88 per cent of those reporting social contact with whites claimed at least one "good friend" ("to whom you can say what you really think") or "close friend" ("to whom you can talk over confidential matters"). Only 10 per cent of those lacking social contact claimed such friendships with white people.

———— The average citizen can have an influence on government decisions.

After testing the scale items for reliability, the distribution of scores was dichotomized at the median.

RACIAL DISSATISFACTION

The attitude of racial dissatisfaction is defined as the degree to which the individual feels he is being treated badly because of his race. A five-item scale was developed to measure this attitude. The questions ask the Negro respondent to compare his treatment (in such areas as housing, work, and general treatment in the community) with various reference groups, such as the southern Negro or the white. Each of the five questions allows a reply on one of three levels: no dissatisfaction, mild dissatisfaction, and intense dissatisfaction. Typical of the items is the following: "If you compare your opportunities and the treatment you get from whites in Los Angeles with Negroes living in the South, would you say you are much better off ———— a little better off ———— or treated about the same as the southern Negro ————?" After a reliability check of the items, replies to the dissatisfaction measure were dichotomized into high and low groups. The cut was made conceptually, rather than at the median, yielding 99 "highs" and 213 "lows" in dissatisfaction.[3]

VIOLENCE WILLINGNESS

The dependent variable of the study is willingness to use violence. Violence is defined in the context of the Watts riot as the willingness to use direct aggression against the groups that are believed to be discriminating, such as the police and white merchants. The question used to capture this outlook is, "Would you be willing to use violence to get Negro rights?" With data gathered

so shortly after the Watts violence, it was felt that the question would be clearly understood by respondents. At the time of data collection, buildings were still smoldering; violence in the form of looting, burning, and destruction was not a remote possibility, but a tangible reality. The violence-prone group numbered eighty-three.

A second measure of violence asked the person if he had ever used violent methods to get Negro rights.[4] Only sixteen respondents of the 312 reported (or admitted) that they had participated in actual violence. As a result of this very small number the item is used as an indicator of trends but is not employed as a basic dependent variable of the study.

SAMPLE

The sample was composed of three-hundred-twelve Negro males who were heads of the household and between the ages of eighteen and sixty-five. The subjects responded to an interview schedule administered by Negro interviewers. They were chosen by random methods and were interviewed in their own homes or apartments. Both employed and unemployed respondents were included in the sample, although the former were emphasized in the sampling procedure (269 employed in contrast to 43 unemployed). The sample was drawn from three major areas of Los Angeles: a relatively middle-class and integrated area (known as the "Crenshaw" district) and the predominantly lower-class and highly segregated communities of "South Central" and "Watts." The sample could be classified as "disproportional stratified" because the proportion of subjects drawn from each of the three areas does not correspond to the actual distribution of Negroes in Los Angeles. For example, it was decided that an approximate fifty-fifty split between middle- and lower-class respondents would be desirable for later analysis. This meant, however, that Crenshaw

[3] With a cut at the median, a good many people ($N = 59$) who were mildly dissatisfied on all five items would have been placed in the "high" category. It was decided that a more accurate description of the "high" category would require the person to express maximum dissatisfaction on at least one of the five items and mild dissatisfaction on the other four.

[4] The question, "Have you ever participated in violent action for Negro rights?" was purposely worded in general terms to avoid accusing the respondent of illegal behavior during the Watts violence. However, racial violence in the United States was somewhat rare at that time, so it is likely that most of the sixteen respondents were referring to participation in the Watts violence.

(middle-class) Negroes were considerably over-represented, since their characteristics are not typical of the Los Angeles Negro community as a whole, and the majority of Los Angeles Negroes do not reside in this, or any similar, area.

RESULTS

We have predicted a greater willingness to use violent methods for three groups: the isolated, the powerless, and the dissatisfied. The data presented in Table 1 confirm these expectations. For all three cases, the percentage differences are statistically significant at better than the .001 level.

The empirical evidence supports our contention that Negroes who are more disengaged from the society, in the structural (isolation) and subjective (powerlessness and racial dissatisfaction) senses, are more likely to view violence as necessary for racial justice than those more firmly tied to the society.

It is one thing to establish a relationship based on action willingness and quite another thing to study actual behavior. Unfortunately, only sixteen of the 312 respondents (5 per cent) admitted par-

TABLE 1   *Percentage Willing to Use Violence, by Social Contact, Powerlessness, and Racial Dissatisfaction*

Variables	Not Willing (%)	Willing (%)	Total (%)
Social contact:*			
High	83	17	100 (N = 192)
Low	56	44	100 (N = 110)
Powerlessness:†			
High	59	41	100 (N = 145)
Low	84	16	100 (N = 160)
Racial dissatis-faction:‡			
High	52	48	100 (N = 98)
Low	83	17	100 (N = 212)

* $\chi^2 = 24.93, P < .001$.
† $\chi^2 = 22.59, P < .001$.
‡ $\chi^2 = 30.88, P < .001$.

NOTE. — In this table and the tables that follow, there are often less than 312 cases due to missing data for one or more variables.

ticipation in violent action for Negro rights. This small number did, however, provide some basis for testing our hypotheses. Of the sixteen who participated in violent action, eleven were isolates while only five had social contact. More impressive is the fact that fifteen of the sixteen "violents" scored high in powerlessness, and thirteen of the sixteen felt high degrees of dissatisfaction. Even with a small number, these are definite relationships, encouraging an interpretation that those who are willing to use violence and those who reported actual violent behavior display the same tendency toward powerlessness, racial dissatisfaction, and isolation.

The next task is to explore the interrelationships among our predictive variables. For example, we have argued that powerlessness has a specific meaning to violence (a low expectancy of changing conditions within the institutional framework) that should be more than a generalized disaffection; that is, we expected our measures of powerlessness and racial dissatisfaction to have somewhat unique effects upon violence.

As a way of noting an interrelationship between our predictive variables, we turn to the test of the isolation-extremism perspective in which the effect of racial isolation upon violence is controlled by powerlessness and dissatisfaction.[5] It will be recalled that we expected the isolated people (with a lower commitment to democratic norms and organized channels) to be more violence-prone when these isolated individuals perceive they cannot shape their destiny within the institutional framework (high powerlessness) or when they perceive differential treatment as Negroes and, as a result, are dissatisfied. It is under these subjective states of mind that a weak attachment to the majority group would seem to be most important to extremism. Table 2, addressed to these predictions, shows our hypotheses to be strongly supported in both cases.

Among the powerless and the dissatisfied, racial isolation has a strong effect upon violence commitment. Conversely, the data show that isolation

[5] The independent variables are moderately intercorrelated. For isolation and powerlessness, the ϕ correlation is .36 $P < .001$; for isolation and disatisfaction, the ϕ is .40, $P < .001$; for powerlessness and dissatisfaction, the ϕ is .33, $P < .001$.

TABLE 2 *Percentage Willing to Use Violence, by Social Contact Controlling for Powerlessness and Racial Dissatisfaction*

| | Percentage Willing to Use Violence | | | |
	Low Power- lessness (%)	High Power- lessness (%)	Low Dis- satisfaction (%)	High Dis- satisfaction (%)
Low contact	23 (N = 31)	53 (N = 78)	23 (N = 47)	59 (N = 63)
High contact	13 (N = 123)	26 (N = 66)	15 (N = 158)	26 (N = 34)
χ^2	P < .20	P = .01	P < .20	P = .01

is much less relevant to violence for those with feelings of control in the system and for the more satisfied (in both cases, significant only at the .20 level).[6]

The fact that isolation (as a cause of violence) produces such a small percentage difference for the less alienated subjects calls for a further word of discussion. Apparently, isolation is not only a stronger predictor of violence for the people who feel powerless and dissatisfied, but is *only* a clear and significant determiner of violence for these subjectively alienated persons. For the relatively satisfied and control-oriented groups, the fact of being isolated is not very important in determining violence. This would suggest that a weak norma- tive bond to the majority group (isolation) is not in itself sufficient to explain the participation of the oppressed minority person in violence and that it is the interaction between isolation and feelings

[6] The .05 level is considered significant in this analysis.

of powerlessness (or racial dissatisfaction) that is crucial for predicting violence.

A final attempt at unification involves the cumu- lative effect of all three of our predictive variables upon violence. Since it was noted that each of the three predictive variables has some effect upon violence (either independently or for specific sub- groups), it seemed logical that the combined effect of the three would produce a high violence pro- pensity. Conceptually, a combination of these var- iables could be seen as ideal types of the alienated and non-alienated Negro. Accordingly, Table 3 ar- ranges the data into these ideal-type combinations.

The group at the top of the table represents the one most detached from society — individuals who are isolated and high in attitudes of powerlessness and dissatisfaction. The group at the bottom of the table is the most involved in the society; these people have intimate white contact, feelings of control, and greater satisfaction with racial condi- tions. The middle group is made up of those with

TABLE 3 *Percentage Willing to Use Violence, by the Combined Effect of Social Contact, Powerlessness, and Racial Dissatisfaction*

	Not Willing (%)	Willing (%)	Total (%)
Ideal-type alienated (low contact, high powerlessness, and high dissatisfaction)	35	65	100 (N = 51)
Middles in alienation	76	24	100 (N = 147)
Ideal-type non-alienated (high contact, low powerless- ness, and low dissatisfaction)	88	12	100 (N = 107)

NOTE. — $\chi^2 = 49.37$; P < .001 (2 d.f.).

TABLE 4 *Percentage Willing to Use Violence by Contact, Powerlessness, and Racial Dissatisfaction, Controlling for Two Geographical Areas and Education*

Independent Variables	Neighborhood		Education	
	South Central–Watts	Crenshaw	Low (High School or Less)	High (Some College)
Low contact	53** (N = 62)	33** (N = 45)	52** (N = 77)	24* (N = 33)
High contact	27 (N = 83)	10 (N = 109)	26 (N = 86)	10 (N = 105)
Low powerlessness	22** (N = 73)	11* (N = 88)	19** (N = 67)	14 (N = 93)
High powerlessness	55 (N = 77)	25 (N = 68)	51 (N = 100)	18 (N = 45)
Low dissatisfaction	26** (N = 81)	12** (N = 130)	22** (N = 96)	12 (N = 114)
High dissatisfaction	53 (N = 68)	39 (N = 28)	59 (N = 73)	17 (N = 24)

* $P < .05$.   ** $P < .01$.

different combinations of high and low detachment. Note the dramatic difference in willingness to use violence between the "ideal-type" alienated group (65 per cent willing) and the group most bound to society (only 12 per cent willing). The "middles" in alienation display a score in violence between these extremes.

Spuriousness

It is possible that the relationship between our predictive variables and violence is due to an intercorrelation with other relevant variables. For example, social class should be related both to violence and to our isolation-alienation measures. In addition, we could expect a greater propensity toward violence in geographical areas where an extreme breakdown of legal controls occurred, such as the South Central and Watts areas (in contrast to the Crenshaw area, where no rioting took place). In such segregated ghettos, violence may have been defined by the inhabitants as a legitimate expression, given their intolerable living conditions, a group definition that could override any effects of isolation or alienation upon violence. In short, it seems essential to control our isolation-alienation variables by an index of social class and by ghetto area.

Because of the rather small violent group, it is necessary to examine our predictive variables separately in this analysis of controls. Table 4 presents the original relationship between each of the independent variables and violence, con-

trolled by two areas of residence: the South Central-Watts area, at the heart of the curfew zone (where violence occurred), and the Crenshaw area, on the periphery (or outside) of the curfew zone (where violent action was rare). In addition, Table 4 includes a control for education, as a measure of social class.

When the ghetto residence of the respondent is held constant, it appears that our independent variables are important in their own right. Education (social class), however, proved to be a more powerful control variable. Among the college educated, only isolation persists as a predictor of violence; powerlessness and racial dissatisfaction virtually drop out. Yet each variable has a very strong effect upon violence among the high school (lower-class) group. In other words, we do not have an instance of spuriousness, where predictive variables are explained away in both partials, but another set of interaction effects — attitudes of powerlessness and dissatisfaction are predictors of violence only among lower-class respondents. These results may be interpreted in several ways. Persons higher in the class structure may have a considerable amount to lose, in terms of occupational prestige and acceptance in white society, by indorsing extreme methods. The college educated (middle class) may be unwilling to risk their position, regardless of feelings of powerlessness and dissatisfaction. These results may further indicate that middle-class norms favoring diplomacy and the use of democratic channels (as opposed to direct aggression) are overriding any tendency toward violence. An extension of this interpretation is that middle-class Negroes may be activists, but non-violent activists, in the civil rights movement. Thus, class norms may be contouring resentment into more organized forms of protest.

CONCLUSIONS

In an attempt to locate the Negro participant in violence, we find that isolated Negroes and Negroes with intense feelings of powerlessness and dissatisfaction are more prone to violent action than those who are less alienated. In addition, isolation has its strongest effect upon violence when individuals feel powerless to control events in the society or when racial dissatisfaction is intensely felt. For those with higher expectations of control or with greater satisfaction regarding racial treatment, isolation has a much smaller and non-significant effect (though in the predicted direction) upon violence. That is, a weak tie with the majority group, per se, appeared insufficient to explain wide-scale participation in extreme action. This study indicates that it is the interaction between a weak bond and a feeling of powerlessness (or dissatisfaction) that is crucial to violent participation.

Viewed another way, the combined or tandem effect of all three predictive variables produces an important profile of the most violence-prone individuals. Negroes who are isolated, who feel powerless, and who voice a strong disaffection because of discrimination appear to be an extremely vola-tile group, with 65 per cent of this stratum willing to use violence (as contrasted to only 12 per cent of the "combined lows" in alienation).

Ghetto area and education were introduced as controls. Each independent variable (taken separately) retained some significant effect upon violence in two geographical areas (dealing with proximity to the Watts violence) and among the less educated respondents. Powerlessness and dissatisfaction, however, had no effect upon violence among the college educated. Several interpretations of this finding were explored.

Applying our findings to the context of the Negro revolt of the last fifteen years, we note an important distinction between the non-violent civil rights activists and the violence-prone group introduced in this study. Suggestive (but non-conclusive) evidence indicates that the participants in organized civil rights protests are more likely to be middle class in origin, to hold considerable optimism for equal rights, and to have greater communication with the majority — this represents a group with "rising expectations" for full equality. In contrast, this study located a very different population — one whose members are intensely dissatisfied, feel powerless to change their position, and have minimum commitment to the larger society. These Negroes have lost faith in the leaders and institutions of the community and presumably have little hope for improvement through organized protest. For them, violence is a means of communicating with white society; anger can be expressed, control exerted — if only for a brief period.

CHAPTER FOUR

Social Processes: Patterns of Interaction and Communication

Role of
Symbols in
Interaction

Man is the only animal with the capacity for rationally coordinating his activities so as to enhance his prospects for achieving designated goals and objectives. Instead of being guided by instincts or by blind subservience to tradition, man can establish social norms designed to regulate his behavior. The secret of man's organizational skill is his ability to use *symbols*. A symbol is any voluntary act, event, or record which through social usage has come to stand for something else. The meanings of symbols are arbitrarily established by social usage. They can stand for objects, events, relationships, or other symbols. Whatever a symbol stands for is the *referent* of that symbol.

Symbols must be distinguished from *natural signs*. Natural signs are historical events over which man has little or no control. They occur regularly in conjunction with subsequent events so that observation of the former results in anticipation of the latter. For example, dark clouds and claps of thunder are signs of rain. By contrast, the words "dark clouds" are a symbol for rain. The essential difference between symbols and signs is that symbols can be produced voluntarily. This enables man, by means of symbols, to discuss events such as rain when the events are not directly present to his senses.

Some symbols stand for objects or events, or for their patterns and sequences. Such symbols have referents in the outside world. The referent for the word "animal," for instance, can be seen, touched, trained, photographed, eaten, and so on. Other symbols, such as the word "leprechaun," stand for imaginary objects that cannot be identified in the flesh as an animal can. As a consequence, the meaning of leprechaun can be designated only in terms of other words or symbols, including drawings, sculptures, paintings, and so on. Symbols that represent other symbols are especially important. Thus, much of logic and mathematics is concerned with the analysis of symbols and their symbolic referents. Logical and mathematical symbols ($=$, $+$, $-$, $\times$) refer to symbolic operations rather than to objects and events in the outside world. Such abstract symbols greatly facilitate the accumulation of knowledge and the growth of science.

Symbols that have acquired conventional meanings within a given society comprise the language of that society. Language includes grammatical rules that tell people how to construct sentences and arguments which make social communication possible. Through language, people can share their experiences and learn from one another. Experiences can be recorded in books and other documents for future analysis and review. In this way the past can be reconstructed and the future contemplated. People's goals and objectives can be precisely formulated, along with plans for their achievement. Alternative courses of action can be examined and evaluated. It seems clear, then, that social organization as we know it today is wholly dependent upon the use of language.

Some
Principles of
Perception and
Cognitive
Organization

The ability to use language does not mean that man has been emancipated from customs and traditions. Language itself is a product of experience and learning. Even man's inventions and innovations are usually relatively minor reorganizations of previous knowledge and practices. There are several reasons for this. First, the meanings of symbols are established by social conventions. They have no intrinsic or inherent meaning. If the word "animal," for instance, were conventionally employed with reference to plants, it would seem entirely natural for us to use the word that way. Thus, man responds to symbols as he does to the rest of his environment. He receives sensory impressions, organizes them so as to give them some meaning, then acts accordingly. The meanings attached to sense impressions depend upon man's experience and learning. This is suggested in the following paradigm of human response.

Sensory input → perceptual organization → motor output

A second reason why man is tied to his past is that there are formal and informal rules governing the assignment of meanings to symbols and to the human experiences symbolized. Man is rarely satisfied by merely observing events that occur. He wants to know how or why they occur. He tries to see law and order in his experiences and observations. He formulates assumptions and theories that enable him to predict and explain the future. Man characteristically jumps to conclusions on the basis of whatever evidence is available.

Consider, for example, the following word:

s ? c i ? l ? g y

The reader will quickly recognize these symbols as comprising the word "sociology," and that the symbol (?) has been substituted for the symbol (o). The context of our preceding discussion makes recognition of the word easy. Studies show that even if certain words in a message are masked by noise, they can easily be recognized if their context is clear enough. For example, the missing word in the following sentence would be recognized even if it were completely obliterated by interference:

"George ——————— was the first President of the United States."

Sometimes formal rules can be employed in assigning meanings to symbolic expressions. For instance, examine the two propositions below:

If A occurs, then B may be expected.
If B occurs, then C may be expected.

Most people can readily go beyond the information given to the inference that:

If A occurs, then C may be expected.

Again, examine the following series of numbers in which one missing number is to be supplied by the reader:

2, 4, ?, 16, 32

As soon as the reader sees that the value of each succeeding number is twice that of its predecessor, he can provide the missing number 8. The context in the last two illustrations suggests the use of formal rules of logic and mathematics. Such rules help us to resolve indeterminate situations. They put our minds at ease by helping us make sense of our observations and experiences. Employment of such formal rules of inference is an essential feature of scientific inquiry.

The above principles of perception and cognitive organization suggest that man often views his world in such a way that its major features tend to be in harmony or balance. Contradictory impressions and unresolved issues seem to be unpleasant. In establishing cognitive balance, we tend to perceive events in such a way that they reinforce our beliefs and attitudes. We respond to situations not as they are but as we perceive them to be. Thus, when Soviet leaders make proposals for world disarmament, we look for possible deceptions and perceive the proposals as carefully planned moves in the Cold War. The same principle is noted in the reactions of people to information on the relation between smoking and lung cancer. Residents of Minneapolis were asked if they thought the relationship between smoking and lung cancer had been proved. The results show that many of the nonsmokers, and only a few of the heavy smokers, believed that the relationship had been proved. People who smoke heavily find it easier to disbelieve that smoking is damaging to their health. In another study, fraternity men were asked to (1) name the men in their group they liked best and liked least, (2) rate themselves on a series of personality traits, and (3) rate the other men on the same series of traits. The evidence indicates that the respondents assumed greater similarity in personality traits between themselves and the people they liked than actually existed. Similar studies show that husbands and wives assume greater similarity between them than actually exists, and this appears to be more true for happily married couples than for those who are not happily married.

It seems "natural" for us to assume that people we like must think and feel as we do. This assumption tends to harmonize or balance our attitudes and impressions. It provides the basic idea in some theories of cognitive balance. These theories help us to predict people's attitudes. Suppose that A and B are close friends. A is a strong supporter of a graduated income tax. He therefore will tend to see B as also favoring such taxes. (See Diagram 1 on page 175.) But if A dislikes B, and if A is a supporter of graduated taxes, he then will tend to see B as opposing them. (Diagram 3.) This is indicated in the following diagrams, where A and B represent two persons and X represents some idea, event, person, or object about which A has a strong opinion. The plus and minus signs represent favorable and unfavorable attitudes of A toward B and X. The broken line at the bottom of each figure illustrates A's perception of B's attitude toward X.

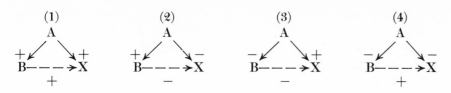

Balanced cognitive states

Note that A's cognitive system is balanced when either all the signs attached to the arrows are positive or only one sign is positive. Otherwise, the system is out of balance. According to the theory, people strive to keep their cognitive systems in balance or to produce balance in systems that are unbalanced.

There is some research evidence that change in people's attitudes tends to occur in such a way as to facilitate cognitive balance. To illustrate, suppose that A has a favorable attitude toward B and also a favorable attitude toward world disarmament. The theory suggests that A would expect B's attitude toward disarmament to be favorable. Now, suppose A hears B make unfavorable comments about disarmament. This puts A's cognitive system out of balance. He can restore balance by rejecting B, by changing his own attitude toward disarmament, or by managing to produce a change in B's attitude. The evidence is that he makes tentative moves in all these directions. While the evidence thus far is by no means conclusive, the theory does seem to have some utility in the understanding of people's perceptions, attitude changes, and interaction patterns.

Communication refers to the processes by which a set of meanings is transmitted from one person or group to another person or group through the use of symbols and gestures. Communication can be analyzed in terms of its source, message content, form, channel or medium, destination, context, goals and objectives, and impact or effect. Research on communication is concerned with the ways in which these factors are interconnected.

Communication and Interaction Processes

The communication *source* is the person, group, or organization that initiates a message. Message *content* is comprised of the ideas, information, or subject matter communicated. It may involve descriptions of observed events, theories and assumptions designed to explain observed events, expressions of opinions and attitudes, or instructions and commands that are directed toward the regulation of human behavior. The *form* of a message must be adapted to its content. Message forms include written or spoken words, Morse code, semaphore signals, music, gestures, and so on. *Channels* include printed texts, graphic displays, films, television, newspapers, radio, phonographic recordings, and similar media. The *destination* of a message is the person, group, organization, or community to which it is directed. *Context* refers to the physical, psychological, social, or cultural conditions surrounding the message. Context, as we have seen, has an important influence on the way a message is interpreted. *Goals* and *objectives* are the purposes for which a message is intended and the anticipated results. Message *impact* or *effect* is determined by the degree to which communication achieves its goal and objectives. Obviously, these factors are frequently connected in subtle and intricate ways. Although there has been a great deal of research on communication, we can indicate here only the most general findings.

Communication always involves the process of *interaction*. Interaction refers to the mutual or reciprocal influences that two or more persons exert on one another through the exchange of symbols, gestures, and so on. The communication source tries to anticipate the responses of the person to whom the message is directed, and prepares the message content and form on the basis of these anticipations. When the receiver gets the message, he interprets and organizes it so as to decide upon its meaning. Of course, the meaning perceived by the receiver may not always be consistent with the meaning intended by the source. Thus, the receiver's response may be different from that intended by the sender. This is why symbols that have conventional and standardized meanings are so important to effective communication.

Much of the communication that occurs in a group or a community involves face-to-face interaction between two persons. Such interaction tends to follow a fairly regular pattern. When strangers interact, they are often very polite and neither interrupts the other. But as they get to know each other, the rate of interaction increases and the interruptions become more frequent. After several hours, the proportion of time each member spends talking usually settles down to a fairly constant amount. The two people approach a stable equilibrium in their interaction pattern. Each person has a relatively constant interaction rate that locates him along a continuum from loquacious to taciturn, even though his behavior is somewhat modified by the characteristics of the person with whom he happens to be interacting in a given situation.

Similar patterns of interaction are observed in small groups comprised of from four to ten or so members. If the group's members are ranked according to the amount of talking each does, a mathematical equation will describe the amount by which participation decreases as rank increases. In addition, the person who sends the most messages is usually the one to whom most of the messages are directed. Again, the person who gives and receives the most messages is likely to direct his comments to the entire group rather than to one specific member. By contrast, the members who give and receive relatively few messages are more likely to direct their comments to a specific person.

Group leaders tend to have high interaction rates. In general, the amount of influence exerted on a group's members varies with the amount of participation. However, two rather distinctive types of leaders have been identified. First, there is the *instrumental* leader whose technical skills and knowledge enable him to help the group achieve its goals and objectives. Second, there are *integrative* leaders who help to boost the group's morale and to solve problems of tension management. In any small group, then, specialized roles tend to develop. Among these are the "instrumental leader," "integrative leader," "follower," and "behind-the-scenes operator." While these roles are not based on any formal rules and regulations, they tend to develop informally in the process of interaction.

Large and complex organizations often find it advisable to *prescribe* channels of communication among their members. For instance, formal rules and regulations make the crew supervisor responsible for the activities of his subordinates. He has authority to make certain decisions for them. The subordinates, in turn, are responsible for carrying out their supervisor's orders and instructions. The supervisor, again, may be responsible to higher management authorities. In relations with these authorities, he may have a subordinate position. The organization's structure — its social positions, channels of communication and authority, and the like — has an important influence on its survival and effectiveness. For this reason a number of experimental studies have attempted to identify the kinds of communication patterns that best serve an organization's instrumental and integrative functions.

In one small-scale experiment, for example, five men were seated around a circular table but were separated from one another by vertical partitions. In the partitions were small slots which could be opened or closed. When the slots were open written messages could be passed through them. By varying the openings, the channels among the five persons could be manipulated so as to produce any desired communication pattern. Four patterns were tested. In the *circular* pattern each person could pass notes to the person on his immediate right and the one on his immediate left. In the *chain* pattern one of the openings was blocked out in order to close one link in the circular pattern. In other words, there were two persons at the end of the chain who could not communicate with each other. The *fork* pattern arranged four of the men in a chain and allowed the fifth member to exchange messages with one inner member of the chain. The *wheel* pattern placed one person at the center of the structure in such a way that he could exchange notes with all four of the other members, but these four could not communicate with one another except through the central person.

The task assigned to the groups in this study was for the members to identify as rapidly as possible a certain symbol held in common by all five members. Each member was given a set of symbols, only one of which was the same in all five sets. Records were kept on the amount of time needed to complete the task, the number of errors, and the number of messages communicated. At the end of the experiment, the members were given a questionnaire to determine how they felt about the communication patterns under which they had operated.

Each communication pattern developed its own special technique for solving the research problem. In the wheel, for example, the peripheral men always sent their information to the central person who discovered the symbol held in common and sent this information back to each peripheral member. In the circle, on the other hand, the members sent repeated messages until each one had all the information and could work out the problem for himself. The different patterns all took approximately the same amount of time to solve the problem. But they differed significantly in the number of errors made. The circle produced the greatest number of errors, while the fork and the wheel had the fewest. Questionnaire responses at the end of the experiment indicated that the men who occupied central positions in the communication patterns enjoyed their work and were recognized as leaders by the others, whereas the men in the peripheral positions had the lowest morale.

Comparison of the circle and wheel patterns shows that the circle was unorganized, unstable, needed the greatest number of messages, made the most mistakes, was leaderless, and was relatively *satisfying* to its members. On the other hand, the wheel pattern was organized, stable, sent few messages, made few mistakes, had a recognized leader, and left four of its five members relatively *dissatisfied* with their jobs. In general, those persons who were recognized as leaders and who felt they were instrumental in solving the problem were the most satisfied. One implication of the study is that efficiency in solving problems is not the only criterion to consider in evaluating alternative communication patterns. It seems that "tall" organizations, in which only a few persons make nearly all the decisions, tend to be deficient in their integrative functions. Relatively "flat" organizations may give the workers a greater sense of participation and accomplishment.

How to attain an appropriate balance between instrumental and integrative functions is a task that confronts all administrators. Also important are questions about the conditions that lead to worker satisfaction, motivation, and conceptions of legitimacy. Accordingly, studies of communication and interaction are having an increasing influence on the structure of modern social systems.

Mass Communication

By *mass communication* we mean the relatively simultaneous exposure of a large, scattered, and heterogeneous audience to messages transmitted by impersonal means from an organized source for whom the audience members are anonymous. The organized sources of mass messages include radio, television, newspapers, magazines, books, motion pictures, and similar media. The capacity of telecommunication systems is increasing tremendously. Microwave systems can process many thousands of messages simultaneously. Electronic devices can read handwriting, transpose spoken into written symbols, and translate communications into many languages. The symbolic equivalent of a person's memory can be stored electronically on a piece of material a few inches square. Satellites in orbit can transmit all kinds of telecommunications instantaneously to any point on the earth's surface. Yet the technology of mass communication is in an early stage of development.

What will be the social effects of this communications "explosion"? Some observers maintain that mass communications are necessarily adapted to the needs and interests of the least sophisticated audience members. They see such media as having a leveling effect that vulgarizes society and fosters social ills such as delinquency and mental illness. Others complain that the mass media are being monopolized by a small group of entrepreneurs who soon will have in their hands the means for "brainwashing" a society. Similarly, the daily diet of TV violence is often blamed for violence on the streets. And some of our political leaders feel that overexposure to the violence of war, as depicted in television news coverage, is largely responsible for negative attitudes toward our foreign military involvements.

There is no essential reason why man's increasing potential for both good and evil should have primarily deleterious results. As used today, mass media seem to be more effective in reinforcing existing habits, beliefs, and attitudes than in working for significant social changes. However, their impact needs further serious study. Among the readings in this chapter, the one by Melvin DeFleur graphically describes the communication system and outlines the main features of many current studies.

PHYSICAL, PERSONAL, SOCIAL, AND CULTURAL DETERMINANTS

26   How the New Suburbia Socializes*

William H. Whyte, Jr.

The conditions under which individuals come together to form small groups and associations is a matter of great interest to social scientists. That it has also been of concern to the general population is attested by such folk sayings as "birds of a feather flock together," "like attracts like," and "opposites marry." Such sayings, of course, tell us little about the actual conditions which lead to the formation of groups. While it is possible to learn more about groups in a laboratory situation, there are also insights to be gained by examining the process of group formation in different types of communities. For example, is there greater group activity among homogeneous populations or among heterogeneous populations? Studies of college housing projects show that in these very homogeneous populations where there is little variation in age, stage of the family cycle, or income, friendships and visiting patterns are largely determined by the physical arrangements of the project — if the placement of apartments, stairs, and paths bring individuals together repeatedly they are likely to become friends. On the other hand, if people living in the next-door apartment use a different stairway and thus offer little contact, they are not likely to be named as friends.

Suburban communities also tend to have homogeneous populations although residents probably differ more from one another than do the students living in university housing projects. The author of

the selection presented here feels that visiting patterns and friendships in the suburbs he has studied develop in much the same way as they do in the housing projects — as a result of spatial arrangements which bring people together. However, on the basis of his report it is not possible to reject completely a psychological explanation for his findings. Perhaps the isolated houses occupied by persons with little participation were selected by individuals who dislike intensive social interaction, whereas the centrally located homes were chosen by persons who like to be involved in all activities. Does this seem to be the likely explanation in this case? How would you design a study which would determine the influence of psychological factors in a situation such as the author describes? Also, if similarity of characteristics is conducive to social interaction and the formation of groups, why is it that there is relatively little "neighboring" among the residents of the apartment house areas in large cities, since these areas also frequently have quite homogeneous populations?

The most striking phenomenon in the new suburbs is that people's friendships, even their most intimate ones, seem predetermined; less on individual personality do friendships depend than on such seemingly inconsequential matters as the placement of a sidewalk, the view out of a picture window, the height of a fence, or the width of a street.

Propinquity, of course, has always been a factor in friendship; after all, you do have to come in contact with people before you can like them. In the new suburbs, however, it has become so powerful a factor that merely by observing certain physical clues of an area a visitor can come amazingly close to predicting who is friends with whom and who isn't. (So close, indeed, that it isn't hard to spot the deviates and the members of the gang.)

. . . As the residents themselves often point out, Park Forest, Illinois, the prototype of the new suburbia, is almost a "laboratory experiment" in social relationships. In designing the rental courts and the homes-for-sale "superblocks" at Park Forest, the architects happened on a basic design that has proved highly functional in shaping people's lives. Just what makes it functional, furthermore, is not too difficult to determine. In

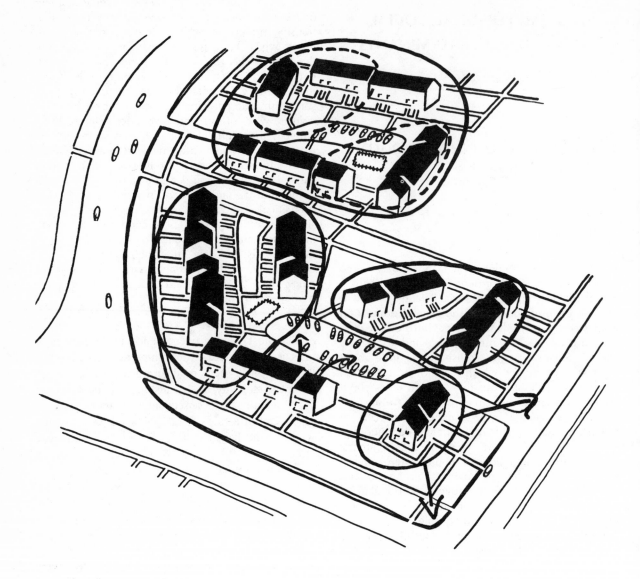

Figure 1

What makes a court clique: *In the rental courts formed around parking bays social life is oriented inward. In the large court at the bottom, for example, wings whose back doors face each other form natural social units. Buildings sited somewhat ambiguously tend to split the allegiance of their inhabitants, or else, like the lonely apartment unit at lower right, isolate them. Smaller courts like the one at the top are usually more cohesive; and though there may be subgroupings, court people often get together as a unit. (Drawing by Miss Miné Okubo, Courtesy of Fortune Magazine)* designing the 105 rental courts the architects staggered the buildings in different fashion in each court; similarly, no two superblocks are laid out exactly alike. By comparing these differences in design with any differences in social activity among areas, one can discover a cause-and-effect relationship.

No two areas have quite the same "character." Some courts have so little *esprit de corps* that the residents get together only occasionally; and in some, feuding and cussedness are chronic. Other courts are notably "outgoing," and though the moving van is constantly bringing in new people and taking out the old ones, the partying, kaffee-klatsching, and the group activity continue un-diminished.

The same is true in the curving superblocks in the homes for sale (price: around $13,000). "We're very lucky here," goes a typical diagnosis. "At the beginning we were so neighborly that your friends knew more about your private life than you did yourself. It's not quite that active now, but it's real friendly — even our dogs and cats are friendly with each other. The street behind us is nowhere near as friendly. They knock on doors over there."

The chance of who happened to land in what block is, of course, important. One of the most habitual mistakes in studying people in groups, let it be conceded, is to forget that they are also individuals, and to treat them instead almost as robots, doing what they do simply because of the external influences of the world around them. But no matter how hard you investigate the effect of individual differences, they fail to explain the social patterns.

Take, for example, a particular group — the forty or forty-five families, say, that live in a cluster of buildings centered around a parking court. Look into the religion of each, their family background, where they were born, how much education they've had, their taste in books and TV, whether or not they drink, what games they like to play. You will find that each one of these considerations somehow affects their friendships. Yet when you try to correlate these factors with the way groups shape up, almost by elimination you are left with only one basic explanation: what really counts is the effect of the physical layout.

THE WELL-DESIGNED GROUP

The way physical design influences social traffic is sometimes capricious; some people, as we will see later, are so ambiguously located that they can never quite be sure who they should be frieids with. By and large, however, the social traffic follows a logical pattern.

It begins with the children. The new suburbs are matriarchies, yet the children are in effect so dictatorial that a term like *filiarchy* would not be entirely facetious. It is the children who set the basic design; their friendships are translated into the mothers' friendships, and these, in turn, to the families'. Fathers just tag along.

Play Areas. Since children have a way of playing where *they* feel like playing, their congregating areas have not turned out to be exactly where elders planned them to be; in the homes area the backyards would seem ideal, and communal play areas have been built in some of them. But the children will have none of them; they can't use their toy vehicles there and so they play on the lawn and pavements out front. In the court areas the children have amenably played in and around the interior parking bay out of traffic's way; the courts' enclosed "tot yards," however, haven't turned out to be functional as was expected; in many courts the older children use them as a barricade to keep the younger children *out*.

It is the flow of wheeled juvenile traffic, then, that determines which is to be the functional door; i.e., in the homes, the front door; in the courts, the back door. It determines, further, the route one takes from the functional door; for when wives go visiting with neighbors they gravitate toward the houses within sight and hearing of their children and the telephone. This crystallizes into the court "checkerboard movement" (i.e., the regular kaffeeklatsch route) and this forms the basis of adult friendships.

Placement of Driveways and Stoops. The ad-joining back porches in the courts and the area around adjacent driveways of homes for sale make a natural sitting, baby-watching, and gossip cen-ter. So strong is the adhesive power of such ad-jacent facilities that people sharing them tend to become close friends even though equidistant neighbors on the other side may have much more in common with them.

Lawns. The front lawn is the thing on which homeowners expend most time, and the sharing of tools, energies, and advice that the lawns provoke tends to make the family friendships go along and across the street rather than over the backyards.

Centrality. The location of one's home in relation to the others not only determines your closest friends; it also virtually determines how popular you will be. The more central one's location, the more social contacts one has. In the streets containing rental apartments there is a constant turnover; yet no matter who moves in or out, the center of activity remains in mid-block, with the people at the ends generally included only in the larger gatherings.

Chronology of Construction. Since a social pattern once established tends to perpetuate itself, the order and direction in which an area is built is an enduring factor. If one side of a street is built first rather than both sides simultaneously, the group tends to organize along rather than across the street. This also helps explain why so little backyard socializing develops; by the time the backyard gets fixed up, the front-lawn pattern has already jelled.

Limitations on Size. One reason it's so important to be centrally placed is that an active group can contain only so many members. By plotting each gathering along any block one discovers that there is usually an inner core of about four to six regulars. Partly because of the size of the living rooms (twenty by fifteen), the full group rarely swells beyond twelve couples, and only in the big functions such as a block picnic are the people on the edges included.

From this one might gather that the rules of the game are fairly simple. They are not. Where, as social leaders chronically complain, do you draw the line?

Physical barriers can provide a sort of limiting point. Streets, for example, are functional for more than traffic; if it is a large street with heavy traffic, mothers will forbid their children to cross it, and by common consent the street becomes a boundary for the adult group. Because of the need for a social line, the effect of even the smallest barrier is multiplied. In courts where the parking bays have two exits, fences have been placed across the middle to block through traffic; only a few feet high, they are as socially impervious as a giant brick wall.

Similarly, the grouping of apartment buildings into wings of a court provides a natural unit whose limits everyone understands. All in all, it seems, the "happiest" groups are those in which no home is isolated from the others — or so sited as to introduce a conflict in the social allegiance of its residents.

Ambiguity is the one thing the group cannot abide. If there is no line the group will invent one. They may settle on an imaginary line along the long axis of the court or, in the homes area, a "barrier" family* will provide a convenient line.

There is common sense behind it. If it's about time you threw a party for your neighbors, the line solves many of your problems for you. Friends of yours who live on the other side understand why they were not invited, and there is no hard feeling.

THE MIDDLE VALUES

People are not yet such pawns of their environment, of course, that physical objective factors are all that determine their social lives. Such characteristics as age have influence. Since most Park Forest couples are in their early thirties, couples much over forty are often so far removed in taste and interests that they do not mesh with the group. Teen-agers are also likely to be lonely.

Whether one drinks or not can be critical; in some courts the groups split along drinking and non-drinking lines, as well as along the usual geographic ones. Bridge playing is another factor; and when those who play bridge a lot speak of neighbors who are more given to pinochle, they often speak with a trace of condescension.

* EDITOR'S NOTE. Barrier families are non-participating or feuding families which are not usually involved in the neighborhood's social gatherings.

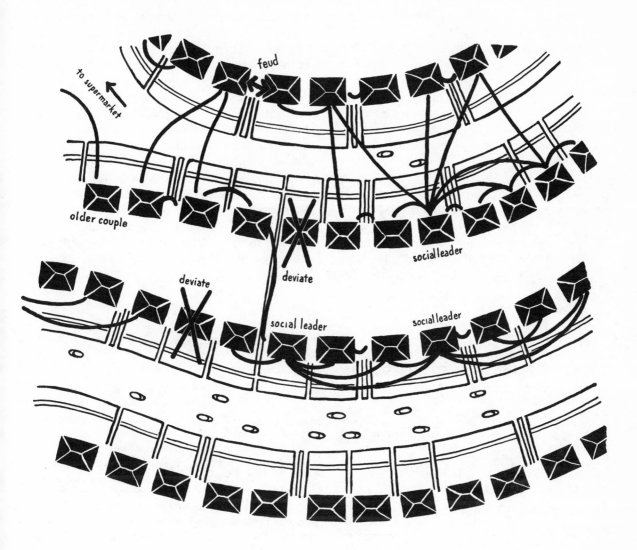

Figure 2

How homeowners get together: *(1) Individuals tend to become most friendly with neighbors whose driveways adjoin theirs. (2) Deviates or feuding neighbors tend to become boundaries of the gang. (3) People in the most central positions make the greatest number of social contacts. (4) Street width and traffic determine whether or not people make friends across the street. (5) People make friends with those in back of them only where some physical feature creates traffic — such as the short-cut pavement one woman on the lower street uses on her way to the supermarket. (Drawing by Miss Miné Okubo, Courtesy of Fortune Magazine)*

But the remarkable aspect of friendship in the new suburbia is how much it transcends such personal characteristics. Despite the great number of occupational and company ties, closest friendships generally have not crystallized this way; after dark, even the car pool loses its pull.

The fact that these different kinds of people can mix so easily is due largely to the great spread of American middle-class values. But it is also due to an active effort the people make to meet one another half way. Just as the Bunco player may put his mind to mastering bridge, so the Ph.D's wife learns to have fun at a coffee; just as the Fundamentalist learns to unbend with a tentative risqué story and beer now and then, so his neighbors tone down their own stories. . . .

This seeking of common values applies markedly to religion. The neighborhood friendship patterns would be impossible unless religious beliefs had lost much of their segregating effect. Indeed, the tolerance has become an almost active one. Several people of other faiths, for example, have joined the National Council of Jewish Women; they like its discussion programs (e.g., the current one on mental health), and they feel no conflict with their own beliefs. The tolerance pervades day-to-day life. "When Will and Ada had to dash East last month — they're devout Catholics — I took care of little Johnny for them," recalls one non-Catholic. "It really tickled me. Here I was picking Johnny up at St. Irenaeus school every afternoon and seeing to it that he said his Rosary every night before he went to bed." Park Forest abounds with such stories, and the good will implicit in them is real. . . .

27   The Nature of Personal Influence*

Paul F. Lazarsfeld · Bernard Berelson

Hazel Gaudet

What are the factors that influence the political decisions of voters? Does a voter choose a certain candidate because of the comments the candidate makes in political speeches? Is the space and time devoted to a candidate by the press and the radio of great importance? Or are voters more influenced by the opinions of their friends and associates? The following study by Paul Lazarsfeld and his associates is based on data collected from a sample of voters in Erie County, Ohio, during the presidential campaign of 1940. According to the evidence, personal contacts were particularly important in influencing the decisions of persons who had not decided for

* From Paul F. Lazarsfeld, Bernard Berelson, and Hazel Gaudet, *The People's Choice,* second edition, New York, Columbia University Press, 1948, pp. 150–158. Reprinted by permission. (Copyright, 1944, 1948, Columbia University Press.)

whom to vote. Some possible reasons for the effectiveness of personal contacts are described.

Remember that television was not a factor in the 1940 election. Today we often think of television as providing an immediacy, intimacy, and personal touch that can be equalled only by face-to-face contact. Had television been available in 1940, would the results of the study have been different? Note that in the 1968 campaign, despite the extensive use of television, a great deal of emphasis was placed on personal contact, including "pressing the flesh," Lyndon Johnson's term for the handshaking ritual. The widespread use of volunteers, such as the students who went from door to door urging people to vote for Eugene McCarthy, also suggests that the study's conclusions are still regarded as valid by politicians despite the technological developments in mass communication since 1940. What is your assessment of the relative importance of communication technology and personal contact in determining political behavior?

The political homogeneity of social groups is promoted by personal relationships among the same kinds of people. But for a detailed and systematic study of the influence of such relationships — the political role of personal influence — a systematic inventory would be needed of the various personal contacts and political discussions that people had over a sample number of days. That would provide an index of personal exposure similar to the indices of exposure to the formal media developed in previous chapters. Such complete data are not available in the present study, but enough information has been collected to indicate the importance of personal relationships so far as their direct political influence is concerned. Our findings and impressions will be summarized without much formal statistical data. The significance of this area of political behavior was highlighted by the study but further investigation is necessary to establish it more firmly.

Personal Contacts Reach the Undecided. Whenever the respondents were asked to report on their recent exposure to campaign communications of all kinds, political discussions were mentioned more frequently than exposure to radio or print. On any average day, at least 10 per cent more people participated in discussions about the election — either actively or passively — than listened to a major speech or read about campaign items in a newspaper. And this coverage "bonus" came from just those people who had not yet made a final decision as to how they would vote. Political conversations, then, were more likely to reach those people who were still open to influence.

For example, people who made up their minds later in the campaign were more likely to mention personal influences in explaining how they formed their final vote decision. Similarly, we found that the less interested people relied more on conversations and less on the formal media as sources of information. Three-fourths of the respondents who at one time had not expected to vote but were finally "dragged in" mentioned personal influence. After the election, the voters were given a check list of sources from which they got most of the information or impressions that caused them to form their judgment on how to vote. Those who had made some change during the campaign mentioned friends or members of their family relatively more frequently than did the respondents who kept a constant vote intention all through the campaign.

The Two-Step Flow of Communications. A special role in the network of personal relationships is played by the "opinion leaders." We noted that they engaged in political discussion much more than the rest of the respondents. But they reported that the formal media were more effective as sources of influence than personal relationships. This suggests that ideas often flow from radio and print to the opinion leaders and from them to the less active sections of the population.

Occasionally, the more articulate people even pass on an article or point out the importance of a radio speech. Repeatedly, changers referred to reading or listening done under some personal influence. Take the case of a retired school teacher who decided for the Republicans: "The country is ripe for a change — Willkie is a religious man. A friend read and highly recommended Dr. Poling's article in the October issue of the *Christian Herald* called, 'The Religion of Wendell Willkie.' "

So much for the "coverage of personal contacts." The person-to-person influence reaches the ones who are more susceptible to change, and serves as a bridge over which formal media of communications extend their influence. But in addition, personal relationships have certain psychological advantages which make them especially effective in the exercise of the "molecular pressures" finally leading to the political homogeneity of social groups. We turn now to a discussion of five such characteristics.

Non-purposiveness of Personal Contacts. The weight of personal contacts upon opinion lies, paradoxically, in their greater casualness and non-purposiveness in political matters. If we read or tune in a speech, we usually do so purposefully, and in doing so we have a definite mental set which tinges our receptiveness. Such purposive behavior is part of the broad area of our political experiences to which we bring our convictions with a desire to test them and strengthen them by what is said. This mental set is armor against influence. The extent to which people, and particularly those with strong partisan views, listen to speakers and read articles with which they agree in advance is evidence on this point.

On the other hand, people we meet for reasons other than political discussion are more likely to catch us unprepared, so to speak, if they make politics the topic. One can avoid newspaper stories and radio speeches simply by making a slight effort, but as the campaign mounts and discussion intensifies, it is hard to avoid some talk of politics. Personal influence is more pervasive and less self-selective than the formal media. In short, politics gets through, especially to the indifferent, much more easily through personal contacts than in any other way, simply because it comes up unexpectedly as a sideline or marginal topic in a casual conversation. For example, there was the restaurant waitress who decided that Willkie would make a poor president after first thinking he would be good. She said: "I had done a little newspaper reading against Willkie, but the real reason I changed my mind was from hearsay. So many people don't like Willkie. Many customers in the restaurant said Willkie would be no good." Notice that she was in a position to overhear bits of conversation that were not intended for her. There are many such instances. Talk that is "forbidden fruit" is particularly effective because one need not be suspicious as to the persuasive intentions of the speakers; as a result one's defenses are down. Furthermore, one may feel that he is getting the viewpoint of "people generally," that he is learning how "different people" think about the election.

Such passive participation in conversation is paralleled in the case of the formal media by accidental exposure, e.g., when a political speech is heard because it follows a favorite program. In both conversation and the formal media, such chance communication is particularly effective. And the testimony to such influence is much more frequent in the case of personal contacts. The respondents mentioned it time and again: "I've heard fellows talk at the plant — I hear men talk at the shop — My husband heard that talked about at work —"

Flexibility When Countering Resistance. But suppose we do meet people who want to influence us and suppose they arouse our resistance. Then personal contact still has one great advantage compared with other media; the face-to-face contact can counter and dislodge such resistance, for it is much more flexible. The clever campaign worker, professional or amateur, can make use of

a large number of clues to achieve his end. He can choose the occasion at which to speak to the other fellow. He can adapt his story to what he presumes to be the other's interests and his ability to understand. If he notices the other is bored, he can change the subject. If he sees that he has aroused resistance, he can retreat, giving the other the satisfaction of a victory, and come back to his point later. If in the course of the discussion he discovers some pet convictions, he can try to tie up his argument with them. He can spot the moments when the other is yielding, and so time his best punches.

Neither radio nor printed page can do anything of the kind. They must aim their propaganda shots at the whole target instead of just at the center, which represents any particular individual. In propaganda as much as in other things, one man's meat is another man's poison. This may lead to boomerang effects, when arguments aimed at "average" audiences with "average" reactions fail with Mr. X. The formal media produced several boomerangs upon people who resented what they read or heard and moved in the opposite direction from that intended. But among the 58 respondents who mentioned personal contacts as concretely influential, there was only one boomerang. The flexibility of the face-to-face situation undoubtedly accounted for their absence.

Rewards of Compliance. When someone yields to a personal influence in making a vote decision, the reward is immediate and personal. This is not the case in yielding to an argument via print or radio. If a pamphlet argues that voting for the opposite party would be un-American or will jeopardize the future, its warning may sound too remote or improbable. But if a neighbor says the same things, he can "punish" one immediately for being unimpressed or unyielding; he can look angry or sad, he can leave the room and make his fellow feel isolated. The pamphlet can only intimate or describe future deprivations; the living person can create them at once.

Of course, all this makes personal contacts a powerful influence only for people who do not like to be out of line. There are certainly some people who gain pleasure from being nonconformists, but under normal circumstances they are probably very much in the minority. Whenever propaganda by another person is experienced as an expression of the prevailing group tendencies, it has greater chances of being successful than the formal media because of social rewards. For example, here is a woman who was for Roosevelt until the middle of the campaign: "I have always been a Democrat and I think Roosevelt has been all right; but my family are all for Willkie. They think he would make the best president and they have been putting the pressure on me." She finally voted for Willkie. This aspect of personal contacts was especially important for women.

The rewards of compliance to other people are learned in early childhood. The easiest way for most children to avoid discomfort is to do what others tell them to do. Someone who holds no strong opinions on politics and hence makes up his mind late in the campaign may very well be susceptible to personal influences because he has learned as a child to take them as useful guides in unknown territory. The young man who was going to vote for Roosevelt because "my grandfather will skin me if I don't" is a case in point.

Trust in an Intimate Source. More people put reliance upon their personal contacts to help them pick out the arguments which are relevant for their own good in political affairs than they do in the more remote and impersonal newspaper and radio. The doubtful voter may feel that the evaluations he reads or hears in a broadcast are plausible, for the expert writer can probably spell out the consequences of voting more clearly than the average citizen. But the voter still wonders whether these are the issues which are really going to affect his own future welfare. Perhaps these sources see the problem from a viewpoint entirely different from his own. But he can trust the judgment and evaluation of the respected people among his associates. Most of them are people with the same status and interests as himself. Their attitudes are more relevant for him than the judgments of an unknown editorial writer. In a formal communication the content can be at its best; but in a face-to-face contact the transference is most readily achieved. For example, here is the case of a young laborer who professed little or no interest in the campaign and who did not even expect to vote until late October: "I've been discussing the election with the fellows at the shop and I believe I'll vote, but I haven't decided yet who for." His constant exposure to the views of his fellow-workers not only brought him to the ballot booth but also brought out his final Democratic vote in line with his colleagues.

A middle-aged woman who showed great interest in the campaign was undecided until late October and then voted for Willkie: "I was talking politics just this morning with a friend, a businessman. He says business will improve if Willkie is elected and that Willkie promises to keep us out of the war. F. D. R. is getting too much power. He shouldn't have a third term." Her friend had apparently run out for her what amounted to a small catalogue of Republican arguments and he was impressive enough to clinch her vote, which had been in the balance throughout the campaign. Her trust in his judgment settled her mind.

Trust in another person's point of view may be due to his prestige as well as to the plausibility of what he has to say or its relevancy to one's interests. It is obvious that in all influences prestige plays a considerable role. The degree of conformity is greater the higher the prestige of the person in our group who seeks to influence us. The plausibility of the consequences he presents will seem greater if he is important. (Of course, the formal media are also important in this respect.) The heightening of trust through the prestige of certain personal contacts was clear in the case of the driver of a bread truck who changed to Willkie because the prominent president of a business firm had done him the honor of persuading him to that direction. Then, too, there is the case of a middle-aged housewife with little education who was for Willkie from May through September, became undecided in October, and finally voted for Roosevelt. She left Willkie because of the statement of people whom she considered authorities: "I talked with a college student from Case, in Cleveland, and students are for Roosevelt because he has helped recreation. I talked, too, with a man from Chicago who is very interested in politics, and he doesn't seem to think that Willkie is a big enough man to handle international affairs."

Persuasion Without Conviction. Finally, personal contacts can get a voter to the polls without affecting at all his comprehension of the issues of the election — something the formal media can rarely do. The newspaper or magazine or radio must first be effective in changing attitudes related to the action. There were several clear cases of votes cast not on the issues or even the personalities of the candidates. In fact, they were not really cast for the candidates at all. They were cast, so to speak, for the voters' friends.

"I was taken to the polls by a worker who insisted that I go."

"The lady where I work wanted me to vote. She took me to the polls and they all voted Republican so I did too."

In short, personal influence, with all its overtones of personal affection and loyalty, can bring to the polls votes that would otherwise not be cast or would be cast for the opposing party just as readily if some other friend had insisted. They differ from the formal media by persuading uninterested people to vote in a certain way without giving them a substantive reason for their vote. Fully 25 per cent of those who mentioned a personal contact in connection with change of mind failed to give a real issue of the campaign as a reason for the change, but only 5 per cent of those who mentioned the formal media omitted such a reason. When personal influence is paramount in this way, the voter is voting mainly for the personal friend, not the candidate.

Practical Implications. In a way the outcome of the election in Erie County is the best evidence for the success of face-to-face contacts. It so happened that for some time the Republican machine in that area worked much more vigorously than its Democratic opponent. When asked whether they knew people who had good ideas about politics, our respondents mentioned considerably more Republican than Democratic local politicians. A few people who did not expect to vote but finally went to the polls mentioned Republican canvassers as the main influence, but we could not trace a similar success for the Democratic machine.

However, one should not identify the personal contacts discussed with the efforts of the professional political machines. These personal contacts are what one might call amateur machines which spring up during elections — individuals who become quite enthusiastic or special groups that try to activate people within their reach. One might almost say that the most successful form of propaganda — especially last-minute propaganda — is to "surround" the people whose vote decision is still dubious so that the only path left to them is the way to the polling booth. We do not know how the budget of the political parties is distributed among different channels of propaganda, but we suspect that the largest part of any propaganda budget is spent on pamphlets, radio time, etc. But our findings suggest the task of finding the best ratio between money spent on formal media and money spent on organizing the face-to-face influences, the local "molecular pressures" which vitalize the formal media by more personal interpretation and the full richness of personal relationships into the promotion of the causes which are decided upon in the course of an election.

In the last analysis, more than anything else people can move other people. From an ethical point of view this is a hopeful aspect in the serious social problem of propaganda. The side which has the more enthusiastic supporters and which can mobilize grass-root support in an expert way has great chances of success.

28 An Experimental Investigation of Group Influence*

Solomon E. Asch

The following classical experiment demonstrates the influence that groups can exert upon their individual members. It shows that even relatively mild forms of group pressure can induce certain persons to misrepresent situations that are obvious under ordinary circumstances, and, in effect, to call white black. How does one explain the errors of perception and judgment that were observed in the study? What are possibly some of the personal and social sources of variation in individual responses to group pressure? Is there anything in the structure of society, the patterns of friendship, or the processes of education that may contribute to the study's outcome? What, if anything, can the social sciences do to enhance the validity of human perceptions, and should anything be attempted in this regard?

The rationale of the investigation[1] I am about to describe was simple and also extreme. We placed a person in the position of a minority of one within a majority that contradicted him about an obvious, easily perceived matter of fact. The object of judgment was present in the field of observation, and the members of the majority were also directly present. The minority and majority were required to announce their judgments publicly. These circumstances generated a conflict within the minority of one, who was the critical subject. The object of the study was to trace the course and outcome of the conflict, and to observe its

* From *Symposium on Preventive and Social Psychiatry,* 15–17 April 1957, Walter Reed Army Institute of Research. Washington, D.C.: U.S. Govt. Printing Office.

[1] This account is based on the following published studies: (1) S. E. Asch, *Social Psychology,* ch. 16, Prentice Hall, 1952; (2) "Effects of Group Pressure upon the Modification and Distortion of Judgments," in *Groups, Leadership and Men* (H. Guetzkow, ed.), Carnegie Press, 1951; (3) "Studies of Independence and Conformity: I. A Minority of One Against a Unanimous Majority," *Psychological Monographs,* Vol. 70, No. 416, 1956.

dependence upon a number of conditions that were systematically varied.

PLAN OF INVESTIGATION

The plan of the investigation required a special kind of majority, one that cooperated with the experimenter. The members of the majority had been instructed in advance to announce judgments (from time to time) that were in fact wrong, and to do so unanimously. This was a *wrong* majority. The critical subject was the only member of the group naïve to these proceedings. Thus, whenever the majority and the minority of one were in disagreement, the former was going contrary to observation and the latter was reporting faithfully.

The object of judgment was of little interest *per se* except for the consequences it engendered. The task was one of matching the lengths of lines under optimal conditions. The group was shown a line, which we will call the standard, and next to it three lines of clearly different lengths, one of which was equal to the standard. The instructions were to select, from among the three comparison lines, the one equal to the standard. The comparison lines were numbered 1, 2, and 3, and the members of the group announced their judgments, by calling out the correct number, in the order in which they were seated. When the judgments were completed, the stimuli were removed and replaced by a new set of standard and comparison lines (see figure 1).

The critical subject was seated toward the end of the group. He always heard all but one of the majority report their judgments before his turn came to respond.

The task of discrimination was easy, the comparison lines differing substantially in length. The errors of the majority were considerable, ranging between ¾ inch and 1¾ inches. Further, the majority was not consistent in its errors on successive occasions; it both underestimated and overestimated. Table 1 contains the lengths of the lines and the judgments of the majority.

The subjects were male college students, ranging in age from 17 to 25; the mean age was 20. They were drawn from three educational institutions. The members of the majority, who numbered in

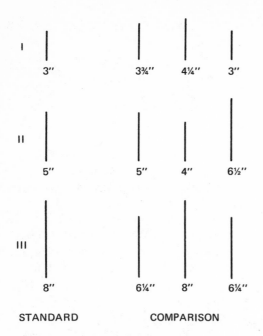

STANDARD   COMPARISON

Figure 1

Critical comparisons

size from 7 to 9, were also students drawn from the same institutions. There were 123 critical subjects.

To complete the present account it should be mentioned that each subject was interviewed carefully at the conclusion of the experiment, and that in the course of the interview a full disclosure and explanation of the reasons for the procedure was made.

Contradictory Demands of Situation. This situation placed contradictory demands upon the critical subject. On the one side was a clearly perceived relation to which he had direct access, and which he had undertaken to judge correctly. On the other side was the unanimous opinion of a majority of peers, whose competence and trustworthiness he had reason to take for granted. Further, the contradiction was irreconcilable; there was no alternative or compromise that might overcome the disagreement. Since there was no discussion during the experiment, there was no possibility of persuading or of being persuaded. The contradiction was also in an important respect understandable; as long as the subject remained naïve, and this was the rule, there was no possibil-

ity of explaining the disagreement. Since the situation was self-contained, it was not easy to refer the disagreement to outer conditions. Finally, the subject was under the necessity of taking a stand. He could not escape, postpone, or delegate responsibility.

These circumstances defined the alternatives open to the critical subject. He could stand by the evidence of his senses, but this was tantamount to declaring that the unanimous majority was in error. Or he could follow the majority, but this he could do only by suppressing the testimony of his experience.

Results

The main results are summarized in Figure 2. (1) Let us note first that a control group, judging the relations in question without the benefit of a misleading majority, was overwhelmingly accurate; under this condition errors comprised less than 1 percent of all judgments. (2) The unanimous majority produced a marked distortion: one-third of the judgments were errors in the direction of the majority. This is an important result when one considers the character of the task and the quality of the subjects. One should not, however, ignore the fact that the preponderance of judgments was independent under this condition of stress. (3) Perhaps more significant was the great

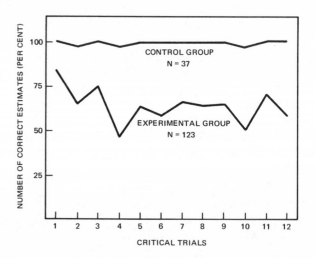

Figure 2

Correct estimates on successive critical trials: experimental and control groups.

TABLE 1   *Majority Responses to Standard and Comparison Lines on Successive Trials. (from Asch.*)*

Trial	Length of standard (in inches)	Length of comparison lines (in inches)			Majority error (in inches)	Type of error
a*	10	8¾	10	8	0	
b*	2	2	1	1½	0	
1	3	**3¾**	4¼	3	+¾	Moderate.
2	5	5	**4**	6½	−1	Do.
c*	4	3	5	4	0	
3	3	**3¾**	4¼	3	+1¼	Extreme.
4	8	**6¼**	8	6¾	−1¼	Moderate.
5	5	5	**4**	6½	+1½	Extreme.
6	8	**6¼**	8	6¾	−1¾	Do.
d*	10	8¾	10	8	0	
e*	2	2	1	1½	0	
7	3	**3¾**	4¼	3	+¾	Moderate.
8	5	5	**4**	6½	−1	Do.
f*	4	3	5	4	0	
9	3	3¾	**4¼**	3	+1¼	Extreme.
10	8	**6¼**	8	6¾	−1¼	Moderate.
11	5	5	**4**	6½	+1½	Extreme.
12	8	**6¼**	8	6¾	−1¾	Do.

* Letters of the first column designate "neutral" trials, or trials to which the majority responded correctly. The numbered trials were "critical," i.e., the majority responded incorrectly. Boldface figures designate the incorrect majority responses. Trials d to 12 are identical with trials a to 6; they followed each other without pause.

range of individual differences. A proportion of the subjects remained independent throughout the experiment; others vacillated between the majority and independence; still others went with the majority as often, or almost as often, as the conditions permitted. The data concerning individual differences appear in Table 2.

The performances of the subjects showed a high degree of internal consistency. Those who were independent in the early part of the experiment tended to remain independent, and similarly for those who went with the majority at the outset.

Effect of Variation in Size of Majority. The effect here described was also studied with majorities differing in size. In successive experiments we varied the size of the opposition from 1 to 15; each condition required, of course, different critical subjects. The results may be summarized as follows: (1) The full effect was obtained with a majority of three. An increase of the majority beyond this point, up to the limit of 15, failed to alter the level. (2) An opposition of two, the smallest majority, reduced the compliance to one-third of the maximum. (3) An opposition of one produced a small but telltale effect. The level of errors was 2.7 percent of all judgments, a slight but nevertheless distinct increase in comparison with the control conditions.

From these findings we may draw a few conclusions. First, the sheer size of majority opposition, while an important condition, is not wholly decisive. Beyond a point that is soon reached, further increases of size are without effect. This statement refers, of course, to the present conditions, but it may have implications for other situations. Second, the data confirm and extend the conclusions reached earlier about the scope of individual differences. There were individuals who

TABLE 2 *Distribution of Errors in Experimental and Control Groups.*

Number of errors	Control group (N = 37)	Group I (N = 70)	Group II (N = 25)	Group III (N = 28)	All experimental groups (N = 123)
		Experimental groups			
0	35	17	5	7	29
1	1	4	2	2	8
2	1	7	1	2	10
3		12	1	4	17
4		3	1	2	6
5		5	2	0	7
6		2	4	1	7
7		3	0	1	4
8		7	4	2	13
9		3	2	1	6
10		4	1	1	6
11		2	0	2	4
12		1	2	3	6
Mean	0.08	4.01	5.16	4.71	4.41
Median	0.00	3.00	5.50	3.00	3.00
Mean percent	0.7	33.4	43.0	39.3	36.8

acted more independently against an opposition of 15 than others who faced an opposition of 2.

DISCUSSION

From a theoretical and from a human point of view the writer is inclined to regard seriously the following experimental variations. The conditions described earlier were retained exactly, except for one detail. There were now two critical subjects in the experimental situation, opposed by a majority of seven to nine. (In a further variation the naïve subject was provided with a "partner" who was instructed to respond accurately without exception.) In short, we altered the situation of the critical subject by putting him in the position of a minority of two. This seemingly small alteration had a profound effect; indeed, it robbed the erring majority of most of its power. Although the critical subjects continued to face the opposition of a substantial majority, they maintained in the presence of a partner a high level of independence.

Not only did conforming responses drop to 10.4 and 5.5 percent, respectively; the degree of compliance of any one subject was strictly curtailed under these conditions. There were very few individuals who went with the majority more than two or three times when another person sided with them. The majority was still exerting a measurable effect, but one that had been drastically reduced.

We conclude that the vulnerability of the minority-of-one condition is to be traced to the special quality of loneness it created. The presence of one other voice testifying to the individual's sense of rightness sufficed to strengthen and protect him from the opposition of an arbitrary majority.

We have spoken of a special, indeed an unusual, situation. It follows that we have studied independence and conformity under highly particular conditions, and that the content and significance of these terms will alter strongly with changing circumstances. It is not hard to think of independence that is irresponsible, of conformity that requires courage. Nevertheless, the present observations make contact with processes of consequence in social life, and investigations of this order may sharpen our thinking and help in finding answers to questions that are important. There are circumstances when the welfare of the individual and the group requires that each should act according to his conviction. Indeed, a human community depends on its members to contribute of their thinking and feeling. When this source of mutual correction and enlightenment is weakened, the social process is disturbed at its foundations; both the individual and the group are damaged.

29   The Development of Social Norms*

Muzafer Sherif

Wherever people live together they tend to develop standardized ways of doing things. They acquire the same speech, similar modes of dress, and fairly uniform beliefs and attitudes regarding a variety of subjects. These habits and customs serve as behavior prescriptions which indicate how the members of the community are supposed to act in different situations. Frequently such standards and prescriptions are called *social norms*.

It is important for the sociologist to learn how social norms arise. Some norms, of course, are established by religious authority or legislative decree. Others may be pronounced by powerful persons backed by force and violence, if necessary. Many of our more important norms arise out of habit and custom; they are simply repetitive and traditional ways of doing things. Fundamental to all norms, however, are social pressures resulting from persons communicating and interacting with each other. Inevitably people make judgments about things and communicate these judgments to others. Subtle though this process of communication may sometimes be, it nevertheless influences our perception of events. Consider, for example, how much our judgment of social issues, politicians, and other public issues and events is conditioned by the attitudes expressed by our associates.

The following study is an attempt to investigate the genesis of a social norm or group judgment. The study clearly demonstrates two important principles of social behavior: (1) our responses to a specific stimulus tend to become standardized; and (2) our responses to, and perception of, a specific stimulus are greatly influenced by group pressures.

Coming to concrete life situations, we find norms wherever we find an organized society, primitive or complicated. These norms serve as focal points in the experience of the individual, and subsequently as guides for his actions. This need not always be a conscious function; many times it is effective without our awareness of it. We see the evidence of its effectiveness by its results, that is, in the behavior of the individual. The daily routine of everyday life is regulated to a large extent by the social norms in each society. As long as life with its many aspects is well settled and runs more or less smoothly from day to day, very few doubt the validity of the existing norms; very few challenge their authority. And the few who challenge them are considered to be doubting Thomases, eccentrics, trouble makers, or lunatics, and are reacted against with varying degrees of scorn or violence.

But when social life becomes difficult and there are stresses and tensions in the lives of many people in the community, the equilibrium of life ceases to be stable, and the air is pregnant with possibilities. Among such stresses may be widespread hunger, or unbearable living conditions due to the rigidity of norms that have come down as survivals from past generations and no longer satisfy the requirements of life, or the ruthless suppression or exploitation of one part of the population by the other. Or such stresses may be due to the alarm aroused by a common real or imagined danger that people face together. Under these delicate conditions the strength of the norms incorporated in the individuals becomes uncertain and liable to break down. Such a delicate, unstable situation is the fertile soil for the rise of doubts concerning the existing norms, and a challenge to their authority. The doubt and the challenge, which no one would listen to before, now become effective. These are times of transition from one state to another. The transition is not simply from the orderliness of one set of norms to chaos, but from one set of norms to a new set of norms, perhaps through a stage of uncertainty, confusion, and at times even violence. In such periods the principles and slogans formulated previously by a then eccentric person or group may be revived by others and propagated easily. Discussions and meetings take place; the interested active parties sharpen their principles and slogans, and endeavor to make these the guides of action for the masses as they urge the people to do their part.

As a result of the strain and stress, of the confusion and uncertainty and feeling of insecurity, there may be action and reaction, apparent stability followed by fresh instability. The outcome is the final emergence or establishment of a stable set of norms having the status of standards. The emergence and standardization of the norms is never an arbitrary process; it is as deterministic as any other lawful process in nature, the causes of which lie in the actual conditions which have given rise to the instability. Henceforth this new set of norms supplants the old ones and becomes the regulator of social life. It suffices us to remember some of the important transitions from one historical period to another in the life of any community with which one is intimately familiar.

Experimental Approach. The study of the process of emergence or standardization of norms in actual life situations is an extremely complicated task. There are so many variables involved that cannot be directly observed. It may, therefore, pay us in the long run to start first with the study of the psychology of norm formation in a general way in a well-controlled laboratory situation. Yet what we shall undertake is really the study of the general psychological process involved in the formation of any norm. The test for such an approach lies in the applicability of the principle reached to the description and explanation of norms found in actual social life. Whether or not this is just one more psychological abstraction or laboratory artifact, which does not have anything to do with the true psychology of the formation of norms that are effective in everyday life, can be decided after it has met facts in the fresh and wholesome air of actualities.

Hypothesis To Be Tested. If a reference point is lacking in the external field of stimulation, it is established internally as the temporal sequence of presentation of stimuli goes on.

Accordingly we raise the problem: What will an individual do when he is placed in an objectively unstable situation in which all basis of comparison, as far as the external field to stimulation is concerned, is absent?

We must first study the tendency of the individual. We must begin with the individual in order to do away with the dualism between "individual psychology" and "social psychology." In this way we can find the differences between individual responses in the individual situation and in the group situation.

Coming to the social level we can push our problem further. What will a group of people do in the same unstable situation? Will the different individuals in the group give a hodge-podge of judgments? Or will they establish a collective frame of reference? If so, of what sort? If every person establishes a norm, will it be his own norm and different from the norms of others in the group? Or will there be established a common norm peculiar to the particular group situation and depending upon the presence of those individuals together and their influence upon one another? If they in time come to perceive the uncertain and unstable situation which they face in common in such a way as to give it some sort of order, perceiving it as ordered by a frame of reference developed among them in the course of the experiment, and if this frame of reference is peculiar to the group, then we may say that we have at least the prototype of the psychological process involved in the formation of a norm in a group.

The Autokinetic Effect. With these considerations clearly in mind, our first task was to find objectively unstable situations that would permit themselves to be structured in several ways, depending on the character of the subjectively established reference points. From among other possible experimental situations that could be used to test our hypothesis, we chose to use the situations that are suitable to produce subjective rhythm and autokinetic effects.

The conditions that produce the autokinetic effect afford an excellent experimental situation to test our hypothesis. We can easily get the autokinetic effect. In complete darkness, such as is found in a closed room that is not illuminated, or on a cloudy night in the open when there are no other lights visible, a single small light seems to move, and it may appear to move erratically in all directions. If you present the point of light repeatedly to a person, he may see the light appearing at different places in the room each time, especially if he does not know the distance between himself and the light. The experimental production of the autokinetic effect is very easy and works without any exceptions, provided, of course, that the person does not use special devices to destroy the effect. For in a completely dark room a single point of light cannot be localized definitely, because there is nothing in reference to which you can locate it. The effect takes place even when the person looking at the light knows perfectly well that the light is not moving. These are facts which are not subject to controversy; anyone can easily test them for himself. In this situation not only does the stimulating light appear erratic and irregular to the subject, but at times the person himself feels insecure about his spatial bearing. This comes out in an especially striking way if he is seated in a chair without a back and is unfamiliar with the position of the experimental room in the building. Under these conditions some subjects report that they are not only confused about the location of the point of light; they are even confused about the stability of their own position.

We have studied the influence of such social factors as *suggestion* and the *group situation* on

the extent and direction of the experimental movement. The study of the extent of the experienced movement permits a quantitative study for the approach to the formation of norms. We shall therefore report on the extent of movement.

Method. The experiments were carried on in dark rooms in the Columbia psychological laboratory. The subjects were graduate and undergraduate male students at Columbia University and New York University. They did not know anything about the physical stimulus set-up, or the purpose of the experiment. There were nineteen subjects in the individual experiment; forty subjects took part in the group experiments.

Individual Experiments. The stimulus light was a tiny point of light seen through a small hole in the metal box. The light was exposed to the subject by the opening of a suitable shutter controlled by the experimenter. The distance between the subject and the light was five meters. The observer was seated at a table on which was a telegraph key. The following instructions were given in written form: "When the room is completely dark, I shall give you the signal READY, and then show you a point of light. After a short time the light will start to move. As soon as you see it move, press the key. A few seconds later the light will disappear. Then tell me the distance it moved. Try to make your estimates as accurate as possible."

The light was physically stationary during the entire time and was not moved at all during any of the experiments.

After the light had disappeared, the subject reported orally the distance through which it had moved as he experienced it. The experimenter recorded each judgment as soon as it was spoken by the subject, writing each one on a separate sheet of a small paper pad. One hundred judgments were obtained from each subject. The subjects reported their estimates in inches (or fractions of inches).

The results unequivocally indicate that when individuals perceive movements which lack any other standard of comparison, *they subjectively establish a range of extent and a point (a standard or norm) within that range which is peculiar to the individual,* that may differ from the range and point (standard or norm) established by other individuals. In other words, when individuals repeatedly perceive movement which offers no objective basis for gauging the extent of movement, there develops within them, in the course of a succession of presentations, a standard (a norm or reference point). This subjectively established standard or norm serves as a reference point with which each successive experienced movement is compared and judged to be short, long, or medium — within the range peculiar to the subject.

To express the point more generally, we conclude that in the absence of an objective range or scale of stimuli and an externally given reference point or standard, each individual builds up a range of his own and an internal (subjective) reference point within that range, and each successive judgment is given within that range and in relation to that reference point. The range and reference point established by each individual are peculiar to himself when he is experimented upon alone.

In the second series of the individual experiments, it was found that once a *range,* and point of reference within that range, is established by an individual, there is a tendency to preserve these in the experiments on subsequent days. A second and third series of 100 judgments each show a median score for a given subject which is very similar to that found in the first series, but with a reduced variability.

Group Experiments. There were eight groups of two subjects each and eight groups of three subjects each. Four groups in each of the two categories started with the individual situation (one whole session for each individual), and then functioned as groups. Four groups in each category started in group situations for the first three sessions on three different days (all subjects of the group being present), and were then broken up and studied in the individual situation.

In order to make the relation of individual members to one another as natural as possible, within the limits of the experimental setting, the subjects were left free as to the order in which they would give their judgments. In fact, they were told at the start to give their judgments in random order as they pleased. Whether the

judgments of the person who utters his first have more influence than the others becomes a study in leadership, which is a further interesting problem. Perhaps such studies will give us an insight into the effect of polarization on the production of norms in a group situation. But from the examination of our results, we can say that the reporting of the judgments has a gradual cumulative effect; aside from whatever influence the first judgment may have on the second or third at a given moment, the judgments of the third individual at a given presentation are not without effect on the subsequent judgments of the first subject in the round of presentations following. Thus the production of an established group influence is largely a temporal affair and not the outcome of this or that single presentation. For a graphic presentation of these data, see Figure 1.

Conclusions. Certain facts stand out clearly from our results. We may summarize these facts in a few paragraphs.

When an individual faces this stimulus situation, which is unstable and not structured in itself, he establishes a range and norm (a reference point) within that range. The range and norm that are developed in each individual are peculiar to that individual. They may vary from the ranges and norms developed in other individuals in different degrees, revealing consistent and stable individual differences. The causes of these individual differences are difficult problems in themselves, the understanding of which may prove to be basic to a satisfactory understanding of our problem. But for the time being it may be worth while to work on our main theme.

When the individual, in whom a range and a norm within that range are first developed in the individual situation, is put into a group situation, together with other individuals who also come into the situation with their own ranges and norms established in their own individual sessions, the ranges and norms tend to converge. But the convergence is not so close as when they first work in the group situation, having less opportunity to set up stable individual norms.

When individuals face the same unstable, unstructured situation as members of a group for the first time, a range and a norm (standard)

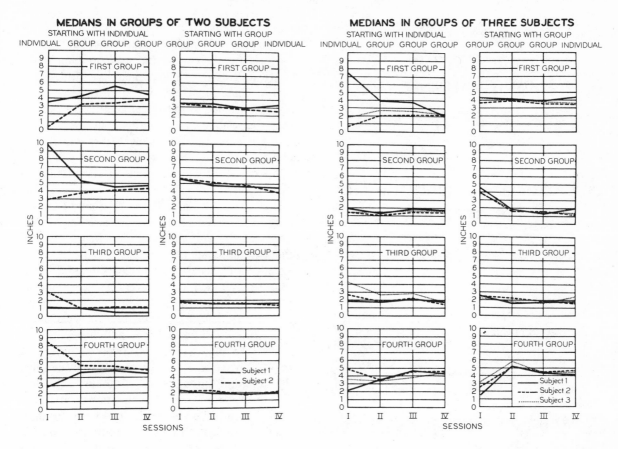

Figure 1

The effect of experience on individual and group response. Where individual sessions came first (I), divergent norms were established, giving rise to "funnel-shaped" figures as a result of the subjects' norms in the subsequent group sessions (II, III and IV). (See left-hand graphs in both figures.) Where the group sessions preceded the individual ones, the convergence of norms was apparent from the first session, and remained throughout, including the (final) individual sessions. (See right-hand graphs in both figures.)

within that range are established, which are peculiar to the group. If, for the group, there is a rise or fall in the norms established in successive sessions, it is a group effect; the norms of the individual members rise and fall toward a common norm in each session.

When a member of a group faces the same situation subsequently alone, after once the range and norm of his group have been established, he perceives the situation in terms of the range and norm that he brings from the group situation.

On the basis of this general principle considered in relation to our experimental results, we shall venture to generalize. The psychological basis of the established social norms, such as stereotypes, fashions, conventions, customs, and values, is the formation of common frames of reference as a product of the contact of individuals. Once such frames of reference are established and incorporated in the individual, they enter as important factors to determine or modify his reactions to the situations that he will face later — social, and even non-social, at times, especially if the stimulus field is not well structured.

INFORMATION AND INFLUENCE

30 Sociability and the Flow of Information*

William Erbe

What is the relationship between gregariousness and possession of information? Are gregarious persons more knowledgeable than those who are social isolates? The following study suggests that the informational advantage of gregarious persons may be due to the fact that they are more likely to be members of groups. In addition, information is communicated more widely in groups that are highly cohesive. The flow of information is enhanced by intensive and extensive interaction.

Research in the field of mass communications in recent years has paid increasing attention to the importance of interpersonal networks of communication in the diffusion of information. Concepts such as "gregariousness" and "integration" have been used in describing the flow of information and influence; sometimes almost interchangeably, without due consideration to nominal definitions of these terms, and the differing implications that these variables might have for communications research.

The study at hand concerns American graduate students and a subject in which they are most vitally concerned: money. The data are taken from a study of a national sample of graduate

* Excerpt reprinted from William Erbe, "Gregariousness, Group Membership, and the Flow of Information," *American Journal of Sociology*, Vol. 67 (March 1962), pp. 502–516, by permission of The University of Chicago Press. Copyright © 1962 by The University of Chicago.

students, conducted in autumn, 1958, by the National Opinion Research Center, the central subject of which was the current financial situation of the American graduate student and his attitudes toward his financial status. We shall use the sample of graduate students to test our counter-hypotheses about the relative effect of gregariousness with the other graduate students versus integration with an informal group of fellow students, in providing the graduate student with information about financial opportunities.

The National Opinion Research Center's sample of graduate students is a two-stage stratified cluster sample of the enrollment of American graduate schools in autumn, 1958. The sample is confined to students in departments which offer the Ph.D. in the "traditional arts and sciences," which means that strictly professional departments and schools of medicine, law, education, etc., are excluded, along with quasi-professional and applied areas such as art, pharmacy and rural sociology. The first step in the sampling was to draw twenty-five schools from the universe of graduate schools offering the Ph.D. in the traditional arts and sciences. Once the universities had been drawn, a quota was assigned to each school and a sample the size of the quota was drawn by random methods from the total enrollment of students studying for advanced degrees in the traditional arts and sciences in the university. The sample of schools and students was drawn in such a way that every student currently enrolled in a department falling in the sample universe had an equal probability of being drawn. The total sample size was set at 3,000, and questionnaires were collected from 2,842 respondents, for a completion rate of nearly 95 per cent.

Gregariousness with other graduate students was measured in the following way: each respondent was asked to indicate the number of students in his department whom he knew "well enough to stop and chat with on the street for a few minutes." We had obtained information from the respective universities on the total enrollment in the student's department. For each size department, a distribution was generated and quartiled, the student being classified according to the quartile of students known in which he fell, for departments the

TABLE 1 *Gregariousness and Integration*

Gregariousness	Percentage Integrated	No.
High (first quartile)	68	(597)
High medium (second quartile)	58	(688)
Low medium (third quartile)	45	(669)
Low (fourth quartile)	22	(678)

size of the department in which he was enrolled.[1] Persons in the first quartile of students known, for each size of department, were classified "high gregarious"; those who fell in the fourth quartile were classified "low gregarious." In addition, students who claimed to know no other students in the department were classified "non-gregarious." They are grouped with the low-gregarious individuals in the following tables.

Each student is classified as being integrated or non-integrated on the basis of his yes-or-no answer to the question: "Do you belong to a group of students which maintains informal contacts outside the classroom?" Group members are self-designated. The size of the sampling interval of a national sample made the gathering of sociometric data impractical.

Table 1 shows the association between gregariousness and integration. We observe that the two variables are highly related. The explanation of this relationship lies beyond the scope of this paper, but two alternative theories might be briefly stated. The first theory holds that gregarious behavior is an expression of a gregarious attitude, the attribute of "sociability" referred to earlier in the paper, and that sociable people who have a great many dyad contacts are more likely to find persons so congenial to themselves as to motivate them to form more permanent social attachments with them. An alternative theory would explain gre-

gariousness in terms of integration; people who have repeated contacts with certain others are more likely to expand the circle of their acquaintance through meetings with friends of their friends from other social environments. At any rate, we may expect that any information or opinion item that correlates with one of these variables will, in all likelihood, correlate with the other.[2]

The items of information which we will use to compare the effects of integration and gregariousness pertain to graduate finances. The first set of questions concerns the kinds of financial aids available to the students in the respondent's department. The respondents were asked: "What is your impression of the chances for graduate students in your department and in your stage of study getting the following?"

1. Teaching assistantships
2. Research assistantships
3. Scholarships and fellowships for tuition "plus"
4. Scholarships and fellowships for full tuition only
5. Scholarships and fellowships for part tuition
6. Part-time jobs of a non-academic type
7. Part-time teaching in night-school or nearby institutions

The second set of responses we shall consider belongs perhaps more in the domain of opinion than of information, although the testimony of graduate students about what might be going on in their department should be classified as extremely informed opinion. The respondents were asked: "From what you know, to what extent do the following criteria influence the allocation of stipends in your department?"

1. Grades
2. Faculty's personal impressions
3. Financial need

For each one of these items the graduate students were presented with a set of precoded answers, ranging from "good" to "not so good" for the financial-aid questions; from "very im-

[1] Gregariousness is controlled for departmental size, since the number of other students known in the department varies with the size of enrolment in the department. Since neither individual integration nor departmental cohesiveness is related to department size, neither is controlled.

[2] This finding also raises the possibility that previous findings in communication studies which show the importance of either gregariousness or group membership show also the importance of the other.

TABLE 2   *Inability to Answer Ten Information and Opinion Questions, by Gregariousness**
(*Percentage Unable to Estimate*)

	Gregariousness			
	High	High Medium	Low Medium	Low
Availability of:				
Teaching assistantships	6 (588)	8 (680)	13 (676)	20 (689)
Research assistantships	11 (584)	14 (670)	18 (663)	25 (687)
Scholarships and fellowships for tuition "plus"	12 (586)	14 (677)	20 (673)	27 (690)
Scholarships and fellowships for full tuition only	21 (580)	22 (671)	25 (670)	30 (685)
Scholarships and fellowships for part tuition	27 (574)	25 (660)	27 (659)	31 (677)
Part-time non-academic jobs	25 (585)	27 (676)	28 (667)	29 (681)
Part-time teaching jobs	31 (583)	34 (673)	39 (664)	40 (679)
Importance for allocation of stipends of:				
Grades	14 (590)	17 (684)	19 (677)	26 (692)
Faculty personal impressions	18 (589)	21 (682)	24 (673)	33 (687)
Financial need	24 (587)	33 (678)	31 (670)	39 (683)

* Numbers in parentheses here and in tables that follow represent percentage base; numbers change from item to item because of different rates of non-response.

portant" to "not important" for the allocation criteria items. In each case, one of the precoded answers was "no idea," and it is this latter category which interests us. A person who circles the "no idea" response for any of these items is admitting a complete lack of information, correct or incorrect; he is unable to say whether the chances for getting this kind of financial aid are good or bad, whether these criteria for the allocation of stipends are important or not important.

On the hypothesis that both gregariousness and integration favor the collection of information, we should predict that persons who are highly gregarious and persons who are integrated will be less likely to answer "no idea" to these items than persons who are not so gregarious and not integrated. Table 2 shows the relationship between gregariousness and the possession of information in these matters. In most of the cases the difference between the most and least gregarious students is about 14 per cent; the exceptions are the questions concerning scholarships just equal to tuition and fees and part-time teaching work, where the difference is 9 per cent, and the questions on part-tuition scholarships and part-time non-academic work, where gregariousness has no effect. The table shows little or no difference between the two upper quartiles, with the third level of gregariousness falling about midway between the most and least gregarious.

Table 3 shows the probability of being uninformed about the same items when group integration is controlled. Again, we note the average difference for response which shows the effect to be about 14 per cent, with the exception of full-tuition scholarships, where the difference is reduced to 8 per cent. As was the case with respect to gregariousness, the questions concerning part-tuition scholarships and part-time non-academic work fail to show the social effect. One response appears to be affected by gregariousness, but not by integration; this is the question on the availability of part-time teaching jobs.

Two of the ten items fail to show the effect of either of the interpersonal variables, and we might speculate on the reasons. In the case of the part-tuition scholarships, it may be that their scarcity makes them unlikely topics of conversation; only 110 respondents (less than 4 per cent of the sample) have such stipends. Scholarships and fellowships which just equal tuition and fees are more common, but not as common as the "tuition plus" stipend, which may also account for the attenuation of the social effect on response concerning the tuition-only scholarship.

On the other hand, more than a thousand of the respondents work some hours on part-time jobs outside the department, so that there is no accounting for the failure of the question on part-time non-academic work to associate with either variable on these grounds. The other non-departmental information item concerning part-time teaching jobs is associated with gregariousness but not with integration.

We will compare the effect of gregariousness with integration on the probability of being informed about these matters by cross-tabulating the percentage of those uninformed against the two variables simultaneously. If the gregariousness effect tends to disappear, we may say that informal group membership is conducive to the possession of information, but not gregariousness; if the integration effect disappears, we may say the opposite. The effects of the two variables are compared in Table 4, where we have omitted the two responses which are not associated with the variables. Here we see that the integration effect remains constant, while the effect of gregariousness virtually disappears among the integrated, and is attenuated among the non-integrated. In seven of the eight comparisons, the likelihood of possessing information is equal to or greater among those who are at the lowest level of gregariousness, but integrated, than for those at the highest level of gregariousness, but not integrated. The sole exception is in the case of the question on part-time teaching, which was not associated with integration at the zero order. Thus, comparing the two extreme analytical types, the information advantage appears to accrue to the cliquish person, as opposed to the "gadabout." The only gregariousness effect retained by this cross-tabulation is a slight and not unexpected tendency for the disparity between the integrated and the unintegrated to be slightly less among the high gregarious than among the low gregarious.

Sociologists generally define a group as "a number of persons in continuous interaction." We suggest that interaction, as such, is not the most important determinant of the strategic position of group members in the flow of information in graduate departments. Interaction is, of course, necessary to the accumulation of information which characterizes group members, but it is not sufficient cause for that accumulation, for persons who engage in extensive interaction with other students in the department are more likely to be "stumped" by questions about conditions in the department than persons who do not have such extensive contacts, but who are members of

TABLE 3 *Inability to Answer Ten Information and Opinion Questions, by Integration (Percentage Unable to Estimate)*

	Integration	
	Integrated	Non-integrated
Availability of:		
Teaching assistantships	4 (1,294)	18 (1,383)
Research assistantships	9 (1,268)	23 (1,368)
Scholarships and fellowships for tuition "plus"	10 (1,283)	25 (1,387)
Scholarships and fellowships for full tuition only	20 (1,273)	28 (1,375)
Scholarships and fellowships for part tuition	26 (1,254)	28 (1,360)
Part-time non-academic jobs	28 (1,285)	26 (1,375)
Part-time teaching jobs	35 (1,278)	37 (1,373)
Importance for allocation of stipends of:		
Grades	12 (1,296)	24 (1,392)
Faculty personal impressions	16 (1,294)	30 (1,382)
Financial need	25 (1,287)	37 (1,375)

TABLE 4   *Gregariousness, Integration, and Inability to Answer Eight Selected Information and Opinion Questions (Percentage Unable to Estimate)*

	Availability of:					Importance of:		
	Assistantships		Scholarships		Part-Time Work Teaching		Faculty Personal Impressions	Financial Need
Gregariousness	Teaching	Research	Tuition "Plus"	Tuition Only		Grades		
Integrated:								
High	3 (398)	7 (394)	8 (395)	19 (390)	30 (393)	12 (399)	14 (399)	21 (397)
High medium	5 (399)	9 (393)	10 (393)	20 (391)	34 (393)	12 (398)	16 (398)	28 (396)
Low medium	5 (296)	11 (290)	13 (294)	20 (292)	40 (294)	13 (297)	17 (295)	23 (294)
Low	7 (149)	10 (149)	9 (148)	20 (147)	41 (145)	15 (149)	22 (149)	33 (148)
Non-integrated:								
High	14 (185)	18 (185)	20 (186)	24 (185)	34 (185)	17 (186)	28 (185)	30 (185)
High medium	13 (275)	21 (271)	18 (277)	24 (273)	34 (274)	23 (279)	28 (277)	40 (275)
Low medium	17 (363)	23 (356)	25 (362)	29 (361)	36 (364)	24 (362)	28 (362)	37 (361)
Low	23 (506)	28 (503)	31 (507)	31 (503)	39 (501)	27 (509)	34 (505)	40 (501)

groups. We submit that the key to the understanding of the advantageous position of group members with respect to the possession of such information lies in the *number* of group members and in the *continuity* of their interaction.

We say their number because, using the imagery of Simmel,[3] every group represents the convergence of a set of social circles: the individual circles of contacts, or role sets, of the members. Every student group is composed of heterogeneous elements: some of the students are integrated with the faculty, other group members have extensive contacts among the student body of the department; some of the members have contacts with faculty and students in other schools, while still other group members may know persons of the administrative staff who have access to special kinds of information. The common knowledge of every member of the group represents a pooling of this information, which is based on resources superior to those of even the most gregarious of individuals.[4] Dyad contacts bring together only two sets of social circles — those of ego and alter. Group participation brings together as many sets of contacts as there are group members. The extent of the difference between the pools of information being tapped is appreciated more if one recalls that each member of a group brings his own set of social contacts to the interaction situation, and that each of these contacts has in turn his own set, so that the difference in size of the resource population tends to grow exponentially as the size of the group is increased. Of course, there may be considerable overlap between the contacts of group members; the more diverse and heterogeneous the contacts of group members, the greater increment in possession of information

[3] Georg Simmel, *The Web of Group Affiliations,* trans. Reinhard Bendix (Glencoe, Ill.: Free Press, 1955). See translator's note, p. 125. The image is more fully developed in the German text (cf. Simmel, "Die Kreuzung sozialer Kreise," in *Soziologie* [Munich: Duncker & Humblot, 1922], pp. 305–44). The translator's comment that "a literal translation of this phrase, 'the intersection of social circles,' is almost meaningless" is perhaps hasty, in the light of the development of set theory in modern algebra. It seems to this writer that Simmel was groping for (and just about making contact with) a conception of the individual representing an intersection of traits derived from association with a unique union of social sets (groups). This article follows this imagery in that it pictures the combined information resources of individuals in interaction as the union of information potential of all the groups with which they are associated.

[4] In connection with the explanation presented here and in the following paragraph, cf. Marjorie E. Shaw, "A Comparison of Individuals and Small Groups in the Rational Solution of Complex Problems," in Maccoby, Newcomb, and Hartley (eds.), *op. cit.* pp. 564–75, and Herbert Gurnee, "A Comparison of Collective and Individual Judgments of Fact," *Journal of Experimental Psychology,* XXI (1937), 106–12.

might be expected. Generally, however, we may expect a group — provided it is larger than a dyad itself — to mobilize a greater informant population than would a casual acquaintanceship.

Although numbers in interaction are the life of a social group, its very special nature lies in the continuity of that interaction, for all populations — even such a sequestered aggregate as a graduate department — are in a state of constant change and realignment. Interruptions and distractions have a tendency to reduce the information levels of integrated and non-integrated alike. We shall illustrate this point with a cross-tabulation of the effect of integration and seniority, number of years the student has been enrolled in the department (Table 5). In this table, we observe (from the base numbers in the parentheses) that seniority and integration are associated. Not surprisingly, there is a tendency for the proportion integrated to grow from the first through the fourth years of graduate study; however, the proportion integrated drops below 50 per cent among students who have been enrolled in the department more than four years. We also note that seniority does tend to confer an advantage with respect to information, but (1) its effect is not as important as that of integration and (2) the effect tends to disappear among those who have been enrolled in the department more than one year, among both in-

tegrated and non-integrated students, and even to reverse slightly in some cases among the students who have been enrolled more than four years.

We attribute this finding to the fact that students who have been enrolled in graduate departments for a long time usually have dropped out somewhere along the way to do something else. The departmental careers of such students contain discontinuities, and they have gotten out of touch with what is happening in the department. The price of keeping in touch is interaction — several hours per week, every week — with other persons in the department, comparing notes, noting the appearance of new opportunities and the closure of old opportunities, correcting erroneous impressions, confirming informed hunches. It is the constant flow of ostensibly petty and trivial details which keeps the integrated student more current on departmental developments.

In conclusion, our data would seem to support two general assertions about the effect of interpersonal relations on the flow of information:

1. Integration with a peer group is conducive to the possession of information, even on a highly salient subject, compared to non-integration.

2. High gregariousness, the maintenance of extensive acquaintanceships with other individuals in the referent population, is also associated with the possession of information, but this effect seems

TABLE 5   *Year of Graduate Study in Department, Integration, and Inability to Answer Nine Selected Information and Opinion Questions (Percentage Unable to Estimate)*

Year in Department	Assistantships		Availability of:		Part-Time Work		Importance of:		
			Scholarships					Faculty Personal	
	Teaching	Research	Tuition "Plus"	Tuition Only	Non-academic	Teaching	Grades	Impressions	Financial Need
Integrated:									
First	7 (447)	14 (444)	12 (446)	18 (444)	31 (446)	41 (442)	17 (447)	23 (445)	31 (445)
Second	2 (332)	6 (325)	11 (329)	20 (326)	29 (329)	37 (326)	9 (335)	12 (334)	21 (334)
Third–fourth	3 (342)	6 (337)	9 (340)	21 (339)	28 (341)	30 (340)	9 (342)	11 (342)	21 (337)
Fifth and later	5 (166)	7 (165)	8 (161)	20 (157)	22 (162)	23 (163)	15 (165)	16 (166)	25 (165)
Non-integrated:									
First	20 (559)	28 (557)	28 (559)	30 (553)	26 (553)	41 (553)	27 (564)	37 (559)	43 (557)
Second	15 (295)	18 (289)	21 (297)	24 (295)	24 (294)	34 (294)	20 (293)	24 (291)	36 (292)
Third–fourth	15 (300)	17 (295)	20 (300)	24 (298)	25 (299)	32 (296)	19 (303)	24 (302)	32 (298)
Fifth and later	19 (203)	26 (201)	29 (203)	32 (202)	30 (202)	35 (203)	25 (204)	27 (204)	34 (200)

to be caused mostly by the fact that highly gregarious persons are also more likely to be group members.

The explanation put forth for these findings was that the group, by bringing together persons whose collective resources of information were greater than those of any individual, and by providing a continuously operating market in which information could be exchanged and verified, constituted a node of such information. Departments in which relatively large numbers of these groups exist constitute a network, such that the integrated individual brings a greater quantity of seemingly reliable information to the group, and the unintegrated individual, through dyad contacts with such persons, is more likely to possess information than his counterpart in a department which is not served by such a network.

31   Power-Dependence Relations*

Richard M. Emerson

Previously, we examined the studies of Asch and Sherif demonstrating the influence of group pressures upon individual behavior. In the next study, individuals who conform to group pressures and those who do not are compared with respect to their motivation, sense of security, and sociometric status. It was found that response to group pressure is associated with sociometric status; conformity tends to be greatest among persons who have either high or low status, while individuals in the middle status categories tend to avoid group pressure. Moreover, people who have high status in their own group and low status in other related groups are inclined toward nonconformity, as are those who have low status in their own group and high status outside. The author concludes that individuals who have high status both in their groups and outside are in powerful positions and are inclined toward conformity because of their "responsible leader" roles, while those whose status is low in their groups and also outside are in dependent positions that demand deference and conformity. Thus, people whose status is uniformly high and those whose status is generally low conform for very different reasons. The author also develops a theory of "power-dependence relations" in an attempt to explain the relationship between status and conformity in a variety of social situations. Is the theory consistent with the findings of Asch, Sherif, and Erbe? Does it add anything to these studies? Does it help explain the current wave of racial demonstrations, riots, and rebellions? Is a special theory of conflict required?

Sherif, Asch, and others have shown that subjects submit to social influence under certain laboratory conditions. Typically, such experiments employ temporary *aggregates* of subjects, among whom no established social relations exist. Hence, in an effort to explain subject behavior, attention tends to be focused upon attributes of persons rather than attributes of interpersonal relations. By contrast, this study was designed to explore interpersonal determinants of conformity or submission to social influence in structured groups, under controlled laboratory conditions.

Three hypotheses were being tested. *Submission to group influence* varies directly with (1) *motivation* toward participation in the group, (2) intensity of group *expectations*, and (3) *status insecurity*. (Status insecurity was defined simply as "uncertainty of acceptance or continued acceptance in status position").

METHOD

To achieve the objectives of this study, it was necessary to find a fairly large number of groups, all very much alike in size and structure, and small enough to be studied in a laboratory situation. With the cooperation of the Minneapolis Boy Scout organization, twenty Boy Scout patrol groups

* Excerpted from *Sociometry*, Vol. 27 (September 1964), pp. 282–298. Reprinted by permission. Copyright © 1964 by The American Sociological Association.

took part. The study was organized as a "distance judging contest," with patrol groups as the competing units.

These twenty patrols, averaging five members each, made up four Boy Scout troops. After a questionnaire had been administered to the entire troop, patrols were taken to the laboratory one at a time to take part in judging tasks. In a completely darkened room, the patrol saw two pinpoints of light about six feet apart and twenty feet away. After ten seconds the right hand light went out, leaving only one light. After ten more seconds a third light came on about midway between the first two, and remained for ten seconds. All stimulus lights then went off and each scout tried to estimate the location of the third light, relative to the two framing lights, on a continuum numbered from 0 (left light) to 100 (right light).

This procedure was repeated five times as *practice trials,* and continued through fifteen more *official trials.* Members' estimates were private, but it was understood that scores would be made public after the task was finished.

Conformity Measure

After each official trial, the experimenter gathered all estimates of light position, went through the motions of averaging them, and then announced a *fictitious group average* before the next trial. Based on considerable pre-testing with light settings and announced averages, plausible averages were presented which were nonetheless clearly in conflict with sensory evidence. Conformity was measured as change in behavior toward the fictitious "group norm."

Motivational Commitment

The initial questionnaire contained a sociometric question, calling for four ordered choices, directed toward any scout in the Troop. In addition, five items were included concerning motivational commitment to the patrol group.

Level of Group Expectation

After the five practice trials, subjects were asked to rate each scout on a five-point scale, indicating how well the group expected that scout to perform in the contest. These ratings were averaged for each subject.

Status Insecurity

In the laboratory session, the first "judging task" asked the subject to guess which scouts might have chosen him in the sociometric question by checking a "yes" or a "no" after each scout's name. In addition, he indicated his certainty or uncertainty about each guess on a four-point scale. These certainty-uncertainty self-ratings were averaged across all ratings.

Results

Table 1 presents correlations among group means on conformity, motivation, percent of choices made within the group, and choices received from outside of the group.

These correlations confirm hypothesis 1. Conformity varies directly with motivation. *In addition,* patrols whose members receive choices from outside the group obtain little conformity from their members.

TABLE 1   *Correlations Among Group Means on Conformity, Motivation, Sociometric Choices Within the Group, and Choices Received from Outside the Group*

Variable	Correlation*			
	1	2	3	4
1. Conformity	—	.60	.42	−.57
2. Motivation	.60	—	.42	−.33
3. Within-group choices (per cent)	.42	.42	—	−.60
4. Out-group choices received	−.57	−.33	−.60	—

* N=20 patrol groups.

TABLE 2   *Mean Conformity Scores for Class Intervals* on Sociometric Status Inside and Outside the Group***

Status Inside the Group	Status Outside the Patrol Group					
	0 to 3		4 to 9		10 plus	
	Score	(n)	Score	(n)	Score	(n)
0 to 3	.49	15	.37	8	−.35	4
4 to 11	.15	18	−.22	9	−.27	9
12 plus	−.42	13	−.34	6	.20	10

* Class intervals were selected to distribute n's as equally as possible, while preserving as many intervals as possible.

** Six subjects were not included for insufficient data.

Hypothesis 2 asserts that conformity varies directly with level of group expectation. Since expectation increases with status ($r = .53$, $N = 88$) we expect to find status differentials reflected in conforming behavior. However, we found no significant relation between expectation and conformity, despite the commonplace character of the hypothesis. But what of status and conformity?

Correlations in Table 1 suggest that the source of sociometric status (in-group or out-group choice received) may make a difference. Hence, Table 2 presents mean conformity for cross-classified status sources. In general, subjects receiving few choices from either source are strong conformers. Subjects receiving many choices from *one* but not *both* sources do not conform. Subjects receiving many choices from both sources conform. This interaction between status sources in Table 2 shows up as a curvilinear relation between conformity and total status. Conformity is found at status extremes.

DISCUSSION

How are these findings to be explained? One interpretation of high status conformity can be eliminated at once. It is sometimes suggested that such conformity is not real, since leaders *set* the norms they "conform" to. However, in this study the experimenter set the norm.

The author initially thought that "status insecurity" might provide the answer. Marginal members might be uncertain of acceptance in the group, and high status members might be uncertain of maintaining status at a level where competition is intense. Our measure of status insecurity, however, failed to correlate either with status or conformity.

An alternative rationale involves a different dynamic at the two status extremes. The peripheral member, who might "know his position" all too well, is nonetheless in a *weak* position, and his behavior might be accordingly deferential. By contrast, the high status member might see his position as defined in part by high group expectations (as indeed it is in these data). Hence, he might "conform" not out of deference but as a "responsible leader," receptive to group demands.

To examine this approach, we divide the subjects into *low* and *high* status groups, using the apex of the conformity curve as a cutting point, and perform linear analysis within each group. We find that *level of expectation* does in fact correlate a little with conformity, and only among the higher status subjects. In addition, we find *motivation* correlated higher with conformity among these subjects. (High status members score higher on motivation, but not significantly so.)

Thus, there are some data suggesting that conformity may be attributable to different sources at the two status extremes, but the leads are tenuous indeed. However, there is one variable in these data which demands attention — *source of sociometric status*. The conforming high status members derive status from out-group choices. (Table 2). Members with comparable in-group status, who receive few out-group choices, are the strongest deviates in the study (Table 2).

To summarize, the data suggest that conformity is related to (1) motivation, (2) low in-group status in the absence of out-group status, and (3) high in-group status *if* accompanied by high out-group status.

In the years following the above study, a theory of power relations was slowly formulated without any special reference to the above findings. It was initially designed to account for processes in large-scale social movements, such as the rise of organized labor, and it was first applied in a study of attitude change in inter-group relations. When it was presented as a step toward a general theory of power, it was noticed for the first time that it might provide an organized explanation for the data presented above.

The central ideas in the theory can be summarized as follows:

Power (Pab). The power of actor A over actor B is the amount of resistance on the part of B which can potentially be overcome by A.

Dependence (Dab). The dependence of actor A upon actor B is (1) directly proportional to A's *motivational investment in goals mediated* by B, and (2) inversely proportional to the *availability* of those goals outside the A-B relation.

(Pab = Dba). The power of A over B is equal to, and based upon, the dependence of B upon A.

The entire theory revolves around these three notions. Since power is based upon the other's dependence, most of the analysis concerns the two variables which determine dependency.

Recognizing the reciprocal character of social relations, involving *mutual* dependency, a *power-dependence relation* is represented as a set of two equations. The relation may be either

$$\text{balanced} \begin{pmatrix} \text{Pab} = \text{Dba} \\ '' \qquad '' \\ \text{Pba} = \text{Dab} \end{pmatrix}$$

$$\text{or unbalanced} \begin{pmatrix} \text{Pab} = \text{Dba} \\ \text{v} \qquad \text{v} \\ \text{Pba} = \text{Dab} \end{pmatrix}^1$$

[1] In an attempt to overcome the cumbersome problem of describing reciprocal ego-alter relations, we adopt the

It is argued that a power balance does not neutralize power, for the relation may be balanced at different *levels* of reciprocal power, leading to a conception of cohesion in social relations or groups.

In an unbalanced relation someone has a *power advantage* (PA) represented as PAab = Pab − Pba. This theory hypothesizes that unbalanced power relations are inherently unstable, generating "tensions of imbalance" [2] which set in motion one or several "balancing operations." A *balancing operation* is a change in the power-dependence relation which moves PA toward zero. It follows from the above propositions that exactly four balancing operations exist:

1. WITHDRAWAL. Decreased *motivational investment* on the part of the weaker member.
2. NETWORK EXTENSION. Increased *availability* of goals for the weaker member outside the relation (extension of the "power network" through formation of new relations).
3. STATUS GIVING. Increased *motivational investment* on the part of the stronger member.
4. COALITION FORMATION. Decreased *availability* of goals outside of the relation for the stronger member ("coalition formation," or collapsing a power network).

While these four operations are suggested logically, they appear to correspond with well-known social processes as suggested by the descriptive names chosen for them. The rest of the theory

formal notation of symbols and subscripts. Pab is read as "the power of A over B," etc. An important feature of this theory is that power is treated as an attribute of a reciprocal A-B *relation* rather than an attribute of a person.

[2] The instability of unbalanced relations can be traced to (a) the fact that any *use of power* will by definition arouse psychological conflict in the recipient, and (b) when power is not actually used, parties nonetheless feel vulnerable in their excessive dependency. The subject involved in an unbalanced relation will likely see the relation as lacking what Homans has called *distributive justice* (George C. Homans, *Social Behavior: Its Elementary Forms,* New York: Harcourt, Brace and World, 1961, pp. 72–78). A study of that concept will show that it can be coordinated closely with the conditions of balance and imbalance.

presented earlier explores some of the implications of these balancing operations in the emergence of group structure, the conversion of power into "authority" and the formation of status hierarchies. Perhaps the most interesting feature of the theory is the concept of "availability" of rewards through alternative social relations, for this notion makes possible a fairly rigorous conception of *power networks.* Change in such structures can be deduced, and from changes in one relation, subsequent changes throughout the network can be deduced.

In the above study of conformity (submission to group influence) we are concerned with a set of n group-member power relations in a group of size n. Conformity should be a function of the member's dependence upon the group. Thus, it should vary directly with *motivational commitment,* and inversely with *availability* of gratification from alternative sources. If sociometric choices received from outside the group are taken as an index of availability, we can deduce the relationships found in Table 1 and the top row of Table 2.

Turning to *status* and conformity, we confront the group's dependence upon the member, in the reciprocal power-dependence relation. The relative power of members (freedom to deviate with impunity?) should increase with *in-group status,* as shown in the left column of Table 2. However, this relation is reversed when high out-group status (*availability*) is added, as shown in the right hand column of Table 2. How can this interaction between *status* and *availability* be explained in our theory?

BALANCING OPERATION 3: STATUS GIVING

Our theory predicts that balancing operations will produce changes, with power advantages converging on zero. Four operations are theoretically possible, but only one of them is feasible at the high status level, in the situation under discussion. That one is number 3, "status giving." Its effect is to increase the dependence of the otherwise independent member, through granting him the special rewards of high status (e.g., prestige, salary increase, etc.). By so doing, the group can keep and control its valued members. In terms of the data presented above, it is most important to note that this balancing operation should affect *only* those members who (a) are highly valued by the group, and (b) are highly valued by other similar groups. Hence, this theory predicts a curvilinear relation between status and conformity, *if and only if* high status members have "status" in alternative groups. This is exactly what the data in Tables 1 and 2 seem to suggest. The crucial variable appears to be the *availability* factor in dependence.

This has been an *ex post facto* account. However, the theory presented was not designed specifically for these data, nor with these data in mind. The dynamics which this theory imputes to conformity patterns among the Boy Scouts are the same dynamics we see in other settings (e.g., the relation between outside "job-offers" and status advancement in academic and business institutions). Sometimes these dynamics are brought to the level of strategy in overt "power-plays," while otherwise they remain implicit, unrecognized by the participants.

ALLIANCE AND OPPOSITION

32   Cooperation and Competition in Small Groups*

Peter M. Blau

In working toward the achievement of their common goals, members of small groups devise or adopt operational procedures which supposedly ensure the success of their efforts. Since these collective ways of behaving frequently develop through trial-and-error efforts during the early stages of group formation, quite similar groups seeking identical goals may differ markedly in the ways in which they behave in relation to these goals. One group may develop a strong leadership organization while another is organized along more democratic lines. The members of one group may have close, congenial personal relations among themselves while members of a second group may be more impersonal and "businesslike" in their relationships. Whatever the collective ways of behaving, these ways tend to become established and habituated responses on the part of the members. Although a group of judges might feel that the ways of one group are more effective in achieving the goal than those of another group, the latter group may show little inclination to imitate the first group. That is, the established ways of the group come to have a value of and in themselves. They are regarded as the right and natural ways of doing things and even though it may be recognized that these are not necessarily the most efficient ways of proceeding, individual members may be pressured to conform.

* Reprinted from Peter M. Blau, "Cooperation and Competition in a Bureaucracy," *American Journal of Sociology*, Vol. 59 (May 1954), pp. 530–535, by permisson of The University of Chicago Press. (Copyright 1954 by The University of Chicago.)

This does not mean that group ways become so fixed that they may never change. They do change and sometimes can be changed deliberately. However, the persistence of established ways is an important characteristic of group behavior.

In the article which follows, the practices of two small groups of interviewers in a public employment agency are described. How did these two groups come to differ so markedly in the competitiveness of their members? What does the author mean when he says these differences call for explanation in sociological rather than psychological terms? Does his evidence support this position?

This paper discusses performance and variations in competitiveness among twelve interviewers in two small sections of a public employment agency. The duties of the interviewers in both sections were essentially alike. They received requests for workers over the phone. The order forms on which job openings were described were filed in a common pool in each section. Most of the official's time was spent interviewing applicants for jobs. After ascertaining the client's qualifications, the interviewer searched the sectional files for suitable vacancies. If an acceptable job was found, he referred the client to it and later phoned the employer to determine whether the client had been hired.

"The statistics which show how many interviews and how many placements each person in the section did are passed around to all interviewers. Of course, you look at them and see how you compare with others. This creates a competitive spirit," said one of the interviewers, voicing the sentiments of most of his fellows. In a period of job shortages, competition took the form of trying to utilize job openings before anybody else did. Interviewers were so anxious to make placements that they even resorted to illicit methods. Said one:

When you take an order, instead of putting it in the box, you leave it on your desk. There was so much hiding of orders under the blotter that we used to ask, "Do you have anything under your rug?" when we looked for an order. You might leave an order you took on the desk, or you might leave it on the desk after you made no referral. . . . Or, you might take an order only partially; you write the firm's name, and a few things; the others you remember.

TABLE 1   *Competitiveness and Productivity in Section A and in Section B*

	Openings Received[a] (1)	Referrals Made by Recipient (2)	Ratio of Referrals to Openings (3)	Competitiveness[b] (4)	Productivity[c] (5)	Number of Placements (6)
Section A:						
Adams	34	19	0.56	3.9	0.70	100
Ahman	62	27	.44	3.1	.49	70
Ajax	40	28	.70	4.9	.97	139
Akers	71	32	.45	3.2	.71	101
Ambros	69	18	.26	1.8	.45	65
Atzenberg	106	43	.41	2.9	.61	87
Auble	10	3	.30	2.1	.39	56[d]
Section B:						
Babcock	16	7	.44	2.2	.53	46
Beers	58	19	.33	1.6	.71	62
Bing	51	16	.29	1.5	.75	65
Borden	17	7	.41	2.1	.55	48[d]
Bush	43	19	0.42	2.1	0.97	84
Section A	392	170	0.43	3.0	0.59	590
Section B	185	67	0.36	1.8	0.67	289

[a] The great differences between interviewers in this column show that some were much more successful than others in inducing employers, or telephone operators, to channel requests for workers to them personally. This form of rivalry does not involve competitive interaction.

[b] Competitiveness index (col. 4): The proportion of job openings received to which the recipient made a referral (col. 3) times the number of members of the section. (This represents the observed divided by the expected frequency of referrals made by the recipient of a job opening.) Base period: First half of April, 1949.

[c] Productivity index (col. 5): The number of placements made (col. 6) divided by the number of job openings available, that is, the number of openings in the section per interviewer. Base period: April, 1949.

[d] The number of placements was adjusted for the two interviewers absent for more than five days during April. Since the sectional numbers of placements were not revised, the values in col. 6 add up to more than the two totals shown.

And you leave it on the pad (of order blanks). You keep on doing this, and all these orders are not in the box.

You can do some wrong filling out. For instance, for a rather low-salary job, you fill out "experience required." Nobody can make a placement on that except you, because you, alone, know that experience isn't required. Or, if there are several openings (on one order), you put the order into "referrals" (file category for *filled* job openings) after you make one placement. You're supposed to put it into "referrals" but stand it up, so that the others can see it. If you don't, you have a better chance of making the next placement than somebody else. And time and again you see four, five openings on one order filled by the same person. (In one case on file, eight out of nine openings on one order had been filled by the same interviewer.)

The major opportunity for competitive monopolization of job openings occurred when they were received from employers. Since illicit practices were concealed from the observer, the extent of competition could not be determined through questioning or direct observation but was betrayed by the record of official transactions. The extent to which an interviewer filled the vacancies he had received over the phone with his own clients in excess of chance expectations furnishes an index of competitiveness. (Col. 4 in Table 1 shows this index; cols. 1–3 present the data on which it is based.)

Structural Conditions and Competitiveness. The members of Section A were more competitive than those of Section B. The last two columns in

Table 1 also show that the interviewer's competitiveness was related to his productivity in Section A (Pearsonian $r = +.92$), but this was not the case in Section B ($r = -.20$). In other words, hoarding of jobs was an effective way to improve an interviewer's placement record only in one of these two groups.

The members of Section B were more cooperative: they discouraged competitive practices by making them ineffective. When they learned about interesting vacancies, they often told one another, but an interviewer who manifested competitive tendencies was excluded from the network of reciprocal information and lost the respect of his co-workers. Any advantage of hoarding jobs was, at least, neutralized by such lack of co-operation, as is indicated by the absence of a relation between competitiveness and productivity in this group. Since competitive practices made an interviewer unpopular and failed to raise his productivity, they were infrequent.

These officials themselves attributed the greater competitiveness in Section A to the ambitiousness of several members: "There is usually one individual who starts it, who becomes a pace-setter. Once it has started, it is too late." The others, so interviewers claimed, have to follow suit. However, the most competitive member of Section A in recounting her reactions when production records were first introduced made it clear that this explanation of competition on the basis of personality characteristics is inadequate:

When they introduced statistics, I realized how fast I worked. I even wanted to drop lower. I didn't mind working fast as long as it didn't show, but when it showed up like that on the record, I wanted to work less. But you know what happened? Some of the others started to compete with each other and produced more than I did. Then I thought to myself, "Since I can do it, it's silly to let them get ahead of me." I'm only human. So I worked as fast as before.

When statistical records made the superior performance of this interviewer public knowledge, she decided to work less, possibly in response to pressures the others had brought to bear upon her. While complaining about her unfair standards, however, the other members of the section also improved their own performance. Consequently, this interviewer, just like the others, felt constrained by colleagues to compete for an outstanding record. One or two members of Section B, on the other hand, were also accused of competitive tendencies, but their colleagues successfully discouraged their expression in monopolistic practices. It is in this sense that the competitive practices of one group and the co-operative practices of the other were social factors, calling for explanation in sociological rather than psychological terms, as Durkheim has long since emphasized.

Differential conditions affected the development of these two groups. First, the supervisor in Section A relied heavily on performance records in evaluating interviewers: "And here, in the production figures, is the answer to the question: How good are you? Here you see exactly how good the work you did was." Interviewers often mentioned the pressure thus exerted: "[Especially] around rating time, you get this competition. You don't care whether the best person gets the job, but you try to make the placement yourself." In contrast, the new supervisor in Section B surprised his subordinates by rating them more leniently than they had expected, and not primarily on the basis of production records. Consequently, as one interviewer reported, "We became less anxious about statistics; another experience like that, and we might forget all about placement credit."

Second, a common professional orientation existed only in Section B. While the members of Section A had been assigned, and had received their training, at different times, the majority of those in Section B received their training together after World War II, at a time when intensive counseling had been stressed, since many returning veterans needed occupational advice. One official said of this period:

When I first came here, in May, 1946, we had a very nice bunch. It was like an all-day consultation; we discussed placements with each other all day long. At that time, the veterans came back, and there was a lot of emphasis on counseling. Nobody asked you how many placements you made, then. The emphasis was on quality, and we consulted with each other all day.

In this situation, the group developed a common professional code, which discouraged speedy placement as constituting defective employment service. In effect, this orientation transformed competitive practices from illegitimate means for desirable ends into illegitimate means for worthless ends. If such practices did occur, they were vigorously opposed on moral grounds as violating the interest of clients. Nevertheless, as will be shown presently, competition could not have been effectively curbed if the supervisor's evaluation practice had engendered acute anxiety over productivity. However, the existence of this code would have made it difficult for the supervisor to judge performance mainly by productivity, since doing so would have stamped him as ignorant of the essentials of good employment service.

No opportunity for the development of a *common* professional code had existed in Section A. Since competitiveness prevailed in this group, the individual whose personal professional standards made him reluctant to compete either became the deviant whose productivity suffered or modified his standards and entered the race with the others.

Third, most members of Section A had been appointed to temporary civil service positions during World War II. They were on probation pending permanent appointments when production records were originally introduced and even afterward remained subject to layoffs due to reductions in staff. Their insecurity led them to strive to impress superiors with outstanding performance. In contrast, all but one of the members of Section B were veterans, whose employment could not be terminated except for cause. As one envious colleague put it, "They felt that nothing could happen to them, because they were veterans, and had super-seniority."

Differences in these three conditions — security of employment, opportunity for the development of a common professional orientation, and the evaluation practice of the supervisor — gave rise to two dissimilar social structures. Productivity was highly valued in Section A and became associated with the individual's standing in the group, while striving for sheer productivity was disparaged in Section B. Thus, whereas the most productive and most competitive member of Section A was considered the best interviewer by her co-workers and was most popular with them, the most productive member of Section B was least respected and least popular. As a result of these structural differences, cooperative norms prevailed only in Section B.

The interviewers in *both* sections disliked working in a competitive atmosphere. A member of Section A said: "If I see that an interviewer keeps orders on her desk, I take them and put them in the box. . . . Of course, you don't make friends that way." Since the majority in this section, including its most popular members, were highly competitive, to antagonize them was to threaten one's own standing in the group. This deterred interviewers from discouraging competitive practices. Antagonizing a deviant, however, does not endanger one's status. Consequently, since a striver was unpopular in Section B, its members could use sanctions freely to combat competitive practices and enforce co-operative norms.

Social Cohesion and Productivity. Table 1 shows that the group most concerned with productivity was less productive than the other group. Fifty-nine per cent of the job openings received in Section A were filled, in contrast to 67 per cent in Section B. The 8 per cent difference is significant on the .01 level. Another implicit paradox is that competitiveness and productivity were directly related for individuals in Section A but inversely related for the two groups.

Anxious concern with productivity induced interviewers in Section A to concentrate blindly upon it at the expense of other considerations. In their eagerness to make many placements they often ignored their relationships with others as well as official rules. Competitiveness in this group weakened social cohesion, while co-operativeness in Section B strengthened it. This difference is further shown by the fact that usually none of the members of Section A spent their rest periods together, whereas all but one of those of Section B, a newcomer when this study was being made, did. Social cohesion enhanced operating efficiency by facilitating co-operation and by reducing status anxiety.

Although the members of both groups had occasion to assist one another, greater effort was required to elicit such co-operation in Section A.

The social interaction that occurred in the office during the twenty-four busiest hours of one week was recorded and classified as official and private contacts, that is, those directly concerned with a specific job or client, and all others. The frequency of an interviewer's official contacts with colleagues was related to his productivity in Section A (rank correlation = +.98) but not in Section B (rank correlation = +.08). This suggests that only interviewers who kept, as one put it, "hopping around all the time" to retrieve job orders that others kept on their desks were able to make many placements in the competitive section. In the cohesive group, on the other hand, the co-operation needed for making placements occurred as a matter of course, and not only in response to special requests. This effort was not required for high productivity.

To maximize his placements, the interviewer in Section A hoarded jobs and simultaneously tried to prevent others from doing so, thereby antagonizing his co-workers, whose co-operation he needed if he was to do well. The members of this section therefore attempted to conciliate colleagues whom their competitive practices had alienated. Often, shortly after having interfered with her operations, an interviewer paid another a compliment about her work or her apparel. The most competitive interviewer was in the habit of taking time out to joke with her co-workers and was proud of making more placements than anybody else, "nevertheless." Actually, this compensating friendliness, which made her popular despite her competitiveness, helped her to be productive.

In Section A, interviewers had to make special efforts at conciliation in order to make placements, but this was not necessary in Section B. At least, this impression is corroborated by the finding that frequency of private contacts with others was also related to productivity in Section A (rank correlation = +.84) but not in Section B (rank correlation = +.13). The members of the cohesive group, whose operating practices did not put colleagues at a disadvantage, did not have to devote time and energy to solicit and encourage co-operation, since it was not extended reluctantly. Their spontaneous co-operation improved operating efficiency.

Social cohesion also lessened the status anxiety

TABLE 2　*Productivity Before and After Rating*

	Section A		Section B
December, 1948	0.64	(619)[a]	0.56 (317)
January, 1949	.70	(941)	.56 (472)
February, 1949 (rating)	.56	(1,342)	.60 (477)
March, 1949	.59	(1,335)	.71 (448)
April, 1949	0.59	(1,001)	0.67 (433)

[a] Numbers in parentheses are the numbers of job openings available on which the productivity index — the proportion of these openings that were filled — is based.

generated by the evaluation system. Such anxiety is most acute in the individual who does not feel integrated in his work group and therefore seeks to derive social recognition from excelling at his task and from approval of superiors. Friendly relations with co-workers made the standing of the individual in the cohesive group independent of his productivity, particularly since fast work was disparaged as a sign of superficial service. The consequent reduction of anxiety in the anti-productivity-oriented group actually raised its productivity.

Fluctuations in productivity illustrate the dysfunction of status anxiety. Section B had not always operated more efficiently than Section A. Its productivity had been lower during the two months preceding the last rating but had abruptly increased then, while that of Section A had declined, as Table 2 shows.

The two groups found themselves in different situations before and after they were rated. The members of Section A were familiar with the rating standards of their supervisor, for she had rated them in previous years. Their anxiety led them to work especially hard immediately before the annual rating. The members of Section B, on the other hand, had never before been rated by their new supervisor. They were also concerned about their record but could not calm their anxiety by concentrating upon certain tasks, because they did not know what the supervisor would stress; the explanation he gave to his subordinates was too vague and adhered too strictly to official procedures to help them to foresee his actual practices. This unfocused anxiety was particularly detrimental to efficient performance. Later, when the interviewers found out that they were not rated primarily on the basis of statistical records, their anxiety largely subsided and their productivity increased. In contrast, the experience of the members of Section A, whose rating was strongly influenced by their production records, intensified their status anxiety, but, when the rating was over, anxiety was no longer channeled into exceptionally hard work, with the result that their productivity declined below that of Section B.

Social cohesion is no guaranty against anxiety in a bureaucracy. Civil service status is too important to officials for them to remain immune to the threat of losing it. But when no such threat is felt, social cohesion reduces anxiety by divesting productivity of its significance as a symbol of status in the work group. Diminished anxiety as well as smoother co-operation then enables those in the cohesive group to perform their tasks more efficiently than the others.

In the absence of social cohesions, competitive striving for an outstanding performance record became a substitute means for relieving status anxiety in Section A. This psychological function of competition is illustrated by the following incident: The interviewers in this section became very irritable, and one of them even became physically ill, when a temporary supervisor, who tried to prevent competitive practices, interfered with their method of allaying anxiety. Status anxiety reduced operating efficiency. Even in the cohesive group, productivity was low when the unknown rating standards of a new supervisor produced acute and diffuse anxiety. Otherwise, however, the cohesive group was more productive, because social cohesion relieved status anxiety by making the individual's standing in the group independent of his productivity. The very competitive striving that undermined the group's cohesiveness also served to lessen the individual's status anxiety in a non-cohesive situation. The hypothesis that the cohesiveness of the group and the competitiveness of the individual in the less cohesive group both reduce status anxiety explains the paradox that the *less competitive group* as well as the *more competitive individual* in the competitive group each was particularly productive.

33 Conflict in a Ghetto*

J. R. Feagin

Some people engage in violence while others, under similar provocation, do not. Why? Is aggressiveness evenly distributed in the population or is it concentrated in certain groups and classes? And, if concentrated, what are the most relevant variables? Such questions are examined in the next study. It presents findings from an opinion poll taken among Negro residents of the Bedford-Stuyvesant area immediately after the 1964 riot. The data suggest that attitudes favorable to violence may be found mainly among the young male residents who are newcomers to the community, who have a relatively low income, and whose education is on either the grammar school or college level. Pro-violent attitudes are also found among persons who read the newspapers regularly, attend church once a month or less, and participate in union activities, lodges, or civil rights groups. Those born in the deep South are less inclined toward violence than are those born elsewhere. Many qualifications of these general findings are given in the report.

The data presented in this exploratory paper are from National Opinion Research Center (NORC) interviews with a "block quota" (modified probability) sample of 200 residents of New York's Bedford-Stuyvesant ghetto shortly after the 1964 riot.[1] The crucial details of the riot can be summarized briefly. The original precipitating

* Excerpted from *Social Problems*, Vol. 15 (Spring 1968), pp. 432–441. Reprinted by permission of The Society for the Study of Social Problems.

[1] I am indebted to NORC for their kindness in making these data available to me. They are of course in no way responsible for the analysis of these data as presented in this paper.

event was a typical one involving the shooting of a Negro boy by a white policeman. The riot initially began in Harlem but soon spread to Brooklyn's Bedford-Stuyvesant section, then occupied by approximately 400,000 Negroes. The two riots lasted six days, involved 8,000 persons, and resulted in 118 injuries and 465 arrests, two-thirds of which were in the Bedford-Stuyvesant ghetto alone.[2] Undoubtedly these crucial events were etched indelibly on the minds of the Negro respondents and provided a context of realism for the poll questions asked by NORC's interviewers.

THE DATA

How extensive was support for violence in the Bedford-Stuyvesant ghetto after the 1964 riot? In response to a key question three-quarters of these Negro respondents indicated they felt that nonviolent means such as sit-ins would be sufficient to enable Negroes to attain equal rights in American society.[3] Most of those interviewed were nonviolence oriented. However, even in this first "hot" summer of the current series 34 respondents, 17 percent of the sample, felt that nonviolent means were not sufficient, and that violent tactics such as riots and fighting were necessary to get equal rights. An additional 7 percent of the sample indicated uncertainty in response to this question. Although the predominant emphasis in this paper will be on the clear-cut responses, data on the uncertain and noncommittal respondents have been included in the tables for the reader's inspection. It could well be argued that some of these respondents were violence oriented, but were unwilling to admit it because of prevailing social pressures.

It should also be noted that there is a positive correlation between general violence orientation and sympathetic attitudes toward a specific instance of violence. Those here classified as violence oriented were considerably more favorable than the nonviolence oriented to the Bedford-Stuyvesant riot which had occurred approximately two weeks before the interviews. They were much more likely than the nonviolence-oriented respondents to be "glad" (or "glad and sorry") that the Bedford-Stuyvesant riot occurred. Sixty-two percent expressed such a view, as compared with 15 percent of the nonviolence-oriented respondents. They were also more likely than the nonviolence supporters to say they felt like joining in that particular riot (24 percent versus 4 percent) and to admit that they had participated in the riot (6 percent versus 0 percent). The two respondents in this sample who admitted participating in the Bedford-Stuyvesant riot were among the violence oriented as above defined. Thus these data clearly suggest that there are several levels of violence orientation. Although in the following analysis I will be discussing violence support at a somewhat general level, these admittedly *post hoc* data do suggest that violence endorsement is the backdrop of riot behavior in a specific situation.

Were violence-oriented Negroes scattered at random throughout the Bedford-Stuyvesant ghetto population? Or did certain groups contain a larger proportion of violence-oriented Negroes than others? If so, which groups? Many guesses about these questions have been made in public discussion. Most of the characteristics discussed below are those frequently mentioned in the mass media and public literature.

On occasion in this public discussion one encounters the assumption, sometimes explicit and sometimes implicit, that it is the older teenagers (or simply "youths") who are the Negroes most likely to be violence oriented.[4] The age data in Table 1 bear out this assumption. As one moves from the 18–24 age bracket, in which one-quarter of the respondents felt violence necessary to the attainment of equal rights, through the other age brackets, the proportion of violence-oriented Negroes goes down systematically to a low of 14.3 percent in the oldest age bracket. The pattern is generally similar for the cumulative data in Column 4 of Table 2. As expected, a larger proportion of young Negroes than of older Negroes were violence oriented; a large proportion of older Ne-

[2] F. C. Shapiro and J. W. Sullivan, *Race Riots: New York 1964,* New York: Crowell, 1964.

[3] The interview question addressed to these ghetto residents was as follows: "Do you think that Negroes will be able to get equal rights, better jobs, and such, by using nonviolent means like sit-ins, or will they have to use violence like riots and fighting to get them?"

[4] J. Cohen and W. S. Murphy, *Burn, Baby, Burn!* New York: Dutton, 1966.

TABLE 1 *Support of Violent and Nonviolent Means by Various Background Variables*

	(1)	(2)	(3)	(4)	(5)	
	Percent Non-violence Oriented	Percent Violence Oriented	Percent Un-certain or Non-committal	Cumula-tive Percent (2)+(3)	Totals	
					Percent	Number
Age						
18–24	64.3%	25.0	10.7	(35.7)	100.0%	(28)
25–34	72.6%	21.0	6.5	(27.5)	100.1%	(62)
35–44	79.4%	14.7	5.9	(20.6)	100.0%	(34)
45+	79.4%	14.3	6.3	(20.6)	100.0%	(63)
Sex						
Male	69.0%	24.1	6.9	(31.0)	100.0%	(87)
Female	81.7%	11.9	6.4	(18.3)	100.0%	(109)
Length of Residence						
Less than a year	44.4%	44.4	11.1	(55.5)	99.9%	(18)
1–4 years	76.7%	18.3	5.0	(23.3)	100.0%	(60)
5–9 years	70.7%	24.4	4.9	(29.3)	100.0%	(41)
10 years or more	85.7%	6.5	7.8	(14.3)	100.0%	(77)
Place of Birth						
Deep South	80.9%	13.2	5.9	(19.1)	100.0%	(68)
Other South	72.9%	20.0	7.1	(27.1)	100.0%	(70)
North and West	68.8%	21.9	9.4	(31.3)	100.1%	(32)
Caribbean	78.3%	17.4	4.3	(21.7)	100.0%	(23)
Other	100.0%	0	0	(0)	100.0%	(3)
Income						
$0–$2999	76.5%	17.6	5.9	(23.5)	100.0%	(34)
$3000–$3999	70.0%	25.0	5.0	(30.0)	100.0%	(40)
$4000–$5999	77.4%	18.9	3.8	(22.7)	100.1%	(53)
$6000 and over	77.8%	11.1	11.1	(22.2)	100.0%	(63)
Education						
8 years or less	76.0%	22.0	2.0	(24.0)	100.0%	(50)
9–11 years	76.6%	15.6	7.8	(23.4)	100.0%	(64)
12 years	78.0%	15.3	6.8	(22.1)	100.1%	(59)
Some college or more	63.2%	21.1	15.8	(36.9)	100.1%	(19)

Note: Missing information on a few respondents results in variations in total N from one background variable to another; choice of categories was restricted by the pre-coded poll data.

TABLE 2 *Support of Violent and Nonviolent Means by*
Several Participation Variables

	(1) Percent Non-violence Oriented	(2) Percent Violence Oriented	(3) Percent Un-certain or Non-committal	(4) Cumula-tive Percent (2)+(3)	(5) Totals	
					Percent	Number
Religious Participation						
Twice a month						
or more	79.0%	14.3	6.7	(21.0)	100.0%	(119)
Once a month						
or less	71.4%	22.1	6.5	(28.6)	100.0%	(77)
Organizational Affiliation						
(Other than church)						
One or more	66.7%	19.3	14.0	(33.3)	100.0%	(57)
None	79.9%	16.5	3.6	(20.1)	100.0%	(139)
Read Newspaper						
Regularly?						
Yes	74.4%	18.1	7.5	(25.6)	100.0%	(160)
No	82.9%	14.3	2.9	(17.2)	100.1%	(35)

groes than of younger Negroes felt nonviolent means to be sufficient.

One note of caution seems necessary at this point. These data do indicate a correlation between age and support of violence; but this should not be taken to mean that most supporters of violence, at least at the general level under consideration here, were in the youngest age bracket. It is clear from a careful examination of the data in Column 2 of Table 1 that only seven of the 34 violence-oriented respondents in the sample were under 25; no less than 14 were over the age of 35; the remainder were between the ages of 25 and 34. A substantial proportion of the violence oriented in this sample were 35 years old or older. In a pioneering study of Negro orientations toward violence after the 1943 Harlem riot, Kenneth Clark found considerable militancy among older Negro interviewees.[5] Although only tentative,

these Bedford-Stuyvesant data also indicate that due recognition should still be given to the support for violence in the older segments of Negro ghetto populations.[6]

A second important characteristic available for these Negro respondents is sex. Public discussions of ghetto violence frequently have suggested that Negro males are more likely to be violence oriented than Negro females. This contention is corroborated by these data, as can be seen in Table 1. Twenty-four percent of the males interviewed believed violent means to be necessary, whereas only 11.9 percent of the females responded in like fashion. The pattern of the cumulative percentages is similar. The proportion of Negro females believing nonviolent means to be sufficient is one of the highest in Table 2.

Another characteristic of these Negro urbanites germane to contemporary discussions is their mi-

[5] K. B. Clark, "Group Violence: A Preliminary Study of the Attitudinal Pattern of its Acceptance and Rejection: A Study of the 1943 Harlem Riot," *Journal of Social Psychology,* 19 (1944), pp. 324–325.

[6] That this is also true of the characteristics of actual riot participants is indicated by data on persons arrested in connection with the Harlem and Bedford-Stuyvesant riots. Sixty-six percent of those arrested were over 21 years of age. Shapiro and Sullivan, *op. cit.,* p. 206.

gration status. Some public appraisals of ghetto riots have implied that recent Southern migrants to urban areas comprise the bulk of the violence-oriented Negroes in our urban areas, presumably because of the frustrations engendered by their encounters with an urban environment.[7] A related view depicts long-term Negro city residents as less likely than newcomers or those who are highly mobile to be violence oriented because of their attachment to the local area. The NORC survey only provides data on length of residence in a given Bedford-Stuyvesant area, thus preventing the differentiation between recent in-migrants from the South, and those who are highly mobile but from Northern points of origin. The available data (Table 1) do show that over 40 percent of those who had resided in their neighborhood for less than a year were violence oriented, as compared to 6.5 percent of those respondents who had been in the area ten years or more. However, the relationship between length of residence and the likelihood of supporting violence is not linear. Twenty-four percent of the intermediate-term (five-to-nine year) residents were violence oriented, a larger proportion than of the one-to-four year residents. Thus the data do give some support to the view that very recent newcomers to a locale, those with the least time to develop meaningful attachments to the community, are the most likely to be violence oriented and to the view that long-term residents are the least likely to be violence oriented. Yet a close inspection of this variable in Table 1 also reveals that a sizable proportion of the violence-oriented Negroes in the sample have lived in their ghetto neighborhoods for five years or more — four in ten among the violence-oriented respondents. For this group it is likely that persisting ghetto conditions, not mobility experiences, are the generators of support for violence.

One other question in the survey is relevant to the issue of Southern origins. Are Southern-born Negroes in ghettos like Bedford-Stuyvesant more likely to be violence oriented than Northern-born Negroes? The data in Table 1 suggest that this is not the case. While 13.2 percent of the "Deep South" respondents believed violence a necessity in the attainment of equal rights, nearly 22 percent of the Northern-born expressed a similar opinion. The proportions of violence-oriented in the "Caribbean" and "Other South" categories fall between those of the other two groups. The pattern for the cumulative percentages in column 4 of Table 1 is similar. A Negro Northerner living in Bedford-Stuvesant was somewhat more likely than his Southern-born counterpart to be violence oriented, a finding which partially corroborates Clark's 1943 data.[8] Admittedly the data on the two preceding characteristics discussed, length of residence and place of birth, are not conclusive, but they do point to the significant presence of relatively long-term Negro residents and Northern-born Negroes among the violence supporters in Negro ghettos.

Data are also available from the NORC survey on the socioeconomic status of these Negro ghetto dwellers. The data in Table 1 show the relationship between gross family income and support of violence. Beyond the $3000 income level the proportion of violence-oriented respondents goes down systematically as income increases. One-quarter of those under Keyserling's "poverty" level of $4000 (but over $3000) were violence oriented, as compared to 18.9 percent of those in the $4000–$5999 bracket and 11.1 percent of those in the highest income bracket. The pattern for the cumulative percentages is roughly similar. These data lend some weight to the argument, frequently heard in the mass media, that violence supporters tend to come from the most disadvantaged strata. However those from families with the lowest incomes deviate somewhat from this pattern: 17.6 percent of those in the lowest income bracket subscribed to violence as a necessary mechanism. The "very poor" were less likely to be violence oriented than the poor just above them. Perhaps these data point to a goal gradient phenomenon. It might be argued that among poor Negroes those closer to the affluent goal are more likely to be violence oriented than others not so close. It should also be noted that half of the 34 violence-oriented Negroes in the sample come from families making incomes above the poverty level of

[7] Governor's Commission on the Los Angeles Riots, *Violence in the City: An End or a Beginning?* Los Angeles, 1965.

[8] Clark, *op. cit.,* p. 326.

$4000. This particular finding suggests that the typical violence supporter in Negro ghettos may not come from the very lowest socio-economic level, although the poor tend to be over-represented among violence supporters.

Another important socioeconomic characteristic relevant to the issue of violence as a mechanism to attain civil rights is education. Table 1 also presents variations in violence orientation by educational attainment. The proportion supporting violence goes down from 22 percent of those Negroes with an eighth grade education or less to 15.3 percent of those with a high school diploma. For Negroes with a 12th grade education or less it does seem that violence support varies inversely with education. However, the college group does not fit into this pattern. Twenty-one percent of the college respondents in the sample saw violence as necessary to attain equal rights; this is roughly the same proportion as of the "eighth grade or less" respondents.[9] The cumulative percentages show a somewhat similar pattern, with the college group having the highest percentage of violence-oriented and ambivalent respondents of the four educational groups.

One additional question on which some light can be shed by the use of these survey data is the question of the isolated ghetto dwellers and support of violence. Are isolated ghetto dwellers more likely than the involved to be violence oriented? One would expect those Negroes strongly committed to a Christian church to be more strongly committed to nonviolent tactics than those who are inactive. The data (Table 2) do lend some support to this expectation. Those who were active church members were less likely to be violence oriented than those who were less active. Fourteen percent of those who attended church twice a month or more often felt violent means to be necessary, as compared to 22 percent of those who attended less frequently. This finding also corroborates Clark's 1943 data. Yet surprisingly enough, about half of the violence-oriented respondents in the sample reported attending church at least twice a month or more often. This finding indicates that the assertion of certain Negro ministers that the "element which riots is not the element which attends church" may be at best a half-truth.[10]

Are Negroes who belong to associations in the community other than the church more likely to be nonviolence oriented than those who are more isolated? The directional differences in the data suggest that this may not be the case. Those who belonged to organizations such as lodges, unions, and civil rights groups were somewhat more likely to be violence oriented than those who were more isolated from this type of local participation. Nineteen percent of those who belonged to one or more such organizations were violence supporters, as compared with 16.5 percent of those who belonged to no such organizations. The cumulative percentages reveal a similar pattern. The data on mass media contact, in this case newspaper reading, confirm this pattern. Those who reported reading newspapers regularly were somewhat more likely to be violence oriented than those who did not. These relatively small percentage differences do not warrant any firm conclusions one way or the other; but they do point to the need for more research on the issue of violence orientation and malintegration into the Negro community.

[9] The militancy of this college group parallels that which Clark found among his college-educated respondents just after the 1943 riots. Clark, *op. cit.*, p. 325.

[10] *Cf.* the comments of the ministers cited in Shapiro and Sullivan, *op. cit.*, p. 65.

MASS COMMUNICATION

34   Mass Media as Social Systems*

Melvin L. De Fleur

In the discussion below the notion of system is applied to the media of mass communication. By describing the major components of the system and their interrelations, the author attempts to explain the "low key" content of these media. Assuming that he is correct in his analysis, what steps would need to be taken to modify the media content and objectives? Should such steps be taken? How and by whom?

. . . A promising approach to understanding the relationship between mass media content and public taste, and for accounting in part for the remarkable continuity in the (low) cultural level of media content is provided by viewing the media as *social systems* which operate within a specific external system — the set of social and cultural conditions that is the American society itself (see Figure 1).

. . . The first major component of the social system of mass communication is the *audience*. . . . The audience is stratified, differentiated, and interrelated in many ways . . . that determine the patterns of attention, interpretation, and response . . . with respect to content of a given type.

. . . Organizations devoted to *research,* to measuring the preferences of media audiences, or to various forms of market research provide informa-

* Excerpts and figure reprinted with the permission of the publisher and of Harper & Row from *Theories of Mass Communication,* copyright © 1966. David McKay Company, Inc., New York, 1966, pp. 145, 151–157.

tion to those responsible for selecting the categories of content that will be distributed to the audience. There is a link, then, between the audience as a component in the system and the market research-rating service organization as a second component. In purely theoretical terms, both components are role systems themselves, and are thus actually subsystems. This is in a sense a one-way link. For very minor (or usually no) personal reward, the audience member selected for study provides information about himself to such an agency. Information flows from the audience component to the research component, but very little flows back. This linkage between components is by comparison relatively simple.

The content itself, of whatever type, flows from some form of *distributor* to the audience. The role system of the distributor component varies in detail from one medium to another. In addition, there are several somewhat distinct subsystems within this general component. First, there are local outlets, which are likely to be in the most immediate contact with the audience. The local newspaper, the local theater, the local broadcasting station play the most immediate part in placing messages before their respective audiences. But inseparably tied to them are other subsystems of this general component. Newspaper syndicates, broadcasting networks, or chains of movie theaters pass content on to their local outlets. The link between these two subsystems is a two-way one. The local outlet provides money and the larger distributor supplies content. Or, the linkage may be that the local outlet provides a service, and the distributor (who is paid elsewhere) provides money.

The relationship between audience and distributor seems at first to be mostly a one-way link. The distributor provides entertainment content (and often advertising), but the audience provides little back in a direct sense. However, it does provide *attention*. In fact, it is precisely the attention of the audience that the distributor is attempting to solicit. He sells this "commodity" directly to his financial backer or sponsor. In addition . . . the audience supplies information to the research component and this is indirectly supplied to the distributor in the form of feedback so that he may gauge the amount of attention he is eliciting. The

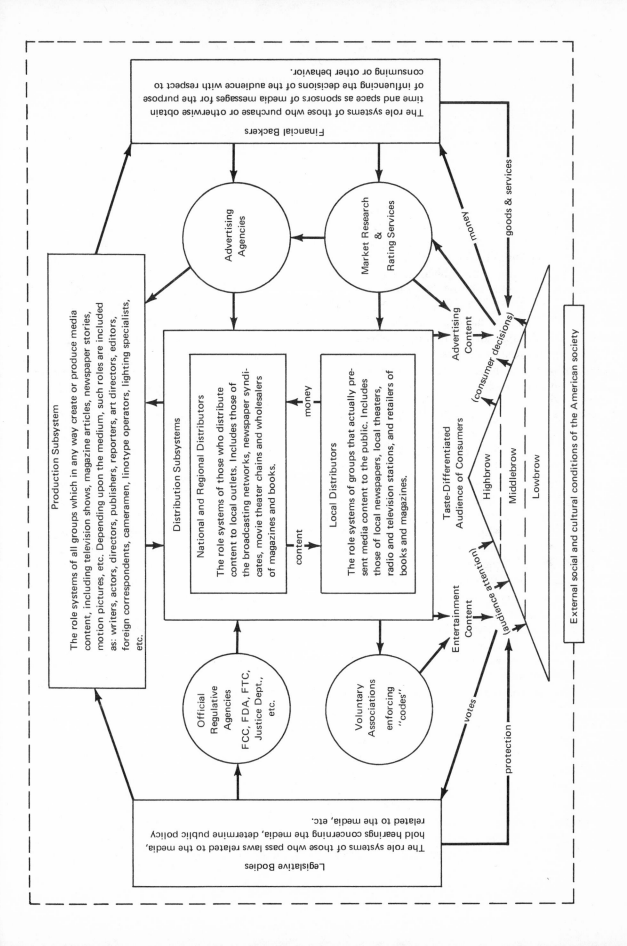

linkages between components grow more complex as we seek the boundaries of the system.

To the audience, the research, and the distributing components, we may add the role system of the *producer* of the content. This component's primary link is with the *financial backer* (or *sponsor*) component and with the distributor, from whom money is obtained and for whom various forms of entertainment content are manufactured. There are a host of subsystems included in this producer component, depending upon the particular medium. Examples are actors, directors, television producers, cameramen, technicians, foreign correspondents, wire service editors, film producers, labor union leaders, publishers, copy editors, clerical staff and many, many more.

Linking the sponsor, distributor, producer, and research organization are the *advertising agencies*. Paid primarily by the sponsor, this component provides (in return) certain ideas and services. For the most part, it provides the distributor with advertising messages. It may have links with the research component as well.

Over this complex set of interrelated components, there are other subsystems that exert *control*. The legislative bodies, at both the state and national level, which enact regulative statutes concerning the media, constitute an important part of such a control component. Another important part of this role subsystem is the official regulative agencies, which implement the policies which have been legislated. The link between the legislative body (control component) and the audience is of course one of votes and public opinion, to which the component is presumably sensitive and dependent. Information lines between audience, legislative bodies, and regulatory agencies are more or less open.

To the regulatory components whose role definitions are found in legal statute can be added the private voluntary associations that develop "codes" and to some degree serve as a control over the distributors. Such distributors provide them with money, and they in turn provide surveillance and other services.

The regulatory subsystems draw definitions of permissible and nonpermissible content from the general set of *external conditions* within which this extremely complicated system operates. Surrounding the entire structure as an external condition are our society's general norms concerning morality, and the expressions that these find in formal law. Similar, although less likely to be incorporated into law, are our general cultural norms and beliefs regarding what will be likely to entertain or otherwise gratify Americans. Thus, we seldom see traditional Chinese opera, but frequently see western horse opera. . . .

. . .

. . . Within the system itself, the principal *internal condition* is, of course, a financial one. Most of the components in the system are occupational role structures, which motivate their incumbent personnel primarily through money. To obtain money, they are all ultimately dependent upon the most central component of all — the audience. Unless its decisions to give attention, to purchase, to vote, etc., are made in favorable ways, the system would undergo severe strain and would eventually collapse.

Almost any dramatic change in the behavior of the audience would cause the most severe disruption in the system for any given medium. . . . Such disruptions are infrequent, but they do occur. The key to heading off dramatic changes in audience behavior, of course, is to provide entertainment content of a type that will satisfy and motivate the largest possible number of audience members to carry out their roles in accord with the needs of the system. Such content will, in other words, *maintain the equilibrium of the system.* The ideal, from the standpoint of the system, is content that will capture the audience member's attention, persuade him to purchase goods, and at the same time be sufficiently within the bounds of moral norms and standards of taste so that unfavorable actions by the regulatory components are not provoked.

The type of entertainment content that seems most capable of eliciting the attention of the largest number of audience members is the more dramatic, low-taste content. Films, television plays, newspaper accounts, or magazine stories that stress physical violence, brutality, sexual gratification, earthy humor, slapstick, or simple melodrama appeal most to those whose educational backgrounds are limited. Their prior socialization has not provided them with sensitive standards for appreciation of the arts or for judging the cultural, educational, or moral merits of a given communication within complex frameworks. In the affluent American society, it is this type of audience member who is by far the most numerous. He has purchasing power in sufficient abundance so that his combined influence on the market can be overwhelming. He is in full possession of the media . . .

What we have called low-taste content is the key element in the social system of the media. It keeps the entire complex together. By continuously catering to the tastes of those who constitute the largest segment of the market, the financial stability of the system can be maintained. The critic who provokes public attention by denouncing media content and socially undesirable behavior may temporarily receive some recognition. He may also achieve some temporary disturbance in the system, or if he is persistent enough he may ultimately even displace some specific form of low-taste content from a given medium altogether. . . .

35 The Weekly Press and the Community*

Alex Edelstein · Otto N. Larsen

In recent years the number of large daily newspapers with city-wide or regional distribution has steadily declined. At the same time there has been a strong upsurge in the number and vitality of weekly newspapers serving limited residential areas within the city. Why are these small weekly papers thriving at a time when large, well-financed papers are unable to survive? It would appear that the weekly neighborhood newspaper must be offering some desirable service to the urban resident that he finds lacking in the great metropolitan daily. Some sociologists believe that the weekly newspaper provides its readers with a sense of neighborhood cohesion and community belonging that cannot be obtained from the metropolitan daily papers. In the following selection a sociologist and a communications authority report on some collaborative research on the contribution of the weekly urban press. Their findings support the idea that these weekly papers play a vital community building role in the modern city. What conditions exist in large cities that would lead residents to value a weekly neighborhood newspaper even when they have access to metropolitan papers? What other agencies or concerns might benefit from emphasizing their local neighborhood affiliation rather than their state or regional character?

The key term in our discussion is "community," for our purpose is to examine the role of the urban weekly as a catalyst for "community" in the sociological sense. Actually, a great variety of meanings and contexts has been attached to the term. Two core meanings stand out, however, from the sociological literature. *"Consensus"* suggests the relationship of those shared and understood values and activities by which the *individual* is perceived by and identifies with others. *"Symbiosis,"* on the other hand, describes the functioning social unit in interdependent terms in the *setting* in which individual and group activities such as employment, protection and education take place. And since the urbanite identifies also with a larger metropolitan community, a communication system is needed to reflect the interdependence of the two environments.

METHOD

The urban weekly studied was the *North Central Outlook,* a free-distribution newspaper delivered to 21,000 households in a high-density residential area in Seattle, Wash. Prior to the field work, a content analysis of a six-month file of the newspaper was undertaken. The categories were devised to be descriptive of the *functional* nature of

* From Alex E. Edelstein and Otto N. Larsen, "The Weekly Press' Contribution to a Sense of Urban Community," *Journalism Quarterly,* Autumn 1960, pp. 489–498. Copyright 1960, *Journalism Quarterly,* University of Minnesota, Minneapolis 14. Reproduced by permission.

the newspaper's content — specifically, the degree to which each content category served to integrate individuals and groups into the community structure.

A departure was made in technique from the usual readership study procedure. Interviewers carried with them a copy of the most recent issue of the newspaper in which *a grouping of several examples* of each content category was clearly outlined in crayon. The interviewer asked, "Do you recall seeing *any items of this kind* in the *Outlook* recently?" This question was followed by others inquiring into (1) the degree to which each category of content produced feelings of *community identification* and (2) the newspaper's effectiveness as a *communication system.*

The sample, an area-cluster design, facilitated the measurement of communicative factors. By sampling clusters of blocks, rather than sampling individual dwelling units, several measures of interpersonal communication were possible, including "back fence" and "front porch" communication.

To carry out the analysis proposed by the theoretical formulation, two major sets of typologies were needed. The first, which we have called "newspaper orientation," classified the audience by its degree of exposure to newspaper content, not by the customary measure of exposure to a single item, but in a broader concept of audience defined by a combination of three measures of exposure:

1. The respondent's claims as to the *frequency* of exposure;
2. How much of the *total content* of the newspaper the respondent said he *usually* reads;
3. The degree of *importance* the respondent attached to his reading, as measured by what he said he would do if the paper were not delivered to him.

An internal measure of the validity of the classifications was incorporated into the research design. Respondents were asked, "How did you first hear about the survey?" The *Outlook* had carried a brief article reporting a "forthcoming survey." If fans were actually the most attentive readers, they would be most likely to have learned of the survey *through the newspaper.* This was validated by the responses. Of the fans, 56.5% first learned

of the survey through the newspaper. Other totals were regulars, 39.7%; moderates, 34.8%; and casuals, 18.0%. A suggestion of the importance attached to the newspaper is shown in the distribution of the 735 respondents by newspaper orientation:

Fans	28.8%
Regulars	26.4%
Moderates	12.1%
Casuals	15.9%
Non-readers	16.8%

More than half the respondents rated either as fans or as regular readers.

The second major typology was defined as "community orientation." Here our items sought to determine the degree to which respondents *identified with* and by their own reports were *integrated into* the social activities and the spatial character of the area. Three measures of "community orientation" are reported here:

1. *Stability of Residence:* At a time when urban areas are undergoing drastic changes and expansion, the length of residence of an individual or family in one area may well be taken as a measure of *social integration.* Qualified further by the economic factor of ownership, there is increasing evidence of the individual's identification with his neighborhood setting.

2. *Image of the Community:* The more that one identifies with a community, the more likely it is that the person will have a positive *image* of it. Thus, respondents were asked to report how much *community feeling* was engendered by specific kinds of newspaper content, so that the newspaper's role in creating, reinforcing or extending community identification could be assessed. Fans, regulars, moderates, casuals and non-readers all were asked if they thought, in the aggregate, if there were more, less or about the same amount of community feeling in their area as compared with other areas. Thus, the relationship between "newspaper orientation" and "community orientation" could be measured.

3. *Social Participation:* It was reasoned that the more a person was *integrated* into the area, the more likely it was that he would demonstrate "gregariousness" or "neighborliness," and that such

TABLE 1 *Newspaper Orientation and Residential Stability**

Newspaper Orientation	Degrees of Residential Stability		
	High (N = 187)	Medium (N = 227)	Low (N = 321)
Fan	41.7%	32.6%	18.7%
Regular	29.4	25.1	25.5
Moderate	8.6	15.9	11.6
Casual	12.3	14.5	19.0
Non-Reader	8.0	11.9	25.2
Totals	100.0%	100.0%	100.0%

* For 8 d.f., $\chi^2 = 59.7$, p < .001.

integration could be related to "newspaper orientation." A Guttman scale of 12 items was used to inquire into the respondent's degree of "neighborliness" or social participation.

Thus, if our measures were effective, a newspaper which was successfully facilitating "community orientation" should reflect in its most loyal readers the attributes of *stability of residence, community identification* and *social participation.*

FINDINGS

A progressive and clear relationship is demonstrated in our findings between *stability of residence* and "newspaper orientation." Table 1 illustrates the degree to which the combined factors of length of residence and ownership are related to exposure to the newspaper. Those who have lived in the community the longest time and are in an ownership status are most likely to be fans, and those who have lived in the community the shortest time and are renters are most likely to be non-readers.

How did the fans compare with those less oriented toward the newspaper in their *image of the community?* Did they demonstrate a stronger identification with the community, or a weaker one, as expressed by degrees of community feeling *produced by content?* Tables 2 and 3 demonstrate a very positive relationship between "newspaper orientation" and image of the community. Those with high "newspaper orientation" report the most "community feeling." Moreover, these respondents credit the newspaper itself with producing that community feeling through exposure to particular kinds of content.

Thus, the measures of stability of residence and community identification demonstrated a positive

TABLE 2 *Newspaper Orientation Related to Perception of "Comparative" Community Feeling**

Community Feeling in Own District Compared with Other Districts	NEWSPAPER ORIENTATION			
	Fans (N = 212)	Regulars (N = 194)	Moderates (N = 89)	Casuals (N = 117)
More	33.8%	28.2%	22.9%	17.8%
Same	38.6	43.6	42.7	36.6
Less	10.6	14.2	16.4	24.0
Don't know	17.0	14.0	18.0	21.6
Totals	100.0%	100.0%	100.0%	100.0%

* For 9 d.f., $\chi^2 = 19.7$, p < .02.

TABLE 3   *Newspaper Orientation and Community Feeling
Attributed to Content**

Degree of Community Feeling Attributed To Content	NEWSPAPER ORIENTATION			
	Fans (N = 212)	Regulars (N = 194)	Moderates (N = 89)	Casuals (N = 117)
Very High	36.5%	31.5%	11.3%	12.0%
High	35.5	33.8	33.4	25.9
Medium	18.4	18.8	29.1	29.8
Low	9.6	15.9	26.2	32.3
Totals	100.0%	100.0%	100.0%	100.0%

* A respondent was given one point if he thought the content "produced" or was "relevant to" community feeling. A maximum of seven points was possible. Those who scored 7–6 points were rated very high; 5–4, high; 3–2, medium; 1–0, low. For 9 d.f., $\chi^2 = 72.7$, $p < .001$.

relationship of "newspaper orientation" to "community orientation," pointing to the urban weekly as a powerful facilitative force for "community" in the sociological sense. This role varied in its impact for various members of the population. Insight is provided into the utility of the community newspaper by examining its audience in terms of sex roles, social and economic status, family size, and age.

1. *Sex Role and Newspaper Orientation:* The neighborhood and the local community may be said to represent the world of the average housewife. She is more likely than her husband to become involved in local activities, and thus can be hypothesized to view the local arena as her preeminent domain. The enrollment of her children into neighborhood schools and their participation in recreational and church activities draw the mother almost irresistibly into the life of the local community. Not only does the local newspaper reflect the range of her social participation, but it also serves as a useful medium for guiding her shopping activities. The relationship of the woman's community role to newspaper orientation is seen in Table 8. Women score significantly higher than men on three measures of exposure.

2. *Education and Economic Status:* While the woman's identification with the local community is reflected in stronger newspaper orientation, it is hypothesized that in the case of some men and women there are broader influences operating to lead these "sophisticates" away from local

orientation and urban weekly newspaper readership. An education and economic status index[1] indicates that high education and economic status may be viewed as a measure of "sophistication" leading away from urban weekly newspaper orientation.

3. *Marital and Family Status:* In the present study, the more active readers were found among the families with the most children, but the progression was not as marked.

Age: Since only adults were interviewed, the age distribution does not extend below 21 years. . . . [The findings] demonstrate a relationship of age to newspaper orientation, with more fans in the oldest age group and more nonreaders in the youngest age group.

We turn now to an examination of the nature of the urban weekly newspaper as a link in a small scale "communication system." The "one-way" nature of the communication has been demonstrated, but a question remains as to how much and what kind of a "flow of information" is generated.

[1] The index was as follows: HIGH — high school graduation or some college and income of $7,500 or more, or some college and income of $5,000 to $7,499; MIDDLE — some high school and income of $7,500 or more, or high school graduation and $5,000-$7,499 income, or some college and income of less than $5,000; LOW — some high school or high school graduation and income of less than $5,000, or some high school and $5,000-$7,499 income. Where either income or education was not reported, the other was used alone.

Two generalized measures of the nature of the communication system were incorporated into the research design. The first, a communicative index, measured the degree to which respondents had discussed with others what they reported they had read in the *Outlook*. The index represents a combined score of communicative activity (discussion) reported on *seven* different categories of content, including advertising . . . high newspaper orientation is related to high communicative activity and low newspaper orientation is reflected in low communicative activity.

The content varied in its communicative "impact" . . . the most exposure was reported to crime and accident news — threats to the community — and the most communicative "impact" was attributed to this kind of content. Generally, the more an item was read, the more likely it was that it would be discussed, and thus incorporated into the communication network of the neighborhood and community.

When an exposure-to-communication ratio was computed, it was demonstrated that the highest ratio of communication to exposure was in the areas of *crime, accidents* and *personal activities,* and that the lowest ratio of communication to exposure was in the categories of *editorials* and *letters to the editor.* News about *organizational activities* and *advertising* made up the middle group. The ratio for each content category is shown below:

Crime	58.2
Accidents	55.5
Personalities	55.4
Advertising	50.6
Organizations	49.1
Editorials	46.9
Letters	45.9

In the aggregate, therefore, it may be stated that about half of the readers of the *Outlook* might be expected "often" or "sometimes" to discuss the content of the newspaper with others.

36 Contradictions in Automobile Advertising*

Jeffrey O'Connell

A point of controversy in contemporary sociology concerns the effects of media content upon audience behavior. Some authorities blame the media for much of the violence in modern society, while others contend that violence in the media has no significant influence upon individual conduct. The research evidence, as revealed in the selections above, is suggestive but perhaps inconclusive. However, the field of advertising provides an excellent arena for testing hypotheses with regard to this issue.

Many advertisers look to the media for assistance in promoting the sale of their products. Yet they often deny that advertising has any influence on the way their products are used after being purchased.

* From Jeffrey O'Connell, "Lambs to Slaughter," *Columbia Journalism Review,* Fall, 1967, pp. 21–28. Reproduced by permission.

Automobile advertising provides an interesting illustration. Traffic accidents may be the number one cause of death among persons in the population between 15 and 25 years of age. Drivers under 25 comprise less than one-fifth of our licensed drivers, but they are charged with responsibility for nearly one-third of the auto accidents. Is there any likely connection between these data and the advertising policies of our automobile manufacturers?

Car makers disseminate widely to young people pamphlets exhorting the teenager to cultivate safe, responsible, courteous driving habits — pamphlets entitled "Good Driving Practices: Courtesy . . . Control, Common Sense" (Chrysler), "How to Earn the Key to Dad's Car" (Ford), "RIGHT behind the wheel" (General Motors). Similarly, they enthusiastically endorse high school driver education to develop, according to the Automotive Safety Foundation, "the attitudes, skills and understanding required in safe . . . driving." According to the foundation: "Today's grim traffic accident statistics reflect hit-or-miss methods of preparing youth for good traffic citizenship."

"Hit-or-miss" is right. At the same time that

the car maker is disseminating these safe driving materials, he is publishing advertisements urging youngsters to hit everything — or everyone — in sight! These are glossy, glamorous ads designed to appeal to the young male car enthusiast in magazines such as *Road and Track, Hot Rod, Motor Trend,* and *Car and Driver.* (These magazines are tremendously popular with teenagers. Any store near a high school is usually stocked with them. In the public library nearest my home, they must be kept under lock and key and yet the librarians still complain that teenage boys manage to pilfer them, so great is their appeal.)

It is most instructive to test the car maker's concern for safety and the fairness of his constant attempt to blame the traffic toll on the "nut behind the wheel" (a favorite Detroit phrase) by comparing quotations from his pamphlets distributed to teenagers and his advertisements aimed at the same group — keeping in mind this is a group whose frightful driving record is caused, according to the car maker, by their "aggressive personality traits and unsound and immature judgment."

(Safe-driving publications)   (Magazine) advertisements

GENERAL MOTORS

[A picture of a roaring lion]

HOW DOES YOUR DRIVING SOUND

. . . We can identify [an immature driver] . . . without even looking — just by hearing the way he drives. A reckless or discourteous driver can be a quiet one, but usually isn't. He tends to make harsh, distinctive noises that reveal his dangerous presence as the rattles, growls, hisses, and buzzes of other menaces. [RIGHT behind the wheel: Articles on Safe Driving from American Youth Magazine, General Motors, p. 24 (1960-61)]

. . . Hulking under the 2 + 2's hood is our whacking great 4 BBL 421. Horsepower — 338. Torque — 459 lb.-ft. Blam . . . For stab-and-steer men, there is a new 3-speed automatic you can lock in any gear. Turbo Hydra-Matic . . . Just straighten right leg, wind tight, move lever. Repeat. Make small noises in your throat. Atta boy tiger! . . . [The 2 + 2 is] just a friendly little . . . saber-toothed pussy cat . . . One of these at fast idle sounds like feeding time at the zoo. [Motor Trend, October 1964, p. 11]

Sometimes a big mouth pays off. The Corvair Monza Spyder's tailpipe . . . makes a throaty growl that

(Safe-driving publications)

Next to a loud and generously used horn, the favorite way for infantile motorists to sound off is with a noisy exhaust. To such drivers, the achievements of the automotive engineers in developing quiet engines represents no progress at all. They love the thrill of power and to them power means noise — lots of throbbing, roaring noise that helps them daydream of being . . . in control of the hottest thing on the road . . . And even during normal cruising, no opportunity must be lost for sudden bursts of speed that produce a gratifying roar. . . .

As one way of rating your own driving ability, check how quietly you drive. The fewer unnecessary noises you make, the sounder your driving.

Those who equate noise with ability are headed for that loudest and worst of all traffic sounds — the crash of metal against metal. [RIGHT behind the wheel, p. 25]

(Magazine) advertisements

pleases people with a feeling for such things. . . . Like any machine that does its job well, the Corvair Spyder looks right . . . and sounds right. [Motor Trend Magazine, February 1964, p. 5]

[A picture of an empty garage at night]

THERE'S A TIGER LOOSE IN THE STREETS

It's late and your bedroom window is open. It's so quiet you can hear the frogs croaking out by the crossroads a good quarter mile away.

After a while a big engined something rumbles by in the night. It checks for a moment at the lights, then swings out onto the highway.

Suddenly a rising moan overrides the rumble as a bunch of extra throats get kicked wide open and start vacuuming air by the cubic acre. The moan gets drowned out in its turn by a booming exhaust note that someone ought to bottle and sell as pure essence of car.

Three times the sound peaks, falls back, peaks again. The last shift into fourth, a throttling back to cruising speed, a dwindle rumble of thunder, and . . . gone. . . . Have you tried one of our 421's

THE 421 MAKERS — PONTIAC [Motor Trend, June 1964, p. 15]

HANDS OFF THE GRAB BAR, CHARLIE, YOU'RE TEARING OUT THE DASH!

The faint shoosh of a seat being depressed. The metallic click of seat belts.

GENERAL MOTORS, Cont'd

A 12-volt starter rasps briefly, followed by a vast convulsion as things mechanical happen in a big way under the hood. The left front fender rises then falls back again as torque prematurely shows its hand. A rumbling boom as of distant thunder. Dust sets to swirling suddenly in the path of a pair of downward pointing exhaust pipes. Someone has just prodded one of our [Pontiac] 421's into fire-in-the-nostrils, show-me-a-road any-road life. . . . [Motor Trend, January 1964, p. 23]

[For infantile motorists] with an unmuffled exhaust normal driving is, of course unthinkable. The engine must be revved up at stops, not idled. Starts must resemble a successful missile launching [RIGHT behind the wheel, p. 25]

A HOWITZER WITH WINDSHIELD WIPERS THE NEW BUICK SKYLARK GRAN SPORT

. . . The Skylark GS . . . is almost like having your own personal-type nuclear deterrent. We've just turned it loose on our dealers. (See the Buick dealers run.) [Motor Trend, March 1965, pp. 48-49]

SON OF GUN THE SKYLARK GRAN SPORT . . .

Ever prodded a throttle with 445-ft. of torque coiled tightly at the end of it?

Do that with one of these and you can start billing yourself as The Human Cannonball. . . .

. . . . The slightly smaller caliber Skylark GS.

Something between a regular Skylark and the Loch Ness Monster. [Motor Trend, April 1965, inside back cover]

AVOID DANGEROUS DRIVING GAMES

Just because you encounter friends along the way to school, don't yield to the impulse to start having a little fun — with automobiles as the game's equipment. Those who treat a car as a toy haven't outgrown playing with toys. Save your exuberance for occasions when "innocent fun" can really be innocent. Keep your competitive spirit for athletics and other school activities where you can gain the limelight for real ability instead of reckless clowning. [RIGHT behind the wheel, p. 14]

A WORD ABOUT THE NOTICEABLE NOVICE
[A picture of a policeman motioning a car to the side of the road]
. . . The novice has certain . . . attributes that make him stand out. A screaming start from the curb as the novice "peels off" is a real attention-getter. In fact, it will earn him a special citation to appear in court in many localities. [The Best Drivers Make It Look Easy, General Motors; unnumbered page, 1964]
The "pro" [driver] knows that anger makes any driver accident prone. A driver in a blind rage is irrational, clumsy and, most of all, unskilled! [The Best Drivers, unnumbered page]

350-hp. CHEVELLE BY CHEVROLET, THE PERFECT SQUELCH
That's a potent squelch to all those others who keep talking about lions, tigers, and such.

A 350 hp squelch goes into any '65 Chevelle you specify. It's that big blue-jowled 327-cubic inch V-8 of song and story, fortified with an extra helping of brute.

. . . Just run your imagination over what [all this performance] does for the welter-weight Chevelle. Not to mention the silencing effect on all those tigers and tamers.

But why rub it in? That's your privilege. Happy squelching. [Motor Trend, February 1965, p. 5]

[A picture of a speeding automobile]
The object in the foreground is a Pontiac 2 + 2. It's what you might call a sudden automobile. Meaning that if it had started accelerating when this sentence began you would now be feeling enormous pressure on your abdomen. [Motor Trend, January 1965, pp. 50-51]

. . . If [Chevelle] . . . doesn't do for your driving what red capes do for bulls, our name isn't Chevrolet Division of General Motors. [Motor Trend, June 1964, p. 3]

Nobody said a nice car can't play mean now and then. . . .

CHEVELLE! BY CHEVROLET [Motor Trend, June 1964, p. 3]

FORD

DRIVING SAFETY: IS IT HARDWARE — SKILL — OR A STATE OF MIND?

Driving has three sides. . . . There are the tangibles — what could be called the nuts-and-bolts. The hardware. These are the features that have been built into the car for greater safety. . . .

But there are even more important sides. They are the skill and state of mind of each driver. It is a matter of knowing or respecting the rules of the road, the rights of others, the capabilities of the car and following the basic rules of driving safety.

You see this state of mind reflected in the comments of the driving experts who have been interviewed for this publication. You see it at Ford Motor Company where there is no let up in the search for ways to increase traffic safety. . . .

We urge you to cultivate a safety state of mind. It is a matter of developing the skills of driving and of *thinking* safety — and turning your thought into positive action. [A Positive View of Good Driving Habits . . . With Expert Tips on Developing Your Personal Safety Program, Ford, Sunday Supplement, appearing in 25 newspapers, January 16, 1966.]

Irvin J. Frey, of Reading, Pennsylvania, is an acknowledged expert [truck driver] in a field where only experts can hold jobs.

"I've noticed too many motorists who are nice, sweet guys at home turn

FOR THE SMOOTHEST BRUTE ON WHEELS, ADD ONE CUBIC INCH TO 427

Everybody knows our 427-solid lifters, headers, double-four-barrels and all. That's a *strong* engine and it comes on like Saturday night in Stanleyville.

Well, we've got a bigger one here — one cube bigger which works out to be 428 cubic inches or 7 Litres, which is its name. But there's a silk shirt over all these muscles. Hydraulic lifters. Single four-valve. 10.5 compression. . . . So now we've got a new kind of car: a brute — but very, very smooth brute. A 97-pound girl can herd this 7-Litre and never know it has 345 horses and 462 pounds-feet of torque — unless she gets mad and stamps her foot.

Then she'll know! . . . [Car & Driver, February, 1966, inside back cover]

[A picture of a car blurred with speed]

THE VELVET BRUTE

This one is a paradox. Up front there's big muscle — 427 cubic inches, two four-barrels, cross-bolted mains, 6,000 rpm and 11.1-to-1 compression — the portrait of Brute Force.

. . . Matter of fact, there just isn't anything else like this Velvet Brute around. Try it — and if you still feel a red-hot performance car ought to ride like a dragster, even that needn't keep you out of a XL. Just run the tires up to 70 pounds and hang on. . . .

Test Drive Total Per-

into terrors when they get behind the wheel," says Frey. "There are several classifications. I call them Kamikazes, who wheel sport cars around as if they were in a road race. [A Positive View of Good Driving Habits, p. 7]

ARE YOU A DUB OR A CHAMP?

An outstanding athlete is not a "grandstander." Do you . . . roar away from a parking place, or race to be the first away from a traffic light? . . .

. . . If you [answer yes] . . . you should change some of your behind-the-wheel habits and your ways of thinking about driving. [Deft Driving, pp. 13, 15]

formance '65 Ford [Motor Trend, January 1965, p. 7]

CYCLONE GT TOP SPINE TINGLER IN THE COMET LINE: CYCLONE GT CONVERTIBLE.

This one will start a glow in any red-blooded American driver. For get-away, there's a new 390 4-barrel V-8 with a high-lift cam. Quite a start. And console-mounted transmission. (The optional 4-speed manual is specially geared for blazing get-away.) . . .

THE BIG BEAUTIFUL PERFORMANCE CHAMPION

MERCURY, COMET GT [Motor Trend, February 1966, back cover]

CHRYSLER

Proper driving attitudes and habits, including the adhering to the rules of the road and driving with courtesy and consideration for others, are every driver's responsibility.

[Care for Your Car for Safe Driving, Chrysler Corp., Automotive Engineering Office, p. 1, March 1963]

We need a new approach to driving. . . . What we need is to build . . . respect. Respect for the power of the car, for the rules of the road, for other people . . . [The Real Fun of Driving!!, Chrysler Motors Corp., p. 3 (1965)]

All of us simply have to work harder at making everybody more safety minded. [The Real Fun of Driving, p. 3]

[A picture of a car turning on a racing strip]

ANIMAL TAMER

(Bring on the Mustangs, Wildcats, Impalas . . . We'll even squash a few Spyders while we're at it.) Dodge has made it a little harder to survive in the asphalt jungle. They just uncaged the Coronet. A hot new Dodge, at a new lower price . . . the new comer that's a real goer.

Your Dodge dealer is waiting for you. Build Coronet the way you want it; Street or Strip.

And then go tame a few tigers. [Motor Trend, November 1964, p. 121]

Beauty and the beast. That's a sleek Dodge Charger with . . . a deep breathing 426 Street Hemi growling under the hood . . . [C]omes on like Genghis Khan. [Motor Trend, May 1966, p. 75]

Many more ads of the same kind can be found in the back issues of any teenage car magazine. Indeed, despite the furor over car safety and despite the assurance to the Congress by vice president John Bugas of Ford, speaking for the industry, that "whatever happened in the past, the industry is now wide-awake [on safety]," advertisements of precisely this kind can be found in *current* issues of teenage car magazines.

At this point, it might be instructive to examine briefly the approach of American Motors.

(Safe-driving publications)

We [at American Motors] believe that the promotion of excessive standards of speed and horsepower, either through participation in racing events or through various forms of advertising is against the public interest.

We consider such promotion not merely inimical to motoring safety itself but also to the sound development of the motor car in all aspects of its full usefulness to the public. [Statement issued by American Motors Corporation, June 1962]

The average motorist normally is quite a responsible person, and most young people are naturally skillful drivers. But we know that speed is attractive to youth . . . as well as to those who have become over-stimulated at a bar.

For the manufacturers themselves to invest competitive passenger-car racing with acceptance and status . . . and to promote their victories and the reason for them . . . would not only tend to authenticate racing on the public thoroughfares — it would *stimulate* it through the glam-

(Magazine) advertisements

AMERICAN MOTORS SHIFTS EMPHASIS TO POWER AND LUXURY
An enthusiastic automobile executive paused the other day while praising a car equipped with a new six-cylinder engine. He leaned across his desk and declared: "That will go from nothing to 60 miles an hour in 13 seconds, and that's better than a lot of V-8's will do."

This tribute to the power of a more lively product did not come from a top official of the Ford Motor Company or the Chrysler Corporation, which have been emphasizing racing to help sell cars. It came, instead, from Roy Abernethy, president of the American Motors Corporation, proponent of the compact Rambler.

Mr. Abernethy's excitement about the new engine may seem out of character for a company that has met huge success by extolling the virtues of an economical car and attacking the "gas guzzling dinosaurs" produced by its competitors. But it underscores a significant change taking place at American Motors.

The car-buying public

(Safe-driving publications)

orous identification of the thrill of power. [Speech by Roy Abernethy, then president, American Motors, before a gathering of advertising and sales executives at Adcraft Club of Detroit, January 18, 1963]

[A picture of speeding cars on a track . . . [To] . . . glamorize and advertise race track speed and wildly excessive horsepower to sell cars . . . *is not in the public interest, and Rambler will have no part in it.*

Reckless glorification of horsepower tempts teenagers to think high-speed driving is 'in' — and safety is 'out'.

It makes irresponsible drivers even more irresponsible.

It contributes to the mounting carnage on the highways all across the nation . . .

. . . We [at Rambler] spend millions on testing, millions more on safety advances.

But not one cent to glorify speed.

We welcome your comments, and invite you to join our crusade for safe motoring. [American Motors advertisement, appearing nationally in newspapers, week of June 1, 1964]

. . . To achieve [total involvement in the field of automotive safety] . . . we need a stronger exercise of leadership at every level. . . .

All of us [in the industry] must continue to try to see and to present the

(Magazine) advertisements

has been shifting its taste toward more racy and expensive cars. Rising affluence has dampened its desire for economic basic transportation. This has damaged American Motors and is forcing the company to sharply alter its image and products.

"We want to move over and let people know we have these things," [Mr. Abernethy] said. "If that's what the people want, we'll give it to them." [The New York Times, September 7, 1964, p. 6.]

[A picture of a speeding Rambler on a race track]
RAMBLER AMERICAN SHOWS ITS NEW MUSCLE! OUTRUNS CORVAIR, DART, FALCON AT DAYTONA. RAMBLER WINS BIG! COMES IN 1, 2 IN CLASS VI ACCELERATION TEST — ONE OF 3 EVENTS IN 1966 PURE OIL PERFORMANCE TRIALS.

This is the car . . . with the newest, biggest, most powerful standard engine in its class — and it shows — out-running Corvair 500, Dodge Dart, Ford Falcon.

This is the car . . . that with automatic transmission, got a tremendous 24.483 miles-per-gallon in the Economy Test. (The only car that could do better, by a scant 0.5 mpg, had such a small engine that it took nearly 4 seconds longer than the American to accelerate from 25 to 70 mph.) [Advertisement appearing nationally, in newspapers, week of January 24, 1966]

(Safe-driving publications)

whole [traffic safety] picture. . . . We cannot afford to point the finger of blame at somebody else or wait for somebody else to lead. The place where responsibility lies is easy to find. Look in the mirror. [Speech by Roy Abernethy, Dealer Highway Safety Meeting, Miami Beach, January 17, 1966]

The result of this turnabout is a proud report by a Rambler dealer in *The Wall Street Journal:* "We're seeing younger people in here asking 'Where's that hot car?' " Other Rambler dealers want still more emphasis on speed and power. Says one California dealer, "Get the biggest engine you can, get on the track and blow up everything in sight."

Henry Ford has said that "the driver is the most important factor [in safety] because, if you drive safely, accidents won't happen."

What can be said about an industry that blames car accidents on unsafe driving and then spends large sums to encourage unsafe driving by the most unsafe drivers?

After I had submitted these ads in testimony before the Congress, Kenneth Ford, the executive editor of *Printer's Ink* (a trade magazine of the advertising industry) took exception in a special report in *Printer's Ink* to my comparing thus the car maker's message in safe driving pamphlets and teenage car ads. Said Ford:

All that sounds pretty devastating . . . [but] actually, it is out of context, willfully scurrilous, and downright vicious. . . . The pamphlets and the ads, as communications vehicles, have two totally different purposes. The first conveys hard information; the second appeals to a "feeling," rather than an actuality. To compare the two is somewhat akin to matching the words against the deeds of a politician.

Concerning Ford's first point, according to the car makers themselves, the crucial problem of young drivers *is* their "feeling" — namely (I cite the car makers again) teenagers' aggressive per-

(Magazine) advertisements

sonality traits, lack of cooperative attitude, and willingness to take undue risks. Thus the pamphlets try to encourage the *right* attitude. All this makes doubly worse any ads that attempt to incite reckless feelings.

As to Ford's second point, perhaps it should not surprise us that, to an adman, "matching words . . . against . . . deeds" is to take words "out of context [and is] willfully scurrilous and downright vicious." To the rest of us, however, a man's words — a politician's or anyone else's — are still a good measure of what his deeds should be.

When the car makers were asked recently to comment on their practice of advertising aimed at the young that encourages unsafe driving, their replies were very revealing.

Said a spokesman for General Motors, "Our ads are by no means all in that [unsafe] vein. We've had quite a campaign on safe driving tips."

A check of the teenage car magazines reveals many stridently irresponsible GM ads for every one concentrating on safe driving tips. But according to GM, the company is justified in having car ads that encourage unsafe driving as long as they are not *all* in that vein!

When asked about the encouragement of unsafe driving in GM's teenage car ads, Gail Smith, the general director of advertising and merchandising for GM, stated: "Naturally in those [hot rod] magazines we use jargon and have an ad appeal which is directed to the young audience. We do not lay undue emphasis on performance but we do make some reference to the car's potential. And we have a safety theme in all our advertising."

But where is the safety theme in the GM ads already quoted?

Smith went on to say that he did not agree with all the GM teenage ads. "When you are with an agency and you write an ad, it is easy sometimes to get carried away," he said. GM, then, advertises in one place that driving a GM car is so dangerous that a driver cannot afford "a moment of inattention," but would have the public believe that GM cannot be expected to control its own advertising of the same cars to exclude unsafe messages.

In responding to questions on teenage ads, a spokesman for Chrysler said: "Chrysler does not feature speed or performance in advertising that is designed for teen age consumption. We do report in newspapers and car buff books our victories in sanctioned races but we make a special point of telling the public that these racing cars are not available to them for purchase, that they are only especially equipped as modified for racing competition."

How, then can Chrysler explain this teenage car ad?

Plymouth Fury, Pace Car. This is the official pace car of the Indianapolis 500. You can buy one just like it . . . It is not a race car. But it has power to spare in its optional 4-bbl. Commando 426 cu.-in. V-8 engine. . . . Put yourself in a Sport Fury soon. We will see you at the checkered flag.

On being asked about its teenage car ads, a spokesman for the Ford Motor Company stated: "We have not been making any substantial changes in our basic advertising philosophy despite the recent safety furor."

Supposedly, according to one press report coming out of Detroit, "the auto industry has calmed down, at least for the moment, its advertising emphasis on hot engines, high horse power, and get-up-and-go cars." As one Chrysler Corporation public relations man explained, "I guess that it is true that some advertising writers get the feeling that Senator Ribicoff is looking over their shoulders as they write their copy." (Senator Abraham Ribicoff of Connecticut heads the Senate subcommittee that focused attention on many phases of the auto safety issue.) But not all advertising writers feel thus constrained — especially at Chrysler. Listen to this Chrysler ad in a teenage car magazine published at the same time as the Chrysler spokesman's remarks:

BOSS HOSS. Dodge Charger with a big, tough 426 . . . Hemi up front makes other steeds look staid. Both for show and go. Charger looks beautifully quick just standing still. And the optional Hemi V-8 supplies a kick to match, with 425 muscular horses. Not a pony or a kitten in the bunch. The hot setup? You bet.

The November, 1966, issue of *Hot Rod* has a GM ad for its Camaro that reads: "CAMARO . . . Its . . . excitement . . . a sporting hustler that's

nothing but lean and forceful." In the same issue, Chrysler advertises its "SPRINT . . . the red-blooded American sports machine. And Ford advertises its "MERCURY CYCLONE . . . The Man's car for men who like their action big!"

Thus, although there has been some toning down of teenage car ads — and, it is true, some adding of safety talk to their texts — improvement is by no means guaranteed as to how long it will last.

In September, 1966, Will Scott, Ford's new director of safety, assured me in conversation that the critics of auto advertising had caused a turnabout in the auto industry's less responsible ads, emphasizing wildness and the like. But within a few days after that assurance from Scott, his own company, the Ford Motor Company, "unleashed" (Ford's word) its new car called the Cougar. At the first showing of the Cougar, it was unveiled "against a background of loud animal roars."

Even more recently Chrysler published this teenage car ad:

BANZAI-I-I*
[Picture of cars blurred with speed]
You've just heard the battlecry of the Belvedere GTX, Hemi-powered, that is 426 cubes, 425 HP, and 490 lbs.-ft of torque — as sung by a 4-speed transmission. And what a commotion they make! Amplified by the Hem's two big AFB-4 barrels.

But then similar war-whoops can be heard from the regular GTX. . . .

Listen, too, to this ad from Plymouth, published within the last few months:

ANNOUNCING THE WILD NEW BARRACUDAS!
These are the sporty new 'Cudas that generate the excitement of a European road race. . . .
These are the cars that live with quickness. . . .
If you want to go the full stormer route, you can order the optional stuff you need. All the way up to a booming 383 cu. in. V-8 which will be ready in plenty of time for Sebring . . .

Interestingly enough, there is an indication that lawyers may soon be reading these advertisements aloud in court. In the summer of 1966, Philip Schemel, age 21, of Springfield, Ohio, brought

* The new Random House Dictionary describes a Banzai attack as "reckless or suicidal."

suit in the United States District Court for the Southern District of Indiana, alleging that he was temporarily paralyzed from the neck down when his car was struck by a Chevrolet Impala going 115 miles an hour. The complaint in Schemel's suit against General Motors for one million dollars read in part:

> . . . Despite the fact that the defendant, General Motors Corporation, knew, or in the exercise of common care and caution should have known, that the public roads and highways in the United States of America were not designed for and were not suitable for automobiles to use them at speeds in excess of 100 miles per hour, that very few, if any, of the drivers operating automobiles on said roads and highways were capable of driving safely at speeds in excess of 100 miles per hour, that the laws of each of the United States of America contemplate maximum speeds of from 60 to 80 miles per hour, and that excessive speeds had killed thousands of drivers of automobiles sold by General Motors Corporation to the ordinary consumer as well as thousands of innocent bystanders, General Motors Corporation not only continued to design, manufacture, sell and distribute automobiles which had more power and which would travel much faster, but General Motors Corporation bragged about how high powered its automobiles were in mass media advertising which has encouraged many irresponsible persons, including [the defendant in this case] . . . to drive at extremely high and dangerous speeds in excess of 100 miles per hour.

The complaint further contended that GM encouraged motorists to drive at excessive speeds by "naming its automobiles names which suggest high speeds such as 'Jetstar' and 'Rocket', all of which has been in wanton disregard for humanity and in sacrifice of the general public for the sole purpose of obtaining astronomical profits . . ."

At the trial level, the complaint was dismissed for failure to state a cause of action. Said the trial judge:

> As to Plaintiff's contention regarding the defendant's alleged method of advertising, it is apparent that if it has the legal right to manufacture automobiles capable of attaining high speeds, it has the right to advertise its merchandise accordingly. Whatever else may be said about it, such advertising is at least truthful. As to the possible adverse effect of defendant's advertising on the driving habits of its customers, it seems to us that such a theory is altogether too speculative to support a legal cause of action.

The trial court's decision was upheld in July, 1967, by a 2-1 decision. It is interesting to note that several of the advertising examples referred to above were used by plaintiff's counsel in his brief filed in this case.

Quite apart from whether lawyers can prove that the wild names were a proximate cause of the resulting accident, surely the effect on a jury of the reading of such names and advertisements may vitally undercut the carmaker's defense in any such case or, in addition, in any products liability case, a contention that in manufacturing its product it was sufficiently concerned about the safety of that product. Such ads could have a particularly devastating effect when the carmakers defend — as they continually do in cases alleging faulty car design — that it was driver error that was the proximate cause of the accident.

CHAPTER FIVE

Socialization: Transactions Between Self and Society

Perhaps the most striking characteristic of human behavior is the frequency and uniformity with which certain acts are repeated. Uniform and repetitive acts are called habits. Habits tend to occur in sets or constellations that fit together in a consistent manner. Excessive drinking of alcohol, for example, is only one aspect of a complex behavior system to which we refer when we use the word "alcoholism." In diagnosing alcoholism we may be equally concerned with the relative absence of alternative modes of self-expression, the fears and anxieties associated with drinking, or the alcoholic's conception of himself as a person who can neither handle his liquor nor get along without it. This means that treatment for alcoholism cannot be directed against the specific act of drinking. To be successful, treatment must be aimed at the modification of a whole array of habits, beliefs, and attitudes.

Behavior and the Individual

How do we explain the uniformity and interdependence of human activities, normal as well as abnormal? Many proponents are found for the theory that man is governed by supernatural forces, that he has a free will, or that his behavior is a product of biological influences. Extreme emphasis on biological factors is reflected in "constitutional psychology" as propounded by William H. Sheldon and his followers. These scholars believe that physique and personality are highly correlated. For instance, they maintain that persons who have soft, round bodies are inclined to be slow-moving, relaxed, even-tempered, sociable, and pleasure-seeking. By contrast, the athletic physique, with its solid construction and rectangular outline, is supposedly associated with an active personality that manipulates people and objects in its search for power and authority. Fragile and delicate bodies, according to the theory, are frequently associated with high-strung, sensitive, cautious personalities that have greater interest in intellectual pursuits than in physical or social activities.

Some Outmoded Theories

The idea that personality is a product of biological forces has considerable support in commonsense observations, folklore, and literature. Santa Claus is usually pictured as a happy, generous person of roly-poly conformation, and variations of the "lean and hungry look" are frequently encountered in literary works. Causal connections are nevertheless difficult to establish in this regard. While Sheldon argues that body type remains constant despite variations in a person's weight, it may be that slow-moving and pleasure-seeking persons develop soft, round bodies because of their food habits and other activities. The actual correlation between physique and personality is still an open question.

Some scholars maintain that natural processes of maturation determine personality development. One of the best-known exponents of this view was the late Arnold Gesell, who used motion picture cameras, hidden observers, and other techniques in charting the stages of human growth from infancy through the first ten or more years of life. Although fluctuations of rapid growth and stability were observed in most children, development tended to follow a typical pattern. The four-year-old, for example, is generally in a period of rapid development. His personality, according to Gesell, grows in scope and complexity as if attempting to keep pace with his rapid physical maturation. He verbalizes constantly, tells tall stories, and tries to appropriate everything for himself. Five years, on the other hand, is the "golden age" of conformity and obedience. At this stage the rate of physical growth levels off temporarily and social development is more orderly. The six-year-old again encounters a difficult period of adjustment. His growth is erratic. His attitudes towards parents and peers are marked by ambivalence and variability; he demands his own way in social relations and is generally hard to handle. At seven, the trend is again toward quieter performance. The child is now inclined to be friendly, passive, and cooperative. The eight-year-old enters another stage of rapid growth, both physically and socially. There is emotional intensity and increased activity marked by tremendous bursts of initiative and spontaneity. Thus, the child's maturation follows a natural cycle comprised of alternating stages of gradual and rapid development.

The behavior and development of most children will tend to fit and thereby to "verify" this theory of maturation. This is especially true if the theory is applied rather loosely to fit specific cases. The four-year-old child whose behavior is similar to that prescribed by the theory for the average three-year-old is described as "maturing rather slowly," while the four-year-old who acts as the theory says a five-year-old should act is regarded as a "precocious" child. Supporters of the theory concede that relative retardation and precocity are frequently observed in children and that fluctuations in development and behavior, in most cases, are nothing for parents to worry about.

Put in the above terms, the theory of maturation is hardly capable of proof or disproof. The theory brings into focus the vicissitudes of growth in most children. It therefore serves as a palliative for parents who are overly concerned that their children may be abnormal in growth and development. The extraordinary appeal of the theory may be due to its therapeutic effect, rather than to its descriptive accuracy or predictive power.

Sociologists deny that human behavior is determined by physical and biological factors alone. They contend that in order to understand behavior we must also take into account the effect of social influences. Man responds to his social environment as well as to his biological needs and to the physical world around him. The social environment is comprised of the groups and organizations to which a person belongs. Groups and organizations are products of social interaction. Their basic function is to coordinate people's activities in the pursuit of certain goals and objectives. Sociologists are interested in how these social systems are established and perpetuated in the careers of individuals — how they are internalized.

The internalization of systems cannot be explained in terms of man's biological heritage or his physical environment. Knowledge of physical and biological factors tells us little about the behavior of a baseball player, an auto mechanic, a parent, or a teacher, for example. We need to know the organizations involved, and the positions and roles assigned to the members. Understanding individual behavior requires knowledge of the structure of social organizations and the impact of this structure on an organization's members.

The uniformity and consistency of behavior reflects the structure of social groups and organizations. If a child is reared in a society that values tradition more highly than social change and invention, he is likely to be punished for failing to conform to social conventions, for challenging sacred beliefs and assumptions, and for innovations in his personal preferences and opinions. Were the same child reared in a modern technological society, he would perhaps be rewarded for his inventiveness and individuality. The way people respond to his behavior, in any case, will reflect the values, beliefs, norms, and sanctions of their social milieu.

The term "social self" refers to a person's perception of his role requirements and his attitudes toward his own roles and the roles of fellow group members. There are two major components of the self. First is a person's *self-conception,* which includes his evaluations of his own aspirations, expectations, and performances, and his evaluations of the attitudes of others toward him. Second is a person's *conception of others,* which includes his evaluation of the attitudes, aspirations, expectations, and performances of other persons who belong to his groups and organizations. The self is a product of group life. It designates modes of behavior acquired through learning and interaction.

Once a particular set of conceptions of self and others has been acquired, a person's behavior tends to confirm and perpetuate these conceptions. The dutiful mother identifies so strongly with her sick child that she suffers with him in his illness. The harassed assistant sublimates his desire to quarrel with his boss by abusing his automobile on his way home from work. The irresponsible college student rationalizes his disinclination to study by explaining that his eyes are tired from too much reading, and takes his girl to the movies. Mechanisms of behavior such as identification, sublimation, rationalization, compensation, and projection, for example, are observed in the behavior of everyone. They are probably necessary for mental health. Nevertheless, many severe behavior disorders develop from the habitual practice of such mechanisms in extreme degree.

The difference between conformity and deviant behavior is largely a matter of degree. Nearly everyone violates some social norms on occasion or experiences thoughts and wishes that are tabu. The relevant issue, from society's standpoint, is the frequency with which a person exhibits such conduct and the degree to which he violates the normative prescriptions. When the members of a community are unanimous in their support of a given norm, the norm tends to be strictly enforced. The nonconformist is ostracized, or punished in some other way. His misbehavior is also likely to be met with personal recriminations and feelings of guilt. Thus, to live in harmony with the group usually requires that we live in harmony with ourselves.

By what means do groups and societies regulate self-development so that people will ordinarily conform to their normative requirements? Conformity, of course, is encouraged by the group's beliefs, values, and especially its sanction system — the rewards and penalties meted out by others. Equally important, however, are the sanctions that result from the person's evaluation of his own behavior. Such personal sanctions (self-inflicted rewards and punishments) are what we mean by voluntary motivation. In general, a person will be motivated to conform to his normative requirements if he (1) perceives the norms accurately, (2) defines the norms as being just and proper, (3) believes that the norms are rewarding and gratifying, (4) anticipates social recognition and approval for conformity, and (5) feels guilty whenever he deviates from the normative requirements. Motivation for conformity depends upon the way a person perceives and defines the roles prescribed for him. Society's task is to control these perceptions and definitions so that the individual will regulate his own behavior in a socially approved manner.

The processes by which an individual learns the values, beliefs, norms, sanctions, and actions of the groups to which he belongs are called, collectively, *socialization.* These are the processes that produce the social self. A human infant at birth does not have a self. He functions with approximately the same repertoire of behaviors as does any other newborn animal. The main difference between the human infant and other animals lies in the tremendous potential of the human organism for the use of symbols and language. That is, the human organism has a vastly superior capacity to produce and utilize many kinds of symbols, including those perceived via the auditory, visual, olfactory, and tactual senses. The use of symbols in communication and interaction permits the deliberate and rational organization of human groups and societies. It also facilitates the indoctrination of individuals in the ways of life prescribed by such groups and societies. Socialization refers to both formal and informal techniques of indoctrination and training.

The social self develops as the child learns to respond appropriately to the many commands and exhortations with which his elders attempt to regulate his behavior. The child learns through interaction with other persons. He sees their gestures, hears their words of encouragement and reproach, and feels their physical punishments and caresses. He is rewarded for imitating their words and actions. Eventually he learns to give himself the same prescriptions that were first given him by his elders and peers. He learns to see himself as others see him. Through this looking-glass self he gains the capacity of self-praise and recrimination. In this way he acquires the values, beliefs, and actions prevalent in the groups to which he belongs.

The looking-glass self explains why people who are traditionally exploited may come to accept the discrimination against them as normal and just, why thieves may acquire great pride in their criminal proficiency, and why the beaten athlete can face a superior adversary with unflinching courage. It also explains the fact that an infant born to American parents and separated from them to be reared among Ubangi children will grow up to express Ubangi beliefs and attitudes. The looking-glass is society's definition of everyday situations, and for most persons there is no other source of social images.

Indeed, society is the means of human survival. The human infant, for example, is completely dependent upon other persons. It can neither feed itself nor defend itself against external dangers. It is without instincts, sentiments, or any other guides to action. Of language, reasoning, and conscience it knows nothing. It is equipped to satisfy certain biological needs by making internal adjustments involving such things as respiration, maintenance of body temperature, regulation of the chemical content of the blood, digestion and absorption of food, and elimination of waste. These adjustments are made by specialized organs that have coordinated functions. But the external sources of food, air, and water, and the sheltered environment needed for the survival and growth, must be provided by outside agents, such as the family, community, and society. More important, the acquisition of social sentiments and skill in the use of symbols requires that children have models in people who have mastered these things. Survival of children as social organisms consequently depends upon sources of almost constant attention, supervision, and affection.

Survival therefore is a social as well as a physiological function. The methods people use in satisfying biological needs may include complicated rituals that have auxiliary social functions. For example, mealtime is much more than a scheduled filling of the stomach. Preparation and serving of food require painstaking care and cooperation among a number of persons and involve necessary rules of order. Mealtime also is the scene of pleasant conversation and story-telling that foster rapport within the group. Many early lessons in patience, self-control, and cooperation are learned at the dining table. Food and drink are used as symbols in honoring courage and accomplishment, in promoting friendship and understanding, and in taking note of important events, such as births, deaths, marriages, and various religious rites. Feasting and drinking ceremonies may be elaborated to the point where the partaking of food is an almost incidental detail. Social prescriptions and expectations are superimposed on man's biological requirements. Many persons would rather die of starvation than to appropriate foods which, according to the norms of the community, do not belong to them. In all societies survival of the group is assigned a higher value than is survival of the individual.

Among the important cultural determinants of personality are the norms regulating child care. The child's earliest social experiences frequently exert a lasting influence on his attitudes and habits. For instance, the indulgent and overly attentive mother can produce in her child dependence, selfishness, and a demanding character. Conversely, the mother who rejects her child may arouse in him attitudes of fear, suspicion, or rebellion. Studies show that infants who suffer from extreme neglect and abuse are inclined to be retarded in the use of their intellectual abilities, slow in the development of their verbal skills, and limited in their capacity to identify with others or to acclimate themselves to changing social demands and responsibilities. The extremely asocial individual who has little conscience and recognizes few normative prescriptions is frequently the product of early parental, and sometimes community, rejection. Variations of personality within a given culture seem to be associated with early experience, especially parent-child and peer-group relations. This raises the question of whether cultures with widely divergent practices of child care may not thereby produce different modal personality types.

There is some support for the contention that different cultures produce different types of personality. For example, studies have been made of the association between basic personality structure and methods of training children among the people of Alor, a small island in the East Indies. The Alorese are characterized as an anxious and suspicious people. They exhibit little ambition, enterprise, or curiosity. Their social relations are often marked by aggressive hostility rather than by mutual trust or affection. These features of basic personality are believed to grow out of techniques of child care, especially the attitudes of independence and neglect demonstrated by Alorese mothers in handling their offspring.

Maternal interest in Alorese children is sporadic, inconsistent, and undependable. Children are usually fed and attended by their older siblings. Also, the

Impact of
Culture on
Socialization

mothers, by constant teasing, tend to irritate their children. Youngsters may be sent on false errands, for instance, and food or other things may be offered them, then withheld. The resultant frustration and anger in the child is regarded by the adults as very amusing. The child's rage produces among the elders displays of laughter and high spirits. As would be expected, the children have frequent temper tantrums. At such times the child may roll on the ground and beat his head into the earth. To this the typical response of the mother is either to ignore the child or to punish him. Eventually, the child, recognizing no reward for his tantrums, discontinues the practice. However, his childhood frustrations may be reinforced in various ways and he may develop symptoms of chronic anxiety, hostility, and revengefulness.

Interconnections between Alorese personality and culture seem to be undeniable. Moreover, such connections between child-care practices and personality development have been noted in other societies. But this does not mean that personality is fixed by early experience or that dramatic changes in an individual's behavior and attitudes rarely occur. Socialization is a continuing process, and the self is highly responsive to changes in a person's social position. Therefore, the behavior of an adult — his aspirations, expectations, and achievements — can be modified by social experiences such as the selection of an occupation, choice of a marital partner, and participation in various groups and organizations.

Early socialization cannot be adequate for the many different positions and roles that people are assigned in their later years. Although some norms are universal and constant throughout the stages of an individual's career, there are also many specialized norms that are attached to a person's educational status, his marital career, his world of work, and many other positions. These norms are acquired

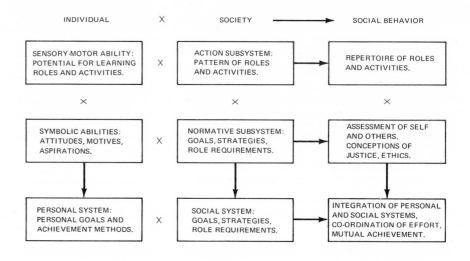

Figure 1

Paradigm of socialization processes. Through social learning the individual acquires a conception of himself as a vital element in the social systems of which he is a member. He internalizes the group's goals and strategies, experiences their virtues and defects, and develops a broader conception of ethics and justice. He contributes in some measure to his social systems and to their integration or disintegration.

through adult socialization, which is a process of learning that continues throughout life, as suggested in Figure 1.

Self-conceptions and perceptions of others inevitably reflect a person's total experience. How to regulate experiences so as to produce the desired results is a problem that confronts every society and culture. It has often been assumed, of course, that man can exert very little influence on the trend of human experience. However, sociologists and other social scientists are learning how social norms can be established or altered, how socialization processes can be redirected, and how societies can be better organized for the pursuit of human goals and objectives. Perhaps it is not too much to expect that man's accomplishments in the physical environment will eventually be rivaled by those in the arena of social action. The potential for social inventions of these kinds is rapidly increasing.

PRIMARY SOCIALIZATION

37 The Social Self*

Alfred R. Lindesmith · Anselm L. Strauss

Every individual, through social participation, acquires a self-conception. Some persons hold themselves in high esteem, are proud, confident, and eager for new experience. Others may feel stupid, anxious, or disgusted with themselves. Such feelings obviously exert great influence on our behavior. These feelings result largely from how well we feel we are doing the things that are expected of us.

Children at an early age become very sensitive to attitudes of approval or disapproval that might be expressed toward them by parents or playmates.

* Reprinted from *Social Psychology*, Revised, by Alfred R. Lindesmith and Anselm L. Strauss, by permission of the authors and The Dryden Press, Inc. (Copyright 1956 by The Dryden Press.) The two excerpts from *Mind, Self, and Society* by G. H. Mead are reprinted here by permission of The University of Chicago Press. (Copyright 1934 by the University of Chicago.)

Play, far from being a random expression of energy, gives the child practice in assuming many of the social roles and responsibilities that will be assigned to him in later years. When the child becomes adept at play, he can join in games and activities which require the concerted effort of a number of persons. It is through the acquisition of social sensibility, the imitation of fellows, and the participation in play activities and games that the child gains the repertoire of social skills necessary for participation in the social world of the adult.

George H. Mead, philosopher and social psychologist, years ago gave some famous lectures on the genesis of personality and the social self. In these lectures Mead elaborated a theory of social maturation that has wide support and popularity even today. The following selection reviews some of Mead's major ideas.

What is meant by role-taking? Discuss the meaning of the "generalized other." When you have finished reading the selection, return to the above questions and answer them carefully according to the theory propounded by the followers of George H. Mead.

G. H. Mead has described graphically how children playfully imitate the roles of elders or associates, and thus gradually develop an ability to see objects, other persons, and themselves from a non-egocentric standpoint. Mead emphasizes what Piaget merely noted in passing, namely, that language is basic in the development of the ability to play roles.

[There are] countless forms of play in which the child assumes the roles of the adults about him. The very universal habit of playing with dolls indicates how ready for expressing, in the child, is the parental attitude, or perhaps one should say, certain of the parental attitudes. The long period of dependence of the human infant during which his interest centers in his relations to those who care for him gives a remarkable opportunity for the play back and forth of this sort of taking of the roles of others. . . . In the play of young children, even when they play together, there is abundant evidence of the child's taking different roles in the process; and a solitary child will keep up the process of stimulating himself by his vocal gestures [spoken words] to act in different roles almost indefinitely. . . . A child plays at being a mother, at being a teacher, at being a policeman; that is, it is taking different roles. . . . We have something that suggests this in what we call the play of animals: a cat will play with her kittens, and dogs with each other. . . . But we do not have in such a situation the . . . taking [of] a definite role in the sense that a child deliberately takes the role of another. . . . He plays that he is, for instance, offering himself something, and he buys it; he gives a letter to himself and takes it away; he addresses himself as a parent, as a teacher; he arrests himself as a policeman. He has a set of stimuli which call out in himself the sort of responses they call out in others. He takes this group of responses and organizes them into a certain whole. Such is the simplest form of being another to one's self. It involves a temporal situation. The child says something in one character and then his responding in another character is a stimulus to himself in the first character, and so the conversation goes on. . . . In that early stage [of childhood] he passes from one role to another just as a whim takes him.[1]

The child's playing at being persons other than himself is paralleled in actual life by the playing of the real roles in which he is involved with parents and playmates. One of the theories of play is that it is a preparation for later adult activity wherein the individual applies the skills that he has acquired. Thus the standards of fair play and the proper attitude toward defeat in competition are often said to be learned on the gridiron or on the "playing fields of Eton." No doubt it is from considerations of this kind

that the widespread absorption of children (and adults) in comic strips and comic books concerns and alarms some, who feel that constant identifications with comic-strip characters of doubtful virtue may lead the children to emulate these fictional "heroes." Without accepting this position one may recognize that this kind of play activity and fantasying gives the child a repertoire of roles and practice in switching from one to the other.

The initial role-taking of the young child is simple and limited, involving only limited and brief fragments of behavior and the imitation of a few specific persons. As the child's circle of acquaintanceship is enlarged, as his mastery of communication develops, and as his real roles multiply in number and become more complex, the role-taking processes become more complicated, as we shall see.

The Generalized Other as an Organization of Others' Role. When the child has developed the ability to grasp the role of one other person at a time, he is on the road to becoming a social being. However, before he can participate in organized adult activity, the child must be able to conceive his own role from the standpoint of all other participants. An illustration will help to make this clear.

Suppose that a group of Air Force men is on a bombing mission. Each man has a definite, assigned general role which involves certain duties and obligations. Each man has a clear conception of his general role as he imagines it from the points of view of all the others. He also has a clear picture of how his own role fits in with the roles of each of the other men.

By contrast, the very young child is able to take the role of only one other person at a time. From this simple kind of role-taking the child eventually develops the ability: (a) to take the roles of all others in the situation, (b) to organize all these roles into an integrated whole, and (c) to view his own behavior from this standpoint. Mead's suggestion of how this learning takes place is as follows:

If we contrast play with . . . an organized game, we note the essential difference that the child who plays

---

[1] G. H. Mead, *Mind, Self, and Society,* University of Chicago Press, Chicago, 1934, pp. 364–65, 150–51.

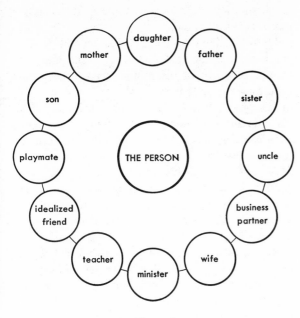

Figure 1

A person learns to look upon his own behavior from the points of view of all these people. He learns their various points of view at different periods in his life, and they have varying importance for the organization of his behavior. (Reprinted from Social Psychology, *Revised, by Alfred R. Lindesmith and Anselm L. Strauss, by permission of the Dryden Press, Inc. Copyright 1956 by The Dryden Press.)*

in a game must be ready to take the attitude of everyone else involved in that game, and that these different roles must have a definite relationship to each other. . . . In a game where a number of individuals are involved . . . the child taking one role must be ready to take the role of everyone else. If he gets in a ball nine he must have the responses of each position involved in his own position. He must know what everyone else is going to do in order to carry out his own play. He has to take all of these roles. They do not all have to be present in consciousness at the same time, but at some moments he has to have three or four individuals present in his own attitude, such as the one who is going to throw the ball, the one who is going to catch it, and so on. . . . The attitudes of the other players which the participant assumes organize into a sort of unit, and it is that organization which controls the response of the individual. . . . Each of his own acts is determined by his assumption of the action of the others who are playing the game . . . he has to have an organization of these roles; otherwise he cannot play the game.[2]

Through his participation in organized games, in play, and in other activities, the child learns to take the role of the participants, and grasps the fact that the roles of others are intertwined. At the same time he comes to see how his own activity within the situation looks from the standpoint of the others. He sees his own role-playing as part of a whole pattern of group activity.

Mead has coined a term for this organization of others' roles; he calls it the "generalized other." He uses this expression because it means that one is taking the related roles of all the other participants rather than the role of just one other person. This concept of the generalized other applies to the organized roles of participants within any defined situation.

The term "generalized other" does not refer to an actual group of people; but rather to a conception or an interpretation which a person derives from his experiences. He then regulates his behavior in terms of these supposed opinions and attitudes of others. He imagines what "people" would say "if they knew" or what they will say "when they know." The term "people" may not have any specific reference to actual persons, but may merely represent the abstract moral standards of his society. These standards widen as role-playing becomes more generalized.

Concept Development and the Organization of Perspectives. The child, like the adult, discriminates between persons, acts, and things in terms of concepts; but the content of his classifications is different from what it will be as he grows more knowledgeable. As new classifications are learned and discovered, old ones change, are revised and qualified. As the child's conceptualizing ability approaches the adult standard his concepts become more numerous and their interrelationships more complex. His ability to play roles and to understand the actions and motives of others develops in a parallel course.

The earlier role conceptions of children are, from the adults' viewpoint, rather curious and

[2] *Ibid.*, pp. 151–152, 154.

often amusing, although in their own way they represent a primitive if incorrect systematization of role. Thus, very young children know there are storekeepers and customers, but they think that the customer buys goods and both he and the storekeeper pay each other. Only the customer buys goods, the storekeeper never does. Monetary activity is confined to buying and selling. Although one storekeeper may help another sell, the distinction between owner and employer is unclear and is not involved in the buying-selling transactions. There are no other roles such as that of manufacturer.[3]

Hartley and his associates[4] have pointed out, in a study of some oddities of children's role conceptions, how the young child is unable to organize certain perspectives properly. Thus a young child conceives of a mother only from one perspective, and denies that mothers can play other roles (that of saleslady, for example). Older children widen the positions from which role-players are viewed until they are able to conceive of any individual as momentarily or permanently playing one role but potentially capable of playing many others. The inflexibility of the very young child, who like Gertrude Stein insists that a mother is a mother is a mother, represents an inability to slide in imagination from perspective to perspective or to organize perspectives into a more inclusive whole.

Hartley's discussion is deficient in that it does not bring out the fact that the young child who cannot conceive of his mother as a saleswoman nevertheless can conceive of her as a daughter of his grandmother. He can do this because in his immature systematization of role concepts, certain roles seem compatible with each other while others do not.

At one step of his concept development the child will deny that two roles are compatible, but later, having grasped their relationship, will agree that they go together. Thus, he will early deny that a teacher can be a storekeeper or vice versa, because each belongs to a different world. Later the child agrees that a teacher could be a storekeeper "after school," but still denies that a storekeeper can be a customer. Still later he sees that a storekeeper can buy in a store and still in a general sense be a storekeeper, but does not yet perceive that the storekeeper must be a customer of manufacturers.

Much of the child's early learning about role relationships occurs in concrete situations where the roles are played out before his eyes. However, most role relationships are rather abstract. Even those relationships that seem most concrete and visible, for example, those between a teacher and a pupil, involve much more than is visible on the surface. Greater maturity and breadth of experience are necessary before the child can be expected to understand the subtler aspects of such relationships.

[3] A. L. Strauss, "The Development and Transformation of Monetary Meanings in the Child," *American Sociological Review,* Vol. 17 (1952), p. 278.

[4] E. Hartley, M. Rosenbaum, and S. Schwartz, "Children's Perceptions of Ethnic Group Membership," *Journal of Psychology,* Vol. 26 (1948), pp. 387–398.

38   Parental Values*

Leonard I. Pearlin · Melvin L. Kohn

The idea that the values parents adhere to in rearing their children differ according to social class is well documented in social research. Middle class parents place more emphasis on self-direction and self-control, while working class parents value conformity and obedience. These differences might be regarded as unique and unexplained aspects of American culture except that comparative studies show similar variations among Italian parents.

Why should these class differences in values be found in two quite different cultures? What is there about the life experience of middle class parents in both Italy and America that leads them to value certain behavior that is quite different from the behavior valued by working class parents? In the following selection the authors seek answers to these questions by examining the different occupational experiences of middle and working class parents. What variations in values might persons acquire in the roles of accountant, national park ranger, garbage collector, service station attendant, astronaut, farmer, bank cashier, policeman, shoe shiner?

The present data from Italy gives us the opportunity to compare the values of American and Italian parents irrespective of their social class. This is the logical place to begin our inquiry, for we can understand the similarities and differences in the effects that social class may have in the United States and Italy only in the context of a more general understanding of the similarities and differences of the two cultures.

METHODS

The present inquiry, conducted in Turin, Italy, during 1962–63, was designed to be comparable to the study of social class and parent-child relationships we conducted in Washington, D.C., in 1956–57.[1] As in the earlier study, interviews were conducted with approximately equal numbers of middle- and working-class parents of fifth-grade children. This was accomplished by over-selecting schools known to have a heavy representation of pupils from middle-class families. Once the schools were selected, the choice of families was made randomly from the rosters of fifth-grade pupils.

Letters were sent beforehand to parents chosen for inclusion, informing them of the nature and purpose of the interviews and the sponsorship of the study. Approximately 85 per cent of those contacted participated. Interviews were completed with 861 individuals. Of these, 341 are with fathers and 520 with mothers. The majority, 628, are husband and wife pairs. The interview schedule itself underwent several pretests and revisions. These pretests, coupled with a number of unstructured qualitative interviews, led to the abandonment of some questions and the inclusion of new ones. At the same time, the pretests provided a further training opportunity for the interviewing staff, all of whom had had some previous experience.

A word about Turin. It is the capital city of the Piedmont region, located in the shadow of the Alps below France. It has long been a principal industrial center. The availability of hydroelectric power has helped make it the fourth largest city of Italy, with a population of over one million. It is economically crucial to the entire country, currently producing 90 per cent of the nation's automobiles and many of its metallurgical and textile products. Historically, it has been an important center of political ferment and activity. Much of the impetus for the reunification of Italy in the middle of the nineteenth century originated in this city; indeed Turin was the first capital of Italy. To this day it has a lively political climate, mirrored by many informal discussion groups in the city's *piazze* as well as by a broad spectrum of trade unions that reflect the principal political currents of the country.

* Excerpted from the *American Sociological Review,* Vol. 31 (August 1966), pp. 466–479. Reprinted by permission. Copyright © 1966 by The American Sociological Association.

[1] For a statement of the design of the earlier study, see Melvin L. Kohn, "Social Class and Parental Values," *American Journal of Sociology,* 64 (January, 1959), pp. 337–351.

TABLE 1   *Proportion of Parents in Italy and the United States Selecting Each Characteristic as One of the Three Most Important, by Social Class*

| | Italy | | | | United States | | | |
| | Fathers | | Mothers | | Fathers | | Mothers | |
Characteristic	Middle-class	Working-class	Middle-class	Working-class	Middle-class	Working-class	Middle-class	Working-class
1. That he is honest	.54	.54	.55	.55	.52	.58	.44	.53
2. That he has good manners	.32*	.44*	.44	.51	.24	.25	.19	.24
3. That he obeys his parents well	.31*	.45*	.36*	.48*	.13*	.39*	.20*	.33*
4. That he acts in a serious way	.25	.18	.18	.20	.00	.03	.00	.01
5. That he has self-control	.23*	.11*	16*	.08*	.20*	.06*	.22*	.13*
6. That he is dependable	.23*	.13*	.21*	.10*	.33*	.08*	.24	.21
7. That he is able to defend himself	.21	.14	.17*	.08*	.02*	.17*	.10	.06
8. That he is ambitious	.19	.17	.21	.19	.17	.08	.07	.13
9. That he be happy	.14*	.07*	.16	.14	.37	.22	.46*	.36*
10. That he be considerate of others	.11	.09	.10*	.03*	.35*	.14*	.39*	.27*
11. That he is affectionate	.10	.12	.13	.12	.02	.08	.05	.04
12. That he is neat and clean	.09	.14	.07*	.14*	.15	.17	.11*	.20*
13. That he is popular with other children	.09	.07	.06	.04	.15	.25	.15	.18
14. That he is a good student	.08*	.24*	.13*	.24*	.07	.19	.15	.17
15. That he is liked by adults	.04	.09	.05	.09	.00	.08	.05	.04
16. That he is curious about things	.03	.01	.02	.01	.13	.08	.18*	.06*
17. That he is able to play by himself	.01	.02	.00	.01	.02	.06	.01	.02
Number of cases	160	148	263	205	46	36	174	165

* Social class difference statistically significant at the .05 level using chi-square test.

NATION, CLASS, AND VALUES

Is social class related to parental values in Italy in much the same way as in the United States? The question requires an examination of the relationship of both nationality and class to parental values. Table 1 presents the value choices of Italian and American fathers and mothers, separately for the middle and working class of each country. The major lessons of this table are two: (1) nationality exerts a profound effect on parental values; (2) despite the considerable difference between Italian and American parental values, social class bears much the same relationship to parental values in both countries.

In some basic respects, the values of Italian and American parents are quite similar. Honesty, for example, is given the highest priority of all the seventeen characteristics in both Italy and the United States. But the rank-order of value choices is substantially different in the two countries. Moreover, regardless of social class, American

parents are more likely than are Italian parents to value happiness, popularity, and consideration; regardless of social class, Italian parents are more likely than are American parents to value manners, obedience, and seriousness. American parents' values are perhaps more child-centered, emphasizing the child's own development and gratifications, while Italian parental values seem more adult-centered, emphasizing the child's conformity to adult standards.[2]

Despite the differences between Italian and American parental values, almost all of the class relationships noted in the United States are found in Italy too. Of the eight characteristics signifi-

[2] One other difference between the two countries is not shown in Table 1. In the United States, working-class parents are more likely to value certain characteristics for girls and others for boys. Italian parents make virtually no distinction between what is desirable for boys and for girls. In fact, the sex of the child makes no difference for anything we shall discuss in this paper. Thus, for simplicity of presentation, the data will not be presented separately for boys and for girls.

cantly related to social class in the United States, six are significantly related to social class in Italy, too,[3] obedience and neatness being more highly valued by the working than by the middle class in both countries, self-control, dependability, happiness and consideration being more highly valued by the middle than by the working class in both countries. In both Italy and the United States, middle-class parents are more likely than working-class parents to value characteristics that bespeak the child's self-direction, and working-class parents are more likely than middle-class parents to value characteristics that bespeak his conformity to external proscription.

The *degree* to which social class is related to parental values in either the United States or Italy should not be exaggerated. The rank-order of middle-class parents' value choices does not differ greatly from that of working-class parents in either country; the difference between the proportions of middle- and working-class parents who value any given characteristic is never very large. What is impressive is that the relationship of social class to parental values is so very nearly identical in the two countries — this despite the considerable cultural difference between the two.

There are two characteristics, self-control and obedience, that seem to us to embody most clearly the essential difference between the middle-class emphasis on self-direction and the working-class emphasis on conformity to external proscription. In fact, these two show a *completely* consistent relationship to social class: in both countries, middle-class mothers and fathers are significantly

more likely than working-class mothers and fathers to value self-control, both for sons and for daughters; in both countries, working-class mothers and fathers are significantly more likely than middle-class mothers and fathers to value obedience, both for sons and for daughters.

It is clear, then, that a high valuation of obedience is not something peculiar to the *American* working class. On the contrary, obedience is more highly valued by working- than by middle-class parents in both countries, and by Italians more than by Americans in both classes. The cumulative effect is that Italian working-class parents are most apt to value obedience, American middle-class parents least so.

And so we have arrived at a rather striking answer to our first question. Not only are the effects of social class much the same in Italy and in the United States; more than that, the conservatism apparent in American working-class parental values, far from being a peculiarly American phenomenon, is even more apparent in Italian working-class values. It seems the lot of the worker that he must accord respect to authority, and teach his children to do so. This is the case with the American worker and even more so with the Italian worker.

THE RELATIONSHIP OF SELF-CONTROL TO OBEDIENCE

Because self-control and obedience most clearly express the essential difference between middle- and working-class values, and because they are so consistently related to social class in both the United States and Italy, we shall focus all further analyses on these two values. We shall search the different occupational experiences characteristic of the two social classes for a possible explanation of middle-class parents' greater valuation of self-control and working-class parents' greater valuation of obedience. This requires a closer examination of the two values.

Self-control and obedience would seem to be antithetical values, in that one stresses control from within and the other conformity to external authority. Yet in another respect they are similar: although they put the locus of control in different places, both stress control. In this respect they

[3] The exceptions are curiosity and ability to defend oneself. Middle-class American mothers, particularly *upper*-middle-class American mothers, value curiosity more highly than do working-class mothers. Not so in Italy. A problem of language may be at issue, for we could find no Italian word equivalent for "curiosity" which was free of the connotation of voyeurism.

In the United States, working-class fathers are more likely than middle-class fathers to value the child's ability to defend himself. In Italy, the middle class is more apt to value the ability to defend oneself. We suspect that in the Italian context, to defend oneself has the connotation, "to be able to take care of oneself in a potentially hostile world."

Two characteristics are not significantly related to social class in the United States but are in Italy — good manners and being a good student. Both are more highly valued by the working man than by the middle class.

TABLE 2   *Distribution of Italian Fathers by Social Class, Valuation of Self-Control, and Valuation of Obedience*

Valuation of Obedience	Valuation of Self-Control							
	Middle-Class Fathers				Working-Class Fathers			
	Highly	Moderately	Not at all	Total	Highly	Moderately	Not at all	Total
Highly	7	12	32	51	5	18	47	70
Moderately	13	29	7	49	3	16	14	33
Not At All	17	7	43	67	8	5	42	55
Total	37	48	82	167	16	39	103	158

stand as one in contrast to such values, for example, as happiness or popularity or being affectionate. It would be well to see to what degree the difference between the two social classes is a matter of a differential valuation of *control,* whatever its source, and to what degree it is a matter of wanting the locus of control to be internal rather than external.

This analysis can be done more precisely with our Italian than with our American data because we secured more information in the Italian study. There we asked parents not only to choose the three most important characteristics from our standard list of seventeen, but also to tell us whether they considered each of the seventeen important or unimportant. This enables us to classify a parent as valuing a particular characteristic *highly* (that is, selecting it as one of the three most important), *moderately* (that is, saying that it is important, but not choosing it as one of the three most important), or *not at all.* With this index, it is possible to see how the valuation of obedience is related to the valuation of self-control. Table 2 presents this for Italian fathers.[4]

For present purposes, there are two basic ways of examining the data of Table 2. The first ignores the source of control, treating self-control and

obedience as equally indicative of an emphasis on *control.* It asks: are middle-class fathers any more or less likely than working-class fathers to emphasize control in their values for their children? Looked at this way, Table 2 shows that virtually identical proportions of middle- and working-class fathers consider both values very important, one very important and the other moderately important, both moderately important, one moderately important and the other unimportant, or neither even moderately important. The conclusion is unequivocal: class differences in the valuation of self-control and obedience are not at all a result of any differential emphasis on control *per se.*

The second way of examining the data of Table 2 is to focus on the differential emphasis on internal as opposed to external sources of control, as exemplified by the relative emphasis given to self-control and obedience. This permits us to specify the difference between middle- and working-class fathers' values more precisely than was possible before. It is not just that working-class fathers are more apt to value obedience and middle-class fathers self-control. More precisely: although fathers of both social classes are disposed to value obedience, working-class fathers are more likely than middle-class fathers to value obedience *highly* and *exclusively,* and to regard self-control as altogether unimportant. Middle-class fathers are more apt to think that self-control is important. In effect, obedience is valued throughout the culture; what differentiates the middle from the working class is that in the middle class self-control has come to be valued too.

[4] The picture is essentially the same for Italian mothers; we shall limit ourselves to the fathers because this is more relevant to the subsequent analyses of the effects of various dimensions of occupation on parental values. Too few of the mothers have jobs to permit a systematic analysis of their occupational situations. Later we shall briefly consider the relevance of fathers' occupational circumstances to their wives' values.

TABLE 3 *Proportion of Italian Fathers Valuing Self-Control and Obedience, by Social Class*

Valuation of Self-Control and Obedience	Middle Class	Working Class
1. Value self-control highly	.22	.10
2. Value self-control moderately	.29	.25
3. Value neither self-control nor obedience	.26	.26
4. Value obedience moderately and self-control not at all	.04	.09
5. Value obedience highly and self-control not at all	.19	.30
Total	1.00	1.00
Number of cases	167	158

$$\chi^2 = 14.2, \text{4 d.f.}$$
$$p < .01$$

Source: Table 2.

Therefore, we shall array the data so as to highlight the contrast between the valuation of obedience alone and of self-control at all. Table 3 presents the data of Table 2 rearranged to show the basic social class comparison most pointedly. At one extreme are the fathers who value self-control highly, followed by those who value self-control moderately. The middle category is comprised of those who attach no value to either. The fourth category is made up of those who value obedience moderately and self-control not at all. The extreme group values obedience highly and self-control not at all. The two classes differ most in the two extreme categories.

In the following analyses we shall combine the five categories into three. Nothing is lost or distorted in thus simplifying the presentation.

THE STRUCTURAL SOURCES OF SELF-DIRECTION IN OCCUPATIONAL EXPERIENCE

We are interested in those dimensions of occupational experience that meet a limited set of conditions: (1) They must be relatively constant aspects of occupation, durable over time, predictable, and patterned. In short, they must be built into the structure of the occupation. (2) They must differ between middle- and working-class occupations — for the only dimensions of occupational experience that will help us to explain class differences in parental values are those that are differentially distributed between middle-class and working-class occupations. (3) They must have *a priori* relevance to the values under scrutiny.

The last is conceptually the most important. Our interest was directed to occupation not only because occupation is so important to social class, but also because we thought that the central difference between middle- and working-class occupations was precisely what seemed to be at issue in the difference between middle- and working-class values: Middle-class occupations require a greater degree of self-direction; working-class occupations, in larger measure, require that one follow explicit rules set down by someone in authority. Our assumption is that the structural requirements of the job are easily transmuted into personal requirements for doing the job well, and that the characteristics one needs in so major a segment of life as one's occupation come to be valued generally — for oneself, and for one's children as well. In particular, jobs that allow, and require, self-direction should lead to high valuation of self-control; jobs that require following the directions established by someone in authority should lead to high valuation of obedience and low valuation of self-control.

Our task then was to specify and index those dimensions of occupation that meet the above conditions and define the overall occupational situation as conducive to self-direction or to conformity to external direction. There seem to be three such dimensions — the closeness of supervision to which a person is subjected, the principal type of work that he does, and the degree to which the job requires self-reliance. These three are closely related empirically as well as conceptually. But since they are analytically distinct, we shall consider them *seriatim* and only then examine their combined effect.

The Closeness of Supervision. A limiting condition for the exercise of self-direction is the closeness of supervision to which one is subjected. Under conditions of close supervision little leeway is possible. On the other hand, freedom from close

TABLE 4   *Proportion of Italian Fathers Valuing Self-Control and Obedience, by Social Class and Closeness of Job Supervision*

Valuation of Self-Control and Obedience	Self-employed	Middle Class			Working Class		
		Loose super-vision	Inter-mediate	Close super-vision	Loose super-vision	Inter-mediate	Close super-vision
Value self-control	.51	.49	.52	.40	.39	.38	.26
Value neither self-control nor obedience	.26	.30	.24	.10	.31	.25	.19
Value obedience, but not self-control	.23	.21	.24	.50	.30	.37	.55
Total	1.00	1.00	1.00	1.00	1.00	1.00	1.00
Number of cases	77	57	17	10	62	48	38
		$\chi^2 = 4.4$, 4 d.f.			$\chi^2 = 6.2$, 4 d.f.		
		$p < .40$			$p < .20$		

supervision, while a condition for self-direction, does not necessarily indicate autonomy. The absence of close supervision might simply indicate a situation where work is so unvaryingly routine that it requires little or no overseeing. In general, however, a situation of close supervision can be taken to mean a limitation on self-direction; we should expect closely-supervised men to be more likely to value obedience and less likely to value self-control for their children, than would less closely-supervised men.

We measured closeness of supervision by three questions, which together form a reasonably satisfactory Guttman scale: (1) How much control does your direct supervisor exercise over your work? (2) Do you feel that you are able to make decisions about the things that have true importance to your work? (3) Do you have much influence on the way things go at your work? The scale pattern is such that men who report that their supervisors exert little or no control over them are likely also to claim decision-making power and considerable influence. Those who are unable to exert influence over their work claim little decision-making power and say they are subject to considerable control.

The relationship between supervision and parental values is stronger for the working class, for only in the working class is any considerable proportion of men subjected to very close super-

vision. Nevertheless, the relationships are essentially the same in the two social classes. (See Table 4.) The more a man feels he is closely directed from above, the more likely he is to value obedience exclusively. The greater the sense of power a man feels he has over the conditions of his work, the more likely he is to value self-control for his children. The self-employed, who are shown separately, are less likely to value obedience alone, and more likely to value self-control, than are any but the least closely supervised of middle-class employees. In sum: in both classes, men who follow orders at work tend to value obedience, those who have greater degrees of freedom in their work situations are more likely to value self-control for their children.

The Principal Component of Work: Things, People, or Ideas

A second dimension of occupation intimately involved in the question of the degree to which one's actions are self-directed is the substance of the work one does. Most working-class occupations deal with things, most middle-class occupations deal with interpersonal relationships or ideas. Work with "things" typically entails the least freedom for independent judgment, work with "ideas" typically entails the most freedom, even necessity, for independent judgment. The manipulation of ideas is necessarily under more direct control of the individual, while the manipulation of things is more easily standardized and regulated by others. Where the task involves ideas, there is a natural opportunity for autonomy of decision and action.

We asked fathers: "In almost all occupations it is necessary to work with ideas, people, and things, but occupations differ in the extent to which they require these types of activities. Considering now a typical day's work, which of these three aspects of work is most important in your occupation?"

The correspondence between social class and whether one works with things, people, or ideas is close, but fortunately for analytic purposes, not complete. There are some middle-class men who deal principally with things, and some working-class men who deal principally with ideas or people. The middle-class men who say that *things* are most important to their work are mostly small entrepreneur-craftsmen, dentists, engineers and highly-trained technicians, managers and sales personnel whose work is very directly related to the manufacture or distribution of hard goods, and a few clerks whose jobs are so routinized that they see themselves as working with things rather than data. The majority of working-class men who say that they work primarily with *people* are in service occupations; the remainder are foremen. Working-class men who say that *ideas* are most important to their work are concentrated in highly skilled jobs. What differentiates them from other skilled workers is that their jobs seem to re-

quire more independence of judgment or evaluation — as in the case of mechanics who specialize in diagnosis, or testers in the automobile factory. In six cases, however, we have no evidence that the job is substantially different from other working-class jobs. Fortunately for the main thrust of our argument, these six men do not account for the relationships we shall present.

Table 5 clearly shows that men who work mainly with things are the least disposed to value self-control, and that men who work mainly with ideas are the most disposed to value self-control. Obedience is most likely to be stressed by those men, whatever their social class, who work mostly with things. The relationships are strong and consistent in both social classes.

The Requirement of Self-Reliance in Work

The degree of supervision to which a man is subject and the type of work he does put limits on the degree of self-direction a job permits. Within these limits, some jobs in fact *require* that a man make independent judgments, take responsibility, invest himself in his work, while others, although they may permit it, do not actually require it. This is the last aspect of self-direction we wish to index: The degree to which the job *requires* self-reliance.

In the interview, fathers were given a list of qualities and asked to indicate, on the basis of their own occupational experience, the rank order of the three that were most important to doing well at their work. For the remainder they were asked

TABLE 5 *Proportion of Italian Fathers Valuing Self-Control and Obedience, by Social Class and Major Component of Work*

Valuation of Self-Control and Obedience	Middle Class			Working Class		
	Things	People	Ideas	Things	People	Ideas
Value self-control	.27	.51	.64	.23	.45	.62
Value neither self-control nor obedience	.45	.26	.21	.29	.16	.27
Value obedience, but not self-control	.28	.23	.15	.48	.39	.11
Total	1.00	1.00	1.00	1.00	1.00	1.00
Number of cases	22	73	58	96	31	26
	$\chi^2 = 9.2$, 4 d.f.			$\chi^2 = 18.7$, 4 d.f.		
	$p < .06$			$p < .001$		

TABLE 6 *Proportion of Italian Fathers Valuing Self-Control and Obedience, by Social Class and Degree of Self-Reliance Required in Work*

Valuation of Self-Control and Obedience	Middle Class				Working Class			
	Least self-reliance	Next least	Next greatest	Greatest self-reliance	Least self-reliance	Next least	Next greatest	Greatest self-reliance
Value self-control	.05	.46	.57	.83	.14	.37	.41	.65
Value neither self-control nor obedience	.58	.26	.24	.00	.33	.28	.21	.21
Value obedience, but not self-control	.37	.28	.19	.17	.53	.35	.38	.14
Total	1.00	1.00	1.00	1.00	1.00	1.00	1.00	1.00
Number of cases	19	50	70	24	36	64	42	14
	$\chi^2 = 30.6$, 6 d.f.				$\chi^2 = 14.0$, 6 d.f.			
	$p < .001$				$p < .05$			

to distinguish between those that were important and unimportant. Four of these items form the dimension "self-reliance." They are: to understand one's self; to be intelligent; to have trust in one's self; and to have a sense of responsibility. The index was formed by giving a weight of four if an item was ranked first in importance, three if it was ranked second, two if it was ranked third, and one if it was considered important even though unranked. These scores were then added for each respondent. Essentially, the higher a man's score, the more his work requires self-reliance. As expected, a man's score on self-reliance is related to his authority situation, and even more closely to

whether he works primarily with ideas, people, or things. It follows that degree of self-reliance is also closely related to social class.

The relationship between the degree to which a man feels that his job requires self-reliance and his values for his children is so large that if job and family were not different realms we would suspect it to be merely tautological. (See Table 6.) Men who think their jobs require a large measure of self-reliance are overwhelmingly more likely to value self-control than are men who do not. Men who think their jobs require little or no self-reliance are overwhelmingly more likely to value obedience.

39 Self Concept as an Insulator Against Delinquency*

Walter C. Reckless · Simon Dinitz

Ellen Murray

One of the facts to be explained by theories of delinquency is that even in communities that have the highest rates most of the youngsters conform to the social norms most of the time. If delinquency were a product of social and cultural forces, why should there be so much conformity in delinquent neighborhoods? The following study attempts to answer this question in terms of self-conceptions of delinquent and non-delinquent youths.

Try to apply the reasoning of this article to young people of college age. Today young people in their teens or twenties are exposed to a wide range of behaviors that our society may generally regard as undesirable. Among persons with equal exposure, some participate and some do not. What determines whether a person begins to use drugs, works out a "living arrangement" with a member of the opposite sex, or starts participating in a weekly "beer bust?" Is "self-concept" a useful tool in helping to understand this phenomenon? What other explanatory concepts might be useful?

This study is concerned with sixth-grade boys[1] in the highest delinquency areas in Columbus, Ohio, who have not become delinquent and who are not expected to become delinquent. What insulates an early teen-age boy against delinquency? Is it possible to identify certain components that enable young adolescent boys to develop or main-tain non-delinquent habits and patterns of behavior in the growing up process?

METHODOLOGY

In order to study the non-delinquent boy, all 30 sixth-grade teachers in schools located in the highest delinquency areas in Columbus were asked to nominate those white boys in their school rooms who would not, in their opinion, ever experience police or juvenile court contact. Treating each nominee separately, the teachers were then requested to indicate their reasons for the selection of a particular boy. Of the eligible students, 192, or just over half, were selected and evaluated by their teachers as being "insulated" against delinquency. A check of police and juvenile court records revealed that 16 (8.3 per cent) of those nominated had some type of law enforcement record, and these boys were eliminated from further consideration. Repeated neighborhood visits failed to locate 51 others. In the remaining cases both the boy and his mother were interviewed.

The 125 "good" boys comprising the final sample were given a series of four self-administered scales to complete. These included, in somewhat modified form, (1) the delinquency proneness and (2) social responsibility scales of the Gough[2] California Personality Inventory, (3) an occupational preference instrument,[3] (4) and one measuring the boy's conception of self, his family,

* From Walter C. Reckless, Simon Dinitz, and Ellen Murray, "Self Concept as an Insulator Against Delinquency," *American Sociological Review*, Vol. 21 (December 1956), pp. 744–746. Used by permission. Copyright © 1956 by the American Sociological Association.

[1] Sixth-grade students were selected for study because they represent the threshold age group for entry into legal and social delinquency. In Columbus, Ohio, the delinquency rate doubles between the ages of 11 and 12. For details on age and census tract rates see John S. Ely, *An Ecological Study of Juvenile Delinquency in Franklin County,* Master's Thesis, The Ohio State University, 1952.

[2] For a detailed description of the delinquency proneness scale see Harrison G. Gough, "Systematic Validation of a Test for Delinquency," reprint of a paper delivered at the annual meeting of the American Psychological Association, September, 1954; Harrison G. Gough and Donald Peterson, "The Identification and Measurement of Predispositional Factors in Crime and Delinquency," *Journal of Consulting Psychology,* 16:1952, pp. 207–212; and Harrison G. Gough, "A Sociological Theory of Psychopathy," *American Journal of Sociology,* 53:1948, pp. 359–366. In correspondence with us, Gough suggested the inclusion of the social responsibility scale as a "partial index of the 'social control' factor in personality . . . (and) an index of delinquency proneness based upon both scales would be a better measure for your study." Both scales were used with Gough's expressed permission and consent.

[3] This instrument was developed in a study of juvenile vulnerability to delinquency. See James E. Morlock, *Predicting Delinquency in a Homogeneous Group of Pre-Adolescent Boys,* Doctoral Dissertation, The Ohio State University, 1947.

and other interpersonal relations.[4] At the same time, though not in the presence of the nominee, the mother or mother-surrogate was interviewed with an open-ended schedule to determine the boy's developmental history, his patterns of association, and the family situation. (Now nearing completion is a comparable study of sixth-grade boys in the same classrooms who were nominated by the same teachers as being likely to come into contact with the police and juvenile court.)

FINDINGS

An analysis of the scores made by these 125 nominees on the delinquency vulnerability (De) and social responsibility (Re) scales seemed to justify their selection as "good" boys. Out of a possible total (De) score of 54, scores ranged from a low of 4 to a high of 34 with a mean of 14.57 and a standard deviation of 6.4. This mean score was significantly lower than that of school behavior problem boys, young delinquents, or reformatory inmates investigated in other studies. In fact, the average De score of the sample subjects was below that obtained in all but one previous study using the same scale.[5]

For a twelve-year-old group, the nominees scored remarkably high on the social responsibility scale. The mean Re score for the group was 28.86 with a standard deviation of 3.60 and a range of 12 to 40 out of a possible 42 points. This mean score was appreciably higher than that achieved by school disciplinary cases, delinquents, and prisoners tested in other studies. The correlation between the two sets of scores was −.605, indicating a significant and negative relationship between delinquency vulnerability and social responsibility as measured by these instruments.

In response to self-evaluation items, the 125 boys portrayed themselves as law-abiding and obedient. Specifically, the vast majority defined themselves as being stricter about right and wrong than most people, indicated that they attempted

to keep out of trouble at all costs, and further indicated that they tried to conform to the expectations of their parents, teachers, and others.[6] The nominees did not conceive of themselves as prospects for juvenile court action or detention,[7] and they stated that their participation in such activities as stealing had been minimal and that their friends were either entirely or almost completely free of police and juvenile court contact.[8] As part of their conformity pattern, the respondents rarely played "hookey" from school and almost without exception indicated a liking for school. Finally, the "good" boys visualized themselves as being about average in ability, activity level, and aggressiveness. When asked "What do you think keeps boys out of trouble?" the respondents listed parental direction (a good home), non-deviant companions, and work, as well as other conventional answers. It would therefore appear that the internalization of these non-deviant attitudes played a significant role in the "insulation" of these boys.

Nominee perceptions of family interaction also appeared to be highly favorable. As noted in a previous paper, the 125 families were stable maritally, residentially, and economically.[9] There appeared to be close parental supervision of the boys' activities and associates, an intense parental interest in the welfare of the children, and a de-

---

[4] This measure was based in part on the Glueck findings concerning family variables and delinquency. See Sheldon and Eleanor Glueck, *Unraveling Juvenile Delinquency,* New York: The Commonwealth Fund, 1950.

[5] Based on data furnished by Gough.

[6] Nearly 60 per cent of the boys thought they were stricter about right and wrong than most people; 85 per cent tried to escape trouble at all costs; 81 per cent stressed their obedience to their parents' wishes, and 81 per cent were concerned with the reaction of friends and others to their behavior. These and other data were based on responses to items in one or more of the four instruments used.

[7] For example, 70 per cent of the boys in answering the questions on the Morlock scale seemed certain that they would never be brought before the Juvenile court; only one respondent believed he would have future contact with the court. Two-thirds indicated certainty about never being taken to jail. Some 57 per cent did not rule out the possibility of becoming policemen.

[8] In only 12 per cent of the cases had any of the friends of these boys experienced police or juvenile court contact.

[9] For a complete discussion of the family backgrounds of the nominees see Walter C. Reckless, Simon Dinitz, and Ellen Murray, "The 'Good' Boy in a High Delinquency Area," accepted for publication in the *Journal of Criminal Law, Criminology, and Police Science.*

sire to indoctrinate them with non-deviant attitudes and patterns. This parental supervision and interest seemed to be the outstanding characteristic of the family profiles. It extended over the entire range of their sons' activities — from friendship patterns, leisure activities, and after school employment to movie attendance and the performance of well-defined duties at home. Thus, as regards companions for example, the mothers almost without exception stated that they knew the boys' friends, that these friends were good boys and that, in fact, the boys couldn't have chosen better companions. The mothers also knew the whereabouts of their sons at almost all times and many insisted on this knowledge.

Despite this intensive supervision, the boys did not feel themselves to be unduly restricted. In general, the nominees appeared satisfied with the amount of parental affection and attention and with the quality of discipline and punishment given them. They viewed their home life as pleasant and their parents as understanding.

Low and high scorers on the delinquency proneness scale and their respective mothers did not differ significantly in their evaluations of these various aspects of family interaction. Of the 22 home background variables tested — ranging from the percentage of boys from broken homes to parental favoritism — none was found to be significantly related to the delinquency proneness scores. This finding was hardly surprising in view of the non-representative character of the sample group and the relatively small amount of variation in the family settings. It may also well be that in defining his interpersonal and family relationships favorably, the "good" boy, regardless of the degree of his "goodness" as measured by various scales, is in fact expressing the positive attitudes and perceptions that are important components in his "goodness."

While there was no appreciable variation in aspects of family interaction between the low and high scorers, the boys as a group and their mothers as a group did differ significantly in some of their evaluations. These differences were largely centered around the activity level of the boys, the definitions of the fairness and severity of parental punishment, and the amount of bickering in the home. Mothers thought their sons to be more active, punishment to be less frequent and severe, and parental tranquility to be more pervasive than did the nominees. Most significantly, perhaps, the mothers expressed less satisfaction with the role played by the boys' fathers than did the boys. Briefly, the mothers pictured their husbands as being relatively aloof and rigid in their affectional relationships with their sons. The nominees, however, could not differentiate between their parents in this regard.

These divergences in perceptions may largely reflect age, sex, and role differences in expectations of what constitutes satisfactory family relationships. Consequently, predictive tables based on the parents' conceptions of the boy and his relationships would necessarily be different in many particulars from those based on the boys' conceptions.

CONCLUSION

"Insulation" against delinquency on the part of these boys may be viewed as an on-going process reflecting an internalization of non-delinquent values and conformity to the expectations of significant others. Whether the subjects, now largely unreceptive to delinquent norms of conduct, will continue to remain "good" in the future remains problematic. The answer to this question, it is felt, will depend on their ability to maintain their present self-images in the face of mounting situational pressures.[10]

While this pilot study points to the presence of a socially acceptable concept of self as the insulator against delinquency, the research does not indicate how the boy in the high delinquency area acquired his self image. It may have been acquired by social definition of role from significant figures in his milieu, such as a mother, a relative, a priest, a settlement house worker, a teacher, etc. It might have been a by-product of effective socialization of the child, which had the good fortune of not misfiring. On the other hand, it may have

---

[10] See Daniel Glaser, "Criminality Theories and Behavioral Images," *American Journal of Sociology*, 61 (March, 1956), pp. 433–444.

been an out-growth of discovery in social experience that playing the part of the good boy and remaining a good boy bring maximum satisfactions (of acceptance) to the boy himself. Finally, there is a strong suspicion that a well-developed concept of self as a "good boy" is the component which keeps middle- and upper-class boys, who live in the better neighborhoods, out of delinquency. The point is that this component seems to be strong enough to "insulate" the adolescent against delinquency in the unfavorable neighborhoods.

ADULT SOCIALIZATION

40 Learning to Belong*

Melvin Seeman

In the following article a leading investigator of alienation reports on the conclusions he can draw from a series of related research projects. His research was conducted in the reformatories, hospitals, and labor unions of several countries. These investigations enable him to specify quite clearly the circumstances under which individuals become alienated from the values, beliefs, and behavior standards of their community. More important, they suggest ways in which people may achieve a sense of belonging. How might these studies be adapted to the campus scene? Under what conditions might we expect students to experience feelings of normlessness and powerlessness?

Most of us in the United States now live in the great faceless conglomerates of population — the large metropolitan areas with their strung-out suburban belts — where who one's neighbors are is largely a matter of accident, and it usually doesn't pay to get closely involved with them because they keep changing. Parents and children are close —

perhaps even closer than before — as long as they live in the same house; but older generations and other relatives drift away, take jobs in other cities, go to retirement homes, have their own interests and associates. Often it seems painful but realistic to conclude that, in the last analysis, you and your family are alone, and the only ones you can really count on for help and support are yourselves. No one else cares.

The American legend has it that not much more than a generation ago it used to be very different. Our fathers lived, mostly, in a golden age of belonging, in the traditional tree-shaded small town or closely-knit neighborhood (complete with the *Saturday Evening Post* version of a colonial-style church at the end of the block). Everyone was friendly and solicitous, and in case of need neighbors by the tens and cousins by the dozens would come running.

For most of us this dream, to the extent that it ever was real, is dead.

It is the dominant theme of "mass theory" in social psychology that such social and personal ties cannot be cut or seriously weakened without major damage — both to us and to the democratic process. Torn loose from so many of our emotional supports and roots — from the guidelines that remind us who we are and what we are worth — we must, so the theme goes, become prey increasingly to feelings of isolation, helplessness, and alienation.

But a theme is not yet a theory. It becomes a theory by being specific about processes — by describing the step-by-step development from cause to effect. How do the feelings of isolation, helplessness and alienation come about and what is their consequence? Mass theory becomes useful when it combines (a) history and social structure with (b) a description of the psychological effects of that structure, those alienative effects which in turn lead to (c) predicted behavior. *Alienation* is the center and the key to mass theory — it is produced by the structure of society, and it produces distinctive behavior.

To describe this process in greater detail:

Historically and *structurally* the old roots and close relationships have practically disappeared and been replaced by anonymity and impersonality in social and personal life, and by bureaucracy and mechanization at work.

Psychologically this must result in *alienation.* Alienation can take a number of forms: feelings of powerlessness, rootlessness, lack of standards and beliefs, and "self-estrangement" (having no clear idea of your personality or place, not even "belonging" to yourself).

Alienation in turn results in *alienated behavior,* such as political passivity, racial and religious prejudice, taking part in movements that promise to usher in the millenium (but have little immediate or practical effect) and the like.

SUCCESS AND FAILURE

Since personal alienation is the key element, psychological theory is crucial to its understanding. In trying to understand and explain these psychological processes, I have found the social learning theory of Julian B. Rotter very helpful. (*Social Learning and Clinical Psychology,* Prentice-Hall, 1954) Rotter's principal contention is that human behavior depends on (1) the degree to which a person *expects* that the behavior will have a successful outcome, and (2) the *value* of that success to the person trying to achieve it. If these factors are powerful, separately or together, the behavior is most likely to occur. Specifically, if a person expects that learning something will help him achieve some goal, and/or he values that goal, he is more likely to learn.

Rotter's theory helps clarify the different meanings of alienation. Let us concentrate on what is probably the most important aspect of alienation in mass society — feelings of *powerlessness,* a person's belief that there is little he can do to bring about what he wants. People conceive of success and failure as being not only due to *external* factors — those that work on a man essentially from the outside and are usually considered beyond his control (luck, fate, "city hall," or "they") — but also *internal* factors, coming from within, which often do give him some control (skills, motives, determination, work).

Rotter and his co-workers argue that most experimental studies in learning usually unwittingly emphasize *external* control — the experimenter himself controls most of the pressures and conditions of the situation, and the subject is really not independent at all. If the subject could feel that he had some personal control over the learning, could relate it to his own needs and self-respect, then the patterns and amounts of learning might be very different.

A number of recent studies have supported this principle. These studies show that when the same learning task is performed in two separate ways, with two sets of instructions — one, for instance, emphasizing the skill and energy required from the learner, and the other stressing the luck or chance aspect of the task (*internal* versus *external* control) — there are striking differences in learning and retention. A person will definitely learn *less* from experiences he conceives to be dominated by outsiders, or by chance, which he feels he cannot influence.

This finding parallels the argument of the followers of mass theory that the isolated individual in "the lonely crowd," subordinated to and intimidated by bureaucracy, becomes convinced of his powerlessness and gives up learning about those things that might affect his future. As a specific example, he becomes apathetic and indifferent to politics — "You can't fight city hall."

Thus, mass society theory and Rotter's social learning theory agree that those persons with greater feelings of powerlessness will not learn as much or as well as those who feel they exercise some control over the factors that influence their lives.

UNIVERSAL ALIENATION

The statement that feelings of powerlessness inhibit knowledge is a basic conclusion about human beings. If true, it should be true not only of a few people, but of many; not only of those in our country but in other nations as well. It should be true not only about one type of learning, but throughout a wide spectrum of learning situations. Providing always, of course, that the learning is *relevant to control* — that it seems to the learner to be giving him a tool he can use to change his condition. Thus, an unemployed man learning how and where best to apply for a job is acquiring *control-relevant* information — while one learning baseball batting averages is not. The alienated can presumably learn escapist and irrelevant information as quickly as anyone — perhaps more quickly.

To test the hypothesis that the connection between feelings of powerlessness and inhibition of learning was generally true of mankind, we conducted several studies on powerlessness and alienation:

  in different institutions (a hospital and a reformatory)
  with different degrees of belonging to a work organization (unorganized versus unionized workers in Columbus, Ohio);
  and in different nations (Sweden and the United States).

Although specific items used in the several studies (hospital, reformatory, Columbus, and Sweden) varied somewhat, in all cases the person was offered a choice between an expression of mastery and one of powerlessness. For example:

  "Many times I feel that I have little influence over the things that happen to me" or "I do not believe that chance and luck are very important in my life";

  "Becoming a success is a matter of hard work; luck has little or nothing to do with it" or "Getting a job depends mainly on being in the right place at the right time."

The study of the hospital, published by John W. Evans and myself in the *American Sociological Review* (1962), and of the reformatory in *American Journal of Sociology* (1963), may be considered as a pair. They were both done in the United States. They sought to find out how feelings of powerlessness are related to lack of knowledge and information, in places where knowledge and information might give the individual some understanding and control of his fate. The hospital study dealt with tuberculosis patients; we found that those with the strongest feelings of powerlessness knew less about health matters than those not so alienated. In the reformatory study, inmates with greater feelings of helplessness learned relatively little when given information about parole, even though it might have helped shorten their confinement.

A third American study with Arthur G. Neal (*American Sociological Review,* 1946) was designed to test whether, as predicted, members of a formal occupational organization, such as a union or professional association, would feel less powerless than non-members. In form and feeling (if not always in fact) joining a vocational association apparently dedicated to a common goal should give a member some feeling of control over his job destiny, and perhaps over broader socio-economic matters as well. Mass theory postulates that the great centers of power — government and the major corporations — are rapidly increasing in size and impersonality. At the same time, and as a consequence, jobs are becoming more specialized, more interchangeable, and the workers are moving more and more from job to job and city to city. This breakdown of personal identification with his work is supposed to make the worker feel more insignificant, expendable, and isolated ("just another cog"). The labor organizations that mediate between him and the great bureaucracies should therefore become more and more important to him, especially as a means of providing him with some sense of control.

ORGANIZED FOR POWER

We picked at random about 800 adult male names from the Columbus, Ohio, city directory, and mailed questionnaires to them designed to explore this relationship between union membership and feelings of powerlessness. About 57 percent answered — 245 manual workers and 216 non-manuals.

The results of the Columbus study were definite. When factors such as age, income, education, and type of job are equal, unorganized workers *do* feel more powerless. This was true of both manual and non-manual workers. (The powerlessness was a little greater for workers who changed jobs most often.) Further, these results were *specific* to powerlessness; that is, a test of the workers' generalized unhappiness (anomie) showed that the unorganized do not feel significantly more despairing about everything (or even most things) than the organized — it is apparently a rather specific sense of *mastery,* but not of well-being in general, that organization membership provides.

On the basis of the Columbus study we could state that feelings of powerlessness do arise among unorganized workers in the United States. But a further demonstration seemed necessary — one that could combine all three elements — organization, powerlessness and knowledge — into a single study; that could show whether these findings were peculiar to America; and that could concentrate on a broader field than health or corrections — the field of politics and international affairs.

Accordingly, a study was designed for Sweden to fulfill these needs, and was carried out by interview (in Swedish) with a sample of the male work force in Malmo. (Malmo is Sweden's third largest city, population about 240,000, with a heavy concentration of commercial and seaport occupations.) A random sample of males aged twenty to seventy-nine was drawn from the official register maintained by government authorities. A total of 558 workers were interviewed.

The interview contained questions on three major variables:

FEELINGS OF POWERLESSNESS. (The individual's expectations of control), proferring the usual choice between items expressing mastery and powerlessness.

ORGANIZATION MEMBERSHIP. Apart from simple membership in a union or other work organization, evidence was gathered on (a) the person's *degree* of participation, and (b) his *involvement* in organizations outside of work.

POLITICAL KNOWLEDGE. A sixteen-item information test dealt with both Swedish politics and international affairs.

When the Swedish data had been collected, checked and evaluated, the differences were found to be consistently and significantly as predicted: *high feelings of powerlessness and low political knowledge were found together among the unorganized workers.* Second, there was a relatively small but predictable difference between those who were officials and those who were simply members of unions.

MASTER OF THE POLITICAL SHIP

These results are clearly consistent with the learning and mass society theses. But before they can be accepted without question, other complicating factors must be eliminated. What about education? Could differences in education be the real underlying cause of the differences in feelings of powerlessness? What about other factors, such as age or job prestige? A close examination of the data, correcting for education and the other elements, makes the result even more emphatic. In Sweden as in the United States, neither education nor other differences obliterated the trend. High powerlessness among the workers appeared to flow from lack of union membership and was intimately related to low political knowledge.

The officers of the unions were shown to have the lowest feelings of powerlessness, and to be highest in political knowledge but was this due to the fact that they were *officers,* and therefore a special kind of member (and also, perhaps, a special breed of cat with different personality characteristics); or was it primarily because they were more involved — "more engaged" — in the affairs of the union, and therefore more capable of exerting control? Would other "more engaged" members (who were non-officers) also be less alienated, and have greater capacity for learning control-relevant information?

"Engaged" members, we decided, would be those who attended meetings regularly, considered the union to be important in their lives, and thought individual members were important and influential in the union. Pitting the scores of such rank-and-file members against the "less engaged" we found a parallel with the overall comparison of organized versus unorganized workers. The relationship is modest but consistent: the greater the personal involvement in union meetings and affairs, the less the feelings of powerlessness; and for the manual workers (who would generally tend to have less education) involvement and amount of political knowledge go together as well. (This picture calls to mind the old socialist ideal of the politically-wise proletarian who spent much time in study and discussion of the political and economic factors that controlled his life, and then organized to do something about them.)

We found, too, that the person's *interest* in political affairs is part of the same picture. Of course, those with more interest in politics have greater knowledge of it; but more important here is the fact that strong feelings of powerlessness go along with low interest. Those who do not feel mastery do not develop interest and do not learn.

This interest, or lack of it, is directly related to union membership — to belonging to an organization that could exert job control. Organized workers were significantly more interested in political affairs than the non-union workers. And this interest, again, was *specific* to what we call *control-relevant* information. The unorganized were *not* totally withdrawn or apathetic; they were just as interested as the organized workers in personal and local affairs and in discussing their work. But the unorganized felt powerless to control their larger destinies — and politics and international affairs represented these larger destinies.

So far, these conclusions agree with both learning theory and mass theory. Men with little hope for success feel powerless, lose interest in, and have difficulty learning control-relevant information.

However, it must be recalled that Rotter's learning theory made a distinction between a person's *expectation* that he can achieve a goal, and the *value* he places on that goal. Theoretically at least, a person will not try very earnestly for a goal he does not value, no matter how sure he is he can get it; contrariwise, he may try very hard, even with little hope of achievement, if he wants the goal badly enough.

In the American reformatory study, knowledge which might have helped the inmate have some control over his future (parole information) and non-control knowledge (descriptive information about the institution) were both offered to inmates tested. We split the subjects into two groups — those who tended to conform to what prison authorities wanted of them, who seemed to value the officially approved goals and behavior set for them (working hard, obeying regulations, making no trouble, trying to meet parole requirements) and those who would not conform. We reasoned that if the inmate did not value parole (as part of the prison system) very highly, then whether or not he believed he could achieve it was not very

important in determining whether he would learn parole information; however if he did value parole, his expectation (or lack of it) that he could determine his own life should affect how much he would study and learn about parole. The results were consistent with this view: generally, those inmates who valued the conventional standards of how to get ahead in the reformatory world, who "conformed," learned more of the parole information than did the "unconventionals." But even in this conforming group, those who felt powerless learned less. We may conclude then that both the *value* of the goal and the *expectation* of achieving it will be reflected in how much learning a man will acquire that relates to the goal.

RISING EXPECTATIONS

Summarizing the overall conclusions of all four studies:

POWERLESSNESS AND ORGANIZATION. A person's feelings of self-reliance and power are tied up with whether he belongs to an organization that has some control over his occupational destiny. If he does belong to such an organization — union, business or professional association — his further feelings of mastery are directly tied up with how actively he works in it — whether he has some control over *its* destiny.

POWERLESSNESS AND LEARNING. The ability to learn and retain knowledge which has some connection with control over an individual's future (politics, parole, or health information) is also directly affected by belonging to a union or other relevant organization, and to a person's alienation. To the extent that he feels powerless to affect his future, he will not learn as well what he needs to know to affect it. And he will not be interested in it — he may even reject it.

To the degree that he *expects* to achieve his goal, he will attend to the associated learning; to the degree that he *values* the goal, he will also be oriented to learn.

The connection between organization membership and powerlessness holds true from nation to nation — it is as true in Sweden, for example, as in the United States.

The connection between powerlessness and learning holds true through many different kinds of organizations (reformatories, hospitals, unions) and many different kinds of control information (parole and health information, politics, international affairs).

These studies are perhaps more important for what they promise than for what they presently accomplish. The promise is that controlled studies of this kind, carried out in various cultures and settings, can establish the validity of arguments and theories about contemporary life which depend upon the idea of alienation. There is much literature of this kind, both inside and outside of social science; and it deals with a wide range of subjects — for example, mass movements, inter-group prejudice, mass communication, and politics. It is a literature which touches a powerful array of basic human values: normlessness and trust, meaninglessness and understanding, self-estrangement and integrity.

The promise is that we can concern ourselves with such large questions about the individual in modern society and test long-held theories that have highly practical consequences — learning what it really means, under various circumstances, to exert control, to sink roots, to find understanding, or even to be oneself.

41 The Western Electric Researches*

George C. Homans

Changes in the social situation frequently have unanticipated effects on human behavior. Political and advertising campaigns sometimes have a "boomerang" effect. Good deeds are sometimes discounted because ulterior motives may be suspected. In sum, the way people respond to a situation depends upon their perception of the situation and not just its objective features. The following study examines employee behavior in a rather complicated work situation.

In reading the selection try to identify the crucial factors in the workers' perceptions and motivations. What lessons can management learn from the study?

Perhaps the most important program of research studied by the Committee on Work in Industry of the National Research Council is that which has been carried on at the Hawthorne (Chicago) Works of the Western Electric Company. This program was described by H. A. Wright and M. L.

Putnam of the Western Electric Company and by F. J. Roethlisberger, now Professor of Human Relations, Graduate School of Business Administration, Harvard University, particularly at a meeting of the Committee held on March 9, 1938. These men, together with Elton Mayo and G. A. Pennock, both members of the Committee, had been intimately associated with the research.[1]

A word about the Western Electric Company is a necessary introduction to what follows. This company is engaged in manufacturing equipment for the telephone industry. Besides doing this part of its work, it has always shown concern for the welfare of its employees. In the matter of wages and hours, it has maintained a high standard. It has provided good physical conditions for its employees; and it has tried to make use of every established method of vocational guidance in the effort to suit the worker to his work. The efforts of the company have been rewarded in good industrial relations: there has been no strike or other severe symptom of discontent for over twenty years. In short there is no reason to doubt that while these researches were being carried out, the morale of the company was high and that the em-

* Reproduced from National Research Council, *The Fatigue of Workers,* by permission of Reinhold Book Corporation, a subsidiary of Chapman-Reinhold, Inc., New York, 1951.

[1] This research has been described in detail in a number of papers and in at least three books. The books are: Elton Mayo, *The Human Problems of an Industrial Civilization* (New York: The Macmillan Company, 1933); T. N. Whitehead, *The Industrial Worker,* 2 vols. (Cambridge: Harvard University Press, 1938); F. J. Roethlisberger and W. J. Dickson, *Management and the Worker* (Cambridge: Harvard University Press, 1939).

ployees, as a body, had confidence in the abilities and motives of the company management. These facts had an important bearing on the results achieved.

The program of research which will be described grew out of a study conducted at Hawthorne by the Western Electric Company in collaboration with the National Research Council, the aim of which was to determine the relation between intensity of illumination and efficiency of workers, measured in output. One of the experiments made was the following: Two groups of employees doing similar work under similar conditions were chosen, and records of output were kept for each group. The intensity of the light under which one group worked was varied, while that under which the other group worked was held constant. By this method the investigators hoped to isolate from the effect of other variables the effect of changes in the intensity of illumination on the rate of output.

In this hope they were disappointed. The experiment failed to show any simple relation between experimental changes in the intensity of illumination and observed changes in the rate of output. The investigators concluded that this result was obtained, not because such a relation did not exist, but because it was in fact impossible to isolate it from the other variables entering into any determination of productive efficiency. This kind of difficulty, of course, has been encountered in experimental work in many fields. Furthermore, the investigators were in agreement as to the character of some of these other variables. They were convinced that one of the major factors which prevented their securing a satisfactory result was psychological. The employees being tested were reacting to changes in light intensity in the way in which they assumed that they were expected to react. That is, when light intensity was increased they were expected to produce more; when it was decreased they were expected to produce less. A further experiment was devised to demonstrate this point. The light bulbs were changed, as they had been changed before, and the workers were allowed to assume that as a result there would be more light. They commented favorably on the increased illumination. As a matter of fact, the bulbs had been replaced with others of just the same power. Other experiments of the sort were

made, and in each case the results could be explained as a "psychological" reaction rather than as a "physiological" one.

This discovery seemed to be important. It suggested that the relations between other physical conditions and the efficiency of workers might be obscured by similar psychological reactions. Nevertheless, the investigators were determined to continue in their course. They recognized the existence of the psychological factors, but they thought of them only as disturbing influences. They were not yet ready to turn their attention to the psychological factors themselves. Instead, they were concerned with devising a better way of eliminating them from the experiments, and the experiments they wanted to try by no means ended with illumination. For instance, there was the question of what was called "fatigue." Little information existed about the effect on efficiency of changes in the hours of work and the introduction of rest pauses. The investigators finally came to the conclusion that if a small group of workers were isolated in a separate room and asked to cooperate, the psychological reaction would in time disappear, and they would work exactly as they felt. That is, changes in their rate of output would be the direct result of changes in the physical conditions of work and nothing else.

The decision to organize such a group was in fact taken. A small number of workers was to be selected and placed in a separate room, where experiments were to be made with different kinds of working conditions in order to see if more exact information could be secured. Six questions were asked by those setting up the experiment. They were the following:

1. Do employees actually get tired out?
2. Are rest pauses desirable?
3. Is a shorter working day desirable?
4. What is the attitude of employees toward their work and toward the company?
5. What is the effect of changing the type of working equipment?
6. Why does production fall off in the afternoon?

It is obvious that several of these questions could be answered only indirectly by the proposed experiment, and several of them touched upon the "psychological" rather than the "physiological" factors involved. Nevertheless, all of them arose out of the bewilderment of men of experience faced with the problem of dealing with fellow human beings in a large industrial organization. In fact, one of the executives of the company saw the purpose of the experiment in even simpler and more general terms. He said that the experiment grew out of a desire on the part of the management to "know more about our workers." In this way began the experiment which is referred to as the Relay Assembly Test Room. With this experiment and the others that followed, members of the Department of Industrial Research of the Graduate School of Business Administration, Harvard University, came to be closely associated.

In April, 1927, six girls were selected from a large shop department of the Hawthorne Works. They were chosen as average workers, neither inexperienced nor expert, and their work consisted of the assembling of telephone relays. A coil, armature, contact springs, and insulators were put together on a fixture and secured in position by means of four machine screws. The operation at that time was being completed at the rate of five relays in six minutes. This particular operation was chosen for the experiment because the relays were being assembled often enough so that even slight changes in output rate would show themselves at once on the output record. Five of the girls were to do the actual assembly work; the duty of the sixth was to keep the others supplied with parts.

The test room itself was an area divided from the main department by a wooden partition eight feet high. The girls sat in a row on one side of a long workbench. Their bench and assembly equipment were identical with that used in the regular department, except in one respect. At the right of each girl's place was a hole in the bench, and into this hole she dropped completed relays. It was the entrance to a chute, in which there was a flapper gate opened by the relay in its passage downward. The opening of the gate closed an electrical circuit which controlled a perforating device, and this in turn recorded the completion of the relay by punching a hole in a tape. The tape moved at the rate of one-quarter of an inch a minute and had space for a separate row of holes for each operator. When punched, it thus consti-

tuted a complete output record for each girl for each instant of the day. Such records were kept for five years.

In this experiment then, as in the earlier illumination experiments, great emphasis was laid on the rate of output. A word of caution is needed here. The Western Electric Company was not immediately interested in increasing output. The experiments were not designed for that purpose. On the other hand, output is easily measured, i.e., it yields precise quantitative data, and experience suggested that it was sensitive to at least some of the conditions under which the employees worked. Output was treated as an index. In short, the nature of the experimental conditions made the emphasis on the output inevitable.

From their experience in the illumination experiments, the investigators were well aware that factors other than those experimentally varied might affect the output rate. Therefore arrangements were made that a number of other records should be kept. Unsuitable parts supplied by the firm were noted down, as were assemblies rejected for any reason upon inspection. In this way the type of defect could be known and related to the time of day at which it occurred. Records were kept of weather conditions in general and of temperature and humidity in the test room. Every six weeks each operator was given a medical examination by the company doctor. Every day she was asked to tell how many hours she had spent in bed the night before and, during a part of the experiment, what food she had eaten. Besides all these records, which concerned the physical condition of the operators, a log was kept in which were recorded the principal events in the test room hour by hour, including among the entries snatches of conversation between the workers. At first these entries related largely to the physical condition of the operators: how they felt as they worked. Later the ground they covered somewhat widened, and the log ultimately became one of the most important of the test room records. Finally, when the so-called Interviewing Program was instituted at Hawthorne, each of the operators was interviewed several times by an experienced interviewer.

The girls had no supervisor in the ordinary sense, such as they would have had in a regular shop department, but a "test room observer" was placed in the room, whose duty it was to maintain the records, arrange the work, and secure a co-operative spirit on the part of the girls. Later, when the complexity of his work increased, several assistants were assigned to help him.

When the arrangements had been made for the test room, the operators who had been chosen to take part were called in for an interview in the office of the superintendent of the Inspection Branch, who was in general charge of the experiment and of the researches which grew out of it. The superintendent described this interview as follows: "The nature of the test was carefully explained to these girls and they readily consented to take part in it, although they were very shy at the first conference. An invitation to six shop girls to come up to a superintendent's office was naturally rather startling. They were assured that the object of the test was to determine the effect of certain changes in working conditions, such as rest periods, mid-morning lunches, and shorter working hours. They were expressly cautioned to work at a comfortable pace, and under no circumstances to try to make a race out of the test." This conference was only the first of many. Whenever any experimental change was planned, the girls were called in, the purpose of the change was explained to them, and their comments were requested. Certain suggested changes which did not meet with their approval were abandoned. They were repeatedly asked, as they were asked in the first interview, not to strain but to work "as they felt."

The experiment was now ready to begin. Put in its simplest terms, the idea of those directing the experiment was that if an output curve was studied for a long enough time under various changes in working conditions, it would be possible to determine which conditions were the most satisfactory. Accordingly, a number of so-called "experimental periods" were arranged. For two weeks before the operators were placed in the test room, a record was kept of the production of each one without her knowledge. In this way the investigators secured a measure of her productive ability while working in the regular department under the usual conditions. This constituted the first experimental period. And for five weeks after the girls entered the test room no change was made in working conditions. Hours remained what they had been before. The investigators felt that this period would be long enough to reveal any changes in output incidental merely to the transfer. This constituted the second experimental period.

The third period involved a change in the method of payment. In the regular department, the girls had been paid according to a scheme of group piecework, the group consisting of a hundred or more employees. Under these circumstances, variations in an individual's total output would not be immediately reflected in her pay, since such variations tended to cancel one another in a large group. In the test room, the six operators were made a group by themselves. In this way each girl received an amount more nearly in proportion to her individual effort, and her interests became more closely centered on the experiment. Eight weeks later, the directly experimental changes began. An outline will reveal their general character: Period IV: two rest pauses, each five minutes in length, were established, one occurring in midmorning and the other in the early afternoon. Period V: these rest pauses were lengthened to ten minutes each. Period VI: six five-minute rests were established. Period VII: the company provided each member of the group with a light lunch in the midmorning and another in the midafternoon accompanied by rest pauses. This arrangement became standard for subsequent Periods VIII through XI. Period VIII: work stopped a half-hour earlier every day — at 4:30 P.M. Period IX: work stopped at 4 P.M. Period X: conditions returned to what they were in Period VII. Period XI: a five-day work week was established. Each of these experimental periods lasted several weeks.

Period XI ran through the summer of 1928, a year after the beginning of the experiment. Already the results were not what had been expected. The output curve, which had risen on the whole slowly and steadily throughout the year, was obviously reflecting something other than the responses of the group to the imposed experimental conditions. Even when the total weekly output had fallen off, as it could hardly fail to do in such a period as Period XI, when the group was working only five days a week, daily output continued to rise. Therefore, in accordance with a sound experimental procedure, as a control on what had been done, it was agreed with the consent of the operators that in experimental Period XII a return should be made to the original conditions of work, with no rest pauses, no special lunches, and a full-length working week. This period lasted for twelve weeks. Both daily and weekly output rose to a higher point than ever before: the working day and the working week were both longer. The hourly output rate declined somewhat but it did not approach the level of Period III, when similar conditions were in effect.

The conclusions reached after Period XII may be expressed in terms of another observation. Identical conditions of work were repeated in three different experimental periods: Periods VII, X, and XII. If the assumptions on which the study was based had been correct, that is to say, if the output rate were directly related to the physical conditions of work, the expectation would be that in these experimental periods there would be some similarity in output. Such was not the case. The only apparent uniformity was that in each experimental period output was higher than in the preceding one. In the Relay Assembly Test Room, as in the previous illumination experiments, something was happening which could not be explained by the experimentally controlled conditions of work.

There is no need here to go into the later history of the test room experiment, which came to an end in 1933. It is enough to say that the output of the group continued to rise until it established itself on a high plateau from which there was no descent until the time of discouragement and deepening economic depression which preceded the end of the test. The rough conclusions reached at the end of experimental Period XII were confirmed and sharpened by later research. T. N. Whitehead, Associate Professor of Business in the Graduate School of Business Administration, Harvard University, has made a careful statistical analysis of the output records. He shows that the changes which took place in the output of the group have no simple correlation with the experimental changes in working conditions. Nor can they be correlated with changes in other physical conditions of which records were kept, such as temperature, humidity, hours of rest, and changes of relay

type. Even when the girls themselves complained of mugginess or heat, these conditions were not apparently affecting their output. This statement, of course, does not mean that there is never any relation between output rate and these physical conditions. There is such a thing as heat prostration. It means only that, within the limits in which these conditions were varying in the test room, they apparently did not affect the rate of work.

The question remains: with what facts, if any, can the changes in the output rate of the operators in the test room be correlated? Here the statements of the girls themselves are of first importance. Each girl knew that she was producing more in the test room than she ever had in the regular department, and each said that the increase had come about without any conscious effort on her part. It seemed easier to produce at the faster rate in the test room than at the slower rate in the regular department. When questioned further, each girl stated her reasons in slightly different words, but there was uniformity in the answers in two respects. First, the girls liked to work in the test room; "it was fun." Secondly, the new supervisory relation or, as they put it, the absence of the old supervisory control, made it possible for them to work freely without anxiety.

For instance, there was the matter of conversation. In the regular department, conversation was in principle not allowed. In practice it was tolerated if it was carried on in a low tone and did not interfere with work. In the test room an effort was made in the beginning to discourage conversation, though it was soon abandoned. The observer in charge of the experiment was afraid of losing the cooperation of the girls if he insisted too strongly on this point. Talk became common and was often loud and general. Indeed the conversation of the operators came to occupy an important place in the log. T. N. Whitehead has pointed out that the girls in the test room were far more thoroughly supervised than they ever had been in the regular department. They were watched by an observer of their own, an interested management, and outside experts. The point is that the character and purpose of the supervision were different and were felt to be so.

The operators knew that they were taking part in what was considered an important and interesting experiment. They knew that their work was expected to produce results — they were not sure what results — which would lead to the improvement of the working conditions of their fellow employees. They knew that the eyes of the company were upon them. Whitehead has further pointed out that, although the experimental changes might turn out to have no physical significance, their social significance was always favorable. They showed that the management of the company was still interested, that the girls were still part of a valuable piece of research. In the regular department, the girls, like the other employees, were in the position of responding to changes the source and purpose of which were beyond their knowledge. In the test room, they had frequent interviews with the superintendent, a higher officer of the company. The reasons for the contemplated experimental changes were explained to them. Their views were consulted and in some instances they were allowed to veto what had been proposed. Professor Mayo has argued that it is idle to speak of an experimental period like Period XII as being in any sense what it purported to be — a return to the original conditions of work. In the meantime, the entire industrial situation of the girls had been reconstructed.

Another factor in what occurred can only be spoken of as the social development of the group itself. When the girls went for the first time to be given a physical examination by the company doctor, someone suggested as a joke that ice cream and cake ought to be served. The company provided them at the next examination, and the custom was kept up for the duration of the experiment. When one of the girls had a birthday, each of the others would bring her a present, and she would respond by offering the group a box of chocolates. Often one of the girls would have some good reason for feeling tired. Then the others would "carry" her. That is, they would agree to work especially fast to make up for the low output expected from her. It is doubtful whether this "carrying" did have any effect, but the important point is the existence of the practice, not its effectiveness. The girls made friends in the test room and went together socially after hours. One of the interesting facts which has appeared from Whitehead's analysis of the output record is that

there were times when variations in the output rates of two friends were correlated to a high degree. Their rates varied simultaneously and in the same direction — something, of course, which the girls were not aware of and could not have planned. Also, these correlations were destroyed by such apparently trivial events as a change in the order in which the girls sat at the workbench.

Finally, the group developed leadership and a common purpose. The leader, self-appointed, was an ambitious young Italian girl who entered the test room as a replacement after two of the original members had left. She saw in the experiment a chance for personal distinction and advancement. The common purpose was an increase in the output rate. The girls had been told in the beginning and repeatedly thereafter that they were to work without straining, without trying to make a race of the test, and all the evidence shows that they kept this rule. In fact, they felt that they were working under less pressure than in the regular department. Nevertheless, they knew that the output record was considered the most important of the records of the experiment and was always closely scrutinized. Before long they had committed themselves to a continous increase in production. In the long run, of course, this ideal was an impossible one, and when the girls found out that it was, the realization was an important element of the change of tone which was noticeable in the second half of the experiment. But for a time they felt that they could achieve the impossible. In brief, the increase in the output rate of the girls in the Relay Assembly Test Room could not be related to any changes in their physical conditions of work, whether experimentally induced or not. It could, however, be related to what can only be spoken of as the development of an organized social group in a peculiar and effective relation with its supervisors.

Many of these conclusions were not worked out in detail until long after the investigators at Hawthorne had lost interest in the Relay Assembly Test Room, but the general meaning of the experiment was clear at least as early as Period XII. A continuous increase in productivity had taken place irrespective of changing physical conditions of work. In the words of a company report made in January, 1931, on all the research which had been done up to that date: "Upon analysis, only one thing seemed to show a continuous relationship with this improved output. This was the mental attitude of the operators. From their conversations with each other and their comments to the test observers, it was not only clear that their attitudes were improving but it was evident that this area of employee reactions and feelings was a fruitful field for industrial research."

At this point the attention of the investigators turned sharply from the test room to the regular department from which the girls had come. Why was the mental attitude of the girls different in the test room from what it had been in the department? In their conversations with one another and in their comments to the observers, the girls were full of comparisons between the test room and the department, very much to the disadvantage of the latter. They felt relief from some form of constraint, particularly the constraint of supervision. They were exceedingly disparaging about the supervisors in the department, although management felt that the department had particularly good supervisory personnel. These facts suggested that the management of the company really knew very little about the attitudes which employees took toward conditions in the plant and very little also about what constituted good supervisory methods. Such was the atmosphere in which the so-called Interviewing Program, the third phase of the work at Hawthorne, was planned. So far the interests of the investigators had been centered on the question of what were good physical conditions of work. Now they shifted definitely in the direction of a study of human relations.

Briefly, the new plan called for interviewing a much larger group of employees than any hitherto studied, with the object of learning more about their feelings and attitudes. A beginning was to be made in the Inspection Branch, representing about 1,600 skilled and unskilled employees in both shop and office work. In the report of January, 1931, the investigators stated that their purposes had been the following: "First, we wanted to know how employees felt about their work and the way they were treated; second, we desired to learn the manner in which the company policies were being applied and the employees' reactions

to them; third, we were hopeful that something would come out of these employee expressions which could be used to develop and improve the training of supervisors."

The supervisors in the Inspection organization were called together, and the project was described to them. Their criticism was invited, and various points in the plan were discussed at this meeting. Five interviewers were chosen from among the supervisors to conduct the interviews. Women were selected to interview women, and men to interview men. The interviewers were not to interview employees whom they knew, since their acquaintanceship might influence what was said. In particular, it was obvious that no one should interview any worker over whom he had administrative authority. Records of the interviews were to be kept, and comments on the working situation were to be set down as nearly verbatim as possible, but all records were to be confidential. The names of the persons interviewed were not to be associated with the records, and any identifying statements were to be omitted. This rule was kept so well that it limited the usefulness of the records. It meant that the details of particular interviews could not be put together to give a picture of an entire working group or department.

In accordance with these plans, the interviewing of employees in the Inspection organization was begun in September, 1928, a year and a half after the beginning of the Relay Assembly Test Room experiment. It was completed early in 1929. So favorable were the results that the decision was made to extend the program to the Operating Branch. For this purpose, the Division of Industrial Research was organized on February 1, 1929, with functions which were stated as follows:

1. To interview annually all employees to find out their likes and dislikes relative to their working status.
2. To study the favorable and unfavorable comments of employees.
   a. To initiate correction or adjustment of causes of unfavorable comments.
   b. To determine upon benefits to be derived from favorable comments and to instigate ways and means of acquiring these benefits.
3. To conduct supervisory training conferences for all supervisors using employee interviews as a basis.

4. To conduct test studies relative to employee relations, fatigue and efficiency.

Obviously a program which called for interviewing annually all employees in a plant in which some 40,000 persons were then working was an ambitious one, and the events showed that it could not be carried through. At the time when the Industrial Research Division was formed, interviews required on the average about a half-hour each. Later, as a result of improvements in the technique of interviewing, they became three times as long. This change alone cut down severely the number of employees who could be interviewed. Nevertheless, in the three years 1928–1930, 21,126 employees were interviewed, more than half of them in the Operating Branch, the rest scattered through other parts of the Hawthorne Works.

The original interviewers had been five in number. The extension of the program made necessary an increase in the staff. For the most part, the new interviewers were chosen from the various branches in which the work was already in progress. In rank they were usually supervisors, and they were taken from their ordinary assignments for a temporary period of about a year. The belief was that such supervisors, with proper instruction, could undertake the interviewing, and that the interviewing experience could be made an important part of their training. Accordingly, as many supervisors as possible were to take part in the work. Besides this temporary personnel, a nucleus staff of permanent investigators was built up, whose duty was to train the new men and take over the more technical aspects of the work, in particular the analysis of the growing body of interview material. The approximate average number of employees involved in the interviewing and analyzing work during 1929 and 1930 was thirty for interviewing and six for analyzing.

The results of the Interviewing Program were interesting from the first. The program was received with enthusiasm by both supervisors and operators. "This is the best thing the Company ever did" and "The Company ought to have done this long ago" were the sort of comments commonly encountered. The employees seemed to enjoy the opportunity of expressing their thoughts. They felt some kind of release, as if feelings which had long been pent up within them had at last found an outlet. Requests for interviews were received, some from the supervisors themselves. Accordingly, the interviewing was extended beyond its original bounds to group and sections chiefs, that is, those supervisors immediately in charge of the rank and file.[2] In the course of their interviews, these supervisors were asked what they thought of the program and its effect. They were in its favor. They felt that it had not embarrassed them, that the employees liked it, and that it ought to be kept up and extended.

Evidence soon accumulated that the interviews not only gave expression to attitudes hitherto pent up but also, in giving them expression, changed them. The report of 1931 explained this rather unexpected result by an analogy: "It has long been known that one who writes a memorandum greatly clarifies his thought upon the material to be presented. Exaggerations, distortions, emotional reactions, defenses, etc., are largely dissolved when thus viewed objectively. In a similar way employees who express their thought and feeling to a critical listener discharge emotional and irrational elements from their minds. Many personal and individual problems and attitudes have been improved by the verbal expression which the interview affords. Taking account of the employees' expressions recorded in twenty thousand interviews, we feel that this value in interviewing cannot be lightly overlooked."

The observation has been made, perhaps too cynically, that in building up good industrial relations it makes little difference what measures are taken to improve working conditions as long as the rank and file realize what the purpose of the measures is. The important factor is the conviction of the workers that the management is concerned about their welfare. Something of this sort Whitehead had in mind when he said of the Relay Assembly Test Room that, though the experi-

---

[2] The name "supervisor" is often given at Hawthorne to all ranks of supervision above the worker. The first-line supervisor, in direct contact with the operators, is the group chief. The three ranks above him are section chief, assistant foreman, and foreman. A foreman is in charge of a department.

mental changes might turn out to have no physical significance, their social significance was always favorable. In the same way in the Interviewing Program, the discovery that management was taking an interest in what they thought and felt was new and stimulating for many of the employees. It may be well to repeat here that the Western Electric Company has a long record of intelligent treatment of its workers, which is reflected in the confidence the workers have in the Company. Without this confidence many of the results of the investigations at Hawthorne could not have been achieved. At the same time the investigations strengthened this confidence.

The effect of the Interviewing Program on the supervisors was not less interesting. The opinion of the management was that supervision improved almost simultaneously with the beginning of interviewing. This improvement was not the result of fear on the part of supervisors that their methods would be disclosed and shown to be faulty. There was apparently no such fear. It was the result rather of an increased knowledge of and interest in workers as individuals and an increased interest in the method of supervision which came from the knowledge that it was being made a subject for research. The records of the interviewers were used as illustrative material for the training of supervisors and for conferences on supervision. An effort was made to see that as many supervisors as possible should have temporary experience as interviewers. Those who took part felt that they acquired a new understanding of the human problems of industry and, not less important, a new understanding of themselves. In fact the two must go together in any study of human behavior. A man can carry his analysis of other men no further than he has carried his analysis of himself. Finally, the men who were most closely associated with the Interviewing Program felt great enthusiasm for the work. They felt that they were acquiring new understanding, that they were free to move wherever the facts led them, and that in the end they would come out with something useful. The Chairman of the Committee pointed out that there seemed to be the same dis-interested curiosity among the investigators as there is in any scientific research laboratory when the work is going well.

The investigators came away from the Relay Assembly Test Room with the feeling that management really knew very little about what constituted good supervision or what the employees thought about their conditions of work. The Interviewing Program was designed to provide such knowledge. It is significant that, in the original plan for the interviews, orders were given that comments on the working situation were to be recorded as nearly verbatim as possible. This material was the sort which was supposed to be important. The interviewers went to their early interviews with something like a series of questions in their heads which they expected the employees to answer. The questions concerned such matters as working conditions, job supervision, and so forth. The interview was to consist in effect of a series of answers to these questions. It is true that the interviewers were cautioned against putting these questions directly to the person being interviewed. Instead they were to enter into conversation with the employee and lead him around to the appropriate subjects only as opportunity served. Nevertheless, the questions existed. Unfortunately for this plan, the discovery was soon made that a series of questions did not form a satisfactory basis for an interview. Questions did produce opinions, but the opinions were of unequal value. For one thing, comments on persons were less likely to produce information on which action could be based than were comments on material conditions of work. Whenever a number of employees working in the same neighborhood complained of cold, smoke and fumes, insufficient locker space, or some other physical source of irritation, an investigation could be made. In many instances the complaints were found to be justified and the conditions were corrected. But complaints about persons and about supervision in general usually had to be disregarded. Investigation showed that they had more reference to the attitudes people took toward situations than to the situations themselves.

42 Backgrounds of Political Activists*

David L. Westby · Richard G. Braungart

It may be comforting to believe that a person's political affiliation reflects a rational analysis of the alternatives followed by selection of the one that best meets his needs and interests. In fact, however, college students tend to have the same political affiliation as their parents. There are exceptions, of course, and it might be anticipated that student political activists would be among those who depart most radically from family political traditions. The following study examines this possibility in trying to identify the characteristics of activists. What are the background factors that distinguish between student activists of the "left" and the "right"? How do you react to the author's deterministic findings? Do you have an alternative hypothesis to suggest?

Recent years have seen the growth and projection of student groups into national politics with an intensity and impact never before experienced in American history. This abrupt turn from the often-criticized juvenile college culture of earlier years has provided sociologists with opportunities to study social movements without leaving their own bailiwick.

Much of the research on student youth movements has found its theoretical point of departure in socialization theory in that it attempts to explain political beliefs and action in terms of family-based experience and family structure.[1] Thus, Maccoby, Mathews, and Morton, in a study of 339 first-time voters, explain the "political conformity" exhibited by some members of their sample in terms of the degree to which their parents exercised control over their youthful activities.[2] In somewhat

similar fashion, Middleton and Putney, in a study of 1440 college youths, endeavored to demonstrate that those "rebelling" against the political positions of their fathers were more estranged from their fathers, especially if the fathers were interested in politics.[3] Generally, the focus of research in this area, with its concentration on socialization patterns in the family, seems to neglect the older class-based model of political beliefs which assumes that the latter are primarily a function of the stratification system.[4]

The present study, based on a relatively small number of student activists, suggests that the class and party of the student's family of orientation may be significant factors in understanding at least certain features of the student movement. It should be clear that we regard the findings presented here as suggestive for further research and definitely not sufficient to establish valid generalizations.

METHOD

Our study focused on "left" and "right" activists in a large public institution in the eastern United States, and was conducted during the spring of 1965. The data reported here deal with class and party backgrounds of the membership bodies of two campus activist organizations, SENSE (Students for Peace) and the Young Americans for Freedom (Y.A.F.), which may be taken to represent the extremes of political opinion on the "left" and "right" respectively. There are other activist groups at the institution in question, especially on the left, but their membership is heavily overlapping with that of SENSE.[5]

---

* Excerpted from the *American Sociological Review*, Vol. 31 (October, 1966), pp. 690–692. Reprinted by permission. Copyright © 1966 by The American Sociological Association.

[1] The general importance of the family in the continuity of party and voting traditions is, of course, a well-established generalization in political sociology.

[2] Eleanor Maccoby, Richard Mathews, and Anton Morton, "Youth and Political Change," *Public Opinion Quarterly*, 18 (Spring, 1954), pp. 23–39.

[3] Russell Middleton and Snell Putney, "Student Rebellion Against Parental Political Beliefs," *Social Forces,* 41 (May, 1963), pp. 377–83.

[4] See, for instance, Paul Lazarsfeld, Bernard Berelson, Hazel Gaudet, *The People's Choice,* New York: Duell, Sloan & Pearce, 1944; Phillip Converse, "The Shifting Role of Class in Political Attitudes and Behavior," in Eleanor Maccoby *et al., Readings in Social Psychology,* New York: Holt, Rinehart & Winston, Inc., 1947; Richard Centers, *The Psychology of Social Class,* New York: Russel & Russell, 1961; and Herbert Hyman, *Political Socialization,* New York: The Free Press of Glencoe, 1959. Of course, practically everything in the Marxist tradition takes this view.

[5] That these two groups represent the extremes of political opinion was demonstrated in a series of attitude items dealing with the present administration policy in

A questionnaire was administered *en masse* to each of the two groups. The first part of the questionnaire consisted of items tapping class backgrounds and related variables, while the second part was composed of a 22-item Likert-type attitude scale dealing with attitudes toward the present war in Viet Nam. The questionnaire was administered to twenty-nine students at a SENSE meeting, to nineteen students at two Y.A.F. meetings, and to 105 students in an introductory sociology class. A few members were absent from these meetings and there is reason to believe that those missing were less extreme and less active.

FINDINGS

Tables 1 through 3 present the origins of SENSE and Y.A.F. members. Table 1 shows a significant difference in median income for the two groups, while Table 2 gives the social class distribution for the two groups, utilizing the Hollingshead Two-Factor Index. The predominantly upper-middle-class high-income origins of SENSE members contrast sharply with the generally low-income and lower-middle- or working-class backgrounds of Y.A.F. members. We shall briefly consider these findings in the light of current stratification theory.

That "revolutionary reactionaries," to use Clinton Rossiter's term, or adherents to the "radical right," should be drawn from the lower-middle and working classes is not surprising if one accepts the "status politics" theory of Hofstadter and others.[6] The "status politics" theory suggests that extreme "right" activists, or "pseudo-conservatives" as Hofstadter prefers to call them, are generally found within status-threatened groups. It is precisely the lower-middle and working classes that are least secure and tend to feel threatened by the upward thrust of new minorities. As Hofstadter wrote in his seminal discussion, "conformity is a way of guaranteeing and manifesting

TABLE 1 *Distribution of Student Activists by Annual Family Income*

	SENSE		Y.A.F.	
Family Income	N	%	N	%
Above median	19	68	4	24
Below median	9	32	13	76
	28	100	17	100

$\chi^2 = 8.36$, d.f. $= 1$, p $< .005$.
Median income: SENSE, \$12,232; Y.A.F., \$6,625.

TABLE 2 *Distribution of Student Activists by Hollingshead's Two-Factor Index of Social Class*

	SENSE		Y.A.F.	
Social Class	N	%	N	%
I, II	15	52	5	26
III	10	35	7	37
IV, V	4	13	7	37
	29	100	19	100

$\chi^2 = 4.60$, d.f. $= 2$, p $< .10$.

TABLE 3 *Distribution of Student Activists by Political Affiliation of Parents*

	SENSE		Y.A.F.	
Political Affiliation of Parents	N	%	N	%
Democrat, Socialist	17	68	5	29
Republican	8	32	12	71
	25	100	17	100

$\chi^2 = 6.03$, d.f. $= 1$, p $< .01$.

Note: A few parents could not be classified by political affiliation because they had none or were independent.

Viet Nam. The groups took overwhelmingly opposed positions on this controversial political issue, while a control group composed of a class of Sociology I students, roughly representative of the student body, fell in between the two, although somewhat closer to Y.A.F. than to SENSE. Mean scores on the attitude scale items, which ranged from 22 (most liberal) to 110 (most conservative), were: SENSE, 37; Sociology I, 72; Y.A.F., 85.

[6] Richard Hofstadter, "The Pseudo-Conservative Revolt — 1955," in Daniel Bell (ed.), *The Radical Right*, New York: Doubleday, 1962, pp. 63–80. In the same volume, see also S. M. Lipset, "The Sources of the 'Radical Right'," and "Three Decades of the Radical Right: Coughlinites, McCarthyites, and Birchers," pp. 259–377.

respectability among those who are not sure that they are respectable enough." [7]

Upper-middle-class status, on the other hand, typically provides the social and economic security that is lacking in the lower-middle and upper-working classes. These latter strata provide a kind of protective belt insulating the upper-middle classes from any immediate challenge on the part of militant lower-status groups. As members of a fully "arrived" stratum, upper-middle-class individuals can afford the luxury of "deviance" from straight-line conformist politics, especially if their position is relatively well-established, and their mobility not too recent. [8]

While this interpretation may seem plausible, it casts a very wide net for a few small fish. Classes are enormous aggregates, while student activists are a small segment of the student body at any university or college. It is important to try to demonstrate which factors *within strata* are decisive in their influence on political action at the extremes of the political spectrum. Table 3 gives the political affiliations of the students' parents and shows a pronounced relationship between left activism and Democratic or Socialist background on the one hand, and Republican background and right activism on the other. In other words, fami-

lies of SENSE members are predominantly high-status Democrats while Y.A.F. members come mainly from low-status Republican families. Within each stratum, it seems, it is party identification and presumably the accompanying ideological orientation that are the more particular factors that predispose students toward political extremism.

Finally, despite their opposed ideological stances, these two groups are similar in one respect — they both exhibit a kind of inconsistency or absence of crystallization. Lenski and others have presented evidence that such types are more insistent upon or receptive to change, more radical as it were, than the highly crystallized. [9] Both the far left and far right press for policies and actions representing considerable departures from those current today.

Generally, student activists seem to be expressing ideological positions that, though extreme, are in the main consistent with the political orientations of their families. It may be that activists are rebelling against their parents, but, if so, it seems to be in a highly selective way in which the intersection of the class structure and the political system is a powerful predisposing force. We think that researchers of the student movement would do well to consider the class and political backgrounds of their subjects.

---

[7] Hofstadter, *ibid.,* pp. 76–77. Our data on the marital status of parents also seem to support the insecurity — conformity relation. Eight Y.A.F. students (46 per cent) came from homes with divorced or widowed parents, while this was true of only 2 (6 per cent) of SENSE members.

[8] We should note that whenever such insulation is absent, as in certain Northern suburban areas and in the South generally, the upper-middle class is as susceptible to right-wing extremist forms of politics as any other group.

[9] Gerhard Lenski, "Status Crystallization: A Non-Vertical Dimension of Social Status," *American Sociological Review,* 19 (August, 1954), pp. 405–13. "Crystallization" is defined as the degree to which positions within two or more ranking systems are congruent. Thus, a white Anglo-Saxon, Protestant doctor making $30,000 a year could be said to be highly crystallized, whereas a Negro doctor making $4,000 would be uncrystallized.

43 Cooling the Mark Out: Adaptations to Failure*

Erving Goffman

We live in a competitive society. Competition means that occasional failure is inevitable for nearly everyone and repetitive failure for many. Since failure is an important component of the social order it may be expected that modes of adaptation to failure will be established and communicated. The following essay provides a perceptive analysis of some of the ways in which people become reconciled to failure.

In cases of criminal fraud, victims find they must suddenly adapt themselves to the loss of sources of security and status which they had taken for granted. A consideration of this adaptation to loss can lead us to an understanding of some relations in our society between involvements and the selves that are involved.

In the argot of the criminal world, the term "mark" refers to any individual who is a victim or prospective victim of certain forms of planned illegal exploitation. The mark is the sucker — the person who is taken in. An instance of the operation of any particular racket, taken through the full cycle of its steps or phases, is sometimes called a "play." The persons who operate the racket and "take" the mark are occasionally called "operators."

The confidence game — the "con," as its practitioners call it — is a way of obtaining money under false pretenses by the exercise of fraud and deceit. The con differs from politer forms of financial deceit in important ways. The con is practiced on private persons by talented actors who methodically and regularly build up informal social relationships just for the purpose of abusing

* Extract from Erving Goffman, "On Cooling the Mark Out: Some Aspects of Adaptation to Failure," *Psychiatry: Journal for the Study of Interpersonal Relations,* Vol. 15 (November 1952), pp. 451–463. Reprinted by special permission of The William Alanson White Psychiatric Foundation, Inc., and the author. Copyright 1952 by The William Alanson White Foundation, Inc.

them; white collar crime is practiced on organizations by persons who learn to abuse positions of trust which they once filled faithfully. The one exploits poise; the other, position. Further, a con man is someone who accepts a social role in the underworld community; he is part of a brotherhood whose members make no pretense to one another of being "legit." A white collar criminal, on the other hand, has no colleagues, although he may have an associate with whom he plans his crime and a wife to whom he confesses it.

The con is said to be a good racket in the United States only because most Americans are willing, nay eager, to make easy money, and will engage in action that is less than legal in order to do so. The typical play has typical phases. The potential sucker is first spotted, and one member of the working team (called the "outside man," "steerer," or "roper") arranges to make social contact with him. The confidence of the mark is won, and he is given an opportunity to invest his money in a gambling venture which he understands to have been fixed in his favor. The venture, of course, *is* fixed, but not in his favor. The mark is permitted to win some money and then persuaded to invest more. There is an "accident" or "mistake," and the mark loses his total investment. The operators then depart in a ceremony that is called the "blowoff" or "sting." They leave the mark but take his money. The mark is expected to go on his way, a little wiser and a lot poorer.

Sometimes, however, a mark is not quite prepared to accept his loss as a gain in experience and to say and do nothing about his venture. He may feel moved to complain to the police or to chase after the operators. In the terminology of the trade, the mark may "squawk," "beef," or "come through." From the operators' point of view, this kind of behavior is bad for business. It gives the members of the mob a bad reputation with such police as have not yet been fixed and with marks who have not yet been taken. In order to avoid this adverse publicity, an additional phase is sometimes added at the end of the play. It is called "cooling the mark out." After the blowoff has occurred, one of the operators stays with the mark and makes an effort to keep the anger of the mark within manageable and sensible proportions. The operator stays behind his team-mates in the capacity of what might be called a cooler and exercises upon the mark the art of con-solation. An attempt is made to define the situa-tion for the mark in a way that makes it easy for him to accept the inevitable and quietly go home. The mark is given instruction in the philosophy of taking a loss.

When we call to mind the image of a mark who has just been separated from his money, we some-times attempt to account for the greatness of his anger by the greatness of his financial loss. This is a narrow view. In many cases, especially in America, the mark's image of himself is built up on the belief that he is a pretty shrewd person when it comes to making deals and that he is not the sort of person who is taken in by anything. The mark's readiness to participate in a sure thing is based on more than avarice; it is based on a feeling that he will now be able to prove to himself that he is the sort of person who can "turn a fast buck." For many, this capacity for high finance comes near to being a sign of masculinity and a test of fulfilling the male role.

It is well known that persons protect themselves with all kinds of rationalizations when they have a buried image of themselves which the facts of their status do not support. A person may tell himself many things: that he has not been given a fair chance; that he is not really interested in be-coming something else; that the time for showing his mettle has not yet come; that the usual means of realizing his desires are personally or morally distasteful, or require too much dull effort. By means of such defenses, a person saves himself from committing a cardinal social sin — the sin of defining oneself in terms of a status while lacking the qualifications which an incumbent of that status is supposed to possess.

A mark's participation in a play, and his in-vestment in it, clearly commit him in his own eyes to the proposition that he is a smart man. The process by which he comes to believe that he cannot lose is also the process by which he drops the defenses and compensations that previously protected him from defeats. When the blowoff comes, the mark finds that he has no defense for not being a shrewd man. He has defined himself as a shrewd man and must face the fact that he is

only another easy mark. He has defined himself as possessing a certain set of qualities and then proven to himself that he is miserably lacking in them. This is a process of self-destruction of the self. It is no wonder that the mark needs to be cooled out and that it is good business policy for one of the operators to stay with the mark in order to talk him into a point of view from which it is possible to accept a loss.

In essence, then, the cooler has the job of handling persons who have been caught out on a limb — persons whose expectations and self-con-ceptions have been built up and then shattered. The mark is a person who has compromised him-self, in his own eyes if not in the eyes of others.

Although the term "mark" is commonly applied to a person who is given short-lived expectations by operators who have intentionally misrepre-sented the facts, a less restricted definition is de-sirable in analyzing the larger social scene. An expectation may finally prove false, even though it has been possible to sustain it for a long time and even though the operators acted in good faith. So, too, the disappointment of reasonable expecta-tions, as well as misguided ones, creates a need for consolation. Persons who participate in what is recognized as a confidence game are found in only a few social settings, but persons who have to be cooled out are found in many. Cooling the mark out is one theme in a very basic social story.

For purposes of analysis, one may think of an individual in reference to the values or attributes of a socially recognized character which he pos-sesses. Psychologists speak of a value as a per-sonal involvement. Sociologists speak of a value as a status, role or relationship. In either case, the character of the value that is possessed is taken in a certain way as the character of the person who possesses it. An alteration in the kinds of attributes possessed brings an alteration to the self-conception of the person who possesses them.

The process by which someone acquires a value is the process by which he surrenders the claim he had to what he was and commits himself to the conception of self which the new value requires or allows him to have. It is the process that persons who fall in love or take dope call "getting hooked." After a person is hooked, he must go through another process by which his new involvement finds its proper place, in space and time, relative to the other calls, demands, and commitments that he has upon himself. At this point certain other persons suddenly begin to play an important part in the individual's story; they impinge upon him by virtue of the relationship they happen to have to the value in which he has become involved. This is not the place to consider the general kinds of impingement that are institutionalized in our society and the general social relationships that arise: the personal relationship, the professional relationship, and the business relationship. Here we are concerned only with the end of the story, the way in which a person becomes disengaged from one of his involvements.

In our society, the story of a person's involvement can end in one of three general ways. According to one type of ending, he may withdraw from one of his involvements or roles in order to acquire a sequentially related one that is considered better. This is the case when a youth becomes a man, when a student becomes a practitioner, or when a man from the ranks is given a commission.

Of course, the person who must change his self at any one of these points of promotion may have profound misgivings. He may feel disloyal to the way of life that must be left behind and to the persons who do not leave it with him. His new role may require action that seems insincere, dishonest, or unfriendly. This he may experience as a loss in moral cleanliness. His new role may require him to forgo the kinds of risk-taking and exertion that he previously enjoyed, and yet his new role may not provide this kind of heroic and exalted action that he expected to find in it. This he may experience as a loss in moral strength.

There is no doubt that certain kinds of role success require certain kinds of moral failure. It may therefore be necessary, in a sense, to cool the dubious neophyte in rather than out. He may have to be convinced that his doubts are a matter of sentimentality. The adult social view will be impressed upon him. He will be required to understand that a promotional change in status is voluntary, desirable, and a natural, and that loss of one's role in these circumstances is the ultimate test of having fulfilled it properly.

It has been suggested that a person may leave a role under circumstances that reflect favorably upon the way in which he performed it. In theory, at least, a related possibility must be considered. A person may leave a role and at the same time leave behind him the standards by which such roles are judged. The new thing that he becomes may be so different from the thing he was that criteria such as success or failure cannot be easily applied to the change which has occurred. He becomes lost to others that he may find himself; he is of the twice-born. In our society, perhaps the most obvious example of this kind of termination occurs when a woman voluntarily gives up a prestigeful profession in order to become a wife and a mother. It is to be noted that this illustrates an institutionalized movement; those who make it do not make news. In America most other examples of this kind of termination are more a matter of talk than of occurrence. For example, one of the culture heroes of our dinner-table mythology is the man who walks out on an established calling in order to write or paint or live in the country. In other societies, the kind of abdication being considered here seems to have played a more important role. In medieval China, for instance, anchoretic withdrawal apparently gave to persons of quite different station a way of retreating from the occupational struggle while managing the retreat in an orderly, face-saving fashion.

Two basic ways in which a person can lose a role have been considered; he can be promoted out of it or abdicate from it. There is, of course, a third basic ending to the status story. A person may be involuntarily deprived of his position or involvement and made in return something that is considered a lesser thing to be. It is mainly in this third ending to a person's role that occasions arise for cooling him out. It is here that one deals in the full sense with the problem of persons losing their roles.

Involuntary loss seems itself to be of two kinds. First, a person may lose a status in such a way that the loss is not taken as a reflection upon the loser. The loss of a loved one, either because of an accident that could not have been prevented or because of a disease that could not have been halted, is a case in point. Occupational retirement because of old age is another. Of course, the loss will inevitably alter the conception the loser has of himself and the conception others have of him, but the alteration itself will not be treated as a symbol of the fate he deserves to receive. No insult is added to injury. It may be necessary, none the less, to pacify the loser and resign him to his loss. The loser who is not responsible for his loss may even find himself taking the mystical view that all involvements are part of a wider con game, for the more one takes pleasure in a particular role the more one must suffer when it is time to leave it. He may find little comfort in the fact that the play has provided him with an illusion that has lasted a lifetime. He may find little comfort in the fact that the operators had not meant to deceive him.

Secondly, a person may be involuntarily deprived of a role under circumstances which reflect unfavorably on his capacity for it. The lost role may be one that he had already acquired or one that he had openly committed himself to preparing for. In either case the loss is more than a matter of ceasing to act in a given capacity; it is ultimate proof of an incapacity. And in many cases it is even more than this. The moment of failure often catches a person acting as one who feels that he is an appropriate sort of person for the role in question. Assumption becomes presumption, and failure becomes fraud. To loss of substance is thereby added loss of face. Of the many themes that can occur in the natural history of an involvement, this seems to be the most melancholy. Here it will be quite essential and quite difficult to cool the mark out. I shall be particularly concerned with this second kind of loss — the kind that involves humiliation.

It should be noted, parenthetically, that one circle of persons may define a particular loss as the kind that casts no reflection on the loser, and that a different circle of persons may treat the same loss as a symbol of what the loser deserves. One must also note that there is a tendency today to shift certain losses of status from the category of those that reflect upon the loser to the category of those that do not. When persons lose their jobs, their courage, or their minds, we tend more and more to take a clinical or naturalistic view of the loss and a non-moral view of their failure. We

want to define a person as something that is not destroyed by the destruction of one of his selves. This benevolent attitude is in line with the effort today to publicize the view that occupational retirement is not the end of all active capacities but the beginning of new and different ones.

A consideration of consolation as a social process leads to four general problems having to do with the self in society. First, where in modern life does one find persons conducting themselves as though they were entitled to the rights of a particular status and then having to face up to the fact that they do not possess the qualifications for the status? In other words, at what points in the structures of our social life are persons likely to compromise themselves or find themselves compromised? When is it likely that a person will have to disengage himself or become disengaged from one of his involvements? Secondly, what are the typical ways in which persons who find themselves in this difficult position can be cooled out; how can they be made to accept the great injury that has been done to their image of themselves, regroup their defenses, and carry on without raising a squawk? Thirdly, what, in general, can happen when a person refuses to be cooled out, that is, when he refuses to be pacified by the cooler? Fourthly, what arrangements are made by operators and marks to avoid entirely the process of consolation?

In all personal-service organizations customers or clients sometimes make complaints. A customer may feel that he has been given service in a way that is unacceptable to him — a way that he interprets as an offense to the conception he has of who and what he is. The management therefore has the problem of cooling the mark out. Frequently this function is allotted to specialists within the organization. In restaurants of some size, for example, one of the crucial functions of the hostess is to pacify customers whose self-conceptions have been injured by waitresses or by the food. In large stores the complaint department and the floorwalker perform a similar function.

One may note that a service organization does not operate in an anonymous world, as does a con mob, and is therefore strongly obliged to make some effort to cool the mark out. An institution, after all, cannot take it on the lam; it must pacify its marks.

The problem of cooling persons out in informal social intercourse is seen most clearly, perhaps, in courting situations and in what might be called de-courting situations. A proposal of marriage in our society tends to be a way in which a man sums up his social attributes and suggests to a woman that hers are not so much better as to preclude a merger or partnership in these matters. Refusal on the part of the woman, or refusal on the part of the man to propose when he is clearly in a position to do so, is a serious reflection on the rejected suitor. Courtship is a way not only of presenting oneself to alter for approval but also of saying that the opinion of alter in this matter is the opinion one is most concerned with. Refusing a proposal, or refusing to propose, is therefore a difficult operation. The mark must be carefully cooled out. The act of breaking a date or of refusing one, and the task of discouraging a "steady," can also be seen in this light, although in these cases great delicacy and tact may not be required, since the mark may not be deeply involved or openly committed. Just as it is harder to refuse a proposal than to refuse a date, so it is more difficult to reject a spouse than to reject a suitor. The process of de-courting by which one person in a marriage maneuvers the other into accepting a divorce without fuss or undue rancor requires extreme finesse in the art of cooling the mark out.

In all of these cases where a person constructs a conception of himself which cannot be sustained, there is a possibility that he has not invested that which is most important to him in the soon-to-be-denied status. In the current idiom, there is a possibility that when he is hit, he will not be hit where he really lives. There is a set of cases, however, where the blowoff cannot help but strike a vital spot; these cases arise, of course, when a person must be dissuaded from life itself. The man with a fatal sickness or fatal injury, the criminal with a death sentence, the soldier with a hopeless objective — these persons must be persuaded to accept quietly the loss of life itself, the loss of all one's earthly involvements. Here, certainly, it will be difficult to cool the mark out. It is a reflection on

the conceptions men have — as cooler and mark — that it is possible to do so.

I have mentioned a few of the areas of social life where it becomes necessary, upon occasion, to cool a mark out. Attention may now be directed to some of the common ways in which individuals are cooled out in all of these areas of life.

For the mark, cooling represents a process of adjustment to an impossible situation — a situation arising from having defined himself in a way which the social facts come to contradict. The mark must therefore be supplied with a new set of apologies for himself, a new framework in which to see himself and judge himself. A process of redefining the self along defensible lines must be instigated and carried along; since the mark himself is frequently in too weakened a condition to do this, the cooler must initially do it for him.

One general way of handling the problem of cooling the mark out is to give the task to someone whose status relative to the mark will serve to ease the situation in some way. In formal organizations, frequently, someone who is two or three levels above the mark in line of command will do the hatchet work, on the assumption that words of consolation and redirection will have a greater power to convince if they come from high places. There also seems to be a feeling that persons of high status are better able to withstand the moral danger of having hate directed at them. Incidentally, persons protected by high office do not like to face this issue, and frequently attempt to define themselves as merely the agents of the deed and not the source of it. In some cases, on the other hand, the task of cooling the mark out is given to a friend and peer of the mark, on the assumption that such a person will know best how to hit upon a suitable rationalization for the mark and will know best how to control the mark should the need for this arise. In some cases, as in those pertaining to death, the role of cooler is given to doctors or priests. Doctors must frequently help a family, and the member who is leaving it, to manage the leave-taking with tact and a minimum of emotional fuss.[1] A priest must not so much save

[1] This role of the doctor has been stressed by W. L. Warner in his lectures at the University of Chicago on symbolic roles in "Yankee City."

a soul as create one that is consistent with what is about to become of it.

A second general solution to the problem of cooling the mark out consists of offering him a status which differs from the one he has lost or failed to gain but which provides at least a something or a somebody for him to become. Usually the alternative presented to the mark is a compromise of some kind, providing him with some of the trappings of his lost status as well as with some of its spirit. A lover may be asked to become a friend; a student of medicine may be asked to switch to the study of dentistry;[2] a boxer may become a trainer; a dying person may be asked to broaden and empty his wordly loves so as to embrace the All-Father that is about to receive him. Sometimes the mark is allowed to retain his status but is required to fulfill it in a different environment: the honest policeman is transferred to a lonely beat; the too zealous priest is encouraged to enter a monastery; an unsatisfactory plant manager is shipped off to another branch. Sometimes the mark is "kicked upstairs" and given a courtesy status such as "Vice President." In the game for social roles, transfer up, down, or away may all be consolation prizes.

A related way of handling the mark is to offer him another chance to qualify for the role at which he has failed. After his fall from grace, he is allowed to retrace his steps and try again. Officer selection programs in the army, for example, often provide for possibilities of this kind. In general, it seems that third and fourth chances are seldom given to marks, and that second chances, while often given, are seldom taken. Failure at a role removes a person from the company of those who have succeeded, but it does not bring him back — in spirit, anyway — to the society of those who have not tried or are in the process of trying. The person who has failed in a role is a constant source of embarrassment, for none of the standard patterns of treatment is quite applicable to him. Instead of taking a second chance, he usually goes away to another place where his past does not bring confusion to his present.

Another standard method of cooling the mark out — one which is frequently employed in conjunction with other methods — is to allow the mark to explode, to break down, to cause a scene, to give full vent to his reactions and feelings, to "blow his top." If this release of emotions does not find a target, then it at least serves a cathartic function. If it does find a target, as in "telling off the boss," it gives the mark a last-minute chance to re-erect his defenses and prove to himself and others that he had not really cared about the status all along. When a blow-up of this kind occurs, friends of the mark or psychotherapists are frequently brought in. Friends are willing to take responsibility for the mark because their relationship to him is not limited to the role he has failed in. This, incidentally, provides one of the less obvious reasons why the cooler in a con mob must cultivate the friendship of the mark; friendship provides the cooler with an acceptable reason for staying around while the mark is cooled out. Psychotherapists, on the other hand, are willing to take responsibility for the mark because it is their business to offer a relationship to those who have failed in a relationship to others.

It has been suggested that a mark may be cooled out by allowing him, under suitable guidance, to give full vent to his initial shock. Thus the manager of a commercial organization may listen with patience and understanding to the complaints of a customer, knowing that the full expression of a complaint is likely to weaken it. This possibility lies behind the role of a whole series of buffers in our society — janitors, restaurant hostesses, grievance committees, floorwalkers, and so on — who listen in silence, with apparent sympathy, until the mark has simmered down. Similarly, in the case of criminal trials, the defending lawyer may find it profitable to allow the public to simmer down before he brings his client to court.

A related procedure for cooling the mark out is found in what is called stalling. The feelings of the mark are not brought to a head because he is given no target at which to direct them. The operator may manage to avoid the presence of the mark or may convince the mark that there is still a slight chance that the loss has not really occurred. When the mark is stalled, he is given a chance to become familiar with the new conception of self

---

[2] In his seminars, Mr. Hughes has used the term "second-choice" professions to refer to cases of this kind.

he will have to accept before he is absolutely sure that he will have to accept it.

As another cooling procedure, there is the possibility that the operator and the mark may enter into a tacit understanding according to which the mark agrees to act as if he were leaving of his own accord, and the operator agrees to preserve the illusion that this was the case. It is a form of bribery. In this way the mark may fail in his own eyes but prevent others from discovering the failure. The mark gives up his role but saves his face. This, after all, is one of the reasons why persons who are fleeced by con men are often willing to remain silent about their adventures. The same strategy is at work in the romantic custom of allowing a guilty officer to take his own life in a private way before it is taken from him publicly, and in the less romantic custom of allowing a person to resign for delicate reasons instead of firing him for indelicate ones.

I have suggested some general ways in which the mark is cooled out. The question now arises: what happens if the mark refuses to be cooled out? What are the possible lines of action he can take if he refuses to be cooled? Attempts to answer these questions will show more clearly why, in general, the operator is so anxious to pacify the mark.

It has been suggested that a mark may be cooled by allowing him to blow his top. If the blow-up is too drastic or prolonged, however, difficulties may arise. We say that the mark becomes "disturbed mentally" or "personally disorganized." Instead of merely telling his boss off, the mark may go so far as to commit criminal violence against him. Instead of merely blaming himself for failure, the mark may inflict great punishment upon himself by attempting suicide, or by acting so as to make it necessary for him to be cooled out in other areas of his social life.

Sustained personal disorganization is one way in which a mark can refuse to cool out. Another standard way is for the individual to raise a squawk, that is, to make a formal complaint to higher authorities obliged to take notice of such matters. The con mob worries lest the mark appeal to the police. The plant manager must make sure that the disgruntled department head does not carry a formal complaint to the general manager or, worse still, to the Board of Directors. The teacher worries lest the child's parent complain to the principal. Similarly, a woman who communicates her evaluation of self by accepting a proposal of marriage can sometimes protect her exposed position — should the necessity of doing so arise — by threatening her disaffected fiancé with a breach-of-promise suit. So, also, a woman who is de-courting her husband must fear lest he contest the divorce or sue her lover for alienation of affection. In much the same way, a customer who is angered by a salesperson can refuse to be mollified by the floorwalker and demand to see the manager. It is interesting to note that associations dedicated to the rights and the honor of minority groups may sometimes encourage a mark to register a formal squawk; politically it may be more advantageous to provide a test case than to allow the mark to be cooled out.

Another line of action which a mark who refuses to be cooled can pursue is that of turning "sour." The term derives from the argot of industry but the behavior it refers to occurs everywhere. The mark outwardly accepts his loss but withdraws all enthusiasm, good will, and vitality from whatever role he is allowed to maintain. He complies with the formal requirements of the role that is left him, but he withdraws his spirit and identification from it. When an employee turns sour, the interests of the organization suffer; every executive, therefore, has the problem of "sweetening" his workers. They must not come to feel that they are slowly being cooled out. This is one of the functions of granting periodic advancements in salary and status, of schemes such as profit-sharing, or of giving the "employee" at home an anniversary present. A similar view can be taken of the problem that a government faces in times of crisis when it must maintain the enthusiastic support of the nation's disadvantaged minorities, for whole groupings of the population can feel they are being cooled out and react by turning sour.

Finally, there is the possibility that the mark may, in a manner of speaking, go into business for himself. He can try to gather about him the persons and facilities required to establish a status similar to the one he has lost, albeit in relation to a different set of persons. This way of refusing to be cooled is often rehearsed in phantasies of the

"I'll show them" kind, but sometimes it is actually realized in practice. The rejected marriage partner may make a better remarriage. A social stratum that has lost its status may decide to create its own social system. A leader who fails in a political party may establish his own splinter group.

All these ways in which a mark can refuse to be cooled out have consequences for other persons. There is, of course, a kind of refusal that has little consequence for others. Marks of all kinds may develop explanations and excuses to account in a creditable way for their losses. It is, perhaps, in this region of phantasy that the defeated self makes its last stand.

DEVIANT SOCIALIZATION

44 Becoming a Marihuana User*

Howard S. Becker

The next selection, a study of how people come to use marihuana, argues that normal and abnormal behavior are acquired in the same way, through a sequence of social experiences during which a person gains a conception of the meaning of the behavior in question and a self-conception that makes the behavior possible. Motivation to engage in a specified type of behavior is learned while practicing the behavior and does not antedate this learning process. Thus, a person does not use marihuana because of some previous motivation but becomes motivated through the use of marihuana. Use of marihuana generally occurs in groups, and the group builds up its own social controls for inducting novices and retaining the habitual users. There develops, as a result, a culture of marihuana usage, a culture that includes customs, beliefs, and other social controls just as any culture does.

After reading the article, describe fully the role

of the marihuana user, including the status prescriptions, language peculiarities, beliefs, practices, and self-conceptions observed among the subjects.

The novice does not ordinarily get high the first time he smokes marihuana, and several attempts are usually necessary to induce this state. One explanation of this may be that the drug is not smoked "properly," that is, in a way that insures sufficient dosage to produce real symptoms of intoxication. Most users agree that it cannot be smoked like tobacco if one is to get high:

Take in a lot of air, you know, and . . . I don't know how to describe it, you don't smoke it like a cigarette, you draw in a lot of air and get it deep down in your system and then keep it there. Keep it there as long as you can.

Without the use of some such technique[1] the drug will produce no effects, and the user will be unable to get high:

The trouble with people like that [who are not able to get high] is that they're just not smoking it right, that's all there is to it. Either they're not holding it down long enough, or they're getting too much air and not enough smoke, or the other way around or something like that. A lot of people just don't smoke it right, so naturally nothing's gonna happen.

If nothing happens, it is manifestly impossible for the user to develop a conception of the drug as an object which can be used for pleasure, and use

* From Howard S. Becker, *Outsiders*, New York: The Free Press, 1963, pp. 46–58. Reprinted by permission.

[1] A pharmacologist notes that this ritual is in fact an extremely efficient way of getting the drug into the blood stream. See R. P. Walton, *Marihuana: America's New Drug Problem* (Philadelphia: J. B. Lippincott, 1938), p. 48.

will therefore not continue. The first step in the sequence of events that must occur if the person is to become a user is that he must learn to use the proper smoking technique so that his use of the drug will produce effects in terms of which his conception of it can change.

Such a change is, as might be expected, a result of the individual's participation in groups in which marihuana is used. In them the individual learns the proper way to smoke the drug. This may occur through direct teaching:

I was smoking like I did an ordinary cigarette. He said, "No, don't do it like that." He said, "Suck it, you know, draw in and hold it in your lungs till you . . . for a period of time."

I said, "Is there any limit of time to hold it?"

He said, "No, just till you feel that you want to let it out, let it out." So I did that three or four times.

Many new users are ashamed to admit ignorance and, pretending to know already, must learn through the more indirect means of observation and imitation:

I came on like I had turned on [smoked marihuana] many times before, you know. I didn't want to seem like a punk to this cat. See, like I didn't know the first thing about it — how to smoke it, or what was going to happen, or what. I just watched him like a hawk — I didn't take my eyes off him for a second, because I wanted to do everything just as he did it. I watched how he held it, how he smoked it, and everything. Then when he gave it to me I just came on cool, as though I knew exactly what the score was. I held it like he did and took a poke just the way he did.

No one I interviewed continued marihuana use for pleasure without learning a technique that supplied sufficient dosage for the effects of the drug to appear. Only when this was learned was it possible for a conception of the drug as an object which could be used for pleasure to emerge. Without such a conception marihuana use was considered meaningless and did not continue.

LEARNING TO PERCEIVE THE EFFECTS

Even after he learns the proper smoking technique, the new user may not get high and thus not form a conception of the drug as something which can be used for pleasure. A remark made by a user suggested the reason for this difficulty in getting high and pointed to the next necessary step on the road to being a user:

As a matter of fact, I've seen a guy who was high out of his mind and didn't know it.

[How can that be, man?]

Well, it's pretty strange, I'll grant you that, but I've seen it. This guy got on with me, claiming that he'd never got high, one of those guys, and he got completely stoned. And he kept insisting that he wasn't high. So I had to prove to him that he was.

What does this mean? It suggests that being high consists of two elements: the presence of symptoms caused by marihuana use and the recognition of these symptoms and their connection by the user with his use of the drug. It is not enough, that is, that the effects be present; alone, they do not automatically provide the experience of being high. The user must be able to point them out to himself and consciously connect them with having smoked marihuana before he can have this experience. Otherwise, no matter what actual effects are produced, he considers that the drug has had no effect on him: "I figured it either had no effect on me or other people were exaggerating its effect on them, you know. I thought it was probably psychological, see." Such persons believe the whole thing is an illusion and that the wish to be high leads the user to deceive himself into believing that something is happening when, in fact, nothing is. They do not continue marihuana use, feeling that "it does nothing" for them.

Typically, however, the novice has faith (developed from his observation of users who do get high) that the drug actually will produce some new experience and continues to experiment with it until it does. His failure to get high worries him, and he is likely to ask more experienced users or provoke comments from them about it. In such conversations he is made aware of specific details of his experience which he may not have noticed or may have noticed but failed to identify as symptoms of being high:

I didn't get high the first time. . . . I don't think I held it in long enough. I probably let it out, you know, you're a little afraid. The second time I wasn't sure, and he [smoking companion] told me, like I asked him for some of the symptoms or something, how would I know, you know. . . . So he told me to sit on a stool. I sat on — I think I sat on a bar stool — and he said, "Let your feet hang," and then when I got down my feet were real cold, you know.

And I started feeling it, you know. That was the first time. And then about a week after that, sometime pretty close to it, I really got on. That was the first time I got on a big laughing kick, you know. Then I really knew I was on.

One symptom of being high is an intense hunger. In the next case the novice becomes aware of this and gets high for the first time:

They were just laughing the hell out of me because like I was eating so much. I just scoffed [ate] so much food, and they were just laughing at me, you know. Sometimes I'd been looking at them, you know, wondering why they're laughing, you know, not knowing what I was doing. [Well, did they tell you why they were laughing eventually?] Yeah, yeah, I come back, "Hey, man, what's happening?" Like, you know, like I'd ask, "What's happening?" and all of a sudden I feel weird, you know. "Man, you're on, you know. You're on pot [high on marihuana]." I said, "No, am I?" Like I don't know what's happening.

The learning may occur in more indirect ways:

I heard little remarks that were made by other people. Somebody said, "My legs are rubbery," and I can't remember all the remarks that were made because I was very attentively listening for all these cues for what I was supposed to feel like.

The novice, then, eager to have this feeling, picks up from other users some concrete referents of the term "high" and applies these notions to his own experience. The new concepts make it possible for him to locate these symptoms among his own sensations and to point out to himself a "something different" in his experience that he connects with drug use. It is only when he can do this that he is high. In the next case, the contrast between two successive experiences of a user makes clear the crucial importance of the awareness of the symptoms in being high and re-empha-

sizes the important role of interaction with other users in acquiring the concepts that make this awareness possible:

[Did you get high the first time you turned on?] Yeah, sure. Although, come to think of it, I guess I really didn't. I mean, like that first time it was more or less of a mild drunk. I was happy, I guess, you know what I mean. But I didn't really know I was high, you know what I mean. It was only after the second time I got high that I realized I was high the first time. Then I knew that something different was happening.

[How did you know that?] How did I know? If what happened to me that night would of happened to you, you would've known, believe me. We played the first tune for almost two hours — one tune! Imagine, man! We got on the stand and played this one tune, we started at nine o'clock. When we got finished I looked at my watch, it's a quarter to eleven. Almost two hours on one tune. And it didn't seem like anything.

I mean, you know, it does that to you. It's like you have much more time or something. Anyway, when I saw that, man, it was too much. I knew I must really be high or something if anything like that could happen. See, and then they explained to me that that's what it did to you, you had a different sense of time and everything. So I realized that that's what it was. I knew then. Like the first time, I probably felt that way, you know, but I didn't know what's happening.

It is only when the novice becomes able to get high in this sense that he will continue to use marihuana for pleasure. In every case in which use continued, the user had acquired the necessary concepts with which to express to himself the fact that he was experiencing new sensations caused by the drug. That is, for use to continue, it is necessary not only to use the drug so as to produce effects but also to learn to perceive these effects when they occur. In this way marihuana acquires meaning for the user as an object which can be used for pleasure.

With increasing experience the user develops a greater appreciation of the drug's effects; he continues to learn to get high. He examines succeeding experiences closely, looking for new effects, making sure the old ones are still there. Out of this there grows a stable set of categories for experiencing the drug's effects whose presence enables the user to get high with ease.

Users, as they acquire this set of categories, become connoisseurs. Like experts in fine wines, they can specify where a particular plant was grown and what time of year it was harvested. Although it is usually not possible to know whether these attributions are correct, it is true that they distinguish between batches of marihuana, not only according to strength, but also with respect to the different kinds of symptoms produced.

The ability to perceive the drug's effects must be maintained if use is to continue; if it is lost, marihuana use ceases. Two kinds of evidence support this statement. First, people who become heavy users of alcohol, barbiturates, or opiates do not continue to smoke marihuana, largely because they lose the ability to distinguish between its effects and those of the other drugs.[2] They no longer know whether the marihuana gets them high. Second, in those few cases in which an individual uses marihuana in such quantities that he is always high, he is apt to feel the drug has no effect on him, since the essential element of a noticeable difference between feeling high and feeling normal is missing. In such a situation, use is likely to be given up completely, but temporarily, in order that the user may once again be able to perceive the difference.

LEARNING TO ENJOY THE EFFECTS

One more step is necessary if the user who has now learned to get high is to continue use. He must learn to enjoy the effects he has just learned to experience. Marihuana-produced sensations are not automatically or necessarily pleasurable. The taste for such experience is a socially acquired one, not different in kind from acquired tastes for oysters or dry martinis. The user feels dizzy, thirsty; his scalp tingles; he misjudges time and distances. Are these things pleasurable? He

isn't sure. If he is to continue marihuana use, he must decide that they are. Otherwise, getting high, while a real enough experience, will be an unpleasant one he would rather avoid.

The effects of the drug, when first perceived, may be physically unpleasant or at least ambiguous:

> It started taking effect, and I didn't know what was happening, you know, what it was, and I was very sick. I walked around the room, walking around the room trying to get off, you know; it just scared me at first, you know. I wasn't used to that kind of feeling.

In addition, the novice's naïve interpretation of what is happening to him may further confuse and frighten him, particularly if he decides, as many do, that he is going insane:

> I felt I was insane, you know. Everything people done to me just wigged me. I couldn't hold a conversation, and my mind would be wandering, and I was always thinking, oh, I don't know, weird things, like hearing music different. . . . I get the feeling that I can't talk to anyone. I'll goof completely.

Given these typically frightening and unpleasant first experiences, the beginner will not continue use unless he learns to redefine the sensations as pleasurable:

> It was offered to me, and I tried it. I'll tell you one thing. I never did enjoy it at all. I mean it was just nothing that I could enjoy. [Well, did you get high when you turned on?] Oh, yeah, I got definite feelings from it. But I didn't enjoy them. I mean I got plenty of reactions, but they were mostly reactions of fear. [You were frightened?] Yes. I didn't enjoy it. I couldn't seem to relax with it, you know. If you can't relax with a thing, you can't enjoy it, I don't think.

In other cases the first experiences were also definitely unpleasant, but the person did become a marihuana user. This occurred, however, only after a later experience enabled him to redefine the sensations as pleasurable:

> [This man's first experience was extremely unpleasant, involving distortion of spatial relationships

---

[2] "Smokers have repeatedly stated that the consumption of whiskey while smoking negates the potency of the drug. They find it very difficult to get "high" while drinking whiskey and because of that smokers will not drink while using the 'weed.' " New York City Mayor's Committee on Marihuana, *The Marihuana Problem in the City of New York, op. cit.*, p. 13.)

and sounds, violent thirst, and panic produced by these symptoms.] After the first time I didn't turn on for about, I'd say, ten months to a year. . . . It wasn't a moral thing; it was because I'd got so frightened, bein' so high. An' I didn't want to go through that again, I mean, my reaction was, "Well, if this is what they call bein' high, I don't dig [like] it." . . . So I didn't turn on for a year almost, accounta that. . . .

Well, my friends started, an' consequently I started again. But I didn't have any more, I didn't have that same initial reaction, after I started turning on again.

[In interaction with his friends he became able to find pleasure in the effects of the drug and eventually became a regular user.]

In no case will use continue without a redefinition of the effects as enjoyable.

This redefinition occurs, typically, in interaction with more experienced users who, in a number of ways, teach the novice to find pleasure in this experience which is at first so frightening.[3] They may reassure him as to the temporary character of the unpleasant sensations and minimize their seriousness, at the same time calling attention to the more enjoyable aspects. An experienced user describes how he handles newcomers to marihuana use:

Well, they get pretty high sometimes. The average person isn't ready for that, and it is a little frightening to them sometimes. I mean, they've been high on lush [alcohol], and they get higher that way than they've ever been before, and they don't know what's happening to them. Because they think they're going to keep going up, up, up till they lose their minds or begin doing weird things or something. You have to like reassure them, explain to them that they're not really flipping or anything, that they're gonna be all right. You have to just talk them out of being afraid. Keep talking to them, reassuring, telling them it's all right. And come on with your own story, you know: "The same thing happened to me. You'll get to like that after awhile." Keep coming on like that; pretty soon you talk them out of being scared. And besides they see you doing it and nothing horrible is happening to you, so that gives them more confidence.

[3] Charen and Perelman, *op. cit.*, p. 679.

The more experienced user may also teach the novice to regulate the amount he smokes more carefully, so as to avoid any severely uncomfortable symptoms while retaining the pleasant ones. Finally, he teaches the new user that he can "get to like it after awhile." He teaches him to regard those ambiguous experiences formerly defined as unpleasant as enjoyable. The older user in the following incident is a person whose tastes have shifted in this way, and his remarks have the effect of helping others to make similar redefinition:

A new user had her first experience of the effects of marihuana and became frightened and hysterical. She "felt like she was half in and half out of the room" and experienced a number of alarming physical symptoms. One of the more experienced users present said, "She's dragged because she's high like that. I'd give anything to get that high myself. I haven't been that high in years."

In short, what was once frightening and distasteful becomes, after a taste for it is built up, pleasant, desired, and sought after. Enjoyment is introduced by the favorable definition of the experience that one acquires from others. Without this, use will not continue, for marihuana will not be for the user an object he can use for pleasure.

In addition to being a necessary step in becoming a user, this represents an important condition for continued use. It is quite common for experienced users suddenly to have an unpleasant or frightening experience, which they cannot define as pleasurable, either because they have used a larger amount of marihuana than usual or because the marihuana they have used turns out to be of a higher quality than they expected. The user has sensations which go beyond any conception he has of what being high is and is in much the same situation as the novice, uncomfortable and frightened. He may blame it on an overdose and simply be more careful in the future. But he may make this the occasion for a rethinking of his attitude toward the drug and decide that it no longer can give him pleasure. When this occurs and is not followed by a redefinition of the drug as capable of producing pleasure, use will cease.

The likelihood of such a redefinition occurring depends on the degree of the individual's participation with other users. Where this participation is intensive, the individual is quickly talked out of his feeling against marihuana use. In the next case, on the other hand, the experience was very disturbing, and the aftermath of the incident cut the person's participation with other users to almost zero. Use stopped for three years and began again only when a combination of circumstances, important among which was a resumption of ties with users, made possible a redefinition of the nature of the drug:

It was too much, like I only made about four pokes, and I couldn't even get it out of my mouth, I was so high, and I got real flipped. In the basement, you know. I just couldn't stay in there anymore. My heart was pounding real hard, you know, and I was going out of my mind; I thought I was losing my mind completely. So I cut out of this basement, and this other guy, he's out of his mind, told me, "Don't, don't leave me, man. Stay here." And I couldn't.

I walked outside, and it was five below zero, and I thought I was dying, and I had my coat open; I was sweating, I was perspiring. My whole insides were all . . . , and I walked about two blocks away, and I fainted behind a bush. I don't know how long I laid there. I woke up, and I was feeling the worst, I can't describe it at all, so I made it to a bowling alley, man, and I was trying to act normal, I was trying to shoot pool, you know, trying to act real normal, and I couldn't lay and I couldn't stand up and I couldn't sit down, and I went up and laid down where some guys that spot pins lay down, and that didn't help me, and I went down to a doctor's office. I was going to go in there and tell the doctor to put me out of my misery . . . because my heart was pounding so hard, you know. . . . So then all week end I started flipping, seeing things there and going through hell, you know, all kinds of abnormal things. . . . I just quit for a long time then.

[He went to a doctor who defined the symptoms for him as those of a nervous breakdown caused by "nerves" and "worries." Although he was no longer using marihuana, he had some recurrences of the symptoms which led him to suspect that "it was all his nerves."] So I just stopped worrying, you know; so it was about thirty-six months later I started mak-

ing it again. I'd just take a few pokes, you know. [He first resumed use in the company of the same user-friend with whom he had been involved in the original incident.]

A person, then, cannot begin to use marihuana for pleasure, or continue its use for pleasure, unless he learns to define its effects as enjoyable, unless it becomes and remains an object he conceives of as capable of producing pleasure.

In summary, an individual will be able to use marihuana for pleasure only when he goes through a process of learning to conceive of it as an object which can be used in this way. No one becomes a user without (1) learning to smoke the drug in a way which will produce real effects; (2) learning to recognize the effects and connect them with drug use (learning, in other words, to get high); and (3) learning to enjoy the sensations he perceives. In the course of this process he develops a disposition or motivation to use marihuana which was not and could not have been present when he began use, for it involves and depends on conceptions of the drug which could only grow out of the kind of actual experience detailed above. On completion of this process he is willing and able to use marihuana for pleasure.

He has learned, in short, to answer "Yes" to the question: "Is it fun?" The direction his further use of the drug takes depends on his being able to continue to answer "Yes" to this question and, in addition, on his being able to answer "Yes" to other questions which arise as he becomes aware of the implications of the fact that society disapproves of the practice: "Is it expedient?" "Is it moral?" Once he has acquired the ability to get enjoyment by using the drug, use will continue to be possible for him. Considerations of morality and expediency, occasioned by the reactions of society, may interfere and inhibit use, but use continues to be a possibility in terms of his conception of the drug. The act becomes impossible only when the ability to enjoy the experience of being high is lost, through a change in the user's conception of the drug occasioned by certain kinds of experience with it.

45 Cats, Kicks, and Color*

Harold Finestone

There are numerous recent studies of juvenile delinquency as a product of group norms, values, and sanctions. One of the most interesting is the following report by Harold Finestone. In reading the selection think of the gang as a delinquent subculture. Try to identify the systems of values, beliefs, norms, and sanctions that foster and protect the action system under analysis. How would you attempt to modify these systems? What are the prospects for success?

Growing recognition that the most recent manifestation of the use of opiates in this country has been predominantly a young people's problem has resulted in some speculation as to the nature of this generation of drug users. Is it possible to form an accurate conception as to what "manner of man" is represented by the current species of young drug addict? Intensive interviews between 1951 and 1953 with over fifty male colored users of heroin in their late teens and early twenties selected from several of the areas of highest incidence of drug use in Chicago served to elicit from them the expression of many common attitudes, values, schemes of behavior, and general social orientation. Moreover, since there was every reason to believe that such similarities had preceded their introduction to heroin, it appeared that it was by virtue of such shared features that they had been unusually receptive to the spread of opiate use. Methodologically, their common patterns

* Excerpt from Harold Finestone, "Cats, Kicks, and Color," *Social Problems,* Vol. 5 (July 1957), pp. 3–13. Reproduced by permission. © 1957 by The Society for the Study of Social Problems.

This investigation was supported by research grant 3M 9030 from the National Institute of Mental Health, Public Health Service, and was carried on under the direction of Clifford R. Shaw and Solomon Kobrin. The writer acknowledges the generous assistance received in the clarification of the problems dealt with in this paper through discussions with Clifford R. Shaw, Henry D. McKay, and Solomon Kobrin, supervising sociologists at the Illinois Institute for Juvenile Research and the Chicago Area Project.

of behavior suggested the heuristic value of the construction of a social type. The task of this paper is to depict this social type, and to present a hypothetical formulation to account for the form it has taken.

No special justification appears to be necessary for concentrating in this paper on the social type of the young colored drug user. One of the distinctive properties of the distribution of drug use as a social problem, at least in Chicago, is its high degree of both spatial and racial concentration. In fact, it is a problem which in this city can be pinpointed with great accuracy as having its incidence preponderantly among the young male colored persons in a comparatively few local community areas. The following delineation of the generic characteristics of young colored drug users constitutes in many respects an ideal type. No single drug addict exemplified all of the traits to be depicted but all of them revealed several of them to a marked degree.

The young drug user was a creature of contrasts. Playing the role of the fugitive and pariah as he was inevitably forced to do, he turned up for interviews in a uniformly ragged and dirty condition. And yet he talked with an air of superiority derived from his identification with an elite group, the society of "cats." He came in wearing a non-functional tie clip attached to his sport shirt and an expensive hat as the only indications that he was concerned with his appearance and yet displayed in his conversation a highly developed sense of taste in men's clothing and a high valuation upon dressing well. He came from what were externally the drabbest, most overcrowded, and physically deteriorated sections of the city and yet discussed his pattern of living as though it were a consciously cultivated work of art.

Despite the location of his social world in the "asphalt jungle" of the "Blackbelt" he strictly eschewed the use of force and violence as a technique for achieving his ends or for the settling of problematic situations. He achieved his goals by indirection, relying, rather, on persuasion and on a repertoire of manipulative techniques. To deal with a variety of challenging situations, such as those arising out of his contacts with the police, with his past or potential victims, and with jilted "chicks," etc., he used his wits and his conversational ability. To be able to confront such contingencies with adequacy and without resort to violence was to be "cool." His idea was to get what he wanted through persuasion and ingratiation; to use the other fellow by deliberately outwitting him. Indeed, he regarded himself as immeasurably superior to the "gorilla," a person who resorted to force.

The image of himself as "operator" was projected onto the whole world about him and led to a complete scepticism as to other persons' motives. He could relate to people by outsmarting them, or through open-handed and often ruinous generosity, but his world seemed to preclude any relationship which was not part of a "scheme" or did not lend itself to an "angle." The most difficult puzzle for him to solve was the "square," the honest man. On the one hand the "square" was the hard-working plodder who lived by routine and who took honesty and the other virtues at their face value. As such he constituted the prize victim for the cat. On the other hand the cat harbored the sneaking suspicion that some squares were smarter than he, because they could enjoy all the forbidden pleasures which were his stock in trade and maintain a reputation for respectability in the bargain.

The cat had a large, colorful, and discriminating vocabulary which dealt with all phases of his experience with drugs. In addition, he never seemed to content himself with the conventional word for even the most commonplace objects. Thus he used "pad" for house, "pecks" for food, "flicks" for movies, "stick hall" for pool hall, "dig the scene" for observe, "box" for record player, "bread" for money, etc. In each instance the word he used was more concrete or earthier than the conventional word and such as to reveal an attitude of subtle ridicule towards the dignity and conventionality inherent in the common usage.

His soft convincing manner of speaking, the shocking earthiness and fancifulness of his vocabulary, together with the formidable gifts of charm and ingratiation which he deployed, all contributed to the dominant impression which the young drug user made as a person. Such traits would seem to have fitted naturally into a role which some cats had already played or aspired to play,

that of the pimp. To be supported in idleness and luxury through the labors of one or more attractive "chicks" who shoplifted or engaged in prostitution or both and dutifully handed over the proceeds was one of his favorite fantasies. In contrast with the milieu of the underworld, the pimp was not an object of opprobrium but of prestige.

The theme of the exploitation of the woman goes close to the heart of the cat's orientation to life, that is, his attitude towards work. Part of the cat's sense of superiority stems from his aristocratic disdain for work and for the subordination of self to superiors and to the repetitive daily routine entailed by work, which he regards as intolerable. The "square" is a person who toils for regular wages and who takes orders from his superiors without complaint.

In contrast with the "square," the cat gets by without working. Instead he keeps himself in "bread" by a set of ingenious variations on "begging, borrowing, or stealing." Each cat has his "hustle" and a "hustle" is any non-violent means of "making some bread" which does not require work. One of the legendary heroes of the cat is the man who is such a skillful con-man that he can sell "State Street" to his victim. Concretely, the cat is a petty thief, pickpocket, or pool shark, or is engaged in a variety of other illegal activities of the "conning" variety. A very few cats are actually living off the proceeds of their women "on the hustle."

The main purpose of life for the cat is to experience the "kick." Just as every cat takes pride in his "hustle," so every cat cultivates his "kick." A "kick" is any act tabooed by "squares" that heightens and intensifies the present moment of experience and differentiates it as much as possible from the humdrum routine of daily life. Sex in any of its conventional expressions is not a "kick" since this would not serve to distinguish the cat from the "square," but orgies of sex behavior and a dabbling in the various perversions and byways of sex pass muster as "kicks." Some "cats" are on an alcohol "kick," others on a marihuana "kick," and others on a heroin "kick." There is some interchangeability among these various "kicks" but the tendency is to select your "kick" and stay with it. Many of these young drug users, however, had progressed from the alcohol to the marihuana to the heroin "kick." Each "kick" has its own lore of appreciation and connoisseurship into which only its devotees are initiated.

In addition to his "kick" the cat sets great store on the enjoyment of music and on proper dress. To enjoy one's "kick" without a background of popular music is inconceivable. The cat's world of music has a distinctive galaxy of stars, and the brightest luminaries in his firmament are performers such as "Yard-bird" (the late Charlie Parker) and disc jockeys such as Al Benson. Almost every cat is a frustrated musician who hopes some day to get his "horn" out of pawn, take lessons, and earn fame and fortune in the field of "progressive music."

The cat places a great deal of emphasis upon clothing and exercises his sartorial talents upon a skeletal base of suit, sport shirt, and hat. The suit itself must be conservative in color. Gaiety is introduced through the selection of the sport shirt and the various accessories, all so chosen and harmonized as to reveal an exquisite sense of taste. When the cat was not talking about getting his clothes out of pawn, he talked about getting them out of the cleaners. With nonchalant pride one drug user insisted that the most expensive sport shirts and hats in the city of Chicago were sold in a certain haberdashery on the South Side. The ideal cat would always appear in public impeccably dressed and be able to sport a complete change of outfit several times a day.

The cat seeks through a harmonious combination of charm, ingratiating speech, dress, music, the proper dedication to his "kick," and unrestrained generosity to make of his day to day life itself a gracious work of art. Everything is to be pleasant and everything he does and values is to contribute to a cultivated aesthetic approach to living. The "cool cat" exemplifies all of these elements in proper balance. He demonstrates his ability to "play it cool" in his unruffled manner of dealing with outsiders such as the police, and in the self-assurance with which he confronts emergencies in the society of "cats." Moreover, the "cat" feels himself to be any man's equal. He is convinced that he can go anywhere and mingle easily with anyone. For example, he rejects the type of music designated "the blues" because for

him it symbolizes attitudes of submission and resignation which are repugnant and alien to his customary frame of mind.

It can be seen now why heroin use should make such a powerful appeal to the cat. It was the ultimate "kick." No substance was more profoundly tabooed by conventional middle-class society. Regular heroin use provides a sense of maximal social differentiation from the "square." The cat was at last engaged, he felt, in an activity completely beyond the comprehension of the "square." No other "kick" offered such an instantaneous intensification of the immediate moment of experience and set it apart from everyday experience in such spectacular fashion. Any words used by the cat to apply to the "kick," the experience of "being high," he applied to heroin in the superlative. It was the "greatest kick of them all."

In the formulation now to be presented the cat as a social type is viewed as a manifestation of a process of social change in which a new type of self-conception has been emerging among the adolescents of the lower socio-economic levels of the colored population in large urban centers. It is a self-conception rooted in the types of accommodation to a subordinate status achieved historically by the colored race in this country, a self-conception which has become increasingly articulated as it responded to and selected various themes from the many available to it in the milieu of the modern metropolis. Blumer's classification of social movements into general, specific, or expressive, appears to provide a useful framework for the analysis of the social type of the cat.

In terms of these categories the cat as a social type is the personal counterpart of an expressive social movement. The context for such a movement must include the broader community, which, by its policies of social segregation and discrimination, has withheld from individuals of the colored population the opportunity to achieve or to identify with status positions in the larger society. The social type of the cat is an expression of one possible type of adaptation to such blocking and frustration, in which a segment of the population turns in upon itself and attempts to develop within itself criteria for the achievement of social status and the rudiments of a satisfactory social life. Within his own isolated social world the cat attempts to give form and purpose to dispositions derived from but denied an outlet within the dominant social order.

What are these dispositions and in what sense may they be said to be derived from the dominant social order? Among the various interrelated facets of the life of the cat two themes are central, those of the "hustle" and the "kick." It is to be noted that they are in direct antithesis to two of the central values of the dominant culture, the "hustle" versus the paramount importance of the occupation for the male in our society, and the "kick" versus the importance of regulating conduct in terms of its future consequences. Thus, there appears to be a relationship of conflict between the central themes of the social type of the cat and those of the dominant social order. As a form of expressive behavior, however, the social type of the cat represents an indirect rather than a direct attack against central conventional values.

It is interesting to speculate on the reasons why a type such as the cat should emerge rather than a social movement with the objective of changing the social order. The forces coercing the selective process among colored male adolescents in the direction of expressive social movements are probably to be traced to the long tradition of accommodation to a subordinate status on the part of the Negro as well as to the social climate since the Second World War, which does not seem to have been favorable to the formation of specific social movements.

The themes of the "hustle" and "kick" in the social orientation of the cat are facts which appear to be overdetermined. For example, to grasp the meaning of the "hustle" to the cat one must understand it as a rejection of the obligation of the adult male to work. When asked for the reasons underlying his rejection of work the cat did not refer to the uncongenial and relatively unskilled and low paid jobs which, in large part, were the sole types of employment available to him. He emphasized rather that the routine of a job and the demand that he should apply himself continuously to his work task were the features that made work intolerable for him. The self-constraint required by work was construed as an unwarranted damper upon his love of spontaneity. The other undesirable element from his point of view was the authoritarian setting of most types of work with which he was familiar.

There are undoubtedly many reasons for the cat's rejection of work but the reasons he actually verbalized are particularly significant when interpreted as devices for sustaining his self-conception. The cat's feeling of superiority would be openly challenged were he to confront certain of the social realities of his situation, such as the discrimination exercised against colored persons looking for work and the fact that only the lowest status jobs are available to him. He avoided any mention of these factors which would have forced him to confront his true position in society and thus posed a threat to his carefully cherished sense of superiority.

In emphasizing as he does the importance of the "kick" the cat is attacking the value our society places upon planning for the future and the responsibility of the individual for such planning. Planning always requires some subordination and disciplining of present behavior in the interest of future rewards. The individual plans to go to college, plans for his career, plans for his family and children, etc. Such an orientation on the part of the individual is merely the personal and subjective counterpart of a stable social order and of stable social institutions, which not only permit but sanction an orderly progression of expectations with reference to others and to one's self. Where such stable institutions are absent or in the inchoate stages of development, there is little social sanction for such planning in the experience of the individual. Whatever studies are available strongly suggest that such are the conditions which tend to prevail in the lower socio-economic levels of the Negro urban community. Stable family and community organization is lacking in those areas of the city where drug use is concentrated. A social milieu which does not encourage the subordination and disciplining of present conduct in the interests of future rewards tends by default to enhance the present. The "kick" appears to be a logical culmination of this emphasis.

The cat is "free" in the sense that he is a preeminent candidate for new forms of social organization and novel social practices. He is attempting to escape from certain features of the historical traditions of the Negro which he regards as humiliating. As an adolescent or young adult he is not fully assimilated into such social institutions as the family, school, church, or industry which may be available to him. Moreover, the social institutions which the Negroes brought with them when they migrated to the city have not as yet achieved stability or an adequate functioning relationship to the urban environment. As a Negro, and particularly as a Negro of low socio-economic status, he is excluded from many socializing experiences which adolescents in more advantaged sectors of the society take for granted. He lives in communities where the capacity of the population for effective collective action is extremely limited, and consequently there are few effective controls on his conduct besides that exercised by his peer group itself. He is fascinated by the varied "scenes" which the big city spreads out before him. Granted this setting, the cat adopts an adventurous attitude to life and is free to give his allegiance to new forms of activity.

It is implicit in the notion of an expressive social movement that, since direct collective action to modify the sources of dissatisfaction and restlessness is not possible, all such movements should appear under one guise, as forms of "escape." Persons viewing the problem of addiction from the perspective of the established social structure have been prone to make this interpretation. It is a gross over-simplification, however, as considered from the perspective of the young drug addict himself. The emergence of the self-conception of the cat is an attempt to deal with the problems of status and identity in a situation where participation in the life of the broader community is denied, but where the colored adolescent is becoming increasingly sensitive to the values, the goals, and the notions of success which obtain in the dominant social order.

The caste pressures thus make it exceedingly difficult for an American Negro to preserve a true perspective of himself and his own group in relation to the larger white society. The increasing abstract knowledge of the world outside — of its opportunities, its rewards, its different norms of competition and cooperation — which results from the proceeding acculturation at the same time as there is increasing group isolation, only increases the tensions. (1)

Such conditions of group isolation would appear to be fairly uniform throughout the Negro group. Although this isolation may be experienced differently at different social levels of the Negro community, certain features of the adaptations arrived at in response to this problem will tend to reveal similarities. Since the struggle for status takes place on a stage where there is acute sensitivity to the values and status criteria of the dominant white group, but where access to the means through which such values may be achieved is prohibited, the status struggle turning in on itself will assume a variety of distorted forms. Exclusion from the "serious" concerns of the broader community will result in such adaptations manifesting a strong element of "play."

Frazier in *Black Bourgeoisie* discusses the social adaptation of the Negro middle class as "The World of Make-Believe."

The emphasis upon "social" life or "society" is one of the main props of the world of make-believe into which the black bourgeoisie has sought an escape from its inferiority and frustrations in American society. This would of make-believe, to be sure, is a reflection of the values of American society, but it lacks the economic basis that would give it roots in the world of reality. (2, p. 237)

In the Negro lower classes the effects of frustrations deriving from subordination to the whites may not be experienced as personally or as directly as it is by the Negro middle class, but the massive effects of residential segregation and the lack of stable social institutions and community organization are such as to reinforce strong feelings of group isolation even at the lowest levels of the society.

It is here suggested that the function performed by the emergence of the social type of the cat among Negro lower class adolescents is analogous to that performed by "The World of Make-Believe" in the Negro middle class. The development of a social type such as that of the cat is only possible in a situation where there is isolation from the broader community but great sensitivity to its goals, where the peer group pressures are extremely powerful, where institutional structures are weak, where models of success in the illegitimate world have strong appeals, where specific social movements are not possible, and where novel forms of behavior have great prestige. To give significance to his experience, the young male addict has developed the conception of a heroic figure, the "ideal cat," a person who is completely adequate to all situations, who controls his 'kick" rather than letting it control him, who has a lucrative "hustle," who has no illusions as to what makes the world "tick," who is any man's equal, who basks in the admiration of his brother cats and associated "chicks," who hob-nobs with "celebs" of the musical world, and who in time himself may become a celebrity.

The cat throws himself into his way of life with a great deal of intensity but he cannot escape completely from the perspective, the judgments, and the sanctions of the dominant social order. He has to make place in his scheme of life for police, lock-ups, jails, and penitentiaries, to say nothing of the agonies of withdrawal distress. He is forced eventually to confront the fact that his role as a cat with its associated attitudes is largely a pose, a form of fantasy with little basis in fact. With the realization that he is addicted he comes only too well to know that he is a "junky," and he is fully aware of the conventional attitudes towards addicts as well as of the counter-rationalizations provided by his peer group. It is possible that the cat's vacillation with regard to seeking a cure for his addiction is due to a conflict of perspectives, whether to view his habit from the cat's or the dominant social order's point of view.

It is this limited, esoteric, character of heroin use which gives to the cat the feeling of belonging to an elite. It is the restricted extent of the distri-bution of drug use, the scheming and intrigue associated with underground "connections" through which drugs are obtained, the secret lore of the appreciation of the drug's effects, which give the cat the exhilaration of participating in a conspiracy. Contrary to popular conception most drug users were not anxious to proselyte new users. Of course, spreading the habit would have the function of increasing the possible sources of supply. But an equally strong disposition was to keep the knowledge of drug use secret, to impress and dazzle the audience with one's knowledge of being "in the know." When proselyting did occur, as in jails or lockups, it was proselyting on the part of a devotee who condescended to share with the uninitiated a highly prized practice and set of attitudes.

The social orientation of the cat, with its emphasis on non-violence, was quite in contrast to the orientation of the smaller group of young white drug users who were interviewed in the course of this study. The latter's type of adjustment placed a heavy stress upon violence. Their crimes tended to represent direct attacks against persons and property. The general disposition they manifested was one of "nerve" and brashness rather than one of "playing it cool." They did not cultivate the amenities of language, music, or dress to nearly the same extent as the cat. Their social orientation was expressed as a direct rather than an indirect attack on the dominant values of our society.

References

1. Myrdal, Gunnar, *An American Dilemma* (New York: Harper & Brothers, 1944), p. 760.
2. Frazier, E. Franklin, *Black Bourgeoisie* (Glencoe, Illinois: Free Press, 1957).

CHAPTER SIX

Distributive Systems:
Differentiation and Stratification

A problem for any social system is the distribution of its rewards and penalties, its opportunities and restraints. In agrarian societies, in which nearly all of man's efforts are devoted to the attainment of a subsistence level of living, the distributive system may be fairly simple. Survival has such a high priority over other values that goods and services are distributed primarily on the basis of need.

However, goods and services are available in a greater supply than is necessary to meet the requirements of survival in modern industrial societies. Their technological capabilities allow much of man's energy to be diverted into the production of various kinds of surpluses, which are distributed according to criteria other than need, depending upon the structure and values of the society in question. A term that encompasses many of these criteria is "power," which may be defined as the probability that a certain individual or group will carry out its desires, despite the opposition of others. Power has many sources and many forms of expression, especially in societies that are advanced technologically and are characterized by pluralistic cultures. In general, then, the greater the degree of technological development and cultural heterogeneity, the greater the complexity of the distributive system.

Variations in the Distribution of Goods and Services

The supply and variety of products to be distributed in a society varies according to the proportion of its energies that can be diverted from activities required for survival. Great differences in the amount of energy available for the production of surpluses are found between societies and within a given society. These surpluses are distributed, on the whole, in accord with a basic law of economics which asserts that:

$$S = \frac{G}{P}.$$

S represents the standard of living, or the average amount of goods and services (usually measured in dollars) available to the individual consumers. G represents the society's gross annual production of goods and services, in dollars. P represents the population of the society. The law holds that the standard of living does not increase unless productivity grows faster than the population.

In 1963 the United States had the highest per capita productivity, $3083, among the 135 nations of the world. Only three other nations — Canada, Sweden, and Switzerland — had a living standard greater than $2000. Among the twenty most productive nations, nineteen are outside Asia, Africa, and Latin America, where the productivity generally ranges between $100 and $300, about one-tenth as great as in the industrialized nations. More than half of the world's 3.5 billion people live in Asia, where the per capita productivity is less than $300, with the exception of Japan, which has a score of $626. India and Pakistan, alone, have 600 million people, and their productivity of $85 means a starvation diet for many.

A similar pattern of deprivation is found in the distribution of many specific goods or services. North America, with 8 per cent of the world's population, has about 23 per cent of its agricultural products, while the Far East has 39 per cent of the population and 16 per cent of the farm produce. The United States, with 6 per cent of the population, consumes one-third of the world's commercial energy, whereas India has 15 per cent of the population and consumes 2 per cent of the energy. The same kind of distribution occurs for variables related to health, life expectancy, and literacy. In the United States, for example, 43 per cent of the population between 20 and 24 years of age attends institutions of higher learning, while in France the percentage is 16, and in Germany, Italy, and Great Britain it is 6. Advanced training in nonindustrial societies is, of course, almost nonexistent.

Furthermore, the gap between "have" and "have-not" societies is apparently increasing. One reason is the tremendous concentration of resources in the industrialized societies. These comprise only 30 per cent of the world's people, but have 75 per cent of the mining production, 90 per cent of the production of gas and electricity, and 90 per cent of the manufacturing. Fiscal resources and managerial know-how are similarly concentrated. In fact, it seems possible, if present trends continue for another decade or two, that the world's third greatest industrial power, after the United States and Russia, will be the US-managed industrial empire in Europe.

Another reason for the growing disparity in the distribution of goods and services is the current trend in the size of the world's population. The greatest increase is found in parts of Africa, in Latin America, and especially in Asia, where many societies will double their population in less than twenty-five years. These are precisely the societies that can least afford any unfavorable changes in their per capita productivity. Unless their fertility is reduced, it seems possible that the lack of space and resources will eventually impose a ceiling on the amount of food and other goods available to the individual consumer, and if such a ceiling is reached the probable result is an increase in the death rate.

However, the problems of distribution are by no means restricted to the inequities observed in different societies. Similar inequities are often found within a given society, and they are frequently as great in industrial societies as elsewhere. Consider the situation in the United States. Population growth is a problem here also. If the current rate of growth were continued for another 2500 years, the population of the United States would outweigh the earth. In addition, the relatively disadvantaged nonwhite population is growing at a rate that is more than 50 per cent greater than the rate of growth in the white population, and the American Indian has a fertility rate nearly twice that of the white population.

In 1964 the median income of United States families was $6600. But it was $4000 more than that for college graduates. It was $3100 lower, on the average, for nonwhite families than for the families of whites, and it was estimated that

34.6 million residents — one out of every seven white Americans and one out of every two nonwhite Americans — had a "poverty level" income. In all, some 8.4 million families, one out of every five, had incomes under $3000.

Education and occupation data revealed similar disparities. Among persons 25 to 34 years of age, for example, 70 per cent of the whites were high school graduates, but only 42 per cent of the Negroes. And the greatest increase in employment, compared with earlier years, was among professional and technical workers, managers, and public officials, all occupations that are relatively inaccessible to untrained or otherwise disadvantaged individuals. By contrast, unskilled labor showed a declining rate of employment. It seems likely that the employment problems of unskilled and poorly educated persons may be further complicated by trends in education which make college training something of a necessity for increasing numbers of job-seekers. Economic and educational disadvantages are frequently cited by the participants as major stimulants in the recent wave of urban rebellions. Thus, the question that faces the community is whether pockets of poverty and deprivation can continue to exist in an affluent society without dire consequences for all.

The Structure of Distributive Systems

The actual distribution of goods and services is only a reflection of the system's operation. Sometimes changes in distribution occur incidentally because of modifications in the environment; a new freeway, park, or playground raises the value of certain properties and lowers the value of others. However, most of the changes that occur in a distributive system seem to be deliberate efforts to rearrange the power relations among the community's members. Numerous devices are used for this purpose, some of them subtle and capable of concealment.

One method of regulating power is by controlling the possession or use of physical objects. Much of man's behavior is organized around utilitarian items such as houses, factories, public buildings, roads, automobiles, tools, and a great variety of personal belongings. Such items are often the focus of attitudes as well as actions. For example, the laborer may become so attached to his outmoded implements that he refuses to adopt newer and more efficient equipment. Or the new automobile may arouse in its owner such feelings of power that he deprives himself of all sorts of things in order to make the monthly payments on it. As a result of man's attachments to such items, the regulation of possession and ownership is a major device of social control in all societies.

However, symbols, especially when written or spoken, have far greater influence and flexibility than do physical objects as instruments of social control. Every word in our language is a symbol that stands for some other object, event, or relationship. And every idea, concept, or belief is a complex of such symbols. Complexes are sometimes organized into *value systems,* which refer to conceptions of what is intrinsically worthwhile, what is right and wrong, and what "ought to be" man's state of affairs or his station in life. Values establish priorities among people's goals and objectives, and provide a foundation for feelings of guilt or approval. Similarly, *belief systems* and *ideologies* refer to different kinds of logic, reasoning, or argument that people use in deciding questions of fact. Sometimes the criterion of truth may be the result of a scientific experiment, while in other cases it may be the argument of a wise person, or what the Bible says. It may be that tested knowledge is gradually replacing traditional beliefs and ideologies as guides to action, but there are very few societies in which much research has been done on the costs and consequences of alternative methods of distributing goods and services. Of all the aspects of social organization, the distributive system seems most frequently to be regarded as sacred and beyond the influence of mundane forces.

It follows that the distribution of goods and services is largely governed by traditional rules dealing with objects, symbols, and systems of symbols. But these rules rarely are "universals" that apply equally to all members of the community. Instead, they are usually "particularistic" in nature; they have different meanings for different persons and in different situations. The right to vote is an example. Rules governing voting nearly always exclude certain individuals or groups. Among those excluded are persons under 21 years of age in most parts of the United States and those who cannot pass a "literacy" test in the South. In order to be reliably employed, particularistic rules must differentiate among people in some way, whether by age, education, sex, citizenship, race, wealth, religion, occupation, or membership in some other group or category.

Social differentiation refers to the diverse positions people occupy in various groups and organizations. Some positions are inherited through the kinship system or by other rules of descent. Others may be attained by demonstrating extraordinary skill and ability or by undergoing prolonged periods of special training. Still others may require rare displays of strength, courage, or integrity. Whatever the method of assignment, a given position always involves special rights or privileges and duties or responsibilities with respect to the operation of a distributive system.

The degree of value attached to a given position determines its *social status*. The arrangement of statuses in a hierarchy of inequalities, ranging from the highest down to the lowest ranks, is called *stratification*. Thus we speak of upper, middle, and lower *social classes,* the wealthy and the destitute, intellectuals and illiterates, and so on. In each case, the way we classify people influences their access to the physical, symbolic, social, and emotional resources of the community.

Economic stratification involves primarily access to money, material goods, and services. Of course, economic inequities may give rise to variations in people's attitudes and values, their opportunities for self-expression and achievement, and their styles of life. Stratification of authority refers to inequities in the right to make decisions affecting others or to carry out one's plans and preferences. Limited authority means that a person is constrained from carrying out his desired course of action; his access to the social and organizational resources of the community is restricted. Stratification of prestige reflects inequalities in the distribution of respect and good will. High status on the prestige dimension means that an individual has easy access to the community's emotional resources. His ideas and opinions are given serious consideration and his efforts at achievement are generally met with friendly assistance.

The distribution of statuses within any given group or community is a powerful determinant of human behavior. Motivation for wealth, authority, and prestige is often taken for granted. Indeed, the person who disavows such interests is frequently viewed with skepticism or scorn. Yet the opportunity to attain high status is severely restricted. Some restrictions are of a personal nature, involving relative skills, abilities, and objectives. Others may grow out of the group's opportunity system; access to various resources may be limited by skin color, religious or political affiliations, social class, and cultural heritage. Sometimes the sex of a person or the order of his birth among his siblings may be important factors.

Even if the group prides itself on its egalitarian values, there is a tendency for differentiation to result in status distinctions. The powerful groups and individuals tend to interact more with one another than with members of the lower classes, to restrict membership in the advantaged classes, and to develop formal and informal norms that perpetuate their positions. Upward mobility is achieved mainly by those members of the lower classes who possess the kinds of power that are valuable to those above. These are chiefly intellectual ability, specialized skills, and the capacity to accomplish difficult tasks that are highly valued by the elite groups.

Although wealth, authority, and prestige tend to be fairly highly correlated, there are numerous exceptions. For example, the *nouveau riche* may have great wealth, but limited authority, and very little prestige. Professional gamblers often have the same set of statuses. Scholars and scientists may have high prestige and influence, but they are likely to be quite low on the other dimensions. Public officials, again, may have great authority and limited economic status. Groups characterized by such status discrepancies are likely to be innovative, rebellious, or otherwise difficult to control.

Another problem is that the status hierarchy may vary from one segment of the community to another. There is often little consensus regarding the traits and activities that should be assigned high or low status. When consensus is lacking, the effectiveness of stratification as a device of social control may be greatly reduced. Accordingly, many attempts have been made to eliminate or to minimize status comparisons. While these efforts have occasionally been instrumental in removing inequities in one or another of the status dimensions, they have not been successful overall. We need to know much more about the whole field of status management before we can control stratification systems.

Conceptions of Justice

In modern societies the rules of distributive systems are often exploited to the advantage of certain groups or individuals. Some common methods by which this occurs are force and the threat of force, legal or traditional authority, and social influence. Thus, some people gain access to goods and services by violent means. Crime is an example, but riot, rebellion, demonstration, and military power are equally important and sometimes more prevalent. Again, many people gain advantages because of the official authority vested in the positions they occupy. Authority, technically speaking, implies the right of a person, by virtue of his position, to control the behavior of others, without regard to their preferences. In capitalistic systems, for instance, the ownership of property gives an individual the legal authority to do with it as he sees fit, except for certain restrictions that are also established by law. By contrast, influence involves the use of personal appeal and persuasion based on informal norms. The prestige a person enjoys also has an effect on his influence. In general, influence denotes an individual's ability to manipulate situations in such a way that others accede to his wishes. "Magnetism," "charm," and "leadership" are terms commonly employed in describing the methods of persons skilled in the use of influence.

While wealth, power, prestige, and other values are distributed in various ways, there is a fairly uniform method of determining the legitimacy of the distribution. This is by the endorsement of the system's officials, with courts of law often serving as the final arbiters in modern societies. It is generally the law, then, that defines justice. But justice is not a response to a particular event, nor is it simply a rule stating what that response should be. Rather, it concerns the entire apparatus by which social values are distributed among a system's members, including the norms

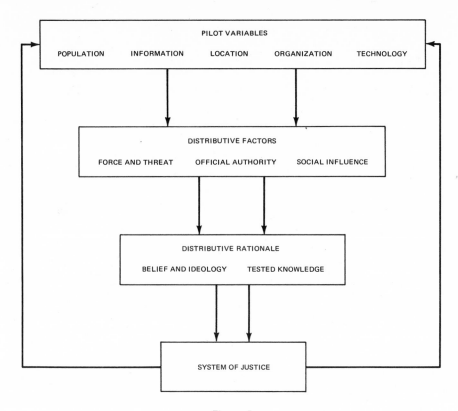

Figure 1

Interrelations of elements in a distributive system. The pilot variables determine the availability of goods and services to be distributed according to the system of justice that operates in any given society or organization. In turn, this distribution has a feedback relationship with the pilot variables.

prescribing the distribution process, the way these norms are implemented in practice, and the degree of correspondence between the norms and the practices. These relationships are outlined in Figure 1.

The traditional system of justice that operates in many societies is confused and inconsistent. Its procedures are not rationalized by their consequences, but by appeal to a supra-empirical authority, usually political or religious. And only the final decisions are ordinarily available for public scrutiny. Their aims, assumptions, and general relationale have minimal visibility. Even the language of justice is often unintelligible, except perhaps to members of the legal profession. Without general understanding and corroboration of its principles, the system is vulnerable to charges of favoritism and discrimination, since disproof of such charges would entail empirical investigations that are regarded as antagonistic to the traditional conception of ultimate power and authority. As a consequence, the administration of justice is often contemplated with suspicion, especially by our alienated minorities and other disadvantaged groups. If the system's norms conflict, or if they are applied inconsistently and to the detriment of certain members, there can be no convincing demonstration of justice; in the long run, there can only be frustration and animosity leading to rebellion against the norm-makers and norm-enforcers.

CLASS AND CASTE

46 Portrait of the Underdog*

Genevieve Knupfer

Members of the lower social classes lack interest and self-confidence in many activities that are regarded as important by the rest of society. This results in their withdrawal from participation in these activities. What are the causes of this failure to participate? How does this withdrawal increase distinctions along class lines? How can the "underdog" be characterized in terms of naïveté, voting behavior, and general knowledge? These are the problems analyzed in the following study of the social activities of members of the lower classes.

. . . The purpose of the present paper is to present some evidence in support of the following hypothesis: that the economic and educational limitations accompanying low status produce a lack of interest in and lack of self-confidence in dealing with certain important areas of our culture; as a result, there is reduced participation — a *withdrawal from* participation in these areas. . . .

The constant interaction of the different factors involved makes it difficult to distinguish between cause and effect. Lack of education and information, of facility in reading and writing, of interest in relatively abstract things; habits of submission, feelings of inferiority, low income, absorption with the problem of mere survival — all these factors continually influence one another, so that we

* Excerpt from *Public Opinion Quarterly,* Vol. 11 (Spring 1947), pp. 103–114. Copyright 1947 by Princeton University. Reproduced by permission.

cannot attempt to show where one begins and the other ends.

Another difficulty for interpretation is that the data on this subject are generally crude. The pattern of limited psychological horizons among the lower as compared with the higher socio-economic groups is certainly not unambiguous. Statistical comparisons show differences between groups, but the differences are not all large, and the groups are heterogeneous. We do not know from such data, for example, what are the different effects of different *types* of low status. In rough classifications of status there may be manual workers, farmers, and small businessmen in the lower group. The over-all figures do not reveal whether or not these different groups react differentially.

Definition of Status. Before presenting the following data, our terms need to be clarified. By "status" we refer to rank position with respect chiefly to income, prestige, and power — one or all of these. "Low" is used in a purely relative sense. The definition varies: sometimes it may be the lower half, sometimes the lower tenth of the population; sometimes it may be measured by income, sometimes by occupation, sometimes by impressionistic ratings. In the case of individual studies cited, a more exact description of the status index used will usually be given.

In order to simplify our language we will use the initials LS and HS for "low status" and "high status." Short cuts in stating statistical comparisons will also be used. Thus, a statement that "the LS person is more inclined to . . ." should be understood to mean "a larger proportion of persons in the lower socio-economic status group. . . ."

The data will be presented in three sections, dealing respectively (*a*) with the differential participation of status groups in social contacts or interaction, both organized and informal, (*b*) with their differential participation in the thought-life of society, and (*c*) with their differential efforts and aspirations to control and to enjoy life.

Participation in Social Life. There is ample evidence to show that LS groups participate in fewer organized activities and know fewer people. As far as membership in clubs and organizations goes, one illustration among many is provided by a study made in Franklin, Indiana (pop. 6,000). The percentage of men in the income class earning less than $100 per month who had no group affiliations at all was eight times as great as that of the men in the higher income class: "In every type of group without exception — church, fraternal, service, recreational, patriotic, political, cultural — membership on the part of the lower income class was markedly lower."

In part the lesser membership is, of course, caused by economic considerations — the cost of membership and of going to meetings, and the many other incidental expenses. There is also the factor of lack of time and energy, due to longer and more strenuous working hours. The explanation most likely to be given by individuals themselves is probably "lack of interest." Of the implications of this lack of interest we shall have more to say later. In some cases there may be a reluctance to mix with persons of higher status. This would operate in the case of organizations which are predominantly middle class. The lower-class mother may hesitate to go to Parent-Teacher Association meetings, being unwilling to meet with women who have more money and education, because of her cheap clothes and her poor grammar. It may be that the relatively high degree of social mobility in this country, and its even greater *ideological* "classlessness," makes the participation of LS persons particularly difficult, because separate organizations are not usually provided for different classes. The great majority of Americans consider themselves middle class and so they are all ostensibly on an equal basis. If they feel themselves too severely handicapped in the competition, they simply withdraw. More investigation is needed to determine which of the factors suggested above actually are most important in different situations.

Studies of participation in civilian defense activities showed that almost all the members were white-collar people. It was the experience of the writer that attempts to bring in manual workers often uncovered an exaggerated fear on the part of the latter of even trying to take the required examination in air raid protection procedures, which was, as a matter of fact, probably well within their capacities to pass.

We might expect to find that LS people compensate for their relative lack of more demanding types of participation by a greater development of informal relationships, just as we find more radio listening among the poor than among the well-to-do, because the latter have so many other opportunities for entertainment and information. But evidence indicates that even in face-to-face contacts LS people are more limited. Informal social activities, such as visiting friends, are more infrequent among them. In Middletown, for example, it was found that 3 per cent of the "business-class" women (who gave the information) said they had no friends whatever, 13 per cent said they had no intimate friends, while for the working-class women the proportions were 13 per cent and 34 per cent respectively. A study of a rural New York community made in 1940–41 brings additional evidence. People were asked "What persons not members of your household do you visit most when away from your business or work?" If two persons in answer to this question mentioned each other, this was called a mutual choice. Mutual choices were regarded as indicating an intimate interpersonal relationship. The community was further divided into 11 prestige groups. The mean number of mutual choices for the highest group was 6, for the lowest 2.

The Foreign and the Distant. Comments made by working-class women on this question in Middletown bring out a corollary of social isolation: suspicion and dread of the foreign, the definition of the foreign being more or less inclusive:

"It doesn't pay to be too friendly."

"I never chum with anyone; it's dangerous."

Whether such reactions are characteristic of LS persons generally is a question which needs further study. Friendliness, solidarity and mutual aid have sometimes been cited as characteristic of the ethic of the underprivileged as opposed to bourgeois competitiveness and self-reliance. Many factors would have to be more precisely determined in order to clarify the issue. There are different types of community, different definitions of "stranger" and "friendliness," and different types of low status groups. The results may well depend on the particular combination of these elements which is involved. Whatever the true interpretation, it seems well established that in many American communities there is a correlation between income and the number of friends or acquaintances an individual associates with.

Moreover, what friendship contacts there are among LS people are apt to be confined to a narrower area. In Middletown, more than half the best friends of the working-class wives, less than a tenth of the friends of the business group, were reported to have been met in the "neighborhood." In a South Dakota town, comparison of the top group with the lowest showed that over 90 per cent of the "Tops" and only 27 per cent of the "Bottoms" exchanged visits with friends outside the immediate neighborhood. It has also been shown that propinquity is more important to the selection of a spouse in the LS group than in the other.

The geographical circumscription apparently attendant upon relatively low socio-economic status is shown in the extent of travel outside the community. In Prairieton, the average lower-class person in the course of a lifetime . . . [had] traveled within a radius of but 145 miles from Prairieton; in contrast the average for upper-class individuals was 1,100 miles.

It is clear that a major factor in the geographical restrictions cited above is the economic one: travel costs money, even within a city. But there may also be a psychological factor: the richer classes have had more chance to cultivate the habit of ignoring obstacles, of conceiving their potentialities generously. They have perhaps acquired the idea that it is worth while to make an effort to choose one's associates freely instead of allowing them to be dictated by circumstances.

Other restrictions in informal social contacts among LS groups appear to be the larger proportion of them which consist of associations with "own kin." In the study of a New York rural community mentioned above, the lowest prestige classes had the highest proportion of mutual choices with their own relatives. A study comparing the political opinions of parents with those

of their (grown-up) children in Cleveland, Ohio, showed less divergence between parents and children in the lower occupational groups than in the higher groups. The reason for this, according to the authors, is that the less privileged individual has less variety of "institutional pulls" outside the family.

Participation in Thought-Life. The lack of reading and writing *facility* as distinct from merely technical literacy is a very important handicap in keeping people isolated from the "thought-life of the group." Although only 6 per cent of the lowest socio-economic group in the United States (the *D* group according to the *ABCD* rating system) do not read newspapers, reading of magazines and books shows sharp socio-economic differentials. In a study of Sandusky, Ohio, based on about 1,600 interviews, respondents were classified into three economic groups. In the lowest socio-economic group, about 35 per cent said they did not read magazines, whereas in the highest group only 7 per cent said they did not. Another group in the same study were asked how many books they had read. Eighty-two per cent of the LS group (*C* and *D* levels) read less than one book a month, while only 59 per cent of the HS group read no more than that.

More significant than the amount of reading are the kinds of material the LS person reads, which, together with data from some public opinion surveys, give us a picture of the differences in interests between socio-economic groups.

A large body of data on magazine reading and radio listening exists as a result of many years of research in this area, undertaken chiefly for commercial purposes. These data show a consistent tendency for LS people to be less interested in "serious" reading and listening. The term "serious," though somewhat vague, is used here for want of a better term. One might try to define it as indicating an interest in subjects whose applicability to one's personal life is not immediately perceptible but which helps one to become a richer person and to see the world more fully.

To take one example among many, a nation-wide survey of women magazine readers showed that more of the "prosperous" read *Time Magazine* than read *True Confessions*. Among the "poor," more read *True Confessions* than read *Time*. Direct questions about reading preferences asked of women readers also showed relatively more interest in fiction, less in public affairs, among the poorer women.

Surveys on radio listening showed similar regularities. Asked "Do you listen to classical music on the radio, such as the Ford Hour or the Metropolitan Opera?", 73 per cent of the HS group, 57 per cent of the LS group, said "yes." Educational programs, serious dramatizations, and programs on public affairs were less listened to by LS groups, according to a Buffalo survey. The most popular programs among a group of people in a Midwestern town were studied. It was found that the programs heard more by LS persons than by HS persons were: comedy and variety, sports, serial stories, religious programs, and service programs.

On the other hand, the HS person heard the following programs more frequently: news, popular music, quiz programs, other than serial dramatizations, serious music and talks, forums and discussions.

Public opinion surveys give a good deal of evidence showing that the LS group has on the whole less interest in international affairs, and in news of any kind, than the HS group. In a survey of attitudes towards Russia, it was found that in the "top 12 per cent" of the population 63 per cent were interested in getting more information about Russia, whereas in the "bottom 12 per cent" only 24 per cent were interested, in spite of the fact that more of the lower group were favorably disposed towards that country. In a study of reactions in one county to the 1940 presidential election, an index of "interest in the election" was devised. Great interest in the election was shown by 33 per cent of the top socio-economic half of the population while only 24 per cent of the lower half displayed a great interest. It is noteworthy that the differences between socio-economic groups in this case are not very great. A presidential election, during the campaign when there is much excitement and publicity about it everywhere, is, of course, less remote than other political issues.

Naturally enough, LS persons are consistently less well informed on a wide variety of subjects. To cite just a few examples: Asked to name the senators of their own state, 69 per cent of the lowest (of three) income groups could name neither, while only 28 per cent of the highest income group were ignorant of both. In another survey, people were asked to pair the names of a list of public figures with their functions. Eighty-four per cent of those who had gone to college knew that Elmer Davis was head of the Office of War Information, while 29 per cent of those with only a grade-school education knew this.

Naïveté and Credulity. Paralleling lack of interest and information, differences in opinion between socio-economic groups show a certain amount of naïveté and credulity among LS persons. Data on this point are more scanty and the differences less pronounced than they were for the points made earlier. In a study of reactions to Boake Carter, the question was asked: "Do you think Carter interpreted the news, or gave you straight news?" More of the LS people thought that Carter gave them straight news. A study of reactions to testimonials in advertisements showed that the LS people less often than the HS believed that the testimonials are paid for. Asked in 1939 whether they thought the war had increased President Roosevelt's chances for re-election, the LS persons were less inclined to believe that it had.

A study of the panic created by Orson Welles' radio drama, "The Invasion from Mars," showed that a relatively larger proportion of the LS group believed the "invasions" to be a reality. "One of the outstanding indices of suggestibility," the authors say, "is the complete absence of awareness that things might be otherwise than they are made out to be." Those who have no relevant standard of judgment into which they can fit an unfamiliar stimulus are inadequately equipped to withstand suggestion. And the narrowed outlook of the LS person, the lack of range in his thought and experience, fail to give him relevant standards of judgment in many areas of life. Some people during the "Invasion from Mars" incident tried to check the truth of what they had heard over the radio. Many, however, did not know how to evaluate evidence, so they ended by accepting what was ostensibly offered them as an interpretation, namely, that the broadcast was news, not fiction. Here we see the effect of the lack of training which is one of the serious forms of underprivilege in LS groups.

"Don't Know." In view of the naïveté and lack of information we have been describing, one might say it is only to be expected that the LS person has so much timidity about voicing an opinion. One of the most consistent results of public opinion polls is the higher proportion of "don't know" and "no opinion" in the LS group. What should the government do to avoid post-war unemployment? Can Russia be trusted? Are there any prominent individuals in this country who might be harmful to our future unless curbed? Could the Germans get rid of the Nazis if they wanted to? (asked in 1944). Should automobile owners be forced to take out insurance against the damage they might do to others? If extra taxes have to be levied should they be sales or income taxes?

On all these questions the LS person is less likely to venture an opinion than the HS person. Of course, he is less well informed about all the issues. But amount of information is probably not the only factor involved. It is not only, we suggest, that the LS person does not know the answer, for most of those who give an opinion probably do not know enough for a rational defense of their views. Very possibly there is another factor: the LS person feels less competent to judge. This implies that he will leave decisions to wiser men. The "wiser" men are those who have been taught that it is more shameful to have no opinion than to have the wrong opinion, who take it for granted that their views are at least as good as the next man's.

The Control and Enjoyment of Life. One might object that perhaps all this apparent lack of interest in and understanding of things not directly related to personal life is merely lack of interest in a certain area, whereas an opposite picture would emerge if we selected different areas for investigation. We might find, for example, that awareness of minute differences in the standings of big league baseball players, or understanding of the workings of political machines in wards, would be much greater among LS persons than among others. However, the areas in modern American life which appear to be relatively closed to the person of low

status are certainly sufficiently important to affect his well-being in a material way.

True, there are large segments of so-called "general information" or upper-class culture which do not seem to serve any purpose other than marking one as a member of a sub-group in the society. For example, the person who has heard of Aeschylus, but knows only that he wrote a play called "Agamemnon," knows nothing which has any bearing on the enrichment of his personal life. But it so happens that the LS persons are also apt to be ignorant of things which do concern them and which might increase their control and enjoyment of life — such as the existence of price ceilings. As we have mentioned, only 6 per cent of even the lowest income group do not read newspapers. Price control legislation was front-page news for a period of time. Moreover, prices are, if anything, of more direct concern to LS persons than to others. Yet a survey made in 1942 showed that fewer of the LS than of the HS knew that price ceilings had been established. The knowledge differential grew with more detailed and exact questions about the workings of the price control system.

The importance of the mental attitude, aside from the mere accessibility of the information, is suggested by the fact that when asked, "Have you seen any ceiling prices displayed in stores or marked on goods?", more of the prosperous than of the poor said "yes." Since most stores have a list of ceiling prices posted, this difference appears to be largely a matter of alertness. The LS person, it would seem, does not see as much of what goes on around him.

Another example of ignorance in a matter which could be detrimental to the LS person is the question of income taxes. Asked how much income tax they thought people should pay at various levels of income, the LS group consistently selected a sum very much smaller than the amount actually paid by people with incomes over $10,000.

Other cases in point include the history of consumer cooperatives, both for information and retail services. By and large, they do not reach the groups who need them most. Birth control practices show the same discrepancy: the poor use less effective contraceptives and use them less frequently. They do not avail themselves readily of the services of birth control clinics even when these are accessible, and even women who express dread of having any more children show an apparent inability to exercise the necessary care and patience in practicing contraception.

These manifestations of a lack of effort to control the environment may spring from deeply ingrained habits of doing what one is told. There is some indication from personality tests that LS persons are more submissive than others, but the evidence is far from definitive.

Indifference to Voting. We do know that there is much more indifference to voting among LS groups. A nationwide survey included a question on voting in the 1944 presidential elections. The sample was divided into three economic groups, the upper fourth, the middle half, and the lower fourth. The proportion of voters in these three groups were, respectively, 84 per cent, 68 per cent, and 53 per cent.

The reasons for non-voting have been described by Lazarsfeld, Berelson, and Gaudet as follows: ". . . three-quarters of the non-voters stayed away from the polls deliberately because they were thoroughly unconcerned with the election. . . . Only a small number of people were kept from the polls by a last-minute emergency. . . . A long-range program of civic education would be needed to draw such people into the orbit of political life, and further studies are needed to unearth the specific nature of their lack of interest."

Is this lack of interest in elections due to a more or less conscious cynicism about their value — a lack of interest in deciding "once every few years which member of the ruling class is to repress and oppress the people through Parliament"? This appears from the facts to be unlikely. In an earlier study of non-voting, Merriam and Gosnell state that general indifference was the chief reason for non-voting, and that "the most common partners of general indifference were ignorance and timidity." Recent research has borne this statement out remarkably well. A series of questions in nationwide polls showed that non-voters are not only less informed about political issues but are less willing to criticize the status quo or even to believe that newspapers should be allowed to criticize "our form of government."

This is not to say that LS persons have fewer complaints about their life than others. A survey on political opinions in Chicago included questions on whether or not respondents were satisfied with the following: their children's opportunities, the kind of work they did, their pay, their treatment at work, their opportunity to enjoy life, and the chance to get ahead. In very case, LS people were more dissatisfied than other groups.

The same study also demonstrated as have many others, that LS groups tend to be more "radical" than HS groups. That is, they tend more to favor social security measures, labor unions, government regulation of business, and to regard it as the rightful function of government to redistribute the wealth more equally. It would seem from this that LS groups do take a rational view of their plight and support measures which would improve their lot. Our picture of mental isolation and withdrawal hardly fits in with these facts. Possibly one might explain the difference as follows: a larger proportion of LS people do not vote, but those who do are alive to their own interests and vote for them. For we cannot be sure when we bring together evidence from various studies showing differences between socio-economic groups, that it is always the same portion of the LS group which displays the given characteristic.

Limited Aspirations. An interesting parallel to the limited efforts of the LS person to control his environment is the apparent fact that he is also limited in what he permits himself to wish for.

When a large sample of people were asked how much income they wanted, it was found that those who had less wished for less. A group of children were given an opportunity to choose Christmas gifts. LS children had fewer desires than the others. High school girls were asked what occupation they would like to enter, as distinct from the occupation they expected to enter. Those from LS groups were less likely than the others to choose such relatively lucrative and interesting professions as medicine and commercial art, and more likely to limit their wishes to such things as stenography and beautician's work.

The low level of aspiration just described connot, of course, be regarded entirely as a handicap. It performs a useful service in making life tolerable for the LS person. Too wide a discrepancy between what one has and what one aspires to would create frustration and discourage effort. Nevertheless, the low level of aspiration may well be, in some cases, a sign of apathy and ingrained acceptance of defeat rather than of adjustment to reality, and may be just as unrealistic as excessive ambition. Studies of unemployed youth showed a tendency for "frightened" youth to go into blind alley jobs, "to crowd into overfilled, unproductive lines of work where they could produce nothing, out of anxiety over unemployment."

Conclusion. In this paper an attempt has been made to present evidence to show that closely linked with economic underprivilege is psycho-logical underprivilege: habits of submission, little access to sources of information, lack of verbal facility. These things appear to produce a lack of self-confidence which increases the unwillingness of the low status person to participate in many phases of our predominantly middle-class culture even beyond what would be a realistic withdrawal adapted to his reduced chances of being effective.

Our theme is summed up by P. F. Lazarsfeld in his conclusion from a study of youth in Austria: "The underprivileged youth has seen less, read less, heard about less, has in his whole environment experienced fewer changes than the socially privileged, and he simply knows of fewer possibilities."

47   Caste in India and the United States*

Gerald D. Berreman

We often assume that social castes are restricted to India and other relatively agrarian societies. The following study, however, shows that caste relations occur in the United States and that the Indian and American caste systems are similar in many ways. The author suggests that we can learn more about caste relations if we examine the similarities of caste systems in different parts of the world than if we emphasize dissimilarities.

Many writers who have contributed to the vast literature on the caste system in India have emphasized its unique aspects and ignored or denied the qualities it shares with rigid systems of social stratification found in other societies. Others have claimed to find caste systems or caste groups in

* Excerpt reprinted from Gerald D. Berreman, "Caste in India and the United States," *American Journal of Sociology,* Vol. 64 (September 1960), pp. 120–127, by permission of The University of Chicago Press. Copyright © 1960 by The University of Chicago.

such widely scattered areas as Arabia, Polynesia, Africa, Guatemala, and Japan. Some observers refer to Negro-white relations in the United States, and particularly in the South, as being those of caste, a usage which others, including C. S. Johnson, Oliver C. Cox, and, more recently, G. E. Simpson and J. M. Yinger, have criticized. This paper will compare the relationship between "touchable," especially twice-born, and "untouchable" castes in India with that between Negroes and whites in the southern United States.

Caste can be defined so that it is applicable only to India, just as it is possible to define narrowly almost any sociocultural phenomenon. Indianists have traditionally held to specific, usually enumerative, definitions. Indeed, the caste system in India has several unique features, among which are its religious aspects, its complexity, and the degree to which the caste is a cohesive group that regulates the behavior of its members. Within India there is considerable variation in the characteristics of, and the relations among, the groups to which the term "caste" is applied.

However, caste can be accurately defined in broader terms. For many purposes similar social facts may be usefully categorized together, despite differences which, while not denied, are not crucial to the purposes at hand. For purposes of cross-cultural comparison this is necessary: for the study of social process, and with the aim of deriving generalizations, caste is a concept which might well be applied cross-culturally. For these purposes a caste system may be defined as a *hierarchy of endogamous divisions in which membership is hereditary and permanent.* Here hierarchy includes inequality both in status and in access to goods and services. Interdependence of the subdivisions, restricted, and/or a degree of cultural distinctiveness might be added as criteria, although they appear to be correlates rather than defining characteristics.

This definition is perhaps best viewed as describing an ideal type at one end of a continuum along which systems of social stratification might be ranged. There can be little doubt that the systems in India and the southern United States would fall far toward the caste extreme of the continuum. It now becomes necessary to look at the differences cited as crucial by those who object to use of the term "caste" in both societies. The objections raised by those interested in structure, relationships, and interaction will be discussed here; the objections of those interested in specific content will be ignored — not because the latter objections are less cogent, but because they are less relevant to the comparison of social systems.

Johnson sees many similarities in the two systems but objects to identifying both as caste, since "a caste system is not only a separated system, it is a stable system in which changes are socially impossible; the fact that change cannot occur is accepted by all, or practically all, participants. . . . No expenditure of psychological or physical energy is necessary to maintain a caste system." Simpson and Yinger agree with Johnson and further object that, in the United States, "we lack a set of religious principles justifying a rigid system of social stratification and causing it to be willingly accepted by those at all levels." Cox lists a number of features of a caste system (i.e., caste in India) which distinguish it from an interracial situation (i.e., Negro-white relations in America), important among which are its "nonconflictive," "nonpathological," and "static" nature, coupled with absence of "aspiration and progressiveness."

Central to these distinctions is that caste in India is passively accepted and indorsed by all on the basis of religio-philosophical explanations which are universally subscribed to, while Negro-white relations in America are characterized by dissent, resentment, guilt, and conflict. But this contrast is invalid, resulting, as it does, from an idealized and unrealistic view of Indian caste, contrasted with a more realistic, pragmatic view of American race relations; Indian caste is viewed as it is supposed to work rather than as it does work; American race relations are seen as they do work rather than as they are supposed, by the privileged, to work. The traditional white southerner, asked to describe relations between the races, will describe the Negro as happy in his place, which he may quote science and Scripture to justify. This is similar to the explanations offered for the Indian system by the advantaged.

The point here is that ideal intercaste behavior and attitudes in India are much like those in America, while the actual interaction and attitudes are also similar. Commonly, ideal behavior and attitudes in India have been contrasted with real behavior and attitudes in America — a fact which has led to a false impression of difference. Similarly, comparisons of race relations in the rapidly changing urban or industrial South with caste relations in slowly changing rural or agrarian India lead to erroneous conclusions. Valid comparison can be made at either level, but must be with comparable data. The impact on intergroup relations of the social and economic changes which accompany urban life seems to be similar in both societies. Recent literature on village India and on the changing caste functions and caste relations in cities and industrial areas presents a realistic picture which goes far toward counteracting traditional stereotypes of Indian caste.

In a study of caste functioning in Sirkanda, a hill village of northern Uttar Pradesh, India, I was struck by the similarity of relations between the twice-born and untouchable castes to race relations in the southern United States. In both situations there is a genuine caste division, according to the definition above. In the two systems there are rigid rules of avoidance between castes, and certain types of contacts are defined as contaminating, while others are noncontaminating. The ideological justification for the rules differs in the two cultures, as do the definitions of the acts themselves; but these are cultural details. The tabooed contacts are symbolically rather than literally injurious as evidenced by the many inconsistencies in application of the rules. Enforced deference, for example, is a prominent feature of both systems. Lack of deference from low castes is not contaminating, but it is promptly punished, for it implies equality. The essential similarity lies in the fact that the function of the rules in both cases is to maintain the caste system with institutionalized inequality as its fundamental feature. In the United States, color is a conspicuous mark of caste, while in India there are complex religious features which do not appear in America, but in both cases dwelling area, occupation, place of worship, and cultural behavior, and so on, are important symbols associated with caste status. The crucial fact is that caste status is determined, and therefore the systems are perpetuated, by birth: membership in them is ascribed and unalterable. Individuals in low castes are considered inherently inferior and are relegated to a disadvantaged position, regardless of their behavior. From the point of view of the social psychology of intergroup relations, this is probably the most important common and distinct feature of caste systems.

In both the United States and India, high castes maintain their superior position by exercising powerful sanctions, and they rationalize their status with elaborate philosophical, religious, psychological, or genetic explanations. The latter are not sufficient in themselves to maintain the systems, largely because they are incompletely accepted among those whose depressed position they are thought to justify. In both places castes are economically interdependent. In both there are great differences in power and privilege among, as well as class differences within, castes and elaborate barriers to free social intercourse among them.

Similarities in the two caste systems extend throughout the range of behavior and attitudes expressed in relations among groups. An important and conspicuous area of similarity is associated with competition for certain benefits or "gains" which are personally gratifying and/or socially valued and which by their nature or under the circumstances cannot be enjoyed by all equally. Competitive striving is, of course, not unique to caste organization; it is probably found to some extent in all societies. It is subject to a variety of social controls resulting in a variety of forms of social stratification, one of which is a caste system as defined here. However, the genesis of caste systems is not here at issue.

The caste system in India and in the United States has secured gains for the groups established at the top of the hierarchy. Their desire to retain their position for themselves and their children accounts for their efforts to perpetuate the system. John Dollard, in his discussion of "Southerntown," identifies their gains as economic, sexual, and in prestige.

In the economic field, low-caste dependence is maintained in India as in America by economic and physical sanctions. This assures not only greater high-caste income but a ready supply of free service and cheap labor from the low castes. It also guarantees the continuing availability of the other gains. In India it is the most explicitly recognized high-caste advantage.

The sexual gain for the southern white caste is defined by Dollard, quoting whom I will substitute "high caste" and "low caste" for "white" and "Negro," respectively.

This arrangement is maintained in the Indian caste system, as it is in America, by severe sanctions imposed upon any low-caste man who might venture to defy the code, by the toleration accorded high-caste men who have relations with low-caste women, and by the precautions which high-caste men take to protect their women from the low castes.

High-caste people gain, by virtue of their caste status alone, deference from others, constant reinforcement of a feeling of superiority, and a permanent scapegoat in the lower castes. Dollard has stated the implications of this gain in prestige. Ideally the high-caste person is paternalistic and authoritarian, while the low-caste person responds with deferential, submissive, subservient behavior. Gallagher might have been describing India rather than America when he noted: "By the attitudes of mingled fear, hostility, friendly domination, and rigid authoritarianism, the white caste generates opposite and complementary attitudes in the Negro caste."

An additional high-caste gain in India is the religious tradition which gives people of high caste promise of greater rewards in the next life than those of low caste. People can increase their rewards in the next life by fulfilling their traditional caste duty. For high castes, this generally results in increasing the economic advantages and prestige acquired in this life, while it requires that the low castes subordinate their own economic gains and prestige in this life to the service and honor of high castes. Thus, for high-caste people, behavior leading to immediate rewards is consistent with ultimate rewards, while, for low-caste people, behavior required for the two rewards is contradictory.

These advantages are significant and recognized reasons for maintenance of the system by the privileged groups. They are expressed in folklore, proverbs, and jokes; for instance, a story tells that, as the funeral procession of an old landlord passed two untouchable women going for water, one hand of the corpse fell from under the shroud and flopped about. One of the women turned to the other and remarked, "You see, Takur Singh is dead, but he still beckons to us." Other stories recount the avariciousness of Brahmins in their priestly role, the hard-heartedness of landlords and the like.

The compensatory gains for low-caste people are cited more often by high-caste advocates of the system than by those alleged to enjoy them. They are gains common to authoritarian systems everywhere and are usually subject to the will of the dominant groups.

As noted above, India is frequently cited as an example of a society in which people of deprived and subject status are content with their lot, primarily justifying it by religion and philosophy. This is the characteristic of caste in India most often cited to distinguish it from hereditary systems elsewhere, notably in the southern United States. On the basis of my research and the literature, I maintain that this is not accurate and therefore not a valid distinction. Its prevalence is attributable in part, at least, to the vested interests of the advantaged and more articulate castes in the perpetuation of the caste system and the maintenance of a favorable view of it to outsiders. The same arguments and the same biases are frequently presented by apologists for the caste system of the southern United States.

In both systems there is a tendency to look to the past as a period of halcyon amity and to view conflict and resentment as resulting from outside disturbances of the earlier normal equilibrium. Alien ideas, or large-scale economic disturbances, or both, are often blamed for reform movements and rebellion. Such explanations may account for the national and regional reform movements which find their advocates and followers primarily among the educated and social elites; they do not account for the recurrent grass-roots attempts, long endemic in India, to raise caste status; for the state of mind which has often led to low-caste defections from Hinduism when the opportunity to do so without fear of major reprisals has presented itself; nor for the chronic resentment and tension which characterizes intercaste relations in even so remote a village as Sirkanda, the one in which I worked.

Among the low or untouchable castes in Sirkanda, there was a great deal of readily expressed resentment regarding their caste position. Specific complaints revolved around economic, prestige, and sexual impositions by the high castes. Although resentment was suppressed in the presence of people of the dominant high castes, it was readily expressed where there was no fear of detection or reprisal. Low-caste people felt compelled to express village loyalties in public, but in private acts and attitudes caste loyalties were consistently and intensely dominant when the two conflicted.

Caste, as such, was not often seriously questioned in the village. Objections were characteristically directed not at "caste" but at "my position in the caste hierarchy."

In the multicaste system of India, abolition of the system evidently seems impossible from the point of view of any particular caste, and a change in its rank within the system is viewed by its members as the only plausible means of improving the situation. Moreover, abolition would destroy the caste as a group which is superior to at least some other groups, and, while it would give caste members an opportunity to mingle as equals with their superiors, it would also force them to mingle as equals with their inferiors. Abolition, even if it could be accomplished, would thus create an ambivalent situation for any particular caste in contrast to the clear-cut advantages of an improvement in rank.

In the dual system of the southern United States where the high caste is clearly dominant, abolition of the caste division may be seen by the subordinate group as the only plausible remedy for their deprived position. Furthermore, they have nothing to lose but their inferior status, since there are no lower castes. There are, of course, Negroes and organized groups of Negroes, such as the black supremacist "Muslims" recently in the news in the United States, who want to invert the caste hierarchy; conversely, there are low-caste people in India who want to abolish the entire system. But these seem to be atypical viewpoints. The anti-caste religions and reform movements which have from time to time appealed with some success to the lower castes in India, for example, Buddhism, Islam, Christianity, Sikhism, have been unable, in practice, to remain casteless. This seems to be a point of real difference between Indian and American low-caste attitudes, for in America objection is more characteristically directed toward the system as such.

In Sirkanda those low-caste people who spoke most piously against high-caste abuses were likely to be equally abusive to their caste inferiors. However, no low caste was encountered whose members did not seriously question its place in the hierarchy. A sizable literature is accumulating concerning castes which have sought to alter their status. Such attempts were made in Sirkanda. A more common reaction to deprived status on the part of low-caste people was what Dollard calls "passive accommodation" coupled with occasional ingroup aggression.

In both America and India there is a tendency for the person of low caste to "laugh it off" or to become resigned. In Sirkanda low-caste people could not avoid frequent contacts with their superiors, because of their proximity and relative numbers. Contacts were frequently informal, but status differences and the dangers of ritual pollution were not forgotten. An untouchable in this village who covered up his bitter resentment by playing the buffoon received favors denied to his more sullen caste fellows. The irresponsible, simple-minded untouchable is a widespread stereotype and one which he, like the Negro, has found useful. Similarly, sullen resignation, with the at-

tendant stereotype of lazy shiftlessness, is a common response, typified in the southern Negro axiom, "Do what the man says." This, too, helps him avoid trouble, although it does little for the individual's self-respect. Aggression against the economically and numerically dominant high castes in Sirkanda was too dangerous to be a reasonable alternative. It was discussed by low-caste people in private but was rarely carried out. Even legitimate complaints to outside authority were avoided in view of the general belief that the high-caste's wealth would insure an outcome unfavorable to the low castes — a belief well grounded in experience.

Since they harbored indignation and resentment, a number of rationalizations of their status were employed by low-caste people, apparently as mechanisms to lessen the sting of reality. Thus, they often attributed their caste status to relative wealth and numbers: "If we were wealthy and in the majority, we would make the high castes untouchable."

Three more explanations of their caste status were consistently offered by low-caste people. These had the effect of denying the legitimacy of their low-caste position:

1. Members of the entire caste (or subcaste) group would deny that they deserved the low status to which they had been assigned. One example:

Englishmen and Muslims are untouchables because they have an alien religion and they eat beef. This is as it should be. We are Hindus and we do not eat beef, yet we, too are treated as untouchables. This is not proper. We should be accorded higher status.

No group would admit to being lowest in the caste hierarchy.

2. People might grant that the caste of their clan, lineage, or family was of low status but deny that their particular group really belonged to it. I have not encountered a low-caste group which did not claim high-caste ancestry or origin. Thus a typical comment is:

Yes, we are drummers by occupation, but our ancestor was a Brahmin who married a drummer woman. By rights, therefore, we should be Brahmins, but in such cases the high castes here go against the usual custom and assign the child the caste of his low-caste parent rather than of his father, from whom a person inherits everything else.

3. A person might grant that his own caste and even his lineage or family were of low status, but his explanation would excuse him from responsibility for it. Such explanations were supplied by Brahmins who, as the most privileged caste and the recipients of religiously motivated charity from all castes, have a vested interest in maintenance of the system and its acceptance by those at all levels. An individual's horoscope would describe him as having been of high caste and exemplary behavior in a previous life and therefore destined for even greater things in the present life. However, in performing some religiously meritorious act in his previous existence, he inadvertently sinned (e.g., he was a raja, tricked by dishonest servants who did not give to the Brahmin the charity he intended for them). As a result he had to be punished in this life with a low rebirth.

Thus, no one said, in effect, "I am of low status and so are my family members and my caste-fellows, and justly so, because of our misdeeds in previous lives." To do so would lead to a psychologically untenable position, though one advocated by high-caste people and by orthodox Hinduism. Rationalizations or beliefs such as these form a consistent pattern — they are not isolated instances. Neither are they unique to the village or culture reported here: the literature reveals similar beliefs elsewhere in North India. They evidently indicate something less than enthusiastic acceptance of caste position and, meanwhile, they perhaps alleviate or divert resentment.

That people remain in an inferior position, therefore, does not mean that they do so willingly, or that they believe it is justified, or that they would not do anything in their power to change it, given the opportunity. Rationalizations of caste status which are consistent and convincing to those who are unaffected or who benefit from them seem much less so to those whose deprivation they are expected to justify or explain. Adherence to a religious principle may not significantly affect the attitudes and behavior to which logic would seem, or to which dogma attempts, to tie it. A comparison of the realities of caste attitudes and interaction in India and the United States suggests that no group of people is content to be low in a caste hierarchy — to live a life of inherited deprivation and subjection — regardless of the rationalizations offered them by their superiors or constructed by themselves. This is one of many points on which further cross-cultural comparison, and only cross-cultural comparison of caste behavior might be conclusive.

It should be evident that the range of similarities between caste in India and race relations in America, when viewed as relations among people, is wide and that the details are remarkably similar in view of the differences in cultural context. Without denying or belittling the differences, I would hold that the term "caste system" is applicable at the present time in the southern United States, if it is applicable anywhere outside of Hindu India, and that it can be usefully applied to societies with systems of hierarchical, endogamous subdivisions whose membership is hereditary and permanent, wherever they occur. By comparing caste situations, so defined, it should be possible to derive further insight, not only into caste in India, but into a widespread type of relations between groups — insight which is obscured if we insist upon treating Indian caste as entirely unique.

48   Farewell to Integration*

W. H. Ferry

The author makes a strong case for the proposition that racial integration in the United States is impossible. He raises the question as to whether aparteid (an ethnically separated minority community) and democratic institutions and practices can be supported by a logically consistent political philosophy. Is his appraisal realistic? Is there a way out of "our nation's most excruciating dilemma," or are we past the point of no return? Is the Separate but Equal doctrine now valid because Black Americans say it is? What are the implications of the challenges in this article for the survival of the white community, the black community, and the United States?

On many fronts the common denominators of poverty, ignorance, and neglect join black and white. I am aware of these intertwinings, as I am of the partial account I shall be offering when I write exclusively in terms of race. Poverty is a black problem, and a large one, but it is not *the* black problem. The same may be said about educational and cultural deprivation. Formulating the race issue in such terms comprises much of the conventional wisdom about the nation's most excruciating dilemma; and this is the heart of the problem.

The conventional wisdom is our way of kidding ourselves about realities, our way of putting a comfortable shoe over raw and ugly bunions. Often it does not matter that we disguise the facts from ourselves. A major import of this article is that it matters very much indeed if we continue to delude ourselves about the actual relations between blacktown and whitetown in the United States. Fooling ourselves about the future of this relationship is among the most dangerous games people play.

* Reprinted with the permission of the author and publisher from *The Center Magazine*, Vol. 1 (March, 1968), pp. 36–40.

My argument moves on three propositions, which I shall set out in turn.

The first is that our major cities, already black, will become preponderantly black in less than a generation.

Philip Hauser's summary in the Fall, 1965 issue of *Daedalus* tells the story:

The Negro has been transformed from a predominantly rural to a predominantly urban resident. . . . By 1960 the concentration of Negroes in [metropolitan areas] had increased to 65% . . . [B]etween 1940 and 1960, Negroes in metropolitan areas more than doubled, increasing by 109% as compared with 50% for whites.

Even more striking . . . is [Negro] concentration *in the central cities of these areas* [my emphasis]. Between 1910 and 1920, the Negro population in central cities of metropolitan areas increased by 40%; between 1920 and 1940, by 83%; between 1940 and 1960, by 123%. Hence, by 1960, of all Negro residents in metropolitan areas, 80% lived in central cities. . . .

Thus between 1910 and 1960, the Negro has been redistributed . . . from rural . . . to urban and metropolitan areas; but within the urban and metropolitan complexes [he] has become and has remained much more highly segregated than was true of white immigrants who flocked there before [him].

This speed-up toward blackening American cities has been accompanied by little discernible consideration — by whites, anyway — of what it will mean when a majority of America's central cities are inhabited by a majority — in some cases perhaps a large majority — of blacks.

One projection is that fifty of our largest cities will by 1970 have majorities of black inhabitants. Another projection says that by 1975 the fourteen largest cities in the United States will have black majorities of 60 to 80 per cent. These projections may turn out to be wrong, but the evidence for them is mounting. Blacks have been moving steadily into the large cities since World War II. Mechanization of Southern farms is pushing them rapidly off the land. Starvation is being systematically employed by Southern whites as a method of chasing blacks from areas where their cheap labor is no longer needed and they become welfare burdens. In forlorn pursuit of community and jobs they go in larger and larger waves to the cities, south, north, east, west.

For the most part our cities are circular in shape, developed in rough concentric circles running outward from a core of offices and governmental centers. The most abject portions of these circles are blacktowns — areas that expand irresistibly with family growth and migrants from rural America. They expand, that is, until they bump into that green and leafy ring closing the circle on all sides, the suburbs. This is a barrier that is virtually unpassable except to a few blacks, a they-shall-not-pass miles thick and getting thicker. So blacktown, no matter how it grows, will have to stop at the signs reading City Limits. Thus, the growing blackness of our central cities is a result ordained by whites, like all major matters affecting blacks.

According to Frances Piven and Richard Cloward in *The New Republic,* blacks will be bilked of political control of the great cities by the rise of metropolitanism — by the emergence of the super-governments they see inevitably consolidating the chief functions and powers of megalopolis. The impetus toward super-government comes from many directions, of which the desire to maintain political ascendancy over black multitudes in the central city is only one. "Metropolitan government," Piven and Cloward say, "will help to [avert impending black control of the cities] by usurping many powers of the city."

They also believe that blacks may be too immature politically and too habituated to white dictation to convert even substantial voting majorities into economic or political power. This thesis is formidable, but it is not conclusive. Divided and unsophisticated the blacks may now be. But these conditions can change with the appearance of a leader or two and the self-confidence generated by a victory or two. I believe Piven and Cloward have also underestimated the capacities and ambitions of a contingent of blacktown not yet on the scene — the thousands now in Vietnam. Blacks may not be able soon to become effective governors, but they will have the numbers and perhaps also the growing will to prevent effective urban government by the traditional forces.

All American cities today, no matter what their ethnic proportions, are ruled by whites for whites. (Cleveland and Gary *may* prove exceptions; the evidence is not yet in.) I discount entirely the presence of token blacks in municipal offices, even in electoral positions. No harm is done by a black alderman who has little influence and no power; he can always be pointed to as an illustration of civic broadmindedness. The issue is not what it *looks* like but what it *is* like. One reads these days of concessions won for blacks by their representatives in City Hall or at the Board of Education. This seems to indicate that the democratic process is working. In reality it indicates only the grudging small price that whites are willing to pay for the large, if temporary, bargain of peace and quiet in blacktown.

No one can seriously maintain that blacktown ever has gotten or is now getting a fair shake from whitetown. Picayune is too strong an adjective to describe even the most advertised aspects of the so-called "progress" of the urban black. It might better be described as a thimbleful of water to a parched man, with another thimbleful promised for some time later, on the condition that he must behave himself.

The white middle-class view, compounded of self-righteousness and paternalism, leads naturally enough to the unbreakable habit of talking about "them" and "us." Thus whites glide smoothly to the conclusion that "we" will somehow rule "them" even when the cities, at least in terms of sheer population, become theirs.

This brings me to a second proposition which is the key to my understanding of the situation. I offer it tentatively even though I am convinced it is valid. If it is, it makes all of our present difficulties trifling and we have before us a problem in statecraft whose dimensions cannot now be imagined.

The proposition is that racial integration in the United States is impossible.

I set forth this proposition without qualification. There are no hidden unlesses, buts, or ifs in it. I shall not deny that in some remote future integration may come about. But I do not see it resulting from the actual present trends and attitudes in American society. It can only be produced by some event overturning these trends. There is no denial in this proposition that there will be a steady betterment in the material situation of blacks. This is even likely. My proposition does, nevertheless, contradict the words of President Johnson that "the promise of America" will be extended to all races and peoples in the nation's slums.

My proposition is sad. Like tens of thousands of other Americans I have supported, organized, and taken part in reformist projects, with integration always beckoning at the end of weary labors. Now such activities must be seen as nothing more than acts of good-will, rather like Peace Corps expeditions into an undeveloped country that look toward the welfare and material progress of the natives but not to their integration with the homeland.

My proposition, in short, smashes the liberal dream. It eliminates the democratic optimistic claim that we are finding our way to a harmonious blending of the races. It changes the words of the marching song to "We Shall *Not* Overcome," for what was eventually to be overcome was hostility and non-fraternity between black and white. My proposition dynamites the foundations of the NAACP, the Urban League, and similar organizations. It asserts that blacktown USA and whitetown USA, for all practical purposes and with unimportant exceptions, will remain separate social communities for as long as one can see ahead. I am not sure, but it may also mean that blacktown will be come a separate political community.

The proposition, I am aware, lends support to Southerners who have been acting on it for hundreds of years. It would seem to place me in the camp of the bigots and locate me with the hopeless. It puts at ultimate zero the efforts of the tough and high-minded who are giving their lives, in the urban bearpits and rural hovels of America, to the dream of equality among men.

Yet I am convinced that integration in the United States is a sentimental, not a doctrinal idea. We came to the idea late in American history, and it disappears readily from the rhetoric of politics — though not from the list of sacred democratic aims — at the first sign of indocility, at the first showing of the rioter's torch. The vast fuss today about improvements in blacktown is not aimed at integration. Few are afflicting us any longer with

such a tiresome lie. All these measures are primarily aimed at the prevention of civic commotions, secondarily at assuaging the conscience of whitetown, and finally at helping the blacks. Priorities tell the story. In the last seven years we have spent $384 billion on war, $27 billion on space, and less than $2 billion on community development and housing.

The United States is a white man's country, conducted according to white customs and white laws for white purposes. And it must be acknowledged that 89 per cent of Americans are non-black. I would not even make the argument that whites should not run the country for their own interests. I would argue that whites do not see, except in perilous self-deceit, that racial integration is one of these interests. I believe that the white attitude toward blacks is generally benign except when black claims intrude on the majority's privileges or peace of mind. Whites have little objection to bettering the condition of black lives as long as it does not cost much, and as long at it leads to the continuance of blacktowns and so does not present the threat of genuine integration at any level. The white condition for black betterment is, to put it simply, separation.

Why is it so hard for us whites to say clearly that we do not want blacks living among us and sharing our world? There must be dozens of reasons playing on one another. One, I suppose, is that we are ashamed to admit we do not subscribe, after all, to a glorious myth. Another is the Christian message that binds us to brotherhood. But as something in our understanding of Christianity made possible the acceptance of slavery, it continues to make possible the shunning of blacks as less worthy than ourselves. Often enough this is accompanied by an aching conscience. So much must be conceded, but it is a conscience that aches amid widespread moral torpor.

Another reason, I suppose, is that after 400 years blacks are still strangers to whites. It is a rare white man who is acquainted with a black, except perhaps for the one who washes his car or shines his shoes. This is not accidental. It has been arranged that way by whites.

A commanding reason, I would guess, is to be found in the mystique of progress, in the belief that by nature everything must somehow improve all the time. Thus, the present degradation of a tenth of our people can be waved aside by referring to better things to come, as come they must to the deserving, perhaps in another century or two or three.

Scientific evidence of black and white likeness, in all qualities except skin color, does not perceptibly alter white attitudes, even among the educated. American liberal thought has, to be sure, on the surface accepted this evidence. Yet we cannot deceive ourselves that there has been any consequential movement of whites toward acceptance of blacks as neighbors, fellow-members of the country club, or potential members of the family. The backlash in the liberal community to ghetto eruptions has been almost as pronounced as that in the suburbs. A certain fragile chumminess has sprung up, notably along the margins of blacktown and whitetown, between the friendly and open-hearted and well-educated on both sides. But this involves a few thousands not millions of people, is far from equality and fraternity, and is no evidence of any important social change.

These encounters do not mark a road to integration but only the nervous response of a few well-intentioned persons either to idealism or to menacing conditions. On close inspection most examples of "successful integration" turn out to be candyfloss. To the vast majority, the black is perceived as belonging to a different order of humanity. This perception is not Southern or Northern but white in character. It is not a perception peculiar to one kind of whiteness, either, but to all kinds, from the lowest "trash" to those most highly situated in society. Hence the terrifying quality, even to the dedicated liberal, of the question, "Would you want your daughter to marry one?"

But I have not yet sufficiently set forth the grounds for my proposition that integration is impossible. In giving up on integration I am not giving up on the blacks but on the whites. Thus, my main evidence runs from the observation I have made about white hypocrisy and obtuseness. We whites cannot imagine what this country looks like from the perspective of blacktown. So we think it must look as it does to us. We cannot imagine the closed doors, the rebuffs, the despair, the second-placeness, the sheer separateness of blacktown. Often with the best of intentions, whites deal with blacks habitually as an inferior species. It is a kind of genteel banditry against the spirit of a people. Blacks are said to have profound psychological difficulties because of their antecedents in slavery. The white memory is similarly tainted; we cannot forget these beginnings either.

But this, it will be said, is what we are starting to get over. I wish it were so; but it just isn't. I fear that I shall not convince those who so insist, but I shall be satisfied to shake their confidence a little, for a great deal depends on getting the issues clear. The black-white situation remains as truly enigmatic today as it was 107 years ago, and the stakes, in my opinion, are the same: the preservation of the Union. If what is needful is to be done, we cannot proceed on illusions, especially illusions about an impossible goal. White America can no longer rationalize its treatment of blacks by "the art of forgiving generously those we have grievously wronged."

Several objections to this position from those who insist that integration is possible must be dealt with. The first points to the apparently successful programs of the armed forces. (I say "apparently" because all I know is that conditions for blacks are better inside the forces than outside, which is not to say much. *Commander's Digest* for September 13, 1967 reported that more than 40 per cent of enlisted blacks said they were dissatisfied with their conditions.) The answer to this objection, in any case, is that we can integrate the nation any time we decide to organize it along military lines.

The second objection is that the young people now agitating on the Vietnam and civil-rights fronts will eventually save us from disunity. The answer is that they will have as little success in achieving integration as they are having in preventing U.S. enormities and escalation in Indo-China, and for the same reasons — the intractable quality of majority opinion.

The third objection is that multiplying affluence will make it possible, once an expensive war is out of the way, rapidly to raise U.S. standards everywhere, especially in blacktown. The answer is that such a program will not be aimed at integration. Anyway, reducing the taxes of whitetown is almost certain to be given a much higher priority by Congress than raising the quality of life in blacktown. Yet, money is not the problem; white-town's attitude is the problem.

The fourth objection is that blacks and whites alike will settle for the desegregation of the community mainly through the gradual absorption of successful and well-known blacks. This sharply misunderstands the hot currents running through blacktown that show no signs of slowing down, and what actually happens. Sprinter Tommie Smith says, "On the track you're Tommie Smith, the fastest man in the world, but off it you are just another nigger."

The last and weightiest objection to my proposition is that, deep in their hearts, white Americans want integration. There is a national will toward it, these objectors say, which will finally prevail because it is rooted in a sense of Judaeo-Christian morality and responsibility to one's neighbors. The answer is that the contrary is the case. Who wants integration? Election results show consistently that at least 60 to 75 per cent of American voters will endorse any proposition that is clearly anti-Negro. The best known example is the result of the Proposition 14 fight in California, where voters decided two to one that blacks should not be protected in their right to buy housing wherever they wished. And even if this customary two-thirds rejection of the black should change to 51 per cent in his favor, would we then say that this showed the triumph of integration? Sadly enough, there is only one place where we have registered even a mild success; we have more or less integrated poverty.

Public and private policy in the United States with respect to blacks is hopelessly confused and ambivalent. Yet each face it shows is authentic in its own way. The howling white mobs in Milwaukee and Chicago are authentic. Programs to improve housing and education in blacktown are authentic. Spotlessly white comic strips are authentic. Lily-white unions are authentic, and so are lily-white corporation offices. Looting and burning in the stews of Newark and Detroit are authentic, as are the Sherman tanks of the Army and the carbines of the National Guard. The sharp cleavage between blacks and whites at the New Politics convention, the country's largest assembly of radicals for many a year, is authentic.

Particularly authentic is the sanguine liberal view of black progress. The liberal view is that patience and persistence will in the end perform the miracle. The enemy is ignorance. Whitetown's resistance, according to this viewpoint, is temporary — stubborn perhaps but penetrable by knowledge and association. The liberal view effectively dismisses what 400 years of subjugation have done to the psyches of both the subjugator and the subjugated, disregards the essentially unchanging positions of blacktown and whitetown, purrs over token accomplishments, and prattles of widespread black advances.

This is nearly the most disastrous myth of all; it is worth examining.

The myth is shattered the moment one looks into the real levels of black opportunity and social mobility; into the real quality of black life and health; into the real cultural and social circumstances of blacktown. The record is clear that after a decade in which integration became enshrined as the true hope of America, blacks are relatively worse off than they were when it opened. In the Fall, 1965 issue of *Daedalus* Rashi Fein showed that blacks consistently are about a generation behind whites. Three quotations are enough to make the point:

In 1964, 16% of Negro males age 20–24 had one or more years of college — the same percentage as among white males age 55–64, most of whom received their college education 35 to 40 years ago. . . .

. . . the Negro male child is born into a world in which his chances of reaching age 20 are about the same as a white's reaching age 37. A Negro girl at birth has the same chance of attaining age 20 as the white girl has of reaching 42 . . .

Today the Negro faces an unemployment situation unknown to the white for almost two and a half decades. What is recession for the white — say, an unemployment rate of 6% — is prosperity for the Negro. He last saw an unemployment rate below 7.5% in 1953. . . .

Undeniably there have been steady gains in blacktown — decreases in infant and maternal mortality, more children attending school longer, and the like — arguments incessantly made by the liberals. It is painful to point out, however, that this is the same argument made by the government of South Africa in defending apartheid.

The point is the constant time lag of twenty years, and often more, between advances in whitetown and blacktown. Though whites believe they should be, the absolute gains of blacktown are not conclusive. Again, the view from below is what counts, and that is of a whitetown gaining steadily on all fronts and leaving blacktown always behind.

Let me put forward the more general testimony in support of my proposition. The race situation in the United States today is marked by growing violence and expressions of hatred and fear on the part of both blacks and whites; growing disillusionment throughout all of blacktown's neighborhoods; increasing belligerency of young blacks and their leaders, and similar belligerency among a wide variety of white spokesmen and organizations; increasing isolation of the black middle class, from whitetown on one side and blacktown on the other; growing uselessness of "treaties" between blacks and whites as black demands become more basic and white resistance more determined.

These signs cannot be regarded as passing inflammations, brought on by irritants like Vietnam. Blacktown's deep discontents have not been provoked by Communists. The outside agitator is whitetown itself. It is important to recognize that separation — non-integration — is the way it has always been. The fostering of the illusion that integration is an achievable goal is bad enough in its effects on blacks, some of whom may still entertain a vision of their children foregathering in total equality under the white yum-yum tree. But the illusion is sinister in its likely consequence for whites. By engaging in it they are leaving themselves unprepared for the grand finale.

My third and final proposition is this: *The United States has at best a few years of grace to think through a political theory that will at once maintain democratic practice and institutions and provide for an ethnically separated minority community.*

Is this possible? From the point of view of history, the practical arrangements would not appear to be difficult. We have been running a separated country for a very long time. But we shall not be permitted to pretend any longer that integration is our end. We shall be relentlessly squeezed by numbers in the cities. No one can assume that blacks in a majority will permit our cities to be governed as they have been governed up to the present. Nor can anyone assume that blacks will automatically permit unofficial control of metropolitan affairs to remain in impregnable board rooms and remote suburbs, though it must be granted that this may happen.

These possibilities indicate some gaping holes in present political theory and practice. It would be more exact to say that they disclose the immense conundrums posed by majoritarianism when the majorities are black. Is whitetown yet ready to take the position that the political ascendancy of blacks must be frustrated, wherever it threatens? What price democratic theory? Blacktown will have something to say about it, since the consent of the governed will still, I would hope, have to be obtained. And it seems to me doubtful that whites, having gone to all the trouble of securing comfortable non-black enclaves, will be ardent to reshoulder the problems they have gone to such trouble and cost to escape.

But even if metropolitanism is successfully invoked, it does not amount to a political doctrine for the governance of a separated nation. Nor does it signify integration. Plato and Aristotle dealt with the issue of a separated group — the slaves — by ignoring them in their constitutions. The ancient wisdom is plainly silly in our situation, for the clamant voices of blacktown, to say nothing of modern understanding of the rights of man, cannot be ignored. Yet a separated nation confronts us, and though I cannot think what a theory for its democratic government might be, I do not claim that it cannot be written. My argument is the contrary: such a theory must be composed. It is just another instance of the proposition that what is necessary has to be possible.

Here and there are some gropings. Milton Kotler, who is no advocate of disintegration, says:

We cannot say that white America governs America for whites, but only for wealthy whites. The fact that poor or middle-class whites may hate Negroes does not establish that they have political power themselves, since their class has no institutional share of state authority. The constitutional solution as it relates to cities is local government in the neighborhoods. These should be constituted with mixed government in which the many and the few share authority. . . .

Robert S. Browne of Fairleigh-Dickinson University, in *Ramparts* (December, 1967), espouses discussion between blacks and whites looking to partition — to separate states. He sees the urgent need to minimize "racial friction by suggesting some fair basis for the separation of the races." Black-white discussions . . . "may lead to two separate nations or it may lead us to some as yet untried type of human community superior to the present system of competing nationalism."

The intellectual task, for that is what it is, has barely been understood, much less undertaken.

There are certain directions which I believe it will be impossible for political theory to take. One will be to rely on science and technology somehow to bail us out of our difficulties, as some now believe technology will overcome the growing pains of mass public education. Thus, it has been seriously proposed that science may be depended upon sooner or later to figure out a way to change black skin to white; and hence we are advised to sweat out our tribulations until that happy day in the laboratory arrives and the nation may become all-white overnight. But what if the pigmentation genius discovers only how to turn white skin to black?

Another direction in which I think it will be impossible for political theory to turn is the establishment of colonies outside the borders of the nation. I place no importance on the tenuous alliances developing here and there between African nations and black Americans. Black resettlement, however, is a notion with respectable forebears, like those of Abraham Lincoln, who toward the end of the Civil War considered four or five schemes for colonization of the blacks, in Africa, the West Indies, and elsewhere. All were put aside with anguish and foreboding. Ours is the inheritance of a problem beyond the reach of the wisest President. It is in any case clear that there can be nothing to the idea of exporting millions of Americans to other shores.

I find equally distasteful, though some political theorists may not, the idea of formalizing the separateness of the races by establishing colonies of blacks within this country. It must be recognized that urban blacktowns already fit most descriptions of colonies. But the idea is blighted from the outset by the obsolescence of colonialism as a respectable political relationship.

Still another direction that political theory may not take is toward systematic repression and violence. There is little doubt that blacktown could be kept in a state of perpetual subjugation by the superior numbers and arms of whitetown. The theory we are seeking is not a plan of battle but a plan for peaceful coexistence. At a minimum the new relationship will have to be based on the understanding that it is aimed at the elevation and self-expression of the blacks, with unstinting white aid and cooperation as requested. It will have to achieve the consent of all parties and the acceptance of non-violent means as the ways of settling disputes.

The relationship must aim at co-respect equally with coexistence. The purpose is to reduce misunderstanding and enmities, not to foment them. The idea is finally for black to achieve the psychological sovereignty, individually and collectively, that whites take for granted. This assignment cannot be deemed impossible. Before the writing of the Constitution many learned men depicted the absolute folly of trying to bring together thirteen colonies of such disparate and competitive backgrounds.

Political theory will have to turn into radically new channels. Here is the ripest of opportunities for the "creative federalisms" of which we have lately heard so much from our Republican friends, though of course they were referring to new understandings among megalopolitan, state, and central governments. The creative federalists concerned about race will start from the fact that the major institutions of society are already arrayed, broadly speaking, on a basis of separation. This is the reason for FEPC's, civil rights laws, and the other legal paraphernalia of anti-discrimination. These legal arrangements assuredly ought not to be tampered with, at least until the creative federalists give us something better, for they provide a sort of demilitarized zone between blacktown and whitetown.

I raise the point about our major institutions, white-owned and directed, because they constitute a peculiar problem for the new federalists. These institutions penetrate and in many ways form the principal structure of blacktown. Supermarkets, chain drugstores, gas stations, were, not by chance, major victims in the civil turmoil in blacktown. There is little reciprocal penetration of whitetown by black institutions. Enterprises owned by soul brothers are few and feeble. Without the economic and political structures of whitetown, blacktown would collapse; but removing black contributions to the structure of the community would have little effect, save perhaps in a few areas in which blacks figure prominently — in welfare departments, in the entertainment industries, and in the national football and baseball leagues.

Let me emphasize again that the theoretical object of this creative federalism will not be that of prescribing another and perhaps more imaginative program aimed at culminating in integration. Nor do I contemplate any form of apartheid (a mischievous word that might well be dropped from the debate), as is evident from my insistence on agreement by all parties to a contract of separation.

The separate state imagined here is not designed to make life easier for whitetown nor to lighten its load. Nor, in its long first stage, does it appear to make life smoother, except psychologically, for blacktown. On both sides the situation initially will be trying in the extreme. Blacks who are visible, equal, organized, and bargaining from positions of strength will for whites be a novel and annoying experience. Blacks will find an autonomous and self-governing community far harder to cope with than any of the ardent separatists have ever suggested.

While we are struggling toward the forms of official separation, probings in blacktown toward indigenous structures must be regarded sympathetically by whites — and from a respectful distance. Many such efforts are under way — foundations, cooperatives, corporations, school districts, self-policing schemes, social and cultural centers. That many are rudimentary is to be expected. Blacktown has had little of the delicious experience of self-determination. Mistakes will be made; but they will be home-made, not inflicted. The very innocence of many current approaches to black autonomy is tempting, especially to white

liberals, whose impulse is to rush in, crying, "Let me help! I know how better than you!" And doubtless this may often be the case. But the stern advice to such well-wishers must yet be, "Stand back, stay away until summoned; and when you are summoned, give the help that is asked for and go away." For the essence is black striving toward selfhood, independence, dignity.

The discovery of the philosophy and machinery for democratic government of a separated country would at first appear to be a constitutional issue. Perhaps, however, it will be found possible to handle it without amending or revising the Constitution. Perhaps all that has to be done is to change the first line of the Constitution henceforth to read, "We, nine-tenths of the people of the United States, in order to form a more perfect Union. . . ." More seriously, it may be a matter for that constitutional penumbra called tacit consent. By this I mean that blacktown and whitetown may, by a series of unacknowledged steps, arrive at a mutual and unstated understanding of the main conditions for maintaining an ethnically divided society. It was tacit consent that until quite recently kept the situation relatively quiet and peaceful.

The first of these steps would be, of course, to let the idea of integration die: by common consent to banish it from the lips of whitetown reformers and politicians and from the expectations of blacktown. Another would be an agreement against humiliation on the one side and disturbance on the other. This would be a wide radiation effect of the agreements against discrimination already legislated. A third step would be increased political autonomy for blacktown, accompanied by markedly stepped-up subsidies from whitetown, which will see blacktown's needs for supplementary help to be at least as important as those of the shipping industry, the corporate farmers, and other veterans of the subsidy trough.

It is doubtless clear that there is next to nothing here about blacktown's reactions to my propositions. This is because I do not know what they are. I mistrust polls of black opinion. Until recently it has made no difference what blacks think. I have never known whether the idea of integration is attractive to blacks. I have idly supposed it was. I know that many blacks have said they wanted integration desperately; others have said that they wanted the right to integration, whether or not they choose to avail themselves of it. I would guess, without any way of knowing whether I am near the mark, that the attitudes in blacktown toward integration might be put in three classes:

The great majority might say, "Integration would be nice, but Whitey's not going to give it — that much is plain from our experience — so we will have to make do until a better arrangement happens."

The minuscule middle class might be saying, "We want integration very much indeed, and sometimes it seems to be coming close. But then it pulls away again, and meanwhile we are becoming more and more cut off from the rest of the blacks."

The young black leaders seem to be saying, "You know what you can do with your integration, Honkey Baby. We want no part of your society and culture; it is corrupt, hypocritical, and brutal."

The question in any case is not how relatively hopeless blacktown may feel about integration but what its outlook might be on the proposition of formal separation. I am impressed by the rising separatism in blacktown, exemplified by statements like those of Malcolm X and his successors. It appears to me to be the last and decisive development in blacktown's outlook on its situation. Along with everything else, events and ideas in blacktown are at an accelerating rate. Since 1954, the year of the *Brown* decision on the schools, the tempo has stepped up. We have passed in these thirteen years through desegregation and integration into nationalism, and now into separatism.

The requirement is to agree on the terms of peaceful coexistence. Unless we can find them, the second Civil War is inevitable. We shall make a great error if we seek these terms amongst the fragments of the integrationist dream. If we in whitetown had ever really wanted integration we would have rushed to achieve it, as we rushed to the moon. If ever integration had a chance, it has receded indefinitely into the clouds of acrimony and self-interest thrown up by urban violence and the promise of a great deal more of the same. For blacktown now will never accept the token of integration for the reality. It will not immigrate into whitetown with its passport stamped "conditional on good behavior as determined by white authorities." What it will do instead is unclear. Its operations are limited. Its capacities are uncertain. What is certain is that it cannot any longer be expected to deceive itself.

A political theory that will embrace our dilemma and provide satisfactory terms for coexistence is not outside our reach. The penalty for failure will be rising violence and bloodshed, and at the end the showdown now being called for by reckless and vindictive men in both towns. And even after such a confrontation nothing will be decided. All the questions will remain. We have muddled through as far as we can go.

I am at the end of a morose tale. It is time to return to the great city, which we have chosen for the black as his habitat and thereby as the locale for the test of the Union. It is here that we shall have to find the replacement for the ideal of integration. Makeshifts may for a while suffice, and bribery has its temporary uses. But finally we shall have to learn how to run a separated society, without the sacrifice of freedom and justice for any man. Since we cannot have integration, we must have something.

OCCUPATIONS AND PROFESSIONS

49 Occupational Prestige: An Empirical Study of Its Correlates*

A. P. Garbin · *Frederick L. Bates*

Statistical methods are often used to identify relationships between variables that cannot be separated experimentally. They are therefore of special importance in social science. An illustration of their use is given in this study of occupational prestige. Thirty occupations were ranked in terms of their prestige. They were then ranked according to twenty specified occupational traits, such as "interesting and challenging work," "intelligence required," etc. The relationships between the occupational traits and the prestige rankings were statistically determined. The results identify traits that are highly correlated with occupational prestige. The same research procedure is employed in a great variety of sociological studies.

Before reading the article, try to anticipate its conclusions. List the traits that are most likely to be highly associated with occupational prestige. Then read the article. Does the original list of traits need modification? Try to account for any errors in the original list. Is it likely that college students differ significantly from other persons in their occupational rankings? How about members of different social classes, or of various ethnic groups?

Sociological theory and research have made it increasingly evident that the understanding of human behavior necessitates a greater knowledge

* Reprinted from *Social Forces*, Vol. 40 (December 1961), pp. 131–136, by permission. Copyright ©, 1961, University of North Carolina Press.

of the system of social rank as it is related to the work activities and occupations which characterize various cultures. Not only is occupational prestige[1] a pervasive value[2] influencing human behavior at the present time, but as society becomes more complex, being characterized by greater heterogeneity and mobility of population, increased secondary interpersonal contacts, urbanization, bureaucratization, and the like, it is very likely that occupational identification will become progressively more significant in displacing "such other status-fixing attributes as ancestry, religious office, political affiliation, and personal character."[3]

As Lawrence Thomas suggests: "Only a beginning has been made on research into possible ingredients of occupational prestige."[4] Caplow holds a similar opinion and makes some pertinent suggestions regarding possible elements involved in the prestige of occupations.[5] Although a number of scholars have recognized the need, there remains a paucity of research undertaken in an effort to discover the ingredients of occupational prestige.[6] The findings of studies which have been done in this area are not as fruitful as would have been the case if certain methodological and measuring procedures had been utilized[7] and a wider scope

[1] Occupational prestige is defined as a social value which is positively evaluated by societal members. It is manifested in the form of sentiments of admiration or deference which some people have with respect to certain work positions.

[2] Williams writes that "values are . . . 'things' in which people are interested — things they want. . . ." Robin M. Williams, Jr., *American Society: a Sociological Interpretation* (New York: Alfred A. Knopf, 1951), p. 375.

[3] Theodore Caplow, *The Sociology of Work* (Minneapolis: University of Minnesota Press, 1954), p. 30.

[4] Lawrence G. Thomas, *The Occupational Structure and Education* (Englewood Cliffs, New Jersey: Prentice-Hall, Inc., 1956), p. 92.

[5] Caplow, *op. cit.,* pp. 52–57.

[6] Only three studies which had appeared at the time of the present research seem worthy of note. Subsequently, the findings of these studies are compared with those of the present investigation.

[7] In this study the following methodological improvements were made: (1) evaluations were indicated in terms of a five-point alternate response scale; (2) a definitive statement was written after each occupation in an effort to clarify the nature of the jobs and increase specificity of the occupational position being evaluated; and (3) in ascertaining the prestige judgments, an effort was made to secure evaluations of the occupational positions (prestige) and not of the individuals (esteem) occupying these positions.

of analysis employed.[8] In addition, certain social-cultural changes which have been magnified within recent years justify further research in this general area.

METHODOLOGY

One way to study prestige and its correlates is to ask a sample of respondents to express their opinions as to the rankings of various occupations with respect to different attributes. This subjective approach ignores the objective ranking of occupations on various measurable attributes in favor of studying the perceived subjective ranking of various respondents. In doing this one approaches prestige as a kind of attitude[9] which is held toward an occupation. It is maintained that this attitude will be more affected by what the attitude holder *believes* to be the ranking of an occupation on various attributes than what the occupation's *actual* ranking may prove to be objectively.

The objective approach might consist of determining prestige on the basis of the amount of actual deference or respect shown practitioners of an occupation as measured by direct observation of behavior. It might further consist of determining the rankings of occupations on various correlates such as income, education required, responsibility to supervise others, etc., on the basis of objective measurement.

In the present study, the subjective approach is employed exclusively. Both prestige and prestige correlates are dealt with in terms of the subjective ratings of respondents.

The sample for this study is composed of 107 freshman students. These students were enrolled in three introductory courses — geography, history, and sociology — at Louisiana State University. Since it is mandatory that all freshmen receive credit in one or another of these courses, we can assume that the attitudes and opinions of the group will represent those of the freshman class as a whole. It is assumed that the written evaluations of these students will reflect, to a large extent, what they have been taught during the socialization process.

The questionnaire technique of gathering data was used to obtain the subjects' attitudes with regard to their prestige evaluations of a selected group of 30 occupations[10] and their expressed evaluations of the occupations in terms of 20 specified occupational traits.[11] These 20 occupational traits constitute some potential correlates of prestige, logically deduced and in several cases empirically discovered by other writers. These traits, as well as the six different aspects of work which they typify, are presented in Table 3.

Respondents were presented with a list of 30 occupations and were asked to rate each occupation in terms of each of the 20 occupational traits listed above and also as to prestige. The ratings were made on a five-point scale which involved the response categories, very high, high, average, low, and very low.[12] The rank order of each of the 30 occupations in terms of prestige and the 20 occupational characteristics was determined by assigning the number 1 to the vocation having the highest mean score, 2 to the next, and so on, with the number 30 being accorded to the occupation having the lowest score.

Rank-order correlations were computed to demonstrate the relationships which exist between

---

[8] Twenty traits of the occupational position are investigated in this study. The number of traits explored in the preceding studies is very limited, often neglecting to investigate what turned out to be significant correlates in the present research. Only one other study of this nature has been conducted in the South, in which relationships were derived between occupational prestige and two other correlates. This study was made in 1934. See W. A. Anderson, "The Occupational Attitudes of College Men," *Journal of Social Psychology*, 5 (November 1934), pp. 435–466.

[9] Attitudes are defined as a "determining tendency, or 'set' which predisposes a person to behave in certain ways toward specific objects or values." Herbert Bonner, *Social Psychology: An Interdisciplinary Approach* (New York: American Book Company, 1953), p. 176.

[10] The occupations are fairly well representative of the vocational range and tend to typify the various conditions and trends in the occupational world.

[11] By occupational traits the writers have reference to certain work characteristics which exist distinct from the occupational positions, but affecting, directly to indirectly, the prerequisites, the nature of the type of performance in the work, and the remunerations, tangible and intangible, of the persons holding these positions.

[12] This is a modification of the Likert Scale. See Rensis Likert, "A Technique for the Measuring of Attitudes," *Archives of Psychology*, No. 140, (June 1932). The use of a five-point alternate response scale made it possible for the percentage rating of each of the occupations in each of the characteristics to be translated into a general score.

the occupational characteristics and the prestige evaluations. High correlations between the occupational characteristics and the occupational prestige ranking indicate that "these traits are either constituents of the prestige stereotype or, at the least, excellent indices of it."[13]

FINDINGS

Hierarchy of the 20 Occupational Prestige Correlates

The basic purpose of this research was to ascertain the relationships between occupational prestige and 20 occupational traits. The association as measured by rank correlation coefficients between each of the 20 occupational traits and prestige is presented in Table 1.

Three of the derived relationships yielded a very high[14] correlation of .90 each. These are the rank-order correlations between prestige and "interesting and challenging work," "intelligence required," and "scarcity of personnel who can do the job." Following are 10 high correlations, extending from .87 between the prestige — "work calls for originality and initiative" correlates, to .71 for the relationship between prestige and "opportunities for advancement." There are five correlates which are moderately related, extending from the prestige — "service to humanity and essential" correlates of .59, to the prestige — "flexible working hours" correlates of .44. The two lowest ranking correlates are the prestige — "safe work" and prestige — "free time on the job" relationships; the former is a low relationship of .35 and the latter is a slight association of .15.

A test of the significance of the 20 correlation coefficients was made in an effort to determine whether or not they might have been produced by

---

13 Thomas, *op. cit.*, pp. 191–192.
14 The strength of the various relationships is described in a manner similar to that suggested by Guilford:

Less than .20	= slight correlation
.20–.39	= low correlation
.40–.69	= moderate correlation
.70–.89	= high correlation
.90–1.00	= very high correlation

See J. P. Guilford, *Fundamental Statistics in Psychology and Education* (New York: McGraw-Hill Book Company, Inc., 1950), p. 165.

TABLE 1 *Hierarchy Rank-order Correlation Coefficients Between Occupational Traits and Prestige Derived from the Evaluation by the Sample Population*

Occupational Trait	Occupational Trait-Prestige Correlation Coefficients
Interesting and challenging work	.90
Intelligence required	.90
Scarcity of personnel who can do the work	.90
Work calls for originality and initiative	.87
Having an influence over others	.86
Regarded as desirable to associate with	.84
Training required	.84
Education required	.83
Responsibility to supervise others	.79
Security	.79
Income	.78
Honorable and morally good work	.75
Opportunities for advancement	.71
Service to humanity and essential	.59
Being one's own boss	.57
Clean work	.51
Dealing more with people than with things	.49
Flexible working hours	.44
Safe work	.35
Free time on the job	.15

chance factors. It was found that all of the coefficients are significant at the .02 level with the exception of the prestige — "free time on the job" coefficient. This may be interpreted to mean that at least some relationship, however weak, exists between prestige and each of the other significantly correlated traits.

Hierarchy of the Correlations Between the Six Occupational Trait Categories and Prestige

A mean trait-prestige correlation was derived for each of the six categories of occupational traits. This was accomplished by computing mean scores of the various related characteristics peculiar to each of the categories. After ranking the mean

TABLE 2   *Hierarchy of the Correlation Coeffi-cients Between Six Occupational Trait Categories and Prestige Derived from the Evaluations by the Sample Population*

Occupational Trait Category	Occupational Trait Category-Prestige Correlation Coefficients
Intellectual and training requirements	.91
Rewards of the work	.91
Interpersonal relations	.87
Intrinsic nature of the work	.86
The working conditions	.49
Individual independence in the work situation	.48

scores, rank-order correlation coefficients were computed between the ranking of occupations for each of these categories of traits and the occupational prestige rank order. The correlations are presented in Table 2.

The highest correlations between mean scores characterize the prestige — "intellectual and train-ing requirements" and prestige — "rewards of the work" relationships, each of which has a correla-tion coefficient of .91. The two lowest correlations are between the prestige — "working conditions" and prestige — "individual independence on the job" correlates, the former being .49 and the latter .48.

Comparison of the Occupational Prestige-Trait Correlations of the Present Study with Previous Research

Coefficients of correlation based on identical or very similar occupational prestige-trait relation-ships were selected from three previous studies to be compared with findings in the present re-search. Because previous studies considered only a very limited number of possible occupational prestige-trait relationships, the number of compar-isons which could be made was limited. Further-more, some of the traits considered in these earlier studies do not have coinciding traits in the present

study. An effort was made in this research to investigate only those traits which were thought to be highly correlated with occupationl prestige.

As is evident from an inspection of Table 3, only one extreme difference in the comparison of the various related correlates exists. Baudler[15] found that the correlation between occupational prestige and "security" was only .22, whereas in the present undertaking the association is a high relationship of .79. However, the latter correla-tion is identical with what Osgood and Stagner[16] found to exist between these two variables. Two other differences stand out when the prestige-income correlates of Osgood and Stagner and of Attneave[17] are compared with the comparable correlate of the present study. Whereas the pres-ent project found the prestige-"income" rela-tionship to be .78, Osgood and Stagner's findings indicated that it was .97; Attneave disclosed that it was a .94 relationship. Baudler's prestige-income correlate of .85 is almost in accord with that of the present study. One of the other large variations is found to exist when Attneave's pres-tige — "dealing more with people than with things" relationship is compared with that of the present study; the relationship derived by Attneave was .64 whereas in this study it is .49.

Minor differences of .06 or less characterize eight of the comparisons between correlates of the three previous studies and comparable cor-relates of the present investigation: Attneave's prestige — "responsibility to supervise others" correlate; Osgood and Stagner's prestige — "se-curity" correlate; Baudler's prestige — "having an influence over others" correlate; Baudler's prestige — "flexible working hours" correlate; Osgood and Stagner's prestige — "intelligence required" cor-relate; Attneave's prestige — "work calls for orig-inality and initiative" correlate; and Baudler's prestige — "service to humanity and essential" correlate.

[15] George Baudler, "A Comparative Study of Fifteen Occupations and Certain Factors of Prestige," unpub-lished study cited in Thomas, *op. cit.,* p. 193.

[16] C. E. Osgood and Ross Stagner, "Analysis of a Prestige Frame of Reference by a Gradient Technique," *Journal of Applied Psychology,* 25 (June 1941), pp. 275–290.

[17] Carolyn Lewis Attneave, "Occupational Prestige: An Experimental Analysis of Its Correlates" (unpub-lished doctor's dissertation, Stanford University, Stan-ford, California, 1951).

DISCUSSION AND CONCLUSION

The question has often been asked as to whether or not prestige is a unitary characteristic. For illustrative purposes, Caplow had five persons rate 45 occupations in terms of several attributes. He found that one factor, that of "behavior control": "the position of the subject with respect to the control of other people's behavior, and their control of his, appears to conform rather well to what is reported as occupational prestige."[18]

Because it was difficult to express the idea of "behavior control" in such a manner that its exact meaning would be conveyed to the respondents, we were unable to include it specifically as one of the occupational traits to be evaluated in this study. However, a combination of two of the traits which were investigated seems to connote about the same meaning. The attitudes of the respondents indicate that these two traits, "having an influence over others" and "responsibility to supervise others," are highly correlated with prestige; the relationships being .79 for the former and .87 for the latter. However, they are not correlated in a one to one relationship. From this we may infer that "behavior control" is not likely to be the only ingredient of prestige. Instead, as our findings conclusively demonstrate, prestige is composed of several ingredients or determined by many indices.[19]

[18] Caplow, *op. cit.*, p. 55.

[19] Caplow comes to the same conclusion as we did. See *ibid.*, p. 57.

TABLE 3 *Comparison of Occupational Prestige-trait Correlations of Present Study with Findings of Three Previous Studies*

Occupational Trait	Osgood and Stagner	Baudler	Attneave	Present Study
Intrinsic nature of the work				
Dealing more with people than with things	—	—	.64	.49
Honorable and morally good work	—	—	—	.75
Interesting and challenging work	.99	—	—	.90
Service to humanity and essential	—	.60	—	.59
Work calls for originality and initiative	—	—	.93	.87
Intellectual and training requirements				
Education required	—	—	—	.83
Education and training required	—	.86	.95	—
Intelligence required	.96	—	—	.90
Scarcity of personnel who can do the job	—	—	—	.90
Training required	—	—	—	.84
Individual independence in the work situation				
Being one's own boss	—	.65	.70	.57
Free time on the job	—	—	—	.15
The working conditions				
Clean work	—	.46	—	.51
Flexible working hours	—	.50	—	.44
Safe work	—	—	—	.35
Interpersonal relations				
Having an influence over others	—	.90	—	.86
Regarded as desirable to associate with	—	.96	—	.84
Responsibility to supervise others	—	—	.82	.79
Rewards of the work				
Income	.97	.85	.94	.78
Opportunities for advancement	—	—	.84	.71
Security	.79	.22	—	.79

Rank-order correlations between the rankings of 20 selected occupational traits in 30 occupations and the prestige ratings of these same occupations reveal that the derived correlation coefficients vary in the extent to which they are associated with prestige. Our findings disclose that three traits are very highly related with prestige, 10 are highly related, five are moderately related, one is lowly related, and one is only slightly related.

On the basis of our data it would appear that there will be a tendency for occupations which have a "very high" or "high" average score or ranking in such traits as "interesting and challenging work," "intelligence required," "scarcity of personnel who can do the job," "work calls for originality and initiative," "having an influence over others," and "education required," to rank "high" or "very high" in the prestige hierarchy.

In enumerating the traits which are "very highly" or "highly" associated with occupational prestige, we do not mean to imply that these are always the only important factors affecting prestige, and that other factors, some of which were not considered in the present study, are unimportant.

Occupational prestige must be visualized as being composed of many interrelated characteristics, some of which may be more important with respect to one occupation than they are to another. That is, the significant ingredients of occupational prestige may not necessarily be the same for all occupations. For example, it is possible for an occupation to be judged very high in certain prestige correlates, and low in equally important correlates. However, the extremely high trait evaluations which an occupation receives may frequently overshadow the negative influence of the low evaluations. Even if we know the extent to which an occupation is characterized by the leading prestige correlates, this does not mean that we will be able to predict with 100 percent accuracy the relative amount of prestige which this occupation will be awarded. We make no claims of being able to do this. However, we do think that, in general, and in most instances, predictions are possible.

In conclusion, as noted earlier, the sample from which the data of this study were collected does limit its generalizability. However, it should be re-emphasized that the attitudes of the freshmen composing this sample are assumed to be fairly well representative of the freshman class as a whole. The symbolically expressed evaluations are expected to indicate the attitudes which are shared by a great many youth.

So similar are the relationships observed in this and other studies that we must conclude that a remarkable degree of consensus must exist in our society on the importance of the various occupational traits. A greater significance may be attached to this apparent similarity in evaluations when we realize how crude the instruments are that have been used in data collection in the various studies and when we recognize the instability and crudeness of the rank-order correlation method which generally has been employed. With such tools, it might be regarded as remarkable if only a general similarity in results emerged, much less the close correspondence observed here. Nevertheless, there is a need for further occupational prestige-correlate research in which the sample is composed of diversified segments of society. In addition, there is a need for more refined measuring techniques. Because several correlates were investigated for the first time in the present study, further evaluations of these traits are needed for comparative purposes. In addition, there are probably other leading correlates which should be empirically investigated.

The major findings of this study may be summarized as follows:

1. The most significant specific correlates of prestige were: "interesting and challenging work" (.90), "intelligence required" (.90), "scarcity of personnel who can do the job" (.90), "work calls for originality and initiative" (.87), "having an influence over others" (.86), "regarded as desirable to associate with" (.84), "training required" (.84), and "education required" (.83).

2. The highest relationships between categories of occupational traits and prestige were: "intellectual and training requirements" (.91), "rewards of the work" (.91), "interpersonal relations" (.87), and "intrinsic nature of the work" (.86).

3. The occupational prestige-trait coefficients of this and three previous studies are very similar.

50 National Comparisons of Occupational Prestige*[1]

Alex Inkeles · Peter H. Rossi

Is it possible to make valid multinational comparisons of occupational prestige? If so, would we find any general areas of agreement? An obvious method would be to construct a list of some fifty occupations and administer such list for rating to a representative sample in selected countries. The authors used a more imaginative method by assembling the results of postwar ratings in six industrial countries — the United States, Great Britain, New Zealand, Japan, Germany, and the Soviet Union. High correlations between the various ratings are found, indicating that within these industrial nations occupations are ranked in a relatively standard hierarchy.

During the latter part of the nineteenth and the first half of the twentieth centuries the factory system of production was introduced, at least on a small scale, to most areas of the world. The factory has generally been accompanied by a relatively standard set of occupations, including the factory manager (sometimes also owner) and his administrative and clerical staff, engineering and lesser technical personnel, foremen, skilled, semiskilled, and unskilled workers. In the factory, authority and responsibility are allocated largely according to the degree of technical or administrative competence required for the job. In addition, the allocation of material and social rewards, the latter generally in the form of deference, is closely adjusted to levels of competence and degrees of authority and responsibility. The pattern of differentiation of authority is undoubtedly functionally necessary to the productive activity of the factory, and it may be that the associated pattern of reward differentiation is also functionally necessary.

* Reprinted from *American Journal of Sociology*, Vol. 61, January 1956, pp. 329–339, by permission of The University of Chicago Press. Copyright © 1956 by The University of Chicago.
[1] We wish to express our appreciation to Edward A. Tiryakian for his voluntary services as research assistant and to Alice S. Rossi for a critical reading.

There is, however, no clear-cut imperative arising from the structure of the factory as such which dictates how the incumbents of its typical statuses should be *evaluated* by the population at large. One possibility is that in popular esteem the typical occupations will stand relative to one another in a rank order strictly comparable to their standing in the formal hierarchy of competence, authority, and reward in the factory. It is also possible, however, that the popular evaluation of these occupations will be quite different. Indeed, where the factory system has been introduced into societies like those of Spain or Japan, with well-established values based on tradition and expressive of the culture, one might expect significant differences between an occupation's standing in the formal hierarchy of the industrial system and its position in the popular ranking scheme.

Thus the interaction of the two systems — the standardized modern occupational system and the individual national value pattern for rating occupations — presents an interesting and important problem in comparative sociology.

We may posit two extreme positions in this interaction, while granting that it might be difficult to find live exponents of either. The extreme "structuralist" would presumably insist that the modern industrial occupational system is a highly coherent system, relatively impervious to influence by traditional culture patterns. Indeed, he might go so far as to insist that the traditional ranking system would in time have to be subsumed under, or integrated into, the industrial system. Consequently, his argument would run, even such occupations as priest, judge, provincial governor, not part of the modern occupational system and often given unusual deference, would come in time to have roughly the same standing relative to one another and to other occupations, no matter what their national cultural setting.

By contrast, an extreme "culturalist" might insist that within each country or culture the distinctive local value system would result in substantial — and, indeed, sometimes extreme — differences in the evaluation of particular jobs in the standardized modern occupational system. For example, he might assume that in the United States the company director would be rated unusually high because of our awe of the independent businessman and large corporations or that in the Soviet Union the standing of industrial workers would be much higher relative to managerial personnel than in Germany, with its emphasis on sharply differentiated status hierarchies. Furthermore, he might argue that the more traditional occupational roles assigned special importance in particular cultures would continue to maintain their distinctive positions in the different national hierarchies. Indeed, he might hold that the characteristic roles of the modern industrial system would come to be subsumed within the traditional rating system, each factory occupation being equated with some traditional occupation and then assigned a comparable rank.

A systematic test of these contrasting positions is not beyond the capacity of contemporary social research. A standard list of occupations — say thirty or forty in number — might be presented for evaluation to comparable samples from countries presenting a range of culture types and degrees of industrialization. The list should contain both standard industrial occupations and the common, but differentially valued, traditional roles (e.g., priest, legislator, etc.).

Data are available which, though far from completely adequate, will carry us a long way beyond mere speculation on these matters. In the postwar years studies of occupational ratings have been conducted in and reported on five relatively industrialized countries: the United States, Great Britain, New Zealand, Japan, and Germany.[2] In addition, the authors have available previously unpublished data for a sixth country, the Soviet Union.

Since these six studies[3] were, on the whole,

undertaken quite independently, our ideal research design is clearly far from being fulfilled. Nevertheless, the data do permit tentative and exploratory cross-national comparisons.

I. The Comparability of Research Designs

The elements of similarity and difference in the six studies may be quickly assessed from the following summary of their essential features:

A. Population studied

United States: National sample of adults fourteen years and over; 2,920 respondents

Japan: Sample of males twenty to sixty-eight years of age in the six large cities of Japan; 899 respondents

Great Britain: Written questionnaires distributed through adult-education centers and other organizations; 1,056 returns (percentage returned unspecified)

U.S.S.R.: Sample of displaced persons, mostly in DP camps near Munich, Germany, and some former DP's now residing on eastern seaboard of U.S.; 2,100 written questionnaires

New Zealand: Sample collected mainly by interviews with inhabitants of town of 2,000, partly by mailed questionnaires (12 per cent returns) sent out to town of 4,000; 1,033 questionnaires and interviews used

Germany: 1,500 Schleswig-Holsteiners: vocational-school students, university students, and male adults (not otherwise specified); adult sample only used here

B. Overlap among occupations studied

Each study involved a different number of oc-

---

[2] Additional studies of occupational prestige are available for the United States and for Australia. The authors decided to restrict the United States data to the most comprehensive study available. The Australian case (Ronald Taft, "The Social Grading of Occupations in Australia," *British Journal of Sociology,* Vol. IV, No. 2 [June, 1953]) was not included in this report because it was felt that little was to be gained by the inclusion of another Anglo-Saxon country.

[3] (1) A. A. Congalton, "The Social Gathering of Occupations in New Zealand," *British Journal of Sociology,* Vol. IV, No. 1 (March, 1953) (New Zealand data); (2) John Hall and D. Caradog Jones, "The Social Grading of Occupations," *British Journal of Sociology,* Vol. I, No. 1 (January, 1950) (Great Britain); (3) National Opinion Research Center, "Jobs and Occupations:

A Popular Evaluation," in Reinhard Bendix and S. Martin Lipset, *Class, Status, and Power* (Glencoe, Ill.: Free Press, 1953) (United States data); (4) the Schleswig-Holstein data are taken from an article published in *Der Spiegel,* June 30, 1954, reporting a study by Professor Karl-Martin Bolte, of Christian-Albrecht University, in Kiel, Germany, to be published early in 1955; (5) Research Committee, Japan Sociological Society, "Report of a Sample Survey of Social Stratification and Mobility in the Six Large Cities of Japan" (mimeographed; December 1952) (the authors are grateful to Professor Kunio Odaka, of the University of Tokyo, for bringing this valuable study to their attention; and (6) the Soviet materials were collected by the Project on the Soviet Social System of the Russian Research Center at Harvard University. The authors plan to publish several articles dealing with the special features of the occupational ratings secured from former Soviet citizens.

TABLE 1 *Number of Identical or Similar Occupations Rated Between Six Countries*

	U.S.	Great Britain	U.S.S.R.	Japan	New Zealand	Germany
United States	. .	24	10	25	24	20
Great Britain	. .	. .	7	14	30	12
U.S.S.R.	. .	. .	. .	7	7	8
Japan	. .	. .	. .	. .	14	19
New Zealand	. .	. .	. .	. .	. .	12
Total occupations studied	88	30	13	30	30	38

cupations, ranging from 88 in the case of the National Opinion Research Center American study to 13 in the Soviet research. Only the New Zealand and the British groups studied exactly the same occupations. Each of the remaining four studies used a different, but partially overlapping, set of occupations.

In order to make comparisons between pairs of countries, each occupation studied in each research was matched, when possible, with an occupation in the data gathered in the other country. In many cases it was necessary to disregard the information about an occupation in one of the paired countries because no comparable occupation was studied in the other. In other instances, in order to increase the number of occupations which could be compared for any given pair of countries, occupations were matched which were only very roughly comparable, e.g., Buddhist priest and minister, or collective farm chairman and farm owner and operator. In most cases, however, a direct correspondence characterizes the pair of occupations which are being equated. The reader is invited to turn to Table 5 (below), where the lists of occupations used from each of the researches are printed. The occupations listed on any row or line were matched. The number of pairs of similar or identical occupations for each cross-national comparison is shown in Table 1.

C. Nature of rating task

United States: Respondents were asked:
. . . Please pick out the statement that best gives your own *personal opinion* of the *general standing* that such a job has. Excellent standing, good standing, average standing, somewhat below average, poor standing."

Japan: Respondents were given a set of thirty cards and asked: ". . . Think of the general

reputations they have with people, and sort them into five or more groups, from those which people think highly of to those which are not thought so well of."

Great Britain: Respondents were told: "We should like to know in what order, *as to their social standing,* you would grade the occupations in the list given to you. [Rate them] . . . in terms of five main social classes . . . ABCDE."

U.S.S.R.: Respondents were asked: "Taking everything into consideration, how desirable was it to have the job of (————) in the Soviet Union? Very desirable? Desirable? So-so? Undesirable? Very undesirable?"

New Zealand: Same as in Great Britain.

Germany: The source is unfortunately not very specific about the rating task assigned. The respondents were apparently asked to rank-order a list of 38 occupations presented as one slate.

D. Computing prestige position

With the exception of the German study, each research presents a "prestige score" for each of the occupations studied. These scores, computed variously, represent in each case the "average" rating given to each of the occupations by the entire sample of raters used. The German study presented only the rank-order positions of the occupations.

One is not sure whether differences between nations are generated by the differences in the questionnaires or the differences in the nations themselves. However, similarities in the prestige hierarchies, particularly when they are striking, are somewhat strengthened by the same lack of comparability in research designs and in the occu-

TABLE 2*   *Correlations Between Prestige Scores (or Ranks) Given to Comparable Occupations in Six National Studies*

	U.S.S.R.	Japan	Great Britain	New Zealand	U.S.	Germany†
U.S.S.R.	. .	.74	.83	.83	.90	.90
Japan	. .	. .	.92	.91	.93	.93
Great Britain	. .	. .	. .	.97	.94	.97
New Zealand	. .	. .	. .	. .	.97	.96
United States	. .	. .	. .	. .	. .	.96
Av. correlation	.84	.89	.93	.93	.94	.94

* See Table 1 for numbers of occupations involved in each comparison.

† All coefficients are product-moment correlations, with the exception of those involving Germany, which are rank-order coefficients.

pations matched to one another. Similarities may be interpreted as showing the extent to which design and other differences are overcome by the comparability among the prestige hierarchies themselves.

II. Comparability of Occupational Prestige Hierarchies

Since each study included some occupations used in another study, it is possible to compare the prestige hierarchies of occupations in pairs of countries by computing correlation coefficients for the scores (or ranks) of occupations. The fifteen correlation coefficients which result are presented in Table 2.[4] It will be seen immediately that the levels of correlation are considerably higher than the magnitude to be expected if there were only rough agreement on placement in the top and bottom halves of the prestige hierarchy. Indeed, twelve of the fifteen coefficients are above .9, and only one is below .8. The three coefficients below .9 all concern the Soviet ratings, which, it will be recalled, involve only a very small number of occupations, maximizing the chances for lower correlations arising from merely one or two "mismatches."

For most of the comparisons, furthermore, the

[4] Note that the correlation coefficients are all product-moment correlations, with the exception of the five coefficients involving the German study, which are rank-order correlations. With the exception noted, these coefficients represent the degree of similarity between the prestige *scores* given to the occupations.

findings go beyond establishing mere comparability of rank orders. With the exception of the correlations involving Germany, each coefficient represents the relationships between prestige *scores* given to the same occupations in two different nations. Hence there is a high relationship between the relative "distance" between occupations, as expressed in score differences, as well. In other words, if, of two occupations, one is given a much lower score than the other by the raters in one country, this difference in prestige scores and not merely crude rank order also obtains in another country.

It should also be noted that these high correlations were obtained by using samples of occupations which were not strictly identical from country to country, including such very crude comparisons already mentioned as that of collective farm chairman and farm owner and operator. One may anticipate that if the occupations studied were more uniform, the similarities of prestige hierarchies from country to country would be even higher.

In other words, *despite the heterogeneity in research design, there exists among the six nations a marked degree of agreement on the relative prestige of matched occupations.* To this extent, therefore, it appears that the "structuralist" expectation is more nearly met than is the expectation based on the culturalist position.

Each of the six nations differs in the extent to which its prestige hierarchy resembles those of other nations. The average of the correlations for each nation, contained in the bottom row of

Table 2, expresses these differences among nations quantitatively. Thus we may see that the American and German occupational prestige hierarchies are most similar to those of other nations, while the Soviet and Japanese hierarchies are most dissimilar. When we consider that the Soviet Union and Japan are, of the six, the more recently industrialized cultures, we may see there some small degree of evidence for the culturalist position.

Furthermore, if we examine the correlations among the three nations which have the closest ties and which share a common historical background and language — Great Britain, the United States, and New Zealand — we find these coefficients to be among the highest in Table 2. Again, the evidence to some extent supports the interpretation of a small "cultural" effect. However, the coefficients in question are not sufficiently distinguished in size from those involving Germany[5] and the three Anglo-Saxon nations to allow much weight to be given to the influence of the common Anglo-Saxon culture. In other words, whatever the national differences between the six, they do not greatly affect the general pattern of the prestige hierarchy.

III. National Patterns of Occupational Prestige

Although the relationships among the six occupational hierarchies are very high, they do not indicate one-to-one correspondences among the national ranks of occupations. Each nation shows some variation from every other, and the international discrepancies may perhaps throw further light on the relationships between social structure, culture, and occupational prestige.

One possibility is that unique aspects of the culture or social structure of a particular country determine distinctive appraisals of a certain type or types of occupation. National differences are thus to be interpreted in a unique fashion for each country.

[5] Since the correlations involving Germany are rank-order correlations, it is difficult to make comparisons of such coefficients with others in Table 1. However, the relationship between rank-order correlations and product-moment correlations is rather high in the upper ranges, and it can be taken for granted that if prestige scores were available for the German ratings, the analysis shown in Table 2 would not be materially altered.

A second possible explanation is that it is the type of occupation which engenders disagreement, some occupations being similarly rated everywhere and others yielding no consistent rating. To some extent these contrasting explanations are similar, respectively, to the culturalist and structuralist positions discussed earlier.

Here again the available data place marked limits on the possibility of a definitive answer, but it is nevertheless feasible for us to go some distance in exploring the problem. In order to obtain some means by which to assess the presence or absence of disagreement among nations, regression equations were computed to predict the prestige positions of the occupations in one country as against the prestige positions of the comparable occupations in each other country. Ten such equations were computed, interrelating the prestige hierarchies in the United States, Japan, Great Britain, New Zealand, and the Soviet Union but excluding Germany, since the published data on that country indicated only the rank order of occupations. Those occupations which lay more than one standard deviation of the estimate off the regression lines were arbitrarily characterized as occupations over which there was a disagreement between the two nations involved.

Applying this criterion, we have, in Table 3, presented the discrepancies in ratings between all the relevant pairs of nations. The columns show the occupations rated higher by a given country in relation to each of the other countries represented in the rows. Reading the table by rows, we find the occupations rated lower by one country than by other nations, not forgetting that each comparison of a pair of countries involves a somewhat different set of occupations from the comparison of ratings for any other two countries. Only a few occupations, such as farmer, teacher, doctor, factory manager, and some form of industrial worker, were rated in all five countries and therefore appear in all the pairs of comparisons. Some occupations, such as judge, were rated in only two countries and therefore appear in only one paired comparison.[6]

Table 3 serves to highlight the special positions

[6] Table 5 will be found a useful aid in this connection, since by reading across the rows of that table one can tell quickly how many times a particular occupation was evaluated and by which national samples.

TABLE 3   *Discrepancies* in the Rating of Matched Occupations by Pairs of Nations*

	Rated Higher in Japan	Rated Higher In U.S.	Rated Higher in Great Britain	Rated Higher in New Zealand	Rated Higher in U.S.S.R.
Rated lower in Japan		Minister, farmer, insurance agent, carpenter	Minister, farmer, insurance agent	Minister, farmer, insurance agent	Accountant
Rated lower in U.S.	Company director, labor leader, reporter (news), street sweeper, shoe shiner		Accountant, chef, street sweeper	Accountant, farmer, truck driver, street sweeper	Engineer, worker
Rated lower in Great Britain	Reporter (news), street sweeper	Civil servant, truck driver, minister, building contractor, electrician		Truck driver	Worker
Rated lower in New Zealand	Reporter (news) street sweeper	Civil servant, building contractor, bookkeeper, electrician, dock worker	Chef, bartender		Worker
Rated Lower in U.S.S.R.	Factory manager, farmer	Scientist, farmer	Farmer	Farmer	

* We consistently designate any cited occupation by the title closest and most familiar to Americans. For example, we used minister in preference to Buddhist priest, electrician rather than fitter (electrical). For the exact titles see Table 5.

held by certain occupations in particular countries. For example, the Japanese Buddhist priest rates lower than a minister in each of the three available comparisons, and this undoubtedly reflects the cultural differences in structure and role between the Buddhist religion in Japan and the Judeo-Christian religion in the three Anglo-Saxon countries. Equally notable is the consistently lower position of farm manager as rated by displaced persons from the Soviet Union. While the occupation collective farm chairman is not strictly comparable to those with which it is matched, there can be no doubt that the displaced persons regard that occupation with a special ambivalence arising out of the position of agriculture in the Soviet economy during the last three decades.

Despite the clarity with which a particular occupation may stand out, it is difficult to find any definite *pattern* characterizing the disagreements expressed by any one country. Of course, such a pattern, if it does exist, may be obscured in our data by the modest number of occupations rated by each country. There are seldom more than one or two occupations of a given type in each of the comparisons, and it is hazardous to assume from the fact, for example, that since the Japanese rate the occupation newspaper reporter higher than Americans, Britishers, or New Zealanders, they would rate occupations *of this type* higher than the other two countries. Nevertheless, it will be noticed that in the country with the largest number of comparisons, the instances of disagreement involve a wide variety of quite disparate occupations. Those rated higher in the United States, for example, range from building contractor to farmer and from scientist to dock worker and appear to have little in common. The same range and absence of a common denominator are shown by the occupations rated lower in the United States. Furthermore, the discrepancies do not consistently appear in all the relevant comparisons: farm owner is out of line in only two out of four comparisons; as to truck driver, the two recorded disagreements go in opposite directions, that occupation being rated higher in comparison with Britain and lower in comparison with New Zealand.

IV. INTERNATIONAL COMPARABILITY OF TYPES OF OCCUPATION

If there is no clear-cut pattern of deviance by country, is there perhaps a tendency for certain types of occupation to be foci of disagreement? Perhaps if we classify occupations according to the features of social structure or culture to which they are most closely related, we may gain further insight into the interaction between culture, social structure, and occupational prestige hierarchies. To explore this question, we grouped all the occupations into seven basic types: industrial, clerical and commercial, professional, political, traditional crafts, agricultural and service occupations.[7] In Table 4 we have indicated the number of international comparisons between pairs among the five countries, again excluding Germany, which could be made involving the occupations in each class of occupations. We have also indicated the proportions of those comparisons which yielded disagreements. Disagreements were recorded on the same basis as in the preceding table, that is, on the basis of predictions from regression equations.

Because our findings so far have so strongly supported the structuralist expectation concerning the influence of industrialization in producing uniformity, our initial expectation may well be that occupations closely allied to the industrial system will enjoy highly comparable standings from country to country, while occupations more remotely connected would be the focus of international discrepancies. Table 4 indicates that industrial occupations do enjoy comparable standing in all five countries. Nevertheless, the *lowest* proportion of disagreements is shown by the professions. In addition, other occupational types,

[7] See note to Table 4 for examples of occupations included in each type.

TABLE 4 *Discrepancies in Prestige Position According to Type of Occupation*

Occupation Types*	Proportion of Discrepancies (Per Cent)	No. of Comparisons
Professional	16	31
Industrial	24	29
Political	25	16
Traditional crafts	27	11
Clerical and commercial	32	37
Agricultural	50	16
Service	63	20

* Examples of occupations included in each type are as follows: *Professional:* doctor, minister, teacher, etc; *industrial:* industrial worker, company director, factory manager, engineer; *political:* judge, civil servant, etc.; *traditional crafts:* bricklayer, carpenter, fisherman; *clerical and commercial:* accountant, bookkeeper, salesman, small entrepreneur, etc.; *agricultural:* farm owner and operator, farm hand; *service:* shoe shiner, barber, porter, streetcar conductor, etc.

such as the political occupations and the traditional crafts, which are not necessarily closely allied to the industrial system, manifested levels of disagreement as low as that enjoyed by the industrial occupations. Only the agricultural and service occupations yield a degree of disagreement which sets them apart from the other occupational groups.

Accounting for these discrepancies appears to require a combination of arguments. In the first place, some types of nonindustrial occupations are easily assimilated to the industrial system. The traditional crafts serve as the prime example here, since the skills involved in such occupations as bricklayer, carpenter, and plumber have a close resemblance to the skills of industrial workers. Indeed, some crafts have been partly incorporated into the industrial system, and, it may be argued, such occupations are easily placed within the hierarchy of industrial occupations and may tend to assume roughly the same position vis-à-vis industrial occupations. Likewise, some professions, such as engineering and applied scientific research, have a most immediate connection with the industrial system, and others, such as architecture, are easily equated with it.

However, closeness or assimilability to the industrial system will not suffice to explain the

TABLE 5

United States Occupation	Score	Germany Occupation	Rank	Great Britain Occupation	Score	New Zealand Occupation	Score	Japan Occupation	Score	U.S.S.R. Occupation	Score
United States:		*Germany:*		*Great Britain:*		*New Zealand:*		*Japan:*		*U.S.S.R.:*	
Physician	93	Doctor	2	Medical officer	1.3	Medical officer	1.4	Doctor	7.0	Doctor	75
State governor	93							Prefectural gov.	3.8		
College professor	89	Univ. professor	1					Univ. professor	4.6	Scientific worker	73
Scientist	89										
County judge	87	High civil servant (Regierungsrat — höherer Beamter)	4	Civil servant	6.0	Civil servant	7.0	Local court judge	4.7		
Head of dept. in state government	87							Section head of a government office	7.2		
Minister	87	Minister (Pfarrer)	6	Non-conformist minister	6.4	Non-conformist minister	5.9	Priest of a Buddhist temple	12.5		
Architect	86	(Elec. engineer)*	10					(Architect)	9.5		
Lawyer	86			Country solicitor	2.6	Country solicitor	3.8				
Member of board of directors of large corporation	86	Factory director (Fabrikdirektor)	5	Company director	1.6	Company director	3.6	Officer of large company	5.5	Factory manager	65
Civil engineer	84	Elec. engineer	10					(Architect)†	9.5	Engineer	73
Owner of factory that employs about 100 people	82							Owner of a small or medium-sized factory	10.2		
Accountant for a large business	81			Chartered accountant	3.2	Chartered accountant	5.7	(Company office clerk)‡	16.1	Bookkeeper	62
Captain in regular army	80	Major (in armed forces)	8							Officer in the armed services.	58
Building contractor	79			Jobbing master builder	11.4	Jobbing master builder	10.7				
Instructor in public schools (teacher)	78	Elem.-school teacher (Volksschullehrer)	11	Elem.-school teacher	10.8	Elem.-school teacher	10.3	Elem.-school teacher	11.7	Teacher	55
Farm owner and operator	76	Farmer (Bauer — mittelgrosser Betrieb)	13	Farmer	7.3	Farmer	8.1	Small independent farmer	16.4	Chairman of collective farm	38
Official of international labor union	75							Chairman of national labor federation	10.8		
Electrician	73										
Trained machinist	73	Skilled industrial worker (Industriefacharbeiter)	24	Fitter (elec.)	17.6	Fitter (elec.)	15.8				
Reporter on daily newspaper	71			News reporter	11.8	News reporter	13.8	Newspaper reporter	11.2		
Bookkeeper	68	Bank teller (bookkeeper in bank)	19	Routine clerk	16.1	Routine clerk	16.4	Company office clerk	16.1	(Bookkeeper)§	62

* Used here only for comparison with Japan. For comparison with other countries, see line beginning "United States civil engineer."

† Architect is the only occupation of a technical nature in Japan and was used here as a comparison only with the Soviet Union.

‡ Used here only for comparison with the Soviet Union. For comparison with other countries, see line beginning "United States bookkeeper."

§ Used there only for comparison with Japan. For comparison with other countries, see line beginning "United States accountant for a large business."

TABLE 5 — Continued

Occupation	Score	Occupation	Rank	Occupation	Score	Occupation	Score	Occupation	Score	Occupation	Score
United States:		*Germany:*		*Great Britain:*		*New Zealand:*		*Japan:*		*U.S.S.R.:*	
Insurance agent	68	Insurance agent	20	Insurance agent	14.6	Insurance agent	16.1	Insurance agent	20.2		
Traveling salesman for wholesale concern	68			Commercial traveler	12.0	Commercial traveler	14.1				
Policeman	67	Postman	23	Policeman	16.1	Policeman	15.5	Policeman	16.4		
Mail carrier	66	Carpenter	18								
Carpenter	65	Non-commissioned officer	31	Carpenter	18.6	Carpenter	17.0	Carpenter	20.2		
Corporal in regular army	60										
Machine operator in factory	60	Machine operator (Maschinen-schlosser-Geselle)	26	(Composite of fitter, carpenter, bricklayer, tractor driver, coal hewer)‖	20.5	(Composite of fitter, carpenter, bricklayer, tractor driver, coal hewer)‖	20.9	Latheman	21.1	Rank-and-file worker	48
Barber	59	Barber	16					Barber	20.5		
Clerk in a store	58	Store clerk (Verkäufer im Lebensmittel geschäft)	28	Shop assistant	20.2	Shop assistant	20.2	Department-store clerk	19.8		
Fisherman who owns own boat	58							Fisherman	22.0		
Streetcar motorman	58	Conductor	33	Chef	13.8	Chef#	21.8	Bus driver	20.9		
Restaurant cook	54			Carter	25.8	Carrier#	20.2				
Truck driver	54			Agricultural laborer	25.5	Agricultural laborer	24.4				
Farm hand	50	Farm laborer (worker)	36	Coal hewer	23.2	Coal hewer	24.7	Coal miner	23.7	Rank-and-file collective farmer	18
Coal miner	49			Dock laborer	27.0	Dock laborer	28.3				
Restaurant waiter	48	Waiter (Kellner)	30	Barman	26.4	Barman	28.3				
Dock worker	47			Road sweeper	28.9	Road sweeper	28.9	Road worker	24.8		
Bartender	44							Shoe shiner	26.9		
Street sweeper	34	(Unskilled laborer)**	38	Bricklayer	20.2	Bricklayer	19.3				
Shoe shiner	33	Bricklayer	27					Owner of a retail store	15.3		
		Clothing-store owner	12	Business manager	6.0	Business manager	5.3				
				Works manager	6.4	Works manager	7.9				
		Tailor	14	News agent and tobacconist	15.0	News agent and tobacconist	15.4	Tailor	17.7		
		Street peddler	35	Tractor driver	23.0	Tractor driver	22.8	Street-stall keeper	24.9		
				Railway porter	25.3	Railway porter	25.3				

‖ Used here only for comparison with the Soviet Union. For comparison with other countries, see individual occupations as they appear later in the table.

As there was no comparable occupation in New Zealand, the occupation substituted was carrier.

** Used here only for comparison with Japan.

relatively stable position of other professions, such as doctor. Nor will it serve to explain the low proportion of disagreement concerning the political occupations. We must recognize that the nations being compared have certain structural and cultural features in common, in addition to the presence of industry. For example, they share certain needs, as for socialization, and values, such as health and systematic knowledge, which insure relatively comparable standing to doctors, teachers, and scientists. Furthermore, all the countries compared have in common the national state, with which is associated a relatively standardized occupational structure ranging from ministers of state to local bureaucrats. In addition, both the professions and the political occupations are highly "visible," and agreement as to their standing is probably facilitated by the relatively objective and easily perceived indexes of power, knowledge, and skill manifested by their incumbents.

The types of occupation which generate the greatest amount of disagreement are highly variant and unstandardized or difficult to assimilate to the industrial structure. Agriculture may be conducted, as in Japan, on relatively small holdings, on collective farms as in the U.S.S.R., or, as in the western plains of the United States, in "agricultural factories." Being a farmer means very different things in each of the five countries, quite unlike the standardized image of the machinist or the factory manager. It can be anticipated, however, that as agriculture tends to be similarly organized in different countries, agricultural occupations will achieve more uniform standing.

The "service" occupations — barber, shoe shiner, chef, street sweeper — show the greatest amount of variation. Many of them antedate the industrial system and are in agrarian as well as industrial societies. They have no fixed position relative to the industrial order, nor are they similar to typical industrial occupations, as are many of the traditional crafts. They therefore appear to be most easily evaluated according to the traditional culture. Personal service in countries like Japan and Great Britain, in which a servant class was historically well developed and benefited from intimate association with an aristocratic upper class,

may still be regarded as not so degrading as in the more democratic societies, such as the United States and New Zealand. In fact, the greatest discrepancy to be found among all the comparisons involves the differences in prestige position accorded to chef in Great Britain as compared with either the United States or New Zealand, although in the case of the former the match was poor, since the comparable occupation was "restaurant cook." As these services come to be organized and mechanized — as in modern laundries or restaurants — they will become more thoroughly integrated into the larger economic order and may in time achieve more strictly comparable status from country to country.

All told, it would appear from this examination of international discrepancies that a great deal of weight must be given to the cross-national similarities in social structure which arise from the industrial system and from other common structural features, such as the national state. The greatest incidence of discrepancies occurs for occupations which are hardest to fit into either the one or the other structure. To this extent the structuralist position which we outlined earlier seems to be more heavily borne out in these data.

V. SUMMARY AND CONCLUSIONS

To sum up, our examination of occupational ratings in six modern industrialized countries reveals an extremely high level of agreement, going far beyond chance expectancy, as to the relative prestige of a wide range of specific occupations, despite the variety of sociocultural settings in which they are found. This strongly suggests that there is a relatively invariable hierarchy of prestige associated with the industrial system, even when it is placed in the context of larger social systems which are otherwise differentiated in important respects. In addition, the fact that the countries compared also have in common the national state and certain needs or values, such as interest in health, apparently also contributes to the observed regularity of the ratings, since both professional and political occupations are foci of agreement. Perhaps the most striking finding is the extent to which the different classes of occupation have been woven together into a single relatively unified occupational structure, more or less common to the six countries. At the same time, there is strong evidence that this relatively standardized occupational hierarchy does not apply without major exception to all occupations in all large-scale industrialized societies. In some instances, important disagreement may arise from the distinctive role of a single occupation in a particular country. In the majority of cases, however, the disagreement appears to involve certain classes of occupation, notably agricultural and service, about which there is only modest agreement. Disagreement probably reflects differences in the length and "maturity" of industrialization in various countries but also clearly results from differentiations in sociocultural systems which may well be relatively enduring.

51 The Situs Dimension in Occupational Structure*

Richard T. Morris • Raymond J. Murphy

Most studies of occupational structure have been concerned with the stratification or vertical aspect. In a pioneering effort the authors suggest that occupational structure is not unidimensional but also possesses a "horizontal" dimension. This horizontal aspect relates to the functional context of an occupation which may differ from the general prestige or vertical dimension. The new concept called "situs" stresses what must be done in a society rather than how they are done. The classification of situses consists of equally valued functional categories of occupations.

The study of social differentiation through the analysis of occupations has long been a major focus of American sociology. The majority of studies of occupational structure, however, have been almost exclusively concerned with the vertical or stratified dimension of the division of labor. It is the purpose of this paper to suggest a theoretical approach and a technique for the systematic analysis of an additional dimension, situs, the horizontal differentiation of occupational structure.

THE VERTICAL DIMENSION

Although considerable disagreement exists in stratification research, there seems to be a high degree of consensus regarding the utility of occupation as an index of socio-economic position. The majority of researchers who use occupation in this way have employed the Edwards census classification[1] or some variant based upon it. This scheme, in its original formulation, classifies occupations into six levels or strata called "social-economic groups":

1. Professional persons
2. Proprietors, managers, and officials:
   2-a. Farmers (owners and tenants)
   2-b. Wholesale and retail dealers
   2-c. Other proprietors, managers, and officials
3. Clerks and kindred workers
4. Skilled workers and foremen
5. Semiskilled workers
6. Unskilled workers:
   6-a. Farm laborers
   6-b, c. Laborers, except farm
   6-d. Servant classes

Edwards attempts to validate this classification as a scale of superior-inferior categories by the use of statistics on median income and educational attainment derived from the 1940 census tabulations. The data show, although with considerable overlapping of ranges, that "the social-economic

* From the *American Sociological Review,* Vol. 24 (April, 1959), pp. 231–239. Reprinted with revised footnotes by permission. Copyright © 1959 by The American Sociological Association.

[1] Alba M. Edwards, *A Social-economic Grouping of the Gainful Workers of the United States,* Washington, D.C., Government Printing Office, 1938.

groups are arranged . . . in the descending order of the social economic status of the workers comprising them and that they do constitute a scale."[2] Edwards' rank-ordering of occupational groups is generally borne out by a number of subsequent studies of occupational prestige and has become a part of the sociologist's stock of "social facts."

We do not wish to raise the question of whether or not occupations are differentially evaluated. Our concern is rather the adequacy of the Edwards scale as a technique with which to analyze and understand the American occupational structure. A perusal of the recent sociological literature suggests a growing dissatisfaction with the Edwards scheme, from the point of view of both its theoretical and methodological characteristics.

Theoretically, there is some question as to whether or not a single rank ordering of occupational groups is an accurate representation of the American occupational structure. Some argue that this notion is an oversimplification of social reality. As Foote sees it, for example, studies of stratification employing this conception have "premised a simple system of ranks organized in a single whole which the scientist could contemplate with indifferent objectivity. But society is not like that; the viewpoint of so-called sociological realism is far from realistic, now if not earlier."[3] Again, Parsons cautions:

It is of the greatest importance that it is only in the broadest sense that this class complex in American society can be made to yield a single unequivocal scale of classes. . . . high business executives, people highly placed in the ascriptive-qualitative functions such as scientists and writers, etc., are extremely difficult to rank relative to each other in any unequivocal way. . . . one of the most notable features of the American system of stratification is its relative looseness, the absence of a clear-cut hierarchy of prestige except in a very broad sense.[4]

The essence of these views seems to be that the American occupational structure may most meaningfully be viewed as consisting of multiple hierarchies — several ladders of occupational status positions instead of one rank order encompassing all types of work. If one accepts this model, it follows that single vertical scales, such as Edwards', are at best a crude representation of reality and at worst a serious distortion of American occupational structure. Certainly, research problems are seriously handicapped through the use of a scale which does not facilitate or permit the analysis of a two-dimensional occupational structure.

Methodologically, the Edwards scale and similar ones suffer from a number of inadequacies, regardless of whether one subscribes to the single or multiple dimensional conception of the occupational system. Those who use the Edwards scale complain about the grossness of the categories; it requires the combination under one head of a heterogeneous collection of occupations which frequently differ in median income, educational prerequisites, social prestige, and nature of work. Consequently, findings based on this type of occupational classification must be fairly rough approximations and subject to considerable variation, and problems of occupational variance and difference within strata often cannot be handled. Kahl makes this point in commenting on a somewhat modified version of the Edwards scale:

The category of managers, proprietors, and officials is probably the least satisfactory for stratification analysis. Obviously the farmers are very different from the urban businessmen, and we must always keep them separate. But the latter category is a hodgepodge, including everybody from pushcart peddlers to bank presidents.[5]

This inadequacy is especially acute when the scale is used as a basis for studying occupational mobility, since much movement is "lost" because of the broadness of the categories.

Such criticisms do not suggest that the Edwards scale has no utility for the student of occupational structure. It has been highly useful, for example, in the analysis of changes in the composition of

[2] Alba M. Edwards, *Comparative Occupation Statistics for the United States,* 1870–1940, Washington, D.C., Government Printing Office, 1943, p. 180.

[3] Nelson N. Foote, "Destratification and Restratification — An Editorial Foreword," *American Journal of Sociology,* 58 (January, 1953), p. 325.

[4] Talcott Parsons, "A Revised Analytical Approach to the Theory of Social Stratification," in R. Bendix and S. M. Lipset, editors, *Class, Status and Power,* Glencoe, Ill., Free Press, 1953, p. 121.

[5] Joseph A. Kahl, *The American Class Structure,* New York, Rinehart, 1957, p. 66.

the labor force through time. Rather, we suggest that changes in scales of this type are necessary if we are to arrive at a more accurate understanding of the nature of American occupational structure, or if we hope to use effectively occupational data in the analysis of stratification. We believe that the inadequacies discussed above can be greatly reduced through the use of an additional dimension — the horizontal — and by making certain corresponding changes in the vertical arrangement of occupational groups. The remainder of this paper concerns the problem of constructing a two-dimensional model of the occupational structure and its utility for stratification and mobility research.

THE HORIZONTAL DIMENSION

Fifteen years ago, Benoit-Smullyan suggested the conceptual difference between stratum and situs. A *stratum* is a category of individuals or positions placed above or below other categories in a hierarchical rank order based upon differential, comparative evaluation. A *situs* (a term coined by Benoit-Smullyan for this purpose) is a category of individuals or positions placed on a level with other categories, all of which are given the same evaluation.

Benoit-Smullyan does not discuss occupational situs distinctions, but rather illustrates the latter with sex and clan differentiation. His conceptual framework may be fruitfully used, however, for establishing the horizontal dimension of occupational structure. Occupational situses, then, are categories of work which are differentiated in some way but are not invidiously compared. The comparison of professionals with unskilled workers is a stratum distinction. The comparison of sales occupations with those in manufacturing is a situs distinction, to the degree that they, as categories, are given equal evaluation.

To satisfy the theoretical model, each situs category should contain occupations ranging from highest to lowest status, cutting through all strata of the occupational structure. Empirically, there may not be equally-extended status ranges of occupations within each situs, but the model, if it is to follow the Benoit-Smullyan conception, must not preclude the possibility of such ranges. Several attempts have been made by sociologists to establish two-dimensional classifications of occupations. However, none of them, in our opinion, has developed a horizontal dimension which meets the situs definition.

In 1949, Warner and his associates proposed a rating scale for occupations which is basically a revision of Edwards' classification, with an additional vertical dimension based on the criteria of skill, size of business, and prestige.[6] In a sense, this is an attempt to transform Edwards' strata into the horizontal dimension — which arrives at a halfway house. The resulting categories are not situses, as here defined, because they are specifically rank-ordered: professionals, proprietors and managers, businessmen, clerks and kindred workers, manual workers, protective and service workers, and farmers. Within each of these categories specific occupations can range from high to low prestige ratings, for example, professionals ranging from physicians to undertakers' assistants, clerks from C.P.A.s to telephone operators, manual workers from contractors to coal miners. As Warner puts it:

> . . . it was decided to treat occupation as a two-dimensional factor and to use the various occupational groups which had been defined by Edwards . . . but to accept the fact that there were gradations within each of these groups with respect to the degree of skill required for the job and the amount of prestige attached to the job. . . . Thus, any category of occupation was not limited to a single rating but could potentially be given a rating of from one to seven, depending upon the degree of skill required for a particular job rather than that associated with a general occupational group.[7]

The resulting classification scheme shows that, due to the nature of the categories, the occupations within each one actually cannot range from one to seven points (that is, from highest to lowest prestige scores). There is a definite staggering or stairstep effect in the arrangement of the categories because professional occupations cannot be found which show the lowest prestige scores, nor manual

[6] W. Lloyd Warner, Marchia Meeker, and Kenneth Eells, *Social Class in America,* Chicago: Science Research Associates, 1949.
[7] *Ibid.,* p. 136.

occupations with the highest scores. The two-dimensional classification thus approaches the notion of situs, but does not fulfill the definition.

Paul K. Hatt picked up the term situs when, in a paper published in 1950,[8] he attempted to establish empirically, through scale analysis of the N.O.R.C. occupational prestige study, a set of equally-evaluated occupational categories. Hatt defines situs (in a subsequent article with Nelson N. Foote):

If it be assumed that jobs and occupations have status values which are hierarchically distributed and, in addition, possess qualities which distinguish them from others without invidious implications, then the occupational structure can be conceived as segmented both horizontally and vertically. The first of these can be called strata and the second situses.[9]

Hatt's constructed situses include: (1) Political, (2) Professional, (3) Business, (4) Recreation and Aesthetics, (5) Agriculture, (6) Manual Work, (7) Military, and (8) Service. As with Warner, it is evident that the Hatt situses do not meet the definition of equal-evaluation. Although he speaks of parallel status ladders, his categories include professions, manual work, and service, which obviously involve evaluative criteria (for example, amount of education) and duplicate Edwards' professional, service, and skill groupings. The result is a series of staggered or overlapping status ladders, which are probably a combined function of the original criterion used (occupation-consumer relationship), the scaling operation itself, and the particular operations selected for the original N.O.R.C. study.

Unlike Hatt's empirically constructed groups, the horizontal classification theoretically requires an equally extended hierarchy of occupations within each situs. It seems to follow from the Benoit-Smullyan definition (and, indeed, from that of Hatt and Foote cited above) that situses *as categories* must be equally evaluated, even though there is a wide status range of *specific occupations* within each group.

Psychologists, concerned with occupations in terms of interest, occupational choice, and the function of work for the individual (and perhaps less preoccupied with vertical structure than sociologists) have developed several systematic multidimensional classification schemes. In 1956, Anne Roe, for example, presented a two-dimensional classification of occupations which meets our requirements for a situs dimension:

In this scheme, every occupation is classified in each of two sets of categories, one called Groups and the other Levels. Group subdivisions indicate the primary focus of activity in the occupation. . . . Classification into Levels depends upon the degree of personal autonomy and the level of skill and training required. . . .[10]

The "Groups" (corresponding to situses) proposed by Roe include: (1) Service, (2) Business Contact, (3) Organization, (4) Technology, (5) Outdoor, (6) Science, (7) General Cultural, and (8) Arts and Entertainment. Roe's six "Levels" (corresponding to strata) are Professional and Managerial (two levels based on degree of responsibility), Semi-professional and Small Business, Skilled, Semi-skilled, and Unskilled.

Roe's Groups satisfy the definition of situs insofar as they allow for extended status ranges within each category and do not form a basis for invidious comparison of categories as a function of the scheme itself. One difficulty with this horizontal classification, however, is that no consistent set of criteria is used to differentiate the Groups:

The focus of an occupation may be on personal interactions, supportive or exploitative, close or more distant, personal or administrative. It may be on activities involved in the first handling of natural resources, or in their conversion into commodities, or in the organizational structures required for these activities. It may be on development and application of knowledge, or the preservation of the institutions and the accumulated knowledge of the culture.

---

[8] Paul K. Hatt, "Occupations and Social Stratification," *American Journal of Sociology,* 45 (May, 1950), pp. 533–543.

[9] Nelson N. Foote and Paul K. Hatt, "Social Mobility and Economic Advancement," *The American Economic Review,* 43 (May, 1953), pp. 371–373.

[10] Anne Roe, *The Psychology of Occupations,* New York: Wiley, 1956, p. 144.

Thus Roe combines in one dimension the criteria of relationship (as Hatt uses it), function, and institutional setting. We believe that a second problem is that the classification inadequately meets the logical criterion of exclusiveness, perhaps because of the mixed criteria used. For example, university and college faculties are included in both the Science and General Cultural Groups, while teachers are assigned to Arts and Entertainment; promoters are included in Business Contact, while ad writers are in Arts and Entertainment; applied scientists are listed in Technology and in Outdoor; the practical nurse is in Service, while the nurse is in Science; taxi drivers are in Service, truck drivers in Technology, while teamsters are in Outdoors.

An adaptation of the Roe classification has been presented by Super.[11] He proposes a three-dimensional classification of occupations, based on an earlier version of Roe's "Groups," the same "Levels" as listed above, and a third dimension of "Enterprise" or institutional setting:

Chemists work in educational institutions, in manufacturing, in agriculture, in government, and in other institutional settings. The same is true of lawyers, of psychologists, of truck drivers, and of clerks. The conditions of work for chemists and clerks vary considerably with the type of enterprise in which they work . . . it is not just pay that varies with the institutional setting, but also the pace of work, type of supervision, security benefits, social life, etc. Hence, it is important to describe occupations in a third dimension, that of the type of enterprise.

Super's Enterprise dimension includes Agriculture-Forestry, Mining, Construction, Manufacture, Trade, Finance, Transport, Services, and Government. In effect this is an adaptation of the Major Industry Groups used by the United States Census. Although our concern here is with a classification of types of work in society and not with the institutional setting of occupations, we believe that this "third dimension" has important sociological implications. It suggests, at least, that even two-

dimensional considerations may be inadequate for the analysis of certain problems in occupational structure.

SITUS CLASSIFICATION

In 1953, the present authors proposed a scheme for the two-dimensional classification of occupations, based upon Benoit-Smullyan's concept of situs. Subsequently a number of modifications of the scheme have been made in an attempt to overcome some of the limitations cited above. Thus, in order to satisfy the specifications of the horizontal dimension of the model, it was necessary to choose a single criterion which theoretically permits equal evaluation of occupational categories. For this reason, the situses were organized primarily in keeping with the principle of societal function.

Theoretically, all legitimate occupations, from street cleaner to architect, are functional for the society, contributing in some degree to its successful operation. But in a society with a complex division of labor no one occupation fully performs any given function (nurses do not completely solve the problem of health in society). Accordingly, a number of occupations may be related to the degree to which they jointly contribute to the fulfillment of a societal function. One of the bases for differential evaluation and reward of occupations is the extent to which they help to fulfill these general requisites. The functions themselves, however, in so far as they are viewed as equally necessary and vital for the maintenance of society, are equally valued. For the purpose of delineating the model, we assume that the prestige distribution of occupations *within* a situs may vary over time and between societies, but the situses themselves, as functional categories, remain stable and equally valued. Following the distinction made by Aberle and his associates, in our situs categories we are stressing *what* must be done in a society, not *how* things are done. The health function, for example, must be carried out, but the nature of the specific occupations charged with contributing to this function may change. It can be argued, of course, that entire functional categories of occupations are differentially valued within a given society and that

[11] Donald E. Super, *The Psychology of Careers,* New York, 1957.

this hierarchy may change over time — thus the relatively higher status of scientific and learned occupations as compared with entertainment occupations, or the shift in the prestige of military occupations from peace to war. By making the assumption in our model of the equivalence of situs categories, and not arbitrarily prejudging the relative position of situs groups, the problem of differential evaluation of function can be subjected to further empirical test.

The situses finally selected bear a close resemblance to the functional categories suggested by Malinowski and others,[12] the chief differences being the proliferation of the productive and distributive functions, as might be expected in a highly industrialized society.

Once the functional categories were established, the criteria of exhaustiveness and exclusiveness were applied on the basis of attempts to fit a large number of specific occupations into the scheme. In each case the tentative assignment to a given situs was based on the nature of the task — what the person in the occupation does, rather than the kind of institution the individual works for, or his associates. Thus, a railroad section-hand was assigned to the Building and Maintenance situs (because he repairs and maintains the right-of-way) rather than to Transportation. The fitting process resulted in several regroupings, combining of situses, and the construction of new situses for the final list. The proposed situs categories, with a brief definition of each, are as follows:

DEFINITION OF CIVILIAN OCCUPATIONAL SITUSES

1. *Legal Authority* — All occupations primarily concerned with the formulation, arbitration, interpretation, or enforcement of the law, including those primarily concerned with the custody of law-breakers.
2. *Finance and Records* — All occupations primarily concerned with the handling of monetary affairs or the processing of records, accounts, or correspondence.
3. *Manufacturing* — All occupations primarily concerned with the fabrication of articles or

the processing of raw materials on a production-line basis.
4. *Transportation* — All occupations primarily concerned with the movement of persons or goods from one location to another.
5. *Extraction* — All occupations primarily concerned with the extraction, procurement, or production of raw materials.
6. *Building and Maintenance* — All occupations primarily concerned with the construction of buildings or other non-massproduced units, or the installation, maintenance, or repair of equipment, property or facilities.
7. *Commerce* — All occupations primarily concerned with the buying, selling, exchange, or marketing of goods or persons.
8. *Arts and Entertainment* — All occupations primarily concerned with the creation of art forms or with the provision of entertainment, recreation, information, or aesthetic satisfaction for the public.
9. *Education and Research* — All occupations primarily concerned with formal instruction or training or with the acquisition of knowledge as an end in itself.
10. *Health and Welfare* — All occupations primarily concerned with the detection, prevention, or alleviation of illness, hazard, or distress.

We do not include the military occupations in this classification because they constitute, we believe, a separate occupational structure with distinctive mobility patterns, income distribution, authority relations, and so on. It would appear, however, that many of the situses listed above could be applied to the military occupational structure. Illegal occupations form another separate and distinctive structure, which is not considered here.

In an attempt to determine the amount of consensus in the placement of occupations in situs categories, and to determine whether or not the descriptions of situs groupings are unambiguous, 40 occupations, selected to represent a broad range of situses and strata (including as well a number of occupations thought difficult to classify), were presented in an alphabetical list to 200 undergraduate students at U.C.L.A. The respondents were asked to classify these occupations according to situs, each of which was defined as

---

[12] Bronislaw Malinowski, *A Scientific Theory of Culture and Other Essays,* Chapel Hill: University of North Carolina Press, 1944, pp. 91 ff.: John W. Bennett and Melvin M. Tumin, *Social Life, Structure and Function,* New York: Macmillan, 1949, pp. 370–377.

THEORETICAL SITUS LOCATION OF SELECTED OCCUPATIONS AND EMPIRICAL LOCATION MADE BY SAMPLE OF STUDENT RATERS

SITUSES

PRESTIGE RANK QUARTILES (Student Ratings) / STRATA	1 Legal Authority	2 Finance & Records	3 Manufacturing	4 Transportation	5 Extraction	6 Building & Maintenance	7 Commerce	8 Aesthetics & Entertainment	9 Education & Research	10 Health & Welfare
1	Supreme Court Justice, Lawyer	City Manager	Owner of a Large Factory	President of a Railroad				Conductor of a Symphony Orchestra	College President	Physician, Minister
2		Banker	Biologist for a Pharmaceutical Company	Airline Pilot	Geologist in an Oil Company	Building Contractor	Advertising Executive, Commercial Artist		Philosopher, County Agricultural Agent	Welfare Worker
3	Policeman	Bookkeeper	Machinist		Farmer, Forest Ranger		Manager of a Hardware Store	Radio Announcer, Singer in a Night Club	Music Teacher	Fireman
4	Prison Guard	Cashier in a Restaurant	Restaurant Cook	Mail Carrier, Truck Driver	Coal Miner	Waiter in a Restaurant, Garbage Collector	Milk Route Man	Barber		

NOTE: Arrows indicate that over 25 per cent of the students placed the occupation in a situs other than that theoretically expected on the basis of situs definitions applied. For those interested, the authors have available a list of a large number of occupations classified by theoretically appropriate situs categories.

above, and to give each occupation a prestige rating, according to the North-Hatt format. The results are summarized in the accompanying table.

Several interesting questions are raised by this pilot study. The occupations on which there was least situs agreement include: waiter in a restaurant, biologist for a pharmaceutical company, garbage collector, barber, city manager, commercial artist, minister, milk route man, and farm owner and operator. The difficulty in placing these occupations unequivocally in the theoretically correct situs appears to stem from at least two situations. The first is that these occupations actually involve, intrinsically, more than one function and these multiple functions are viewed as equally important to the job. (Almost any occupation can be said to serve a number of secondary functions.) For example, the minister may be equally concerned with instruction or training and with the alleviation of distress; the commercial artist may be equally concerned with the production of an art form as an end in itself and with how well the art will sell a product; the waiter may be equally occupied with maintenance of the tables, carrying food, and with sales (pushing the roast beef); the milk route man may be equally a salesman and a truck driver. *Situs ambiguity* may be an important cue to the dynamics of changing occupations, conflicting self-images of people so employed, and impending specialization and breakdown of occupations into sub-tasks.

The second reason for multiple or incorrect situs placement probably is the existence of a different public image, a misunderstanding or lack of knowledge about what an individual actually does in an occupation. (This lack of clarity is often due to insufficient specification of the occupation.) The city manager is perceived by some students as primarily a legal position; the biologist for a pharmaceutical company is seen as being primarily concerned with health and welfare (perhaps an instance of the effectiveness of institutional advertising); the farmer is viewed as being primarily engaged in selling his products rather than producing them; the barber and the garbage man are seen as operating in the health field. (These data on public images of the functions of occupations are themselves sociologically provocative.)

Notwithstanding the situs ambiguity of some oc-cupations, the fact remains that the students were able to classify a majority of the occupations, using our definitions of situs, clearly and correctly. It should be emphasized, however, quite aside from these tentative findings of a pilot study, that even if a national survey of situs perception were carried out, the results would neither validate nor invalidate the situs classification presented here. The utility of situs analysis does not rest upon whether the public sees or thinks in terms of these occupational categories. The scheme will stand or fall, be further adjusted or rejected, on the basis of how well it can facilitate the prediction, or help in the understanding, of social behavior.

THE UTILITY OF SITUS ANALYSIS

Several research problems are suggested by the systematic introduction of the situs dimension in the occupational structure. First, it is possible to reanalyze by *situs* the tremendous mass of data collected for the purpose of showing relationships between occupational *strata* and such correlates as political attitudes, fertility, modes of socialization, patterns of expenditure, and associational behavior. This may be either a one-way or two-way secondary analysis: by situs alone or by situs and stratum simultaneously. A comparison of strata correlates and situs correlates suggests another potentially useful research area.

We hypothesize that situses, as well as strata, form characteristic sub-cultures expressed in common values, norms, understandings, and attitudes. We are not suggesting that strata analysis be ignored or replaced, but that it be elaborated and refined by the addition of situs analysis. The basic prediction here is that the functional context of an occupation may make as much difference for the behavior or life style of the incumbent as the general prestige or socio-economic level of that occupation. As with strata, occupational situses may be expected to influence formal and informal group membership, common interests, goals, tastes, and so on. It may well be that people use occupational situs categories as reference groups in addition to strata or instead of them: "There's no business like show business."

The study of mobility is also subject to both primary and secondary analysis using the situs dimension.[13] This area provides a number of problems: the relative amounts of and relationship between vertical and horizontal (situs) mobility; differential mobility barriers in the various situses; shifts in occupational structure as reflected in situs mobility; generational *versus* career mobility patterns in relation to situs changes; the incidence of situs mobility in different strata. With reference to the latter problem we have developed an "I" hypothesis: that situs mobility is greatest at the top and bottom of the occupational structure where skills are most interchangeable. Horizontal mobility aspiration is another potentially rewarding field of study. For example, aspirations may vary with age in a "U" curve: widest in scope with school-age children, decreasing as the adult settles himself in a specialized job, increasing again as the person becomes older.

[13] Natalie Rogoff, *Recent Trends in Occupational Mobility,* Glencoe, Ill.: Free Press, 1953.

The study of occupational role (the social psychology of occupations) is enlarged and informed by the application of situs analysis. As suggested above, situs ambiguity on the part of members of an occupation, or as seen by the general public, is perhaps a good indication of a change in the occupation, role conflict within an occupation, or problems of marginality.[14]

It is hoped that the situs categories presented here will be refined and corrected as the result of further theoretical or empirical work. Certainly serious classificatory problems remain in the scheme. We believe, however, despite errors in detail in the two-dimensional model, that the systematic inclusion of the situs dimension in occupational research warrants the serious consideration of sociologists.

[14] Thelma H. McCormack, "The Druggist's Dilemma: Problems of a Marginal Occupation," *American Journal of Sociology,* 61 (January, 1956), pp. 308–315.

SOCIAL MOBILITY

52 Social Mobility and Social Isolation: A Test of Sorokin's Dissociative Hypothesis*

Robert A. Ellis · W. Clayton Lane

A popular folk myth exists that one of the major avenues for upward social mobility of an individual is admission into a high status university. What are

* Excerpted from the *American Sociological Review,* Vol. 32 (April, 1967), pp. 237–253. Reprinted by permission. Copyright © 1967 by The American Sociological Association.

the personal and social consequences of this experience? The authors study upwardly mobile youth who have been screened for their 'middle-class' characteristics and for their academic and social promise in high school. They encountered a disproportionate share of isolating experiences and personal strain both as viewed through the eyes of institutional observers and as realized in personal experience. Three hypotheses are advanced for explaining the process: the compensatory hypothesis, the ameliorative hypothesis, and the dissociative hypothesis. The findings of this research support the latter. What are the implications of this paper for the new thrust of prestige colleges and universites for a more 'representative' (central city) student bodies?

The stratification system generally operates in our society to bind persons to the class circumstances to which they are born. Nevertheless, in any given generation a number of individuals do free themselves of the restraints of their class of origin and change their position in the social structure. Just what consequences these shifts in status have for the individual, especially where major mobility is involved, has been a matter of recurring concern but little consensus.

One line of thought portrays the upwardly mobile as isolated, lonely individuals who, because of their ascent, find themselves unable to form satisfactory personal relationships in their new environment. This point of view — what we term the *dissociative hypothesis* — was introduced by Sorokin over a quarter of a century ago. Although in discussing the effects of mobility Sorokin mentions such benefits to society as increased creativity and adaptability, he points out that they come at a psychological cost to the individual. Part of this cost is an experience of rootlessness, for upward mobility is a disruptive social experience that, to use Sorokin's terms, "diminishes intimacy and increases psychosocial isolation and loneliness." The mobile man in contemporary society he thus depicts as one who is unattached to anything or anybody.[1]

An alternative view, the *compensatory hypothesis,* has been advanced by psychoanalytically oriented social scientists. They treat social isolation as more the cause than the effect of upward mobility. Status strivings, from this standpoint, are evoked to compensate for social deprivation arising from childhood and early adolescent experiences. While those who rise in the social structure may, as adults, encounter inordinate difficulties in establishing close ties with others, this isolation is construed as only "a continuation of [the same] superficial, impermanent primary group relations" that originally motivated them to alter their class circumstances.

Still another approach is to be found in the *ameliorative hypothesis* set forth in reference group theory. An upward shift of one's class position is acknowledged to have a potentially disruptive effect, but one that is not inevitable. The disruptive tendencies can be substantially ameliorated, if not alleviated entirely, by prior social experiences. Conceiving anticipatory socialization to be the usual mechanism for achieving upward mobility, proponents of this hypothesis contend that lower-class persons who have had opportunity to absorb the values, norms, and judgmental standards of the middle class to which they aspire

should easily gain acceptance by that segment of society.[2]

In essence, then, these represent three competing interpretations of the personal consequences of upward mobility. The dissociative hypothesis stipulates that a prolonged period of estrangement is the normal, direct consequence of upward mobility. Conversely, social isolation is treated in the compensatory hypothesis as a concomitant of mobility, but not a direct consequence, and in the ameliorative hypothesis as a potential consequence of mobility, but not a normal one. The validity of these hypotheses remains, however, to be demonstrated.

Methodologically, a test of Sorokin's hypothesis against its two theoretical alternatives requires capturing upwardly mobile individuals at a time of major status transition. This would permit determining whether a significant step in upward mobility is, in fact, accompanied by a period of social dislocation. If social isolation is a result, independent evidence needs to be gathered as to whether this isolation can be attributed either to (1) earlier inability to form effective social relationships or (2) the absence of effective anticipatory socialization.

RESEARCH PROBLEM

This paper endeavors to provide such a test by examining a situation of extreme mobility. We draw upon findings from a panel research undertaken at Stanford University over a complete undergraduate sequence to ascertain the intellectual and social adjustment students make to college life. As the discussion makes clear, the elaborate institutionalization of behavior at Stanford, plus the wide discrepancy between the past and present status circumstances of the upwardly mobile, make it an excellent natural experimental setting for testing the effects of social mobility.

Of primary interest in this inquiry are the highly selected students who come to Stanford from lower-class backgrounds. Clearly in the minority at this university, constituting only three percent

[1] Pitirim A. Sorokin, *Social Mobility,* New York: Harper & Bros., 1927, pp. 522–525.

[2] Robert K. Merton, *Social Theory and Social Structure* (Rev. Ed.), Glencoe, Ill.: The Free Press, 1957, pp. 254–255, 265–266, 384–385.

of the total undergraduate student body, they are upon matriculation confronted with the task of assuming full-time residence in what, from their perspective, may seem an alien and stressful social environment. Stanford is, in terms of its personnel, policies, and values, a predominantly upper-middle-class institution. Moreover, it is a highly competitive setting. This partially results from the characteristically upper-middle-class emphasis put on striving for achievement. In part, it is the direct consequence of admissions procedures that recruit youths who have been eminently successful in high school, having in the majority of cases been outstanding leaders in both scholastic and non-scholastic endeavors.

Yet this is not a world for which such lower-class youth as these are unprepared. The joint circumstances of self- and institutional selection have operated to bring to Stanford students from lower social backgrounds who have already adopted a middle-class reference group and many of its attendant norms and values.[3] It is nevertheless problematical (1) whether their anticipatory socialization into middle-class practices and beliefs enables them to be readily assimilated into the Stanford undergraduate society; and (2) if not, whether the social estrangement that results is attributable to a chronic inability on their part to establish effective primary group ties.

METHOD

The subjects for this report consist of 126 male undergraduates who entered Stanford as first-year freshmen in the fall of 1958. Of these, 99 were selected by means of a standard probability sample. Designated the Regular Sample, it furnishes a reliable and accurate estimate of the characteristics of the Stanford undergraduate population. The remaining 27 students represent an oversample taken of all lower- and lower-middle-class freshmen not originally contained in the Regular Sample so as to compensate for the underrepresentation of persons from these social levels in the student body. The oversample is used to aug-

ment the Regular Sample whenever the factor of social class is analyzed.

Social-class background was determined by the Index of Class Position (ICP), a two-factor intercommunity measure of stratification developed and validated specifically for research on college populations.[4] ICP is based on the two components of father's occupation and the student's subjective identification of the class position of the family. This index yields a six-class scale ranging as follows:

Social Class	Nominal Designation
I	Upper
II	Upper-Middle
III	Middle-Middle
IV	Lower-Middle
V	Upper-Lower
VI	Lower-Lower

For a student to be categorized in the lower stratum by ICP, his father would have to be employed in a blue-collar occupation, and the student would have to perceive the family as being in the working or lower class.

Since background factors other than social class might be presumed to alienate individuals from their peers, appropriate controls were imposed. Race, ethnicity, and age were controlled by sample exclusion, so that non-whites, foreign-born, and persons over 20 and under 17 were eliminated from the sample frame, a step that resulted in only a negligible reduction of the parent universe. Non-Protestants among the Stanford student body were too few to permit systematic partialling of the effects of Catholic, Jewish and Protestant backgrounds. Nevertheless, all class differences obtained for the Regular Sample were recomputed for only the Protestants in the sample so as to insure that the effect of religion did not spuriously contribute to the results. All class differences reported below have been found to stand up independently of the effect of religion. Finally, the

---

[3] See Robert A. Ellis and W. Clayton Lane, "Social Mobility and Career Orientation," *Sociology and Social Research,* 50 (April, 1966), pp. 280–296.

[4] Robert A. Ellis, W. Clayton Lane and Virginia Olesen, "The Index of Class Position: An Improved Intercommunity Measure of Stratification," *American Sociological Review,* 28 (April, 1963), pp. 271–277.

incidence of broken homes among Stanford students was found to be evenly distributed among the social classes, and thus required no special treatment.

Data on social background, as well as all other information gained through students' self-reports, were obtained from hour-long interviews held early in the freshman year and, so long as the students remained in college, at the end of the freshman, sophomore, and senior years — which for some involved a time span of up to seven years. Two additional sources of data were provided by administrative records and by judgments made of the students by other persons with the opportunity to observe and evaluate them in a social context. Included among the latter were high school teachers, dormitory counselors, and college administrators.

These outside judgments furnish an especially vital datum. Their use permits us to avoid exclusive reliance on individual self-reports, which may very well mask the more sensitive social and personal side-effects of upward mobility. Moreover, since these evaluations span the time from high school to the senior year at Stanford, they help make it possible to pinpoint the pre-mobility characteristics of the students and then to discern over an extended period the social impact that results from their movement in the social structure.

Finally, we should emphasize the strategic nature of the Stanford setting which allows us to concentrate on persons taking a major step in upward mobility.

PRE-COLLEGE POTENTIAL FOR SOCIAL SUCCESS

Our first concern is with the social potential exhibited by lower-class students prior to the time they come to Stanford. Is there early indication that they lack the skills necessary for making an effective social and personal adjustment to college life?

By their record of extracurricular accomplishments in high school, it is readily evident that social maladjustment is the exception, characterizing no more than 5 to 10 percent of all class V and VI students. It is much more the rule for the upwardly mobile to be the prototype of the much-fabled "All-American Boy." They have been able to combine a record of scholastic excellence with a prominent leadership role in the non-scholastic activities of high school life and even in the community at large. Not infrequently, these youngsters have achieved scholastic distinction as class valedictorian or National Merit Scholarship holder, while at the same time accumulating a series of nonscholastic honors, such as leadership in extracurricular organizations, class or student body officership, and major athletic awards. Many, in addition, have held offices that would bring them to the attention of the community at large, as, for example, in the City Youth Council or Junior Red Cross. In addition, almost half of the lower class were recipients of such "general honors" as American Legion Award for Outstanding Citizen of the Year or Senior Voted Most Likely to Succeed. Of equal significance is the fact that their record of leadership in nonscholastic endeavors falls only slightly below that of Stanford undergraduates in general: 64 percent of class V and VI students, as compared to 76 percent of the Regular Sample, have had the kind of awards and offices that would stamp them as outstanding leaders in the student culture. Consequently, their high school accomplishments not only mark these class V and VI students as atypical of other persons coming from their background, but also indicate that they have essentially the same potential for social success as students coming to Stanford from higher status levels.

Tabulation of these items shows that class V and VI students are viewed by high school administrators as slightly more motivated and able than other Stanford freshmen to do academic work — a finding that is not too surprising since almost all lower-class freshmen come to Stanford on scholarships.

It is also clear from the high school reports that these lower-class youth are thought to possess the social potential to fit into the Stanford undergraduate culture. Slightly more than half are regarded as having been good leaders in the high school student body, a result comparable to that obtained for the Regular Sample. Furthermore, they are even more likely than other Stanford freshmen to be judged free from those "personal or social problems . . . that would interfere with academic and personal success at Stanford," and not a single lower-class student is reported as being "more likely than the typical student" to be experiencing such problems. Moreover, in spite of their families' socio-economic status — which almost inevitably was the subject for comment in the high school's report — the students from classes V and VI are described as possessing those personal and social characteristics which stamp an individual as "middle class." Almost without exception they are described as: (1) generally neat and clean in appearance, (2) responsible and trustworthy in social and academic affairs, (3) likely to accept suggestions and corrections gracefully, (4) respectful and cooperative toward teachers and school officials, and (5) able to get along well with students and be respected by them.

Thus, from both their high school records and the judgments of high school personnel, it is clear that before they enter Stanford these upwardly mobile youth are not the socially inept, constrained individuals that the compensatory hypothesis of upward mobility would imply. Nor do they give evidence of having missed the significant anticipatory socialization into middle-class practices and beliefs that the ameliorative hypothesis suggests would pave the way for their making an easy and effective adjustment to the new social world they are entering.

Let us now turn our attention to the social reaction made to these students at the time they enter Stanford and over the course of the undergraduate years. Does the reaction by the other Stanford students indicate that the upwardly mobile encounter special difficulty in gaining social acceptance in this new milieu?

SOCIAL REACTION TO THE UPWARDLY MOBILE

Initial Reaction

The task of selecting undergraduate judges is simplified by Stanford's practice of having 24 undergraduate counselors assigned as residents to the freshman dormitory, one to approximately every 30 freshmen. After the initial list of applicants is screened by the administration, these counselors, known at Stanford as "freshman sponsors," are elected to their post each year by the preceding group. Their role in the dormitory consists partially of acting as institutionally approved socializing agents. They are expected to interpret the undergraduate culture for the new students and to serve as a prototype of the model Stanford undergraduate. Their job also requires acting as agents of social control in maintaining house discipline and reporting signs of trouble to the administration.

Apart from convenience, two basic advantages accrue from using sponsors as judges. First, they typify the core upper-middle-class undergraduate society faced by students coming from lower social strata. Second, they are by virtue of the functions of their role put in a position to know the incoming students intimately — a premise well borne out by the data. High agreement is found between sponsors and students on their expectations of how the student will fare in college (e.g., getting very good grades, joining a fraternity, being an important person in school affairs, being a good athlete, etc.).

The sponsors' evaluations of the students in their charge were obtained through individual interviews held two months after the start of the school year. The number of students judged by each sponsor ranged from 3 to 11, the median being 5.

One measure of the extent to which lower-class students are integrated into the undergraduate culture was provided by gauging the sponsors' own personal reaction to the students in their charge. Sponsors were asked whether they, themselves, had found any of these students "difficult to know or to understand as a person" and, if so, why? From their replies, two different categories of "difficult" students can be identified:

1. Those who are socially withdrawn (e.g., "he keeps to himself.")
2. Those whose attitudes are in some way interpreted as peculiar (e.g., "he has a don't-give-a-damn attitude.")

As the findings show, the phenomenon of social withdrawal is concentrated disproportionately in the lower class where one-third of the students are perceived as socially isolated, withdrawn individuals.

TABLE 1   *Social Class Differences Among Students Reported by Sponsors as Social Isolates and/or Unpopular Early in Freshman Year (%)*

(N)	Social Class					Regular Sample (99)
	I (12)	II (49)	III (27)	IV (16)	V and VI (22)	
Social isolates and/or unpopular	33	16	15	44	64[a]	23

[a] One-tailed χ^2_c (1 d.f.) $=12.00$; $P < 0.001$ when classes V and VI are compared with Regular Sample.

A second measure of social estrangement was obtained by having the sponsors make percentile estimates of the popularity the students in their charge would eventually enjoy by the time they are seniors.

When the results on unpopularity and withdrawal are combined, as has been done in Table 1, we are in the best position to appraise the initial social impact of upward mobility. Despite the earlier data indicating that the lower class had in high school made a dramatic shift to a middle-class reference group and, at that time, given evidence of fully the same potential for social success as students from the Regular Sample, once the lower class enter Stanford they are quickly reacted to as marginal individuals on campus. Fully two-thirds of the lower class are perceived as failing to become integrated into the undergraduate society.

Subsequent Reaction

That this experience of estrangement is not a transitory phenomenon is shown by the data in Table 2, where we present the social reaction to the students at the end of freshman year and during the later undergraduate years. For these data, it was necessary to turn to administrative records. Throughout the time a student is an undergraduate, Stanford compiles a series of confidential reports that carefully chronicle his academic and social progress. Of particular importance are the detailed comments provided on the student's ability for getting along with others, his personal traits, and the extent and kind of involvement he manifests in social life and extracurricular activities.

Use of these confidential reports as a data source yields essentially the same definition of social isolation as relied upon in the preceding section. The

TABLE 2   *Social Class Differences in Negative Social Reaction Made to Students Later in Their Undergraduate Career (%)*

	Social Class					Regular Sample
	I	II	III	IV	V and VI	
End of Freshman Year						
Social isolates	00	21	09	25	38	17
Unpopular	11	12	05	00	12	08
Social isolates and/or unpopular	11	27	14	25	50[a]	23
(N)	(9)	(33)	(22)	(12)	(16)	(71)
Later Undergraduate Years						
Social isolates	12	18	25	38	64	24
Unpopular	12	06	07	00	29	06
Social isolates and/or unpopular	25	24	25	38	79[b]	29
(N)	(8)	(34)	(16)	(13)	(14)	(66)

[a] One-tailed χ^2_c (1 d.f.) $=3.65$; $P < 0.05$ when classes V and VI are compared with Regular Sample.
[b] One-tailed χ^2_c (1 d.f.) $=10.18$; $P < 0.001$ when classes V and VI are compared with Regular Sample.

fact that a student may be depicted as quiet and shy is not, by itself, sufficient to classify him as socially isolated. He is categorized as socially isolated only when there are explicit statements that he has withdrawn from his peers.[5]

Inspection of Table 2 reveals that as a group the upwardly mobile do not succeed in overcoming the social barriers initially encountered. At the end of freshman year, still one-half of class V and VI students are depicted as social isolates or as unpopular in the eyes of their classmates. Moreover, in later undergraduate years, when they have moved out of the freshman dormitory to which they were assigned on a random basis and taken up residence in new quarters and with friends more of their own choosing, an even greater proportion of them encounter social difficulties. Seventy-nine percent are reported during this later period to be socially isolated or rejected by their peers.

The exact extent of their estrangement in their new surroundings is best seen by examining Table 3, which summarizes the findings obtained over the undergraduate years. As the results show, the vast majority (77 percent) of class V and VI students have at some point in their undergraduate career encountered difficulty in establishing effective peer-group relations. For a few, the social disruption that occurs is of relatively short duration, lasting less than a year. For 60 percent of the upwardly mobile, however, the period of social

TABLE 3 *Summary of Negative Reactions to Lower-Class Students Throughout the Undergraduate Years (%)*

Reacted to as Social Isolates and/or Unpopular	Classes V and VI	Regular Sample
At Least Once While at Stanford		
Percent	77[a]	35
(N)	(22)	(99)
For One Year or More		
Percent	60[b]	19
(N)	(20)	(91)
For the Entire Period at Stanford		
Percent	40[c]	10
(N)	(20)	(91)

[a] One-tailed χ^2_c (1 d.f.) $=11.25$; $P<0.001$.
[b] One-tailed χ^2_c (1 d.f.) $=12.44$; $P<0.001$.
[c] One-tailed test of exact probability yields a P of 0.003.

dislocation lasts at least a year or longer; and for 40 percent, it continues unabated throughout the time they are at Stanford. Thus, for many, although not for all, the price of social mobility is social isolation.[6]

Perceived Success in College

A fuller comprehension of the social disadvantage at which the upwardly mobile find themselves in their new surroundings is gained by examining

---

[5] The following three examples illustrate the kind of statements relied on for categorizing students as socially isolated.

> John had trouble adjusting to college life. It took him nearly the entire year to become accustomed to being away from home. He tended to live quite unaware of activity around him. In fact, he did not converse with anyone at length. It is only in the past few weeks he has begun to come out of his shell.
>
> He is not well integrated in house activities. Only recently has he begun to be seen often with his roommate. He is the only fellow in the dorm who did not come to our cottage [the faculty resident's] for our evening get-togethers. [The sponsor notes: "He seems to let the group go its own way as long as he can go his."]
>
> I cannot say I know him well, although he has been one of my charges (certainly, one of my brighter ones) all year long. He is extremely independent, quiet in a forceful rather than a meek way, his relations with his neighbors are polite but minimal, and he keeps his own counsel.

[6] That this isolation is the consequence of mobility, not its precursor, is clearly revealed by the sharp and abrupt contrast between the lower-class students' pre-college potential for social success and their actual college experiences. This conclusion is further underscored by findings obtained on twelve lower-class boys who had been specifically singled out in their high-school recommendations as "good leaders." Consistent with these recommendations, the majority had either been major officers in the student body or had held important positions in student government. Those who had not done so had distinguished themselves by major accomplishments in extracurricular activities or in athletics. By all indications, none should have experienced inordinate difficulty in adjusting socially to college life. Yet, once they enter Stanford there is a sharp reversal in their social fortunes. Eight out of the twelve are reported at some juncture in their undergraduate career as socially isolated or rejected by their peers; and for six, this period of estrangement lasts a year or more.

TABLE 4   *Social Class Differences in Sponsors' Expectations of Achievement in Four Selected Spheres of the Student Role (%)*

Achievement Expectations (N)	Social Class					Regular Sample (99)
	I (12)	II (49)	III (27)	IV (16)	V and VI (22)	
Join a fraternity	75	67	63	56	36[a]	64
Get very good grades	25	55	52	69	50	53
Be a good athlete	33	24	41	19	32	28
Be an important person in school affairs	8	24	19	6	5	18
Success in one or more role spheres	92	88	93	88	82	88
Success in both scholastic and nonscholastic roles[b]	8	39	37	38	14[c]	33

[a] One-tailed χ^2_c (1 d.f.) $=4.46$; $P<.05$, when classes V and VI are compared with the Regular Sample.

[b] Nonscholastic success is defined as a person who is expected to join a fraternity, be a good athlete, and/or be a very important person in school affairs.

[c] One-tailed χ^2_c (1 d.f.) $=2.46$; $P\approx.05$.

Table 4, which presents the sponsors' expectations early in the freshman year of the success students in the sample would later attain in four areas of undergraduate achievement: scholastic, extracurricular, athletic, and social life (i.e., fraternity membership). It can be seen that some measure of successful accomplishment is expected of most freshmen, regardless of their class of origin. Moreover, students from classes V and VI are viewed as not handicapped in the scholastic and athletic spheres of undergraduate life where success depends more upon technical proficiency than upon social skills. It is only when successful accomplishment requires some degree of social facility that social class considerations loom as important. One such instance is fraternity membership, which is seen to decline consistently with class position — and abruptly so for class V and VI students. The latter are deemed half as likely as other undergraduates to make a fraternity, a prediction which, if true, would importantly shape their social experiences on campus. Similarly, only a negligible minority of lower-class students are expected to attain a position of prominence in school affairs, this being viewed as mainly the domain of classes II and III.

The findings on perceived success in college, thus, temper what might otherwise be an overly bleak picture of the upwardly mobile. While the data continue to emphasize the failure of the lower class to find ready social acceptance among their peers, they reveal that the opportunity for success is not closed to them in college. Rather, their success is perceived to lie in those spheres where achievement is largely a matter of technical proficiency.

BEHAVIORAL EVIDENCE OF SOCIAL ISOLATION

The evidence so far has been based on observations by others officially in a position to be in close contact with the students and familiar with their progress in college. Their judgments, reflecting as they do the prevailing norms of the Stanford culture, give us considerable insight into the social dislocation that accompanies upward mobility. Nevertheless, it is germane to inquire whether or not the portrait that is gained of the lower class has its counterpart in the actual social and academic experiences of the students. Is there independent behavioral evidence that students from the lower class do not gain social acceptance from their peers? Do their actual accomplishments in college take on the segmental pattern predicted by the freshman sponsors?

Social Acceptance

One indicator of peer acceptance on campus is living-group affiliation. In spring of the freshman year, the student is faced with the choice of joining a fraternity, joining an eating club, or remaining independent. An eating club, an institution distinctive to Stanford (at least in its function), gives the student an intermediate option between the highly organized group life characterizing fraternity living and the socially autonomous existence of being an independent. Like the fraternity, the eating club is a socially exclusive organization electing its own members. Members of each eating club eat together in their own dining hall but, unlike fraternity members, do not live together in a separately established house. Instead, members of all eating clubs are quartered in a common dormitory. The eating club thus provides companionship, and a sense of belonging to a chosen group without the total strictures of organized fraternity life. In this way, eating-club life also contrasts sharply with the dormitory existence facing independents who are more prone to look upon their living quarters as a "boarding house" than as a place for social companionship.

As may be seen, a student's affiliation with a living group provides a rough index of his popularity among his peers. Regardless of whether student popularity is measured by sponsors' estimates early in the freshman year or by admissions office ratings of students' "personal potential" for Stanford, fraternities are found to recruit the most popular students on campus, and eating clubs, those intermediate in popularity. In turn, those who remain independents receive the lowest ratings of popularity.

Social class differences in living-group affiliation offer striking evidence of the extent to which the upwardly mobile are out of the mainstream of undergraduate society. Three-fourths of students in all social classes except V and VI manage to join either a fraternity or an eating club, with one-half affiliating with a fraternity. In contrast, only 45 percent of the lower class join a fraternity or an eating club, and only 20 percent a fraternity. Even their acceptance into a fraternity or an eating club does not necessarily signify that the upwardly mobile have made a successful adjustment to the social demands of undergraduate life. Some have, but the majority fail to become integrated into the living group. Instead, they later appear in administrative records as "loners" — persons who do not mix with the other members of the

house or club. Yet those who remain independent are not exempted from the necessity of having to cope with living in an upper-middle-class environment, for class II students still constitute the model group in the dormitories reserved for independents.

A second indicator of social acceptance on campus is popularity with the opposite sex. Dating is such an elaborately institutionalized facet of campus life that, as Willard Waller long ago noted, it serves as a sensitive barometer of an undergraduate's informal standing in the college peer group.[7] Moreover, the gradient of dating desirability is so clearly recognized and adjusted to on the college campus that it can be an especially traumatic event for the student to perceive himself — and have others perceive him — as one who is unable to get a date. Yet the same barriers that set the lower class apart from other college males also appear to restrict their relationships with college coeds. Information to this effect was obtained by asking students in each of the four interviews how often each month they have coffee and study dates and how often each month they have other kinds of dates. No effort was made to restrict answers to dates with Stanford coeds, though in the majority of cases the dates were with girls attending Stanford. In all four interviews, a substantial minority of the upwardly mobile report being in a situation of not dating.[8] That this situation is clearly in evidence during freshman year, before students have a chance to affiliate with fraternities or eating clubs, rules out

[7] Willard Waller, "The Rating and Dating Complex," *American Sociological Review,* 2 (October, 1937), pp. 727–734.

[8] Undoubtedly, financial factors contribute to the social plight of the lower class, but a simple economic interpretation is not feasible. Seventy-one percent of class V and VI students report owning or having access to a car while they are at college — a figure that is somewhat, but not materially, less than that obtained for the Regular Sample, 86 percent of whom own or have access to a car. Students from the lower class, on the other hand, are handicapped by having considerably less money per month than class I and II students to spend for recreational purposes. (The median amount of spending money available to class V and VI students is $18; for students in classes I and II, $51 and $40.) Nevertheless, they are no more handicapped than students from classes III and IV, who have a similar restricted budget for recreational purposes but do not encounter the same barriers to fraternity membership and dating behavior.

TABLE 5 *Social Class Differences in College Accomplishments (%)*

(N)	Social Class					Regular Sample
	I (12)	II (49)	III (27)	IV (16)	V and VI (22)	(99)
1. Area of Success						
Scholastic	0	18	15	12	32[a]	16
Athletic	8	4	7	19	9	5
Social	33	22	30	25	5[b]	25
Extracurricular	33	39	15	6	18	28
2. Pattern of Success						
Scholastic or athletic	8	22	22	31	41[c]	21
Social or extracurricular	50	43	33	31	18[d]	39
Success in any area	58	57	52	38	50	53

[a] One-tailed test of exact probability yields $P=.09$ when classes V and VI are compared with the Regular Sample.
[b] One-tailed test of exact probability yields $P=.02$ when classes V and VI are compared with the Regular Sample.
[c] One-tailed χ^2_c (1 d.f.) $=2.76$; $P<0.05$ when classes V and VI are compared with the Regular Sample.
[d] One-tailed χ^2_c (1 d.f.) $=2.16$; $P<0.05$ when classes V and VI are compared with the Regular Sample.

considering the low frequency of dating to be a side effect of living group affiliation.

Success Achieved in College

A more balanced picture of the impact of upward mobility is gained by examining the students' record of accomplishment in college. In each interview from the end of freshman year to the time they left college (in some cases, seven years later) a continuing inventory was taken of students' activities, achievements, and awards in all areas of undergraduate endeavor. This information was subsequently checked against calss yearbooks and a variety of administrative records. Besides insuring completeness and accuracy, this check made it possible to include in the final inventory those achievements realized after the terminal spring interviews (e.g., honors and awards conferred at graduation and awards received for spring sports). Using a procedure closely patterned after the High School Achievement Scale referred to above, we classified students as to whether they had been highly or very highly successful in four main spheres of undergraduate life: scholastic, athletic, extracurricular, and social (i.e., achievements centering around the living group). Students classified as successful were ones who had clearly gained general recognition on campus for being top scholars or athletes, being very important per-

sons in school affairs, or being elected leaders of their living group.

The findings reveal what may be best described as a qualified success story for the upwardly mobile. (See Tables 5 and 6.) They are as likely as students from more favored backgrounds to compile a record of outstanding accomplishment over the undergraduate years. Their achievements, however, take on the segmental pattern predicted originally by the freshman sponsors, being concentrated disproportionately in scholastic and athletic endeavors rather than in the realm of social and extracurricular pursuits. The latter is, instead, the domain of class I and II students who together hold 69 percent of the major positions of social and extracurricular leadership on campus.

RESPONSE TO ESTRANGEMENT

Evidence of Alienation

As Table 6 makes clear, the successful attainments of the upwardly mobile have been realized at a social cost. Nine of the 11 who are successful have undergone the estranging experience of moving abruptly from a situation of peer acceptance to one where they are socially isolated or rejected for an extended period. That they are not impervious to this reversal of their social fortunes is

TABLE 6 *Attainments, Social Experiences, and Role Stresses of Upwardly Mobile Who Achieve Success in College*

Student	Inventory of Attainment[a]	Social Experiences[b]		Evidence of Alienation[c]
		First Year	Later Years	
A	*Scholastic:* 1. Phi Beta Kappa, 2. graduation with great distinction, 3. departmental honors.	—	—	Continuous pattern
B	*Scholastic:* 1. graduation with distinction.	—	— to +	None
C	*Scholastic and Extracurricular:* 1. graduation with distinction, 2. election to student legislature.	—	+	Intermittent pattern
D	*Scholastic:* 1. departmental honors.	—	— to +	Intermittent pattern
E	*Athletic:* 1. three varsity letters in major sport.	+	—	None
F	*Athletic:* 1. three varsity letters in minor sport.	—	—	None
G	*Scholastic and Extracurricular:* 1. Phi Beta Kappa, 2. Tau Beta Kappa, 3. graduation with distinction, 4. scholastic award from national professional society, 5. vice president and treasurer of undergraduate professional society, 6. secretary of campus voluntary association.	0	0	None
H	*Scholastic:* 1. Phi Beta Kappa, 2. graduation with great distinction.	— to +	—	Initial response
I	*Extracurricular:* 1. editor of major campus publication.	—	No data	Continuous pattern
J	*Social and Extracurricular:* 1. rush chairman and social chairman of eating club, 2. one of five elected to major legislative post.	+	+	Continuous pattern for first two years
K	*Scholastic:* 1. graduation with distinction.	—	—	Initial response

a Graduation with distinction at Stanford is an honor comparable to graduating *magna cum laude* at other universities; graduation with great distinction is comparable, in turn, to graduating *summa cum laude*.

b Data on social reaction to students are coded for freshman year and later undergraduate years as follows: — = student perceived as socially isolated and/or unpopular, 0 = student perceived as having average acceptance among peers, + = student perceived as popular among peers.

c Alienation is defined by the student's reporting in one or more interviews that he has experienced difficulty at Stanford in "feeling you are a nobody." The patterns of answers are coded as follows: (1) none, (2) initial response [in first interview only], (3) intermittent response [in four interviews], (4) continuous pattern for first two years [but not in senior-year interview], and (5) continuous pattern [reported in all four interviews].

shown by the feeling of self-alienation that emerges. As is true of the upwardly mobile in general, two-thirds of those in classes V and VI who have been outstandingly successful report experiencing difficulty at college in "feeling you are a nobody" — a response given only by a minority of the Regular Sample.

Interrupted Pattern of Academic Achievement

Not surprisingly, the social shock of their mobility experience appears to have had a temporarily adverse effect on their performance in the classroom. As may be seen from Table 7 their grades in freshman year suffer, but in a subtle fashion. Compared to other undergraduates, they do not perform poorly on the average. Nevertheless, it is only in the freshman year that they fail to maintain the relatively superior academic record realized both in high school and in the later undergraduate years. Thus their interrupted pattern of academic achievement appears to serve as apt testimony both to the disruptive consequences of upward mobility and to the resilience of those who succeed in achieving upward mobility.

CONCLUSIONS

The findings detailed above offer convincing confirmation for Sorokin's dissociative hypothesis of upward mobility against its two competing

TABLE 7 *Pattern of Scholastic Achievement by Lower-Class and Other Stanford Undergraduates*

	Median GPA				
	High School	First Year	Second Year	Third Year	Fourth Year
Varied N[a]					
Classes V and VI	3.89	2.34	2.81	3.12	3.13
Regular Sample	3.64	2.37	2.66	2.62	2.93
diff.	+.25	−.03	+.15	+.50	+.20
Constant N[b]					
Classes V and VI	3.88	2.56	2.81	3.12	3.13
Regular Sample	3.64	2.47	2.67	2.62	2.93
diff.	+.24	+.09	+.14	+.50	+.20

[a] N varies by interview phase. For classes V and VI, N = 22, 22, 18, 16, and 15; for Regular Sample, N = 98, 98, 90, 77, and 77.

[b] Analysis is limited to students who complete the undergraduate sequence at Stanford. N for classes V and VI = 15; for Regular Sample, N = 77.

alternatives. The high potential for social success manifested by the lower class before coming to college, plus the evidence we have of their having already made a behaviorally significant shift to a middle-class reference group, rule out the possibility of attributing their social difficulties in their new upper-middle-class surroundings either to a chronic inability on their part to form socially effective relationships with their peers or to the absence of anticipatory socialization. The extended period of estrangement the lower class has undergone, their interrupted pattern of scholastic performance, as well as their own response of self-alienation, clearly attest to the disruptive effects of social mobility. Whether such disruptive effects also accompany mobility achieved through different institutional channels or through educational settings having different institutional arrangements poses significant questions for future empirical research, but ones that lie outside the realm of the present inquiry.[9]

[9] This does not imply that the present findings have no application beyond the Stanford setting. Though considerable caution needs to be exercised in generalizing beyond these parameters, it is our expectation that similar social difficulties will be encountered by lower-class youth at other prestige college and universities in which students must assume residence in a predominantly upper-middle-class environment if they are to avail themselves of the intellectual, economic, and social advantages such schools have to offer.

53 Class and Opportunity in Europe and the United States*

Seymour Martin Lipset · Natalie Rogoff

This article examines the popular notion that Europe, as compared to the United States, has a frozen class structure which keeps people from rising out of the social classes to which they were born. The evidence is that the popular notions are largely mythical and that opportunities for upward social mobility have by no means been eliminated.

The new sociology has in recent years effectively destroyed a number of hallowed myths. Studies of election campaigns have demolished the civics-textbook image of the independent voter who decides the election after weighing all the arguments — we now know that the "independent voters," the men who make up their minds at the last moment, are for the most part the least informed and least interested section of the electorate, as Paul F. Lazarsfeld, Bernard Berelson, and Hazel Gaudet show in their book *The People's Choice* (Columbia University Press). In a recently published study, *Psychosis and Civilization* (The Free Press), Herbert Goldhamer and Andrew Marshall indicate that the almost universally accepted belief that insanity has increased during the past century is untrue. And in the November 1953 issue of COMMENTARY, William Petersen assembled the evidence from a number of studies to demolish the myth that opportunity to rise in the social scale in the United States is shrinking. Examining, among other things, the survey data on the relationship between the occupational status of fathers and sons, Mr. Petersen concluded that the rate of social mobility is probably at its all-time high today, with more people rising above the occupational status of their fathers than ever before in American history.

* Reprinted from *Commentary*, by permission; copyright © 1954 by the American Jewish Committee.

I

If one were to find fault with Mr. Petersen's demonstration that America is still a land of opportunity, we think it would be in his implicit assumption that the United States has a higher rate of social mobility than other countries. High mobility is a relative term; we call the American rate "high" in comparison with what is assumed to be the "low" rate obtaining in the rigid, closed societies of Europe. But is this assumption, traditional and universal though it be, justified, or is it another one of those myths waiting to be destroyed by sociological analysis?

Until recently we simply did not have the data to answer this question. In the last few years, however, sociologists in Germany, France, Great Britain, Finland, Italy, The Netherlands, Sweden, and Japan have made studies of social-mobility rates based on random samples of national populations. Unfortunately, it is not easy to compare these studies with one another, for in almost every country different systems of classifying occupations were employed. But every study (except the British) does differentiate between manual and non-manual (white collar, professional, managerial, etc.) occupations, and most (except the British and the Italian) separate rural from urban occupations.

Thus broad comparisons are possible; and having made them, we can hardly doubt that all of the European societies for which we have data, except Italy, actually have "high" rates of social mobility, if by a high rate we mean one comparable to the American. In each country, a large minority is able to rise above the occupational position of their fathers, while a smaller but still substantial minority falls in occupational status. Indeed, the data indicate hardly any substantial difference in the rates of mobility among France, Great Britain, Germany, Finland, Sweden, *and* the United States. In our opinion, even if the data were completely comparable, they still would not show a great difference among these six countries. The Italian data, it is true, indicate a somewhat lesser rate of mobility in that country than in the other six, but even here the difference does not appear to be great.

Three of the studies — the American, French, and German — permit a statistical comparison if we reduce the occupational classifications to three groupings: manual, non-manual, and farm. The table below compares the proportion of sons in each country who remained in the occupational groupings of their fathers, and the proportion that shifted into different groupings — that is, it compares the occupational "destinations" of men of similar origins in each society. Thus, the first column of the table shows that of 100 sons of American non-manual workers, 71 are themselves engaged in non-manual work, 25 in manual work, and 4 in farming. Notice how similar are the figures for non-manual workers' sons in France and the United States and that the pattern of movement of manual workers' sons in all three countries is well-nigh identical.

There can be no doubt that the data from these three studies refute any claim that social mobility in the United States is on the whole markedly greater than in Europe, where family status allegedly limits positions open to sons.

There is, however, a significant difference revealed in the table below between the United States and the other countries: while the majority of the sons of American farmers have shifted to non-agricultural occupations, in France and Germany seven farmers' sons out of ten stay on the land.

That is, the American urban economy has offered many more opportunities than the European, drawing large numbers of people from rural areas into cities, with the result that the number of people engaged in farming in the United States has declined at a far greater rate than in France or Germany. But this is not so much a reflection of the difference in the rate of social mobility between America and Europe, of any severer limitations imposed by class origins in Europe — after all, the pattern of occupational distribution for the sons of manual and non-manual workers remains approximately the same in France, Germany, and the U. S.; rather it reflects a difference in what is called the "opportunity structure" in these countries. Not the alleged rigidity of European lines — Europe's supposed lower rate of social mobility — but the ability of the expanding American urban economy to absorb much larger numbers of the sons and daughters of the American countryside, explains why America is more of a land of opportunity than Europe.

We have looked at the different social "destinations" of men of the same social origins. Now let us consider the different social origins of men who have arrived at the same destination. This is the conventional approach to the study of social and political elites, but it is just as enlightening when used to examine the origins of *all* strata in society.

We find that there is more movement from the manual worker and farm class into clerical, managerial, and professional jobs in the U. S. than abroad. A larger proportion (52 per cent) of American non-manual workers have manual or farm backgrounds than do their French and German counterparts (35 per cent and 30 per cent respectively). But this is only the other side of the above-mentioned decline of the proportion of Americans engaged in agriculture. The larger movement of Americans into the class of non-manual workers is due, again, not to *a higher rate of social mobility as such,* but to a greater increase in the proportion of non-manual "opportunities" in the U. S., which have expanded at a faster rate than in Europe.

Returning again to the comparison of social mobility patterns, we should like to buttress our conclusion that much of Western Europe has as open a class structure as the U. S. with data from

Father's Occupation	Son's Occupation		
	Non-Manual	Manual	Farm
United States			
Non-Manual: 100%	71	25	4
Manual: 100%	35	61	4
Farm: 100%	23	39	38
France			
Non-Manual: 100%	73	18	9
Manual: 100%	35	55	10
Farm: 100%	16	13	71
Germany			
Non-Manual: 100%	80	20	—
Manual: 100%	30	60	10
Farm: 100%	12	19	69

Son's Occupation	Father's Occupation			
	Aarhus, Denmark			
	I	II	III	IV
I — Professionals, Bus. Exec. & Self-Employed	38%	23%	14%	32%
II — Clerical & Sales	20	28	12	12
III — Manual	41	48	73	52
IV — Farm	1	1	1	4
	Indianapolis			
I	33%	21%	10%	11%
II	29	42	17	15
III	38	37	72	70
IV	—	—	1	4

two provincial cities, Indianapolis, Indiana, and Aarhus, Denmark.

It is clear that there is no substantial difference in the social mobility patterns of Aarhus and Indianapolis. The sons of manual workers have about the same chance of rising in both communities.

The Indianapolis study was primarily designed to find out whether mobility in the U. S. has decreased over time. As Mr. Petersen notes in his article, it demonstrates conclusively that the rate of social mobility in Indianapolis remained constant between 1910 and 1940. Happily, we have a somewhat similar comparison for a European city. One of the earliest quantitative studies of social mobility (Federico Chesaa, *La Transmissione Ereditoria delle Professione,* Fratelli Bocca, 1912) was made in Rome using marriage license statistics for 1908. In 1950 another survey of Rome was made using a representative sample of the population. (This study by Alessandro Lehner is reported in a paper presented to the 1953 meeting of the International Sociological Association.) These two studies suggest the same conclusion as the Indianapolis study: mobility rates have hardly varied in the forty-year period.

There are also a number of studies, made during the 20's, of social mobility in Germany, and these, too, indicate a rate of social mobility (both upward and downwards) which is not much below contemporary findings. The largest single study was made by the German white-collar workers'

union, which secured questionnaire data from over 90,000 white-collar workers in the late 1920's. Almost a quarter of the males in this group, 23.9 per cent, came from working-class families.

To sum up, our evidence suggests that in the United States, France, and Germany, somewhere between a fifth and a quarter of those with fathers in white-collar occupations become manual workers, whereas about one-third of those whose fathers are manual workers rise to a non-manual position, and that this has been the state of affairs since before the First World War.

II

Two questions present themselves. First, why do all the countries for which we have data exhibit similar patterns of social mobility? And second, why did everyone agree in seeing great differences in social mobility between Europe and America when the data in fact show none?

The answer to the first question is relatively simple. In each of these countries, the so-called new middle (white collar) class has grown at the expense of the rural population, and to a lesser extent of the manual working-class population, though this development has gone very much further and faster in the U. S. than in Europe. The "second industrial revolution" has brought about an increase in administrative, office, and paper work rather than in the number of industrial workers. More and more people are needed in each country to manage industry, distribute goods, provide the services required for leisure activities, and run the welfare state. Thus there has to be "upward" mobility within each society.

A second factor that tends to produce upward mobility is a differential fertility — the tendency of those with more money to have fewer children. While shifts in the economic structure have expanded the proportion of the non-manual prestige occupations, the families in such occupations have not been begetting their proportionate share of children. Consequently, even if every son of a high-status family keeps that status, room is left for others to rise into it.

There is also the fact that the ever growing cities in modern industrial countries cannot replenish and enlarge themselves except by receiving a steady stream of migrants from the countryside who take the least desirable positions. The implications of this fact emerge clearly from two studies, one of Stockholm, and the other of a San Francisco area.

In the first study ("Social Mobility in Sweden," a paper presented to the International Sociological Association at Liège in August 1953), two Swedish social scientists, Gunnar Boalt and Carl-Gunnar Jannsson, determined the name and father's occupation of every boy in the fourth grade of the Stockholm public schools in 1936. By checking these same names against the Stockholm electoral register for 1949, they were able to discover the occupations of 94 per cent of the 1936 schoolboy group. To their surprise, 69 per cent were employed in non-manual occupations; over half of the sons of manual workers had entered non-manual work, though the group was only about twenty-four years old in 1949.

The question naturally arose as to where the manual workers of Stockholm came from, since most of the children of manual workers were no longer in that class. To answer this, Boalt and Jannsson went back to the electoral register and recorded the occupations of all males born in 1925, the year in which their original group had been born. Comparing "natives" (those in Stockholm schools in 1936) with "migrants" (those who had *not* been in Stockholm that year), they found that over two-thirds of the "migrants" were manual workers, as compared with less than one-third of the "natives." Comparable findings are also reported for Finland.

This clearly suggests the existence of a cycle in which the children of workers in metropolitan areas are able to climb higher on the occupational ladder while their places below are taken by migrants from smaller communities and rural areas. A similar pattern in the U. S. was detected in a study of social mobility in Oakland, California, conducted by the Institute of Industrial Relations of the University of California. The smaller the community in which one was brought up, the greater the likelihood of remaining a manual worker. (In the U. S., the migrants taking up the lower positions in the rapidly growing cities come from Puerto Rico, Mexico, and Canada, as well

as from the smaller American cities and the countryside.)

Since urban expansion is also characteristic of Western Europe, this pattern of migrants taking up the lower positions is probably uniform. No wonder the rate of social mobility differs so little at the present time among these countries.

III

Given the evidence that the social structure of the U. S. is actually no more fluid than that of Western Europe, the problem remains of explaining why everyone thinks that it is. This is a complex question. We have answered it in part by distinguishing between social mobility as such, and fundamental changes in the "opportunity structure" caused by the rapidly expanding American economy. Thus the precipitous decline in the absolute and relative size of the American farm class, the other side of which is a sharp increase in the number and proportion of non-manual urban occupations, has been mistakenly attributed to a more fluid class structure in the U. S. But this is only part of the answer. The rest of the answer is to be sought in two things: the differences in total national income and its distribution between the U. S. and Western Europe, and the different value systems of the American and European upper classes.

Income, in every class, is so much greater in America, and the gap between the living styles of the different social classes so much narrower that in effect the egalitarian society envisaged by the proponents of high social mobility is much more closely approximated here than in Europe. While Europeans rise in the occupational scale as often as we do, the marked contrast between the ways of life of the different classes continues to exist. Thus, in the United States, workers and middle-class people have cars, while in Europe only the middle class can own an automobile. In the world as a whole, the wealthier countries tend to have a more equitable distribution of income among their social and occupational groups than do the poorer ones, contrary to the view that sees the rich getting richer and the poor poorer under capitalism. (This more equal distribution of income has nothing to do with social mobility, strictly defined: a high rate of social mobility is compatible with wide discrepancies in standards of living, as we find in India and the Soviet Union today.)

This is what one might call the real, or material, explanation of the impression that the European class structure is rigid and the American fluid. However, there is also an "ideological" explanation, and this has not perhaps been given its due weight.

Until the emergence of the Communist societies, the U. S. was the only country in which the predominant conservative as well as liberal ideology asserted the equality of all men. Ideological egalitarianism in the U. S. has not denied or even challenged existing differences in rank and authority. It has, however, insisted that such differences are only justifiable as a reward for demonstrated ability: able men can and should rise. While family background and inherited social position play a role in the U. S., eminent businessmen of even upper-class background point in self-justification to the humble youthful origins from which they have risen. Walter Chrysler entitled his autobiography *The Story of an American Workman,* and a recent magazine advertisement by the Crown-Zellerbach Corporation, one of the largest West Coast businesses, boasts that it started in a push-cart in the streets of San Francisco in 1870.

In Europe, on the other hand, the conservatives, at least until the present century, have rejected egalitarianism. Aristocratic values have patterns of inherited privilege and position are still upheld by much of the upper class of Great Britain, Germany, France, and many other countries. Thus the European conservative would wish to minimize the extent of social mobility. We would hazard that in much of Europe successful individuals of lower-class provenance would seek to conceal rather than publicize their origins.

In the previously cited French survey of social mobility, this motive is considered a problem affecting the very data. The author of the survey says that "it is precisely among those who have experienced the greatest social mobility that reticence [in the interview] may be of most significance. One interviewer, commenting on the refusal of an interview by a respondent, adds: 'I think it was a question of self-esteem; though he is an industrialist, his father was a white-collar worker, and his grandfather's origins were humble.' "

Then, too, advocacy of equality in European society has largely been the function of the left, whose chief charge against capitalist society is that equal opportunity does not exist and class mobility is not possible. Thus European conservatives and radicals both find it to their interest to deny the existence of significant opportunity to rise out of one's class in Europe. In America, on the other hand, the conservatives argue that it has existed and still exists, and the radicals disagree with them solely as to whether there is sufficient opportunity, or whether the rate of mobility is declining.

This is undoubtedly an illustration of W. I. Thomas's sociological dictum, "If men define things as real, they are real in their consequences." Whatever the actual rate of social mobility has been in Europe, it has been *experienced* by Europeans (and Americans) as low; and this illusory conviction of a lack of mobility has served as one of the major stimuli to political activity.

Is it possible that occupational mobility means less in Europe because there is more snobbery there, and one does not move up *socially* as fast, or as far, as one moves *occupationally?* Such data as we have do not support this view. We have German and American data on marriages between persons classified according to their occupations, the former being based on all marriages in the state of Bavaria in 1927, and the latter on Philadelphia marriage licences for the years 1913 to 1916.

One would have expected that the differences between the value systems of the European and American upper classes discussed above would make for higher barriers to interclass marriage in Europe. In fact, however, if the limited and partly non-comparable data for Bavaria and Philadelphia are typical of European and American patterns, such differences do not exist. Indeed, the similarities in interclass mobility patterns revealed by the above table are in some ways more startling than the similarities in occupational mobility patterns considered earlier.

Husband's Occupation	Occupations of Marriage Partners Bavaria and Philadelphia			
	Bavaria 1927 Wife's Occupation		Philadelphia 1913–1916 Wife's Occupation	
	Non-Manual	Manual	Non-Manual	Manual
Non-Manual	59%	21%	60%	23%
Manual	41	79	39	77

Other evidence also suggests that social snobbery in Europe is perhaps not as strong a barrier as many believe. A recent British study reports little difference in the rates of marriage across class lines between Great Britain and America when occupations of the fathers of husbands and wives are compared. (David V. Glass, ed., *Mobility in Britain,* Routledge and Kegan Paul, 1954.) The fact that intermarriage between Jews and Gentiles tends to be higher in Western Europe than in America (see "Jewish-Gentile Intermarriage: Facts and Figures," by Herschel Shanks, in COMMENTARY, October 1953) also suggests that status restrictions may be lower under certain conditions abroad than in this country. It may be argued, in fact, that the more aristocratic and secure an upper-status group, the less emphasis it places on exclusiveness. Thus the patterns of rigid upper-class exclusion of *nouveau riche* families, which W. L. Warner has suggested is characteristic of the highest status groups in American society, may reflect the insecurity which is felt in a highly mobile society where no one can feel that he has a permanent and irrevocable place in the upper class.

But why is it that successful Americans, who are more open about their lower-status origins than successful Europeans, nevertheless seem to show great concern about origins in evaluating a man's status? The answer may lie in the ability of men and groups successfully to uphold contradictory values in different life contexts. In economic contexts, ability is on the whole the criterion; in social contexts, inherited qualities. A recent study of race tensions among automobile workers exposes clearly this human ability to maintain "contradictory" attitudes. Dietrich Reitzes

reports (in *Journal of Social Issues,* Vol. IX, No. 1, 1953) that many of the workers who strongly favored equal job rights for Negroes took part in organized efforts to keep Negroes out of their residential neighborhoods.

IV

Our finding that no significant differences exist between the rates of occupational mobility in America and industrially advanced European countries suggests a need to modify the long held assumption that a large socialist movement and class-conscious proletariat have not developed in the U. S. because of the high rate of American social mobility as compared with the presumed low European rate. Ambitious sons of lower-class fathers are able to rise in *all* Western societies.

What then makes for the difference in political behavior? Apparently, for one thing, the differences in total income as between America and Europe and the degree to which the different classes share equally in that income, and the different definitions of the class structure. Socialism developed in countries whose dominant groups traditionally accepted rigid class differentiation as a basic social value. Marxist doctrine, with its emphasis on class differences, reflected the realities of European society; it reflected less and less of the realities of the American status system as the productivity of the American economy surged upwards. The socialists in Europe did not have to underline the large variations in rewards for different services; this was, and is, an obvious feature of most non-American societies. It is the American assumption of egalitarianism, combined with the 20th-century fact of the greater economic productivity and more equal distribution of income and prestige symbols, that prevents the building up of proletarian class-consciousness in this country.

Further evidence for this general thesis may be found in the fact that there was greater working-class radicalism and class-consciousness in 19th- and early 20th century America than exists today. In the 19th century, the income and consumption gap between the urban classes was much greater than at present. And we find that workers were much more likely to respond to class appeals than today. The slogan, "a rich man's war and a poor man's fight," arose during the Civil War, not during the First or Second World Wars. Local labor and radical parties had greater success between 1865 and 1914 than they have had since. Trade unions were much more outspokenly anti-capitalist in the earlier period. The assembly line and mass production, with the higher wages and more equal distribution of wealth that they make possible, are thus probably more responsible for the development of the American "classless" society than trends in social mobility.

CHAPTER SEVEN

Systems Under Stress: Deviance
and Disorganization

A popular contention holds that discord and corruption are inevitable consequences of modernization, and that the maintenance of traditional social controls is essential if we are to avoid ultimate chaos. Proponents of this view tend to favor only those social changes which, like stricter law enforcement, are designed to strengthen the traditional order. Opponents, by contrast, maintain that many of our traditions actually impede progress and that social reform and reconstruction are necessary for the attainment of desired objectives. Moreover, they often view the deviant, disabled, or otherwise disadvantaged members of the community as potential allies in the struggle for reform.

This conflict between traditional and utopian ideologies is well documented in history, ancient as well as modern. But resolution of the conflict awaits the development of more reliable knowledge about the anticipated and unanticipated consequences of many current reform efforts. Decisions on social problems may be relatively simple in preliterate societies where few strategies are available and a vocabulary for differentiating among problems is lacking. Most modern societies have an extensive repertoire of strategies for handling such problems, yet there is little evidence that one strategy is superior to another in many cases. For some observers, the lack of conclusive evidence seems to justify the notion that social problems should be treated as moral or legal issues and that empirical considerations are of minor importance. Others argue that more research is needed and that solutions to problems can be found if we can agree on the relevant questions. Some reasons for this dilemma are examined below.

System Impairment

The functioning of a social system may be impaired in various ways. Disruptions may result from wars, epidemics, mass migration, economic depressions, and numerous other changes in the environment. Impairment may also occur because the system's strategies are based on erroneous assumptions; knowledge may be insufficient for a viable blueprint to be formulated. Or the system may be hampered by the *deviant behavior* of its members — that is, the members may have inaccurate perceptions of their role requirements, or they may engage in deliberate nonconformity. Finally, the system may be *disorganized;* the norms may be in conflict with one another or there may be discrepancies between the normative and the action subsystems. At the present stage of social and cultural development, it may be that deviance and disorganization are our chief problems of social control.

B. PERSONAL SYSTEM	A. SOCIAL SYSTEMS	
	NORMATIVE SUBSYSTEM	ACTION SUBSYSTEM
	A1. PRESCRIPTIONS	A2. PERFORMANCES
B1. PRESCRIPTIONS	A1, B1	A2, B1
B2. PERFORMANCES	A1, B2	A2, B2

Figure 1

Relationships between deviance and disorganization. The social system is disorganized if there are contradictions in A1 or A2, or if there are conflicts between A1 and A2. Deviance implies that B1 is not consistent with A1, or that B2 is not consistent with A2. In a disorganized system (A1 does not agree with A2), the conforming individual must exhibit discrepancies between his personal prescriptions (B1) and his own performances (B2).

Disorganization appears in many varieties. One is conflict between prescriptions and performances. Conflict between avowed and actual objectives is evidenced by a system which is designed for a given purpose but operates primarily to perpetuate itself. For example, it is argued that our courts and other control agencies are sometimes more interested in preserving their authority than in curbing the amount of deviant behavior. Similarly, the prescribed strategies may be vastly different from those practiced. Thus, our police and courts may sometimes operate under a policy of negotiated justice which makes the penalties prescribed for law violations a rarity in practice.

Disorganization may also occur among the normative prescriptions themselves. Goals may be inadequately defined, contradictory, lacking a pattern of relative values, or without tangible criteria for measuring the degree of their attainment. Strategies may be inconsistent, infeasible, or founded on false information. Roles may be incompatible or mutually exclusive, and so on. Such disorganization is often found in our prisons and other correctional institutions, where the goals of therapy, punishment, deterrence, and social protection may be mutually exclusive, or where the norms of the inmate society may be in conflict with the official rules and regulations.

Whenever disorganization occurs deviant behavior is inevitable. Unless the prescriptions are consistent and compatible, behavior that conforms to one norm must violate another. It follows that an individual's failure to conform to his role requirements may sometimes be due to defects in the social system, even though we may ordinarily try to explain the deviance in terms of the individual's characteristics.

Figure 1 presents a greatly simplified account of the relationships between deviance and social disorganization. In an organized system, prescriptions are in agreement with actions (A1 agrees with A2), while disorganization is evidenced by discrepancies within the normative subsystem (A1), the action subsystem (A2), or between these subsystems (A1 does not agree with A2). Deviant behavior occurs when an individual's prescriptions or performances are not in accord with those of his group (B1 disagrees with A1, or B2 disagrees with A2). Conformity of course implies agreement between the individual and the group. This means that in a disorganized system the individual must exhibit the discrepancies that prevail in the social system in order to conform.

Not all deviance is destructive to the group's welfare. Moralists are people who pattern their prescriptions and performances after the group's prescriptions exclusively (B1 and B2 agree with A1), whereas those whose prescriptions and performances are consistent with the action subsystem (B1 and B2 agree with A2) are pragmatists. Both moralists and pragmatists may be classified as deviants if the social system is disorganized.

The figure helps us to understand why deviance may be at a minimum in stable societies and why it may sometimes serve a useful purpose. Social change, whether approved or disapproved, frequently involves the efforts of deviant individuals who strive for new definitions of social objectives or new strategies for achieving them. Historically, moralists have at times been dominant in numbers and influence, while at other times pragmatists have prevailed. Thus, it is not deviance per se but its impact upon the social system that determines the group's reaction, although most researchers and officials alike have directed their attention toward the control of the undesired varieties.

Research on deviance has been modeled largely after the germ theory of disease and its assumptions concerning single causes and specific treatments. However, the model seems inappropriate in this case, even though the theory contributed significantly to the control of communicable diseases. The causes of deviance are mostly social, not physical, and they involve complex feedback relationships between social and personal systems. Deviance has its highest incidence among people who are confronted by discrepant social norms, who occupy inconsistent positions in a variety of disassociated groups, or who are lacking in social affiliations and socializing experiences.

Treatment aimed only at changing the deviant individual is therefore likely to be ineffective. This is suggested, for example, by experience in the rehabilitation of retarded persons who may acquire proficiency in occupations such as meat cutting or machine repair, but who may nevertheless fail to gain acceptance in the community because they have trouble in cooperating with fellow workers, communicating across the counter with customers, or playing their nonoccupational roles in the broader society. Such inadequate performance may often be partly due to the attitudes of the community's members who may shun the deviants and exclude them from essential socializing activities. Thus, treatment may have to be applied to the people who do the excluding as well as to those who are excluded.

Deviance therefore should not be defined as a property of any given individual. We must also take into account society's reaction to its members' characteristics. This reaction, instead of being a direct consequence of the members' characteristics, depends in part upon society's norms, its conceptions of what is desirable and undesirable, its facilities for identifying undesirable traits or characteristics, and its beliefs and assumptions concerning the propriety of different methods of treatment and control. The norms of the social system are always an essential factor in the definition, identification, and treatment of deviance.

Reactions to system impairment vary greatly in time and place, depending upon the state of the pilot variables. Still most of these reactions can be classified under a few general headings. Some of the most important, historically, are listed below.

Toleration refers to a society's failure to detect its members' offenses, or to the nonrecognition of offenses that are detected. All forms of unofficial action may be included in this category.

Exclusion involves capital punishment, banishment, imprisonment, ostracism, and all other methods by which a society prevents its deviant individuals from participating in certain activities.

Rehabilitation includes the use of therapy, training, or other reform measures in an attempt to change the deviant person while maintaining his involvement in his group or community.

Reconstruction implies the revision of a society's normative or action subsystems, resulting in a redefinition of deviance or a rearrangement of the social structure that assigns people's positions, defines their privileges and responsibilities, or regulates their access to information and other resources.

There is some overlap among these reactions, of course, but they can usually be differentiated by their goals and strategies, both as prescribed and as practiced.

Toleration and exclusion are low feedback options which try to solve the problem of impairment by denying the offense or by eliminating the offender. Neither method calls for any drastic changes in the social system. These options seem to prevail in simple, stable, isolated societies in which people are relatively self-sufficient and the division of labor is uncomplicated. By contrast, rehabilitation and reconstruction are relatively high feedback options, usually calling for rather extensive revisions of social norms and practices. Such high feedback options are prevalent in times of social upheaval or in dynamic societies characterized by an intricate division of labor, elaborate programs of education and training, a high degree of interdependence among members, a pluralistic culture, and easy access to neighboring societies.

Ordinarily, the low feedback methods seem least disruptive of the social order. In fact, toleration seems to be almost universally preferred, especially if the offenses are minor and the victims willing to have the matter settled informally. Even in urban societies, most criminal infractions escape official attention or, in one way or another, avoid some of the impact of the prescribed penalty. In addition, toleration is espoused by many researchers and officials who feel that formal action, by labeling and otherwise stigmatizing the offender, tends to encourage nonconformity.

The extent of toleration varies according to a society's methods of status management. For example, the offenses of large organizations or of professional and white-collar workers may often be handled in civil courts and the violators may be permitted to seek private therapy instead of receiving public punishment. Also, our official stance toward organized crime has long been one of nonrecognition, concealment, or denial; if this protective attitude were abandoned, it would force the overhaul of much criminological theory, which is based primarily on studies of theft, robbery, assault, and similar offenses that are included in the conventional definition of crime.

But even among conventional crimes, toleration may be more prevalent in the middle and upper classes than in the lower classes. This is evidenced by compari-

sons of self-reported offenses and official actions. Self-reports suggest little variation by class or several other status variables. Official actions are nevertheless far
more frequent in the disadvantaged groups. Some observers try to explain these
differences in terms of discriminatory practices by the police, courts, and other
authorities, but the data do not support such a simple conclusion. Class, race, and
many other differences tend to disappear if we take into account variables such as
the attitude or the demeanor of the suspected offenders. Authorities are inclined
to be severe in dealing with belligerent or recalcitrant individuals and lenient with
those who seem contrite and compliant, regardless of class, race, or other symbol
of status. Demeanor, of course, is correlated with status, probably because of
differences in training and experience. But the best studies, by holding the status
variables constant, show that it is attitude, more than status, which determines the
reaction of society.

Toleration and exclusion are close partners in the traditional strategy of control.
When official action is imperative, the most prominent method of control, even in
modern societies, is exclusion. This is especially the case for those occupations and
institutions that can regulate the entrance and exit of their members. Thus, the
lawyer, doctor, teacher, or minister who violates the norms of his profession is
often disbarred from further membership. Although he may remain in the community, his exclusion from the profession is usually complete and permanent.
Moreover, the professions and other preferred positions are frequently connected
by unspoken rules of reciprocity so that exclusion from one of these positions
means, for practical purposes, exclusion from all of them. For example, the disbarred lawyer is not likely to be accepted for training in medicine or social work,
and even the youth who is expelled from school may find his relations with religious
and other institutions similarly affected.

What we have, then, is a policy of multiple exclusions which again serves as a
device for status management. It places a ceiling upon the positions that are accessible to persons who have been ejected from preferred positions because of their
norm violations. There is little evidence on the strength of these barriers against
social mobility, but it seems clear, from a systems viewpoint, that management of
status has priority over rehabilitation of these offenders, and that neither the aims
nor the methods of rehabilitation are employed, to any great extent, in the operation of our middle class institutions.

Rehabilitative efforts have therefore been reserved largely for persons whose inadequacies, apart from their deviance, may prevent them from attaining even the less
valued social positions. Despite the lofty objectives they proclaim, these efforts are
designed primarily to help deviant individuals achieve positions of marginal ac-
ceptability, but not preferred ones. There are exceptions to this rule, no doubt,
but they tend to be more conspicuous than frequent. Society's position seems to
be that people who need rehabilitative services should not attain a higher station
in life than those who receive no special help. As a result, rehabilitation may
constitute somewhat of an obstacle to outstanding achievement and self-realization.
The person who is excluded from the professions may face a barrier of lesser
magnitude.

However, the aggressive pursuit of rehabilitation leads almost inevitably to
efforts at social reconstruction. The focus is not only on the deviant person, but also
on his friends and associates, his family, and his community. Reconstruction involves proposals for changing the system by eliminating some of the main sources

of strain and disorganization. Yet such proposals are strongly resisted because they are likely to disrupt the present machinery of status management. Further, most societies have little experience in planning and implementation of rational systems on any large scale, and efforts along these lines are only beginning.

Social reconstruction occurs more or less continuously, whether planned or not. The rate of change is no doubt faster in modern societies, where a pluralistic culture provides norms of sufficient diversity to satisfy people of heterogeneous backgrounds. This means there may be different conceptions of right and wrong, and even the official version of propriety may be unclear and inconsistent. The definition of legitimacy is changed whenever people can find an acceptable rationalization for a new or a formerly deviant way of doing things. Hence, the prohibition of liquor was abolished on the grounds that "people who want to drink will do it anyway," and the same kind of argument is used for legalization of gambling, registration of firearms, and control of numerous other activities.

Sometimes the rationalizations are accepted by the entire community, but in other cases they may be restricted to certain groups or individuals. During World War II some segments of the business community violated Office of Price Administration regulations because they were regarded as "unconstitutional restrictions" and "invasions of private business." Similarly, many conventional criminals are sustained in their illegal practices by the assumption that "everybody has a racket," "the real criminals never get sent to prison," and "only suckers work." If a person defines the "establishment" as "corrupt" or "prejudiced," this justifies his rebellion. The greater the resistance he encounters, the greater is the motivation to continue his efforts in a "just" cause. In this way deviants' status may be legitimated for themselves and their associates.

Consider, also, the rationalizations of the authorities who deal with deviant persons. Crime is commonly regarded as a deliberate act for which the offender alone is responsible. It reflects a pervasive and usually permanent defect in the offender's character, as evidenced in the motto: "Once a criminal, always a criminal." Punishment and stigma are believed to benefit the offender and to deter. Officials therefore are expected to exhibit, publicly and forcefully, their repugnance against the violation and the violator. Most of the community's conforming members are influenced by the same prescriptions.

As a result, the offender is officially assigned a position characterized by the imputations mentioned. This position may restrict his activities and limit his access to legitimate opportunities. For example, there is no concept in everyday language referring to a legitimate position for ex-convicts. Of course, many offenders do achieve legitimate positions in numerous occupations, including correctional administration, but the maintenance of these positions usually entails concealment of their ex-offender status.

Scientific research is needed to clarify the rationalizations of authorities and deviants alike, and to test them by logical and empirical methods. Obviously, the rationalizations of most criminals are not the properties of individuals, but of groups and subcultures that reward and reinforce their deviant behavior. They are symptoms of social disorganization, not of personal inadequacy, and their influence is not likely to be eradicated by rehabilitative efforts directed at the deviant individual alone. However, authorities' rationalizations are also group products; and if they are inadequate, they too might encourage deviance. Indeed, the evidence, is that both offenders and officials tend to overestimate the antisocial char-

Rationalization
and the
Legitimation of
Action

acteristics of the offenders, while both groups perceive officials as being more authoritarian than they are in fact. The spiralling of such mutual misperceptions, if unchecked, may lead almost inevitably to conflict that could be avoided if the factual information were readily available.

The conflicting goals and strategies of our social control agencies reflect a more fundamental disorganization in the broader society. Where such disorganization occurs, the target of reform and reconstruction must not be the isolated individual, but society itself. Much research on social systems will be necessary before we can engage in reconstructive efforts with any great prospects for success.

CULTURAL, SOCIAL, AND PERSONAL ASPECTS OF NONCONFORMITY

54 Continuities and Discontinuities in Cultural Conditioning*

Ruth Benedict

All culture must somehow recognize the fact that throughout his lifetime the individual is required to play a succession of frequently contrasting social roles. Perhaps the most universally observed are the sex roles, which differentiate behavior expected of males and that expected of females, and the age roles, which differentiate behavior expected of infants, children, youths, adults, and the aged. The discontinuity of the life cycle, from birth to death, and the contradictions inherent in some of the

* Reprinted by special permission of The William Alanson White Psychiatric Foundation, Inc., and Patrick Mullahy from *A Study of Interpersonal Relations*, edited by Patrick Mullahy and published by Thomas Nelson and Sons, New York. Copyright, 1949, by Heritage Press. (Originally published in *Psychiatry*, 1938, 1: 161–167.)

above roles are an inescapable fact of nature. Every man, to fulfill his potentialities, must first play the role of child and then the role of father. In the first instance, he is dependent upon others for his existence, whereas in the latter case he must provide sustenance and security for others. The contrast is definite, often hard.

The ways in which age and sex roles are defined and enforced vary greatly from culture to culture. In some societies the transition from one role to another receives adequate preparation and occurs with little emotional stress. Elsewhere, the transitions may be abrupt and shocking to the persons involved. Generally, transitions are easy to make if they do not involve a process of "unlearning" that which was essential in the performance of the preceding role. Discontinuities occur when aspects of a new role are inconsistent with, or contradictory to, the old. Many investigators believe that such discontinuities are a major cause of anxiety and mental illness.

The following article examines some of the continuities and discontinuities of the conditioning process in several cultures, including ours.

I shall select for discussion three contrasts that occur in our culture between the individual's role as child and as father: (1) responsible–non-responsible status role; (2) dominance–submission; (3) contrasted sexual role. It is largely upon our cultural commitment to these three contrasts that the discontinuity in the life cycle of an individual in our culture depends.

Responsible–Non-responsible Status Role. The techniques adopted by societies which achieve continuity during the life cycle in this sphere in no way differ from those we employ in our uniform conditioning to three meals a day. They are merely applied to other areas of life. We think of the child as wanting to play and the adult as having to work, but in many societies the mother takes the baby in her shawl or carrying net to the garden or to gather roots, and adult labor is seen even in infancy from the pleasant security of its position in close contact with its mother. When the child can run about it accompanies its parents still, doing tasks which are essential and yet suited to its powers, and its dichotomy between work and play is not different from that which its parents recognize, namely the distinction between the busy day and the free evening. The tasks it is asked to perform are graded to its powers and its elders wait quietly by, not offering to do the task in the child's place. Everyone who is familiar with such societies has been struck by the contrast with our child training. Dr. Ruth Underhill tells me of sitting with a group of Papago elders in Arizona when the man of the house turned to his little three-year-old granddaughter and asked her to close the door. The door was heavy and hard to shut. The child tried, but it did not move. Several times the grandfather repeated, "Yes, close the door." No one jumped to the child's assistance. No one took the responsibility away from her. On the other hand there was no impatience, for after all the child was small. They sat gravely waiting till the child succeeded and her grandfather gravely thanked her. It was assumed that the task would not be asked of her unless she could perform it, and having been asked the responsibility was hers alone just as if she were a grown woman.

The essential point of such child training is that the child is from infancy continuously conditioned to responsible social participation while at the same time the tasks that are expected of it are adapted to its capacity. The contrast with our society is very great. A child does not make any labor contribution to our industrial society except as it competes with an adult; its work is not measured against its own strength and skill but against high-geared industrial requirements. Even when we praise a child's achievement in the home we are outraged if such praise is interpreted as being of the same order as praise of adults. The child is praised because the parent feels well disposed,

regardless of whether the task is well done by adult standards, and the child acquires no sensible standard by which to measure its achievement. The gravity of a Cheyenne Indian family ceremoniously making a feast out of the little boy's first snowbird is at the furthest remote from our behavior. At birth the little boy was presented with a toy bow and arrow and from the time he could run about serviceable bows suited to his stature were specially made for him by the man of the family. Animals and birds were taught him in a graded series beginning with those most easily taken, and as he brought in his first of each species his family duly made a feast of it, accepting his contribution as gravely as the buffalo his father brought. When he finally killed a buffalo, it was only the final step of his childhood conditioning, not a new adult role with which his childhood experience had been at variance.

Dominance–Submission. Dominance–submission is the most striking of those categories of behavior where like does not respond to like but where one type of behavior stimulates the opposite response. It is one of the most prominent ways in which behavior is patterned in our culture. When it obtains between classes, it may be nourished by continuous experience; the difficulty in its use between children and adults lies in the fact that an individual conditioned to one set of behavior in childhood must adopt the opposite as an adult. Its opposite is a pattern of approximately identical reciprocal behavior, and societies which rely upon continuous conditioning characteristically invoke this pattern. In some primitive cultures the very terminology of address between father and son, and more commonly, between grandfather and grandson or uncle and nephew, reflects this attitude. In such kinship terminologies one reciprocal expresses each of these relationships so that son and father, for instance, exchange the same term with one another, just as we exchange the same term with a cousin. The child later will exchange it with his son. "Father–son," therefore, is a continuous relationship he enjoys throughout life. The same continuity, backed up by verbal reciprocity, occurs far oftener in the grandfather-grandson relationship or that of mother's brother–sister's son.

From the point of view of our present discussion, such kinship conventions allow the child to put in practice from infancy the same forms of behavior which it will rely upon as an adult; behavior is not polarized into a general requirement of submission for the child and dominance for the adult.

It is clear from the techniques described above by which the child is conditioned to a responsible status role that these depend chiefly upon arousing in the child the desire to share responsibility in adult life. To achieve this little stress is laid upon obedience but much stress upon approval and praise. Punishment is very commonly regarded as quite outside the realm of possibility, and natives in many parts of the world have drawn the conclusion from our usual disciplinary methods that white parents do not love their children. If the child is not required to be submissive, however, many occasions for punishment melt away; a variety of situations which call for it do not occur. Many American Indian tribes are especially explicit in rejecting the ideal of a child's submissive or obedient behavior. Prince Maximilian von Wied who visited Crow Indians over a hundred years ago describes a father's boasting about his young son's intractability even when it was the father himself who was flouted; "He will be a man," his father said. He would have been baffled at the idea that his child should show behavior which would obviously make him appear a poor creature in the eyes of his fellows if he used it as an adult. Dr. George Devereaux tells me of a special case of such an attitude among the Mohave at the present time. The child's mother was white and protested to its father that he must take action when the child disobeyed and struck him. "But why?" the father said, "he is little. He cannot possibly injure me." He did not know of any dichotomy according to which an adult expects obedience and a child must accord it. If his child had been docile he would simply have judged that it would become a docile adult — an eventuality of which he would not have approved.

Child training which brings about the same result is common also in other areas of life than that of reciprocal kinship obligations between child and adult. There is a tendency in our culture to regard every situation as having in it the seeds of a dominance–submission relationship. Even where dominance–submission is patently irrelevant we read in the dichotomy, assuming that in every situation there must be one person dominating another. On the other hand, some cultures, even when the situation calls for leadership do not see it in terms of dominance–submission. To do justice to this attitude it would be necessary to describe their political and especially their economic arrangements, for such an attitude to persist must certainly be supported by economic mechanisms that are congruent with it. But it must also be supported by — or what comes to the same thing, express itself in — child training and familial situations.

Contrasted Sexual Role. Continuity of conditioning in training the child to assume responsibility and to behave no more submissively than adults is quite possible in terms of the child's physiological endowment if his participation is suited to his strength. Because of the late development of the child's reproductive organs continuity of conditioning in sex experience presents a difficult problem. So far as their belief that the child is anything but a sexless being is concerned, they are probably more nearly right than we are with an opposite dogma. But the great break is presented by the universally sterile unions before puberty and the presumably fertile ones after maturation. This physiological fact no amount of cultural manipulation can minimize or alter, and societies therefore which stress continous conditioning most strongly sometimes do not expect children to be interested in sex experience until they have matured physically. There need be no discontinuity, in the sense in which I have used the term, in such a program if the child is taught nothing it does not have to unlearn later. In such cultures adults view children's experimentation as in no way wicked or dangerous but merely an innocuous play which can have no serious consequences.

It is this physiological fact of the difference between children's sterile unions and adults' presumably fertile sex relations which must be kept in mind in order to understand the different mores which almost always govern sex expression in children and in adults in the same culture. A great many cultures with preadolescent sexual license require marital fidelity and a great many which value pre-marital virginity in either male or female arrange their marital life with great license. Continuity in sex experience is complicated by factors which it was unnecessary to consider in the problems previously discussed. The essential problem is not whether or not the child's sexuality is consistently exploited — for even where such exploitation is favored, in the majority of cases the child must seriously modify his behavior at puberty or at marriage. Continuity in sex expression means rather that the child is taught nothing it must unlearn later. If the cultural emphasis is upon sexual pleasure, the child who is continuously conditioned will be encouraged to experiment freely and pleasurably, as among the Marquesans; if emphasis is upon reproduction, as among the Zuni of New Mexico, childish sex proclivities will not be exploited, for the only important use which sex is thought to serve in his culture is not yet possible to him. The important contrast with our child training is that although a Zuni child is impressed with the wickedness of premature sex experimentation he does not run the risk as in our culture of associating this wickedness with sex itself rather than with sex at his age. The adult in our culture has often failed to unlearn the wickedness or the dangerousness of sex, a lesson which was impressed upon him strongly in his most formative years.

Discontinuity in Conditioning. Even from this very summary statement of continuous conditioning the economy of such mores is evident. In spite of the obvious advantages, however, there are difficulties in its way. Many primitive societies expect as different behavior from an individual as child and as adult as we do, and such discontinuity involves a presumption of strain.

Many societies of this type, however, minimize strain by the techniques they employ, and some techniques are more successful than others in ensuring the individual's functioning without conflict. It is from this point of view that age-graded societies reveal their fundamental significance. Age-graded cultures characteristically demand different behavior of the individual at different times of his life and persons of a like age-grade are grouped into a society whose activities are all oriented toward the behavior desired at that age. Individuals "graduate" publicly and with honor from one of these groups to another. By this means an individual who at any time takes on a new set of duties and virtues is supported not only by a solid phalanx of age mates but by the traditional prestige of the organized "secret" society into which he has now graduated. Fortified in this way, individuals in such cultures often swing between remarkable extremes of opposite behavior without apparent psychic threat.

Our chief interest here is in discontinuity which primarily affects the child. In many primitive societies such discontinuity has been fostered not because of economic or political necessity or because such discontinuity provides for a socially valuable division of labor, but because of some conceptual dogma. The most striking of these are the Australian and Papuan cultures where the ceremony of the "Making of Man" flourishes. In such societies it is believed that men and women have opposite and conflicting powers, and male children, who are of undefined status, must be initiated into the male role. In central Australia the boy child is of the woman's side, and women are taboo in the final adult stages of tribal ritual. The elaborate and protracted initiation ceremonies of the Arunta therefore snatch the boy from the mother, dramatize his gradual repudiation of her. In a final ceremony he is reborn as a man out of the men's ceremonial "baby pouch." The men's ceremonies are ritual statements of a masculine solidarity, carried out by fondling one another's *churingas,* the material symbol of each man's life, and by letting out over one another blood drawn from their veins. After this warm bond among men has been established through the ceremonies, the boy joins the men in the men's house and participates in tribal rites. The enjoined discontinuity has been tribally bridged.

I have chosen illustrations of discontinuous conditioning where it is not too much to say that the cultural institutions furnish adequate support to the individual as he progresses from role to role or interdicts the previous behavior in a summary fashion. The contrast with arrangements in our culture is very striking, and against this background of social arrangements in other cultures the adolescent period of *Sturm und Drang* with which we are so familiar becomes intelligible in terms of our discontinuous cultural institutions and dogmas rather than in terms of physiological necessity. It is even more pertinent to consider these comparative facts in relation to maladjusted persons in our culture who are said to be fixated at one or another pre-adult level. It is clear that if we were to look at our social arrangements as an outsider, we should infer directly from our family institutions and habits of child training that many individuals would not "put off childish things"; we should have to say that our adult activity demands traits that are interdicted in children, and that far from redoubling efforts to help children bridge this gap, adults in our culture put all the blame on the child when he fails to manifest spontaneously

the new behavior or, overstepping the mark, manifests it with untoward belligerence. It is not surprising that in such a society many individuals fear to use behavior which has up to that time been under a ban and trust instead, though at great psychic cost, to attitudes that have been exercised with approval during their formative years. Insofar as we invoke a physiological scheme to account for these neurotic adjustments we are led to overlook the possibility of developing social institutions which would lessen the social cost we now pay; instead, we elaborate a set of dogmas which prove inapplicable under other social conditions.

55   Kibbutz in Crisis*

Ivan Vallier

Local problems sometimes result from changes in the community that are independent of changes in the larger society. Famine, pestilence, or the death of a local leader are some examples. But problems connected with trends and changes in the larger society are far more common. This is true of Mayeem Kareem, an agricultural commune in Israel, as indicated in this selection. Israel's vigorous industrialization has stripped the kibbutzim (communes) of some important functions and has substituted the new goal of maximizing production. Note the resulting cultural and organizational problems. Have similar issues occurred in America's agricultural communities? What implications does this study have for the many new nations that are emerging around the world?

INTRODUCTION

The societal-subsystem relationship, a major point of articulation between macroscopic social

* Excerpt from Ivan Vallier, "Structural Differentiation, Production Imperatives and Communal Norms: The Kibbutz in Crisis," *Social Forces,* 40, 3 (March 1962), 233–242. Reproduced by permission. Copyright ©, 1962, University of North Carolina Press.

processes and concrete systems, is a promising but relatively undeveloped area of sociological inquiry. This paper deals with one such relationship, the Israeli society and the agricultural communes (*kibbutzim*). The focus is on an empirical pattern of internal difficulties that presently characterizes these communes, frequently referred to as the "kibbutz crisis," and takes into account two levels of social structure: a level between the kibbutzim and the wider society and a level between one kibbutz and its several subsystems.

THE SOCIOLOGICAL FEATURES OF THE KIBBUTZ

The kibbutz is a unique small-scale system dominated by the values of fraternity and equality. The fraternal, horizontal emphasis encourages close, informal relationships. The equality standard discourages hierarchy and privilege, thereby reducing vertical social differentiation. The key institutional patterns (collective property, cooperative labor, shared distribution, direct democracy, communal dining, collective nurseries, and mutual responsibility) articulate the central values with the exigencies of daily life. Solidarity and informality are the expected bases of member-member relationships.

The kibbutz's way of life is comprehensive for the individual. All of his social relationships (except for occasional trips to the city) are consummated with others who occupy the same formal status position: member-comrade or member-equal. Spiro refers to the kibbutz as a *gemeinschaft*. It is a system viewed by the members as morally right, therefore a set of institutional arrangements valued as an end in itself.

Structurally these systems are highly interdependent. Small modifications in any key relational area have important repercussions throughout the total system. Consequently the kibbutz's normative base restricts the types of structural solutions that can be effected for solving the system problems under changing conditions. Innovations that create status differences, power positions, and unequal privileges have to be carefully guarded against. It is true, however, that some required activities are more problematic for the integration and stability of the norms than others. Production, for instance, is one of the most threatening activities in its sociological implications for it requires the instrumental organization of resources, the legitimation of hierarchically-arranged leadership roles, the disciplining of a labor force, and the routine assignment of differentially rewarding tasks. Various mechanisms, including task rotation, have been instituted to minimize the potentially disruptive consequences of production work. But with the use of these integrative devices, some sacrifice in production effectiveness has to be accepted. To follow a policy of strict rotation means, in actuality, that members not especially qualified to assume key instrumental positions eventually take a turn. Weber has pointed to the relationship between communal norms and instrumental activities as follows: "Communistic systems for the communal or associational organization of work are unfavorable to calculation and to the consideration of means for obtaining optimum production; because . . . they tend to be based on the direct feeling of mutual solidarity."

STATEHOOD AND CHANGE: THE KIBBUTZ'S DILEMMA

The 225 communes, with a membership of more than 80,000, are a fully integrated sector of the society's institutional order and have contributed positively in many ways to Israel's growth and international distinction. However, the kibbutz members have always faced to some degree the dilemma of maintaining a unique normative base and, at the same time, maximizing production goals. Yet the intensity of this dilemma has varied with the change in the kibbutzim's relationship to the larger society.

In the period preceding statehood, 1918 to 1948, this internal dilemma was largely latent owing to the fact that the kibbutzim (as defense posts, immigrant training depots, cultural centers, models of grass-roots communism, and agricultural proving grounds) served a strategic multifunctional role. Hence they were not evaluated by strict standards of economic rationality. During this intense colonization period the kibbutzim were valued for their contribution to diverse goals and correspondingly received great amounts of financial support and positive prestige rewards without having to meet standards of production effectiveness. Land, long-term credit, trained personnel, wholesale trading stores and co-operative markets were made available to the kibbutzim through the wider co-operative structure that formed the basis of the Jewish community. As Barber rightly argues, the kibbutzim benefited greatly from this external support.

With the establishment of the Israeli state in 1948, major structural changes took place in rapid sequence. The Israeli society, geared to reaching major goals effectively, entered a phase of widespread structural differentiation. In this period of major change, the original multifunctional kibbutz was placed in a more specialized role. The bulk of the kibbutzim's quasi-military duties were transferred to the newly-formed Defense Force and their immigrant-training responsibilities were given to units developed for this purpose. In like manner, the kibbutzim's important symbolic role, as pioneer elite, was generalized to the society as a whole. By virtue of their significant land holdings and the agricultural know-how of the members, the kibbutzim's functional position was pared down to one of economic primacy.

In the competitive, instrumentally-oriented post-state period, pressures from the higher councils of government planning and economic policy-making have been placed on all production units. Efficiency teams and productivity institutes were formed to iron out production problems in order to raise levels of output. The kibbutzim, dominating the agricultural sector, were caught in this instrumental push.

The responses of the individual kibbutzim to these pressures have varied. Those aligned with the moderate political parties have attempted to integrate their activities with the trend of events in the larger society. In other cases, particularly among the kibbutzim of the more radical Mapaam group, the communal institutions have been held to with vigor. Nevertheless, the overall picture is one of developing internal strains with several observable results: intermember conflicts, chronic dissatisfactions, moral disillusionment, and membership withdrawals. Serious commentators on this state of affairs speak of "the kibbutz crisis." In a review of these evaluations which attempt to spell out the reasons for this crisis, three major points of view can be discerned: (1) the "evolutionists," who argue that the communal settlement was a good idea at one time but now it has served its purpose and must therefore be replaced with other social forms; (2) the "perfectionists," who claim that the "crisis" is due to a change in the moral fabric of the kibbutz member, that he has changed from a strong idealist to a satisfied family man; and (3) the "anti-collectivists," who see the "crisis" as a result of an inherent incongruity between man's needs and the closed, restrictive, communal life.

These several explanations do not, from my point of view, take into account sufficiently the sociological setting of the "crisis," *viz.,* the relationship between the functional position of the kibbutzim in the larger society and the implications of this instrumental role for their internal functioning. Fortunately, a prolonged field study of one kibbutz made by the author during this "crisis" period provides first-hand materials that bear importantly on a fuller understanding of the consequences of a changing societal-subsystem relationship.

PRODUCTION IMPERATIVES IN THE KIBBUTZ

Mayeem Kareem, the kibbutz studied, is a typical communal settlement of the middle Mandate period. This settlement was established in the 1930's by a group of young German Jews who had trained for agricultural work in the European youth organization of the Jewish Federation of Labour. Membership of Mayeem Kareem in 1954 totalled 375: 160 adult members, 150 children, 20 grandparents, and the remainder, youth groups and agricultural trainees.

Mayeem Kareem's economy consisted of intensive agriculture and several service operations. Ten major divisions, including cereal crops, a dairy, banana plantations, fish ponds, a grain mill, poultry houses, and vegetable gardens, formed the focus of the production operation. In the few years preceding the study, Mayeem's economy had developed both in size and complexity, requiring differentiation along both the skill and power dimensions.

In the course of the year's field work, nine months were spent living and working in the commune. Although intensive interviews were obtained from a sample of 30 adult members, most of the information pertinent to this article was gained through continuous observation and indirect questioning during actual work in various branches of the economy.

Throughout the study, two main problems focused the research: (1) changes occurring in the institutional patterns having to do with increasing production effectiveness and (2) the consequences of these changes for other important aspects of the kibbutz system. The success of the complex economic enterprise required the effecting of several structural changes that contradicted the basic normative expectations of the members. Five of the most important changes are here described.

Criteria For Allocating Personnel To Work Roles

As the economic organization of the kibbutz grew increasingly complex and specialized, the standards for assigning members to occupational roles were modified. The work preferences of the members were increasingly subordinated to the instrumental requirements of the production program. Priority was increasingly placed on the members' differentiated skills, special training and general performance capacity. One of the most important managers made this principle explicit: "The community must give the jobs to the most capable."

The Decision-Making Process

The kibbutz general assembly, consisting of the entire adult membership, is the institutional arena for discussing and deciding on all matters that affect the total system. All members are equally privileged to present a point of view in the weekly meetings. Decisions are reached by a majority of those present.

With the multiplication of occupational activities and production divisions, issues frequently arise from day to day that demand immediate attention and/or appraisal in light of specialized knowledge. In these cases, referral to the general assembly means considerable delay. To avoid this drag, many decisions are made outside the assembly. A veteran member put it this way: "When the farm was small, there were many problems put before the general assembly which would be impossible now. Taking out five pounds used to be a decision of the members, now one thousand can be taken out by a special committee." The acceptance of responsibility for making *minor* decisions outside the general assembly in the interest of settling an issue and sustaining the production work has led to the making of *more important* decisions in a similar way. In Mayeem Kareem the bulk of decision-making regarding the planning and policy of the economy were being made in a few small committees which had earlier functioned as advisory or implementing groups. One member commented as follows: "The *meshek* (farm operation) has changed and the various committees get more rights." In the interest of effectiveness, the executive farm committee, the secretariat, and several "ad hoc" committees were assuming a larger and larger role in areas of importance that were legitimately the responsibility of the general assembly. As one member volunteered, "Last year important decisions were being made by the farm committee 'unofficially.' " Clearly, the demands of the production operation placed considerations of decision-making efficiency over those of equality and diffuse responsibility. Mayeem Kareem had not only created new production divisions and new occupational roles but had also shifted functional responsibilities to structures not originally intended to carry them.

The Incipient Formation Of An Elite Leadership Group

In kibbutz ideology, all members are equal. This equality means, among other things, that all members have equal responsibilities to serve both as leaders and as ordinary laborers. Rosenfeld has shown, however, that even in the kibbutzim talent rises to the top because of the demand for leadership capacity. In Mayeem Kareem the development of an elite group among top coordinating and managerial positions was in evidence. However, this group was not a solid, exclusive, self-conscious stratum.

The members who occupied these top roles were identified for a five-year period, 1949–1954. From a membership of more than 150 adults, Mayeem Kareem had given the top leadership responsibilities for the five-year period to 31 members, less than a fifth of those eligible. And among these 31 top leaders, one person had seven key roles in the five-year period, five members had each held five roles, three had had four key roles, and five others had occupied three key roles.

Adoption Of Formal Communication Techniques

The publication of a weekly news sheet, "The Yomim," represented another innovation in Mayeem Kareem. This news sheet provided the members with pertinent information on decisions made or developments pending. The news sheet gave an account of the main topics currently under consideration by the central committee and a breakdown of the members' votes. Other topics included were crop sales, production results, and equipment acquisitions. This news sheet functioned to provide the members with a wider understanding of the production activities in the kibbutz. In earlier years the members had known "what was going on." Increases in complexity of operation and the segmentation of work activities led to communication gaps. Members of one economic division were often unaware of the problems and/ or accomplishments of other divisions. The kibbutz in a period of rapid expansion had grown beyond the sphere of comprehension of the individual member. Specialization, hurried schedules, and an increase in production efforts worked against the informal patterns which had functioned effectively only a few years earlier.

Hired Laborers

The fifth change Mayeem Kareem was making in this post-state production era centered on the recruitment of additional laborers. Mayeem, at the time of the study, had practiced the policy of hired laborers for one year. It represented, therefore, a very recent change, but one that was most conspicuous. Since the principle of self-labor was so dominant in the kibbutz value system, this form of exploitation had been avoided in every way.

The number of hired laborers working in Mayeem Kareem varied with the season. For example, during the harvest period as many as 25 or 30 were employed. About 15 men were hired on a more permanent basis. However, even these were not contracted for a specific time. They were strictly defined as "temporary" help. These hired laborers made up a very valuable, low-status, mobile work force for the commune. The hirelings were expected to work a full nine-hour day in any division which needed them. At all times there existed a clear-cut division between the members and the hired laborers with respect to the type of work assigned.

TYPES OF COMPLICATIONS AND STRAINS ATTENDING CHANGES

Periods of change are inevitably periods of stress and strain. Modifications in social structure have unanticipated consequences, not all of which are positive for the system. Under pressure to raise production effectiveness, steps were taken in Mayeem Kareem to allocate resources more effectively. This entailed changes, the most important of which have been briefly described above.

The second focus of the field work was on the difficulties and problems that followed from the adjustments in the instrumental sub-system. These are defined as a series of complications attending the changes in the production operation. The four most important ones are as follows:

Inflexibility Of The Labor Force

With increased specialization, the chances for occupational tenure increased. Under these con-ditions, members became attached to their jobs and to the differential privileges gained from them. When the production schedule had to be changed and members reallocated, the members assigned to the more specialized and rewarding jobs showed an unwillingness to move quickly into other work roles critical for the completion of a job. Tractor drivers, for example, demonstrated strong resistance when the work manager assigned them to uncompleted manual work.

The need for occupational specialization in the production operation led to worker-job identifications which interfered with the redistribution of the labor force when the work schedule had to be shifted unexpectedly. The exigencies of agricultural production require a flexible work force, yet if this operation is large and complex, specialization is also needed. By emphasizing the latter imperative, Mayeem Kareem indirectly encouraged a set of worker attitudes blocking labor mobility and quick reassignment.

Reduction Of Worker Satisfactions For the Unskilled Member

Paralleling the semi-skilled and skilled workers' attachments and satisfactions were the dissatisfactions on the part of the members who lacked special training or leadership ability. Increasingly, the unskilled workers found themselves members of a labor reservoir viewed as a ready source of energy for the many difficult and less attractive jobs that seemed to abound in the kibbutz. These members realized the implications of this status: that their opportunities for assignment to more rewarding jobs were very small. On those occasions when an unskilled member asked for a less difficult job he would receive the answer: "But you can't handle it well." If he asked for the privilege of learning the skill, the usual answer was "We can't take the time now. Maybe next year." For the most part the kibbutz had to informally postpone this kind of on-the-job training for this would take away a needed laborer and would generally complicate the reassignment of jobs to members who were already proficient. It was not simply a decision to hold the aspirant back but rather that the system did not allow the degree of "resource waste" necessary for training the new man.

Dissatisfaction Of Women

A third consequence of the more rational use of production resources was the gradual exclusion of women from direct production tasks. Although the kibbutzim's ideology places unusual emphasis on sexual equality in all spheres excepting the reproductive, it is gradually recognized that women cannot carry the same burden of work in the field as the men. This pattern in the Israeli communes has been discussed elsewhere, but not in the context of the theoretical problem examined here. Hence, the characteristics of the pattern in Mayeem Kareem should be noted. Out of the total of 84 adult women, only one worked regularly in the field. A second woman assisted with the poultry, a third worked in the dairy. Other than these, the women's occupations were limited to one of the following spheres: laundry, kitchen, dining room, serving room, children's houses (including teaching and nursing).

The symptoms of the women's dissatisfactions came out in direct verbal criticisms, through a pattern of work tardiness, in heated conflicts with the work assigner, and in worker-worker squabbles during the day. The women, socialized to an equality-dominated system, were consistently faced with facts to the contrary. This discrepancy was given a semblance of meaning by relating the pattern to the requirements of the economy and to the "good of the whole kibbutz." But this surface explanation did not prove strong enough to suppress the negative feelings many of the women expressed.

The "Refusal Pattern" — Responsibility Without Power

Paralleling the dissatisfactions and tensions arising from the emergence of divisions in Mayeem Kareem's labor force of equals is the problem of exercising delegated authority and its implications for motivating members to fulfill key leadership positions having to do with management, organizing production activities, allocating scarce resources, and assigning members to work tasks. This is a phenomenon of serious proportions and one which appears to be on the increase.

The members who serve as leaders occupy positions which are legitimated but not fully insti-tutionalized, *viz.,* the positions are only reluctantly accorded a place in a system based on equality and voluntary co-operation. As the force of production goals makes greater inroads on the kibbutz's internal activities, these leaders gain increased responsibility. Yet the added burdens of leadership are not accompanied by proportional increases of formal power. Even though a manager is given full responsibility to delegate, sanction, and direct, he is empirically involved in a web of solidary, affective, equalitarian expectations which dampen the sharp, straightforward exercise of authority.

The members who accept the task of directing community operations are made responsible for successful achievement and yet are limited in the use of controls. A branch manager cannot lower a member's wages if he fails to perform. Nor can he "fire" him. The responsibility of balancing heavy work requirements with communal norms, i.e., "expected solidarity and equality," complicates the effectiveness of the leader's efforts. This is essentially the problem of discipline versus affectivity, a latent dilemma in all communal systems but a major source of strain when an attempt is made to increase an accustomed pace of instrumental performance.

Strains attend leadership in the kibbutz because leaders experience contradictory expectations, "You should be responsible and effective, but you should not exercise power." If the leader fails to guide his division or activity to success, he is criticized for incompetence. Similar responses from others occur, on the other hand, if the leader is "authoritarian" and severe. This leadership dilemma and the concurring strain leads many members to withdraw from community responsibility. This reluctance to accept public positions may be referred to as the "refusal pattern."

The refusal pattern takes shape when the general assembly meets to elect members to the central positions. The members who are unwilling to accept these posts use a variety of excuses: lack of ability ("someone else can do it better than I"); commitment to other responsibilities ("I am already serving on the Housing Committee"); health, family troubles, or the lack of a replacement ("who will do the job I now have?"). Interviews covering this topic of community responsibility indicated the following characteristics of the pattern: (1) there was unanimous agreement among the members questioned that the refusal pattern existed; (2) the members noted that the refusal pattern had increased over the recent years both in frequency and scope; and (3) the amount of refusal varied with the type of position that was being reassigned. Refusals were principally related to positions which required the member to take action or make decisions which had consequences for the whole community and thereby placed the occupant in "the public's eye" where his everyday actions and long-term efforts were easy to evaluate. These positions, in addition, usually required the member to give up or sacrifice some of his non-occupational interests, including after-hours time and family associations. In short, criticism is feared and leadership responsibility is perceived as separating one from the informal community and his family-leisure hours.

Those who were willing to fulfill leadership roles, meaning that they had the capacity to tolerate public disapproval and evaluation, were constantly or continually allocated by the community to the public hot spots. In this pattern there tended to be a tacit agreement on the part of the refusing members that those in charge could go ahead and run the show. This led to a withdrawal of support from the leaders and to a retreat from an equal share of communal responsibility. The over-all picture of these central positions indicated that only a minority of the members were willing to undertake the heavy responsibilities and this increased the rank-and-file versus elite cleavage in the community. The nonleaders were apprehensive about accepting responsibility yet resented the pattern that was emerging. This pattern of political apathy and its stratification consequences increased in turn both the responsibility and the strain of the occupants. The basic principles of the kibbutz were being violated, and no easy solution was at hand.

A SOCIOLOGICAL INTERPRETATION OF THE CRISIS

Mayeem Kareem during the post-state period is encountering serious internal problems. The research points clearly to these difficulties as having developed in relation to increased task responsibilities connected to the pressures for raising the effectiveness of production activities. Mayeem Kareem's economy requires a complex division of labor. The intensity and scope of the total production operation are forcing changes in the structure of power, in the organization of work, and in the occupational role system. These adjustments are helping the kibbutz achieve its short-run production goals. But since these developments toward formality, hierarchy, specialization, and diversity have taken place within a communal institutional framework, the entire system has been affected. Basic changes in the instrumental subsystem have had repercussions for other aspects of the collective life. Intermember tensions have developed in those instances where the communal norms are subordinated to more instrumental considerations. Communication patterns on an informal level are breaking down. Cliques are developing in the wider community along lines that reflect the various members' positions in the occupational system. Leaders in the work situation tend to seek the companionship of other division leaders during leisure hours. The over-all solidarity of the kibbutz can no longer be taken for granted. *Mayeem Kareem is attempting to carry out a complex production operation within the institutional limits of an extreme communal pattern.* The crucial relationship between the instrumental requirements of the commune and its ideal institutional basis has become a major source of strain.

It is the conclusion of this paper that the kibbutzim's complex internal strains are closely related to the incongruence between the communal norms governing the kibbutzim and their functional position in the wider society. It does not appear that the sociological problem of the kibbutzim can be understood by limiting the analysis to the internal features. The kibbutzim are, from the wider society's standpoint, mainly production units. The new structures that were established in the period following the formation of the Israeli state in 1948 took over many of the more expressive functions that the kibbutzim had helped to carry during the Mandate period. Structural differentiation led to the specialization of concrete groups or collectivities along key functional lines. The kibbutzim, as a group of units, were "specialized" relative to the adaptive problem and are now primarily units of the economy.

In discussing the problem of structural differentiation, Parsons states that with respect to the value pattern of a societal subsystem "Its direction of differentiation is defined by the primary function of the subsystem for the larger system of which it is a part." A business firm, for example, belongs to the economy and, on a higher level, to the adaptive or instrumental subsystem. The business firm's function is to produce a certain type of goods or services. The roles that are institutionalized within this production unit are those which stress performance, specificity, discipline, and universalism. The business firm's main value pattern is, therefore, appropriate to the subsystem in which it is located. The business firm, in its instrumental role, is integrated in terms of norms which stress "economic rationality." The kibbutz, in its present instrumental role, is a communal system integrated on the basis of "moral-integrative" values, the polar opposite of those functional for the firm. In explaining the difficulties that are presently being encountered by the kibbutzim, it is important to consider this difference. These communes, because of a unique historical situation, illustrate a sociological problem which may be referred to as "value pattern inappropriateness." The norms or values governing role relationships in the kibbutzim are not appropriate to the production tasks they are now emphasizing.

I interpret this incongruity or inappropriateness between the kibbutzim's functional role and their institutionalized value patterns as one of the basic sociological factors which has given rise to the difficulties or "crisis" within the kibbutz. Production imperatives, hypothetically, always pose problems for communal systems. In the kibbutz, however, these production imperatives are exaggerated. This emphasis has increased the potential for conflict between the values and the instrumental subsystem.

56 Conversion to a Deviant Perspective*

John Lofland · Rodney Stark

Groups and communities everywhere develop ideological justifications for their way of life, more or less organized perspectives which provide a comprehensible picture of man's place in the world. When a person exchanges one such perspective for another, we refer to the process as an example of conversion. Conversion often involves a shift from one popular perspective to another that has equal community support, from Catholicism to Humanism, from conservative to liberal, from artist to scientist, and so on. However, the frequent emergence of extremist organizations shows that sometimes an individual will relinquish a popular perspective for one that is almost universally condemned. Below is a study of the conversion process in a small religious cult that predicted restoration of the Garden of Eden by 1967. The authors formulate a general theory of conversion that may have relevance to the study of deviant perspectives in many fields of behavior.

....

In this paper we shall outline a model of the conversion process through which a group of people came to see the world in terms set by the doctrines of one such obscure and devalued perspective — a small millenarian religious cult. Although it is based on only a single group, we think the model suggests some rudiments of a general account of conversion to deviant perspectives. But the degree to which this scheme applies to shifts between widely held perspectives must, for now, remain problematic.

* Excerpted from the *American Sociological Review*, Vol. 30 (December, 1965), pp. 862–875. Reprinted by permission. Copyright © 1965 by The American Sociological Association.

BACKGROUND

Our discussion is based on observation of a small, millenarian cult headquartered in Bay City,[1] a major urban center on the West Coast. This "movement" constitutes the American following of a self-proclaimed "Lord of the Second Advent," a Mr. Chang, who has attracted more than 5,000 converts in Korea since 1954. The "Divine Precepts," the doctrine Chang claims was revealed to him by God, concerns a complete "Restoration of the World" to the conditions of the Garden of Eden by 1967. The message was brought to this country by Miss Yoon-Sook Lee, a graduate of Methodist seminaries, and a former professor of social welfare at a large, church-supported, women's college in Seoul.

In 1959 Miss Lee arrived in a university town (here called Northwest Town) in the Pacific Northwest, and in two years gained five totally committed converts to the Divine Precepts (hereafter referred to as the D.P.). In December, 1960, after difficulties with local clergymen and public opinion, largely touched off when two female converts deserted their husbands and children, the group moved to Bay City.

By mid-1963, 15 more converts had been gained and by the end of 1964 the cult numbered more than 150 adherents. Converts were expected to devote their lives to spreading "God's New Revelation" and preparing for the New Age theocracy which God and a host of active spirits were expected to create on earth shortly. Typically the converts lived communally in a series of houses and flats, contributed their salaries from menial jobs to the common treasury, thus supporting Miss Lee as a full-time leader, and gave all their spare time to witnessing and otherwise proselytizing.

In this brief report, analysis will be limited to the single problem of conversion.[2] Under what conditions and through what mechanisms did persons come to share the D.P. view of the world, and, conversely, who rejected this perspective?

The logical and methodological structure of the analysis is based on a "value-added"[3] conception. That is, we shall offer a series of seven (more or less) successively accumulating factors, which in their total combination seem to account for conversion to the D.P. All seven factors seem necessary for conversion, and together they appear to be sufficient conditions.

The sequential arrangement of the seven conditions may be conceived in the imagery of a funnel; that is, as a structure that systematically reduces the number of persons who can be considered available for recruitment, and also increasingly specifies who is available. At least theoretically, since the mission of the cult was to "convert America," all Americans are potential recruits. Each condition narrows the range of clientele: ultimately, only a handful of persons responded to the D.P. call.

Typically, and perhaps ideally, the conditions develop as presented here, but the temporal order may vary. The ordering principle is *activation,* rather than temporal occurrence alone: the time of activation is the same whether a condition exists for a considerable time prior to its becoming relevant to D.P. conversion or only develops in time to accomplish conversion.

Data were gathered through participant observation in the cult from early 1962 to mid-1963. Further information was obtained from interviews with converts, their acquaintances, families, and work-mates; with persons who took some interest in the D.P. but were not converts; and with a variety of clergymen, officials, neighbors, employers and others in contact with the adherents. Less intensive observation was conducted through mid-1964.

Although complete data pertinent to all seven steps of the conversion model were not obtainable for all 21 persons who were classified as converts by mid-1963, full information on all seven factors was available for 15 converts. All the available data conform to the model. In presenting biographical information to explicate and document the model, we shall focus on the most central of

---

[1] All names that might compromise converts' anonymity have been changed.

[2] Other aspects of the cult's formation, development, maintenance and proselytization procedures are analyzed in John Lofland, *Doomsday Cult,* Englewood Cliffs, N.J.: Prentice-Hall, 1966.

[3] Neil J. Smelser, *Theory of Collective Behavior,* New York: The Free Press of Glencoe, 1963, pp. 12–21. See also Ralph Turner, "The Quest for Universals in Sociological Research," *American Sociological Review,* 18 (1953), pp. 604–611.

the early converts, drawing on material from less central and later converts for illustrations. The converts were primarily white, Protestant, and young (typically below 35); some had college training, and most were Americans of lower middle-class and small-town origins.

CONVERSION OPERATIONALLY DEFINED

How does one determine when a person has "really" taken up a different perspective? The most obvious evidence, of course, is his own declaration that he has done so. This frequently takes the form of a tale of regeneration, about how terrible life was before and how wonderful it is now.[4] But verbal claims are easily made and simple to falsify. Indeed, several persons who professed belief in the D.P. were regarded as insincere by all core members. A display of loyalty and commitment, such as giving time, energy, and money to the D.P. enterprise, invariably brought ratification of the conversion from all core members, but to require such a display as evidence of "actual" conversion overlooks four persons who made only verbal professions but were universally regarded as converts by core members. To avoid this difficulty two classes or degrees of conversion may be distinguished: *verbal converts,* or fellow-travelers and followers who professed belief and were accepted by core members as sincere, but took no active role in the D.P. enterprise; and *total converts,* who exhibited their commitment through deeds as well as words.

Up to a point, the same factors that account for total conversion also account for verbal conversion and initially we shall discuss the two groups together. Later we shall attempt to show that verbal conversion is transformed into total conversion only when the last stage in the conversion sequence develops.

A MODEL OF CONVERSION

To account for the process by which persons came to be world-savers for the D.P., we shall investigate two genres of conditions or factors. The first, which might be called *predisposing conditions,* comprises attributes of persons *prior* to their contact with the cult. These are background factors, the conjunction of which forms a pool of potential D.P. converts. Unfortunately, it has become conventional in sociology to treat demographic characteristics, structural or personal frustrations, and the like, as completely responsible for "pushing" persons into collectivities dedicated to protest against the prevailing social order. These factors are not unimportant, but a model composed entirely of them is woefully incomplete. The character of their incompleteness is expressed by a Meadian paraphrase of T. S. Eliot: "Between the impulse and the act falls the shadow." The second genre of conditions is this shadowed area, the situational contingencies.

Situational contingencies are conditions that lead to the successful recruitment of persons predisposed to the D.P. enterprise. These conditions arise from confrontation and interaction between the potential convert and D.P. members. Many persons who qualified for conversion on the basis of predisposing factors entered interpersonal relations with D.P. members, but because the proper situational conditions were not met, they did not become converts.

With these two classes of factors in mind, we may turn to a discussion of the first and most general of predisposing conditions.

1. Tension. No model of human conduct entirely lacks a concept of tension, strain, frustration, deprivation, or other version of the hedonic calculus. And, not surprisingly, even the most cursory examination of the life situations of converts before they embraced the D.P. reveals what they at least *perceived* as considerable tension.[5]

This tension is best characterized as a felt discrepancy between some imaginary, ideal state of affairs and the circumstances in which these people saw themselves caught up. We suggest that acutely felt tension is a necessary, but far from sufficient condition for conversion. That is, it creates some disposition to act. But tension may be resolved in

---

[4] Peter Berger has given us a delightful characterization of the reconstructive functions of such tales. See his *Invitation to Sociology,* New York: Doubleday Anchor, 1963, Ch. 3.

[5] We conceive this tension as subjective to avoid judgments about how tension-producing the "objective" circumstances actually were, attending instead to the way these circumstances were experienced.

a number of ways (or remain unresolved); hence, that these people are in a tension situation does not indicate *what* action they may take.

Just as tension can have myriad consequences, its sources can also be exceedingly disparate. Some concrete varieties we discovered were: longing for unrealized wealth, knowledge, fame, and prestige; hallucinatory activity for which the person lacked any successful definition; frustrated sexual and marital relations; homosexual guilt; acute fear of face-to-face interaction; disabling and disfiguring physical conditions; and — perhaps of a slightly different order — a frustrated desire for a significant, even heroic, religious status, to "know the mind of God intimately," and to be a famous agent for his divine purposes.[6]

....

2. Type of Problem-Solving Perspective. Since conversion to the D.P. is hardly the only thing people can do about their problems, it becomes important to ask what else these particular people could have done, and why they didn't. Because people have a number of conventional and readily available alternative definitions for, and means of coping with, their problems, there were, in the end, very few converts to the D.P. An alternative solution is a perspective or rhetoric defining the nature and sources of problems in living and offering some program for their resolution. Many such alternative solutions exist in modern society. Briefly, three particular genres of solution are relevant here: *the psychiatric, the political* and *the religious.* In the first, the origin of problems is typically traced to the psyche, and manipulation of the self is advocated as a solution. Political solutions, mainly radical, locate the sources of problems in the social structure and advocate reorganization of the system as a solution. The religious perspective tends to see both sources and solutions as emanating from an unseen and, in principle, unseeable realm.

The first two secular rhetorics bear the major

weight of usage in contemporary society. No longer is it considered appropriate to regard recalcitrant and aberrant actors as possessed of devils. Indeed, modern religious institutions tend to offer a secular, frequently psychiatric, rhetoric concerning problems in living. The prevalence of secular definitions of tension is a major reason for the scarcity of D.P. converts. Several persons, whose circumstances met other conditions of the model, had adopted a psychiatric definition of their tensions and failed to become converts. In one exaggerated instance, an ex-GI literally alternated residence between the D.P. headquarters and the psychiatric ward of the veterans' hospital, never able to make a final decision as to which rhetoric he should adopt.

All pre-converts were surprisingly uninformed about conventional psychiatric and political perspectives for defining their problems. Perhaps those from small towns and rural communities in particular had long been accustomed to define the world in religious terms. Although all pre-converts had discarded conventional religious outlooks as inadequate, "spiritless," "dead," etc., prior to contact with the D.P., they retained a *general propensity to impose religious meaning on events.*

Even with these restrictions on the solutions available for acutely felt problems, a number of alternative responses still remain. First, people can persist in stressful situations with little or no relief. Second, persons often take specifically problem-directed action to change troublesome portions of their lives, without adopting a different world view to interpret them.

....

Third, a number of maneuvers exist to "put the problem out of mind." In general these are compensations for or distractions from problems in living: e.g., addictive consumption of the mass media, pre-occupation with child-rearing, or immersion in work. More spectacular examples include alcoholism, suicide, promiscuity, and so on.

....

In any event, we may assume that many persons with tensions not only explore these possible strategies, but succeed in some cases in "making it,"

---

[6] It is currently fashionable to reduce this last to more mundane "real" causes, but it is not necessary here to pre-judge the phenomenology.

and hence, are no longer potential D.P. recruits.[7]

3. Seekership. Whatever the reasons, preconverts failed to find a way out of their difficulties through any of the strategies outlined above. Their need for solutions persisted, and their problem-solving perspective was restricted to a religious outlook, but all pre-converts found conventional religious institutions inadequate as a source of solutions. Subsequently, each came to define himself as a religious seeker, a person searching for some satisfactory system of religious meaning to interpret and resolve his discontent, and each had taken some action to achieve this end.

Some hopped from church to church and prayer group to prayer group, pursuing their religious search through relatively conventional institutions. A male convert in his early twenties recounted:

My religious training consisted of various denominations such as Baptist, Methodist, Congregationalist, Jehovah's Witnesses and Catholicism. Through all my experiences, I refused to accept . . . religious dogma . . . because it was Truth I was seeking, and not a limited belief or concept.

Others began to explore the occult milieu, reading the voluminous literature of the strange, the mystical and the spiritual and tentatively trying a series of such occult groups as Rosicrucians, Spiritualists and the various divine sciences.

....

Or, the seeker might display some amalgam of conventional and unusual religious conceptions, as illustrated by a male convert's sad tale:

I was reared in a Pentecostal church and as a child was a very ardent follower of Christianity. Because of family situations, I began to fall away and search for other meanings in life. This began . . . when I was about 12 years old. From that time on, my life

was most of the time an odious existence, with a great deal of mental anguish. These last two years have brought me from church to church trying to find some fusion among them. I ended up going to Religious Science in the morning and fundamentalist in the evening.

Floundering about among religions was accompanied by two fundamental postulates that define more specifically the ideological components of the religious-seeker pattern. Although concrete pre-convert beliefs varied a good deal, all of them espoused these postulates about the nature of ultimate reality.

First, they believed that spirits of some variety came from an active supernatural realm to intervene in the "material world." Such entities could, at least sometimes, "break through" from the beyond and impart information, cause "experiences" or take a hand in the course of events.

Second, their conception of the universe was teleological, in the sense that beyond all appearances in the "sensate world" exists a purpose for which every object or event is created and exists. The earth is as it is to meet the needs of man, for example, and man manifests the physical structure he does to do the things he does. More important, man himself as a phenomenon must "be on earth" because, somewhere, sometime, somehow, it was decided that *homo sapiens* should "fulfill" a purpose or purposes. Accordingly, each person must have been "put on earth" for some reason, with some sort of "job" to perform.

Beliefs were typically no more specific than this. The religious seeking itself was in terms of finding some more detailed formulation of these problematically vague existential axes.

A few words on the general question of the importance of prior beliefs in effecting conversion are necessary at this point. A number of discussions of conversion have emphasized congruence between previous ideology and a given group's "appeal"[8] while others treat the degree of congruence as unimportant so long as the ideology is

---

[7] Our analysis is confined to isolating the elements of the conversion sequence. Extended analysis would refer to the factors that *in turn* bring each conversion condition into existence. That is, it would be necessary to develop a theory for each of the seven elements, specifying the conditions under which each appears. On the form such theory would probably take, see Ralph Turner's discussion of "the intrusive factor," *op cit.,* pp. 609–611.

[8] E.g., H. G. Brown, "The Appeal of Communist Ideology," *American Journal of Economics and Sociology,* 2 (1943), pp. 161–174; Gabriel Almond, *The Appeals of Communism,* Princeton: Princeton University Press, 1954.

seen as embodied in what appears to be a successful movement.[9] Both views seem extreme.[10]

Our data suggest that only the two gross kinds of congruence that make up the ideology of religous seekership are necessary for conversion to the D.P. Presumptively important items, such as fundamentalist Christianity, millenarian expectations, and hallucinatory experience were far from universal among pre-converts. Most pre-converts believed in a vaguely defined "New Age" that would appear gradually, but they *became* apocalyptic pre-millenarian only upon conversion.

The role of these gross points of congruence is suggested in the substantive D.P. appeals to pre-converts. Active spirits were rampant in their view of reality. Converts lived with an immediate sense of unseen forces operating on the physical order (e.g., the weather) and intervening in human affairs — in relations among nations, in the latest national disaster, and in their own moment-to-moment lives. Nothing occurred that was not related to the intentions of God's or Satan's spirits. For persons holding a teleological conception of reality, the D.P. doctrine had the virtue of offering a minute and lawful explanation of the whole of human history. It systematically defined and revealed the hidden meaning of individual lives that had lacked coherence and purpose, and of course, it explained all hallucinatory behavior in terms of spirit manifestations. These spirits had been preparing the pre-convert to see the truth of the D.P.

Although acute and enduring tensions in the form of frustrated aspirations is not an ideological component, in the sense of being a more abstract postulate about the nature of reality, it should be noted here, in relation to the matter of congruence, that the D.P. also offered a proximate and major solution. Converts were assured of being virtual demi-gods for all eternity, beginning with a rule over the restored and reformed earth in the immediate future. By 1967 God was to impose the millennium upon earth, and those who converted early, before the truth of this message became self-evident, would occupy the most favored positions in the divine hegemony. Converts particularly stressed this advantage of conversion in their proselytization: "those who get in early," as one member put it, "will be in on the ground floor of something big."

Religious seekership emerges, then, as another part of the path through the maze of life contingencies leading to D.P. conversion. It is a floundering among religious alternatives, an openness to a variety of religious views, frequently esoteric, combined with failure to embrace the specific ideology and fellowship of some set of believers.[11] Seekership provided the minimal points of ideological congruence to make these people available for D.P. conversion.

4. The Turning Point. The necessary attributes of pre-converts stated thus far had all persisted for some time before the pre-converts encountered the D.P.; they can be considered "background" factors, or predispositions. Although they apparently arose and were active in the order specified, they are important here as accumulated and simultaneously active factors during the development of succeeding conditions.

We now turn to situational factors in which timing becomes much more significant. The first of these is the rather striking circumstance that *shortly* before, and *concurrently* with their encounter with the D.P., all pre-converts had reached or were about to reach what they perceived as a "turning point" in their lives. That is, each had come to a moment when old lines of action were complete, had failed or been disrupted, or were about to be so, and when they faced the opportunity (or necessity), and possibly the burden, of doing something different with their lives.[12]

---

[9] E.g., Eric Hoffer, *The True Believer,* New York: Mentor, 1958 (copyright 1951), p. 10.

[10] Cf. Herbert Blumer, "Collective Behavior" in Joseph B. Gittler (ed.), *Review of Sociology,* New York: Wiley, 1957, pp. 147–148.

[11] For further suggestive materials on seekers and seeking see H. T. Dohrman, *California Cult,* Boston: Beacon, 1958; Leon Festinger, Henry Riecken and Stanley Schacter, *When Prophecy Fails,* Minneapolis: University of Minnesota Press, 1956; Sanctus De Santis, *Religious Conversion,* London: Routledge and Kegan Paul, 1927, esp. pp. 260–261; H. Taylor Buckner, "Deviant-Group Organizations," unpublished M.A. thesis, University of California, Berkeley, 1964, Ch. 2. For discussion of a generically similar phenomenon in a different context, see Edgar H. Schein, *Coercive Persuasion,* New York: Norton, 1961, pp. 120–136, 270–277.

[12] Everett C. Hughes, *Men and Their Work,* Glencoe: Free Press, 1958, Ch. 1; Anselm Strauss, "Transformations of Identity," in Arnold Rose (ed.), *Human Behavior and Social Processes,* Boston: Houghton Mifflin,

Turning points in general derived from recent migration; loss of employment . . . and completion, failure, or withdrawal from school. Perhaps because most converts were young adults, turning points involving educational institutions were relatively frequent. Illustrations . . . are a graduate student who has just failed his Ph.D. qualifying examinations, two second-semester college seniors who had vague and unsatisfying plans for the future, and a seventeen-year-old who had just graduated from high school. Recovery from or the onset of an illness, marital dissolution and other changes, extant or imminent, . . . were relatively infrequent. The significance of these various turning points is that they increased the pre-convert's awareness of and desire to take some action about his problems, *at the same time giving him a new opportunity to do so.* Turning points were situations in which old obligations and lines of action were diminished, and new involvements became desirable and possible.

5. Cult Affective Bonds. We come now to the contact between a potential recruit and the D.P. If persons who go through all four of the previous steps are to be further drawn down the road to full conversion, an affective bond must develop, if it does not already exist, between the potential recruit and one or more of the D.P. members. The development or presence of some positive, emotional, interpersonal response seems necessary to bridge the gap between first exposure to the D.P. message and accepting its truth. That is, persons developed affective ties with the group or some of its members while they still regarded the D.P. perspective as problematic, or even "way out." In a manner of speaking, final conversion was coming to accept the opinions of one's friends.[13]

It is particularly important to note that conversions frequently moved through *pre-existing* friendship pairs or nets.

Subsequent conversions also followed friendship paths, or friendships developed between the pre-convert and the converts prior to conversion.

Bonds that were unsupported by previous friendships with a new convert often took the form of a sense of instant and powerful rapport with a believer.

Although a potential convert might have some initial difficulty in taking up the D.P. perspective, given the four previous conditions *and* an effective tie, he began seriously to consider the D.P. and to accept it as his personal construction of reality.

6. Extra-Cult Affective Bonds. One might suppose that non-D.P. associates of a convert-in-process would not be entirely neutral to the now immediate possibility that he would join the D.P. group. We must inquire, then, into the conditions under which extra-cult controls are activated through emotional attachments, and how they restrain or fail to restrain persons from D.P. conversion.

Recent migration, disaffection with geographically distant families and spouses and very few nearby acquaintances made a few converts "social atoms"; for them extra-cult attachments were irrelevant. More typically, converts were acquainted with nearby persons, but none was intimate enough to be aware that a conversion was in progress or to feel that the mutual attachment was sufficient to justify intervention.

In many cases, positive attachments outside the cult were to other religious seekers, who, even though not yet budding converts themselves, encouraged continued "investigation" or entertain-

1962, pp. 67–71. Cf. the often-noted "cultural dislocation" and migration pattern found in the background of converts to many groups, especially cults.

[13] Cf. Tamatsu Shibutani, *Society and Personality,* Englewood Cliffs, N.J.: Prentice-Hall, 1961, pp. 523–532, 588–592. Schein (*op. cit.,* p. 277) reports that "the most potent source of influence in coercive persuasion was the identification which arose between a prisoner and his more reformed cellmate." See also Alan Kerckhoff, Kurt Back and Norman Miller, "Sociometric Patterns in Hysterical Contagion," *Sociometry,* 28 (1965), pp. 2–15.

ment of the D.P. rather than exercising a counter-vailing force. Indeed, such an extra-cult person might be only slightly behind his friend in his own conversion process.

In the relatively few cases where positive attachments existed between conventional extra-cult persons and a convert-in-process, control was minimal or absent, because of geographical distance or intentional avoidance of communication about the topic while the convert was solidifying his faith. Thus, for example, a German immigrant in his early thirties failed to inform his mother in Germany, to whom he was strongly attached, during his period of entertainment and only wrote her about the D.P. months after his firm acceptance. (She disowned him.)

During the period of tentative acceptance, and afterwards, converts, of course, possessed a rhetoric that helped to neutralize affective conflicts. An account by a newly converted soldier in Oklahoma conveys the powerful (and classic) content of this facilitating and justifying rhetoric:

I wrote my family a very long detailed but yet very plain letter about our movement and exactly what I received in spiritual ways plus the fact that Jesus had come to me himself. The weeks passed and I heard nothing but I waited with deep trust in God.

This morning I received a letter from my mother. She . . . surmised that I was working with a group other than those with the "stamp of approval by man." She . . . called me a fanatic, and went on to say: "My fervent constant prayer is that time will show you the fruitlessness of the way you have chosen before it consumes you entirely. A real true religion is deep in the heart and shines through your countenance for all to see. One need not shout it to the house tops either."

At first it was the deepest hurt I had ever experienced. But, I remember what others in [the D.P.] family have given up and how they too experienced a similar rejection. But so truly, I can now know a little of the rejection that our beloved Master experienced. I can now begin to understand his deep grief for the Father as he sat peering out of a window singing love songs to Him because he knew that the Father would feel such grief. I can now begin to feel the pain that our Father in heaven felt for 6,000 years. I can now begin to see that to come into the Kingdom of heaven is not as easy as formerly thought. I can now see why many are called but few are chosen. I began to understand why men will be

separated, yes even from their families. I begin to see the shallowness of human concern for God as a Father and their true blindness. Oh my heart cries out to Our Father in greatful [*sic*] praise and love for what He has given.

....

Where there were emotional attachments to outsiders who were physically present and cognizant of the incipient transformation, conversion became a "nip-and-tuck" affair. Pulled about by competing emotional loyalties and discordant versions of reality, such persons were subjected to intense emotional strain.

....

When extra-cult bonds withstood the strain of affective and ideological flirtation with the D.P., conversion was not consummated. Most converts, however, lacked external affiliations close enough to permit informal control over belief. Affectively, they were so "unintegrated" that they could, for the most part, simply fall out of relatively conventional society unnoticed, taking their co-seeker friends, if any, with them.

7. *Intensive Interaction.* In combination, the six previous factors suffice to bring a person to *verbal conversion* to the D.P. but one more contingency must be met if he is to become a "deployable agent,"[14] or what we have termed a *total convert.* Most, but not all, verbal converts ultimately put their lives at the disposal of the cult. Such transformations in commitment took place, we suggest, as a result of intensive interaction with D.P. members, and failed to result when such interaction was absent.

Intensive interaction means concrete, daily, and even hourly accessibility to D.P. members, which implies physical proximity to total converts. Intensive exposure offers an opportunity to reinforce and elaborate an initial, tentative assent to the D.P. world view, and in prolonged association the perspective "comes alive" as a device for interpreting the moment-to-moment events in the convert's life.

The D.P. doctrine has a variety of resources

[14] On the concept of the "deployable agent" or "deployable personnel" in social movements see Philip Selznick, *The Organizational Weapon*, New York: The Free Press, 1960 (copyright 1952), pp. 18–29.

for explicating the most minor everyday events in terms of a cosmic battle between good and evil spirits, in a way that placed the convert at the center of this war. Since all D.P. interpretations pointed to the imminence of the end, to participate in these explications of daily life was to come more and more to see the necessity of one's personal participation as a totally committed agent in this cosmic struggle.[15]

Reminders and discussion of the need to make other converts, and the necessity of supporting the cause in every way, were the main themes of verbal exchanges among the tentatively accepting and the total converts, and, indeed, among the total converts themselves. Away from this close association with those already totally committed, one failed to "appreciate" the need for one's transformation into a total convert.

In recognition of this fact, the D.P. members gave highest priority to attempts to persuade verbal converts (even the merely interested) to move into the cult's communal dwellings.

When one of them began to waver in his faith, unwavering believers were fortunately present to carry him through this "attack of Satan."

Most verbally assenting converts were induced

[15] Cf. Schein, *op. cit.*, pp. 136–139, 280–282.

out of his tenuous state, through contrived or spontaneous intensive interaction, within a few weeks, or more typically, a few months. In a few instances the interval between assent and total commitment spanned a year or more. When the unmarried older sister of the German immigrant mentioned above came to entertain the D.P. perspective, some 11 months of subtle and not-so-subtle pressures were required to get her to leave her private apartment and move into a communal dwelling. Within two months she went from rather lukewarm belief to total dedication and subsequent return to Germany as a D.P. missionary.

Thus, verbal conversion and even a resolution to reorganize one's life for the D.P. is not automatically translated into total conversion. One must be intensively exposed to the group supporting these new standards of conduct. D.P. members did not find proselytizing, the primary task of total converts, very easy, but in the presence of persons who reciprocally supported each other, such a transformation of one's life became possible. Persons who accepted the truth of the doctrine, but lacked intensive interaction with the group, remained partisan spectators, who played no active part in the battle to usher in God's kingdom.

57 Conformity and Commitment*

Charles A. Kiesler

The following report corroborates the results of research by Asch, Sherif, Emerson, and others with regard to the influence that groups may have on their individual members. But it also adds another variable to the analysis of group effects, and that

variable is commitment, the individual's desire for continued involvement with the group or the expectation that involvement will bind the members in a realization of their mutual destiny. The data suggest that commitment and response to group pressure have a complex but significant relationship.

Should I go along with the group?

We have all confronted this question, consciously or not, in one form or another at some time in our multiple relationships with groups at work, in school, in social life, at play, even in the bosom of the family. Will we conform to go along with what others think is right?

People often talk of conformity in the abstract

— and like sin in the abstract, they are usually against it. But men face *concrete* situations and decisions every day, often under considerable pressure. What do they do? When will a man change his attitudes and behavior to adjust? To what extent will he change them? What does conformity in this context actually mean? The word conformity implies one of three views of adaptive behavior:

The first view (the most popular) holds that conformity is an enduring personality characteristic — that organization men are essentially born, not made, so their seduction to conformity comes without strain.

The second view holds that conformist behavior is a kind of tactic — a superficial "going along with the crowd" because of necessity or temporary advantage — without essential change of private opinion.

The third is something of a middle ground, although closer to the second. It holds that a conforming individual may actually come to change his private as well as his public opinions and attitudes as a result of continued disagreement with the group; and that this change will last.

In the first view, the natural conformer will try to be like others in most things, finding his satisfactions and support not in personal uniqueness or integrity but in a group identification. There is a germ of truth in this belief. People do wish to be "correct" and in agreement. To some extent we all look to others to validate our opinions. We tend to pick up our cues on proper behavior and personal worth from others. This influence is pervasive and important. After all, the great majority of people conform in rules and customs or our civilization would be impossible.

However, there is little evidence that mankind tends to polarize around two distinct breeds, conformist and non-conformist. People vary in their dependence on, or independence of, the opinions and attitudes of others. They vary in their internal needs and in their perceptions. Thus conformity depends not only on personality and experience, but also on how we analyze our situations.

The second and third views shift emphasis from personality to the situation and how it is perceived.

The second type of conformer goes along with the crowd overtly — while keeping his real disagreement private from the group in question. He is not convinced — he merely pretends he is, whether for convenience or to serve some higher goal. For instance, if a subject in an experiment is told that he and the group would be given $50 if they agreed on some issue, agreement will usually come soon enough.

DOES SHE OR DOESN'T SHE?

This second view of conformity is called *compliance*. Its forms and rationalizations are many. People may want to be tactful and considerate, and so pretend to believe things they do not; they may want to get something unpleasant over with as soon as possible; they may be animated by greed or malice; or, as with Galileo disavowing belief in the Copernican theory before church authorities (while, legend has it, muttering to himself, "It's true all the same"), they may simply consider that a certain amount of lip service is a necessary price for peace and the chance to go one's own way in most things. A complier, among friends, may express very different opinions from those he expresses before the group with which he complies.

There has been much research on compliance, most notably that of Solomon Asch and his associates. In Asch's experiments subjects were shown two lines and asked which was longer. When alone, they almost never made a mistake. But in the rigged company of others who insisted that the shorter was longer, one-third went along. Presumably they still believed their eyes, and only their public, but not their private, opinions conformed.

The third view, a logical next step after compliance, has most concerned my students and myself in the last several years. It states that not only the overt opinion, but the private one as well, can be changed as a result of disagreement. Certain consequences follow that would not follow from compliance alone and that do not depend on the presence of the group. If a person changes his opinion, his behavior and attitudes will be changed whether the group is around or not. And this change should last.

Of course, people do not change their opinions easily. They must be motivated to do it. Research has shown that one important motivation is approval — if someone feels that others generally agree with him and find him attractive, he is likely to adjust his opinions to theirs on some issue.

But prior research did not prepare us for a finding in our own work that is more important to us. Our experiments have shown that *commitment* — in this case the expectation by a person that he must continue working and associating with a particular group — is also a major factor in opinion change and conformity to that group's standards. (Elsewhere J. Sakumura and I have defined commitment as "a pledging or binding of the individual to behavorial acts." This is a perfectly reasonable, if somewhat limited, view of commitment, and could include more subjective meanings, such as dedication or resolve. We have evidence that commitment is not, in and of itself, a motivation to change or resistance to change; but the *effect* of commitment is to make particular cognitions, or perceptions, more resistant to change.)

Let us briefly review the complicated experimental procedure that led to this outcome.

The subjects, all volunteers, were told that they would be assigned to discussion groups designed to test how strangers can work together for common goals. Each was told he had to return for four successive one-hour sessions. However, some were told they would continue with the same groups for all sessions (were, in effect, committed to them) while others were told they would be switched later to different groups and had no anticipation of working with the same people all the time.

After a session each privately gave his "first impressions" of the others. He also discussed and ranked various objects by his preferences, including some modern paintings. Each subject was then given bogus information about how others rated him ("Perhaps you would like to see what others thought of you. . . .").

Thus some are told that others find them very attractive, average, or unattractive. All subjects are told that the others disagree with their rankings of the objects. Then each is asked to rerank the objects — " . . . just for the institute; the group will never see them."

Note that every relevant variable is manipulated: the anticipation of continuing with the group; the extent of disagreement; how attractive the group finds each one. The individuals were completely taken in, very serious about cooperating, and unaware that they were being manipulated. (After the experiment the subjects were informed of its purpose, and the manipulation was explained. We found them intrigued, interested, and not offended.)

Under such controlled and cooperative circumstances we could be precise about what factors produced our results and confident that the results could be reliably applied to others. Our studies also demonstrated that:

— the less others like us, the less we like them;

— the less we like them, the less they affect our opinions.

The more we impressed upon a subject that the group didn't like him, the more he indicated that he didn't like them either, and the less he changed his opinion to conform with what we told him theirs was. This much was predictable from other work. However, we found an important exception created by the factor of *commitment*. Results were not the same in those cases when the person was committed to continue associating with the same group.

A committed person — like the noncommitted — generally modified his own opinions when he felt there was a high expression of attraction from the others. They both also modified them, though somewhat less, when the attraction was moderate. *But at the extreme — when least attracted — the committed person (but not the uncommitted) changed his opinions almost as much as the highly attracted did!*

This fascinating finding is not easily accounted for in current psychological theory. The subject does not like the group; they apparently do not like him; yet they have large influence on him. It is passive influence — they do not overtly try to influence him at all, yet they do. Only the individual knows that he disagrees; the group, presumably, does not know he disagrees and would never know unless he brought it up himself. It is a safe position for him to be in, to disagree as much as he pleases privately without external consequence. Yet his opinion changes to meet what he has been told theirs is.

But this is true only if he must continue with the group. If he is not so committed the group does not influence him at all, and the relationship between attraction and opinion change proceeds in the predictable straight line.

Further, this opinion change is stable — it lasts. But the obvious suspicion that anyone capable of such change must be a well-oiled weathervane, swinging around to accommodate any new wind, is wrong.

THE DEVIATE ALLY

This was well illustrated when we told the committed but low-attracted person that he had an ally (a "deviate ally") who agreed with his original opinion in spite of the rest of the group. Previous studies have demonstrated that if a person who disagrees with a group finds he has even one ally, he will stick by his guns and hold out. But with the committed, low-attracted person it depended on *when* he found out about this ally. If he found out before he had changed his opinion, he stood fast, as expected — opinion change under these circumstances was near zero. But if he found out *after* he had accepted and expressed his new opinion, the ally had little effect. Moreover, he tended to resent this new-found "friend" and even to build up an active dislike for him. Of those who found out about this ally early, before change, 58 percent liked him best in the group. But of those who discovered him late, after change, only 14 percent said they liked him best, and 13 percent said they liked him least.

Let us analyze the implications of this finding a little further. First, they definitely limit the concept that greater attraction must inevitably lead to greater private acceptance; they illustrate at least one significant condition under which it does not. Second, they illustrate how important commitment is for understanding the behavior of groups and of individuals within groups. Commitment obviously can make a difference in attitudes, conclusions, and behavior generally.

It must be reemphasized that commitment makes this difference only when there is very little (or even negative) attraction to the group — the person doesn't like them or the situation, and he doesn't want to keep on, but feels he must. Obviously, therefore, this change of attitude is not what the subject really prefers — it is used only when all other avenues of psychological escape are closed off.

How can we account for this reversal — which seems contrary not only to prior research but to "common sense" as well?

This process can loosely be described in the following way: If a person feels out of harmony with some others or with a group, he has certain alternative methods of response for self-protection or counterattack. He can reject the group — decide to have nothing to do with it, and break off as soon as possible. Or he can devalue it — say that its opinions, importance, and members are of no particular consequence, not worth agreeing with.

There is some evidence that people will act this way if they do not feel bound to continue with the others. But these alternatives are not available to someone who is committed. He must somehow make his peace with them — and with his own concept of himself as someone who acts from conviction.

APPEASEMENT AND AGGRAVATION

This is not peace at any price. It is not bland and superficial conformity. As our findings indicate, the important peace is within the subject himself. Also, it takes the long view — it considers consequences for the whole length of the commitment. A person not committed to continue can afford to practice "appeasement" — to bend to immediate pressures in the hope that they will pass. The committed must be much more cautious.

Thus commitment does not only and always tend toward agreement and the easing of tensions.

It can lead as well toward sharpened conflict *in the short term,* if this seems necessary for long-term benefits. People who must cooperate cannot forever sweep unpleasant things under the rug.

For instance, how should an individual react to someone else's unpleasant habits or overbearing manners? He can pretend to ignore them once or a very few times. But what if they must keep associating? He may face the same problem at each meeting — aggravated by time and apparent acceptance. This *would* be appeasement in its classical form.

I am now collaborating with Sara Kiesler and Michael Pallak on a series of experiments designed to answer such questions. Specifically, how will people react to a social faux pas made by another? Folklore — in fact, many of the precepts of formal etiquette — suggest we try to save the offender's "face" and "gloss things over" when he is annoying or embarrassing us.

Our data analyses are not yet complete. But so far we have found what we expected. The *un*committed will tend to ignore the faux pas in a private confrontation with the offender; but something very different occurs among people who must continue association. Committed subjects were quite blunt about privately calling the offender's attention to his acts, reproving him, trying to get him to change. They apparently feel compelled to face the problem *now,* rather than keep on suffering from it.

We often notice parallel behavior between husband and wife, people who could hardly be more closely committed. They may reprove each other for acts that each would tolerate without comment from strangers. We usually consider this a sign of breakdown of marriage ties. But could not, as our studies imply, something of the reverse also sometimes be true — a desire to clear away potential sources of friction to make for an easier and more sincere relationship?

It is unfortunate that the effects of commitment have not been given more study, and we can hope that more research will come soon. Any factor that can influence people to change convictions and attitudes is a major force in human behavior and must be reckoned with.

A Note on The Study

This article represents the culmination of a series of studies on consistency, conformity, and commitment. However, it deals primarily with two recent studies.

The first of these, conducted by myself and Lee H. Corbin in 1965, used 180 volunteers, sorted into six-man discussion groups as part of the requirements of an introductory psychology course. Subjects did not know each other personally. They were told of interest by the (fictitious) American Institute for Small Group Research in how strangers worked out certain tasks. They were supposed to rate 10 abstract paintings which, they were told, had previously been rated by experts; theoretically, the individuals and group that came closest to the experts would win cash prizes. Half were made to feel that they would continue with the same group through four sessions; the other half were made to understand that the composition of their groups could and might change and that in time each would have some choice about who would be included in his final group analysis. Half, therefore, felt they would be continuing on with the others, with the problems in adjustment and conformity that this might entail; and the other half should, theoretically, have felt more free of this continuing social pressure.

The second major study, conducted by myself, Mark Zanna, and James De Salvo at Yale and published in 1966, was quite similar in design and procedure. The subjects, however, were 198 high school boys who volunteered to take part in five- and six-man discussion groups. They had been recruited from newspaper advertisements and record shops and did not know one another.

The final study mentioned in this article, by myself, Sara Kiesler, and Michael Pallak, is still in process, and data analyses are not yet complete. Its findings, therefore, while very suggestive, are still tentative.

CONTRADICTIONS AND CONSEQUENCES

58   The Hasher: A Study of Role Conflict*

Louis A. Zurcher, Jr. · *David A. Sonenschein*

Eric L. Metzner

Below is a participant observation study of the "college man" who plays the role of "hasher" in a sorority and the conflicting expectations that result. Some common methods of avoiding conflict are institutionalized in the informal society of hashers, and these patterns of avoidance must be learned and enacted if an individual hasher is to gain membership in the society. Thus, the mechanisms of avoidance and defense, although they are implemented by individuals, have a social definition and origin, and they are legitimated by group pressures. The analytical framework employed in this study can be applied to numerous situations familiar to college students and some of its implications can be further tested in terms of the reader's own experience.

The individual entering college for the first time has, through exposure to a popularized and dramatized stereotype, come to perceive the status of "college man" as incorporating the following characteristics and role expectations: (1) a young man who deserves a white-collar or "clean" occupation of more than average prestige, (2) a sophisticate, above average in intelligence, taste, and *savoir faire* — able to smoke a pipe with an air of casual indifference, (3) a "lover," a "man of the world" who dominates and manipulates the tender young coeds, (4) a "hail fellow well met"

* From *Social Forces,* Vol. 44, June 1966, pp. 505–514. Reproduced by permission.

who can, at any time spontaneously join in an impromptu frolicsome venture. These expectations are repeatedly reinforced in the informal academic setting.

Hashers at the subject university are male college undergraduate students who are employed as attendants in the kitchens of sororities and fraternities (in this paper, we will focus our attention on the unique social situation of the sorority hasher). In return for their work, hashers are given meals and, in some cases of additional responsibility, a few dollars a month. The job consists of setting tables; washing and drying dishes, silver, and utensils; cleaning up the kitchen; mopping floors; disposing of garbage; general handy work; and, on occasion, carrying luggage for the girls. As it can be seen, the tasks are in general very similar to those of the "K. P." of military fame.

Even though it is part-time work, the job of hasher can be classified as what Becker calls a "service occupation."[1] According to Becker, the service occupations are "distinguished by the fact that the worker in them comes into more or less direct and personal contact with the ultimate consumer of the product of his work, the client for whom he performs the service. Consequently, the client is able to direct or attempt to direct the worker at his task and to apply sanctions of various kinds. . . ."[2] Becker sees as characteristic of such jobs that the workers consider "the client unable to judge the proper worth of the service and resent bitterly any attempt on his part to exercise control over the work. A good deal of conflict and hostility arises as a result, and methods of defense against outside interference become a preoccupation of the members."[3]

The hasher occupies the lowest level in the functional work hierarchy of the kitchen. At the top of the hierarchy is the house mother, then the cooks (in order of longevity), the head hasher, and finally, the hashers themselves (in order of longevity). This chain-of-command is rigidly enforced — a policy not unusual in an organized kitchen work setting. Whyte, for example, describes the elaborate restaurant kitchen status sys-

[1] Howard S. Becker, "The Professional Dance Musician and His Audience," *The American Journal of Sociology,* 57 (September 1951), pp. 136–144.
[2] *Ibid.,* p. 136.
[3] *Ibid.,* p. 136.

tem in which even the kinds of vegetables worked with and the levels of food preparation are related to position in the staff hierarchy.[4] Orwell writes of the rigid caste system existing in the hotel restaurant where he was employed, in which the staff "had their prestige graded as accurately as that of soldiers, and a cook or waiter was as much above a kitchen helper as a captain above a private."[5] The hasher in the sorority house, since he is the low man on the totem pole, is expected to accept without question the assignments handed out by the cooks and by the head hasher (though there is considerably more latitude for complaining or "bitching" about a task assigned by the latter). Furthermore, as part of his job, the hasher is expected to be neat, quietly efficient, and at all times polite to the girls. He is not to speak with them when serving (unless asked a question), and, by house rule, he is not to attempt to date them during his off-duty hours.

The position of hasher in a sorority thus brings with it the behavioral expectations of (1) menial or "dirty" work, (2) low prestige, (3) a marked lack of sophistication, and (4) manifest subservience to and strict social distance from a group of college coeds.

It appears, therefore, that the individual who must enact both the role of college man and hasher experiences conflict, and it will be seen that this conflict manifests itself in the way the hashers perceive themselves, the way they behave in the work situation, their attitudes toward and behavior with the girls for whom they work, and the attitudes of the girls toward and their behavior with the hashers. Furthermore, components within the informal organization of the work situation will be observed to provide the individual with group-structured defenses to the role conflict. These defenses become an integral part of the hasher role enactment and are learned along with the formal requirements of the job.

PROCEDURE

The two junior authors (one a senior in cultural anthropology and the other a senior in psychol-

ogy), both of whom had been hashers in a total of five different sororities for three years previous to the present study, observed as participators[6] in the hasher group of a large, campus housed, nationally affiliated sorority (85 girls, ten hashers). The systematic observations were conducted during the course of ten months, a little more than the full academic year. The participant observers, cognizant of the hypotheses and familiar with role theory, kept daily records of relevant attitudes, behaviors, statements, and patterns of interaction of (1) the hashers, (2) the sorority girls, and (1) and (2) *vis-à-vis* each other. The three authors met several times a week to discuss the data and to focus attention for the periods of observation to follow.[7]

The subject sorority was one of the largest on the university campus. At the time of the study, and for a number of years before, the subject sorority was not among those considered by the students to be popular or "in," but rather among those considered to be "unreal." Furthermore, and perhaps to be expected because of the girls' awareness of the relatively low status of their house in the Panhellenic system, the social distance maintained between the members and the hashers was rigid and extreme.

The work setting of hashers in this particular sorority house would be, the authors felt, one in which there was a high degree of role conflict, and one in which the defenses to such conflict would be clearly manifested.

---

[6] The two junior authors occupied the role of "complete participator" in Gold's continuum of participant-observers. That is, they themselves were hashers, and members of the work group were not aware of the fact that they were being observed. See Raymond L. Gold, "Roles in Sociological Field Observations," *Social Forces,* 36 (March 1958), pp. 217–223.

[7] In addition to the work by Gold cited above, the authors are indebted to the following for various participant-observer techniques: Howard S. Becker, "Problems of Inferences and Proof in Participant-Observation," *American Sociological Review,* 23 (December 1958), pp. 652–660; Mortimer Sullivan, Stuart Queen, and Ralph Patrick, "Participant Observation as Employed in the Study of a Military Training Program," *American Sociological Review,* 23 (December 1958), pp. 660–667; Jackson Toby, "Variables in Role Conflict Analysis," *Social Forces,* 30 (March 1952), pp. 323–327; Roger Heyns and Ronald Lippitt, "Systematic Observational Techniques," in Gardner Lindzey (ed.), *Handbook of Social Psychology,* Vol. 1 (Cambridge, Mass.: Addison-Wesley, 1954), pp. 370–404.

---

[4] W. F. Whyte, *Human Relations in the Restaurant Industry* (New York: McGraw-Hill Book Co., 1948).

[5] George Orwell, *Down and Out in Paris and London* (London: Secker and Warburg, 1933), p. 70.

Conclusions based upon the data from participant observation in the subject sorority provided the framework for a series of open-ended interview questions.[8] Though the main focus of this investigation was the case study analysis of a specific conflict engendering work situation (in one sorority), interviews were conducted with 48 hashers, 50 members, and 21 staff personnel of

[8] The purpose of the open-ended interviews was to explore, in sororities other than the subject house, the following broad phenomena: What did the hashers think of their jobs? How did they get along with the girls? What did the girls think of the hashers? How did the house mothers and the cooks view the interaction between the hashers and the girls? What were the formal house rules and expectations relevant to the hasher work situation?

In each interview situation, at least the following questions were asked with the intent being to get the respondents talking, and to probe with further, more specific questions when the opportunity arose: (1) *Hashers:* What do you think of the job of hasher? Advantages? Disadvantages? When is the job most enjoyable? When is the job least enjoyable? Why did you choose hashing as a part-time job? Do you intend to continue hashing while you are a student? What do you think of the girls in this sorority? What do you think their attitude is toward the hashers? How do the hashers and girls get along, generally? Have you worked for any other houses? If so, how do the work situations compare? What is your idea of a "good house" for which to work? A "bad house?" Do you do any extra things for the girls in this house? Do you represent them in intramural sports? Do any of the hashers in the house date a member? Would you recommend the job of hasher to a good friend? (2) *Girls:* What do you think of the job of hasher for a college man? What do you think of the hashers in your own sorority? What is your idea of a "good hasher?" A "bad hasher?" How do you think the hashers and the members get along, generally? What are the names of the hashers who work in your sorority house? How do you think the hasher crew of your house compares with those of other houses? Do you think the members should date hashers? Have you ever dated a hasher? Do you ever find it difficult to get a hasher to do what you ask him to do? Do you have a "turn-about" day? Tell me about it. (3) *House Mothers and Cooks:* What do you think of the job of hasher for a college man? What is your idea of a good hasher employee? A bad hasher employee? Are there any particular work or disciplinary problems that you have with the hashers? How, in general, do the girls get along with the hashers? The hashers with the girls? What is your opinion of hashers and members dating? Is there a formal or informal house rule against such dating? What is the hasher turnover rate in this house? Have you worked for other houses? If so, how do the hashers here compare with those in the others? Are there any differences among the houses with which you have been associated in the way the hashers and the girls get along? In this sorority, do you have a "turn-about" day? Tell me about it.

seven of the remaining 13 sororities on the university campus, thus attempting to establish the degree, if any, to which the conclusions could be generalized. Including the subject sorority house, the sample consisted of: two "large" houses (65 or more members, eight to ten hashers, and two full-time cooks); three "medium" houses (50-65 members, six to eight hashers, and two cooks on separate shifts); and three "small" houses (less than 50 members, five or fewer hashers, and one full-time cook). Independent of size, the eight sorority houses in the sample varied in prestige (indicated by the number of "rushees," number of student body and club offices held by members, number of queens, cheerleaders, pompon girls, etc., and by student opinion). Two were high prestige or "top" houses; four were of average prestige; and two were low prestige or "loser" houses. It was felt that this sample of sororities was fairly representative of the entire university population of houses, though at the onset, since the authors were aware of the limitations of participant observation and open-ended, informal interviews, no sweeping generalizations were intended.

Results and Discussion

It is immediately apparent to the observer that the hasher is not proud of his work and that he prefers not to be identified with the job. As MacIver has pointed out, men in our society tend to be judged according to the work which they pursue,[9] and the stereotype representing the occupational levels similar to that of the hasher is distasteful to the aspiring college man. Table 1 presents the mean prestige ranks assigned by 276 freshman and sophomore students in basic social science classes to ten part-time jobs typically held by male college students. As indicated in the table, the male students, on the average, rank the job of hasher last. The female students rank the jobs of off-campus restaurant helper and movie usher lower than the job of hasher. None of the student evaluators were fraternity or sorority members.

The college student has, in general, a middle-

[9] R. M. MacIver, *Society: A Textbook of Sociology* (New York: Rinehart & Co., 1937).

TABLE 1 *Mean Prestige Ranks Assigned by Lower Division Students to Ten Typical Part-Time Jobs Held by Male College Students*

Part-time Job	Average Rank By Sex	
	Males (N = 112)	Females (N = 164)
Bellboy	6.8	6.8
Grocery Clerk	5.9	5.8
Life Guard	4.0	3.5
Hasher	7.4	7.0
Stock Clerk	4.9	5.0
Gas Station Attendant	6.1	6.0
Off-campus Restaurant Helper	7.1	7.1
Reader	2.8	2.6
Library Assistant	3.4	2.9
Movie Usher	6.6	7.5

class view of work — that is, work should enhance one's prestige, provide for the realization of one's talents, and be satisfying and desirable in itself. This view is in contrast to that of the lower class which sees work as an unpleasant but necessary means of securing food and shelter, and as being neither interesting nor desirable in itself.[10] To the members of the lower class who must pursue such "drudgery," the college student imputes low intelligence, irresponsibility, and generalized inferiority.[11] The hasher then finds himself in the unique situation of having middle-class definitions and expectations of work, but performing tasks and conforming to expectations which clearly are representative of a lower-class job.

When in a position in which he must profess the nature of his employment, the hasher's admission is inevitably quickly followed by a qualifying statement: "It's a means to an end," "I'm just doing this until I find something more suitable," "It's the only job I could get with hours that won't interfere with my class schedule," and so on. The *temporary* nature of the job is stressed, and a

point is made of demonstrating to the questioner that the hasher's primary role is that of student. (Table 1 indicates the high student ranking of the "scholarly" student related jobs of reader and library assistant.) The hasher's friends and acquaintances are often observed to ask him why he does such work, thus indicating a violation of their expectations of him as a college man. Sometimes a hasher will describe, with a leer, his job as an opportunity to "get near all those girls," and will gloss over the unpleasant realities of his task. In fact, some of the hashers interviewed stated that they initially took the job with the hope that they would "get the inside track" to a covey of coeds. This hope, of course, vanished in the face of the blunt reality of sorority girl-hasher social distance.

In the subject sorority house, there is a formal rule forbidding dating between the hashers and the sorority girls, and social intercourse within the house is maintained at as impersonal, employer-employee level as possible. Fraternization has been discouraged to the point where the girls and the hashers both feel uncomfortable if they have to interact on a level other than that called for by the job.

The no-dating rule in the subject sorority has been rigidly followed only for the last two years. The older hashers often speak of those "good old days a couple of years ago" when the girls were "somehow much nicer." Pertinent here is the hasher's definition of the sorority member who is a "good kid." In every case interviewed, the hasher's description of this ideal sorority girl centered on the attribute of "naturalness" — that is, a tendency to "be herself" and not to "look down" on the hasher, thus not stressing his subservient role. A good house to work for is one in which you are "treated like a human being." Good kids and good houses, then are those that treat the individual less like a hasher and more like a college man. W. F. Whyte observed that a conflict situation resulted among restaurant personnel when persons of high status had their activities initiated by persons perceived by them to be of lower status.[12] Many of the hashers are upper

[10] Krech, Crutchfield, and Ballachey, *op. cit.*, p. 283.

[11] Helen M. Davidson, F. Reissman, and Edna Meyers, "Personality Characteristics Attributed to the Worker," *Journal of Social Psychology*, 57 (June 1962), pp. 155–160.

[12] W. F. Whyte, "The Social Structure of the Restaurant," *American Journal of Sociology*, 54 (January 1949), pp. 302–310.

classmen, yet they must take orders from and wait on freshman girls. Any sorority member who minimizes this status threat is appreciated by the hasher as a "good kid."

Whyte also noted that in the restaurant under his observation it was not uncommon for female employees to initiate the action of male employees — e.g., waitresses giving orders to male cooks. Since in our society the male sex role generally includes the expectation that he be the originator of action between the sexes, that he dominate in heterosexual interpersonal relations, Whyte saw the role reversal in the restaurant as a key source of employee dissatisfaction. He cites a number of occasions where male employees contrived ways to avoid having to receive direct orders from female employees.[13] Similarly, in an analysis of some of the factors contributing to alienation from work, Blauner observed that "jobs differ in the degree to which they permit the particular 'manly virtues' that in our society are deemed appropriate to a 'real man.' "[14] One of the factors Blauner emphasizes is the degree to which the job allows sexual expression and status dominance with respect to women. It can be seen that the job of hasher includes both the sex role reversal that Whyte viewed as disruptive of the work situation and the lack of sexual expression and status dominance over women that Blauner saw as being a contributing factor to alienation from work. (Note, as indicated in Table 1, the high prestige position of the life guard, a very masculine job.)

The kitchen, called "The Inside" by the hasher, is his stronghold — within it he is in close association with other like-situated individuals. In the dining room, "The Outside," are "them," the girls. Interaction through the swinging doors might best be described as studied aloofness on the part of the girls and overt hostility on the part of the hashers. Orwell writes of the "double door between us (kitchen help and waiters) and the dining room" and contrasts the spontaneity of emotion, the relative relaxation, and the we-feeling

of the kitchen with the controlled, tense, and guarded interaction with the customers. "It is an instructive sight," continues Orwell, "to see a waiter going into a hotel dining room. The set of his shoulders alters; all the dirt and hurry and irritation have dropped off in an instant. He glides over the carpet, with a solemn priest-like air."[15] Scott describes a similar phenomenon in the paddock, the private world of the professional jockeys and handlers. According to Scott, when in the paddock with his peers, the jockey or the handler "can no longer fake his behavior . . . The paddock represents that point where ordinary vigilance in role deception cannot be sustained."[16] Becker's description of the deliberately maintained self-isolation of the dance-band musician provides an interesting parallel to the hasher's kitchen stronghold. Becker observes that "the musician is, as a rule, spatially isolated from the audience, being placed on a platform barrier that prevents any direct interaction. This isolation is welcomed because the audience, being made up of squares, is felt to be potentially dangerous . . . Musicians, lacking the usually provided physical barriers, often improvise their own and effectively segregate themselves from their audience."[17]

The hasher, of course, is not able to isolate himself from the "clients" as readily as the dance-band musician or even the professional waiter. He must interact with the girls in the sorority house, on the campus, and often in the classroom. Neither is he so obligated, on the other hand, to restrain himself from insulting the "clients." Though hashers are formally expected to be polite to the girls "no matter what," and though they are still bound by the "gentleman" expectation for college men, they often are not subtle in their demonstrations of displeasure with the girls.

The girls very often refer to the individual as "hasher," rather than by given name, and are quite free with orders and criticism. Any praise usually takes on a condescending tone — "nice hasher," "nice boy," and so on. The girl's view of the hasher in the subject sorority house is revealed by

[13] *Ibid.*, pp. 305–307.

[14] Robert Blauner, *Work, Self, and Manhood: Some Reflections on Technology and Identity,* paper read at the annual meeting of the American Sociological Association, Montreal, Canada, September, 1964.

[15] Orwell, *op. cit.,* p. 86.

[16] Marvin B. Scott, "A Note on the Place of Truth," *Berkeley Journal of Sociology,* 8 (June 1963), p. 38.

[17] Becker, *op. cit.,* p. 142.

the fact that one of the initiation requirements for a pledge is that she sing a love song to a hasher while he sits on her lap. This is taken to be one of the initiation rites that "humbles the pledges." (Ironically, the hashers themselves use this as a kind of initiation rite for entrance into their informal work group. That is, the newest hasher is the one who is made available to the pledge for the love song, and after he has been so used, he is told by his fellow hashers that he now knows "what working in the sorority is really like.")

The hashers seem to get much satisfaction from "getting the girls goats." The kitchen often resounds with gleefully shared exclamations like "Boy, did I get *her* mad!" and "I sure told *her* off!" Spilling of food while serving, ignoring an order, sharp answers to criticism, and any other verbal aggression is rewarded with the plaudits of the other hashers — "That'll show them"; "That'll shape her up!" While in the kitchen the hashers will often deliberately make noises (loud talking, whistling, banging of pots and pans) with the intent of disturbing the girls. In the subject sorority, the hashers will save the food scraps from the preparation phase of the meal, and while the girls are eating will overload the garbage disposal unit and convulse with laughter as the mechanism emits loud and excruciating gurgles, whines, and crunches. "It's hard to tell," reported one chuckling hasher, "which garbage disposals sound the worst — the ones out in the dining room, or the one in the kitchen."

Orwell describes the kitchen personnel's disdain for the customer of the hotel restaurant — a disdain developed as a defense against the "superiority" of the customer. One waiter told Orwell that, "as a matter of pride, he had sometimes wrung a dirty dishcloth into the customer's soup before taking it in, just to be revenged upon a member of the bourgeoisie."[18] Another waiter scolded Orwell, "Fool! Why do you wash that plate? Wipe it on your trousers. Who cares about the customers? They don't know what's going on. What is restaurant work? You are carving a chicken and it falls on the floor. You apologize, you bow, you go out; and in five minutes you come back by another door — with the same chicken.

That is restaurant work!"[19] So also is it hasher revenge. Besides the deliberate casualness toward dropped food and the amused "what they don't know won't hurt them attitude," on numerous other occasions in the subject sorority minor assaults were made on foods to be served to the girls — e.g., a marble tossed into a gelatin and grape salad mold; a small amount of grass thrown in with cooking spinach ("for those cows"); each dinner roll "thrown around the bases" from one hasher to another before it was placed in the serving basket; a drop or two of blood from the cut finger of a hasher splashed into a pot of soup ("This ought to make those bloodsuckers happy!"); green food coloring added to the milk; salt shaker tops loosened so they would fall off in the girls plates; etc. The action themselves are, of course, less significant than the glee with which they are shared by the hashers who are "getting to the girls."

An extremely interesting phenomenon revealed by the participant observation (and confirmed in other than the subject sorority by interviews) is the nature of the derisive terms the hashers have for the girls. Almost always, the names have animal referents, and the animal is most often the pig — "Here they come, let's slop the troughs"; "Soueee" and "Oink-Oink" grumbled (on the kitchen side of the swinging door) as the hashers walk out of the kitchen to serve the food; "What do the pigs want now"; "Let's go clean out the feeding pens"; "Mush, you huskies!" The records contain a startling number of this kind of statement, as well as many other derogatory comments about the girl's manners, breeding, and femininity. It would appear that the hashers are projecting feelings of their own "low born" position upon the girls. It is almost as if they are saying, "See, we aren't so bad, look at those slobs out in the dining room!"

The physical appearance of the sorority girls is also called into question by the hashers. "They've all had their faces remodeled, and they still can't get dates." "A guy would have to be pretty hard up to take out one of these dogs." "They must have an 'ugly requirement' in order to get into this sorority." The hasher lets his peers

---

[18] Orwell *op. cit.,* p. 113.

[19] *Ibid.,* p. 114.

know that even if he *could* date one of the girls in the sorority, he wouldn't. Thus is some modicum of control gained by the hasher over the emasculating "no dating" situation.

Within the kitchen, escape mechanisms of various sorts are everywhere apparent. Horseplay is the order of the day, with episodic food throwing and water splashing bouts, word fads, running "in group" jokes, and general zaniness. Of particular interest are the sets of activities which the hashers in the subject sorority house referred to as "bits." A "bit" is a relatively organized session of play-acting, originally arising spontaneously, and having a central theme and roles for each of the hashers. During the "bit" everything in the work setting, people, actions, and utensils, would be made a part of the scene, and the hashers would adopt the argot relevant to the situation enacted. For example, the "bit" for one work session staged the kitchen and dining room as a hell ship, with the hashers cast as the mutineers, the girls as "Powdered Pirates," and the cooks as "Ahab" and "Bly." Knives became "harpoons," the dinner meat became "salt horse," going out into the dining room was "walking the plank," one abundantly endowed sorority sister became the "treasure chest," and so on. In another session the kitchen was part of the Third Reich, with cooks "Goebbels" and "Goering" sending the hasher "Pots and Pans Panzer Corps" out to face the girls, who were now cast as "Storm Troopers" and "Girdled Gestapo." Serving the food was making a "Blitzkrieg," chicken was a "Luftwaffe Loser," and "bravery under fire" while in the dining room was rewarded with lettuce leaf medals at an "awards ceremony." "Bit," if contagious enough, would go on for more than one work session or even more than one day. Often the same "bit" would be recurrent, returning for replay every few months and year after year (e.g., the science fiction or horror movie "bit," the gangster "bit," and the western hero-villain "bit").

It would appear that the "bit" serves a number of functions for the hashers. It is, not unlike the therapeutic applications of psychodrama and role playing, an opportunity for a more or less legitimized expression of hostility. It serves also as a distraction from the repetitive drudgery and potential boredom of the hasher's work tasks, allowing him, in effect, to be more creative and expressive while on the job. Furthermore, the "bit," while affecting the hashers' enactment of an interconnecting and interdependent set of fantasy roles, serves to tighten the cohesion of the informal work group. As one hasher said, not without pride, "When we've got our own laughs going for us, this job is no sweat." Lastly, it would seem that the hasher welcomes the relatively clearly defined and uncomplicated roles of the "bit." Even if the play-acting roles are acknowledged fancy and are ephemeral, they are less ambiguous, less conflict-ridden, and less distasteful than his actual work role.

Other forms of symbolic withdrawal from the hasher work situation are also common. In the subject sorority house, the threats to quit, to leave the field, ran about 20 per week. Rarely did any hasher go through the entire week without stating his intention to quit next week. Each new work day brought with it a new challenge to "finish up faster than yesterday, and get the hell out of here."

In the kitchen, stories of the "I am a great lover" variety are daily bantered about by the hashers, expressed in a fashion that seems to insist "away from here, I really do manipulate and dominate the coeds." Many joking references and comic routines concerning homosexuality are observed, the hashers themselves using a falsetto voice or feigning homosexual characteristics. The homosexual routine does, in fact, at times represent itself with the elaborateness of a "bit." Such behavior is often seen in social environments where the masculine role is perceived by males to be threatened. Elkin, for example, describes clinically the need for overt erotic expression manifest among members of Army barracks.[20] Zurcher describes the "salty language" and "sea stories" of sexual conquest among recruits isolated in the Naval Training center.[21] Following Blauner's lead

---

[20] H. Elkin, "Aggressive and Erotic Tendencies in Army Life," *The American Journal of Sociology,* 51 (March 1946), pp. 408–413.

[21] Louis A. Zurcher, "The Naval Recruit Training Center: A Study of Role Behavior in a Total Institution," *Sociological Inquiry,* in press.

mentioned above, it may be that the emphasis on sexual topics during the work sessions is an effective means whereby the hashers can put some of their sex role expectations back into the job.

On those nights when the girls bring male guests to the sorority house, the hashers are especially belligerent. Venomously, the hashers comment about the dates the girls have — "I wonder if she's paying him a flat fee, or by the hour." "God, she must have robbed a grave to get him!" On such occasions, the role conflict of the hasher is exacerbated, since he must wait on college *couples.* Some hashers flatly refuse to work at these times. Others will agree to work in the kitchen, but refuse to wait on table.

The conflicts and resultant reactions thus far reported are seen, as indicated by the interview material, to be typical of the hasher-in-sorority situation, though the degree of conflict and defense varies from house to house. The interview material also revealed that two hasher groups would enter intramural athletic contests as representatives of their sororities, but the remaining six groups steadfastly refused to do so. The key variable influencing the degree to which the hashers would thus agree to identify with the sorority appeared to be the degree of status differentiation in the house — those with more rigid "class" lines, thus with a situation that emphasized the hasher-college man conflict, are not identified with and are not represented. The two sorority houses represented in intramural sports by their hasher groups are more informal and relaxed in hasher-member interaction.

It appears that the degree of social distance between hashers and members is less a function of the size of the house than a function of its relative status on the campus. The "loser" sororities apparently have greater need to maintain class lines within their houses than do the "top" sororities. This relationship was difficult to assess and is cautiously presented, considering the techniques used in this study and the fact that the work setting of the hasher is affected by other variables — e.g., the managerial styles of the house mothers and the cooks. The significant point is that, in *all* the houses considered here, there was evidence of some degree of social distance between the hashers and the girls, of hasher role conflict, and of the hashers' need to abate that conflict.

Most of the sororities permit a yearly "turnabout" day, during which the girls wait on the hashers. Such role reversals are seen in other social groups that have a sharp status differential and restricted social interaction — e.g., Naval vessels (enlisted men take over the ship for a few hours when it crosses the Equator);[22] military academies (lower classmen are allow to command the upper classmen for a day);[23] asylums and prisons (skits in which patients and inmates mimic the staff members).[24] Such behavior can be taken to be a clear indicator of the awareness of and resentment of status inferiority.

[22] Louis A. Zurcher, "The Sailor Aboard Ship: A Study of Role Behavior in a Total Institution," *Social Forces,* 43 (March 1965), pp. 389–400.

[23] Sanford Dornbusch, "The Military Academy as an Assimilating Institution," *Social Forces,* 33 (May 1955), pp. 316–321.

[24] E. Goffman, *Asylums* (New York: Doubleday & Co., 1961).

59 Strain in Role Sets*

J. Diedrick Snoek

Modern society is characterized by an intricate division of labor and a complex social organization is required to maintain some continuity among diverse work roles. It seems reasonable that such complexity and diversity may be associated with the strains and tensions reported by workers. The outbursts of crying waitresses have thus been explained in terms of the strains and stresses found in the waitress-customer relationship, and the firing of baseball managers has been described as an adaptation to a situation in which the demand for a winner conflicts inevitably with the fact that most teams are losers. The following study reports findings concerning the relationship between strain and organizational complexity. It suggests that the sources of strain may be classified as: Conflicts in which incompatible role requirements must somehow be reconciled; overload, the piling up of demands from all sources in excess of the worker's capacity for coping with stress; ambiguity and uncertainty related to communication failure, infractions against informal norms, and the anticipation of behavioral irregularities; finally, the worker may find it necessary to exert influence upon his fellows without having the legitimate authority that may be required. What are the main conflicts, overloads, ambiguities, and authority problems in the organization of a modern university? Which of the major positions — president, dean, professor, or student — are the most vulnerable to strain? By what means can the main sources of strain be minimized?

This paper represents an attempt to relate the experience of tension in the work role to one structural feature of all such roles, namely, the diversity of interests and loyalties represented in the role set.

The term "role set" was introduced by Merton to designate the total complement of role relationships in which a person becomes involved by virtue of occupying a particular social position.[1] Following Rommetveit, we shall call all those persons who complement a given person's role in this sense his "role senders," to designate their function of communicating and enforcing the relevant role expectations.[2] In a formal organization the role senders to a given office need not be under the same administrative authority; indeed, from the management's point of view, some role senders may have no discernible (or legitimate) relationship with the office at all. But from the point of view of role analysis, any person who is actively concerned with the officeholder's performance presumably holds expectations regarding his role. To illustrate from Whyte's example, the cook, the supervisor, the barman, the pantry helper, the customer, and the other waitresses, all have expectations about how the waitress should behave, and they will communicate these expectations in their behavior toward her.

Both Merton and Goode have pointed out that any role set possesses a potential for conflict to the extent that members of the set occupy different social positions.[3] The key to the waitress' problems lies in the fact that her role requires her to relate to people in an unusually large variety of complementary roles. In the simplest case, one's job requires contact with only one complementary role, that of the supervisor. In the more usual case, role relationships have to be maintained with several others, including especially co-workers as well as a supervisor and perhaps subordinates. The waitress' role fits well up on the scale of diversification, inasmuch as it calls for a complex balancing of relationships with at least five classes of role senders: supervisor, customer, fellow waitresses, pantry personnel, and the barman. We can characterize a role set as more or less *diversified* to the extent that it involves the maintenance of a variety of role relationships. It should be

* Excerpted from J. Diedrick Snoek, "Role Strain in Diversified Role Sets," *American Journal of Sociology,* Vol. 71, January 1966, pp. 363–372, by permission of The University of Chicago Press. Copyright © 1966 by The University of Chicago.

[1] See Robert K. Merton, "The Role Set: Problem in Sociological Theory," *British Journal of Sociology,* VIII (June 1957), 113 ff.

[2] Ragnar Rommetviet, *Social Norms and Roles* (Minneapolis: University of Minnesota, 1954).

[3] See Robert K. Merton, *Social Theory and Social Structure* (Glencoe, Ill.: Free Press, 1957); and William J. Goode, "A Theory of Role Strain," *American Sociological Review,* XXV (1960), 483–96.

possible to arrive at a measure of role-set diversity by counting the number of different classes of role senders with whom relationships must be maintained. The concept of a class of role senders is introduced here to take account of the equivalence of all role relationships involving subordinates, for example. The dimension of diversity, therefore, refers to the number of different relationships that must be maintained, not to the number of persons with whom the officeholder must interact.

The greater the diversification of a role set, the greater the possibility of intrarole conflicts, because each class of role senders is apt to develop expectations that are more attuned to its own organizational goals, norms, and values than to the total requirements of the officeholder's role. Gross, Mason, and McEachern have demonstrated such conflicts in their study of school superintendents.[4] Kahn, Wolfe, Quinn, and Snoek also pointed to this source of difficulty in their study of role conflicts in industry, arguing that conflict is especially likely to occur in so-called boundary positions, that is, positions for which some of the role senders are located in a different role system, whether this be another unit in the same organization or another organization entirely.[5] Accordingly, the first hypothesis to be examined is that role strain, in the sense of felt difficulty in job performance, will be more common in jobs requiring the individual to maintain a highly diversified set of role relationships.

A second factor of interest is the size of the organization in which the individual is employed. Organizational size bears upon the rationale just presented in that we would expect the typical phenomena of bureaucratization to be maximally present in large-scale organizations.[6] One of the major unintended consequences of bureaucratization is the increase in rule-bound, inflexible behavior on the part of the organization's members, resulting in difficulty in meeting the needs of the organization's clients. This result should increase the conflict potential for relations with extra-organizational role senders as well as for relations among different units of the organization which were intended to serve each other. A second and related feature of bureaucratization is what Selznick has called the "bifurcation of interests" among departments of the organization, produced by each department's commitment to its own goals and maintenance.[7] Again, where departments develop to some extent their own goals for the organization and their own rules of procedure, the relations among role senders representing different departments should hold greater potential for conflict. A second hypothesis, therefore, is that role strain is more common in large than in small organizations, particularly in those positions that require highly diversified role-sender contacts.

SAMPLE AND PROCEDURES

The data for this study are drawn from a series of questions included in a national sample survey conducted by the University of Michigan's Survey Research Center during 1961. In this study respondents were chosen to represent all adults over eighteen years of age living in private households. Interviews were conducted with 1,300 such persons. For purposes of the present analysis, however, we selected only those people in the sample who reported that they were wage and salary workers and who were working more than twenty hours per week at the time of the survey — a total of 596 persons altogether. Comparison of the present sample with figures reported by the U.S. Census Bureau for the year 1960 revealed no significant differences in terms of age, sex, education, or occupational distribution.

[4] Neal Gross, Ward Mason, and Alexander McEachern, *Explorations in Role Analysis* (New York: John Wiley & Sons, 1958).

[5] Robert L. Kahn, Donald M. Wolfe, Robert P. Quinn, and J. Diedrick Snoek, *Organizational Stress* (New York: John Wiley & Sons, 1964), chap. v.

[6] One recent investigation of the relation between organizational size and bureaucratization asserts that small organizations many on many dimensions of comparison be as "bureaucratic" as large ones (Robert H. Hall, "Bureaucracy and Small Organizations," *Sociology and Social Research*, XLVIII [1963], 38–46). However, several of the small organizations in Hall's study were local branches of very large ones, and larger organiza-

tions clearly had higher scores on some of the dimensions of bureaucratization that Hall employed, e.g., "systematization of rules governing the rights and duties of positional incumbents."

[7] This discussion rests heavily upon the analysis of theories of bureaucracy offered by James G. March and Herbert A. Simon in *Organizations* (New York: John Wiley & Sons, 1958).

The variable used as an indicator of role strain in this study was the Job Related Tension Index (JRT), developed at the Survey Research Center. Scores on this index are derived from a list of fifteen common problems on the job. The interviewer introduced the items by telling respondents:

All of us occasionally feel bothered by certain kinds of things in our work. I'm going to read a list of things that sometimes bother people, and I would like you to tell me how frequently you feel bothered by each of them.

Respondents then reported on a five-point scale the frequency with which they felt bothered by each of the following:[8]

1. Feeling that you have too little authority to carry out the responsibilities assigned to you
2. Being unclear on just what the scope and responsibilities of your job are
3. Not knowing what opportunities for advancement or promotion exist for you
4. Feeling that you have too heavy a work-load, one that you can't possibly finish during an ordinary workday
5. Thinking that you'll not be able to satisfy the conflicting demands of various people over you
6. Feeling that you're not fully qualified to handle your job
7. Not knowing what your supervisor thinks of you, how he evaluates your performance
8. The fact that you can't get information needed to carry out your job
9. Having to decide things that affect the lives of individuals, people that you know
10. Feeling that you may not be liked and accepted by the people you work with
11. Feeling unable to influence your immediate superior's decisions and actions that affect you
12. Not knowing just what the people you work with expect of you
13. Thinking that the *amount* of work you have to do may interfere with how *well* it gets done

14. Feeling that you have to do things on the job that are against your better judgment
15. Feeling that your job tends to interfere with your family life

It is assumed that a high average tendency to report feeling troubled by the variety of problems on the list reflects a high level of emotional tension associated with the job. In earlier studies it has been shown that the items intercorrelate significantly with each other and that each item correlates with total scale scores more than with any other item. High index scores have been found to be significantly associated with an objective measure of role conflict as well as with job dissatisfaction and a variety of mild neurotic symptoms.[9] Getzels and Guba used a very similar measure, labeled "intensity of felt conflict," in a study of role conflict among military instructors, and reported it to be significantly associated with ratings of ineffective teaching performance.[10] In short, JRT seems to measure a variety of difficulties in job performance, close to the conceptual meaning of role strain as discussed by Goode.[11]

The classification of diversity of role-sender contacts was based upon the question: "How often do you have something to do as part of your job with each of the following groups of people?" Five classes of role senders were defined for the respondent: (1) Your boss or other people over you; (2) People you supervise, directly or indirectly; (3) Others who work in the same department as you do; (4) Others who work in the same company, but not in the same department; (5) Outsiders who have business with your company. In addition, the respondent was asked about any other class of contacts he could mention, and this was counted as a sixth class if the contacts he named could not be reclassified into any of the

---

[8] The answer "Doesn't Apply" was also printed on the card shown to respondents. It was used frequently by self-employed persons, but rarely by wage and salary workers. To take account of such instances, however, the index score used in this study is the mean frequency based on the number of items that the respondent thought applied to his job.

[9] See Donald M. Wolfe and J. Diedrick Snoek, "A Study of Tensions and Adjustment under Role Conflict," *Journal of Social Sciences*, XVIII (1962), 102–21; and Kahn *et al., op. cit.* See also Bernard Indik, Stanley E. Seashore, and Jonathan Slesinger, "Demographic Correlates of Psychological Strain," *Journal of Abnormal and Social Psychology*, LXIX (1964), 26–38.

[10] Jack Getzels and Egon Guba, "Role, Role Conflicts and Effectiveness: An Empirical Study," *American Sociological Review*, XIX (1954), 164–75.

[11] William J. Goode, *op. cit.*

earlier categories. Frequency of contact was reported on the five-point scale reported earlier.

Two questions were asked to obtain information about the size of the organization where the respondent was employed. The first of these was intended to establish the size of the plant where respondent worked ("About how many people work at the same place where you work?"). The second question obtained the respondent's best estimate of the total number of persons employed by his company ("Does the company [organization] you work for employ other people besides the ones that work at the same place you do?" IF YES: "To the best of your knowledge, about how many people work for your company [organization] altogether?"). For all companies of more than 100 persons, interviewers also ascertained the name of the organization. The figures reported by the respondents for these organizations were later checked against standard business references.[12] Figures for roughly two-thirds of the companies named could be verified in this way. Few corrections of respondents' estimates proved necessary. In this analysis we shall be concerned with *company size* rather than *plant size,* on the assumption that many of the distinctive features and processes of a large-scale organization probably make themselves felt even in smaller plants belonging to it. Nevertheless, company size is only a very crude operational index of the intended conceptual variable, bureaucratization.

A series of questions attempting to locate each respondent in his organization's chain of command did not yield useful data, because it classified all but a few respondents at the fourth level from the top or lower. This failure is further testimony to the growing importance of the large-scale organization as the most common working environment for Americans today. Instead we shall classify respondents in terms of an implied rank ordering of level of supervisory responsibility, according to whether they have no such responsibility, have some subordinates but all of them under their direct supervision, or have both direct subordinates and indirect responsibility for others.

DIVERSITY OF ROLE-SENDER CONTACTS

Scores on the JRT index have a possible range from 1.0 to 5.0. The frequency distribution of scores is markedly skewed, 16.4 per cent of the sample obtaining the lowest score of 1.0 and an additional 36.9 per cent scoring between 1.1 and 1.5. Since the greatest interest pertains to the high scorers, "high tension" has been defined arbitrarily as a score of 1.6 or higher for purposes of the present analysis.[13]

Table 1 shows the relations between job-related tension and frequency of interaction with each of the five predefined classes of role senders. For four out of five classes of role senders, there is a marked but not necessarily linear relationship between frequency of contact and the prevalence of high tension. In all cases, the greatest increment in high-tension cases occurs in the comparison of those who have no contacts with those who have some contact or more with each class of role senders. This is true even for the case of interaction with superiors, although the number of respondents who report a total absence of daily contacts with their superiors is so small that the difference between them and the remaining respondents might easily have arisen by chance alone.

In the case of contact with subordinate role senders (*line B*), the more frequently the respondent interacts with subordinates, the greater the likelihood that he will have a high tension score. But interaction with other kinds of role senders — those not hierarchically related to the respondent — is most tension-producing when it occurs with a frequency less than the maximum possible on our scale. When the five classes are compared in terms of the over-all levels of tension associated with them, no single class of contacts stands out as significantly more tension-producing than any other. We may summarize the data in Table 1 by concluding that, with the exception of contact with superiors, jobs that require any kind of daily contact with subordinates, with other organization members — whether in one's own de-

---

[12] Mainly, *Moody's Industrial Manuals* (New York: Moody's Investors Service, 1961).

[13] The separation of the JRT distribution comes close to a median split, "high tension" scores starting at the 53d percentile.

TABLE 1   *Percentage of High-Tension Cases in Relation to Frequency of Interaction with Five Cases of Role Senders**

Class of Role Senders	"How Often during the Day Do You Have Something To Do as Part of Your Job with Each of the Following Groups of People?"						
	Never (Inap.)†	Rarely	Some- times	Rather Often	Nearly All the Time	χ^2	P
A. Your boss or other people over you	38 (21)	47 (125)	48 (171)	51 (145)	54 (133)	2.6	N.S.
B. People you supervise directly or indirectly	33 (340)	57 (28)	52 (46)	64 (72)	69 (110)	55.5	< .001
C. Others who work in your depart- ment	38 (157)	50 (62)	51 (130)	58 (106)	42 (141)	14.0	< .01
D. Others in your company, but not in the same department	35 (200)	46 (137)	59 (135)	54 (77)	51 (51)	14.6	< .01
E. Outsiders who have business with your company	34 (278)	64 (66)	59 (71)	65 (69)	47 (108)	38.1	< .001

* In this as in the following tables the number of cases in each cell is shown in parentheses. Total number of cases in each row does not always add up to 596 because of N.A.'s.

† Cases coded Inap. have been combined with those coded Never.

partment or outside it — or with outsiders who have business with one's organization, are apt to be more tension-producing than those that do not.

Let us now ask whether roles that require the maintenance of contacts with many classes of role senders (high diversity) show a greater incidence of high tension than those which involve only a moderate or small number of such relationships. The question is answered in Table 2. The result strongly supports the hypothesis that there is a significant association between tension on the job and interaction with a diversified set of role senders.

TABLE 2   *Percentage of High-Tension Cases in Relation to Role-Set Diversity*

	No. of Classes of Role Senders with Whom Respondent Maintains Contact in His Job				
	1–2	3	4	5	6
Per cent	25	34	45	65	80
N	(144)	(138)	(136)	(98)	(88)

NOTE: χ^2 (excluding N.A.'s): 83.3; 4 d.f.; $P < .001$.

SUPERVISORY RESPONSIBILITY

The data collected also permitted the analysis of the relationship between job-related tension and supervisory responsibility. In an earlier study on a much smaller sample, Wolfe and Snoek found tension to be associated with both supervisory responsibility and organizational rank.[14] In this sample, 42 per cent of those who have direct supervision over some people and 75 per cent of those who have both direct supervisory responsibility over some and indirect responsibility for others have high tension scores, as compared with only 36 per cent among those without any supervisory responsibility.

Since people with diversified role sets carry supervisory responsibility noticeably more often than those in low-diversity role sets, we may well ask whether the greater prevalence of tension among supervisors is not associated almost exclusively with the diversity variable. As Table 3 shows, supervisors appear more likely to report high tension even when we control for the effects of the diversity variable. In the remainder of the

[14] Wolfe and Snoek, *op. cit.*

TABLE 3 *Percentage of High-Tension Cases in Relation to Supervisory Responsibility and Role-Set Diversity*

Supervisory Responsibility	Low Diversity (1–2)	Moderate Diversity (3–4)	High Diversity (5–6)
None:			
Per cent	20	36	63
N	(127)	(200)	(70)
Direct, indirect, or both:			
Per cent	67	49	77
N	(12)	(67)	(113)

NOTE: χ^2 for tension in relation to supervisory responsibility: low diversity: 12.01 (corrected for continuity), $P < .01$; moderate diversity: 3.75, $P < .10$; high diversity: 4.23, $P < .05$.

analysis, supervisory responsibility will therefore be treated as an independent contributor to tension.

COMPANY SIZE

Let us turn now to the variable of company size, with its implications for increased complexity of organization and difficulty of co-ordination among adjacent offices. Table 4 shows that high tension is relatively more common in large organizations than in smaller ones. Table 5 shows that the differences in tension level associated with company size tend to disappear when we control for the respondent's level of role-set diversification, except in the case of those with the highest level of diversification. The same reduction of

TABLE 4 *Percentage of High-Tension Cases in Relation to Company Size*

	Estimated No. of Employees Working for Respondent's Company				
	1–9	10–49	50–499	500–4,999	5,000+
Per cent	29	45	42	56	54
N	(85)	(95)	(141)	(96)	(183)

NOTE: χ^2 (excluding N.A.'s): 18.5, 4 d.f., $P < .001$.

TABLE 5 *Prevalence of High Tension in Small and Large Companies,* Controlling for Role-Set Diversification and Supervisory Responsibility*

Company Size	Level of Role-Set Diversity†		
	Low (1–2)	Moderate (3–4)	High (5–6)
Small (< 500):			
Per cent	27	40	64
N	(96)	(201)	(114)
Large (≧ 500):			
Per cent	26	39	85
N	(38)	(72)	(72)

Company Size	Level of Supervisory Responsibility‡		
	None	Direct Only	Direct and Indirect
Small (< 500):			
Per cent	35	57	68
N	(281)	(84)	(40)
Large (≧ 500)			
Per cent	38	73	86
N	(124)	(40)	(29)

* χ^2: small versus large (high diversity, 9.3, $P < .01$).
† χ^2: role-set diversity (small company, 31.3, $P < .001$; large company 45.7, $P < .001$).
‡ χ^2: supervisory responsibility (small company, 24.1, $P < .001$; large company 30.1, $P < .001$).

differences between small and large companies appears in the second half of Table 5, when we control for supervisory responsibility. None of the apparent differences in tension level between those working in small as opposed to large companies reaches the 5 per cent level of significance in this case.

Focusing on the previously established relationship between level of diversification and tension, the results show that it appears in both small and large companies. The same is true for the relationship between supervisory responsibility and tension. In short, the prevalence of high tension increases as a function of both role-set diversification and supervisory responsibility, regardless of company size. The over-all greater prevalence of tension in large companies is in large part attributable to the fact that one finds more role-set diversification and also more supervisors in large than in small organizations.

If our earlier reasoning is correct, we would also expect that whatever possibilities for role strain are implicit in role-set diversification would be realized more often in organizations with a higher level of bureaucratization. Using company size as a crude indicator of bureaucratization, the results give tentative support to this hypothesis in that high role-set diversification is associated with a significantly higher level of tension in large than in small companies.

SOME DEMOGRAPHIC CORRELATES OF TENSION

The first column of Table 6 shows the prevalence of high tension in relation to sex, age, and

TABLE 6 *Prevalence of High Tension by Age, Sex, and Education*

	Crude Prevalence* (Per Cent)	Standardized Prevalence† (Per Cent)	Base N
Age:			
18–24	42	43	64
25–34	53	51	169
35–44	49	50	148
45–54	43	43	128
55–65+	35	37	92
Sex:			
Male	51	48	384
Female	38	43	219
Education			
Grade school (0–8)	32	39	144
High school (9–12)	43	44	284
College (13+)	63	52	170

* χ^2 (crude rates): age: 24.4, $P < .001$; sex: 18.5, $P < .001$; education: 32.1, $P < .001$.

† Standardized for role-set diversity and supervisory responsibility; χ^2 calculated on standardized rates fails to show significant associations.

education. High tension tends to be more common among males than females, among the younger than among the older age groups, and among college-educated than among high-school- or grade-school-educated groups. These findings are in accord with those published by Indik, Seashore, and Slesinger, who reported the demographic correlates of job-related tension among a very large population of employees of a single company.[15]

It is, of course, possible that the apparent association of tension with age, sex, and education can be attributed to differences among these demographic groups in the distribution of role diversity and supervisory responsibility. The second column of Table 6 shows the relationship between tension and each of the demographic variables after the figures have been adjusted to take account of the influence of role diversity and supervisory responsibility.[16] A comparison of the crude and standardized prevalence figures shows that, especially in the case of sex and education, the degree of association between the demographic variable and tension is substantially reduced after role diversity and supervisory responsibility have been taken into account. Chi-square values calculated on the adjusted figures fail to reach the 5 per cent level of confidence, although the trends noted in the crude figures are still apparent. The reduction of tension differentials is especially apparent in the case of sex and education, but less so in the case of age. In short, the high prevalence of tension observed among men and among college-educated persons can apparently be attributed in large part to the fact that the jobs held by these persons are more likely to involve role-set diversification and supervisory responsibility.

[15] Indik *et al.*, *op. cit.*

[16] The standardized figures have been calculated by the so-called indirect method, set forth in George W. Barclay, *Techniques of Population Analysis* (New York: John Wiley & Sons, 1958), pp. 161–66. Tension-prevalence rates for the total sample, subdivided into six groups defined by three levels of diversity and two levels of supervisory responsibility, were used as the standard.

60 Status Consistency and Cognitive Dissonance*

James A. Geschwender

A major source of deviant behavior, as we have seen, is the incompatibility of the various roles assigned to persons who occupy a variety of positions in complex societies. Several theories have been constructed to organize the vast amount of information available on this subject. The following paper analyzes some of these theories and attempts to find certain points of agreement from which behavioral predictions can be made. An impressive array of theoretical uniformities and behavioral predictions is the result.

The concept of status consistency (status crystallization or status congruence) is gradually assuming greater prominence in the literature of social stratification. Its major weakness lies in its use as a structural characteristic predicting behavioral consequences without an explicitly stated social-psychological theory of motivation to account for these predictions. Three such theories have been proposed. They are Homans' Theory of Distributive Justice,[1] Zaleznik's Theory of Social Certitude,[2] and Sampson's Principle of Expectancy Congruence.[3]

The last-named is an attempt to explain the findings of status consistency research within the framework of Festinger's Theory of Cognitive Dissonance.[4] Sampson's approach is similar to that of Zaleznik but has the advantage of being more general. However, it is still incomplete as it does not adequately explain all consequences of status inconsistency. It is suggested herein that the Theory of Distributive Justice can bridge this gap if it can be integrated into a dissonance framework. Two attempts to do this have been made.[5] However, they represent mere beginnings as they are limited as to degree of specification and detailed analysis. The present paper hopes to complete the task and to spell out in some detail further implications of the combined theory.

The strategy of attack will be to briefly describe the Theory of Social Certitude and the Principle of Expectancy Congruence, to relate them to each other, and to evaluate this combination. The Theory of Distributive Justice will then be described and integrated into dissonance theory. This combination will subsequently be evaluated as to its ability to explain the empirical findings of status consistency and further theoretical implications will be derived.

SOCIAL CERTITUDE AND EXPECTANCY CONGRUENCE

The essence of the Theory of Social Certitude is the assumption that each status position carries with it a set of behavioral expectations regarding both the behavior of the occupant of said position and the behavior of all persons with whom he interacts. Each individual occupies several positions and possesses several sets of behavioral expectations which may either reinforce or contradict one another.

The status consistent possesses sets of behavioral expectations which either reinforce or are consistent with one another. A condition of social certitude exists and social relations are fluid and satisfying. The status inconsistent possesses sets of expectations which conflict with one another. A condition of social certitude does not exist. Anxiety is produced for all concerned and social relations are hampered and unsatisfying. This sets in motion forces tending toward the creation of status consistency.

---

* From *Social Forces*, Vol. 46, December 1967, pp. 160–171. Reproduced by permission.

[1] George C. Homans, *Social Behavior: Its Elementary Forms* (New York: Harcourt, Brace & Co., 1961).

[2] A. Zaleznik, C. R. Christenson, and F. J. Roethlisberger, in collaboration with George C. Homans, *The Motivation, Productivity, and Satisfaction of Workers* (Cambridge: Harvard University Press, 1958), pp. 56–66.

[3] Edward E. Sampson, "Status Congruence and Cognitive Consistency," *Sociometry*, 26 (June 1963), pp. 146–162.

[4] Leon Festinger, *A Theory of Cognitive Dissonance* (Evanston, Illinois: Row, Peterson & Co., 1957).

[5] James A. Geschwender, "Explorations in the Theory of Social Movements and Revolutions," unpublished manuscript; and C. Norman Alexander, Jr., and Richard L. Simpson, "Balance Theory and Distributive Justice," *Sociological Inquiry*, 34 (Spring 1964), pp. 182–192.

The Principle of Expectancy Congruence and the Theory of Social Certitude have much in common. The major difference between them is that the former is stated within the framework of the more general dissonance theory while the latter stands alone. Sampson bases his analysis upon the following assumption:

Let us make the assumption that one aspect of each position — or set of positions — along a given status dimension consists of certain expectations for the behavior of the occupant of that position. Thus, for example, a person ranking high in education may meaningfully be said to have certain expectations held by others and by himself for his behavior. A similar parallel between rank position and expectation can be drawn for other dimensions along which persons can be ranked.[6]

From this point, the analysis is identical to that proposed by Zaleznik. Incongruent expectations are a problem for everyone and interfere with interaction. Congruent expectations simplify interaction. Thus, there is a pressure on all participants to create and maintain a congruence of expectations. This is why status inconsistency is an undesirable state which produces pressure toward changing the situation.

EVALUATION OF SOCIAL CERTITUDE AND EXPECTANCY CONGRUENCE

The Principle of Expectancy Congruence has the advantage of being derivable from a more general theory of motivation. This makes it more attractive than the Theory of Social Certitude as it may be more easily related to findings in other areas. However, the ultimate test of any theory is how well it explains empirical findings. It is at this point that the principle breaks down.

Research has demonstrated a relationship between status inconsistency and tendencies toward social isolation, mobility striving, political liberalism, psychosomatic symptoms of stress, and preference for changes in the social order or actual attempts to bring about these changes. This research will be discussed below. Some of these findings are explainable within an expectancy congruence approach and some are not.

The frustrations and anxieties produced by a lack of expectancy congruence might easily produce psychological symptoms of stress. They might interfere with social interaction and produce a tendency for inconsistents to withdraw into social isolation. They might also produce mobility strivings to achieve a state of expectancy congruence. However, this approach does not do a very good job of explaining the status inconsistent's preference for a change in the social order and predisposition for participation in social movements. Actually, mobility strivings are only partially explained. This approach does not supply us with any means of predicting which response to inconsistency a status inconsistent will be likely to select. An expanded theory which integrates the Theory of Distributive Justice into dissonance theory might perform this function.

THE THEORY OF DISTRIBUTIVE JUSTICE

An author can usually state his own ideas better than someone else can summarize or paraphrase them. Thus, it is best to quote Homans' description of his theory:

A man in an exchange relation with another will expect that the rewards of each man will be proportional to his costs — the greater the investments, the greater the profits. . . . Finally, when each man is being rewarded by some third party, he will expect the third party, in the distribution of rewards, to maintain the relation between the two of them. . . . . The more to a man's disadvantage the rule of distributive justice fails of realization, the more likely he is to display the emotional behavior we call anger . . . men are regarded by the attainment of justice, especially when just conditions are rewarding in other ways. For instance, I am more likely to demand justice when justice would bring me more money than when it would bring me less. . . . Not only do men display anger, or less predominantly, guilt when distributive justice fails in one way or the other, but they also learn to do something about it. They learn to avoid activities that get them into unjust exchanges; they learn to emit activities that are rewarded by the attainment of justice. . . .[7]

---

[6] Sampson, *op. cit.,* p. 153.

[7] Homans, *op. cit.,* pp. 332–333.

Homans suggested that certain status dimensions could be viewed as investments into a social situation while others could be viewed as rewards received from that situation. The four dimensions that Lenski utilized in his analysis of status consistency may be classified according to this framework. Education and ethnicity may be seen as investment dimensions. There are universalistic norms in American society which lead one to expect that he will be rewarded in terms of his level of education. There are also particularistic norms which lead one to expect that he will be rewarded in terms of his ethnic status. Thus, education may be classified as an achieved investment and ethnicity as an ascribed investment.

Occupation and income may be viewed as reward dimensions. Income is clearly a reward as it determines one's standard of living. Occupation may also be seen as a type of reward. Some occupations are preferable to others in terms of the amount of physical labor demanded by them, the cleanliness of the work, and the amount of individual autonomy allowed. Thus, occupation may be classified as a social reward and income as a material reward.

Using these definitions, it could be concluded that a state of distributive justice exists when individuals who possess greater investments (higher education and/or ethnicity) also possess greater rewards (higher occupation and/or income). Those persons whose investments are higher than rewards (level of occupation and/or income below level of education and/or ethnicity) will experience a felt injustice and feel anger. It is reasonable to assume that this anger may be directed against the society which fails to maintain distributive justice and may lead to behavior designed to change society in order to eliminate this inequity.

Those persons whose investments are lower than their rewards (education and/or ethnicity below level of occupation and/or income) would experience a felt injustice and feel guilt. It may be assumed that individuals who are over-rewarded will not attempt to reduce guilt feelings by lowering their reward level. It is more likely that they will develop a political philosophy which, if implemented, would ameliorate the consequences of being short-changed for those who are under-

rewarded. They might also develop a philosophy which defines ascribed investments as irrelevant to rewards. In short, they may become political liberals. If educational investment is the low dimension, they may either attempt to raise their level of education to one consistent with rewards received or else develop a definition of education as being "ivory tower" and impractical, which would lead to anti-intellectualism. It is to be noted that the Theory of Distributive Justice is not equipped to handle an explanation of the consequences of either investment (education-ethnicity) or reward (occupation-income) inconsistencies.

RELATION OF DISTRIBUTIVE JUSTICE TO DISSONANCE THEORY

It is possible to incorporate the Theory of Distributive Justice into dissonance theory with the addition of a few assumptions. We may assume that every individual includes within his cognitive set cognitions concerning his status level in the educational, occupational, ethnic, and income hierarchies. We may assume that he possesses cognitions defining education as an achieved investment, ethnicity as an ascribed investment, occupation as a social reward, and income as a material reward. We may also assume that he possesses cognitions which define the proper relation that should hold between investment and reward dimensions. This definition of the proper relation between investments and rewards would be based upon the individual's perception of that relation which normally exists in society.

Thus, experiencing a state of felt injustice is reduced to experiencing cognitive dissonance resulting from inconsistency among simultaneously held cognitions. The empirical consequences of felt injustice may be seen as behavioral attempts to reduce dissonance.

This may be combined with Sampson's assumption that each status position carries with it expectations regarding behavior that should be forthcoming from, or directed toward, the occupant of that position. Congruent sets of expectations facilitate the development of satisfying patterns of social interaction and incongruent sets of expectations impede this development. Thus, status inconsistency leads to the development of cognitive dissonance, and attempts to cope with this inconsistency represent behavioral attempts to reduce dissonance. Other behavioral responses may be non-coping responses indicating an inability to reduce dissonance. Dissonance theory, thus expanded, may enable us to explain the empirical consequences of status inconsistency which have been observed and to predict others not yet observed.

EVALUATION IN RELATION TO FINDINGS

The research literature has demonstrated six different types of responses to status inconsistency. These are enhanced mobility striving, withdrawal into social isolation, psychosomatic symptoms of stress, political liberalism, preference for and attempts to change the social order, and prejudice. The findings in each of these areas of research will be considered separately and in relation to the foregoing theoretical approach.

Mobility Striving

Benoit-Smullyan proposed the existence of a status equilibration process.[8] He stated that individuals are ranked or have status on three major dimensions: the economic, political, and prestige hierarchies. These types of status are analytically distinguishable and often empirically independent, but there is a tendency for one to be transformed into the others through a status equilibration process.

Implicit in Benoit-Smullyan's analysis is the assumption that possession of discrepant statuses in different hierarchies creates strain for individuals and causes them to follow a course of action designed to bring their statuses into line with one another. This assumption was not tested. Fenchel *et al.,* did attempt to test this hypothesis with an undergraduate population at CCNY.[9] They had the students rate themselves as to their general standing in five potential reference groups

and as to where they would like to stand. The difference between the two ratings was taken as an index of status striving. The hypothesis was supported as the students did tend to strive for a common ranking in all reference groups.

Homans reinterpreted one of his earlier studies into a framework which lends support to the equilibration hypothesis.[10] This was a study of female clerical workers and involved two categories of jobs — cash posters and ledger clerks. The line of promotion was from cash poster to ledger clerk. The general evaluation was that the position of ledger clerk was a better job, carried more responsibility, and conveyed more status. However, the same salary was paid to both positions. Ledger clerks protested demanding that they be paid more than the cash posters as would befit their more important jobs. They were status inconsistent because their material rewards were not comparable to their occupational status. They were attempting to reduce dissonance by raising their lower-ranking status to a level consistent with their higher-ranking one.

The literature does not deal with variations in response by pattern of status inconsistency. However, it does yield implications for it. It suggests that persons experiencing dissonance resulting from status inconsistency may attempt to reduce this dissonance by altering their ranking on one or more of the dimensions of status. This would not be equally possible for all types of inconsistents. Persons who are low ethnically but high on the other dimensions could not normally be expected to alter their ethnic status through individual mobility. But a person who is high in education and low in occupation and/or income might hope to reduce dissonance through hard work, individual effort, and mobility on the occupational and/or income dimensions. More will be said about this below.

Political Liberalism

Lenski studied the relationship between status inconsistency and political liberalism.[11] A sample of persons were asked their views toward a gov-

[8] Emile Benoit-Smullyan, "Status, Status Types, and Status Interrelations," *American Sociological Review,* 9 (April 1944), pp. 151–161.

[9] Gerd H. Fenchel, Jack H. Monderer, and Eugene H. Hartley, "Subjective Status and the Equilibration Hypothesis," *Journal of Abnormal and Social Psychology,* 46 (October 1951), pp. 476–479.

[10] Homans, *op. cit.,* pp. 237–242.

[11] Gerhard E. Lenski, "Status Crystallization: A Non-Vertical Dimension of Social Status," *American Sociological Review,* 19 (August 1954), pp. 405–413.

ernment-sponsored health insurance program, price controls, and a general extension of governmental powers. Their responses were classified along a continuum of liberalism. The more liberal responses were found to be associated with low status consistency. Democratic voting was taken to be an indication of relative liberalism and was found to be associated with low status consistency.[12]

Both of these associations held when general status levels were controlled. Certain patterns of inconsistency were more closely associated with liberalism than others. A person of low ethnic status and high income, occupational, or educational status tended to be more liberal than the reverse combinations. Individuals with low educational and high occupational statuses tended to be more politically liberal than did those with the opposite combination. An inconsistent with high occupational and low income status was more likely to be liberal than was the reverse combination. In fact, the high income–low occupation inconsistent was less likely to be liberal than were consistents.

Lenski's findings have been interpreted as indicating that status inconsistents may be prone to engage in social movements designed to bring about major changes in society. This may be erroneous. The particular items that Lenski used to measure political liberalism appear to be more closely related to a mild reformist perspective as might be incorporated into a welfare state or great society philosophy rather than the type of outlook that would motivate a person to join a social movement with more sweeping aims.

These findings suggest that a person who experiences dissonance resulting from status inconsistency may try to reduce his dissonance through the development of a liberal political outlook. The relationship of particular types of inconsistents to political liberalism is suggestive. Inconsistents with low educational and high occupational statuses and inconsistents with low ethnic and high occupational or income statuses are types of inconsistents categorized above as over-rewarded. Their investment dimensions are lower than their reward dimensions. They would be expected to feel guilt. Their attempts to reduce dissonance might be expected to take the form of attempting to ameliorate the consequences for others of their getting more than their share, and to develop a belief that ethnicity should not be related to rewards. Both of these are indications of political liberalism.

The inconsistent with low ethnicity but a high educational status represents a different type. He has brought his achieved investment to a level higher than his ascribed investment. In this sense, he is a success. One might expect that, in this sample, this type of inconsistent is also high on reward dimensions. This is based on the fact that inconsistents with high education and low occupation are lower on the liberalism scale. Thus, they may also be over-rewarded and react as the others described above. However, I would suggest that we reserve judgment of this type of inconsistent. It might be necessary to know his position on reward dimensions before making any predictions about him. Similarly, we should reserve decision on the two types of reward inconsistents (high income–low occupation and high occupation–low income). It is difficult to draw any conclusions regarding the relative importance of income and occupation as types of rewards.

Social Isolation

Lenski also studied the relationship between status inconsistency and tendencies toward social isolation.[13] He found that status inconsistents were less likely than status consistents to interact with neighbors and fellow workers outside of business hours, to be members of voluntary associations, to be regular participants in those voluntary

[12] Kenkel's retest of this hypothesis produced results which did not support it. See William F. Kenkel, "The Relationship Between Status Consistency and Politico-Economic Attitudes," *American Sociological Review,* 26 (June 1961), pp. 365–368. However, this retest was severely criticized. See Gerhard E. Lenski, "Comments on Kenkel's Communication," *American Sociological Review,* 26 (June 1961), pp. 368–369. Lenski maintained that Kenkel erred in using different indices of status. His lack of results may have resulted from not using those that Lenski believed had a central place in American society. For the purposes of the present analysis, it will be useful to assume that Lenski's criticisms are correct.

[13] Gerhard E. Lenski, "Social Participation and Status Crystallization," *American Sociological Review,* 21 (August 1956), pp. 458–464.

associations in which they were members, and less likely to report sociable motives (noneconomic reasons) for those voluntary ties that they had. No attempt was made to analyze the relation between types of inconsistency and tendency toward social isolation.

Homans provided data which suggest that this tendency toward social isolation may not always be voluntary.[14] He found that the status inconsistent members of a work group were high on initiating interaction for others but were low on the receipt of interaction from others. Generally the interaction that they initiated took the form of horseplay or joking. Homans suggested that joking may be the reaction of the inconsistent to the insecurities in the situation, while the reaction of others is a tendency to avoid the inconsistent.

These results are explainable with the assumptions that Sampson makes in his Principle of Expectancy Congruence. Status inconsistency creates a situation in which there exist conflicting sets of behavioral expectations. This interferes with the development of fluid tension-free interaction. Thus, interaction becomes unpleasant and tends to be broken off. It may be possible that the earliest stage of this process is found in other persons avoiding the inconsistent and in the inconsistent resorting to joking. Withdrawal on the part of the inconsistent may represent the final acceptance on his part of the impossibility of creating satisfying patterns of interaction. Suicide is the most extreme form of withdrawal, and Gibbs and Martin found a relationship between status inconsistency and propensity toward suicide.[15]

Preference for Social Change

Lenski postulated that status inconsistents might be prone to react against society by participating as leaders in social movements and that a society with widespread status inconsistencies was unstable and generated pressures toward change.[16] However, he never empirically tested this proposition. Benoit-Smullyan made a similar suggestion when he stated, "There are historical grounds for supposing that when legal, customary, or other barriers seriously hamper the equilibrating tendency, social tensions of revolutionary magnitude may be generated."[17] He cited as evidence the fact that support for the Nazi Party came from large classes of persons who became impoverished but retained their former prestige statuses.

There are other historical examples of status inconsistents who have supported social movements. Frazier noted that Negro support for organizations like the Urban League and the NAACP tends to come from middle-class Negroes.[18] Lipset pointed out that urban middle-class leaders in the C.C.F. tended to come from minority groups, while the urban middle-class leaders in the Liberal and Conservative Parties tended to come from the Anglo-Saxon majority group.[19] Michaels noted that middle-class Jews were quite prominent in European Socialist parties.[20] These last three examples are all of status inconsistents whose ethnic status was lower than their occupational status. It is worth noting at

---

[14] George C. Homans, *Sentiments and Activities* (Glencoe, Illinois: The Free Press, 1962), p. 100.

[15] Jack P. Gibbs and Walter T. Martin, "Status Integration and Suicide," *American Sociological Review,* 23 (April 1958), pp. 140–147. For other research documenting the fact that status inconsistency interferes with the development of free communications and satisfying interaction see Stuart Adams, "Status Congruency as a Variable in Small Group Performance," *Social Forces,* 32 (October 1953), pp. 16–22; Ralph V. Exline and Robert C. Ziller, "Status Congruence and Interpersonal Conflict in Decision-Making Groups," *Human Relations,* 12 (April 1959), pp. 147–162; and Arlene C. Brandon, "Status Congruence and Expectations," *Sociometry,* 28 (September 1965), pp. 272–288.

[16] Lenski, "Status Crystallization . . . ," p. 412.

[17] Benoit-Smullyan, *op. cit.,* p. 160. For supporting documentation see also William Kornhauser, *The Politics of Mass Society* (Glencoe, Illinois: The Free Press, 1959), p. 181. Lipset cites unpublished research by Robert Sokol which found a relationship between perceived status discrepancy and support of McCarthy, but patterns of discrepancy were not discussed. See Seymour M. Lipset, "Three Decades of the Radical Right," in Daniel Bell, *The Radical Right* (New York: Anchor Books, 1955), p. 403.

[18] E. Franklin Frazier, *Black Bourgeoisie* (Glencoe, Illinois: The Free Press, 1959), pp. 98–104.

[19] Seymour M. Lipset, *Agrarian Socialism* (Berkeley: University of California Press, 1950), p. 191.

[20] Robert Michels, *Political Parties,* (trans.) Eden and Cedar Paul (New York: Dover Publications, 1959), pp. 260–261.

this point that the examples show low ethnicity–high occupation inconsistents supporting leftist movements and high occupation–low income inconsistents supporting rightist movements.

Ringer and Sills found a high proportion of status inconsistents among political extremists in Iran. They were overrepresented among the extremists on the revolutionary left and the nationalistic right.[21] The inconsistents were of a high educational level and only a moderate economic status. The degree of inconsistency was sharpest for the revolutionary left. Both types of extremists were anti-colonialist and this common antagonism to vestiges of colonialism may have been more important in attracting adherents than their left-right differences. These data shows a tendency for under-rewarded inconsistents with a high level of education to take an extremist position in reacting against the social order. The data regarding the NAACP, C.C.F., and Jewish socialists show over-rewarded inconsistents with a low ethnic status taking a more moderate reformist position when reacting against the social order.

Goffman related status inconsistency to preferences for change in power distributions within society.[22] Status inconsistency was measured using the educational, occupational, and income hierarchies. Preference for change was measured by asking respondents to check their perceptions of the amount of influence in the conduct of national affairs presently held by, and the amount of influence that they prefer be held by, state governments, big business, labor unions, businesses that were not big, and the national government. Status inconsistents exhibited a greater preference for change than did status consistents. This relation held with general status levels controlled. No attempt was made to analyze differences between status types. It is not possible to discuss the left-right direction of these preferences for change without knowing more detail about the responses than Goffman provided.

These findings suggest that there is reason to believe that status inconsistents may attempt to reduce dissonance by reacting against the social order, or at least by expressing a preference for a change in the present distribution of power within society. They further suggest that under-rewarded inconsistents are more likely than over-rewarded inconsistents to take an extreme reaction against the social order. This is predictable from the assumptions incorporated into dissonance theory from the Theory of Distributive Justice. Homans states that anger is a stronger emotion than guilt. The angry (under-rewarded) inconsistent would be expected to experience a sharper form of dissonance and a more extreme reaction than would guilty (over-rewarded) inconsistents.

Psychosomatic Symptoms

Elton Jackson studied the relationship between status inconsistency and the exhibition of psychosomatic symptoms.[23] Consistency was measured in terms of the ethnic, educational, and occupational status dimensions. He found a significant relationship between status inconsistency and the exhibition of psychosomatic symptoms. He also found a significant difference between types of inconsistents.

Jackson noted that two types of inconsistents (high ethnicity combined with either low occupation or low education) had high rates of psychosomatic symptoms, while the opposite types (low ethnicity combined with high education or high occupation) did not have symptom rates which differed from that of status consistents. He noted that Lenski had found the two types of status inconsistents with high symptom rates to exhibit only a slight tendency toward political liberalism and the two types with low symptom rates to exhibit strong tendencies toward political liberalism.

[21] Benjamin B. Ringer and David L. Sills, "Political Extremists in Iran," *Public Opinion Quarterly,* 16 (Winter 1953), pp. 689–701.

[22] Irwin W. Goffman, "Status Consistency and Preference for Change in Power Distribution," *American Sociological Review,* 22 (June 1957), pp. 275–288.

[23] Elton F. Jackson, "Status Consistency and Symptoms of Stress," *American Sociological Review,* 27 (August 1962), pp. 469–480. Dunham has also found that persons with high education and low occupation exhibit a tendency toward both schizophrenia and psychopathies, though he raises questions regarding the causal direction. See H. Warren Dunham, Patricia Phillips, and Barbara Srinivasan, "A Research Note on Diagnosed Mental Illness and Social Class," *American Sociological Review,* 31 (April 1966). pp. 223–227.

He suggested that the important determinant is the relationship between achieved and ascribed ranks. Those with high ascribed and low achieved ranks are likely to see themselves as failures and to develop high psychosomatic symptom rates. Persons with low ascribed and high achieved ranks are likely to see themselves as successes — they have made it despite their ethnic handicap. Thus, they will direct their response to stress outward. This will take a political form for many.

The major difficulty with this interpretation of political and psychosomatic responses as alternative ways of reacting to inconsistency is that it does not seem to apply equally well to all types of inconsistents. Jackson included in his table, but did not discuss, psychosomatic symptom rates and tendencies toward political liberalism for high occupation–low education and high education–low occupation inconsistents. Both types of inconsistents have symptom rates higher than consistents and also exhibit a stronger tendency toward political liberalism. The one possible support for viewing political and physical reactions as alternative responses comes from the fact the symptom rates for these two types of inconsistents are lower than those with high physical, low political responses and their tendency toward political liberalism is less than those with high political, low physical responses. Possibly these results show a tendency for some persons experiencing this type of inconsistency to react physically and others to react politically.

Jackson advanced one other tentative proposition that bears examination. He found male inconsistents with high occupation and low educational statuses to have a symptom rate much higher than did status consistents. Those males who had high educational and low occupational statuses exhibited a symptom rate lower than that of status consistents. He suggests that mobility opportunities might explain this. The latter type of inconsistent is likely to see the possibility of future mobility bringing about consistency, while the former type cannot look forward to this possibility. More mobility would simply cause greater inconsistency. Jackson indicated elsewhere the existence of the relation of mobility possibilities

and age.[24] Younger inconsistents, who had status profiles which could become consistent through mobility, had lower levels of psychosomatic symptoms than older inconsistents with similar profiles. This could indicate that with advanced age mobility would be defined as less likely and persons would give up striving and develop physical responses.

Jackson's major contribution came in demonstrating that failure to reduce dissonance through either mobility or political reactions might force one to attempt to live with dissonance. Dissonance is tension-producing and, in the absence of dissonance-reducing behavioral attempts, might easily produce a physical response leading to psychosomatic symptoms.

Prejudice

There is currently very little research relating status inconsistency to prejudice.[25] However, we can draw indirect inferences regarding this relationship if we accept membership in the Ku Klux Klan as an indication of racial prejudice. Vander Zanden has pulled together the names and occupations of 153 members of the Klan.[26] Ninety-eight of these were found in occupations (skilled labor, marginal businessmen, and marginal white-collar occupations) which are the occupations in

[24] Elton F. Jackson, "Status Consistency, Vertical Mobility, and Symptoms of Stress," unpublished Ph.D. dissertation, University of Michigan, 1960, p. 95.

[25] See Donald J. Treiman, "Status Discrepancy and Prejudice," *American Journal of Sociology,* 71 (May 1966), pp. 651–664. Treiman attempted to evaluate the relative utility of a status consistency and an additive hypothesis for the explanation of prejudice. He concluded that the additive hypothesis was adequate for the explanation of prejudice without making the complex assumptions involved in a status consistency hypothesis. His treatment is unsatisfactory for three reasons. First, he limited himself to a consideration of education — income inconsistents. Second, he used family income rather than individual income. This does not give an individual status profile as one does not know how many people contribute to total family income. Third, and most important, he used a system of classification which produced some "inconsistents" which could be more accurately classified as consistents. This does not mean that his findings are necessarily wrong — merely that they are questionable.

[26] James W. Vander Zanden, *Race Relations in Transition* (New York: Random House, 1965), pp. 42–43.

which Negroes are making the greatest inroads.[27] The rest are transportation workers, semiskilled or unskilled laborers. These are occupations in which whites have been receiving competition from Negroes for many years. It is reasonable to assume that in the South, the status attributed to an occupation declines with increases in the proportion of Negroes. Thus, KKK members are status inconsistent because their occupational status fails to come up to their high ethnic status.

If membership in the KKK is not accepted as a valid indication of racial prejudice, it certainly is an indication of willingness to express and/or act out hostility toward members of a racial minority. Thus, we can see that under-rewarded status inconsistents may attempt to reduce dissonance by directing hostility against members of a minority group.

DISCUSSION

It would appear that all research findings to date dealing with consequences of status inconsistency can be explained within the framework of an expanded version of dissonance theory. This would require combining the initial premises of the theory with Sampson's assumptions and a series of assumptions derived from the Theory of Distributive Justice. A brief statement of the assumptions would go as follows:

1. All persons hold sets of cognitions which include some that are reality-based, some which are definitional, and some that are normative. Reality-based cognitions describe the existing state of affairs while normative cognitions describe the state of affairs which should exist.

2. Any set of cognitions may stand in a relation of dissonance, consonance, or irrelevance depending upon the internal relations which hold among reality-based and normative cognitions. If the conjunction of a reality-based and a normative

cognition implies another reality-based cognition in the set then a state of consonance exists. If this conjunction implies the negation of another reality-based cognition in the set then a state of dissonance exists. If this conjunction implies neither another reality-based cognition nor the negation of one in the set then a state of irrelevance exists.

3. Reality-based cognitions will include perceptions of one's status in the educational, occupational, income, and ethnic hierarchies. They will also include perceptions of behavior expected from, and expected to be directed toward, the occupants of positions in each of these hierarchies. Definitional cognitions will include the definition of ethnicity as an ascribed investment, education as an achieved investment, occupation as a social reward, and income as a material reward. Normative cognitions will include beliefs regarding the proper relation that should exist among the various status positions. Particularly, they will include the belief that rewards received should be proportional to investments. Possession of a higher level of ascribed investments than achieved investments will be defined as failure. The reverse combination will be defined as success.

4. Dissonance is an upsetting state and will produce tension for the individual. This tension will lead to an attempt to reduce dissonance by altering cognitions, adding new cognitions, or deleting old ones. Attempts to alter reality-based cognitions will involve attempting to change the real world. Attempts to alter normative cognitions will involve attempts to change evaluations of the real world and will take place within the cognitive system.

5. Status inconsistents whose rewards received are less than believed to be proper for their investments will feel anger and inconsistents whose rewards exceed investments will feel guilt. Anger is a sharper form of dissonance than guilt. The perception of failure produces a sharper form of dissonance than the perception of success. The intensity of dissonance-reducing behavior will be directly proportional to the sharpness of dissonance.

6. Dissonance-reducing attempts will take the form of coping responses, attempts to change the real world, when possible. When coping responses

---

[27] For a description of these inroads see James A. Geschwender, "Social Structure and the Negro Revolt: An Examination of Some Hypotheses," *Social Forces,* 43 (December 1964), pp. 248–256; James A. Geschwender, "Desegregation, the Educated Negro, and the Future of Social Protest in the South," *Sociological Inquiry,* 35 (Winter 1965), pp. 58–68.

are not possible, dissonance-reducing attempts will take the form of attempting to withdraw from interaction. When neither changing the real world nor withdrawal from it is possible, dissonance will remain and the tension will be manifested in psychosomatic symptoms.

7. Dissonance-reducing attempts will move from the simple to the complex. That is, the simplest types of alterations in reality that would reduce dissonance will be attempted first. If these attempts are unsuccessful, a shift will be made to increasingly complex attempts. The simplest form of altering reality is to attempt to change one's own status through individual mobility. Downward mobility would create sharper dissonance by causing a comparison with rewards received in the past, and therefore believed possible, and rewards currently received. Thus, only upward mobility would be a dissonance-reducing move. The next most simple form of altering reality is to strike out against individuals and categories of individuals (e.g., prejudice and discrimination). The most complex form of attempting to change reality is attempting to alter society. The simplest form of withdrawal is social isolation, and the most complex form of withdrawal is suicide.

| SOCIETAL REACTION |
| TO IMPAIRMENT |

61 Discrimination in Handling Delinquents*

Robert M. Terry

It is often contended that members of minority groups and persons with limited economic means are the objects of discriminatory policies in our system of justice. But the research findings are not clear on this issue. Some, but not all, minorities have a very high rate of criminal arrest and conviction. However, these rates may reflect variations in the frequency of law violations, differences in the visibility and social impact of the offenses, or discriminatory practices. Or some combination of these influences, and others, may occur. Several studies suggest that racial and economic traits are not highly associated with the treatment accorded offenders if the type of offense and the demeanor of the offender are taken into account. One such study is reported below. How do you interpret the findings? Does the evidence deny the charge of discrimination? If not, how do you explain the results? What kinds of further studies are needed?

In a study of the screening of juvenile offenders by the police, this writer found that sex, ethnicity, and socio-economic status were related with statistical significance to the type of disposition accorded. When control variables were introduced, however, these relationships became negligible.[1] Therefore, serious questions arise concerning the validity of the common assertions that control agencies base decisions upon the offender's sex, ethnicity, or socio-economic status. Further research should investigate intensively and systematically the possible relationships between these variables and the severity of sanctions accorded by control agencies.

THE PROBLEM

This study focused on the screening of juvenile offenders by three control agencies. Juveniles whose behavior has been identified and defined as delinquent may become involved subsequently in the legal-judicial process, including the police, the

* From Robert M. Terry, "Discrimination in the Handling of Juvenile Offenders by Social-Control Agencies," *Journal of Research in Crime and Delinquency*, 4 (July 1967), pp. 218–230. Reproduced by permission.

[1] Robert M. Terry, *Criteria Utilized by the Police in the Screening of Juvenile Offenders*, University of Wisconsin, unpublished master's thesis, 1962.

probation department, and the juvenile court. At each stage, decisions are made with respect to possible dispositions or sanctions of varying severity. Thus, it is possible to test hypotheses at each stage of the screening process. For the purposes of this research, it was assumed that the commonly held notions were accurate, and the following hypotheses were proposed:

Hypothesis 1: The severity of sanctions accorded juvenile offenders is positively related to the "maleness" of the offender.[2]

Hypothesis 2: The severity of sanctions is positively related to the offender's minority status. The ethnic groupings used as measures of the degree of minority status are (1) Anglos, (2) Mexican-Americans, (3) Negroes.[3]

Hypothesis 3: The severity of sanctions is negatively related to the offender's socio-economic status. Socio-economic status, as measured by the use of the Minnesota Scale for Paternal Occupations, includes (1) lower status, (2) middle status, (3) upper status.[4]

Police actions are ranked as follows with respect to severity: (1) release, (2) referral to a social or welfare agency, (3) referral to the county probation department, (4) referral to the State Department of Public Welfare. Release is the least serious type of disposition since it indicates there will be no further action taken by social-control agencies.

[2] This was deemed proper in view of the fact that, in the existing criminological literature, males are regarded as being much more severely sanctioned.

[3] Minority status may be viewed as an indicator of social distance between offenders and agents of social control. "Anglos" include all Caucasians with the exception of Mexican-Americans, whose status is regarded as higher than that of Negroes for two reasons: (1) Several of them are members of the community's social-control agencies while no Negroes are so employed. (2) There is less overt discrimination in the community under study against Mexican-Americans than against Negroes. During the period under study, Negroes were not permitted to stay in the community's major hotels or eat in a number of establishments and were more segregated in housing.

[4] Lower status consists of Classes V, VI, and VII of the Minnesota Scale, middle status consists of Classes III and IV, and upper status consists of Classes I and II. See "The Minnesota Scale for Paternal Occupations," University of Minnesota Institute of Child Welfare, Minneapolis, undated pamphlet.

Referral to a social or welfare agency results in counseling in a "nonauthoritarian" setting. Referral to the county probation department calls for adjudication of the offender as a delinquent by the juvenile court or, minimally, for action to be taken by the probation department to prevent further misbehavior. Finally, referrals to the State Department of Public Welfare represent direct calls for the institutionalization of the offender by the police.

Probation department action consists of four ranks: (1) release, (2) placement under informal supervision, (3) referral to the juvenile court, (4) waiver to the criminal court. Release is the lease severe disposition made by the probation department. Somewhat more severe is placement under informal supervision (probation), in which the offender must comply with certain rules and regulations under the threat of possible further legal action. Referral to the juvenile court involves the filing of a petition and a formal court hearing. This makes commitment to an institution a distinct possibility and minimally involves adjudication of the offender as a delinquent. Finally, waiver to criminal court is a probation-department recommendation whereby the judge usually signs the waiver on the basis of information provided by the probation department. The offender whose offense is waived to the criminal court is held responsible for his actions and is subject to the same punitive sanctions as an adult.

Although a variety of dispositions are available to the juvenile court, the judge in the community in which this research was undertaken utilized only two kinds: (1) placement under formal supervision and (2) institutionalization. Institutionalization is obviously more severe than placement under formal supervision in that it removes the offender from his home and subjects him to the regimentation and discipline of a correctional institution.

DATA

The study was made in a heavily industrialized Midwest community of slightly less than 100,000. Basic data included information obtained from records on file in the police Juvenile Bureau, with respect to the nature of the offense; the offender's prior record; personal, behavioral, and situational characteristics; and disposition by the police. Probation-department records were utilized to ascertain the dispositions accorded by both the probation department and the juvenile court. Since records of control agencies generally do not indicate the socio-economic status of an offender, parents' occupations were obtained from city directories for this purpose.

To include a sufficient number of offenders from the juvenile court stage it was necessary to utilize a universe rather than a sample of offenses; thus, all offenses during 1958–1962 on file in the Juvenile Bureau were included in the research. Several kinds of offenses and offenders were eliminated, including children under six years of age, nonresidents of the community, traffic offenses (subject to different handling), and "information" cases (juveniles who were victims of an offense or had information about offenses or offenders but were not otherwise involved). The resulting "universe" included 9,023 juvenile offenses which had resulted in contact with the police. Of these, 775 were referred to the probation department; only 246 appeared in the juvenile court.

The principal statistical measure used was Kendall's rank order correlation coefficient, tau. This measure seems particularly appropriate since the variables can be viewed meaningfully as ordinal and the measure can be generalized to a partial rank order correlation coefficient ($tau_{xy.z}$), thus permitting the introduction of control variables where warranted. Since this study did not utilize a sample, in the strictest sense, assessing the significance or relationships became important. Previous research indicated that relationships in this area are frequently of relatively small magnitude. This may be attributed, in part, to the fact that a large number of independent variables may be important. In view of this, hypotheses in which $+.10 > tau > -.10$ were rejected except when the matrix indicated that the direction of the relationship was consistent for each category of the independent variable despite the introduction of control variables.[5]

ADEQUACY OF THE DATA

The adequacy of police records is crucial to this analysis since citation in these records is prerequisite to appearance at any of the three stages of the legal-judicial process. Recording of juvenile offenses by the police had to be such that unforeseen biases would not enter the data. Fortunately, offenses which result in police contact with juveniles appear to be recorded without bias.

First, when anyone other than the police is the complainant, the offense automatically becomes a part of the record; officers at the complaint desk attach numbers to every complaint received and fill out standard forms recording information on the nature of the offense, its location, the time reported, etc. Of the 9,023 offenses 83.9 per cent were reported by persons other than the police, indicating that a sizable proportion had been recorded without bias.

The second grouping of offenses consists of those in which the police themselves are the complainant. In late 1957, the chief of police instituted a "street-level" policy in which officers were encouraged to dispose of minor offenses by releasing the juveniles to their parents without undue recourse to the Juvenile Bureau; however, they were ordered to record and report *all* delinquent offenses to the Juvenile Bureau together with the usually recorded information. Juveniles were told the Juvenile Bureau would contact them and their parents if investigation or action was to be carried further. The result was an increase in the number of delinquent offenses on file in the police records in 1958, which can be attributed to the greater reporting and recording of minor offenses. While we have no way of proving that this kind of police contact is inclusive, it appears to be relatively accurate and adequate.

RESULTS

Each hypothesis was tested three times since we were concerned with three successive and separate stages of the legal-judicial process.

---

[5] Although only significant effects will be reported, the following variables were used as controls in each of the tests of hypotheses: age of offender, seriousness of offense, number of previous offenses committed, complainant, delinquency rate of area of residence, degree of commercial or industrial development of the area in which the offense occurred, degree of involvement with adult offenders, degree of involvement with offenders of the opposite sex, and the number of individuals involved in the commission of the offense.

TABLE 1 *Sex and the Severity of Disposition*

Police Disposition	Female	Male
	(n = 1,611)	(n = 7,411)
Released	84.9%	89.7%
Referred to Social or Welfare Agency	7.4%	0.8%
Referred to County Probation Dept.	7.4%	8.8%
Referred to State Dept. of Public Welfare	0.3%	0.7%
Total	100.0%	100.0%
tau = −.05		

Probation Disposition	Female	Male
	(n = 119)	(n = 656)
Released	27.7%	30.0%
Informal Supervision	46.2%	28.6%
Referred to Juvenile Court	25.3%	32.9%
Waived to Criminal Court	0.8%	8.5%
Total	100.0%	100.0%
tau = .07		

Juvenile Court Disposition	Female	Male
	(n = 30)	(n = 216)
Formal Supervision	23.3%	40.3%
Institutionalized	76.7%	59.7%
Total	100.0%	100.0%
tau = −.11		

Sex

Table 1 shows the relationships found to exist between the offender's "maleness" and the severity of the disposition. In the case of the police, the relationship, although relatively small (tau = −.05), was in the direction opposite to that which had been hypothesized. The reason appears to be that girls, much more than boys, are likely to be referred to social and welfare agencies. If we account for the disproportionate number of female referrals to social and welfare agencies, most of the relationship may be explained in terms other than sex. The data provide a plausible explanation. While girls account for only 17.9 per cent of all offenses, they represent nearly half of the sex offenses and incorrigibility cases. Nearly 70 per cent of all referrals to social and welfare agencies are in this category. Thus, the apparently greater severity in dealing with girls stems from their disproportionate commission of offenses which result in referral to social and welfare agencies. While

the hypothesis must be rejected, an alternate hypothesis, suggesting a negative relationship between the severity of police action and the "maleness" of the offender is not warranted.

Table 1 indicates a positive relationship (tau = .07) between the "maleness" of the offender and the severity of probation department disposition. Again, the relationship is relatively small. When the seriousness of the offense committed and the number of previous offenses committed are controlled, the existing relationship is reduced in magnitude (tau$_{xy.z}$ = .04 and .04, respectively). The relationship may be largely accounted for in terms of the influence of these two variables. First, while girls are heavily over-represented among offenses for which informal supervision is most likely to be accorded (sex offenses and incorrigibility), boys are heavily over-represented among offenses for which referral to the juvenile court is most likely (burglary, auto theft, homicide, and robbery) and among those offenses which result disproportionately in waiver to criminal court (disorderly conduct, liquor offenses, assault, violent property damage, homicide, and robbery).

In addition, boys are heavily over-represented among offenders who have committed seven or more previous offenses, which further explains the disproportionate waiver of boys to the criminal court. Girls are heavily over-represented among offenders who have committed from one to four previous offenses. This type of record is most likely to result in placement under informal supervision.

The seriousness of the offenses and the number of previous offenses appear to account for most of the relationship between the "maleness" of the offender and the severity of the probation department disposition. In view of this, the hypothesis was rejected.

Finally, a *negative* relationship of significant magnitude was found between the "maleness" of the offender and the severity of juvenile court dispositions (tau $= -.11$), indicating that females are more likely to be institutionalized than males. When the degree of involvement with the opposite sex and with adult offenders was controlled, the existing relationship was reduced (tau$_{xy.z} = -.07$ and $-.08$, respectively), indicating that girls are more often cited for offenses involving the opposite sex and adults, both of which are more likely to result in institutionalization. When the number of previous offenses was controlled, however, the negative relationship between "maleness" and severity of juvenile-court disposition was enhanced (tau$_{xy.z} = -.18$), indicating that females are more severely sanctioned than males even though they tend to have less extensive records of prior delinquent behavior. These results led to the rejection of the hypothesis; an alternate was posited, maintaining that a negative relationship exists between the "maleness" of the offender and the severity of juvenile court sanctions.

The reason why girls are more severely dealt with in the juvenile court (but not, apparently, at earlier stages in the process) can only be suggested. The appearance of a girl in juvenile court may be taken more seriously since it frequently indicates that she has failed to conform after previous measures have been taken or that the offense is serious enough to warrant adjudication as a delinquent; personal and situational characteristics

justify the severe action the court may take.[6] Such factors perhaps are considered much more seriously in the case of girls since they may be less compatible with the female role.

Degree of Minority Status

Table 2 presents the relationships that exist between the degree of the offender's minority status and the severity of disposition. A positive relationship was found to exist between the offender's minority status and police sanctions, although it was very small (tau $= .02$). The most salient difference was the over-representation of Mexican-Americans among referrals to the county probation department. A review of the data indicates that this may result from their over-representation in the commission of the offenses for which referrals to the county probation department are most common. Although Mexican-Americans commit only 7.1 per cent of all offenses, they commit 12.5 per cent of the homicide and robbery, 7.5 per cent of the auto theft, 11.6 per cent of the burglary, and 9.0 per cent of the assault and violent property damage offenses. The relationship between degree of minority status and severity of police disposition is negligible when the seriousness of the offense is held constant (tau$_{xy.z} = .00$). These results led to the rejection of the hypothesis at this level.

The severity of disposition of offenders of varying minority status by the probation department also indicates a negligible relationship (tau $= .01$). Only the percentage waived to the criminal court increased as the degree of minority status increased and the differences were very small. The hypothesis as it applies to the probation department stage of the screening process was rejected.

A positive relationship was found to exist between the degree of minority status and the severity of juvenile court sanctions, although it was again of small magnitude (tau $= .04$). This relationship appears to be a function of the more severe dispositions accorded Negro offenders. A review of the data reveals, however, that Negroes are under-represented among offenders who have committed two or fewer previous offenses and are

---

[6] See Terry, *op. cit. supra* note*, pp. 242–55.

TABLE 2 *Degree of Minority Status and the Severity of Disposition*

Police Disposition	Anglo	Mexican-American	Negro
	(n = 7,282)	(n = 637)	(n = 1,104)
Released	89.1%	84.0%	89.5%
Referred to Social or Welfare Agency	2.1%	1.4%	1.7%
Referred to County Probation Dept.	8.2%	14.4%	7.7%
Referred to State Dept. of Public Welfare	0.6%	0.2%	1.1%
Total	100.0%	100.0%	100.0%
tau = .02			

Probation Disposition	Anglo	Mexican-American	Negro
	(n = 598)	(n = 92)	(n = 85)
Released	28.7%	37.0%	28.2%
Informal Supervision	32.9%	26.0%	25.9%
Referred to Juvenile Court	31.9%	28.3%	34.1%
Waived to Criminal Court	6.5%	8.7%	11.8%
Total	100.0%	100.0%	100.0%
tau = .01			

Juvenile Court Disposition	Anglo	Mexican-American	Negro
	(n = 191)	(n = 26)	(n = 29)
Formal Supervision	39.3%	38.5%	31.0%
Institutionalized	60.7%	61.5%	69.0%
Total	100.0%	100.0%	100.0%
tau = .04			

over-represented among offenders having more extensive prior records of delinquent behavior. When the number of previous offenses committed is controlled, the relationship in question is reduced (tau$_{xy.z}$ = .02). In view of this, the hypothesis at the juvenile court stage of the screening process was rejected.

Socio-Economic Status

A negative relationship was posited between the socio-economic status of the offender and the severity of disposition accorded (Table 3). At the police level, a negative relationship was found, although it was relatively small (tau = —.04). While the differences exist in the hypothesized direction, the similarities are perhaps even more noteworthy. When the seriousness of the offense and the number of previous offenses were con-

trolled, the relationship is slightly reduced (tau$_{xy.z}$ = .02). In view of this, the hypothesis at the juvenile court stage of the screening process was rejected.

A negative relationship was posited between the socio-economic status of the offender and the severity of disposition level, a negative relationship was found, although it was relatively small (tau = —.04). While the differences exist in the hypothesized direction, the similarities are perhaps even more noteworthy. When the seriousness of the offense and the number of previous offenses were controlled, the relationship is slightly reduced (tau$_{xy.z}$ = —.03), reflecting the slight tendency for lower-status juveniles to commit the more serious types of offenses as well as to have more extensive prior records of delinquent behavior. Therefore, it is doubtful that the police utilize

TABLE 3 *Socio-economic Status and the Severity of Disposition*

Police Disposition	Lower	Middle	Upper
	(n = 6,415)	(n = 1,861)	(n = 737)
Released	88.1%	90.0%	92.4%
Referred to Social or Welfare Agency	2.2%	1.9%	0.8%
Referred to County Probation Dept.	9.1%	7.5%	6.7%
Referred to State Dept. of Public Welfare	0.6%	0.6%	0.1%
Total	100.0%	100.0%	100.0%
tau = −.04			
Probation Disposition	**Lower**	**Middle**	**Upper**
	(n = 588)	(n = 138)	(n = 49)
Released	29.0%	30.4%	24.5%
Informal Supervision	30.1%	32.6%	40.8%
Referred to Juvenile Court	31.8%	31.9%	30.6%
Waived to Criminal Court	8.2%	5.1%	4.1%
Total	100.0%	100.0%	100.0%
tau = −.02			
Juvenile Court Disposition	**Lower**	**Middle**	**Upper**
	(n = 187)	(n = 44)	(n = 15)
Formal Supervision	35.8%	43.2%	53.3%
Institutionalized	64.2%	56.8%	46.7%
Total	100.0%	100.0%	100.0%
tau = −.09			

socio-economic status as a criterion in referral. The hypothesis was rejected at this level.

The severity of probation-department disposition is also related negatively to the offender's socio-economic status, although the magnitude of the relationship was even less than at the police level (tau = −.02). Variations appear to result from the prior records of the offenders. Middle- and, especially, upper-status offenders are more likely than lower-status offenders to have committed only one or two previous offenses or none at all. Lower-status offenders are much more likely to have committed seven or more previous offenses. When the number of previous offenses is controlled, the relationship between socio-economic status and severity of probation department disposition is negligible ($tau_{xy.z}$ = .00). In view of this evidence, the hypothesis was rejected.

A negative relationship was found to exist between socio-economic status and severity of juvenile court dispositions (tau = −.09), consistently

in the expected direction. However, when the number of previous offenses was controlled, the relationship was drastically reduced ($tau_{xy.z}$ = −.02), indicating that lower-status offenders are more likely to have committed a greater number of previous offenses than middle- and upper-status offenders. The large reduction in the magnitude of the relationship would seem to indicate that lower-status offenders are accorded more severe dispositions not because they are lower-status individuals, but because of differences in prior records of delinquent behavior. (The prior record of delinquent behavior appears to be the most significant criterion utilized by the juvenile court in the screening of offenders.) Therefore, the hypothesis was rejected at this level.

CONCLUSION

The evidence indicates that the severity of disposition is not a function of the degree of minority status of the juvenile offender or his socio-economic status. The sex of the offender was found to be directly relevant at only one of the three stages of the screening process and, in that instance, the relationship was in a direction opposite to that expected. These findings clearly contradict the assertions commonly made by students of criminal and delinquent behavior.

Obviously, generalization of this research must be regarded with caution. The findings are limited in that we have studied the disposition of offenders in a single community, utilized rather crude measures of socio-economic status, have not con-

trolled for variations in the population which appears in the police records in the first place, and have concerned ourselves with decision-making by a limited number of control agents. However, the findings certainly warrant further research.

While males, Mexican-Americans, Negroes, and lower-status offenders are over-represented in correctional institutions, probation departments, courts, and police records, this over-representation does not, on the basis of the evidence examined in this study, appear to be a direct result of these characteristics. The over-representation of these individuals is not the result of discrimination by control agencies.

62 Alternatives to a Deadly Showdown*

Muzafer Sherif

For the first time in history man has the capability of destroying civilization. We live, as the author of the following selection suggests, under "the ominous shadow of a deadly showdown." One consequence of this is that social scientists have developed a research interest in methods of conflict resolution. The next paper describes some of the research and outlines proposals for the control of international conflict. What are some of the problems and assumptions involved in using small group research as a basis for policy proposals on an international level? Can you think of research designs that would be more relevant to the suggestions made by the author?

For some years, the world has lived in the ominous shadow of a deadly showdown. The consequences of such a tragic climax have been vividly described by the creators of weapons themselves. These grim consequences have led many to search

for measures to avoid a showdown and to reduce the conflicts which are at its roots.

Among the various measures advocated are the following:

Various models of deterrence, that is, up-to-date models of the old "balance of power."

Conferences of leaders and their representatives to negotiate differences.

Programs of person-to-person contact, such as exchange of persons and conferences of students, scientists, businessmen, artists and teachers.

Dissemination of information designed to correct erroneous views of each other held by the parties in conflict.

There is at least one condition necessary if any of these measures are to be effective — the provision of a broad *motivational* basis for contacts, communication, and negotiation. If such a broad motivational basis is created any one of these measures, except the first, permits creative alternatives to a deadly showdown. I will touch on these measures and their variants in context. First, however, I should make it clear why I do not regard the first — namely, deterrence — as a creative solution.

As C. N. Barclay, British military author, stated in the *New York Times Magazine* of May 5, 1963: "The deterrent is the modern version of the balance of power, employed in the past — not very successfully — to keep the peace in Europe. The difference lies in the fact that failure to keep the peace in the days of conventional weapons . . . was not universally fatal. Failure with nuclear weapons, on the other hand, would be catastrophic for all mankind" (p. 17). Let us not be misled by new trappings or the use of high speed computers. A rose by any other name smells as sweet, and deterrence smells like a preliminary to war. In contrast, the aim of the other measures is to reduce conflict, not maintain it.

THE RESEARCH BACKGROUND

Whatever a social psychologist such as myself can contribute to the search for alternatives to a headlong plunge into mass destruction must rest on the research and theory in his specialty. I will, therefore, mention briefly the factual basis for my conclusions.

Fifteen years ago, we began a program of research on conflict between human groups and its resolution. Hunches, or hypotheses if you like, were based on existing research and on cases of conflict between groups of all sizes and description. Our hunches concerned conditions *sufficient* for the development of conflict between groups, along with the hostile acts and attitudes that accompany it, and conditions *necessary* for the subsequent reduction of the conflict and change of the participants' attitudes. Three experiments were conducted, each continuing 24 hours a day for nearly a month.

Here, I will not go into details of the experiments, which will be of interest mainly to fellow social psychologists and which are readily available in print. A brief summary, however, may be in order as point of departure for the focus of this paper.

The experiments started with two bunches of unacquainted and very similar individuals, brought to a summer camp. By presenting them with situations where pulling together with one's fellows led to desired ends, we soon had two genuine groups — each with its own recognized leader, name, and local customs. Once the groups formed, a series of events was introduced in which the victory of one group inevitably meant defeat for the other.

Over a period of time, as predicted, the two groups became hostile toward each other; they called each other names; they disliked each other intensely, and they began to fight. This unfortunate outcome was a necessary preliminary to the study of various measures in reducing conflict between groups.

There are some similarities between these experiments and real life. First, the entire experience was very natural for the individuals studied, and the problems they faced were very real to them. They cared a great deal about their groups and their vicissitudes. Second, like many groups in real life, behavior toward the other group was not regulated by rules enforced by some superior authority. The groups formulated their own ways of relating to each other.

Being experiments, however, these studies were necessarily in miniature. The groups were small, as they had to be to have experimental control of their habitat. The members were young boys; since then, however, similar results have been obtained by other investigators working with adults. Still, there is a genuine problem of whether or not one is justified in drawing analogies between what happened to these small groups and what happens to large and powerful nations. I leave this to your judgment and, ultimately, to the outcome of future research conducted on a larger scale.

SUPERORDINATE GOALS

I shall now venture to state some things we learned from these experiments about intergroup conflicts and its reduction. A variety of measures were proposed for the reduction of conflict and were tried out in the experiments. One of these turned out to be a *necessary* condition for the avoidance of violent alternatives.

This necessary condition is the existence of "superordinate goals." Superordinate goals are those ends greatly desired by all those caught in dispute or conflict, which cannot be attained by the resources and energies of each of the parties separately, but which require the concerted efforts of all parties involved. Even in our miniature experiments, we found that a *series* of superordinate goals was required if concerted effort was to become general, and if hostility was to turn to friendly interchange between groups. Even at this level, the reduction of intergroup conflict is not a one-shot affair. A series of superordinate goals has a cumulative effect, which provides a broad motivational base on which person-to-person contacts, information, and conferences between leaders or representatives can become effective.

Communication must be opened between groups before prevailing hostilities can be reduced. But person-to-person contact and communication without goals which are urgent, compelling, and highly appealing to *all* groups involved frequently serve only as mediums for further accusations and recriminations. The discussion or the negotiation gets bogged down, directly or indirectly, in the fruitless question of "Who's to blame?" for the existing state of affairs.

The experiments revealed a dynamic sequence resulting in a vicious circle, with each side justifying its own actions and casting blame on the other side. For this to happen, it was sufficient to have two groups, each pitted against the other for a goal that can be won only if one group fails. It is also pertinent to note that individual members need not in any way be neurotic or sinful for the vicious circle to occur.

In the experiments, the groups were from the same culture and the members were as similar in background and appearance as possible. Shall we then, attribute their behavior to universal human nature? Since we arranged the conditions which started this vicious circle and since we later successfully altered it, there is no justification for assuming that this is "just the way of human nature."

When the groups in our experiments were in conflict, considering each other as enemies, each adopted a policy of deterrence. In addition to security measures designed to conceal their possessions and locations, weapons were improvised from available resources and were hoarded "in case" they were needed. Banners were destroyed and raids on each other's property were conducted in stealth as a show of power. It may be, therefore, that deterrence is a way of conducting conflict rather than a preserver of the peace, as it is sometimes represented.

GROUP CONFLICTS AND STEREOTYPES

In the course of encounters between the groups, each individual — whether leader or appointed representative or rank-and-file — acted as a loyal, responsible member of his group. Being loyal and responsible, in this case, meant that he directed his energies and efforts against the rival. The unfavorable qualities, the derogatory stereotypes attributed to the other group, as derogatory stereotypes were the *products* of this process, and were not an initial condition for it. One's own group was endowed with favorable qualities which were self-justifying and even self-glorifying. The rival group was assigned stereotyped traits which justified its treatment as an enemy. Since this is a *product* of inter-group conflict, and is not its initial cause, attempts to remove the stereotyped conceptions in and of themselves — through information, pleas for fair-mindedness or justice — are ordinarily rather futile and fruitless.

Once hostile attitudes and unfavorable stereotypes of another group are stabilized, they influence the manner in which individual members see and size up events. Each side sees the actions of the other through the colored glasses of hostility, which filter out the favorable colors in which we see ourselves and our friends. Undoubtedly, this filtering process affects the judgment of *negotiators* and *representatives*. For example, in one experiment, an individual holding a high position in his own group decided, with the best of motives, that the time had come to negotiate peaceful relations with the hostile group. He was received by them as an enemy who sought to mislead them with pretended expressions of reconciliation. His departure was accompanied by a hail of "ammunition" collected by the group "in case" they were attacked — in this case, green apples.

THE LEADER REJECTED

Equally interesting was the fate of this individual, who had made reasonable attempts at reconciliation, when he returned to his own group. Far from being received as a hero, he was chastized for even making the attempt. This is but one of many examples of the fact that leadership, representation, and negotiation between groups are governed primarily by and operate within the bounds acceptable in each group. If he is to negotiate effectively, a leader or his delegate must remain a part of his own group. In order to do so, he must act in ways that his fellow members regard as acceptable and decent, in terms of their group's definitions. The realistic alternatives that a leader or negotiator can consider, therefore, are limited. Not all possible alternatives that are logically conceivable, or even rational, are realistically available. The realistic alternatives are those that are clearly acceptable to members of his own group at the time. In large groups, where negotiations may be conducted in secret, a leader has somewhat more latitude. But there is not one leader in the world today who could remain in power after committing his group to a course clearly unacceptable to the members.

How can the blinding stereotypes and self-justifications of groups in conflict change, and how can the vicious circle stop, if the groups do not accept the regulation of some still larger body? Many methods are effective in the context of a series of superordinate goals, which are felt as urgent by *all* parties involved.

New Communication Possible

When contacts between persons involve superordinate goals, communication is utilized to reduce conflict in order to find means of attaining common goals. True and favorable information about the other group is seen in a new light, and then the probability of this information being effective is enormously enhanced.

When groups cooperate toward superordinate goals, their leaders are in a position to take bolder steps toward greater mutual understanding and trust. Lacking superordinate goals, however, genuine moves by a leader to reduce intergroup conflict may be seen by his own group as out-of-step and ill-advised. He may be subjected to severe criticism and even to a loss of faith. Where there are superordinate goals, however, these encourage a leader to make moves to advance cooperative efforts. He can more freely delegate authority, and negotiation can proceed more effectively. The

decisions reached are more likely to receive support from other group members.

Various measures suggested for reducing intergroup conflict acquire new significance and effectiveness when they become part and parcel of joint efforts directed toward goals with real and compelling value for all groups concerned. The development of such superordinate goals provides the necessary motive. It is needed to lift the heavy hand of the past, with its entrenched stereotypes and vicious circle of "Who's to blame?", and to work out procedures for cooperation.

Over a period of time, the procedures of groups working toward superordinate goals are generalized to new problems and situations. In time, the process should assume organizational forms. If the tasks of building such organizations seem formidable, they are certainly no more formidable than those which a modern war would impose. There can be no doubt that man's potentialities can be realized better in the course of such efforts than in the vicious circle of assigning blame for the present state of affairs, in pursuing old fears, old hostilities, old conflicts — with their awesome possibilities in this present world.

Beyond the Experiments

In considering the possibility of superordinate goals in international affairs, we must pass beyond our experiments. For in our experiments, superordinate goals emerged in problem situations that involved the deprivation of vital necessities or the achievement of a venture much-desired by all. They were not matters for interpretation, and they did not require experts with different opinions about the "facts" to offer conjectures. The conditions giving rise to superordinate goals in our experimental groups were compelling and immediate — right in front of their eyes, a naked necessity for all to see and feel.

Debating Human Survival

In the thousand-fold complex problems engulfing the people of the world today, there seems to be a debate about one goal which should be overriding — human survival. There is debate among scientists as well as policy-makers about the range of weapons of destruction and their carriers; about the radius of destruction in population centers; about whether 100 million or 500 million people would perish or be mutilated; about which peoples and places would be involved; about how many and what kind of shelters are required for survival as human beings, if they survive; about the effects of radiation on the present and future generations of children. Such debates continue as though we were splitting hairs instead of talking about millions of human lives.

In the midst of these debates, the problem of human survival is obscured; instead of human survival emerging as an all-embracing superordinate goal, its urgency is muffled. Yet human survival is the most inclusive superordinate goal. It provides the needed motivational basis for:

> making possible the effective negotiations of leaders toward the abolishment of nuclear warfare as an alternative;

> communication and information to be effective toward abandonment of war as a means of furthering national or ideological policy — *any* national or ideological policy;

> exchange of persons across national lines to be occasions for understanding rather than promoting the vicious circle of "Who's to blame?"

But, for all of these, human survival has to be felt as a necessity — like the air we breathe, the food we eat, the danger sign that we heed when near high explosives.

A DECLARATION FOR HUMAN SURVIVAL

One effective first step toward the recognition of human survival as a superordinate goal may be a universal *declaration* for human survival and development, including in vivid word and picture, the horrors of nuclear war, its cost in life, its destruction of human civilization and culture, and the ever-present dangers of radiation to those who survive. Some experts on communication conclude that people do not listen to threats, pointing to studies showing that the threat of cancer is not sufficient to cause people to stop smoking. However, we know that when people of a country learn of a genuine threat to the lives and well-being of their country, even in the newspapers, they do have a strong desire for survival and the removal of the threat; and all sectors of society pull together for this purpose. Human survival is a positive goal for all peoples, and the common threat to all today has not been presented with comparable urgency.

As we all know, declarations have been made by groups of scientists, by professional bodies, and even by heads of governments and military men of stature. What is intended here is not just another declaration at a single conference, or in a few newspapers, or in an occasional policy statement. What is intended here is an agreement — especially by policy-makers of the major powers — that a universal declaration for human survival, which also conveys in understandable terms what nuclear warfare means, has their full support. Of course, even this is not sufficient.

Such universal declaration for human survival as a recognized superordinate goal needs the support of all religious bodies which ask for prayers for peace, so that the universal declaration for human survival will be part of their daily and weekly exercises. All organizations, boards and regents directing policies at university, high school and grade school levels in every country, who profess to have at heart the well-being and development of the younger generation as civilized human beings, should make such a universal declaration an integral part of their educational programs. Owners and directors of the mass media of communication in all countries — who profess public responsibility in enlightening and informing — should feature prominently and repeatedly such a universal declaration for human survival as a cherished goal. At the cost of appearing naive, I also propose that political parties in all countries who profess their concern with peace on earth and the brotherhood of man should include this universal declaration as an integral part of their platforms — even if this be the only plank they share in common.

If through these means, human survival becomes a superordinate goal for the majority of peoples of the world, then nuclear war may be out-of-bounds in their eyes as an alternative in national or ideological policies. Being out-of-bounds in terms of cherished goals of the people for survival and development as human beings, the attempts of demagogues to fish in muddied waters, to dramatize issues and events out of all proportion, will fall on deaf ears. Leaders will be charged with staying within the bounds of the cherished goals of their peoples.

A New Framework for Cooperation

I do not suggest at all that a universal declaration could settle the problems underlying international conflicts. I do propose it as a *first* step toward eliminating nuclear war as an alternative that any leader could consider. The underlying conflicts, however, can be affected to the extent that the nations of the world and their citizens engage in common enterprises which each sees as being for the benefit of all, regardless of their differences.

The differences between nations may seem so great today that the possibility of common concerns seems slim. I am inclined, however, to find merit in the observation by Eugene Rabinowitch (*Bulletin of the Atomic Scientists,* February, 1963) that there are such areas, and that "the cultural and scientific areas are the least controversial and most suitable for international cooperation" at present (p. 7). The implications of our own research also support his contention that such cooperation should be, not merely an exchange of persons, but "common enterprises" jointly initiated and carried out on a large scale.

In brief, the implication of our research is that when superordinate goals are concretely perceived and emotionally felt by members of groups in conflict, they do tend to cooperate, to pull together their resources and energies to attain them. A series of such efforts over a period of time is effective in reducing their hostilities, changing their unfavorable images of each other, and producing a climate in which creative alternatives to mutual extinction can be explored. The exploration of creative alternatives may be more effective than the prevailing policy of contending parties at present, in which strategists attempt to figure out probabilities of deterrence. This policy of deterrence contains the constant hazard of getting out of hand because of even a small miscalculation or misinformation at this or that particular point.

Inter-nation Universities

A final word on committing the knowledge, resources, and efforts of major parties in conflict to common, large-scale projects, as part of a process directed toward the superordinate goal of human survival on the level of the cultures attained through centuries. Such common and interdependent projects could include, for example, joint efforts by cosmonauts, technicians, and researchers of nations aimed at the conquest of space. Such projects could include inter-nation universities, in which the faculty consists of scholars and scientists who have outgrown the 19th century conception of national ways of life and ideological divisions as closed systems. These are only examples already proposed by various authors such as Charles E. Osgood and Eugene Rabinowitch. In joint meetings of scholars and scientists dedicated to human survival, and the survival of human cultures across national and ideological lines, a whole series of such common and interdependent ventures could be imaginatively worked out.

The involvement of talents, resources and effort in joint and interdependent *new* projects is less liable to misinterpretations as trickery or propaganda moves. In the more direct political and military areas where parties already have entrenched stands, sometimes fixed as national norms or stereotypes, the likelihood of misinterpreting the motives and moves of the other side is greater. However, once a new series of joint and interdependent projects is underway, active involvement in it is likely to be conducive to an atmosphere of good faith, in which the negotiating parties will not be suspect at every turn and twist of occasion.

CHAPTER EIGHT

Institutions: Legitimation of System Linkages

Norms are important because of their regulative influence on human conduct. They define the behavior expected of an individual in nearly all repetitive situations. If we note the behavior of a given person, for example, we find that several recurrent activities consume a large share of his time and energy. His schedule of working, sleeping, eating, and playing varies only slightly from day to day. But we should not assume that norms leave no room for individual variations. There are many styles of dress, speech, work, recreation, social and civic activity, and so on. Each person tends to develop his own patterns in these activities; one gets to be known as a "hippy," while another is a "square." So long as their variations stay within the community's tolerance limits, people generally pay little attention.

The amount of variation tolerated by the community depends upon the mode of behavior in question. Some activities, such as speech or dress, have wide areas of tolerance and receive relatively few sanctions. The term "folkways" refers to such permissive patterns in which informal expectations and unofficial sanctions prevail. Some other activities are regarded as important to the group's survival. These are regulated by formal prescriptions, often called "mores," and are sanctioned by official methods. Among the mores in modern societies are statutes dealing with a wide range of activities, from the preparation and distributions of food and drink to the handling of the sick and the dead, and from the care and training of children to the conditions of labor, the preservation of life and property, and the support of law and order. In general, the mores support the notion that survival of the group or community is more imperative than the survival of the individual.

Emphasis on group survival is reflected by the fact that few, if any, societies have a universal prohibition against the taking of human life. Nearly all societies identify certain conditions under which the elimination of selected persons is condoned or even encouraged. The taking of human life may be regarded as reprehensible murder if the act represents a threat or challenge to the community or its leaders. But the elimination of the aged or the incompetent, the destruction of disloyal persons or the group's enemies, and the practice of abortion, for example, engender little public complaint in many societies. In fact, the taboo against incest appears to have wider application. Ordinarily, the most severe sanctions are directed against persons who violate formal norms concerned with sex behavior

Linkages among Personal and Social Systems

429

and the integrity of the family, the inheritance or utilization of power or property, and the transmission of belief and knowledge. These sanctions and the norms they enforce reveal the essential requirements of community life: the need for law and order; the definition and regulation of property and possessions; rules of descent and inheritance; responsibility for the care and rehabilitation of the weak or the helpless; and protection against strangers or enemies. While the basic needs of all communities are very similar, the methods employed in meeting these needs are almost infinitely varied.

Norms may vary in duration as well as in content. Their duration may range from temporary *fads* and *fashions* to relatively permanent *customs*. Fads and fashions are noted in slang expressions, styles of dress, automobile design and equipment, architecture, and many other modes of behavior. Although temporary, they may have strong support while in vogue. They gain their power from the frequency and intensity of their operations and from the social contagion with which they spread through various groups and communities. Customs survive over longer periods of time. They often deal with large systems, such as the family, religion, government, and the economy. For example, in Western culture, mate selection, family membership, and economic activities are regulated by customs such as the dating complex, single family residences and marketplace bargaining.

Customs are frequently reinforced by emotionally toned symbols — the Madonna, the Christmas tree, gifts, or by elaborate ceremonies — and especially by *traditions*. Traditions are formalized accounts of a group's experience and destiny, real or imagined. Customs and traditions expose successive generations of people to repetitive social situations in which behavior prescriptions are precisely formulated and strongly sanctioned. Generally, the more ancient the customs and traditions, the more powerful is their impact upon the group's members.

Functions of Institutions

Institutions are vast social systems organized around certain cultural objectives. More specifically, an institution is a relatively enduring configuration of prescriptions, beliefs, and practices regarded as essential for the maintenance of a society, its structure, and its basic values. Institutions that come readily to mind are the family, religion, government, education, and the economy. Each has a distinctive task to perform, and if any should fail in its performance, society would be seriously affected.

The family is concerned with procreation, child care and training, affective relations, and the regulation of sexual behavior. If the human race did not procreate, it would soon disappear. However, procreation is always strictly controlled by norms that prescribe and legitimize certain patterns of sexual behavior while prohibiting other activities. In our society, for instance, the official norms hold that sexual activities are legitimate only if they occur within the rules of monogamous marriage. Such rules may help people to control their biological propensities and maintain harmonious relations with other persons. The informal norms, by contrast, allow wider variation in sexual practices.

People in all societies need to coordinate their efforts in the production of economic goods such as food, clothing, and shelter. The economic institution is serviced by subinstitutions just as the family is serviced by the subinstitution of marriage. Economic subinstitutions include the money system, credit, the marketplace, banking, and the stock exchange.

The institution of government is concerned with processes of community decision-making and the execution of official decisions. It strives for the consensus necessary both for harmony within the community and for protection against external dangers. The state, political parties, the electoral ballot, and so on, are subinstitutions of government.

Religion also is concerned with establishing an *esprit de corps* among the community members. Its prescriptions help to maintain peace of mind by regulating relations between man and the unknown. Religious beliefs hold man accountable to himself, to his fellows, and often to his deities; they provide plausible explanations for many of the imponderables of life and death.

Schools and other educational institutions help indoctrinate children, and sometimes adults, in the group's traditions, its beliefs, and its practices. The institution of science regulates man's pursuit of knowledge. Welfare institutions may protect the weak against the strong and provide for relief from disasters or other emergencies. Various other institutions could be identified.

The number and variety of institutions depends upon the degree of social organization within the society in question. Where there is a complex division of labor, there will be many institutions, and vice versa. Whatever their number and variety, the institutions of a society are always interdependent. Change in one of them will inevitably affect operation of the others, as is observed in the way stock market fluctuations influence governmental policies on foreign exchange.

The interrelationships among institutions can be compared with a wheel, its hub, spokes, and rim. The structure and function of each part is geared to the structure and functions of the remainder. The family, which is the focal institution and the first with which the individual becomes familiar, is like the hub of the wheel. Radiating from the hub are the spokes — religion, government, education, science, welfare, the economy, and so on. The rim delineates the boundary of the community in which the various institutions operate. Subinstitutions — courtship, marriage, money, credit, the market, schools, sects and churches — provide a network of interconnections among the spokes of the wheel. When the entire structure is operating smoothly, the parts are almost indistinguishable.

Institutions establish a close connection between the individual and his society. They provide a set of rules and regulations that minimizes the need for personal decisions. From cradle to grave, they provide a pattern of life that specifies the individual's goals and objectives, prescribes legitimate means for achieving the objectives, and sanctions the individual according to his performance. They tend to be localized in certain physical facilities such as the home, the church, the school, the factory, and so on. They incorporate utilitarian objects — furniture, tools, equipment — and distinctive symbols — the cross, the flag, the coat of arms — that reinforce the operation of their normative and action subsystems. This kind of institutional structure is illustrated in Figure 1.

Institutions are differentiated and formalized as a society becomes more complex. So long as order and conformity prevail, a society has little reason to question its institutions and values. This argument is sometimes used to explain the social and moral stability of simple agrarian societies that were governed for thousands of years by tradition and the "cake of custom." In these societies, laws and other prescriptions were often regarded as divine decrees and were applied as "universals" to nearly all members of the community. Generally, the social positions occupied by people from birth to death were ascribed on the basis of kinship, sex, age,

Institutional Interrelation-ships

INSTITUTION	FUNCTIONS	POSITIONS	SUBSYSTEMS	PHYSICAL AND SYMBOLIC TRAITS
FAMILY	PROCREATION PRIMARY SOCIALIZATION IDENTITY OF SELF REGULATION OF SEX AND AFFECT	FATHER MOTHER CHILD	DATING MARRIAGE LEGAL DESCENT	HOUSING AND FURNISHINGS PROPERTY AND POSSESSIONS WEDDING RING, WILL, EMBLEM
ECONOMY	PRODUCTION AND DISTRIBUTION OF GOODS PROFIT DIVISION OF LABOR	EMPLOYER WORKER CONSUMER MANAGER	MARKET MONEY CREDIT STOCKS	FACTORY AND EQUIPMENT BANKS AND CREDIT OFFICES CREDIT RATING TRADEMARK
GOVERNMENT	ACHIEVING CONSENSUS DETERMINING PUBLIC POLICY ENFORCING LAWS	CITIZEN OFFICIAL VOTER PARTY MEMBER	STATE PARTY ELECTION POLL DRAFT	PUBLIC WORKS AND BUILDINGS CONSTITION AND LAWS FLAG, MILITARY UNIFORM
RELIGION	PEACE OF MIND COOPERATIVE ATTITUDES FAITH IN FUTURE	PASTOR MEMBER ACOLYTE POPE NUN	SECTS SEMINARY COUNCIL OF CHURCHES	CATHEDRALS AND TEMPLE CROSS, ALTAR, ICON BIBLE, TESTAMENT
EDUCATION	LEARNING SOCIALIZATION KNOWLEDGE INDOCTRINATION	TEACHER STUDENT DEAN CUSTODIAN	P.T.A. SCHOOL BOARD CURRICULUM ATHLETICS PUBLICATIONS	SCHOOLS, LABORATORIES BOOKS AND LIBRARIES DIPLOMAS AND DEGREES GRADES AND HONORS

Figure 1

Some of the elements of selected institutional systems. Institutions are vast social systems that coordinate various kinds of elements in the pursuit of certain general cultural objectives. Some examples are listed here.

and other variables over which the individual could exercise little influence. Membership in such societies was established at birth, and strangers were rarely admitted.

Often the extended family was the center of social activities — the unit of residence, of economic production, of child care and training, of religious and other ceremonial observances, and of nearly all the activities that bind people together. Community boundaries did not ordinarily reach beyond a few families that shared the same interests, traditions, and practices. Consequently, community relationships tended to reinforce and strengthen the same traditional prescriptions that regulated family affairs.

Rule by tradition places great reliance upon consensus as a means of social control. For consensus to be achieved, there must be a uniform focus of attention and a standardized way of perceiving things that are of important daily concern. Some things of concern in traditional societies, of course, are physical objects, such as the familiy's possessions, the tools and weapons employed in defense and survival, the fields and pastures that may be held in common by the community's members, and the magical devices used on ceremonial occasions. Other things are less tangible, but probably even more important: common values, beliefs, and attitudes; common history, legends, and traditions; and common habits and practices observed by all. Thus, the members of traditional societies have many interests in common, and these mutual interests are often embedded in a monolithic normative system that integrates the peoples' activities and preserves the social order. Consensus, stability, and conformity are the key characteristics of such a social system.

This kind of traditional order has been repeatedly disrupted and reconstructed in the modernization of contemporary societies. All spheres of life have been affected by the increasing division of labor, the differentiation and specialization of social roles, and the substitution of social contracts for traditional rules and regulations. Many of the family's functions, for example, have been assumed by new institutions that were established specifically to meet society's growing and changing interests in fields such as education, industry, recreation, religion, welfare, and professional services. Modernization has drastically revised older patterns of work and production, making irrelevant many of the traditional skills and diminishing the security long attached to agricultural and manual labor. Political power has been largely removed from the local community, undermining the status of the former elite and speeding the trend toward centralization of government.

In all this, the "universal" norms of the traditional era have given way to numerous "specialties" and "alternatives" that call for distinctive skills and training. Occupations and other social positions have been opened to individual achievement, and this requires that individuals make numerous important decisions during their careers. As a result, the interdependence and mutual destiny of peoples may be far greater in modern societies than in earlier times.

Many of these trends are continuing at an increasing pace, expanding man's effective environment, and establishing an interdependence among nations and continents that was previously unthinkable. For example, the communications explosion, with its growing capacity for storing, retrieving, analyzing, and transmitting information of all kinds, has aggravated relations between "developed" and "undeveloped" countries by increasing the awareness of inequalities in income and opportunity that exist throughout the world. Man's expanded social environment enhances the prospects for the exchange of goods and services, the transmission of experience and knowledge, and the adoption of selected features of alternative modes of life. But it also may complicate some problems of social control, such as protecting the identity of the individual, maintaining the integriy of the community as a social system, and preserving harmonious relations among groups and communities that have divergent beliefs and interests. Modernization, with its increasing interdependence, mass communications, and growing population size and density, may tend to make social problems far more visible and more destructive in their impact upon the community than ever before.

Social change and planning therefore seem inevitable in modern society. All societies attempt to organize and coordinate their activities so as to bring about social changes which otherwise might not occur. These deliberate attempts to regulate social changes may be carried out through totalitarian governments such as those of Soviet Russia. But they occur also in societies such as those in England, Canada, and the United States. Some of the most dramatic attempts at rational planning are found in Japan, India, China, and the newly emerging nations of Africa. In these societies the desire for rapid modernization provides an added incentive for large-scale planning. Their attempts often underscore the interrelationships among the various parts of their social structure.

Frequently, change in one part of a society produces unanticipated consequences in other parts. However, the demand for controlled change is so great that these efforts are not likely to be terminated because of occasional failure. Man has learned that he is capable of organizing his affairs. He can, under favorable circumstances at least, produce normative systems that enhance prospects for achieving his objectives. This is one reason for the increasing effort to involve sociologists and other scientists in programs of social planning and control.

FAMILY: LINKAGE BETWEEN GENERATIONS

63 China's Traditional Family*

Shu-Ching Lee

The interdependence of institutions is clearly shown in the following description of the Chinese family. The traditional family, which persisted through 2,000 years without any substantial change, was thoroughly integrated with education, religion, economics, and politics, and indeed tended to serve as the center for all these types of activities. Technological changes in the early twentieth century, however, accompanied a rapid disintegration of the traditional family among the modern-educated intellectuals in the large cities and trade ports, and the emergence of the conjugal family as a sharp competitor. Under the impetus of the present political and social revolution the destruction of this system has penetrated to all groups of society and to the vast interior.

THE FAMILY AS AN INSTITUTION

As a rule, life in the large family centers on consanguinity, whereas life in the small family centers on matrimony. The Chinese family defi-

* Excerpt from Shu-Ching Lee, "China's Traditional Family: Its Characteristics, and Disintegration," *American Sociological Review,* Vol. 18 (June 1953), pp. 273–280. Reproduced by permission. Copyright © 1953 by the American Sociological Association.

nitely constitutes an institutionalized type of the former. Its fundamental characteristics are stability, continuity, and perpetuation through generations. A long period of living together by a number of persons in the same household naturally develops some peculiar ways of life which are called the family's tradition. In order to preserve this tradition, each family generally sets up its own rules, written or unwritten, to discipline its members. Both the tradition and the rules are important means of maintaining the family as an institution.

The family tradition, composed of a variety of minute manners unique to each family, gives its members a strong feeling of *esprit de corps.* This tradition is conscientiously kept intact and proudly transmitted through generations. When strengthened by the cult of ancestor worship, it becomes the code of conduct and permeates the minds of family members. It determines the proper relations between members of the family, inheritance of the family's property, and succession to a title, an occupation, or even a craft. In traditional China, the complex of family etiquette, which distinguished members of a good family from those of a poor one, was generally taken by society as a yardstick of the prosperity and the status of a family.

In intellectual families, the spirit of tradition is codified into a written constitution, or the family laws,[1] which enable the patriarch to regulate behavior of the family members. His power and authority extend far into the realm of what the West would consider to be personal matters of an individual. The question arises as to how this power and authority can be maintained, especially after members have reached maturity. Aside from moral sanction and the social pressure exerted by the community, a crucial answer to this question

[1] The book which is used to record these codified rules is called the *chia-li-p'u.* Cf. Y. K. Leong and L. K. Tao, *Village and Town Life in China,* London: George Allen & Unwin, 1915, pp. 7, 24 and 70–71.

is the inheritance of or succession to the patrimony or craft. In traditional China when education was not socialized, the means of securing a livelihood was primarily transmitted within the family. Not only was the tangible property such as land, house, and livestock largely inherited, but in addition such crafts or skills as brewing, weaving, drug-making, or painting were also acquired through the father-son relationship. If a son wanted to be a legal heir for any of these, the first duty he learned in childhood was to obey the family's rules, or better still, to live up to the family's traditional spirit. It must be remembered further that severe punishment could be inflicted on a wayward son, including hauling to the ancestral hall, flogging, ostracism, or even execution upon the consent of the elders of the agnate clan.

FUNCTIONS, ROLES, AND STATUS

The way in which the members of a Chinese family are trained or disciplined can best be understood by an examination of the functions and roles assigned by Confucian traditions to each category of different relations within the family. As a primary institution, the family takes no account of any individual, but places all its emphasis on the identification of individual members with the established roles according to consanguineous or matrimonial principles.

The basic relatives of a family are, of course, parent and child, husband and wife, and brothers and sisters; the rest are only extended forms of these three relationships. The father is a patriarch (or a "stern sovereign" as the Chinese refer to him) whose solemn duty, besides representing the family in financial and other matters in the community, is to make sure that no member violates the family's established traditions and rules and that nothing happens to lower the family status. Naturally, he loves his sons and daughters just as much as his wife does, but socially he, as a patriarch, is traditionally entrusted with the responsibility for the rightful and proper conduct of other members in the family and also for their success in society. The proverb, "spare the rod, spoil the child," illustrates well the situation. In fulfilling his duty, the father has to exercise his authority to punish a misbehaving member in order not only to correct him (or her) but to maintain harmony and order in the household. Because of this, he is generally *respected,* but rarely *loved.*

Confucian doctrine, especially as amended by the scholars of the former Han Dynasty, inculcates two principles with regard to the roles of the father and the mother; that of *esteem* and that of *affection.* The father commands his descendants' esteem and the mother, their love. The chief responsibility of the former is to discipline and provide for the education of his children, while to his wife is entrusted their care and rearing. It is quite beyond the mother's role to punish her sons, except to warn the stubborn ones that "If you continue to do such and such things I am going to report to your father." Difficulties arise, however, when the father dies early and leaves no brother in the family to take care of disciplinary measures. Many a distinguished family has been ruined by such unfortunate circumstances.

According to the established convention in traditional China, the husband as a husband has no clearly defined role, except to support his wife; his position is found in other connections such as a son or as a father. This does not mean that he cannot assert authority over his wife — very often he does. The wife's place in the family deserves lengthy discussion. As one who has been brought up in a different family and different circumstances, she is more or less a stranger. She becomes the wife of a husband whom she may have never met before marriage and assumes the role of an active member of his family. In contrast to the situation in a conjugal family, her affiliation with her husband's family is considered to be far more important than the simple fact of her being a spouse. Because of this, she is rigidly required to comply with the traditions and rules of the family into which she has married, no matter how disagreeable and unreasonable they may be to her. Should she have difficulty in getting along with the family, not to mention any misconduct on her part, her husband, regardless of what his feelings may be, is forced to repudiate her to maintain the integrity of the family institution.

MARRIAGE AND THE SELECTION OF A MATE

Since marriage in traditional China means taking a new member into the family rather than simply getting a wife for a husband, marriage is defined in the Confucian Classics as "to make a union between two persons of different families, the object of which is to serve, on the one hand, the ancestors in the temple, and to perpetuate, on the other hand, the coming generation." It must be arranged through "the orders of the parents and the words of the go-between." Among young boys and girls, dating is unknown and romantic love nonexistent — both seem to be the devices for a conjugal union, not for an institutional family.

In the Western world the choice of a mate, based on mutual compatibility, is made in the light of life-long companionship. In the traditional society of China, however, a wedding was not considered as a matter between two individuals, but rather as a conjugation between two families, and, therefore, personal adjustment between husband and wife constitutes only a minor factor in the selection of a spouse. With regard to a wife, consideration was chiefly centered on the following three qualifications: (1) capability of bearing children, (2) compliance with the family's traditions and rules, and (3) ability to endure household drudgery. It is readily seen that these qualities can be more or less objectively estimated; or at least, they are not so subtle as "personal compatibility" which the Western husband and wife may not be able to determine at the moment of marriage.

Under the large family system, a child is born into a group, a primary institution, and brought up in a milieu where, through personal contact and intimate reactions to each other, young and old, identification with and conformity to the family and its rules become more or less a natural process of integration. Members of a lower generation address members of the one immediately above reverently as fathers and mothers, and address each other as brothers and sisters. It is the feeling of "we" (not of "I" as in the family of the Western world), which is cherished, cultivated, and finally incorporated in the personality of the grown-up adults. "A Chinese," wrote Leong and Tao, "does not live for himself and for himself alone. He is the son of his parents, the descendant of his ancestors, the potential father of his children, and the pillar of the family." [2]

Observation of the cardinal virtue, filial piety and obedience, is exhorted in the name of the ancestors, rewarded by the inheritance of the patrimony, and reinforced by the family traditions and rules which sanction punishment of any offender. It is the binding force of this virtue and of its far reaching effects that has reduced juvenile delinquency to a minimum in the Chinese family; and it is also this aspect of life which leads an able American observer to remark: "Of almost no moral law in any civilization can be more confidently said that it is not honored in the breach. In fact it has become so deeply ingrained, so firmly interwoven in the unconscious, as to constitute almost a biological principle." [3]

The cultivation of a strong "we" feeling in family life naturally engenders an equally strong pride in the family. This pride is very persistent and popular among the high standing families, and has led not only to friendly relations and marriage arrangements, but also to family feuds and even bloody conflicts between families or clans in traditional China. The implications of this concept go far beyond the family's locality. When any member of the household has succeeded in gaining an official position, it is both his duty and his honor to get jobs for other members, capable or incapable, through his association and influence. A brilliant son may be supported not only by the resources of his immediate family, but many a large and prosperous clan generally makes practice of raising enough funds to support a gifted member to gain fame and position. This is done mainly on the ground that members of the entire family or clan may all be benefited some day.

The Family in Transition

The foregoing is a brief and generalized description of the traditional family system in China. Since the advent of Western influence in China a century ago, however, this traditional and time-honored system has begun to decay with ever-increasing speed. Modern education and the importation of Western ideas have gradually weakened the hold of Confucian teaching upon which most of the family ethics are based. Urbanization,

[2] Leong and Tao, *op. cit.,* p. 68.

[3] Nathaniel Peffer, *China: The Collapse of a Civilization,* New York: John Day Co., 1930, p. 39.

together with the creation of job opportunities and of better living quarters for middle and upper classes, have affected a great number of people through a loss of traditional values.

This transition which has taken place in the Chinese family represents but a phase of a world-wide trend. It is a shifting of the center of family life from consanguinity to matrimony, or to adopt Dr. E. W. Burgess' terminology, from institution to companionship. The social change in China which has thoroughly shaken the traditional structure of society has shifted the emphasis of the family to comradeship. The whole process may be described in the following three stages:

(1) *The decline of the large family system.* The changes of socioeconomic environment since the turn of the century have brought about many effects fatal to the traditional family system in China. The intellectuals who have the responsibility of upholding the traditional model of the family are no longer interested in traditional ways of life. The rise in the cities and trade ports of the new group of "upstarts" in the form of compradors, big merchants, and warlords, rendered the situation in the family still worse. One common characteristic of this group of people is a weakness of conviction and virtue, traditional or Western, and yet an exploitation of all the privileges that work in their own favor under the old system. For instance, many of these parvenus, irrespective of their occupations, have not only bought domestic maids but also taken one or more attractive concubines of obscure and often disreputable orgin, even though their formally married wives may still be alive and have borne to them many sons to bear the family names. They, as family heads, continue to exercise power and authority over their offspring in accordance with the prerogatives of the old patriarchy, but it now devolves upon the public schools and colleges to provide their education. In the household, because of heterogeneity of cultural background, enforcement of family rule is very difficult, and bitter dissensions and even licentious relations between family members and others are frequent.

In the villages, the breakdown of the large households is not so much the work of outside cultural impact as it is of the profound effects of economic forces. The ever-growing decay of the rural economy has forced many of the peasants' sons or daughters to leave home and to seek jobs elsewhere, and thus has reduced the family size to a minimum. Although the family of the landlord class is still relatively big and continues to be managed more or less along the traditional pattern, its educated sons or daughters, after completing their schooling, are most likely to stay away from home and set up their own small families in the cities.

(2) *The emergence of the conjugal family.* The real conjugal family in which the members live together both in spirit and in form is largely a phenomenon of the large cities and is found among Westernized intelligentsia. Failure to make distinctions between form and spirit has caused many writers, Western as well as Chinese, to exaggerate the prevalence of the conjugal type of family.[4] The poor peasants in the villages may live in nominally conjugal families, but the way in which their wives and children are treated and disciplined is fundamentally traditional. The modernized professional is the only one whose economic independence from the support of the old household gives him freedom to marry the girl he loves, and whose college-educated wife cannot tolerate even a day of the mother-in-law's meddling in her business. Under the influence of modern education, the young talk about the out-datedness of the traditional family, and vigorously demand the right to choose their own mates, to set up their own conjugal families in the cities, and to live in their own way without interference.

(3) *The emancipation of women.* The destruction of the traditional family structure was accelerated by the revolutionary tide which has swept over China since 1946. The family system has been the target for heavy attack by the Chinese Communists. The spirit of family collectivism in terms of "we" feeling and group solidarity seems to have been shifted to apply to the Party and the nation, while the low status of women, together with the frequent maltreatment of wives, concubines, daughters-in-law, and domestic maids, have been used to point out the evils of the traditional family system. In mass meetings and public trials, mistreated women are encouraged to voice their grievances against their husbands, parents-in-law, and others. These latter persons are severely con-

[4] Cf., for instance, the statistics gathered by Olga Lang in her *Chinese Family and Society*, New Haven: Yale University Press, 1946, pp. 134–54.

demned, and can scarcely escape some punishment. Enslaved maids begin to settle accounts with their former owners by demanding wages covering all past years.

The attempt of the Peking regime to bring about a fundamental revolution in the family system is being implemented by inculcating in the minds of people, and especially of the youth, new ideas with regard to marriage and family. All the traditional family ethics and Confucian virtues are discarded as vestiges of feudalism. Families are urged to sign "a pact of patriotism" under which all individual members pledge their allegiance to the nation, and not to any particular persons within the family. Hence, newspapers often report open trials, in which a wife accuses her husband, or a son or daughter brings charges against the father. Marriage is no longer taken as a matter involving two families as in traditional China, nor between two individuals as in the Western world, but a spiritual union of two comrades of different sexes; and the first task of the couple is to strengthen and cherish their commonly shared belief of communism, and then to engage in production to build a new society. The prospect of success of this indoctrination campaign cannot at present be estimated, but one thing seems certain: familism and the large family system as known historically are irretrievably gone from the land of the Middle Kingdom.

64 Family Structure and Educational Attainment: A Cross-National Analysis*

Glen H. Elder, Jr.

What is the relationship between family structure and the educational achievement of adolescents? Is the pattern of parental dominance a positive or a negative factor in the development of the potential of youth? What clues does this study yield which can help the present college generation in its relations with both older and younger generations? The author has analysed the results of approximately 1,000 interviewees age 18 and over in the United States, Great Britain, West Germany, Italy, and Mexico. The study shows clearly that parental domination in adolescence was negatively associated with the probability of reaching secondary school in all five nations.

Family structure is one of the more important determinants of achievement motivation and skills. Many of the personal qualities and skills that enable children to meet standards of excellence — self-reliance, competent judgment, provlem-solving ability, and a questioning mind — are acquired in parent-child relations providing guidance and yet allowing the child freedom to develop independent mastery and responsible decision-making.[1] Parental dominance, on the other hand, often produces passivity, rebelliousness, and dependency. Domination is characterized by "a rigidity or inflexibility of purpose, . . . an unwillingness to admit the contribution of another's experiences, desires, purposes of judgment in one's determining of goals which concern others." Responsibility and confidence in independence are acquired through guided opportunities in independent problem solving and activity, and parental domination during late childhood and in adolescence largely denies these experiences.

Conjugal role patterns, affecting as they do family relations and climate, also influence the

* Excerpted from the *American Sociological Review,* Vol. 30 (February 1965), pp. 81–96. Reprinted with revised footnotes by permission. Copyright © 1965 by The American Sociological Association.

[1] Glen H. Elder, Jr., *Family Structure and the Transmission of Values and Norms in the Process of Child Rearing,* unpublished Ph.D. dissertation, University of North Carolina, 1961. See also Murray H. Straus, "Conjugal Power Structure and Adolescent Personality," *Marriage and Family Living,* 24 (February, 1962), pp. 17–25.

acquisition of self-confidence and mastery in children. The most negative effects are associated with wife-dominance. In a recent study, American adolescents who described their mothers as dominant in family decision-making tended to be relatively low on autonomy and academic motivation.[2] Devereux *et al.* found that American and West German pre-adolescent boys in extremely wife-dominated families were rated by teachers and peers as more selfish, incompetent, excitable, and dependent than boys from any other type of family.

This paper reports a cross-national study of the effects of parent-child and conjugal role patterns on level of educational attainment. Most research on the effects of parental dominance on motivation and achievement level has been conducted in the U.S., so that the effects of family structure on educational achievement in other societies are to some extent unknown.[3] The data for the present analysis are drawn from a study of political behavior in the U.S., Great Britain, West Germany, Italy, and Mexico.[4] Interviews were obtained from approximately 1,000 adults, ages 18 and over.

These nations represent considerable diversity of culture and of educational opportunity. Individual achievement and competition are core themes in American culture, and are more prominent in Great Britain and West Germany than in Italian and Mexican cultures. On the other hand, cultural support for male dominance in family, economic, and political affairs is more pronounced in Italy and Mexico than in the other countries. Italy and especially Mexico also stand apart from the other countries in the development of human resources through education. These variations define in part the general context in which I shall assess the relation between family structure and educational attainment.

The control parents exercise over adolescent sons and daughters ranges from complete subordination of the child to no regulation over the child's behavior. Both extremes have negative effects on the development of achievement motivation and skills. Among adolescents living in central areas of Ohio and North Carolina those who were dominated by their parents and prevented from acquiring decision-making experience lacked interest in school, academic motivation, and plans for additional education.

To a lesser extent this pattern was characteristic of youth given little parental guidance and supervision. Girls and boys who participated, under parental guidance, in decisions concerning their own activities attained the highest levels of academic motivation and achievement.

These results suggest the following hypothesis: in each of the five nations, *educational attainment is negatively related to the degree of parental dominance in adolescence.*[5]

The effects of dominance on the development of ability and motivation to achieve are heavily contingent on which parent is dominant. For boys, paternal dominance and maternal overprotection have the most negative effects. Furthermore, in

[2] See Edward C. Devereux, Jr., "Children of Democracy: on the Consequences for Children of Varying Patterns of Family Authority in the United States and West Germany," summary of a paper presented to the 7th International Seminars on Family Research, Washington, D.C., September 1962: Edward C. Devereux, Jr., Urie Bronfenbrenner and George J. Suci, "Patterns of Parent Behavior in America and West Germany: A Cross-National Comparison," *International Social Science Journal*, 14 (1962), pp. 488–506.

[3] Studies in Japan, Brazil, Germany and Turkey have corroborated American findings regarding the effects of paternal dominance on achievement, motivation. See David C. McClelland, *The Achieving Society, Princeton,* N.J.

[4] These data were obtained in 1959 and 1960 by Gabriel Almond and Sydney Verba for a study of political behavior in these five countries. See *The Civic Culture,* Princeton: Princeton Universty Press, 1963.

[5] The measure of educational attainment is the percentage reaching secondary school. An index of parent-youth relations was constructed from the following two items: "As you were growing up, let's say when you were around 16, how much influence do you remember having in family decisions affecting yourself?" (*2,* much influence; *1,* some; *0,* none at all. Other and "don't know" responses not scored.) "At around the same time, if a decision were made that you didn't like, did you feel *free* to complain, did you feel a little *uneasy* about complaining, or was it *better not* to complain?" (*2,* felt free; *1,* felt a little uneasy; *0,* it was better not to complain. Other and "don't know" responses not scored.) The index score, ranging from 0 to 4, is the sum of the two component scores. In the following analysis, scores 3 and 4 indicate *democratic* parent-child relations, and scores 0, 1, and 2 indicate authoritarian relations. (The data did not permit a measure of parental permissiveness.) The two component items are highly correlated; 3 x 3 tables based on the total sample in each nation yielded the following gamma coefficients. U.S., .61; Italy, .63; West Germany, .65; Great Britain, .56; Mexico, .46.

an authoritarian, father-dominated family boys seem to receive little achievement training from father.

In the present samples, father-dominance in parent-youth relations tends to reflect husband-dominance in conjugal relations: the average "Q" coefficient is .38. A similar positive association was obtained in most age, sex and nationality sub-groups. Respondents who reported being excluded from decision-making during adolescence were also more likely to report that father was the chief decision-maker on matters pertaining to discipline. To a limited extent, then, a parent-dominated home tends to indicate father dominance in family relations generally.

Research on the effects of conjugal role patterns indicates that achievement among American boys is highest in the "equalitarian" household and lowest in wife-dominated homes.[6] Boys in a small sample from a New England high school were most likely to have upwardly mobile occupational aspirations when mother and father shared family authority.[7] Similar results for boys have been observed in samples of second generation Italians and Jews,[8] and a study conducted by Gill and Spilka among Mexican-American youth indicates that in a "masculine" culture, wife-domination has negative effects on academic achievement, particularly for boys.[9]

These findings suggest that parent-youth and conjugal relations jointly affect adolescent achievement. Accordingly, my second hypothesis is that *high educational attainment is most prevalent among persons who report democratic relations with their parents and equalitarian relations between mother and father*. In his study of second-generation Italian and Jewish boys in the Boston area, Strodtbeck found that those who experienced democratic relations with their parents and reported equality between parents were most likely to value independent mastery and achievement.[10] Variation in this relationship by sex is difficult to predict because most research has been conducted with boys, but both achievement pressures and educational opportunities are less commonly experienced by girls. Given educational opportunities and encouraged to take advantage of them, girls' achievement should be similarly affected by the same family structural patterns.

Power variations in the parent-child relationship should have a greater effect on adolescent achievement than role variations in the marital relationship. In a study of high school students, the joint effects of structural variations in parental and conjugal relations on academic motivation were assessed in an analysis of variance (with social class and sex controlled), and in three of four sub-groups, variations in parent-youth relations accounted for substantially more of the variation in the desire to achieve.[11] The third hypothesis, then, is that *parent-youth relations have a greater effect on educational attainment than conjugal role patterns.*

Responses to the question, "How far did you get with your education?" ranged from no education to various types of higher education. For the present analysis, high educational attainment is defined as having reached secondary school. (Note that this does not necessarily imply *completion* of secondary school.) For Italian respondents, junior was distinguished from senior high school; I used the percentage reaching junior high school as the index of achievement, so that the percentage of Italian respondents reaching secondary school is slightly inflated. The proportion who reached 12 years of education was used as the index in the U.S., since it seems to be comparable to reaching secondary school in the other four nations.

Opportunities for secondary education vary substantially among the five countries in this study, and this variation is most notable among girls. In

[6] Elder, *Adolescent Achievement and Mobility Aspirations,* Chapel Hill, N.C., Institute for Research in Social Science, 1962.

[7] Donald G. McKinley, "Class, Resulting Family Structure, and the Socialized Child," a paper read at the American Sociological Association meetings, Washington, D.C., September 1962.

[8] Fred Strodtbeck, "Family Interaction, Values and Achievement," in David C. McClelland, *et al., Talent and Society,* Princeton, N.J., 1958.

[9] Lois J. Gill and Bernard Spilka, "Some Non-intellectual Correlates of Academic Achievement Among Mexican-American Second School Students," *Journal of Educational Psychology,* 53 (June, 1962) pp. 144–149.

[10] Strodtbeck, *op. cit.,* See also Elder, *Adolescent Achievement and Mobility Aspirations, op. cit.*

[11] Elder, *Adolescent Achievement and Mobility Aspirations, op. cit.*

West Germany and Great Britain the percentages of 15–19 year olds enrolled in secondary school were 18.2 and 16.8, respectively, and slightly less than half of all students were girls. In the U.S., the rate of secondary enrollment is about 90 per cent. In contrast, 7.8 per cent of the Italian 15–19 year olds were enrolled in secondary school, and less than 40 per cent of these students were girls. Secondary enrollment in Mexico was well below the Italian rate, and less than 33 per cent of the students were girls. Thus, the opportunity for secondary education is currently available to relatively few Mexican and Italian youth, though it was available to even fewer in the 1920's, 30's and 40's. Between 1950 and 1960, the secondary enrollment rate in Mexico doubled, yet less than 10 per cent of youth 15–19 years old are currently enrolled in secondary school.

These cross-national variations do not seriously limit the present analysis, since relations between variables *within* each nation are of primary interest, not comparisons of single indicators across nations. Of course, the strength of these relationships will itself vary with differences in the structure of education, and as a partial control for within-nation variations in educational opportunities, I have used socio-economic status and size of birthplace. Educational opportunities tend to be more available to urban and middle-class youth; rural residence, in particular, is a relatively accurate index of low educational opportunity.[12]

The influence of educational opportunity on educational attainment is illustrated in the recently completed Robbins Report on Higher Education in Great Britain. A multiple regression analysis indicated that persistence in school and entrance to institutions of higher education were most influenced by local opportunities to attend grammar school and parents' education. Persistence in school was measured by the number of the 17-year-olds at school in January, 1960 as a percentage of 13-year-olds at school in January, 1956 in each Local Education Authority. Zero-order correlation coefficients between this index and percentage in grammar school, father's education, and

father's occupation were .82, .66 and .65, respectively. The degree of inequality of educational opportunity across the 145 Local Education Authorities in England and Wales is shown by the range in school persistence rates — 27.9 to 2.5.[13]

Value-orientations also influence the relation between family structure and educational attainment. American studies have found that individualistic, competitive achievement is valued highly by urban, middle-class, and Protestant or Jewish families.[14] Familism, acceptance of social position, and a belief that events affecting oneself are externally determined tend to be more prevalent among rural, working-class, and Catholic families. Parental dominance also tends to be more common in the latter categories, and evidence in several countries indicates that the educational attainment of youth from these families is relatively low. In the present analysis, place of birth, and social class will be used as indicators of cultural orientation.[15]

RESULTS

Birthplace, Parent-Youth Relations, and Educational Attainment

Educational attainment in part reflects the availability of schooling and in part, the motivational

---

[12] Glen H. Elder, Jr., "Achievement Orientations and Career Patterns of Rural Youth," *Sociology of Education,* 37 (Fall, 1963), pp. 30–58.

[13] Lord Robbins' Committee on Higher Education, Higher Education: *The Demand for Places in Higher Education,* London: Her Majesty's Stationery Office, 1963, App. 1, Sec. 3.

[14] For social class and religious variations, see Gerhard Lenski, *The Religious Factor,* New York: Doubleday, 1961, and Herbert J. Gans, *The Urban Villagers,* New York: The Free Press of Glencoe, 1962. For rural-urban differences, see Elder, "Achievement Orientations and Career Patterns of Rural Youth," *op. cit.*

[15] In lieu of a measure of childhood social class, the interviewer's four-point rating of adult social class is used. (Information on occupation was not available for all respondents.) A rating of 1 or 2 was defined as middle class, 3 was defined as working class and 4 indicated lower class. Interviewers were instructed to classify each respondent according to his economic status in the community or area in which he resides. The most commonly used criteria for this classification were housing, occupation, family status and size, income, and comforts and luxuries. To standardize the proportions of respondents rated 1, 2, 3, and 4 in each area, 1's and 2's were to equal the top 16 per cent of the community, the 3's the middle 52 per cent and the 4's the bottom 32 per cent.

TABLE 1   *Per Cent Who Reached Secondary School, by Age, Sex, Parent-Youth Relations and Place of Birth*

Place of Birth	Type of Parent-Youth Relations	Men		Women	
		18–40	41+	18–40	41+
United States					
Rural	Authoritarian	(26) 46	(75) 22	(24) 58	(92) 26
	Democratic	(41) 66	(48) 39	(49) 67	(74) 49
Urban	Authoritarian	(22) 82	(39) 44	(35) 60	(39) 41
	Democratic	(69) 88	(43) 42	(58) 77	(47) 51
Great Britain					
Rural	Authoritarian	*	(32) 19	*	(31) 16
	Democratic	(29) 48	(20) 32	(23) 48	(41) 15
Urban	Authoritarian	(58) 50	(82) 31	(59) 41	(101) 22
	Democratic	(102) 60	(91) 48	(112) 57	(91) 30
West Germany					
Rural	Authoritarian	(35) 11	(71) 10	(40) 2	(83) 2
	Democratic	(37) 27	(32) 19	(36) 20	(23) 9
Urban	Authoritarian	(45) 24	(59) 15	(59) 10	(70) 11
	Democratic	(60) 47	(43) 33	(53) 32	(52) 25
Italy					
Rural	Authoritarian	(48) 38	(45) 20	(49) 22	(60) 3
	Democratic	(39) 51	(37) 38	(32) 50	(30) 17
Urban	Authoritarian	(61) 54	(58) 22	(60) 28	(58) 26
	Democratic	(50) 60	(26) 58	(40) 60	(24) 29
Mexico					
Rural	Authoritarian	(45) 11	(45) 4	(127) 9	(82) 5
	Democratic	*	(34) 12	(25) 12	
Urban	Authoritarian	(126) 19	(58) 7	(217) 20	(118) 8
	Democratic	(57) 63	(33) 42	(93) 31	(40) 8

* Fewer than 20 cases.

and intellectual capacities of the child. Since both the quality and availability of educational facilities differ substantially between rural and urban areas, the relation of parental dominance to achievement is evaluated with place of birth controlled. Places of birth defined as "rural" include communities of 5,000 population or less, and urban birthplaces include all larger communities. (Exceptions to this classification will be noted.)

Parental dominance is inversely related to the likelihood of reaching secondary school in each of the five countries, with age, sex, and birthplace controlled (see Table 1). Of the 36 possible comparisons, 33 are in the predicted direction. The degree of association between parent-youth relations and education is quite similar in each of the five nations: average percentage differences range from 13 per cent for Great Britain to 19 per cent for Italy.

The effects of parental dominance tend to be most pronounced among the urban-born in every nation except the U.S. Although these differences are frequently neither large nor entirely consistent, the data generally conform to other data showing that educational opportunities are much more favorable in urban places.[16] Not only do rural residents in each of the five nations have less access to primary and secondary education, but, typically the education they receive is lower in quality. Table 2 shows that entrance to secondary school is more common among the urban-born, especially in Mexico. Very few rural-born Mexicans, male or female, have reach secondary school. Yet even under these conditions parent-youth relations have some effect on educational attainment. The fact that the effect of parent-youth relations is markedly stronger among urban-born Mexicans indicates that in a favorable social and educational context a motivating family environment substantially encourages social advancement.

The combined influence of age, sex, birthplace and parent-youth relations is best revealed by comparing the educational attainment of persons with the most and least favorable characteristics, i.e., compare young democratically-reared, urban-born men with older authoritarian-reared, rural-born women, in Table 2. Percentages reaching

[16] UNESCO, *Rural Education,* Vol. 14, No. 3, 1962.

secondary school are: U.S. 88 vs. 26 per cent; Great Britain, 60 vs. 16 per cent; Italy, 60 vs. 3 per cent; and Mexico, 63 vs. 5 per cent.

Social Class, Birthplace, Parent-Youth Relations, and Educational Attainment

Substituting adult social class for childhood social class involves several assumptions. Youth who experience democratic relations with parents as well as achievement training are likely to be achievement-oriented, and therefore are apt to be upwardly mobile. Youth who are dominated are likely to be non-mobile or downwardly mobile. Thus, lower- and working-class youth who experience achievement training in childhood and adolescence should be more apt to move into the middle class than youth of comparable status who are dominated. According to this reasoning, the relation between parent-child relations and education should be weakest among lower-class adults, slightly stronger among working-class adults, and strongest among middle-class adults, in part because of the assumed relation between dominance and vertical mobility, and in part because educational opportunities improve as one ascends the class hierarchy.

These expectations are generally confirmed. The relation between parental control and educational attainment is generally stronger in the middle than in the working class. No consistent relationships were observed in the lower class because only an extremely small proportion reached secondary school, and in the Mexican sample the number of Mexicans rated middle-class was too small to permit analysis. Among working-class persons in all five nations, dominance appears to have had pronounced effects on educational achievement.

Analysis of the relation between parental dominance and achievement, with birthplace and social class controlled, is restricted to the U.S., Great Britain, and West Germany, due to the paucity of middle-class Mexican and Italian respondents. The index of parent-youth relations is related to educational attainment in the expected direction in all but one of the 18 subgroups. The relationship is generally stronger in the working class and particularly in the middle class than it is in the lower class. Among rural-born, lower-class adults, the effects of authority patterns tend to be weak-

TABLE 2 *Per Cent Who Reached Secondary School by Birthplace and Family Structure*

	Type of Parent-Youth Relation	Rural Conjugal Pattern		Urban Conjugal Pattern	
		Husband Decides	Both Decide	Husband Decides	Both Decide
United States	Authoritarian	(77) 34	(91) 29	(38) 50	(43) 61
	Democratic	(39) 55	(117) 59	(32) 60	(111) 76
Great Britain	Authoritarian	(36) 28	(67) 25	(54) 36	(75) 40
	Democratic	(24) 33	(106) 38	(62 47	(169) 53
West Germany	Authoritarian	(73) 8	(135) 5	(83) 19	(108) 14
	Democratic	(38) 11	(68) 26	(57) 26	(106) 44
Italy	Authoritarian	(88) 18	(72) 26	(111) 32	(78) 29
	Democratic	(62) 47	(53) 37	(45) 58	(63) 53
Mexico	Authoritarian	(79) 5	(132) 7	(137) 13	(243) 12
	Democratic	(27) 4	(35) 14	(54) 32	(132) 39

est and the likelihood of reaching secondary school least.

Extremes in both support and opportunity for education occur in rural lower-class and urban middle-class environments. This contrast is most evident in the Italian and Mexican samples. Almost none of the rural-born lower-class Italians and Mexicans reached secondary school, compared with over half the Italians and over one-third of the middle-class Mexicans who were born in communities larger than 5,000 in population. In addition to low educational opportunity, data reviewed above show that authoritarian parent-child relations are also more prevalent in rural, lower-class environments, and least common among urban middle-class families. The fact that lack of educational opportunity and parental dominance both characterize rural lower-class environ-ments constitutes an imposing problem for the development of human resources.

Another negative factor in these rural areas is the prevalence of *countervailing conditions* that thwart the development of abilities and achievement motivation. The early induction of children into the farm labor market is one such factor, and frequent absence from school is one consequence of the intensive use of child labor. In the U.S., child labor means absence from school most prominently among children in migrant farm families.

Conjugal Relations, Parental Authority and Educational Attainment

Since most relevant studies have found that equalitarian conjugal relations are associated with high occupational achievement among boys, I hypothesized that adults who report democratic relations with their parents *and* equalitarian relations between parents during adolescence are most likely to have reached secondary school. To assess conjugal decision making patterns, answers to the following question were used: "We're interested in how decisions were made in your family when you were a child, let's say when you were 16. Here's a list of ways of making family decisions. By and large, how were decisions made in your family?" Response categories were: "By and large, father made the decisions"; By and large, mother made the decisions"; "Both parents acted together"; and "Each parent acted individually." (If mother and father were not present, the response was coded "other.") Since responses other than father-dominance and the equalitarian pattern were too few to permit analysis, these cases have been excluded, leaving four possible variations in perceived family structure: families are father-dominated or equalitarian and parent-youth relations may be recalled as either authoritarian or democratic.[17] To distinguish the effects of family structure, birthplace is held constant.

In all nations except Italy, adults who report equalitarian relations between their parents and democratic parent-youth relations are indeed most likely to have reached secondary school. And in all five nations the likelihood of reaching secondary school is consistently low among persons with authoritarian parents regardless of the pattern of decision making between mother and father. The index of parent-youth relations is more strongly and consistently related to educational attainment than the two conjugal patterns; of 20 possible comparisons between authority patterns, 19 show percentage differences in the expected direction. The only relatively consistent effects of conjugal relations appear among democratically-reared

persons, with the percentage reaching secondary school tending to be largest among persons reporting equalitarian relations between parents. The weak effects of the conjugal pattern may reflect various flaws in the data; it is also reasonable to suppose that in fact conjugal relations have relatively little effect independently of parent-child relations. Recent American research suggests, however, that "either wife-dominance in the family or autocratic parental control in child-rearing, or both in combination, are relatively unlikely to promote high educational aspirations among boys." [18]

As noted, family structure has a different effect on the probability of reaching secondary school among Italians. Among both rural and urban respondents, those who describe their fathers as dominant in conjugal relations, and report democratic relations with their parents, are most likely to have reached secondary school. A similar reversal occurred among Mexican men. This slight reversal may be due in part to a cultural pattern of male dominance in which submission of husband to wife is considered evidence of weakness. From his intensive study of five Mexican families, Oscar Lewis concludes ". . . that in the strongly male-oriented Mexican culture, only men who are aging, impotent, homosexual, or 'bewitched' are unable to carry out the authoritarian role of the husband." [19]

Family Structure and Educational Attainment: A Summary Assessment

The Analysis up to this point has indicated that the relation between family structure and educational attainment depends heavily on educational opportunity and values. Among rural-born Mexicans and Italians, for instance, educational achievement is extremely low and conjugal and parent-youth relations have very little effect on achievement.

---

[17] The relative prevalence of each type of conjugal pattern in each nation is difficult to determine because the proportion of respondents who gave "other" and "don't know" responses varies. Among respondents who are 18–40 years old, the percentages indicating a husband-dominant pattern in the U.S., Great Britain, West Germany, Italy and Mexico are, for men: 23, 24, 42, and 26; and for women: 14, 19, 26, 33 and 22. On wife dominance, the percentage reporting wife-dominance are, for men: 11, 15, 12, 16, and 6; and for women: 11, 18, 19, 21, and 11. The percentage giving the equalitarian response is around 50 in each sample.

[18] Charles E. Bowerman and Glen H. Elder, Jr., "Variations in Adolescent Perception of Family Power Structure," *American Sociological Review,* 29 (August, 1964), pp. 551–567.

[19] Oscar Lewis, *Five Families,* New York: Basic Books, 1959, p. 17. See also William Madsen, *The Mexican-Americans of South Texas,* New York: Holt, Rinehart & Winston, 1964.

A summary assessment of the effects of conjugal and parent-youth relations, with all test factors simultaneously controlled, would be helpful at this point, but limited sample sizes seriously restrict the number of variables that can be simultaneously controlled in tabular cross-classifications. To surmount this limitation, a multiple regression analysis with dummy variables was used.[20] This procedure permits simultaneous control of all test factors by statistically adjusting subclass percentages for the effects of all other variables together. No assumptions concerning the linearity of the effects of each factor are required, but the technique does have the sizable disadvantage, for our purposes, of ignoring interaction and estimating only the main effects. For example, this procedure assumes that the effects of parent-youth relations are the same for each size of birthplace, though the data previously shown clearly indicate that this assumption is false. Nevertheless, an overview of the main effects of perceived family structure with residence, social class, and religion controlled is valuable at this point. Table 3 shows the adjusted percentages derived from this analysis for American and West German men ages 18 through 40. (Region of birth was included in the analysis because some regions, such as the American South, offer less educational opportunity.) Variations in the percentage reaching secondary school are generally small for all variables except adult social class, which is obviously closely related to educational attainment.

Conjugal patterns do not affect educational attainment appreciably, particularly in the U.S. sample. In the German sample, men from equalitarian homes are more apt to reach secondary school than are men from husband-dominant homes, while those who report mother dominance are least likely to have reached secondary school. This finding corresponds to research findings reported earlier, but results from the U.S. sample tend to run in the opposite direction. In either case, however, the number of respondents reporting wife-dominance is simply too small to obtain reliable estimates of variation. Parent-youth relations have considerably more influence on achievement in both samples, but the percentage differences are relatively small.

Social class and size and region of birthplace reflect both educational opportunity and the value attached to education; thus, their effects on achievement are naturally greater than those of the index of parent-youth relations. Religious affiliation, however, has very little effect on achievement in the West German sample. American Catholics, on the other hand, are slightly more likely to have reached secondary school than Protestants. Even with social class and region controlled, educational attainment varies markedly by size of birthplace; conditions relevant to educational achievement are strongly linked to community size, even in highly industrialized nations.

The principal conclusion to be drawn, then, is that the independent influence of culture and the opportunity-structure on educational attainment exceeds that of perceived family structure among younger American and West German men. This result suggests feasible strategies in the development of human resources.

Parental domination is but one factor determining achievement; educational and vocational opportunities, as well as the expectations of significant others outside the family, are also important. "The key to the unlocking of potential is always found in the first instance in the widening of opportunity."[21] And yet, full utilization of opportunity is also contingent on ability and motivation. To elevate educational attainment, whether among youth in the American South or among rural Italians, not only must educational facilities be improved and made more widely available, but the kind of family relations conducive to achievement, and the value attached to education relative to other goals must be encouraged as well. Many patterns are possible: in one, changes in educational and economic opportunities may alter ideology, values and aspirations, and these newly acquired orientations may, in turn, change traditional family patterns.

The introduction of schools and industries to

[20] For a description of this technique, see Alan B. Wilson, "Analysis of Multiple Cross-Classifications in Cross-Sectional Designs," revision of a paper presented to the American Association for Public Opinion Research, Excelsior Springs, Missouri, May, 1964. See also J. W. Morgan *et al., Income and Welfare in the United States,* New York: McGraw-Hill, 1962, Appendix E.

[21] Eli Ginsberg, *The Negro Potential,* New York: Columbia University Press, 1956, p. 12.

TABLE 3 *Perceived Family Structure and Per Cent Who Reached Secondary School, with Place and Region of Birth, Social Class and Religion Controlled: Adjusted Percentages for Sub-Classes in a Multiple Classification Analysis*

Categorical Variables	U.S. Men Ages 18–40		West German Men Ages 18–40	
	N	Adjusted Percentage	N	Adjusted Percentage
1. Family Structure				
A. Conjugal Role Pattern				
1. Father dominant	37	72.2	46	27.8
2. Mother dominant	19	76.9	23	13.4
3. Equalitarian	80	73.4	103	32.5
B. Parent-Youth Relations				
1. Authoritarian	47	65.6	80	23.7
2. Democratic	107	77.7	97	34.0
2. Educational Opportunity and Values				
A. Region of Birth				
1. United States				
East	51	78.9		
Central	59	71.6		
South	37	63.4		
West	9	*		
2. West Germany				
Schleswig-Holstein			24	32.2
N. Rhine Westphalia			56	16.9
Hesse			38	23.1
Bavaria			22	31.6
B. Place of Birth				
1. Less than 5,000	69	62.8	78	15.8
2. 5,000 to 100,000	52	78.1	55	36.1
3. 100,000 and over	42	78.8	57	33.9
C. Adult Social Class				
1. Middle	32	86.0	33	64.9
2. Working	112	74.8	129	24.4
3. Lower	19	30.4	29	0.0
D. Religion				
1. Protestant	104	68.5	100	27.7
2. Catholic	37	75.2	83	26.5
	Total N[b]	Grand Per Cent	Total N[b]	Grand Per Cent
	168	71.8	191	27.2

* Fewer than 10 cases. In this table adjusted percentages for two sub-classes are based on 19 cases each, despite the 20-case rule applied in all preceding tables except Table 3.

[a] The rank of each of the six variables was not computed because primary interest was in examining the effects of the two family-structure indices with the four test factors simultaneously controlled.

[b] Total N refers to the total number of respondents in the two subgroups. Summation of the cases in each response class of each variable will result in smaller totals due to non-response and omitted responses (e.g., Jews, under Religion).

rural areas frequently initiates a whole series of improvements in the development of human potential. The influx of technicians and managerial personnel, and their families, adds a more educated element and a source of potential leadership to the community. As non-agrarian employment opportunities increase, schooling is apt to acquire greater relevance and importance in the minds of youth and their parents. More and better education may develop a tradition of going to school and, ultimately, ideological support for education. These and other changes resulting from social and economic development directly widen the life opportunities of youth and should eventually alter family relations, in both present and future generations, creating family environments more conducive to the development of achievement motivation and skills.

Oscar Lewis has described how education, accompanied by other aspects of modernization, generated greater interest in schooling for children; elevated aspirations, and fostered changes in child-rearing practices in the Mexican village of Tepotzlan. "Younger and more educated parents," according to Lewis, "punish more lightly, permit more play, and send their children to school for as long as possible." Even where traditional family organization and values inhibit social change, educational and economic opportunities can be manipulated *directly* — a form of intervention that is seldom possible in family and other social relations.

65 Romanticism and Motivation to Marry in the United States, Singapore, Burma, and India*

George A. Theodorson

How do students in different cultures react to the romantic syndrome characteristic of American mate selection? This study examines and analyzes the degree of acceptance of the American type orientation among the most highly educated and Westernized classes in Chinese Singapore, Burma, and India in comparison to like groups in the United States. These societies differ in social organization, degree of industrialization-urbanization, and in value systems.

The impact of industrialization on traditional values in non-Western societies has long been a subject of interest for social scientists as well as political leaders. There has been much discussion of whether traditional values, even in modified form, will be able to withstand the onslaught of Westernizing influences.[1] The effect of these Westernizing influences on values associated with the family is particularly crucial because of the central position of the institution of the family in maintaining the traditional social structure.

The study presented in this paper deals with respondents drawn from an urbanized, educated, and Western-influenced segment of three non-Western societies, Chinese Singapore, Burma, and India. Their attitudes toward the husband-wife relationship first will be analyzed to determine whether the impact of industry, urban culture and Western education has led to their abandonment of the traditional contractual orientation to marriage in favor of the romantic orientation, characteristic of modern American society,. Secondly, the relationship between romanticism and motivation to marry will be considered. This paper is not primarily concerned with changes in specific family norms, for example those regulating the position of women. Rather it is concerned with a broader value-orientation, contractualistic or

* From *Social Forces,* 44, September 1965, pp. 17–27. Reproduced by permission.

[1] See George A. Theodorson, "Acceptance of Industrialization and Its Attendant Consequences for the Social Patterns of Non-Western Societies," *American Sociological Review,* 18 (October 1953), pp. 477–484.

romantic, which conceivably may change or remain constant despite changes in more specific norms.

In Singapore, Burma, and India, the mass media have spread the ideals of romanticism. In all three cultures the educated youth in particular are being exposed to the romantic ideal in motion pictures, books, magazines, newspapers, and American popular songs.[2] Popular writers in these countries have expressed concern (and some alarm) about changes in traditional attitudes toward marriage and particularly about the rise of unrealistic romantic expectations of the future marriage relationship on the part of modern youth. We shall start, therefore, with the following hypothesis: Due to the impact of industrialization, urbanization, Western education, and the concomitant changes and pressures accompanying these forces, no differences will be found between Indian, Burmese, and Singapore Chinese students and American students on attitudes reflecting the ideals of a romantic orientation toward marriage.

It should be recognized from the outset, however, that these three Asian groups represent three different combinations of two highly significant analytical variables — degree of contractualism of the traditional culture and degree of cultural change. Considering the first of these two variables, the degree of contractualism in marriages was very high in the traditional cultures of China and India. Parents selected suitable mates for their children on the basis of economic and social (e.g., caste in India) considerations. Since the young couple frequently did not know each other prior to marriage, romantic love played no part as the basis for marriage. In China, love before marriage was severely condemned. Romance was considered a potential enemy of filial obedience, which could create tensions destructive of family unity.[3] In India, even romantic love between husband and wife was considered dangerous, for it might cause the husband to neglect his duties

toward his parents.[4] The tie between mother and son was considered more central and of deeper emotional involvement than the tie between husband and wife.

In traditional Burmese culture there was a greater element of romanticism in marriage than in India or China. Parents arranged the marriages of their children, but usually with the children's consent. The young man and woman knew each other before marriage, usually having seen each other frequently at social gatherings. In fact the young man or woman quite properly might initiate marriage proceedings by speaking to his or her parents, who, if they approved of the match, would then speak to the other parents either directly or through a matchmaker. Marriage based on romantic love was not a widespread traditional pattern, but when romantic love did occur it might be seriously considered in arranging a marriage. There was courtship, but under direct parental supervision. In the case of parental objection to a marriage, elopement was a formally disapproved but usually accepted pattern often adopted by romantically inclined young couples. However, while the element of romanticism was present, traditional Burmese expectations nevertheless were primarily contractualistic. Close scrutiny was kept over unmarried daughters, and young men and women were not permitted to be alone together. A dowry was paid by the groom to the bride's parents. As in the Indian family, the closest emotional attachment was expected to be between mother and son rather than between husband and wife.

The second analytical variable to be considered is degree of cultural change. Of these three Asian societies, Burma has experienced the least change. In India there is evidence of striking changes from traditional attitudes in regard to divorce, widow remarriage, intercaste marriage, and equality of the sexes. However, by far the greatest change from traditional patterns has occurred among the Singapore Chinese. According to Shu-Ching Lee there was a rapid de-

[2] Noel P. Gist, "Mate Selection and Mass Communication in India," *Public Opinion Quarterly,* 17 (Winter 1953), p. 482: David Mace and Vera Mace, *Marriage: East and West* (Garden City, New York: Doubleday & Co., 1959), pp. 138–142.

[3] Mace and Mace, *op. cit.,* p. 134.

[4] Aileen D. Ross, *The Hindu Family in its Urban Setting* (Toronto: University of Toronto Press, 1961), p. 161.

cline in the strength of the institutional family among modern educated intellectuals in the large cities of China in the early twentieth century. Since then ". . . the destruction of this system has penetrated to all groups of society and to the vast interior."[5] The Singapore Chinese have experienced family change not only insofar as they come from a background of change in China, but also because of their peculiar circumstances in Singapore. The Singapore Chinese immigrants, mostly from a rural background, experienced the impact of sudden urbanization. Secondly, they found themselves in a very heterogeneous situation, despite the fact that the majority of the population of Singapore is Chinese (78 per cent in 1947) and mostly from Fukien and Kwangtung Provinces. These provinces are very diverse, and consequently there are many dialects, subdialects, and sub-sub-dialects represented. One of the most common expressions heard among the Singapore Chinese reflects a consciousness of their heterogeneity: "We Singapore people are very mixed up." Thirdly, the Singapore Chinese are more mobile than they normally would be in China because a family's house cannot be its ancestral home. These factors have not by any means led to an eradication of the traditional family system, but they have led to greater change and susceptibility to modern influences than in Burma or India.

In considering these two analytical variables together, it may be seen that the Singapore Chinese have a highly contractualistic cultural tradition but have experienced the greatest social change. The Indians also with a highly contractualistic cultural tradition have experienced decidedly less social change. The Burmese have had the least social change, but they also have the least contractualistic cultural tradition of these three Asian groups.

PROCEDURE

The Cross-Cultural Study

The data presented in this study are drawn from responses to a questionnaire completed by 4,006 students in the United States, Burma,

---

[5] Shu-Ching Lee, "China's Traditional Family, Its Characteristics and Disintegration," *American Sociological Review,* 18 (June 1953), p. 272.

India, and Singapore. The distribution of respondents is as follows: 1,324 students, 748 men and 576 women, from two universities in northeastern United States; 486 students, 249 men and 237 women, from the largest university in Burma; 1,240 students, 1,038 men and 202 women, from nine universities in northern India; 956 students from the university and three institutes in Singapore. Of the 956 Singapore respondents only those identifying themselves as Chinese — a total of 797, 510 men and 287 women, are included in this study. The students in the four cultural groups came from diverse curricula, with no concentration of majors in one field in any of the four groups. Burmese respondents included a larger proportion of Christians (26 per cent) than are found in the total population of Burma. However, in the responses discussed in this paper there were no significant differences between Buddhists and Christians except in the one instance specifically noted below.

A basically identical questionnaire containing background questions and a series of attitude statements to which respondents indicated whether they strongly agreed, agreed, were uncertain, disagreed, or strongly disagreed, was used for all four cultural groups. For the Asian respondents high competence in English made it unnecessary to translate the questionnaire. In the case of India, where an expression might be confusing the Hindi equivalent was inserted in parentheses. The use of respondents in Burma, India, and Singapore who know English and are highly educated not only assures their understanding of the questions and familiarity with Western conceptions, but also increases the likelihood of obtaining the greatest deviation from traditional norms. These respondents are drawn from the segment of society most Westernized and most likely to have been influenced by ideas of romantic love.

The Indices of Romanticism

In this paper five indices are used to measure romanticism. These indices were chosen to measure crucial value differences which distinguish a romantic from a contractual orientation toward marriage.

In analyzing the literature on romanticism one

finds overwhelming emphasis on physical attraction as a crucial element in the romantic complex. In discussing romantic love Parsons and Bales speak of the emphasis on "overt, specifically feminine attractiveness, with strong erotic overtones . . ." [6] Burgess and Locke write, "In romantic love the emphasis is upon sexual attraction, personal beauty, and emotional response." [7] Smith tells us that romantic love is "based on overwhelming sex attraction" [8] and that "Glamour is closely associated with romantic love . . ." [9] Harsh and Schrickel state, ". . . to love and be loved one must want intensely to possess and be possessed sexually. To that end attractive physical appearance becomes a *sine qua non*." [10] Two aspects of this emphasis on physical attraction may be distinguished. One is an emphasis on physical attraction, with strong erotic overtones, as a criterion of mate selection. The other aspect involves an emphasis on a woman's maintaining an attractive physical appearance after marriage. Recognizing these two aspects of physical attraction in romantic love, Parsons writes, "The . . . pattern . . . of the 'glamour girl,' has a tendency to predominate in the relations of the sexes in the premarital period, being deeply rooted in the youth culture. The fact that in our family system the stability of marriage must rest mainly on personal sentiment creates a tendency for this to carry over into marriage and into the adult feminine role." [11] In this paper two indices are used to measure these two aspects of the romantic value of physical attraction. They are: "The person I marry must be sexually stimulating" and "A woman should be as concerned about her appearance after marriage as she was before."

A second major value in the romantic complex is the ideal of companionship between husband and wife based on a sharing of thoughts and actions, with each confiding in the other. Burgess and Locke, recognizing companionship and "freedom of communication and action" as crucial elements in romantic love, write:

> One method of gauging the depth of love of a couple is by determining the extent and intimacy of communication and behavior. In the love relationship the person may exercise even a higher degree of freedom of confiding and of acting than in a close friendship. [12]

Winch regards a belief in mutual sharing as an essential condition for mate selection to be based on romantic love. He points out that ". . . in middle-class America we have come to regard marriage as the relationship *par excellence* for the sharing of experience, of feelings, and hence of gratification." [13] He goes on to show that this belief which means in effect that "the marital dyad . . . [is] culturally defined as a congeniality group and the spouse as a friend" is a crucial factor in the romantic approach to mate selection. The ideal romantic pair does not want to withhold secrets from each other. In contrast, under a contractual system it is usually considered proper and desirable for a husband and wife not to discuss certain matters and not to share all thoughts. Each sex may be expected to live certain areas of life apart from the opposite sex. In this study those respondents who accept the ideal of total voluntary confiding will not agree with the statement, "Sometimes it is wise not to completely confide in your mate (life-partner)."

As romanticism involves the ideal of companionship between husband and wife, so it also necessarily includes a conception of the husband and wife as equal partners. Parsons points out that a marriage relationship which rests ". . . primarily on affective attachment for the other person as a concrete human individual, a 'personality' rather than on more objective considerations of status . . . puts a premium on a certain kind of mutuality and equality. . . . Each is a

[6] Talcott Parsons and Robert F. Bales, *Family, Socialization and Interaction Process* (Glencoe, Ill.: The Free Press, 1960), p. 24.

[7] Ernest W. Burgess and Harvey J. Locke, *The Family* (New York: American Book Co., 1953), p. 327.

[8] Ernest A. Smith, *American Youth Culture* (New York: The Free Press of Glencoe, 1962), p. 117.

[9] *Ibid.*, p. 123.

[10] Charles M. Harsh and H. G. Schrickel, *Personality Development and Assessment* (New York: The Ronald Press Co., 1950), p. 248.

[11] Talcott Parsons, "The Social Structure of the Family," in Ruth Nanda Anshen (ed.), *The Family: Its Function and Destiny* (New York: Harper & Bros., 1949), p. 198.

[12] Burgess and Locke, *op. cit.*, p. 325.

[13] Robert F. Winch, *Mate-Selection* (New York: Harper & Bros., 1958), p. 70.

fully responsible 'partner' . . ." He goes on to say, "Surely the pattern of romantic love which makes his relation to the 'woman he loves' the most important single thing in a man's life, is incompatible with the view that she is an inferior creature, fit only for dependency on him." [14] Moreover, according to Benedek, the type of "psychobiological interaction" idealized in romantic love rests on an assumption of equality between the man and woman.[15] In a partnership of equals neither partner is expected to sacrifice more than the other. In contrast, in the traditional contractualism of China, India, and Burma it was considered proper for a wife to sacrifice in every way possible for her husband.[16] In this study respondents who believe that marriage is a partnership of equals based on equality of sacrifice will not agree with the statement, "Generally speaking a woman has to sacrifice more in marriage than a man."

A final essential characteristic of the romantic value complex is a de-emphasis on the fulfillment of specific expectations in the marriage relationship, and in its place an emphasis on generalized feelings of affection and trust which are combined with an idealization of the future marriage partner. Contractualism involves an orientation toward a future spouse in which the expected pattern of role relationship between husband and wife is based on the "mores, religion, and law" of the cultural group. Definite, culturally defined norms of proper behavior are expected of a future mate whoever he (or she) may be. In contrast, in the case of romanticism the details of the proper marriage relationships are not as specifically determined by societal norms, but are to a much greater extent determined by the particular individuals in interaction with each other. Norms are largely dyadic and based on mutual agreement. Therefore the romantic demands of a prospective mate are relatively few

in terms of formal universalistic expectations. Parsons contrasts the traditional, contractual conception of the marriage relationship which gives primary emphasis to "matters of objective status and obligations to other kin" with the romantic conception which emphasizes "subjective sentiment." Parsons goes on to explain that in the contractual marriage relationship "Very definite expectations in the definition of the different roles, combined with a complex system of interrelated sanctions, both positive and negative, go far to guarantee stability and the maintenance of standards of performance." Since this is lacking in the American kinship system Parsons suggests that romanticism provides a "functionally equivalent substitute in motivation to conformity with the expectations of the role. . . ." "Hence it may be suggested that the institutional sanction placed on the proper subjective sentiments of spouses, in short the expectation that they have an obligation to be "in love,' has that significance." [17] This means, in effect, that the romantic attitude toward one's future spouse holds that he (or she) will do "the right thing" because "he loves me" not because of societal norms and sanctions. This belief is strengthened by the romantic tendency to idealize one's future spouse, a romantic tendency often discussed, and by the romantic myth of a mysterious predetermined destiny for each other. Thus the romantic emphasis is on trust, on the voluntary fulfillment of one's role because of love. As Parsons says, ". . . affective devotion . . . is linked to a presumption of the absence of any element of coercion." Respondents who accept the ideal of the absence of coercion, the romantic value of trust with role fulfillment based on love will not agree that "A husband is obliged to tell his wife where he has been if he comes home very late."

RESULTS

The results are summarized in Table 1. Table 1 presents normed indices based on the observed proportion of each group of respondents who agree (or do not agree if not agreeing indicates a

---

[14] Talcott Parsons, "The Kinship System of the Contemporary United States," *Essays in Sociological Theory Pure and Applied* (Glencoe, Ill.: The Free Press, 1949), pp. 245–246.

[15] Therese Benedek, "The Emotional Structure of the Family," in Anshen, *op. cit.,* p. 210.

[16] Mace and Mace, *op. cit.,* p. 67; Ross, *op. cit.,* pp. 105–06; John F. Cady, *A History of Modern Burma* (Ithaca: Cornell University Press, 1958), p. 62.

[17] Parsons, "The Social Structure of the Family," *op. cit.,* p. 184.

TABLE 1 *Acceptance of Romanticism*

	MEN			
	Americans	Singapore Chinese	Burmese	Indians
Physical attractions: As a criterion of marriage choice	133*	103	—	75
Physical attraction: Importance for wife after marriage**	164	84	88	65
Confiding valued in marriage (marriage as companionship)	168	100	86	54
Equality of sacrifice in marriage (marriage as a partnership)	160	94	88	63
Trust: No compulsory explanation by husband	137	81	80	87
	WOMEN			
	Americans	Singapore Chinese	Burmese	Indians
Physical attraction: As a criterion of marriage choice	130	78	—	44
Physical attraction: Importance for wife after marriage**	134	81	77	57
Confiding valued in marriage (marriage as companionship)	138	67	65	81
Equality of sacrifice in marriage (marriage as partnership)	158	62	76	17
Trust: No compulsory explanation by husband	161	54	43	57

* $\dfrac{\text{observed proportion}}{\text{expected proportion}} \times 100$

** Based on proportions strongly agreeing.

All differences between American and Singapore Chinese men, American and Burmese men, American and Indian men, American and Singapore Chinese women, American and Burmese women, and American and Indian women are statistically significant by both the chi-square test (of frequency distributions) and the Kolmogorov-Smirnov D test (one-tailed — of cumulative percentage distributions) with p's below .001 on all five indices.

romantic orientation) with each statement divided by the proportion of that group that would be expected to agree (or not agree) — that is the proportion the group is of the total number of men or women — multiplied by 100. Thus in all cases a higher index score indicates a more romantic orientation. On all five indices American respondents are significantly more romantic (at the .001 level) than any of the three Asian groups. This is true of both men and women. However, the three Asian groups tend to follow a consistent pattern with the Singapore Chinese most romantic, the Burmese intermediate, and the Indians least romantic.

Physical Attraction

The Indian and Singapore Chinese respondents show significantly less concern with physical attraction as a criterion of mate selection than do American respondents. An overwhelming majority of Americans agree that "The person I marry must be sexually stimulating." In contrast, a majority of the Indians do not agree. Many more Indian women disagree than agree. The Singapore Chinese are in an intermediate position. It was not permissible to ask this question in Burma.

This difference between the Indian and American respondents does not reflect a more puritanical attitude on the part of the Indians. Traditional Indian culture stressed the importance of sex in marriage. Moreover, 79 per cent of the Indian men and 68 per cent of the women agree that "Sex is one of the most important aspects of marriage." This is an even greater proportion of agreement than among the Americans. (Sixty-two per cent of the American men and 55 per cent of the women agree.) Indian respondents do not refuse to recognize the role of sex, rather they are less concerned with physical attraction as a criterion in mate selection. Thus they tend to believe that concern with sex should follow rather than precede marriage.

The Americans also place greater emphasis on the desirability of a wife's maintaining continued concern with her physical attractiveness. The Americans express almost unanimous agreement with the statement, "A woman should be as concerned with her appearance after marriage as she was before marriage." While the Indians, Burmese, and Singapore Chinese are not opposed to a wife's maintaining an attractive appearance, they are far less likely than the Americans to strongly agree. This is not a crucial and highly valued norm for them as it is for the romantically oriented Americans.

Confiding

Indian, Burmese, and Singapore Chinese respondents show significantly less acceptance than do American respondents of the romantic ideal of total voluntary confiding in marriage. A majority of the Indians, Burmese, and Singapore Chinese express a belief, characteristic of a contractual system, in the desirability of a husband and wife not discussing certain matters and not sharing all thoughts. A particularly large proportion of the Indian men agree that it is wise not to confide (82 per cent). This is in accordance with the findings of Ross who reports in her study of India that husbands frequently withhold secrets from their wives and that there is very little companionship between husbands and wives even in the cities.[18]

Equality of Sacrifice

An overwhelming majority of the Indians (90 per cent of the women) agree that "Generally speaking, a woman has to sacrifice more in marriage than a man." In contrast, more Americans (a majority of the men) disagree than agree. A majority of the Burmese and Singapore Chinese agree, but the lower percentage of the Indians places them in an intermediate position. (Among the Burmese, more Buddhists, 65 per cent, than

[18] Ross, *op. cit.*, pp. 127 and 159.

Christians, 50 per cent, agree.) Responses to this question do not differentiate between traditional and modern evaluations of the desirability of feminine sacrifice. Agreement on the part of the Indians, Burmese, and Singapore Chinese, first of all may represent approval of the traditional Indian, Burmese, and Chinese point of view that it is proper for a woman to sacrifice more than her husband. On the other hand, feminists may also agree, feeling that while it is not morally right, it is nevertheless true that women must sacrifice more than men. However, the question does differentiate between the romantic and the non-romantic orientation. The majority of Indian, Burmese, and Singapore Chinese respondents do not accept the romantic view that marriage involves equal sacrifice for husband and wife.

Trust: Role Conformity Through Affection

Indian, Burmese, and Singapore Chinese respondents show a greater orientation in terms of specific expectations, whereas American respondents show a greater emphasis on the ideal of trust. Significantly more Indians, Burmese, and Singapore Chinese than Americans agree that "A husband is obliged to tell his wife where he has been if he comes home very late." There is a particularly striking difference between the women in the strongly agree category. Only 14 per cent of the American women strongly agree compared to 39 per cent of the Singapore Chinese, 44 per cent of the Indian, and 47 per cent of the Burmese women. Whether or not an American wife would in fact like an explanation if her husband came home late, the significantly lower percentage of American agreement must be understood primarily in terms of a projection of the romantic ideal. The Indian, Burmese, and Singapore Chinese responses indicate the persistence of a contractualistic orientation, with concrete universal expectations rather than a romantic orientation with an emphasis on trust.

The five indices point to a rejection of the null hypothesis. Despite the impact of industrialization, urbanization, and Western education, despite changes in specific traditional family norms and despite the sexual frustrations which result from delayed marriage combined with premarital sexual taboos, Indian, Burmese, and Singapore Chinese

TABLE 2   *"Ideally, if it were up to you, would you like to get married?"*

	Yes	No	N.A.	Total	Number
MEN					
Americans	86.5%	1.6%	11.9%	100%	748
Singapore Chinese	86.9	8.8	4.3	100	510
Burmese	81.5	8.8	9.7	100	249
Indians	50.0	19.6	30.4	100	1038
WOMEN					
Americans	94.4%	1.4%	4.1%	100%	576
Singapore Chinese	80.5	12.5	7.0	100	287
Burmese	75.5	18.6	5.9	100	237
Indians	48.5	28.2	23.3	100	202

American and Singapore Chinese men: $\chi^2 = 30.97$; d.f. $= 1$; p $<.001$
American and Burmese men: $\chi^2 = 28.73$; d.f. $= 1$; p $<.001$
American and Indian men: $\chi^2 = 181.41$; d.f. $= 1$; p $<.001$
American and Singapore Chinese women: $\chi^2 = 49.01$; d.f. $= 1$; p $<.001$
American and Burmese women: $\chi^2 = 85.02$; d.f. $= 1$; $<.001$
American and Indian women: $\chi^2 = 181.21$; d.f. $= 1$; p $<.001$

respondents have maintained a contractualistic value-orientation toward marriage and basically have not accepted the ideals of the romantic orientation. However, the three Asian groups are not equally contractualistic. On the five indices they follow a rank order directly related to the two analytical variables discussed above. The Singapore Chinese, who have experienced the most social change are the least contractualistic. The Burmese, with the least contractualistic cultural tradition, rank second. The Indians express the most contractualistic value-orientations.

ROMANTICISM AND MOTIVATION TO MARRY

Since the publication of E. W. Burgess' paper on romanticism and family disorganization in the nineteen twenties, most sociological analysis has emphasized the dysfunctions of romanticism. However, there also has been some recognition of possible positive functions of romanticism. Parsons suggests that romanticism may serve a positive function in motivating choice of a marriage partner in the absence of coercion or a system of arranged marriages.[19] This function also is mentioned by Waller and Hill who see romanticism

functioning as a motivation to marriage counteracting certain pressures of modern life against marriage.[20] The data in this study tend to support this hypothesis. More specifically these data suggest that romanticism may function to promote a greater motivation to marry than does contractualism during a period of rapid social change.

A significantly greater percentage of the American respondents than of the Indian, Burmese, and Singapore Chinese respondents express a desire to marry. The difference is particularly great among the women, with 28 per cent of the Indian women, 19 per cent of the Burmese women, 13 per cent of the Singapore Chinese women, and only one per cent of the American women not wishing to marry. (Table 2.) The large percentage of Indian respondents who do not wish to marry reflects the strains in the Indian family and a radical departure from traditionalism. Marriage, according to the traditional Indian conception was accepted as a natural, necessary and inevitable part of life. For women, a husband was the only means for respectable status in this world and salvation in the next.[21] The proportion of Burmese respondents who do not wish to marry, although

[19] Parsons, "The Kinship System of the Contemporary United States," *op. cit.,* p. 241.

[20] Willard Waller and Reuben Hill, *The Family* (New York: The Dryden Press, 1951) p. 174–175.
[21] Ross, *op. cit.,* p. 154.

less than the Indians, also indicates a weakening of the traditional system. One of the five specific duties of parents, according to Burmese Buddhism, is to provide their children with suitable wives and husbands, while one of the duties of children is to maintain the lineage and tradition of the family.[22] It has been noted in the literature that Western education has increased the number of unmarried men and women in Burma. In traditional Chinese culture also marriage was regarded as essential. A girl's life was without significance unless she married and had a son. In the tradition of Mencius, of the three unfilial acts, the worst is to have no posterity.[23] Thus, in all three cultures traditionally motivation to marry was supported by strong sanctions. The large percentages of respondents in these cultures expressing a desire not to marry indicate a decline in the strength of traditional motivations for marriage.

The greater motivation to marry of the American respondents suggests a possible positive function of the romantic approach to marriage under conditions of rapid social change. The continuing contractualistic orientation of the Indian, Burmese, and Singapore Chinese respondents may be less functional than the romantic orientation in maintaining high morale toward marriage in an urban setting amid rapid social change. In the contractualistic orientation marriage expectations are in keeping with institutionally expected norms. In a period of rapid social change, with the emerging of new definitions to challenge the old ones, demoralization may be greater with a contractual orientation than with the more fluid romantic orientation. During periods of social change, traditional expectations come into conflict with new expectations, as for example, husband dominance vs. equalitarian husband-wife relationships. (Men may fear feminist wives, while women may fear patriarchical husbands.) Various traditional and modern norms are unevenly accepted by the two sexes, as well as by different individuals. In the romantic marriage, the rejection of traditional universalistic definitions of the marriage relationship may provide less confusion and demoralization because the definition of what is proper is primarily to be decided through husband-wife interaction. This may eliminate much of the possibility of a conflict of past family traditions with newly emerging definitions. The problem of defining the precise relationship is ultimately and ideally to be decided only in marriage and in the dyadic relationship itself.

It might be suggested that the larger proportion of Asian women not wishing to marry is due to the greater career orientation of college women in these countries than in the United States. However, it must be recognized that while only one per cent of the American women do not wish to marry, obviously a far larger percentage than this are career oriented. Romanticism permits the combination of a career for the wife with marriage far more readily than does contractualism. It is the contractual orientation placing as it does primary emphasis on the performance of traditional role expectations that makes marriage unattractive to career minded women. Thus whether or not Asian college women are more career oriented than American college women does not diminish the significance of the relationship between romanticism and motivation to marry. Quite clearly, the difference in desire to marry of the men is not a matter of a difference in career orientation.

In considering the relationship between romanticism and motivation to marry suggested by the data presented in this paper, it must be recognized that group correlations are not synonymous with individual correlations.

However, it is not possible with these data to establish for each cultural group significant positive individual correlations between romanticism and motivation to marry. In the case of the American respondents there are too few who do not wish to marry to permit any significant comparison. In the contractualistically oriented societies, factors such as poor opportunity to find romantically oriented marriage partners may adversely affect the motivation to marry of romantically oriented individuals. The specific factors involved are beyond the scope of the data available in this study, but provide a valuable area for further investigation.

---

[22] Cecil C. Hobbs, Christian Education and the Burmese Family, unpublished master's dissertation, Colgate-Rochester Divinity School, 1942, pp. 76–77.

[23] Shu-Ching Lee, *op. cit.*, p. 275; Mace and Mace, *op. cit.*, pp. 28–29.

TABLE 3 *Romanticism and Disinterest in Marriage*

MEN		
	Mean of Romanticism Indices	Desire Not to Marry
Americans	152	14
Singapore Chinese	92	69
Burmese	85	73
Indians	69	209
WOMEN		
	Mean of Romanticism Indices	Desire Not to Marry
Americans	144	12
Singapore Chinese	68	111
Burmese	65	167
Indians	51	304

As Menzel has pointed out, group correlations, while not establishing individual correlations, may in themselves provide valuable information. In Table 3 it may be seen that there is a perfect inverse rank order correlation for the four cultural groups (in the case of both the men and the women) between the means of the five normed indices of romanticism and normed index scores of desire not to marry. These data suggest that romanticism promotes a milieu in which, despite the absence of traditional pressures, and despite the conflicts inherent in rapid social change, marriage is highly valued and viewed optimistically. It is significant to know that a greater degree of optimism toward marriage permeates a culture in association with the diffusion of the ideals of romanticism regardless of the nature of the psychological relationship between romanticism and motivation to marry in various social and cultural contexts.

It is recognized, of course, that we are concerned here with a highly Westernized segment of the three Asian cultures studied, and it is not suggested that traditional pressures motivating a desire to marry are equally weakened in the population at large.

CONCLUSION

Indian, Burmese, and Singapore Chinese respondents, although from the segment of their societies most subject to Western influences, do not show an acceptance of the American type of romantic orientation to marriage. Consistently large significant differences were found between the American respondents on the one hand, and the Indian, Burmese, and Singapore Chinese respondents on the other hand, on attitudes reflecting the romantic or contractualistic orientation to marriage. Singapore Chinese attitudes were closest to the romantic American attitudes, with the Burmese attitudes next, and the Indian attitudes the most contractualistic. This has been explained in terms of the interaction of two analytical variables — degree of contractualism in the traditional cultures and degree of cultural change.

The data also support Parsons and Waller and Hill's hypothesis that romanticism functions to maintain high motivation to marry with the decline of traditional sources of motivation. The data suggest that contractualism when combined with the rejection of traditional norms may be less functional than romanticism in maintaining high motivations to marry. The four cultural groups follow the same rank order on romanticism and on desire to marry. This relationship requires further and more specifically focused investigation.

RELIGION: LEGITIMATION OF MORAL VALUES

66 Is There An American Protestantism?*

Charles Y. Glock · Rodney Stark

Nearly all Americans say they believe in God, but not necessarily the same God. Even among Protestants there is much diversity in defining the requirements for "salvation," for "improper acts," and for beliefs in the divinity of Jesus. Although some divergence in point of view exists within a denomination, there are clear patterns of belief which characterize certain denominations or sects. This article suggests that Catholic-Protestant contrasts are inconsequential when compared to differences found among Protestants. Can there be, in fact, an American Protestantism?

"Do you, personally, believe in God?" To this recurrent question on Gallup polls, 97 per cent of Americans answer "Yes." Supported by such findings, commentators on contemporary American life are unanimous in asserting that all but an insignificant fraction of Americans believe in God.

Another prevalent judgment about religious life in this country is that all Americans are coming to believe pretty much in the same things. The primary feature of American religion today seems to be no longer its diversity — based on the existence of several hundred Christian bodies — but its unity of outlook. Furthermore, the recent series of denominational mergers has fostered rising hopes for a general ecumenicalism.

* From *Religion and Society in Tension* by Charles Y. Glock and Rodney Stark. © 1967 Rand-McNally. Reproduced by permission.

We believe this assertion is much too premature. We mean to raise a much more basic question: Have such changes really taken place? Is there really a "common core" belief in American Protestantism? Do the 97 per cent of Americans who believe in God believe in the *same* God?

Our extensive survey shows that there are still a great many basic differences of belief among Protestant denominations in America.

The notion that American religion has undergone doctrinal agreement rests on two main premises:

That the old disputes (such as adult versus infant baptism) have lost their force and relevance; that nobody much believes in, or cares about, the idiosyncracies that once rent Christendom.

That the demise of these historic differences leaves Americans in general agreement, sharing in the essential core of Christian (and Judaic) teachings. That is, Americans now are in consensus on such bedrocks of faith as the existence of an all-powerful, personal God, the moral authority of the Ten Commandments, and the New Testament promise of salvation.

But systematic evidence supporting these premises has been extremely scanty. Important and sweeping assertions about American religion need more careful examination, and firmer evidence. So we shall draw upon empirical data from our study of Christian church members to see to what extent American religion really is homogeneous.

SUPERNATURALISM

As noted at the outset, American adults report a virtually unanimous belief in God. But what do they believe *about* God? And to what *degree* do they believe?

Table 1 demonstrates definitely that Americans are anything *but* unanimous in their beliefs about God; and that the distinctions are not only sharp between individuals, but between demoninations as well.

Only 41 per cent of the Congregationalists indicated unquestioning faith in a personal God. (Table 1.) This rises to 60 per cent of the Methodists, 63 per cent of the Episcopalians, about 75

TABLE 1   *Belief in God*   "Which of the following statements comes closest to what you believe in God?"

	Congregationalists	Methodists	Episcopalians	Disciples of Christ	Presbyterians	American Lutherans	American Baptists	Missouri Lutherans	Southern Baptists	Sects	Total Protestants	Catholics
"I know God really exists and I have no doubts about it."	41%	60%	63%	76%	75%	73%	78%	81%	99%	96%	71%	81%
"While I have doubts, I feel that I do believe in God."	34	22	19	20	16	19	18	17	1	2	17	13
"I find myself believing in God some of the time, but not at other times."	4	4	2	0	1	2	0	0	0	0	2	1
"I don't believe in a personal God, but I do believe in a higher power of some kind."	16	11	12	0	7	6	1	0	1	1	7	3
"I don't know whether there is a God and I don't believe there is any way to find out."	2	2	2	0	1	*	0	1	0	0	1	1
"I don't believe in God."	1	*	*	0	0	0	0	0	0	0	*	0
No answer	2	*	1	4	*	2	2	0	0	1	1	1
Number of respondents	(151)	(415)	(416)	(50)	(495)	(208)	(141)	(116)	(79)	(255)	(2326)	(545)

Note: Asterisk denotes less than ½ of 1 per cent.
Some columns fail to sum to 100% due to rounding error.
The number of respondents shown for each denomination in this table is the same for all other tables.
American Lutherans include The Lutheran Church in America and the American Lutheran Church.
Sects include The Assemblies of God, The Church of God, The Church of Christ, The Church of the Nazarene, The Foursquare Gospel Church and one independent Tabernacle.

per cent among the center denominations, and is virtually unanimous among Southern Baptists and members of the fundamentalist sects. Overall, 71 per cent of the Protestants endorsed the orthodox position, as compared with 81 per cent of the Roman Catholics.

The second line shows that most of those who rejected unquestioning faith did not hold a different image of God, but were uncertain in their belief. They conceived of a personal divinity, but had doubts about his existence. Denominational differences here too are marked: 34 per cent of the Congregationalists doubted; but only 1 per cent of the Southern Baptists.

The fourth question is especially interesting, for it indicates a different conception of God, rather than mere doubt. Again, contrasts are striking: 16 per cent of the Congregationalists, 11 per cent of the Methodists, 12 per cent of the Episcopalians — and *none* of the Southern Baptists — substituted some kind of "higher power" for a personal God.

Two per cent of the Congregationalists, Episcopalians, and Methodists were agnostics, and 1 per cent of the Congregationalists said they did not believe in God at all.

If the first four lines are added, then 98 per cent of both Protestants and Catholics may be said to believe to some extent in some kind of God. Superficially, this supports the Gallup figures. But the Gallup poll implication of uniformity and piety are entirely misleading.

Gallup studies also report that American Christians are virtually unanimous in believing Jesus Christ to be the Divine Son of God. But this faith too needs to be qualified.

Table 2 shows important contrasts in belief in the divinity of Jesus. Denominational differences are virtually identical to those in the belief of God. Only 40 per cent of Congregationalists had *no doubts* that "Jesus is the Divine Son of God." This rose abruptly to 99 per cent of Southern Baptists. The total Protestant figure is 69 per cent versus 86 per cent for Catholics.

CONCEPTS OF SIN

Unlike the supernatural, sin is related directly to the nature of man. Acceptance of man as sin-ful by nature increases in the usual pattern (Table 3), from the more liberal denominations on the left to the more conservative ones on the right; however, compared to differing beliefs in the supernatural, the spread is generally more even.

But on the acceptance of "original sin" ("A child is born into the world already guilty of sin"), there are some abrupt departures from the spectrum: those denominations with a liturgical or "high church" tradition are readily distinguishable by their willingness to accept this belief. Original sin cannot be absolved by personal efforts, but only through the church, especially those churches which emphasize ritual. Thus, the ritualistic Episcopalian church stands out sharply from the liberal group, and the American Lutherans from the other center groups. The strongly ritualistic Catholic church contrasts greatly with the Protestants in general, 68 per cent to 26 per cent.

It is clear that a general relationship exists between belief in original sin and theological conservatism, so that Lutherans are much more likely to hold this view than Episcopalians; yet the marks of the formal doctrine show up all across the table. Thus, on the left of the table the traces of old doctrinal differences on original sin may still be detected, while on the right these differences retain much of their old force.

SALVATION

What of the central concern and promise of all Christianity: salvation?

FAITH. Christians have long battled over the question of whether faith *and* works were necessary to be saved; but there has been no argument that faith at least was absolutely required. The central tenet of this required faith is belief in Jesus Christ as the divine son of God who died to redeem men from their sins. Some Christian traditions hold that more is necessary ("Faith without works is dead"); but all agree that there is no salvation outside of Christ.

However, we have seen that members of American denominations do not all believe Jesus divine. Therefore, it is not surprising to find them also disagreeing over whether belief in Christ is absolutely necessary for salvation.

TABLE 2 *Belief in the Divinity of Jesus* "Which of the following statements comes closest to what you believe about Jesus?"

	Congregationalists	Methodists	Episcopalians	Disciples of Christ	Presbyterians	American Lutherans	American Baptists	Missouri Lutherans	Southern Baptists	Sects	Total Protestants	Catholics
"Jesus is the Divine Son of God and I have no doubts about it."	40%	54%	59%	74%	72%	74%	76%	93%	99%	97%	69%	86%
"While I have some doubts, I feel basically that Jesus is Divine."	28	22	25	14	19	18	16	5	0	2	17	8
"I feel that Jesus was a great man and very holy, but I don't feel Him to be the Son of God any more than all of us are children of God."	19	14	8	6	5	5	4	0	0	*	7	3
"I think Jesus was only a man, although an extraordinary one."	9	6	5	2	2	3	2	1	1	*	4	1
"Frankly, I'm not entirely sure there was such a person as Jesus."	1	1	1	0	1	*	0	0	0	0	1	0
Other and no answer	3	3	2	4	1	0	2	1	0	1	2	2

TABLE 3 *Sin*

	Congregationalists	Methodists	Episcopalians	Disciples of Christ	Presbyterians	American Lutherans	American Baptists	Missouri Lutherans	Southern Baptists	Sects	Total Protestants	Catholics
"Man can not help doing evil."												
Completely true	21	22	30	24	35	36	63	62	37		34	22
Probably true	36	36	34	36	35	30	20	14	15		31	29
Probably not or definitely not true	39	38	31	38	25	15	13	22	42		30	43
"A child is born into the world already guilty of sin."												
Completely true	2	7	18	6	21	23	86	43	47		26	68
Probably true	2	4	7	2	7	9	4	3	3		6	10
Probably not or definitely not true	94	87	71	90	68	65	9	55	46		65	19

In the liberal groups, only a minority consider faith in Christ "absolutely necessary." (Table 4.) Among the conservative and fundamentalist groups, however, there is almost complete consensus about the necessity of faith in Christ for salvation. Overall, 65 per cent of Protestants and 51 per cent of Roman Catholics gave this answer.

It seems likely that among all Protestant groups, persons who accept the promise of eternal salvation beyond the grave are also likely to feel that this eternal reward is contingent upon belief in Christ as savior.

All denominational groups are less likely to feel that one must hold "the Bible to be God's truth" in order to be saved. Overall, the pattern follows the now familiar increases from left to right, with one notable exception. The Southern Baptists had been most unanimous in their assertion of traditional Christian positions, yet they are not importantly different from the center on the importance of Bible literalism. This probably reflects the great emphasis they put on Christ as the primary source by which one attains grace.

WORKS. Having become accustomed to increases from left to right in proportions of those holding faith necessary for salvation, it comes as a surprise to see these trends reverse in Table 5.

Table 5 deals with the necessity of *works*. Those denominations weakest on the necessity of faith for salvation are the strongest on the necessity of "doing good for others." In fact, the proportions of people on the left who think doing good for others is required for salvation is higher than those of the same groups who think faith in Christ absolutely necessary. More people in the liberal churches believed in the absolute necessity of doing good than believed in life after death. On the other hand, the conservative groups do not give "good deeds" any special importance in the scheme for salvation.

We suggest that these responses on "doing good" by those who essentially reject the traditional notion of salvation represent their desire to ratify the ethical components of their religious outlook. Indeed, ethics are likely *the* central component of their religious beliefs.

Turning to the matter of tithing, it is clear that Christians in general are not inclined to connect this with salvation. Only 14 per cent of the Protestants and 10 per cent of the Roman Catholics thought tithing absolutely necessary.

Improper Acts

American Christians no longer regard drinking as a certain road to damnation (Table 6). Only 8 per cent of Protestants and 2 per cent of Catholics thought it was. Only among the Baptists and the followers of fundamentalist sects did more than a handful attach temperance to their scheme of salvation.

Virtually no Protestants (only 2 per cent) thought the practice of artificial birth control would prevent salvation, but perhaps even more interesting and surprising, *less than a quarter of the Catholics held this view*. Whether or not Catholics approve of birth control, more than three-quarters of them are unwilling to agree it carries the supreme penalty of damnation.

The last two items in Table 6, dealing with racial discrimination, seem especially interesting, and repeat the pattern of evaluation of good works. On virtually all other "barriers to salvation," the conservative and fundamentalist bodies have been most likely to see them as absolutely necessary. However, on questions of racial discrimination and anti-Semitism, the Southern Baptists are the *least* likely of all religious groups to see them as relevant to salvation. Thus, while 27 per cent of the Southern Baptists thought cursing would definitely prevent salvation, only 10 per cent of them viewed anti-Semites as disqualified from entrance into God's Kingdom, and only 16 per cent saw racial discrimination as a definite barrier. On the other hand, while only 13 per cent of the Congregationalists thought that taking the name of the Lord in vain would definitely prevent salvation, 27 per cent thought that racial discrimination and 23 per cent that anti-Semitism would be barriers. Perhaps an even more suggestive contrast appears when we consider that about half of the members of all denominations thought it necessary to "love thy neighbor."

To sum up the findings on salvation: Christian denominations in America differ greatly in their beliefs about what a man must do to be saved. While most denominations give primary importance to faith, the liberal Protestant groups are

TABLE 4   *Requirements for Salvation: Faith*

	Congregationalists	Methodists	Episcopalians	Disciples of Christ	Presbyterians	American Lutherans	American Baptists	Missouri Lutherans	Southern Baptists	Sects	Total Protestants	Catholics
"Belief in Jesus Christ as Saviour." Absolutely necessary	38	45	47	78	66	77	78	97	97	96	65	51
"Holding the Bible to be God's truth." Absolutely necessary	23	39	32	58	52	64	58	80	61	89	52	38

TABLE 5   *Requirements for Salvation: Works*

	Congregationalists	Methodists	Episcopalians	Disciples of Christ	Presbyterians	American Lutherans	American Baptists	Missouri Lutherans	Southern Baptists	Sects	Total Protestants	Catholics
"Doing good for others" Absolutely necessary	58%	57%	54%	64%	48%	47%	45%	38%	29%	61%	52%	57%
"Loving thy neighbor" Absolutely necessary	59	57	60	76	55	51	52	51	41	74	58	65
"Tithing" Absolutely necessary	6	7	9	12	10	13	16	7	18	48	14	10

TABLE 6   *Barriers to Salvation: Improper Acts*

	Congregationalists	Methodists	Episcopalians	Disciples of Christ	Presbyterians	American Lutherans	American Baptists	Missouri Lutherans	Southern Baptists	Sects	Total Protestants	Catholics
"Drinking liquor." Definitely prevent salvation	2	4	2	0	2	2	9	1	15	35	8	2
"Practicing artificial birth control." Definitely prevent salvation	0	0	2	2	1	3	1	2	5	4	2	23
"Discriminating against other races." Definitely prevent salvation	27	25	27	34	22	20	17	22	16	29	25	24
"Being anti-Semitic." Definitely prevent salvation	23	23	26	30	20	15	13	22	10	26	21	20

inclined to favor good works. Protestants in a ritualistic tradition and Roman Catholics place greater emphasis on the sacraments and other ritual acts than do those from low-church traditions.

UNITY AND REALITY

To return to the questions posed at the beginning of this article: Is religion in modern America accurately characterized as unified? Do such concepts as "common core Protestanism," and "common American religion" bear any important resemblance to reality?

We suggest that they do not. Differences in the religious outlooks of members of the various denominations are both vast and profound. On the basis of our data it seems obvious that American religion has indeed undergone extensive changes in recent decades, but it seems equally obvious that these changes have been greatly misperceived and misinterpreted.

Has American religion become increasingly secular? As noted, many commentators claim that the mystical and supernatural elements of traditional Christianity have been replaced by a demythologized (ethical rather than theological) religion.

In light of the data, important changes of this kind have indeed occurred to *some* American denominations. We have no comparable data on the past; but compelling historic grounds exist for assuming that the typical Episcopalian or Congregationalist in the mid-19th century firmly believed such tenets as the Virgin Birth and the Biblical miracles. If true, obviously secularization has indeed taken place in these religious bodies, for only a minority of them adhere to these beliefs today. On the other hand, among the Southern Baptists and the various sects, commitment to traditional Christian theology has been virtually impervious to change. The fact that these more evangelical and traditionalist denominations have been growing at a faster rate than the mainline denominations suggests that two simultaneous and divergent trends have been taking place:

Many people have been staying with or turning to "old-time" Christianity.

Others have been, to some extent, changing

their theological outlook away from the supernatural and miraculous toward a more naturalistic view.

These opposed trends seem to hold significant implications for the future.

THE NEW DENOMINATIONALISM

Historically, the schisms in Christianity were largely marked by subtle doctrinal distinctions, and disagreements on proper ritual or organization. All observers generally agree that these issues have lost much of their relevance and divisive potential in contemporary America. Our data confirm these judgments.

But the data also suggest that new and generally unnoticed splits have appeared in Christianity that may well hold greater potential for division than the old disputes.

Earlier disagreements were bitter; nevertheless they took place among men who usually shared belief in such basic components of Christian theology as the existence of a personal and sentient God, the Saviorhood of Christ, and the promise of life-everlasting.

But today, our data indicate, the fissures which map what might well be called the "New Denominationalism" fragment the very core of the Christian perspective. The new cleavages are not over such matters as how to properly worship God — but whether or not there is a God it makes any sense to worship; not whether the bread and wine of communion become the actual body and blood of Christ through trans-substantiation, but whether Jesus was divine at all, or merely a man. These disagreements, it must be emphasized, are not only between Christians and secular society, but exist *within* the formal boundaries of the Christian churches themselves.

How, therefore, can we account for all the hope and talk about general ecumenicalism? For those groups close together to begin with, such a possibility may well exist. At least there seem no overwhelming theological barriers to merger. But how are we to interpret exploratory talks between Roman Catholics and Episcopalians, or between Methodists and Baptists? Do the participants in the ecumenical dream simply misperceive one another's theological position, or do they consider such matters unimportant? Perhaps both of these factors are operating; but there are also signs that church leaders are becoming more aware of the doctrinal chasms that separate them.

THE PROTESTANT SPECTRUM

At least four and probably five generic theological camps can be clearly identified afong the American denominations. The first, the *Liberals,* comprises the Congregationalists, Methodists, and Episcopalians, and is characterized by having a majority of members who reject firm belief in central tenets of Christian orthodoxy. It is likely that the changes that have gone on in these bodies, since they are among the highest status and most visible Protestant groups, have largely produced the impressions that Protestantism in general has shifted toward a secular and modernized worldview.

The second group, the *Moderates,* is composed of the Disciples of Christ and the Presbyterians. This group is less secularized than the Liberals, but more so than the *Conservatives,* who are made up of the American Lutheran group and the American Baptists. The *Fundamentalists* include the Missouri Synod Lutherans, the Southern Baptists, and the host of small sects.

Because of historic differences with Protestant-ism, the Roman Catholics are perhaps properly left to form a fifth distinct group by themselves. But on most theological issues, both those presented here and many more, the Roman Catholics consistently resemble the Conservatives. Only on special Protestant-Catholic issues such as Papal infallibility (accepted by 66 per cent of the Roman Catholics and only 2 per cent of the Protestants) were the Catholics and the Conservatives in any extensive disagreement.

Merging the denominations to form these five major groups is the greatest degree of clustering that is statistically permissible. It seems very unlikely that ecumenical clustering could result in fewer.

Finally, the data seriously challenge the common practice of contrasting Protestants and Roman Catholics. Protestant-Catholic contrasts are often large enough to be notable (and often, too, remarkably small), but they seem inconsequential compared to differences found among the Protestant groups. The overall impression of American Protestantism produced when members of all denominations are treated as a single group (the "Total Protestant" column in the tables) at best bears resemblance to only a few actual Protestant denominations. Indeed, in some instances these "average Protestants" do not closely correspond to *any* actual denomination.

---

67 Theology and the Position of Pastors on Public Issues*

Benton Johnson

* Excerpted from the *American Sociological Review,* Vol. 32 (June 1967), pp. 434–442. Reprinted by permission. Copyright © 1967 by The American Sociological Association.

In the previous study we learned of the multiple groupings in American Protestantism. Benton Johnson, the author of this paper, has made fundamental investigations of the relationship between theological position and partisan voting. This study is designed to test the hypothesis that the theological divisions within Protestantism have implications not only for party choice, but also for political ideology. Johnson measures the attitudes of Methodist and Baptist clergymen in Oregon on such diverse issues as federal aid to education, racial segregation, the income tax, participation of the United States in the United Nations, capital punishment, and foreign aid.

The data to test our hypotheses were obtained from responses to questionnaires mailed to Methodist and Baptist pastors of Oregon in the spring and summer of 1962. Eighty-two percent of the Methodist pastors responded; seventy-one percent of the Baptist pastors returned their questionnaires.

All respondents were asked to place themselves within one of the following theological categories: liberal, neo-orthodox, conservative, or fundamentalist. Six percent of the Baptist respondents and 18 percent of the Methodist respondents declined to check any of these categories and have therefore been excluded from this analysis. We have combined the conservative and fundamentalist respondents into a single category which we have labeled conservative.

The respondents were asked to report their opinions on six public issues. Three criteria governed the selection of these issues. The first criterion was that the issue be a currently debated one. The second was that the resolution of the issue involve judicial or legislative action. The third was that there be a liberal and a conservative position on each issue. The six issues selected were federal aid to public education, racial segregation, the federal income tax, United States participation in the United Nations, capital punishment, and foreign aid. Respondents were asked to indicate whether they favored or opposed each one of these policies. Their responses were then classified as either liberal or conservative.

Our denominations can be fairly accurately ranked in terms of the prevalence of liberal and conservative theological views among their clergy. The Methodist Church is clearly the most liberal of our denominations. Its conservative pastors form a small and dwindling minority. The American Baptist Convention ranks next in proportion of pastors who have liberal or neo-orthodox views. Even though, as our data indicate, American Baptists in Oregon are overwhelmingly conservative in theology, the denomination as a whole contains an influential liberal and neo-orthodox element. The Southern Baptist Convention ranks next. There are a few liberal Southern Baptists, but the denomination itself is predominantly conservative. The two small ethnic Baptist bodies and the Conservative Baptist Association of America are the least liberal of our denominations.

A preliminary inspection of Table 1 shows that the basic relationship between theology and position on each public issue remains intact even when denomination is controlled. This may be seen by comparing the responses of the Methodist pastors of the two major theological groups. In all cases,

the Methodist conservatives are less likely to take a liberal stand and more likely to take a conservative stand than are their liberal and neo-orthodox colleagues. The table also shows that with three minor exceptions no category of conservative respondent is more liberal or less conservative on any issue than are the Methodist liberals and neo-orthodox. We do not, of course, know how liberal and neo-orthodox pastors would have responded had there been any among our other denominations.

Table 1 also shows that the response pattern of the theological conservatives does vary by denomination. But this variation is not independent of the content of the specific issues themselves. On three issues, federal aid to education, segregation and the income tax, there are only minor and seemingly random denominational differences in the proportion of conservative respondents taking a conservative or a liberal stand. But the data on the three other issues strongly support our proposition concerning denominational milieu. This pattern is most strikingly apparent on the issue of capital punishment. At the one extreme, only 20 percent of the conservatives of the most liberal-minded denomination are in favor of it. At the other extreme, fully 88 percent of the Conservative Baptists favor it. The percentage difference between the two denominations is equally striking when the proportions opposing capital punishment are compared. On the issue of the United Nations there is a difference of 64 percentage points between the most and the least liberal denomination, and a difference of 35 points between the most and the least conservative denomination. And although there is only an 8 point range in conservative responses on the issue of foreign aid, the range of liberal responses is 37 points. In all cases in which the range of liberal or conservative responses among the theological conservatives exceeds 30 percentage points, the most conservative denomination is the Conservative Baptist and the most liberal denomination is the Methodist. Moreover, as we predicted, in all such cases the American Baptists are more conservative and less liberal than the Methodist conservatives in their response pattern. With only one exception they are followed in order of decreasing liberalism and increasing conservatism by the Southern Baptists,

TABLE 1 *Percentage Distribution of Liberal, Neo-Orthodox, and Conservative Pastors on Six Public Issues, by Denomination*

Issue	Liberal and Neo-Orthodox Methodist (N = 94)	Conservative				
		Methodist (N = 25)	American Baptist (N = 23)	Southern Baptist (N = 33)	North American and General Conference Baptist (N = 13)	Conservative Baptist (N = 101)
Federal aid to education						
For	63	48	48	40	46	40
Against	20	40	31	36	23	47
Undecided	16	12	17	15	23	8
NA, other	1	0	4	9	8	5
Racial segregation						
For	1	4	4	0	0	8
Against	98	88	92	91	77	70
Undecided	1	8	4	3	23	17
NA, other	0	0	0	6	0	5
The income tax						
For	95	80	83	76	77	75
Against	4	16	0	9	8	7
Undecided	0	4	4	0	0	6
NA, other	1	0	13	15	15	12
U.S. participation in the United Nations						
For	98	92	87	58	46	28
Against	1	4	4	21	31	39
Undecided	1	4	9	18	23	29
NA, other	0	0	0	3	0	4
Capital punishment						
For	6	20	26	70	61	88
Against	85	68	31	9	8	3
Undecided	8	12	26	18	31	6
NA, other	1	0	17	3	0	3
Foreign aid						
For	97	80	78	64	62	43
Against	2	8	9	12	15	16
Undecided	1	12	13	12	15	26
NA, other	0	0	0	12	8	15

the two ethnic Baptist bodies, and the Conservative Baptists.

But there is one fact about the response patterns of the theological conservatives that casts doubt on such an interpretation and in turn suggests an alter-native explanation. This fact is the extremely high proportion of conservatives of all denominations who take a liberal stand on the issue of racial segregation. If simple working-class authoritarianism underlies the response pattern of the well insulated theological conservatives, one would expect them to favor segregation and to differ sharply in their position from respondents in the more liberal denominations. But as a matter of fact almost no one in any of our denominations supports racial segregation. Now liberals are very favorably disposed toward the rights of Negroes and they are currently more active than theological conservatives in efforts to secure these rights, but a humanitarian concern for the Negro was historically shared by *both* branches of ascetic Protestantism outside the South. Our conservative respondents' solicitude for the Negro not only reflects a liberal frame of mind; it can also be interpreted as reflecting a *traditionalist* posture.

It is possible to interpret the well-insulated conservatives' response pattern on the issues of capital punishment, foreign aid and the United Nations in a similar light. Like segregation, these issues do not affect the personal fortunes of many people but, unlike segregation, a liberal stand on them does violence to certain traditional Protestant commitments. It was widely held among 19th century Protestants that the United States as a nation had been uniquely called to set an example of Protestant piety to the world. This optimistic teaching inspired the efforts of evangelists, foreign missionaries, and Christian social reformers, and it imparted a sacred aura to America's independence, its institutions, and its laws. But the events of history have frustrated many of these earlier hopes. Liberal Protestants long ago abandoned this particularistic image of the United States, but many fundamentalists have reacted with defensiveness and alarm as the hope of realizing a Christian America has become dimmer.

Many conservative Protestant leaders have opposed the social philosophy of the liberals, to be sure, but their primary objection has been to the liberals' abandonment of the supernatural foundations of theology. This abandonment was, after all, a more serious threat to traditional Protestants than anything that was going on in the political realm, and it was a response to this abandonment that brought the fundamentalist movement into being in the first place. There are good reasons for assuming, therefore, that, whereas consensus among liberals and neo-orthodox is greatest on social issues, consensus among fundamentalists is

greatest on purely theological issues. Put differently, it is probable that having a liberal political outlook is much more important for liberals and neo-orthodox than having a conservative political outlook is for fundamentalists.[1] If this is so, we may more easily understand why Protestant conservatives seem more susceptible to liberal political influences than Protestant liberals are to conservative political influences.

DISCUSSION AND CONCLUSION

Our studies have shown that theology is a good predictor of the political attitudes and behavior of ascetic Protestant pastors and laymen. There seems little doubt that Protestant liberals and conservatives tend to take different positions on a variety of political matters. The relationship between theology and political preference is modified by a number of other factors, but it has not disappeared or changed direction when these factors have been taken into account. It seems appropriate now to ask what role theology has actually played in initiating and sustaining the political commitments of the members of these two divisions of Protestantism. We began these studies by assuming that these commitments had their origin in theology. It seemed plausible, for example, in light of the Weber thesis, that the Republican preferences of 19th century Protestants and their lineal descendants, the fundamentalists, originated in an affinity for industrial capitalism that was implicit in their theological beliefs. Such an affinity may exist, but it is clearly not a sufficient condition for the formation of Republican political commitments. Lipset has pointed out, for example, that until the eve of the Civil War the revivalist or "sectarian" branch of Protestantism, including the Methodists and Baptists, generally sided with the Democrats despite that party's anti-business policies.[2] Moreover, for reasons that seem fairly ob-

[1] There is evidence for this assertion in the fact that regional and national meetings of denomination in which liberals predominate are much more likely than meetings dominated by conservatives to pass resolutions on a wide variety of public issues.

[2] Seymour Martin Lipset, "Religion and Politics in the American Past and Present," in Robert Lee and Martin E. Marty (eds.), *Religion and Social Conflict,* New York: Oxford University Press, 1964, pp. 69–126.

vious, the southern denominations never formed Republican attachments in spite of the fact that their theological positions were virtually the same as those of their sister denominations in the north. Finally, although Negro religion is predominantly ascetic Protestant and most Negro denominations remain theologically traditionalist, the Negro vote has gone overwhelmingly to the Democratic party since the time of the New Deal. Moreover, the Republican allegiance of Negroes before 1932 probably had little to do with a theologically based affinity for capitalism. Clearly, theology has not alone been responsible for the political norms of these Protestant groups. Historical data cannot tell us much about the relationship between liberal theology and liberal politics because liberalism is a recent movement and it cuts across denominational lines. But there is such a great diversity in the content of the various modernist theologies that one wonders how political liberalism can be equally derived from all of them.

Our data show that the political norms of two distinct Protestant subcultures are different in certain respects. These subcultures can be identified by theological names but we have grounds for rejecting theology as the sole or even the major source of these norms. Where, then, do these political commitments come from? We can only guess at the answer. It seems plausible that the major source of the political views of liberal religious leaders is simply their common commitment to humanistic social values and their common interest in translating these values into policy positions on specific issues.[3] The source of the political norms of Protestant conservatives is probably a common interest in safeguarding traditional beliefs, values and policy positions within an en-

vironment that is perceived to be actively hostile. Conservatives appear most interested in preserving their theologies against modern heresies, but many of them are also interested in preserving other traditional commitments of their religious subculture. The origin of these other commitments is a matter for historical investigation.

The existence of important political and perhaps value-orientational differences among Protestant liberals and conservatives leads us to propose that these two divisions of American Protestantism be treated as distinct socio-religious groups in Lenski's sense of the term.[4] This is to say that sociologists should look on them as subcultures whose members have a common identity, communicate disproportionately with one another, and share many norms that are not shared with outsiders. Because liberals and conservatives have a common heritage from the not too distant past, and because they do not seriously restrict their members' outside participations, they are no doubt alike in many respects and their attitudes and behavior in some spheres of life are probably little different from the attitudes and behavior of others in their immediate environment. But in view of their many differences in outlook and the long-standing antagonism between them, it is a good bet that investigation will reveal that political issues are not the only matters on which these two groups differ. Indeed, it is our guess that sociologists will find the distinction between liberal and conservative group membership the single most useful one to make in their researches into the behavior of American Protestants.

[3] John Scanzonia has recently argued that the liberal clergy should be regarded as an innovating elite within American Protestantism. See his "Innovation and Constancy in the Church-Sect Typology," *American Journal of Sociology,* 71 (November, 1965), pp. 320–327.

[4] Gerhard Lenski, *The Religious Factor,* New York: Doubleday, 1961, pp. 17–21, 300–308. See also Andrew M. Greeley, "A Note on the Origins of Religious Differences," *Journal for the Scientific Study of Religion,* 3 (Fall, 1964), pp. 21–31. See also Benton Johnson and Richard H. White, "Protestantism, Political Preference, and the Nature of Religious Influence: Comment on Anderson's Paper," *Review of Religious Research,* 9 (Fall, 1967), 28–35, for a further development of this perspective.

EDUCATION: LEGITIMATION OF KNOWLEDGE AND SKILLS

68   Adolescent Subculture and Academic Achievement*

James S. Coleman

Our educational system has been established to prepare growing members of society for effective participation in adult life. How does the system define effective preparation? Is academic excellence its primary concern? And, if so, do the divergent goals of the students themselves prevent realization of the school's aims? Or does the system itself emphasize other types of achievement?

Industrial society has spawned a peculiar phenomenon, most evident in America but emerging also in other Western societies: adolescent subcultures, with values and activities quite distinct from those of the adult society — subcultures whose members have most of their important associations within and few with adult society. Industrialization, and the rapidity of change itself, has taken out of the hands of the parent the task of training his child, made the parent's skills obsolescent, and put him out of

* Excerpt from James S. Coleman, "The Adolescent Subculture and Academic Achievement," *American Journal of Sociology,* Vol. 65 (January 1960), pp. 337–347. Used by permission of the author and the publisher. Copyright 1960 by The University of Chicago.

The research discussed in this paper was carried out under a grant from the United States Office of Education; a full report is contained in "Social Climates and Social Structures in High Schools," a report to the Office of Education. The paper was presented at the Fourth World Congress of Sociology, Milan, Italy, September 1959.

touch with the times — unable to understand, much less inculcate, the standards of a social order which has changed since he was young.

By extending the period of training necessary for a child and by encompassing nearly the whole population, industrial society has made of high school a social system of adolescents. It includes, in the United States, almost all adolescents and more and more of the activities of the adolescent himself. A typical example is provided by an excerpt from a high-school newspaper in an upper-middle-class suburban school:

> Sophomore Dancing
> Features Cha Cha
>
> SOPHOMORES, this is your chance to learn how to dance! The first day of sophomore dancing is Nov. 14 and it will begin at 8:30 A.M. in the Boys' Gym. . . .
>
> NO ONE is required to take dancing but it is highly recommended for both boys and girls. . . .
>
> If you don't attend at this time except in case of absence from school, you may not attend at any other time. Absence excuses should be shown to Miss ———— or Mr. ————.

In effect, then, what our society has done is to set apart, in an institution of their own, adolescents for whom home is little more than a dormitory and whose world is made up of activities peculiar to their fellows. They have been given as well many of the instruments which can make them a functioning community: cars, freedom in dating, continual contact with the opposite sex, money, and entertainment, like popular music and movies, designed especially for them. The international spread of "rock-and-roll" and of so-called American patterns of adolescent behavior is a consequence, I would suggest, of these economic changes which have set adolescents off in a world of their own.

Yet the fact that such a subsystem has sprung up in society has not been systematically recognized in the organization of secondary education. The theory and practice of education remains focused on *individuals;* teachers exhort individuals to concentrate their energies in scholarly directions, while the community of adolescents diverts these energies into other channels. The premise of the present research is that, if edu-

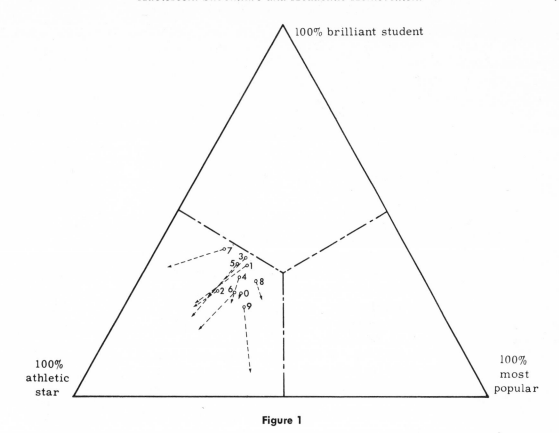

Figure 1

Positions of schools and leading crowds in boys' relative choice of brilliant student, athletic star, and most popular.

cational goals are to be realized in modern society, a fundamentally different approach to secondary education is necessary. Adults are in control of the institutions they have established for secondary education; traditionally, these institutions have been used to mold children as individuals toward ends which adults dictate. The fundamental change which must occur is to shift the focus: to mold social communities as communities, so that the norms of the communities themselves reinforce educational goals rather than inhibit them, as is at present the case.

The research being reported is an attempt to examine the status systems of the adolescent communities in ten high schools and to see the effects of these status systems upon the individuals within them. The ten high schools are all in the Midwest. They include five schools in small towns (labeled *0–4* in the figures which follow), one in a working-class suburb (*6*), one in a well-

to-do suburb (*9*), and three schools in cities of varying sizes (*5, 7,* and *8*). All but No. *5,* a Catholic boys' school, are coeducational, and all but it are public schools.

The intention was to study schools which had quite different status systems, but the similarities were far more striking than the differences. In a questionnaire all boys were asked: "How would you most like to be remembered in school: as an athletic star, a brilliant student, or most popular?" The results of the responses for each school are shown in Figure 1,[1] where the left corner of the triangle represents 100 per cent saying "star athlete"; the top corner represents 100 per cent saying "brilliant student"; and the right corner represents 100 per cent saying "most popular."

[1] I am grateful to James A. Davis and Jacob Feldman, of the University of Chicago, for suggesting such graphs for presenting responses to trichotomous items in a population.

Each school is representedly a point whose location relative to the three corners shows the proportion giving each response.

The schools are remarkably grouped somewhat off-center, showing a greater tendency to say "star athlete" than either of the other choices. From each school's point is a broken arrow connecting the school as a whole with its members who were named by fellows as being "members of the leading crowd." In almost every case, the leading crowd tends in the direction of the athlete — in all cases *away* from the ideal of the brilliant student. Again, for the leading crowds as well as for the students as a whole, the uniformity is remarkably great; not so great in the absolute positions of the leading crowds but in the direction they deviate from the student bodies.

This trend toward the ideal of the athletic star on the part of the leading crowds is due in part to the fact that the leading crowds include a great number of athletes. Boys were asked in a questionnaire to name the best athlete in their grade, the best student, and the boy most popular with girls. In every school, without exception, the boys named as best athletes were named more often — on the average over twice as often — as members of the leading crowd than were those named as best students. Similarly, the boy most popular with girls was named as belonging to the leading crowd more often than the best student, though in all schools but the well-to-do suburb and the smallest rural town (schools *9* and *0* on Fig. 1) less often than the best athlete.

These and other data indicate the importance of athletic achievement as an avenue for gaining status in the schools. Indeed, in the predominantly middle-class schools, it is by far the most effective achievement for gaining a working-class boy entrée into the leading crowd.

Similarly, each girl was asked how she would like to be remembered: as a brilliant student, a leader in extracurricular activities, or most popular. The various schools are located on Figure 2, together with arrows connecting them to their leading crowd. The girls tend slightly less, on the average, than the boys to want to be remembered as brilliant students. Although the alternatives are different, and thus cannot be directly compared, a great deal of other evidence indicates that the girls — although better students in every school — do not want to be considered "brilliant students." They have good reason not to, for the girl in each grade in each of the schools who was most often named as best student has fewer friends and is less often in the leading crowd than is the boy most often named as best student.

There is, however, diversity among the schools in the attractiveness of the images of "activities leader" and "popular girl" (Fig. 2). In five (*9, 0, 3, 8,* and *1*), the leader in activities is more often chosen as an ideal than is the popular girl; in four (*7, 6, 2,* and *4*) the most popular girl is the more attractive of the two. These differences correspond somewhat to class background differences among the schools: *2, 4, 6,* and *7,* where the activities leader is least attractive, have the highest proportion of students with working-class backgrounds. School *9* is by far the most upper-middle-class one and by far the most activities-oriented.

The differences among the schools correspond as well to differences among the leading crowds: in schools *2, 4,* and *6,* where the girls as a whole are most oriented to being popular, the leading crowds are even more so; in the school where the girls are most oriented to the ideal of the activities leader, No. *9,* the leading crowd goes even further in that direction. In other words, it is as if a pull is exerted by the leading crowd, bringing the rest of the students toward one or the other of the polar extremes.[2] In all cases, the leading crowd pulls away from the brilliant-student ideal.

If, then, it is true that the status system of adolescents *does* affect educational goals, those schools which differ in the importance of academic achievement in the adolescent status system should differ in numerous other ways which are directly related to educational goals. Only one of those, which illustrates well the differing pres-

---

[2] This result could logically be a statistical artifact because the leaders were included among students as a whole and thus would boost the result in the direction they tend. However, it is not a statistical artifact, for the leading crowds are a small part of the total student body. When they are taken out for computing the position of the rest of the girls in each school, schools *2, 4, 6,* and *7* are still the most popularity-oriented, and school *9* the most activities-oriented.

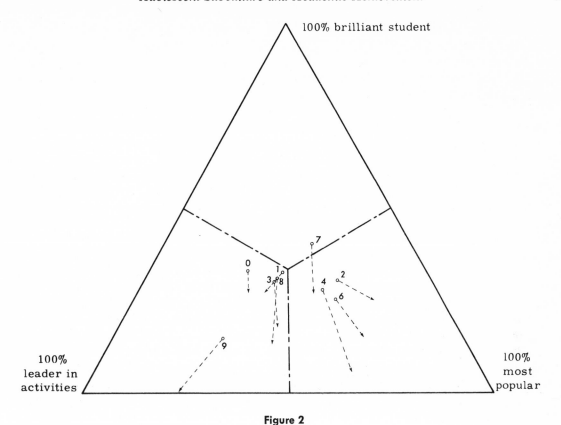

Figure 2

Positions of schools and leading crowds in girls' relative choice of brilliant student, activities leader, and most popular.

sures upon students in the various schools, will be reported here.

In every social context certain activities are highly rewarded, while others are not. Those activities which are rewarded are the activities for which there is strong competition — activities in which everyone with some ability will compete. — In such activities the persons who achieve most should be those with most potential ability. In contrast, in unrewarded activities, those who have most ability may not be motivated to compete; consequently, the persons who achieve most will be persons of lesser ability. Thus in a high school where basketball is important, nearly every boy who might be a good basketball player will go out for the sport, and, as a result, basketball stars are likely to be the boys with the most ability. If in the same school volleyball does not bring the same status, few boys will go out for it, and those

who end up as members of the team will not be the boys with most potential ability.

Similarly, with academic achievement: in a school where such achievement brings few social rewards, those who "go out" for scholarly achievement will be few. The high performers, those who receive good grades, will not be the boys whose ability is greatest but a more mediocre few. Thus the "intellectuals" of such a society, those defined by themselves and others as the best students, will not in fact be those with most intellectual ability. The latter, knowing where the social rewards lie, will be off cultivating other fields which bring social rewards.

To examine the effect of varying social pressures in the schools, academic achievement, as measured by grades in school, was related to I.Q. Since the I.Q. tests differ from school to school, and since each school had its own mean I.Q. and its own variation around it, the ability of high performers (boys who made *A* or *A* — average)[3] was measured by the number of standard deviations of their average I.Q.'s above the mean. In this way, it is possible to see where the high performers' ability lay, relative to the distribution of abilities in their school.[4]

The variations were great: in a small-town school, No. *1,* the boys who made an *A* or *A* — average had I.Q.'s 1.53 standard deviations above the school average; in another small-town school, No. *0,* their I.Q.'s were only about a third this distance above the mean, .59. Given this variation, the question can be asked: Do these variations in ability of the high performers correspond to variations in the social rewards for, or constraints against, being a good student?

Figure 3 shows the relation for the boys between the social rewards for academic excellence (i.e., the frequency with which "good grades" was mentioned as a means for getting into the leading crowd) and the ability of the high performers, measured by the number of standard deviations their average I.Q.'s exceed that of the rest of the boys in the school. The relation is extremely strong. Only one school, a parochial boys' school in the city's slums, deviates. This is a school in which many boys had their most important associations outside the school rather than in it, so

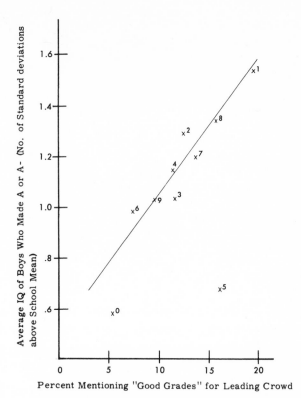

Figure 3

I.Q.'s of high achieving boys by importance of good grades among other boys.

that its student body constituted far less of a social system, less able to dispense social rewards and punishments, than was true of the other schools.

Similarly, Figure 4 shows for the girls the I.Q.'s of the high performers.[5] Unfortunately, most of the schools are closely bunched in the degree to which good grades are important among the girls, so that there is too little variation among them to examine this effect as fully as would be desirable.

---

[3] In each school but *3* and *8,* those making *A* and *A* — constituted from 6 to 8 per cent of the student body. In order to provide a correct test of the hypothesis, it is necessary to have the same fraction of the student body in each case (since I.Q.'s of this group are being measured in terms of number of standard deviations above the student body). To adjust these groups, enough *6*'s were added (each being assigned the average I.Q. of the total group of *6*'s) to bring the proportion up to 6 per cent (from 3 per cent in school *3,* from 4 per cent in school *8*).

[4] The I.Q. tests used in the different schools were: (*0*) California Mental Maturity (taken seventh, eighth, or ninth grade); (*1*) California Mental Maturity (taken eighth grade); (*2*) SRA Primary Mental Abilities (taken tenth grade); (*3*) California Mental Maturity (taken ninth grade; seniors took SRA PMA, which was tabulated as a percentile, and they have been omitted from analysis reported above); (*4*) Otis (ninth and tenth grades; taken eighth grade); Kuhlman Finch (eleventh and twelfth grades, taken eighth grade; (*5*) Otis (taken ninth grade); (*6*) California Mental Maturity (taken eighth grade; (*7*) California Mental Maturity (taken eighth grade); (*8*) Otis (taken ninth or tenth grade); and (*9*) Otis (taken eighth grade).

[5] For the girls, only girls with a straight-*A* average were included. Since girls get better grades than boys, this device is necessary in order to make the sizes of the "high-performer" group roughly comparable for boys and for girls. Schools differed somewhat in the proportion of *A*'s, constituting about 6 per cent of the students in the small schools, only about 3 per cent in schools *6* and *7,* 1 per cent in *8,* and 2 per cent in *9.* In *8* and *9,* enough girls were added and assigned the average grade of the *7* (*A*—) group to bring the proportion to 3 per cent, comparable with the other large schools. The difference, however, between the large and small schools was left.

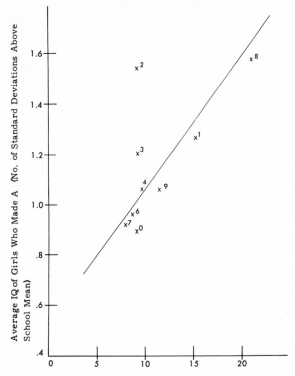

Figure 4

I.Q.'s of high achieving girls by importance of good grades among other girls.

School *2* is the one school whose girls deviate from the general relationship.

The effect of these values systems on the freedom for academic ability to express itself in high achievement is evident among the girls as it is among the boys. This is not merely due to the school facilities, social composition of the school, or other variables: the two schools highest in the importance of scholastic achievement for both boys and girls are *1* and *8*, the first a small-town school of 350 students and the second a city school of 2,000 students. In both there are fewer students with white-collar backgrounds than in schools *9* or *3*, which are somewhere in the middle as to value placed on academic achievement, but are more white-collar than in schools *7* or *4*, which are also somewhere in the middle. The highest expenditure per student was $695 per year in school *9*, and the lowest was little more

than half that, in school *4*. These schools are close together on the graphs of Figures 3 and 4.

So much for the effects as shown by the variation among schools. As mentioned earlier, the variation among schools was not nearly so striking in this research as the fact that, in all of them, academic achievement did not count for as much as other activities. In every school the boy named as best athlete and the boy named as most popular with girls was far more often mentioned as a member of the leading crowd, and as someone to "be like," than was the boy named as the best student. And the girl named as best dressed, and the one named as most popular with boys, was in every school far more often mentioned as being in the leading crowd and as someone "to be like," than was the girl named as the best student.

The relative unimportance of academic achievement, together with the effect shown earlier, suggests that these adolescent subcultures are generally deterrents to academic achievement. In other words, in these societies of adolescents those who come to be seen as the "intellectuals" and who come to think so of themselves are not really those of highest intelligence but are only the ones who are willing to work hard at a relatively unrewarded activity.

The implications for American society as a whole are clear. Because high schools allow the adolescent subcultures to divert energies into athletics, social activities, and the like, they recruit into adult intellectual activities people with a rather mediocre level of ability. In fact, the high school seems to do more than allow these subcultures to discourage academic achievement; it aids them in doing so. To indicate how it does and to indicate how it might do differently is another story, to be examined below.

Figures 1 and 2, which show the way boys and girls would like to be remembered in their high school, demonstrate a curious difference between the boys and the girls. Despite great variation in social background, in size of school (from 180 to 2,000), in size of town (from less than a thousand to over a million), and in style of life of their parents, the proportion of boys choosing each of the three images by which he wants to be remembered is very nearly the same in all schools. And

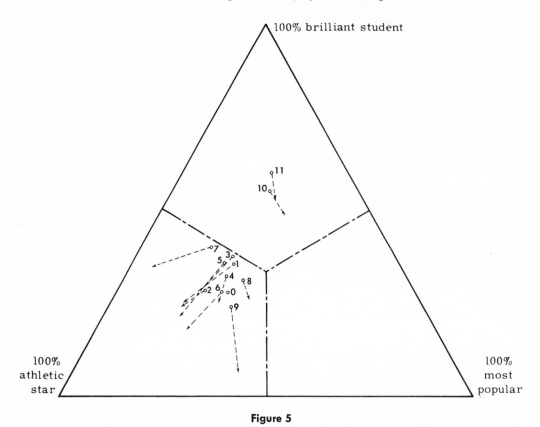

Figure 5

Positions of schools and leading crowds in boys' relative choice of brilliant student, athletic star, and most popular (two private schools [10, 11] included).

in every school the leading crowd "pulls" in similar directions: at least partly toward the ideal of the star athlete. Yet the ideals of the girls in these schools are far more dispersed, and the leading crowds "pull" in varying directions, far less uniformly than among the boys. Why such a diversity in the same schools?

The question can best be answered by indirection. In two schools apart from those in the research, the questionnaire was administered primarily to answer a puzzling question: Why was academic achievement of so little importance among the adolescents in school 9? Their parents were professionals and business executives, about 80 per cent were going to college (over twice as high a proportion as in any of the other schools), and yet academic excellence counted for little among them. In the two additional schools parental background was largely held constant, for they were private, coeducational day schools

whose students had upper-middle-class backgrounds quite similar to those of school 9. One (No. *10*) was in the city; the other (No. *11*), in a suburban setting almost identical to that of No. 9. Although the two schools were added to the study to answer the question about school 9, they will be used to help answer the puzzle set earlier: that of the clustering of schools for the boys and their greater spread for the girls. When we look at the responses of adolescents in these two schools to the question as to how they would like to be remembered, the picture becomes even more puzzling (Figs. 5 and 6). For the boys, they are extremely far from the cluster of the other schools; for the girls, they are intermingled with the other schools. Thus, though it was for the boys that the other schools clustered so closely, these two deviate sharply from the cluster; and for the girls, where the schools already varied, these two are not distinguishable. Furthermore, the leading crowds of boys in these schools do not pull the ideal toward the star athlete ideal as do those in almost all the other schools. To be sure, they pull away from the ideal of the brilliant student, but the pull is primarily toward a social image, the most popular. Among the girls, the leading crowds pull in different directions and are nearly indistinguishable from the other schools.

The answer to both puzzles, that is, first, the great cluster of the boys and now, in these two additional schools, the greater deviation, seems to lie in one fact: the boys' interscholastic athletics. The nine public schools are all engaged in interscholastic leagues which themselves are knit together in state tournaments. The other school of the first ten, the Catholic school, is in a parochial league, where games are just as hotly contested as in the public leagues, and is also knit together with them in tournaments.

Schools *10* and *11* are athletically in a world apart from this. Although boys in both schools may go in for sports, and both schools have interscholastic games, the opponents are scattered private schools, constituting a league in name only. They take no part in state or city tournaments and have almost no publicity.

There is nothing for the girls comparable to the boys' interscholastic athletics. There are school activities of one sort or another, in which most girls take part, but no interscholastic games involving them. Their absence and the lack of leagues which knit all schools together in systematic competition means that the status system can "wander" freely, depending on local conditions in the school. In athletics, however, a school, and the community surrounding it, cannot hold its head up if it continues to lose games. It *must* devote roughly the same attention to athletics as do the schools surrounding it, for athletic games are

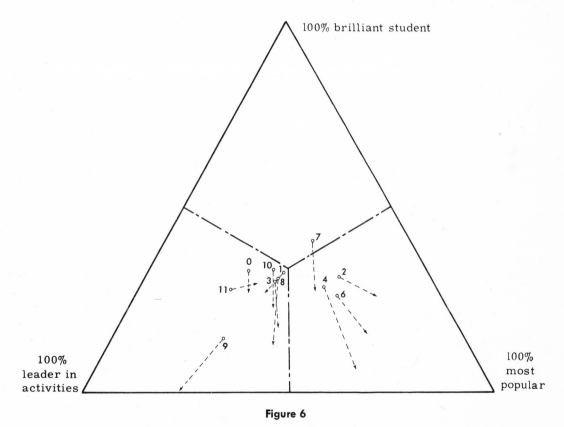

Figure 6

Positions of schools and leading crowds in girls' relative choice of brilliant student, activities leader, and most popular (two private schools [10, 11] included).

the only games in which it engages other schools and, by representation, other communities.

These games are almost the only means a school has of generating internal cohesion and identification, for they constitute the only activity in which the school participates *as* a school. (This is well indicated by the fact that a number of students in school *10,* the private school which engages in no interscholastic games, has been concerned by a "lack of school spirit.") It is as a consequence of this that the athlete gains so much status: he is doing something for the school and the community, not only for himself, in leading his team to victory, for it is a school victory.

The outstanding student, in contrast, has little or no way to bring glory to his school. His victories are always purely personal, often at the expense of his classmates, who are forced to work harder to keep up with him. It is no wonder that his accomplishments gain little reward and are often met by ridiculing remarks, such as "curve-raiser" or "grind," terms of disapprobation which have no analogues in athletics.

These results are particularly intriguing, for they suggest ways in which rather straightforward social theory could be used in organizing the activities of high schools in such a way that their adolescent subcultures would encourage rather than discourage, the channeling of energies into directions of learning. One might speculate on the possible effects of city-wide or statewide "scholastic fairs" composed of academic games and tournaments between schools and school exhibits to be judged. It could be that the mere institution of such games would, just as do the state basketball tournaments in the midwestern United States, have a profound effect upon the educational climate in the participating schools. In fact, by an extension of this analysis, one would predict that an international fair of this sort, a "Scholastic Olympics," would generate interscholastic games and tournaments within the participating countries.

69 The "Cooling-Out" Function in Higher Education*

Burton R. Clark

Ever since Goffman called attention to the "cooling-out process," students of sociology have become particularly interested as to how the disappointment in expectation is handled by both the disappointed person and those responsible for the disappointment. In England, for example, the crucial time in the academic life of a child comes at age eleven when the traditional ability-aptitude-achievement test is given. Those with the top 12 per cent to 18 per cent test scores are selected for grammar schools and, perhaps, eventual college-university careers. The other more than 80 per cent go to secondary modern schools to prepare to enter the job market at age 15. For these students the "cooling-out process" is well structured. In the United States with its "open-door" admission practices, the process is more complex. This study deals with the "cooling-out process" in American community colleges.

A major problem of democratic society is inconsistency between encouragement to achieve and the realities of limited opportunity. Democracy asks individuals to act as if social mobility were universally possible; status is to be won by individual effort, and rewards are to accrue to those who try. But democratic societies also need selective training institutions, and hierarchical work organizations permit increasingly fewer persons to succeed at ascending levels. Situations of opportunity are also situations of denial and failure. Thus democratic societies need not only to motivate achievement but also to mollify those denied it in order to sustain motivation in the face of disappointment and to deflect resentment. In the

* Excerpted from the *American Journal of Sociology,* Vol. 71 (May 1960), by permission of The University of Chicago Press. Copyright © 1960 by The University of Chicago.

modern mass democracy, with its large-scale organization, elaborated ideologies of equal access and participation, and minimal commitment to social origin as a basis for status, the task becomes critical.

The problem of blocked opportunity has been approached sociologically through means-end analysis. Merton and others have called attention to the phenomenon of dissociation between culturally instilled goals and institutionally provided means of realization; discrepancy between ends and means is seen as a basic social source of individual frustration and recalcitrance. We shall here extend means-ends analysis in another direction, to the responses of organized groups to means-ends disparities, in particular focusing attention on amelioriative processes that lessen the strains of dissociation. We shall do so by analyzing the most prevalent type of dissociation between aspirations and avenues in American education, specifying the structure and processes that reduce the stress of structural disparity and individual denial. Certain components of American higher education perform what may be called the cooling-out function, and it is to these that attention will be drawn.

The Ends-Means Disjuncture

In American higher education the aspirations of the multitude are encouraged by "open-door" admission to public-supported colleges. The means of moving upward in status and of maintaining high status now include some years in college, and a college education is a prerequisite of the better positions in business and the professions. The trend is toward an ever tighter connection between higher education and higher occupations, as increased specialization and professionalization insure that more persons will need more preparation. The high-school graduate, seeing college as essential to success, will seek to enter some college, regardless of his record in high school.

A second and allied source of public interest in unlimited entry into college is the ideology of equal opportunity.[1] Strictly interpreted, equality

[1] Seymour Martin Lipset and Reinhard Bendix, *Social Mobility in Industrial Society* (Berkeley: University of California Press, 1959), pp. 78–101.

of opportunity means selection according to ability, without regard to extraneous considerations. Popularly interpreted, however, equal opportunity in obtaining a college education is widely taken to mean unlimited access to some form of college.

Many other features of current American life encourage college-going. School officials are reluctant to establish early critical hurdles for the young, as is done in Europe. With little enforced screening in the pre-college years, vocational choice and educational selection are postponed to the college years or later. In addition, the United States, a wealthy country, is readily supporting a large complex of colleges, and its expanding economy requires more specialists. Recently, a national concern that manpower be fully utilized has encouraged the extending of college training to more and different kinds of students. Going to college is also in some segments of society the thing to do; as a last resort, it is more attractive than the army or a job. Thus ethical and practical urges together encourage the high-school graduate to believe that college is both a necessity and a right; similarly, parents and elected officials incline toward legislation and admission practices that insure entry for large numbers; and educational authorities find the need and justification for easy admission.

A commitment to standards is encouraged by a set of values in which the status of a college, as defined by academicians and a large body of educated laymen, is closely linked to the perceived quality of faculty, student body, and curriculum. The raising of standards is supported by the faculty's desire to work with promising students and to enjoy membership in an enterprise of reputed quality — college authorities find low standards and poor students a handicap in competing with other colleges for such resources as able faculty as well as for academic status. The wish is widespread that college education be of the highest quality for the preparation of leaders in public affairs, business, and the professions. In brief, the institutional means of the students' progress toward college graduation and subsequent goals are shaped in large part by a commitment to quality embodied in college staffs, traditions, and images.

Students who pursue ends for which a college education is required but who have little academic ability gain admission into colleges only to encounter standards of performance they cannot meet. As a result, while some students of low promise are successful, for large numbers failure is inevitable and *structured*. The denial is delayed, taking place within the college instead of at the edge of the system. It requires that many colleges handle the student who intends to complete college and has been allowed to become involved but whose destiny is to fail.

RESPONSES TO DISJUNCTURE

What is done with the student whose destiny will normally be early termination? One answer is unequivocal dismissal. This "hard" response is found in the state university that bows to pressure for broad admission but then protects standards by heavy drop-out. In the first year it weeds out many of the incompetent, who may number a third or more of the entering class. The response of the college is hard in that failure is clearly defined as such. Failure is public; the student often returns home. This abrupt change in status and in access to the means of achievement may occur simultaneously in a large college or university for hundreds, and sometimes thousands, of students after the first semester and at the end of the freshman year. The delayed denial is often viewed on the outside as heartless, a slaughter of the innocents. This excites public pressure and anxiety, and apparently the practice cannot be extended indefinitely as the demand for admission to college increases.

A second answer is to sidetrack unpromising students rather than have them fail. This is the "soft" response: never to dismiss a student but to provide him with an alternative. One form of it in some state universities is the detour to an extension division or a general college, which has the advantage of appearing not very different from the main road. Sometimes "easy" fields of study, such as education, business administration, and social science, are used as alternatives to dismissal. The major form of the soft response is not found in the four-year college or university, however, but in the college that specializes in handling students who

will soon be leaving — typically, the two-year public junior college.

In most states where the two-year college is a part of higher education, the students likely to be caught in the means-ends disjuncture are assigned to it in large numbers. In California, where there are over sixty public two-year colleges in a diversified system that includes the state university and numerous four-year state colleges, the junior college is unselective in admissions and by law, custom, and self-conception accepts all who wish to enter.[2] It is tuition-free, local, and under local control. Most of its entering students want to try for the baccalaureate degree, transferring to a "senior" college after one or two years. About two-thirds of the students in the junior colleges of the state are in programs that permit transferring; but, of these, only about one-third actually transfer to a four-year college.[3] The remainder, or two out of three of the professed transfer students, are "latent terminal students": their announced intention and program of study entails four years of college, but in reality their work terminates in the junior college. Constituting about half of all the students in the California junior colleges, and somewhere between one-third and one-half of junior college students nationally,[4] these students cannot be ignored by the colleges. Understanding their careers is important to understanding modern higher education.

THE REORIENTING PROCESS

This type of student in the junior college is handled by being moved out of a transfer major to a one- or two-year program of vocational, business, or semiprofessional training. This calls for the relinquishing of his original intention, and he is induced to accept a substitute that has lower status in both the college and society in general.

In one junior college [5] the initial move in a cool-

[2] Burton R. Clark, *The Open Door College: A Case Study* (New York: McGraw-Hill Book Co., 1960), pp. 44–45.

[3] *Ibid.,* p. 116.

[4] Leland L. Medsker, *The Junior College: Progress and Prospect* (New York: McGraw-Hill Book Co., 1960), Chap. iv.

[5] San Jose City College, San Jose, Calif. For the larger study see Clark, *op. cit.*

ing-out process is pre-entrance testing: low scores on achievement tests lead poorly qualified students into remedial classes. Assignment to remedial work casts doubt and slows the student's movement into bona fide transfer courses. The remedial courses are, in effect, a subcollege. The student's achievement scores are made part of a counseling folder that will become increasingly significant to him. An objective record of ability and performance begins to accumulate.

A second step is a counseling interview before the beginning of the first semester, and before all subsequent semesters for returning students. "At this interview the counselor assists the student to choose the proper courses in the light of his objective, his test scores, the high school record and test records from his previous schools." [6] Assistance in choosing "the proper courses" is gentle at first. Of the common case of the student who wants to be an engineer but who is not a promising candidate, a counselor said: "I never openly countermand his choice, but edge him toward a terminal program by gradually laying out the facts of life." Counselors may become more severe later when grades provide a talking point and when the student knows that he is in trouble. In the earlier counseling the desire of the student has much weight; the counselor limits himself to giving advice and stating the probability of success. The advice is entered in the counseling record that shadows the student.

A third and major step in reorienting the latent terminal student is a special course entitled "Orientation to College," mandatory for entering students. All sections of it are taught by teacher-counselors who comprise the counseling staff, and one of its purposes is "to assist students in evaluating their own abilities, interests, and aptitudes; in assaying their vocational choices in light of this evaluation; and in making educational plans to implement their choices." A major section of it takes up vocational planning; vocational tests are given at a time when opportunities and requirements in various fields of work are discussed. The tests include the "Lee Thorpe Interest Inventory" ("given to all students for motivating a self-appraisal of vocational choice") and the "Strong Interest Inventory" ("for all who are undecided about choice or who show disparity between accomplishment and vocational choice"). Mechanical and clerical aptitude tests are taken by all. The aptitudes are directly related to the college's terminal programs, with special tests, such as a pre-engineering ability test, being given according to need. Then an "occupational paper is required of all students for their chosen occupation"; in it the student writes on the required training and education and makes a "self-appraisal of fitness."

Tests and papers are then used in class discussion and counseling interviews, in which the students themselves arrange and work with a counselor's folder and a student test profile and, in so doing, are repeatedly confronted by the accumulating evidence — the test scores, course grades, recommendations of teachers and counselors. This procedure is intended to heighten self-awareness of capacity in relation to choice and hence to strike particularly at the latent terminal student. The teacher-counselors are urged constantly to "be alert to the problem of unrealistic vocational goals" and to "help students to accept their limitations and strive for success in other worthwhile objectives that are within their grasp." The orientation class was considered a good place "to talk tough," to explain in an *impersonal* way the facts of life for the overambitious student. Talking tough to a whole group is part of a soft treatment of the individual.

Following the vocational counseling, the orientation course turns to "building an educational program," to study of the requirements for graduation of the college in transfer and terminal curriculum, and to planning of a four-semester program. The students also become acquainted with the requirements of the colleges to which they hope to transfer, here contemplating additional hurdles such as the entrance examinations of other colleges. Again, the hard facts of the road ahead are brought to bear on self-appraisal.

If he wishes, the latent terminal student may ignore the counselor's advice and the test scores. While in the counseling class, he is also in other courses, and he can wait to see what happens. Adverse counseling advice and poor test scores may not shut off his hope of completing college;

[6] San Jose Junior College, *Handbook for Counselors,* 1957–58, p. 2. Statements in quotation marks in the next few paragraphs are cited from this.

when this is the case, the deterrent will be encountered in the regular classes. Here the student is divested of expectations, lingering from high school, that he will automatically pass and, hopefully, automatically be transferred. Then, receiving low grades, he is thrown back into the counseling orbit, a fourth step in his reorientation and a move justified by his actual accomplishment. The following indicates the nature of the referral system:

Need for Improvement Notices are issued by instructors to students who are doing unsatisfactory work. The carbon copy of the notice is given to the counselor who will be available for conference with the student. The responsibility lies with the student to see his counselor. However, experience shows that some counselees are unable to be sufficiently self-directive to seek aid. The counselor should, in such cases, send for the student, using the Request for Conference blank. If the student fails to respond to the Request for Conference slip, this may become a disciplinary matter and should be referred to the deans.

After a conference has been held, the Need for Improvement notices are filed in the student's folder. *This may be important* in case of a complaint concerning the fairness of a final grade.

This directs the student to more advice and self-assessment, as soon and as often as he has classroom difficulty. The carbon-copy routine makes it certain that, if he does not seek advice, advice will seek him. The paper work and bureaucratic procedure have the purpose of recording referral and advice in black and white, where they may later be appealed to impersonally.

A fifth step, one necessary for many in the throes of discouragement, is probation: "Students [whose] grade point averages fall below 2.0 [C] in any semester will, upon recommendation by the Scholarship Committee, be placed on probationary standing." A second failure places the student on second probation, and a third may mean that he will be advised to withdraw from the college altogether. The procedure is not designed to rid the college of a large number of students, for they may continue on probation for three consecutive semesters; its purpose is not to provide a status halfway out of the college but to "assist the student to seek an objective (major field) at a level on which he can succeed." An important effect of probation is its slow killing-off of the lingering hopes of the most stubborn latent terminal students. A "transfer student" must have a C average to receive the Associate in Arts (a two-year degree) offered by the junior college, but no minimum average is set for terminal students. More important, four-year colleges require a C average or higher for the transfer student. Thus probationary status is the final blow to hopes of transferring and, indeed, even to graduating from the junior college under a transfer-student label. The point is reached where the student must permit himself to be reclassified or else drop out. In this college, 30 per cent of the students enrolled at the end of the spring semester, 1955–56, who returned the following fall were on probation; three out of four of these were transfer students in name.

This sequence of procedures is a specific process of cooling-out;[7] its effect, at the best, is to let down hopes gently and unexplosively. Through it students who are failing or barely passing find their occupational and academic future being redefined. Along the way, teacher-counselors urge the latent terminal student to give up his plan of transferring and stand ready to console him in accepting a terminal curriculum. The drawn-out denial when it is effective is in place of a personal, hard "No"; instead, the student is brought to realize, finally, that it is best to ease himself out of the competition to transfer.

COOLING-OUT FEATURES

In the cooling-out process in the junior college are several features which are likely to be found in other settings where failure or denial is the effect of a structured discrepancy between ends and means, the responsible operatives or "coolers"

[7] Erving Goffman, "Cooling the Mark Out: Some Aspects of Adaptation to Failure," *Psychiatry*, XV (November, 1952), 451–63. Goffman's original statement of the concept of cooling-out referred to how the disappointing of expectations is handled by the disappointed person and especially by those responsible for the disappointment.

cannot leave the scene or hide their identities, and the disappointment is threatening in some way to those responsible for it. At work and in training institutions this is common. The features are:

1. *Alternative achievement.* — Substitute avenues may be made to appear not too different from what is given up, particularly as to status. The person destined to be denied or who fails is invited to interpret the second effort as more appropriate to his particular talent and is made to see that it will be the less frustrating. Here one does not fail but rectifies a mistake. The substitute status reflects less unfavorably on personal capacity than does being dismissed and forced to leave the scene. The terminal student in the junior college may appear not very different from the transfer student — an "engineering aide," for example, instead of an "engineer" — and to be proceeding to something with a status of its own. Failure in college can be treated as if it did not happen; so, too, can poor performance in industry.

2. *Gradual disengagement.* — By a gradual series of steps, movement to a goal may be stalled, self-assessment encouraged, and evidence produced of performance. This leads toward the available alternatives at little cost. It also keeps the person in a counseling milieu in which advice is furnished, whether actively sought or not. Compared with the original hopes, however, it is a deteriorating situation. If the individual does not give up peacefully, he will be in trouble.

3. *Objective denial.* — Reorientation is, finally, confrontation by the facts. A record of poor performance helps to detach the organization and its agents from the emotional aspects of the cooling-out work. In a sense, the overaspiring student in the junior college confronts himself, as he lives with the accumulating evidence, instead of the organization. The college offers opportunity; it is the record that forces denial. Record-keeping and other bureaucratic procedures appeal to universal criteria and reduce the influence of personal ties, and the personnel are thereby protected. Modern personnel record-keeping, in general, has the function of documenting denial.

4. *Agents of consolation.* — Counselors are available who are patient with the overambitious and who work to change their intentions. They believe in the value of the alternative careers, though of lower social status, and are practiced in consoling. In college and in other settings counseling is to reduce aspiration as well as to define and to help fulfil it. The teacher-counselor in the "soft" junior college is in contrast to the scholar in the "hard" college who simply gives a low grade to the failing student.

5. *Avoidance of standards.* — A cooling-out process avoids appealing to standards that are ambiguous to begin with. While a "hard" attitude toward failure generally allows a single set of criteria, a "soft" treatment assumes that many kinds of ability are valuable, each in its place. Proper classification and placement are then paramount, while standards become relative.

IMPORTANCE OF CONCEALMENT

For an organization and its agents one dilemma of a cooling-out role is that it must be kept reasonably away from public scrutiny and not clearly perceived or understood by prospective clientele. Should it become obvious, the organization's ability to perform it would be impaired. If high-school seniors and their families were to define the junior college as a place which diverts college-bound students, a probable consequence would be a turning-away from the junior college and increased pressure for admission to the four-year colleges and universities that are otherwise protected to some degree. This would, of course, render superfluous the part now played by the junior college in the division of labor among colleges.

The cooling-out function of the junior college is kept hidden, for one thing, as other functions are highlighted. The junior college stresses "the transfer function," "the terminal function," etc., not that of transforming transfer into terminal students; indeed, it is widely identified as principally a transfer station. The other side of cooling-out is the successful performance in junior college of students who did poorly in high school or who have overcome socioeconomic handicaps, for they are drawn into higher education rather than taken out of it. Advocates of the junior college point to this salvaging of talented manpower, otherwise lost to the community and the nation. It is indeed a function of the open door to let hidden talent be uncovered.

Then, too, cooling-out itself is reinterpreted so as to appeal widely. The junior college may be viewed as a place where all high-school graduates have the opportunity to explore possible careers and find the type of education appropriate to their individual ability; in short, as a place where everyone is admitted and everyone succeeds.

The students themselves help to keep this function concealed by wishful unawareness. Those who cannot enter other colleges but still hope to complete four years will be motivated at first not to admit the cooling-out process to consciousness.

Once exposed to it, they again will be led not to acknowledge it, and so they are saved insult to their self-image.

In summary, the cooling-out process in higher education is one whereby systematic discrepancy between aspiration and avenue is covered over and stress for the individual and the system is minimized. The provision of readily available alternative achievements in itself is an important device for alleviating the stress consequent on failure and so preventing anomic and deviant behavior. The general result of cooling-out processes is that society can continue to encourage maximum effort without major disturbance from unfulfilled promises and expectations.

POLITICS: LEGITIMATION OF POWER AND AUTHORITY

70 The People's Choice*

Paul F. Lazarsfeld · Bernard Berelson
Hazel Gaudet

In an earlier article (#27), we considered the role of personal contacts in the influencing of those persons who had not decided for whom to vote. As stated then, this is obviously only one factor in this classic study of how the voter makes up his mind in a presidential campaign. The current selection from the Erie County (Ohio) Study deals with the

social differences between Republicans and Democrats in terms of socio-economic status, religious affiliation, and age; these factors, in turn, are used to develop an index of political predisposition. The article further discusses the cross-pressures facing those who have not made up their minds, and illustrates some of the factors which bring about activation on the matter.

For the student who wants to know how the survey was conducted, a brief account of the research method plus a short account of the setting of the study (the crucial time of 1940) is given.

Do the "class differences" between the political parties in 1940 hold true today? Does the situation in Erie County parallel the one in your community? What findings in this study should influence political campaigns of today?

The survey was done in Erie County, Ohio, located on Lake Erie between Cleveland and Toledo. This county was chosen because it was small enough to permit close supervision of the interviewers, because it was relatively free from sectional peculiarities, because it was not dominated by any large urban center although it did furnish an opportunity to compare rural political opinion with opinion in a small urban center, and because for forty years — in every presidential election in the twentieth century — it had deviated very lit-

* Excerpts from Paul F. Lazarsfeld, Bernard Berelson, and Hazel Gaudet, *The People's Choice,* second edition, New York, Columbia University Press, 1948, pp. 3–5, 13–14, 16–27, 56, 60–61, 65–70, 84–85. Used by permission. (Copyright 1944, 1948, Columbia University Press.)

Time Table	May	June	July	August	September	October	November
		REPUBLICAN CONVENTION		DEMOCRATIC CONVENTION		ELECTION	
Interview Number	1	2	3	4	5	6	7
Group Interviewed	Total Poll (3000)	Main Panel 600	Main Panel 600	Main Panel 600	Main Panel 600	Main Panel 600	Main Panel 600
			Control A 600	Control B 600		Control C 600	

Figure 1

Outline of the Erie Study.

tle from the national voting trends. Because of the diversity of American life, there is no such thing as a "typical American county." But it is not unlikely that Erie County was as representative of the northern and western sections of the country as any similarly small area could be. In any case, we were studying the *development* of votes and not their distribution.

In May, 1940, every fourth house in Erie County was visited by a member of the staff of from twelve to fifteen specially trained local interviewers, chiefly women. In this way, approximately 3,000 persons were chosen to represent as closely as possible the population of the county as a whole. This group — the poll — resembled the county in age, sex, residence, education, telephone and car ownership, and nativity.

From this poll, four groups of 600 persons each were selected by stratified sampling. Each group was closely matched to the others and constituted, in effect, a miniature sample of the whole poll and of the county itself. Of these four groups of 600, three were reinterviewed only once each — one in July, one in August, and one in October. They were used as "control-groups" to test the effect that repeated interviewing might have on the panel. At the same time they provided a larger sample (1,200 respondents) on a variety of important questions asked at the control points. The fourth group — the panel — was interviewed once each month from May to November.

The Setting of the Study. On November 5, 1940, the people of the United States went to the polls to elect a president to lead them through the crucial years of the war. Hitler's blitzkrieg was in full swing. He had already taken over Austria, Poland, and Czechoslovakia, and during the pre-election period his armies marched through the Low Countries and conquered France. Just before the election, his ally Italy invaded Greece. The United States traded some old warships to Britain for naval and air bases in the Atlantic. Military conscription was begun. The wholesale suppression of civil rights in the totalitarian countries highlighted the picture of a nation democratically choosing a leader amid free discussion.

Social Differences Between Republicans and Democrats. Any practical politician worth his salt knows a great deal about the stratification of the American electorate. It is part of his every-day working equipment to know what kinds of people are likely to be dyed-in-the-wool Republicans or traditional Democrats. He would not be in business long if he did not know who was most susceptible to the arguments of either party.

Today, in most sections of the country, the politician can count on the banker, the business manager, the farmer, the bishop and a good many of his flock to vote Republican. In the same way, he knows that the immigrant, the working man,

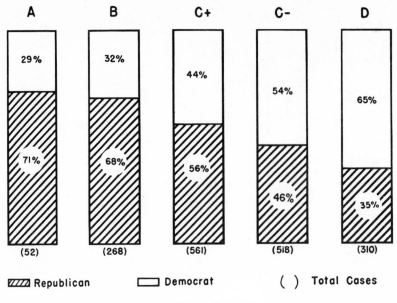

Figure 2

Voting behavior by socio-economic status. Those high in socio-economic status (SES level) are more likely to vote Republican than Democratic.

the priest and most of his parishioners — particularly those in cities — constitute the mainstay of the Democratic party outside the Solid South.

The features by which the politician differentiates a Republican and a Democrat, then, seem to be economic status, religion, residence, and occupation. To these can be added a fifth — age. Tradition has it that youth shuns the conservative, in politics as well as in clothes, music, and manners.

For the most part, the study of Erie County's voting behavior in 1940 confirms this voice of experience. But it does more than merely lend scientific status to common-sense knowledge. By systematizing the knowledge, by giving an actual measure of the influence of each of these factors of stratification, the study places them in their proper rank-order and brings out their interdependence.

The Role of Socio-Economic Status. Before discussing the role which socio-economic status plays in the composition of the two major political parties, let us consider the index by which we measure this characteristic.

Public opinion research customarily makes use of interviewers' ratings of socio-economic status. For convenience let us refer to them as SES ratings. Interviewers are trained to assess the homes, possessions, appearance, and manner of speech of the respondents and to classify them into their proper stratum in the community according to a set quota. The people with the best homes, furniture, clothes, etc., i.e., the ones with the most money, would be classed as A's; and the people at the other extreme would be D's. In Erie County, the quota was approximated in the following distribution: A, 3%; B, 14%; C+, 33%; C−, 30%, and D, 20%.

There are a number of general considerations implied in such a classification which can only briefly be summarized here. The first question concerns the reliability of such a classification procedure. Would two independent tests yield the same results? We have some evidence on this question. Experiments have shown that two sets of ratings, representing two independent appraisals of the same subjects by the same interviewers but spaced three weeks apart, have a correlation of .8. When the same subjects are observed by two different interviewers, the correlation goes down to .6 or .7. Although there is some variation, then, the ratings provide a fairly stable classification.

But do these ratings classify people so that the result corresponds to general experience? Again there is evidence to show that the SES ratings are closely related to the material possessions of the respondents. The higher the rating, the higher the average income, the average number of expensive household articles owned, and so on.

These SES ratings are closely related to the educational level of the subjects. Also, the higher ratings go to business and professional people, while the lower ones are given mainly to workers and manual laborers.

Now, to what extent did the SES levels differentiate party vote? To what extent did people on the various levels support the Republicans or the Democrats? The answer is that there were twice as many Republicans on the A level as on the D level. And with each step down the SES scale, the proportion of Republicans decreases

and the proportion of Democrats correspondingly increases.

As a first basis for further classification (Figure 3), we can use the occupations of our respondents. On each SES level, the "upper" occupational groups — professionals, business men, clerical and commercial people — were more Republican than the "lower" groups (skilled mechanics, factory workers, and manual laborers).

However, once people are classified by the general SES index, the further classification by occupation does not refine the groups very greatly. In other words, people of the same general socio-economic status have about the same political attitudes regardless of their occupations.

Religious Affiliation and Age. In Erie County there was another factor which was no less important than SES level. That was religious affiliation.

Sixty per cent of the Protestants and only 23 per cent of the Catholics had Republican vote intentions in May. At first glance, this might

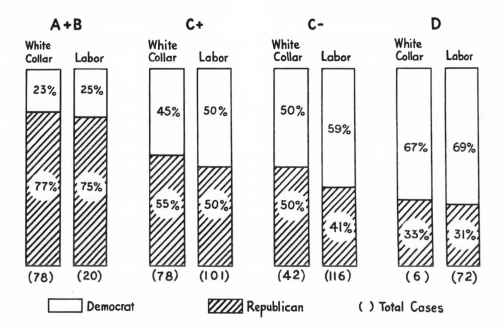

Figure 3

Voting behavior by occupation and by socio-economic status. Fewer laborers than white-collar workers vote Republican, but if SES level is held constant, occupation makes little difference.

appear to be a spurious result. As a group, Catholics are ordinarily lower in economic status than Protestants and hence this result may simply reflect SES levels. But it does not. On each SES level, religious affiliation plays an important role in determining political affiliation (Figure 4).

This difference between Protestants and Catholics may have several explanations. Perhaps it was due to differences in the national origins of the religious groups. In the big cities, the Irish, Polish, and Italian people — most of whom are Catholic — have strong ties with the Democratic party. But this is not adequate to explain the voting behavior of Erie County Catholics. For there was only one nationality group, other than the Anglo-Saxon, of any appreciable size in Erie County — the German. The religious composition of this group was the same as that of the rest of the population residing in Erie County.

But that attempt at explanation, unsatisfactory in itself, contains the germ of another hypothesis which undoubtedly has greater validity. The Catholics have traditionally been affiliated with the Democratic party through the waves of Irish, Italian, and Polish immigration. Many Democratic party leaders have been Catholics — note these recent chairmen of the national committee: Raskob, Farley, Flynn, Walker, Hannegan — and Al Smith, the Democratic candidate in 1928, is the only Catholic ever nominated for the Presidency. The political affiliation of the Catholics is explained, to some extent, by this simple historical fact.

The differences in the political inclinations of the two religious groups serve to introduce the relationship between age and vote preference. Legend has it that older people are more conservative in most things, including politics, both because they like to perpetuate their own idealized past and because they have more to conserve. By the same token, younger people are more liberal, more receptive to change. If one accepts the common stereotypes — that the Republican party is more "conservative" and the Democrats more "liberal" — then the legend seems to hold for Erie County in 1940.

In May, 50 per cent of those below 45 years of age, but 55 per cent of those over 45 intended to vote Republican. However, this result does not hold for the Protestants and Catholics separately. Only among the Protestants were the older people more Republican. Among the Catholics, the relationship was reversed: the older people were more Democratic. This refinement of the relationship between age and political preference probably has two explanations. First, the younger people, who are generally less church-influenced than their elders, show less influence of religion upon vote. Thus young Protestants are less Republican than old Protestants and young Catholics less Democratic than old Catholics. And secondly, the myth that age brings political conservatism — here shown to be incorrect — may apply in another sense. Like appetite, custom grows by what it feeds on. The religious factors which influence vote preference are intensified through the years so that they carry more weight for the elderly. They have a longer time to exercise their influence, to indoctrinate the respondent, to affect him through the common elements. In other words, advancing age may not bring *political* conservatism but it does bring *social* conservatism.

An Index of Political Predisposition. To this point, we have isolated two major influences upon vote: the SES level and religious affiliation. And incidentally, we have seen that the political effect of age differs for Catholics and Protestants. A number of other factors were investigated, but only one proved statistically significant: there were 14 per cent more Republican voters in the rural part of the county than in Sandusky, the one large industrialized town with a population of 25,000.

Other differences were less important. Women were somewhat more inclined to favor the Republican party. The same was true for better-educated people, but education is so highly related to SES level that it is hard to say whether the influence of education alone would be distinguishable if a more refined economic classification were used.

The multiple correlation between vote and the social factors discussed above is approximately .5. But the greatest part of the predictive value of all these factors derives from three factors: SES level, religion, and residence. Of all rich Protestant farmers almost 75 per cent voted Republican, whereas 90 per cent of the Catholic laborers living in Sandusky voted Democratic.

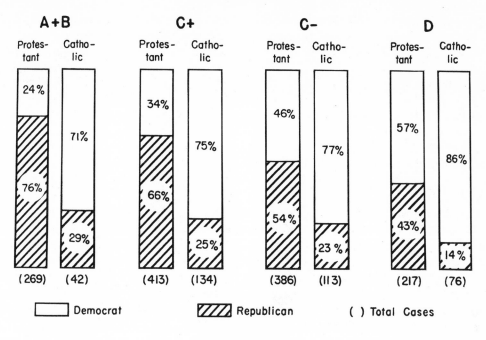

Figure 4

Voting behavior by religious affiliation and by socio-economic status. Religious affiliation splits vote sharply. This cannot be attributed to the fact that Catholics in this country are, on the average, lower in SES level than Protestants. The relationship between vote and religious affiliation holds true on each SES level.

In order to use these factors in a simple way, we constructed an index of political predisposition (IPP) so that the respondents could be classified on a scale ranging from those with strong Republican predispositions at one extreme to those with strong Democratic predispositions at the other. While an index is, of course, cruder than a coefficient of multiple correlation, it does serve to distinguish easily among the votes of people with different combinations of personal characteristics (Figure 5). The proportion of Republicans falls off consistently and significantly from one extreme of political predispositions to the other. And thus a simple combination of three primary personal characteristics goes a long way in "explaining" political preferences.

There is a familiar adage in American folklore to the effect that a person is only what he thinks he is, an adage which reflects the typically American notion of unlimited opportunity, the tendency toward self-betterment, etc. Now we find that the reverse of the adage is true: a person thinks, polit-

ically, as he is, socially. Social characteristics determine political preference.

Cross-Pressures and Time of Decision. Previously we have indicated that there were a number of factors differentiating Republican and Democratic voters. Each of these factors could be considered a "pressure" upon final vote decision. We found the Protestant vote allied to the Republicans and the Catholic vote more strongly Democratic. We found that individuals on the higher SES levels tended to vote Republican and their poorer neighbors to vote Democratic. In other words, a vote decision can be considered the net effect of a variety of pressures.

Now what if these individual factors work in opposite directions? Suppose an individual is *both* prosperous and Catholic? How will he make up his mind? Or suppose he belongs to the Protestant faith and lives in a poor section of the community? Which of the conflicting influences will win out? People who are subject to contra-

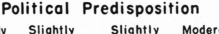

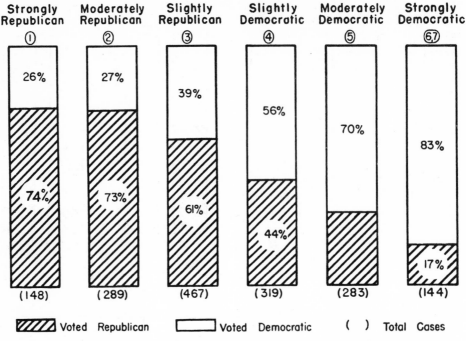

Figure 5

Voting behavior by political predisposition and by socio-economic status. High SES level, affiliation with the Protestant religion, and rural residence predispose a voter for the Republican party; the opposites of these factors make for Democratic predisposition. Summarized in an index of political predisposition (IPP), their effect is illustrated by the high correlation with vote intention.

dictory and opposing influences of this kind are said to be under cross-pressures.

The Effect of Cross-Pressures. Whatever the source of the conflicting pressures, whether from social status or class identification, from voting traditions or the attitudes of associates, the consistent result was to delay the voter's final decision. The voters who were subject to cross-pressures on their vote decided later than the voters for whom the various factors reinforced one another. And of all the cross-pressures which we have identified the single most effective one in delaying vote decision was the lack of complete agreement within the family.

Why did people subject to cross-pressures delay their final decisions as to how they should vote? In the first place, it was difficult for them to make

up their minds simply because they had good reasons for voting for both candidates. Sometimes such reasons were so completely balanced that the decision had to be referred to a third factor for settlement. The doubt as to which was the better course — to vote Republican or to vote Democratic — combined with the process of self-argument caused the delay in the final vote decision of such people.

In the second place, some of the people subject to cross-pressures delayed their final vote decisions because they were waiting for events to resolve the conflicting pressures. In the case of conflicting personal characteristics, such resolution was hardly possible but in other cases a reconciliation of conflicting interests might be anticipated. A person might hope that during the campaign he could convince other members of his family, or even more, he might give the family every chance to bring him around to their way of thinking. And the family often does just that. Or, again, he might wait for events in the campaign to provide him with a basis for making up his mind. Although there is a tendency toward consistency in attitudes, sometimes the contradiction was not resolved and the voter actually went to the polls with the cross-pressures still in operation.

Such conflicting pressures make voters "fair game" for the campaign managers of both parties, for they have a foot in each party. They are subject to factors which influence them to vote Republican and others, perhaps equally strong, which influence them to vote Democratic.

From this particular point of view, the heavy campaigning of both parties at the end of the campaign is a good investment for both sides — to the extent to which it can be effective at all.

The Types of Changes. People delayed their final vote decisions either because they did not have enough interest in the election to push through to a definite choice or because the selec-

tion of a candidate put them in a difficult situation, containing elements favorable to both sides. But the process of delay did not work identically for all of them. Some people were "Don't Know's" until sometime during the campaign and then definitely decided on their vote. Others decided early in the campaign for one of the candidates, then had a period of doubt when they became undecided or even went over to the other side, and finally came back to the original choice. Still others changed from one particular party to the other. In short, the people who did not make up their minds until some time during the campaign proper differed in the ways in which they came to their final vote decision. In this sense, the three main kinds of changers were the following (the figures are percentages of the voters as a whole):

28% Crystallizers: They are people who had no vote intention in May but later acquired one; they went from "Don't Know" to Republican (14 per cent) or from "Don't Know" to Democrat (14 per cent).

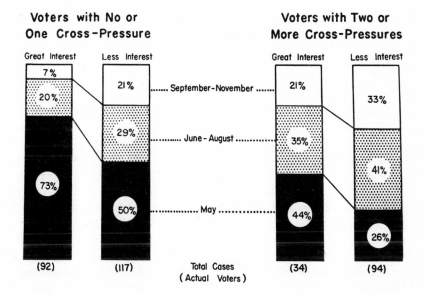

Figure 6

Vote decision by cross-pressures and by interest in election. Both cross-pressures and lack of interest delay the final vote decision. Their joint effect is especially strong. Separately, they show about equal strength.

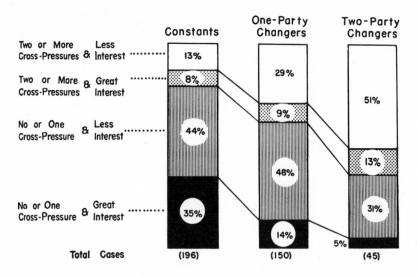

Figure 7

Vote intentions by degree of interest and cross-pressures. The less interest people have and the more cross-pressures to which they are subject, the more variable are their vote intentions.

15% Waverers: They are people who started out with a vote intention, then fell away from it (either to "Don't Know" or to the other party) and later returned to their original choice. Most of them went from a party to "Don't Know" and then back to the original party (11 per cent: Republicans, 5.5 per cent; Democrats, 5.5 per cent), and others from a party to the other party and then back to the first party (4 per cent: Republicans, 1 per cent; Democrats, 3 per cent).

8% Party Changers: They are people who started out with a vote intention and later changed to the other party, finally voting for it. They went from Republican to Democrat (2 per cent) or from Democrat to Republican (6 per cent).

Time of Final Decision and the Changers. As the campaign wore on, what kinds of changers were still left to be convinced, once and for all?

The three kinds of changers — the crystallizers, the waverers, and the party changers — all came to their final decision some time after May, but not all at the same time. Actually, the crystallizers decided much earlier than the others; 68 per cent had settled their vote by August as against only 48

per cent of the party changers and 46 per cent of the waverers.

But the waverers — the people who left the party of their original choice but later came back and voted for it — comprise a special group because, as we noted above, there were two different kinds of waverers. There were those who wavered only to indecision and there were those who wavered all the way to the other party. This "distance" of the wavering is significant both for time of final decision and, as we shall see, for the roles of interest and cross-pressures. The indecision waverers definitely decided much earlier than the party waverers (57 per cent by August as against 14 per cent). If, then, we divide the changers into two groups — the one-party changers (crystallizers and indecision waverers) and the two-party changers (the straight party changers and the party waverers) — we find that the people who intended sometime during the campaign to vote for both parties took much longer to reach a final vote decision than those who varied only between one of the parties and indecision. Almost two-thirds of the two-party changers did not definitely decide until the last period of the campaign; almost two-thirds of the one-party changers definitely decided by August. As the campaign went into its last weeks, the people who were still to make up their minds, relatively speaking, were those who had been in the camp of the opposition earlier.

Interest, Cross-Pressures, and the Changers. What were the roles of interest in the election and cross-pressures in voting background for these groups of voters who had arrived at their final vote decision in different ways? Did these two influential factors differentiate such voters?

The story is clear. There was a steady decrease of interest and a steady increase of cross-pressures from constants to one-party changers to two-party changers. The people who changed their position during the campaign but never enough to move into both parties stood between the constants and the two-party people. In other words, the more interest and the fewer conflicting pressures a person had, the more he tended to decide once and for all early in the game and never change his mind thereafter. If a person had somewhat less interest and somewhat more cross-pressures, then he tended to doubt longer and oftener than the constants but he slid back only to a tentative "don't know" and never far enough to get into the other camp. Only those people who had much less interest and many more conflicting pressures actually vacillated between the two parties.

The Personality Traits of the Changers. The personalities of the different kinds of voters can be compared on the basis of ratings made by our interviewers. After the fourth interview, by which time the interviewers had become reasonably well acquainted with the respondents, each member of the panel was rated on a graphic rating scale covering ten personality characteristics readily observed during interviews.

On almost all traits, the constants were rated superior to voters who changed in any way. Constants were reported to be more self-assured, better informed, more cooperative, and broader in their interests. All the traits correspond to their greater enthusiasm for the political campaign. All the changers, on the other hand, showed a limited range of community contacts and interests in their personality ratings as well as in other measures indicated previously. This underlines the finding

that the campaign itself is progressively waged in order to win the less interested and less involved, the "withdrawn" individuals living within narrower horizons.

The waverers were distinguished by a higher rating on "fair-mindedness" which probably grew directly out of their hesitation and reservations. In addition, the waverers seemed to suffer somewhat more from emotional maladjustment as evidenced in more unhappiness and lack of self-assurance. It is a well known psychological pattern for uneasiness to lead to floundering about in areas not directly related to the distress.

The ratings on the party changers indicated that the direction of the change has to be taken into account. There were no personality characteristics which distinguished the party changers as such. In personality, the party changers resembled the adherents of the party they changed *to* more than the adherents of the party they changed *from*.

Some Illustrations of Activation. The whole process of activation is rather complex and our respondents were not likely to be aware of it themselves. The following case is a typical example, from our interviews, of how the expression of political predispositions came about. This respondent is a Protestant store owner with an SES level of B, living in a rural part of the county. In the first months of the campaign period he could not decide which candidate he favored. He thought Roosevelt had been a good president, had instituted many important reforms, and had "kept us from the internal revolution that they said was threatening the country." He also stated that "if times were different, Willkie might be good." But his Republican predisposition naturally led him to propaganda favorable to the Republican party. And by September, constant reading of a newspaper which came out for Willkie had brought him into line with others of his social group: *"Now that he (Willkie) has come out and said what he was for* — defense is the most important thing — I plan to vote for him . . . I also like his business program of trying not to interfere with business or burden business with taxes. *I have been reading the texts of Willkie's speeches* in the *Cleveland Plain Dealer.*"

Another way to trace the role of activation is to

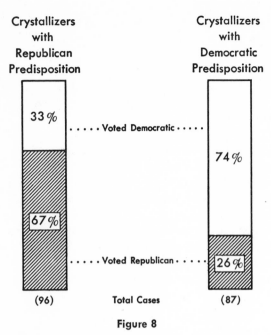

Figure 8

Predisposition to vote by final vote decision. Predisposition, as measured by the IPP scale, permits us to predict subsequent vote decisions of people who originally are undecided.

see how the same argument takes different forms for respondents of differing backgrounds. One of the slogans in favor of Willkie was that he represented the American ideal of the poor boy who made good. The following three quotations illustrate how Willkie became all things to all men:

Well-to-do Railroad Foreman, Retired: "He is a *business man* and that is what will most likely put the nation back on its feet. Roosevelt is all politician, and I wouldn't vote for anybody for a third term anyhow. . . ."

Poor Unemployed Musician: "Willkie is *for the poor people* . . . I have been reading how he was a poor farmer boy and worked for 75 cents a day tending cows and how he was for the poor people. He has got to be president of some big company just through hard work. . . ."

Well-to-do Woman Engaged in Farming: "I am against the third term and since reading Wilkie's life in the *Farm Journal* I am rather sure I will vote for him. I was waiting for both conventions

before deciding. I am greatly impressed by an article in the *Farm Journal* that Willkie started as a poor boy and now owns *four farms* valued at $88,000."

It seems, incidentally, that the social function of such stereotypes can be better understood in the light of the internal and subjective selection of influences. A campaign argument will be particularly successful if a variety of meanings can be read into it. From this picture of a man who started humbly and became successful any of three different elements may be brought to the fore: The poor people can feel that he will not have forgotten them, the rich people can be convinced that he will take care of their interests, and the middle-class voters can be attracted by the implications of hard work and thrift which are so prominent in their own ideology. One may speak of structured and unstructured stereotypes. The former are too well defined to be useful. The unstructured are catch-alls into which each voter reads the meanings he desires.

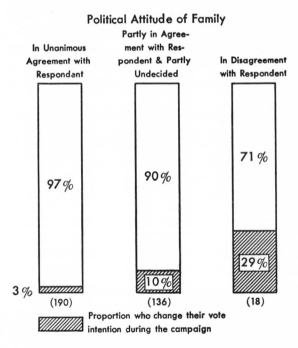

Figure 9

Variability in vote intentions by family homogeneity. The less homogeneous the family is with respect to their votes, the more the members of the family tend to change their minds.

71 Characteristics of Voters and Non-Voters*

Seymour Lipset

Political participation, like participation in other types of institutional behavior, varies with other social characteristics in predictable ways. These relationships are found in the United States and are very similar throughout the Western democracies.

Voting is the most commonly used index of political participation. To what extent does voting behavior reflect real political concern? To what extent does it indicate political effectiveness?

Patterns of voting participation are strikingly the same in various countries: Germany, Sweden, America, Norway, Finland, and many others for which we have data. Men vote more than women; the better educated, more than the less educated; urban residents, more than rural; those between 35 and 55, more than younger or older voters; married persons, more than unmarried; higher-

status persons, more than lower; members of organizations, more than non-members.[1] These differences are, however, narrowing in many countries, like Sweden, for example, especially in regard to age and sex differences.[2]

As an example of the character of these differences we may look at contemporary Germany where both regular sample surveys and a very large sample of the entire voting population taken in 1953 by the German Bureau of Statistics report consistent differences. Male voting in Germany increased with education and with income. Among farm owners and the self-employed 90 per cent voted in the previous election. The lower-paid among manual workers voted at a 78 per cent rate. Within each occupational category, the better-paid voted more. Also, when the workers

[1] The best single compendium and study of political participation is Herbert Tingsten, *Political Behavior: Studies in Election Statistics* (London: P. S. King & Son, 1937). A summary of generalizations on voting turnout.

[2] See Dankwart A. Rutow, *The Politics of Compromise* (Princeton: Princeton University Press, 1955), pp. 137–39. Since voting participation has steadily increased in Sweden from 1924 onward (from a low in that year of 58 per cent to a high in 1948 of almost 83 per cent), part of the decline of differences between groups is undoubtedly due to the increases in all groups rather than direct social influences on particularly low voting groups.

TABLE 1 *Social Characteristics Correlated with Voting Turnout*

HIGHER TURNOUT	LOWER TURNOUT
High income	Low income
High education	Low Education
Occupational groups:	Occupational groups:
Businessmen	Unskilled workers
White-collar employees	Servants
Government employees	Service workers
Commercial-crop farmers	Peasants, subsistence farmers
Miners	
Whites	Negroes
Men	Women
Middle-age people (35–55)	Young people (under 35)
Older people (over 55)	
Old residents in community	Newcomers in community
Workers in western Europe	Workers in United States
Crisis situations	Normal situations
Married people	Single
Members of organizations	Isolated individuals

TABLE 2 *Social Factors Affecting Rates of Voting Turnout*

1. The relevance of government policies to the individual:
   a. Dependence on government as one's employer
   b. Exposure to economic pressures requiring government action
   c. Exposure to government economic restrictions
   d. Possession of moral or religious values affected by government policies
   e. Availability of relevant policy alternatives
   f. General crisis situations
2. Access to information:
   a. Direct visibility of effects of government policies
   b. Occupational training and experience making for general insight
   c. Contact and communication
   d. Amount of leisure
3. Group pressure to vote:
   a. Underprivilege and alienation
   b. Strength of class political organization
   c. Extent of social contacts
   d. Group norms opposing voting
4. Cross-pressures
   a. Conflicting interests
   b. Conflicting information
   c. Conflicting group pressures

were considered by level of skill, fewer of the unskilled than the skilled and semi-skilled voted. These differences are significant in view of the unusual size of the samples.[3] They will be discussed later, in terms of the main social factors which seem to explain them best, but it may be noted here that many of the explanations for lower voting among the lower-status groups coincide with the various experiences associated with low-status occupations, that have been cited to account for authoritarian values.[4] In addition, many distinct factors rarely occur on the group level except in combination with others operating in the same direction. This makes the task of isolating causal variables difficult.

The small group of farm laborers in the national German sample was the most apathetic segment of the population. Many of the factors which will be singled out for analysis as separately tending to reduce the voting rate of a social group combine in the case of the farm laborers. They are generally less educated, under-privileged economically, socially isolated, and in close personal contact (especially in Germany, where the farmers are largely peasants, not large absentee landowners) with their employer. They are little exposed to the mass media, and few are members of unions or other voluntary organizations. In 1953, 48 per cent of the farm laborers interviewed were "indifferent" about the outcome of the election, as compared to 28 per cent of the urban manual workers and 16 per cent of the farm owners.[5]

[3] See Erich Reigrotski, Sozsale Verflechtungen in der Bundes-republik (Tubingen, J. C. B. Mohr, 1956), pp. 63–68 for these figures. See also Juan Lanz, The Social Bases of German Politics (Ph.D. dissertation, Department of Sociology, Columbia University, 1958).

[4] The effects of low status in creating authoritarian predispositions, as well as withdrawal and apathy, have been analyzed in Chap. IV, "Working-class Authoritarianism."

[5] See Juan Lanz, *op. cit.,* pp. 747 ff. The actual differences in voting in 1949 were much less since 75 per cent of the farm laborers voted as compared to 87 per cent of the farmers and 83 per cent of the nonfarm workers, but it is quite likely that in Germany there is a widespread feeling of moral obligation to vote, but not such a strong norm regarding interest in, or knowledge of, the candidates and the issues. On other measures of interest, the farm laborers were consistently lower than other occupational groups. A sample of 12,000 cases from five American national surveys found that

Thus, farm laborers and domestic workers are the social groups most likely to have an extremely low voting rate, and this is borne out by available data from many countries.

Some descriptive differences in voting turnout which have been located in a multitude of studies

---

service workers, subject to essentially the same conditions as the farm laborers, had the lowest voting rate (56 per cent). See G. M. Connelly and H. H. Field, "The Non-Voter, Who He Is, and What He Thinks," *Public Opinion Quarterly*, 8 (1944), pp. 175–87.

are listed in Table 1. The specific explanations for these differences may be summarized under four very general explanatory propositions. A group will have a higher rate of voting if (1) its interests are strongly affected by government policies; (2) it has access to information about the relevance of political decisions to its interests; (3) it is exposed to social pressures demanding voting; (4) it is not pressed to vote for different political parties. A further classification of these factors found in concrete social groups is presented in Table 2.

72 Alienation and Political Participation: Some Research Findings*

Fredric Templeton

In this study the author analyzes the political implications and consequences of the alienated individual. He shows that alienation has very little to do with whether a respondent identified himself as a Republican or as a Democrat. Attitudes toward Negroes, toward the community power structure (the political establishment), and toward the federal government are measured and examined. Particular attention is directed to contrasts between the situation at the national and at the local levels.

Political sociologists have long used alienation as one of their more important theoretical constructs. Different theorists have defined it in quite different ways, but, nonetheless, in one guise or another, alienation is a predictable element of most sociological and many psychological theories of political behavior. Furthermore, considerable recent work has been done on developing a consistent definition of alienation and on specifying

* From Fredric Templeton, "Alienation and Political Participation: Some Research Findings," *Public Opinion Quarterly*, Vol. 30 (Summer 1966) pp. 249–261. Copyright 1966 by Princeton University. Reproduced by permission.

empirical measures of particular types of alienation.

This paper reports findings from a local survey of 1960 voting behavior pertinent to the discussion of the ramified political consequences of alienation. We shall first present data indicating the influence of alienation upon the voting patterns of individuals in the 1960 national elections and upon their orientations toward the Federal government. These findings will then be compared with the orientations of individuals toward their local political system and their voting patterns on local political issues. From these comparisons we shall attempt to present a consistent discussion of the differential role played by alienation in conditioning individual political participation.

STUDY DESIGN

The data presented below were gathered in structured interviews with a probability sample of individuals living in Berkeley, California, between November 1 and November 7, 1960. The sample was initially designed for a study conducted by the California State Department of Public Health. From this initial sample of approximately 600 dwelling units, a sum sample of 250 randomly selected. Interviewers were instructed to contact the individuals living in the dwelling unit next door to the one included in the Department of Public Health sample. Each interviewer received an equal quota for male and female respondents. Three callbacks were required before the interviewer was permitted to interview a substitute respondent. Of the 240 interviews completed, 239 were usable.

Interviewers were drawn from a graduate-level research methods course given by the sociology department of the University of California. Each interviewer received extensive instruction in interviewing techniques prior to the collection of the data. Since approximately sixty interviewers were used, the distortion of findings attributable to the inadequacy of any particular interviewer was minimized. The degree to which the sample adequately represents the population of Berkeley can be suggested by a comparison of the two items included in both the survey and the 1960 United States *Census of Housing*. These two comparisons are presented in Table 1. In both cases the figures are within 4 percentage points of one another.

The measure of alienation used in this study was one version of Srole's Anomia Scale. Individuals who obtain a high anomia scale score may be considered alienated in the sense that they have indicated that they believe that their society is a pretty poor place to live. Furthermore, it seems unlikely that the present findings would be appreciably modified by using one of the other currently available measures of alienation. Previous research indicates that similar results are produced whether one uses Srole's scale or measures of "powerlessness," "political alienation," or "sense of political efficacy." [1] Even theoretically distinct types of alienation have been found to be both highly interrelated and similarly related to most important status variables.

TABLE 2 *Status and Alienation (in per cent)*

| Status Indicators | Alienation | | | |
	High	Low	Total	(N)
Race:				
Negro	76	24	100	(25)
White	39	61	100	(140)
Occupation:				
Manual	60	40	100	(40)
Nonmanual	31	69	100	(106)
Education:				
0–12 years	57	43	100	(51)
13–15 years	32	68	100	(31)
16 or more years	25	75	100	(64)
Class identification:				
Working or lower	58	42	100	(38)
Upper or middle	32	68	100	(100)
Interviewer's SES estimate:				
Lower 2 quartiles	53	47	100	(68)
Upper 2 quartiles	27	73	100	(78)

FINDINGS

Status. As in the case of every piece of research bearing upon the relationship, social status was found to be negatively related to alienation. This relationship held irrespective of the particular indicator of status used. As the figures in Table 2 indicate, individuals with high alienation scores were found disproportionately among Negroes,[2] manual workers, those with less than

TABLE 1 *A Comparison of Survey Estimates and Data from the 1960 United States Census of Housing (in per cent)*

	Survey (239)	Census (39,686)
Racial occupancy of Berkeley homes:		
White	82	78.1
Nonwhite	18	21.9
Total	100	100.0
Ownership of Berkeley homes:		
Home owned by occupant	48	44.0
Home rented by occupant	52	56.0
Total	100	100.0

Source: *U.S. Census of Housing: 1960, Vol. III, City Blocks*, Series HC(3), No. 26, Bureau of the Census, 1961.

[1] Compare findings presented in Meier and Bell, "Anomie and Differential Access in Achievement of Life Goals," *American Sociological Review*, Vol. 24, No. 2, 1962, pp. 189–201; Horton and Thompson, "Powerlessness and Political Socialism: A Study of Defeated Local Referendums," *American Journal of Sociology* 67, No. 5, 1962, pp. 485–493; and Angus Campbell, Gerald Guren, and Warren E. Miller, *The Voter Decides*, Evanston, Row, Peterson, 1954, pp. 187–194.

[2] Because of the very high level of alienation found among Negro respondents, they were excluded from further analysis. Thus subsequent findings are not biased by the inclusion of a large proportion of alienated Negroes in the blue-collar category.

a college education, those who identify with the working or lower classes, and those who were identified by interviewers as being in the lower two quartiles of socio-economic status. Furthermore, more detailed analysis indicated that the relationship of each of these indicators of status to alienation was partially independent of the effects of the others.[3] Therefore, subsequent tables will present figures separately for white-collar and blue-collar workers. This is an admittedly crude form of statistical control, but given the sample size it was as much as could be done.[4] Other background variables, such as age and sex, showed no consistent relationship to alienation independent of social status and will be ignored in the following discussion.[5]

National politics. At first glance, alienated respondents did not seem to differ materially from nonalienated respondents in terms of their national political behavior. Alienation had very little to do with whether a respondent identified himself as a Republican or a Democrat. It did not play a significant role in determining whether a respondent had voted for President Eisenhower or Governor Stevenson in 1956. Nor did it show any appreciable relationship to 1960 presidential voting intentions. These comparisons are presented in Table 3.

To say that alienation had little influence on

[3] Because of the sample size, these tests were far from exhaustive. Each indicator of status was related to alienation partially independently of each of the others taken separately.

[4] The tables presented below are very similar to those which would be produced were education substituted for occupation as a control variable. White-collar workers include all those employed in professional, semi-professional, managerial, proprietor, official, clerical, and sales occupations. Blue-collar workers include skilled, semi-skilled, and unskilled workers. Individuals with anomia scores of over 4 were classified as alienated. The findings are essentially the same, however, irrespective of the cutting point chosen for dichotomizing Srole's scale. The exclusion of Negroes, nonclassifiable occupations, and uncodeable alienation scores reduced the sample size to 146 respondents. Subsequent tabulations are based on that total, though the N's for each table will vary somewhat because of nonresponse. It need hardly be emphasized that the sample is very small for multivariate analysis and the findings must therefore be taken as tentative.

[5] This finding is also consistent with those of previous investigators. See, in particular, Meier and Bell, *op. cit.*

TABLE 3 *Social Class, Alienation, and National Political Behavior (in per cent)*

	Nonmanual Alienation		Manual Alienation	
	Low (73)	High (33)	Low (16)	High (24)
Democrats	39	34	53	50
Voted for Stevenson in 1956	37	33	44	50
Intend to vote for Kennedy in 1960	45	39	44	43

political identification and 1956 and 1960 presidential voting, is not, however, to say that alienation is irrelevant to national politics. In particular, it has been suggested that though the voting of alienated and nonalienated citizens is roughly similar, the quality of their participation, expressed by their voting, is distinctly different.[6] Irrespective of whether one is a Democrat or a Republican, he can perceive his electoral choice as either a vote for the more qualified and desirable candidate or a vote for the lesser of two evils. Thus, radically different stances toward the political process can produce reasonably similar results. According to Levin and Eden, an alienated "lesser evil" orientation toward voting is intimately related to a tendency to view politics in terms of morality rather than in terms of more traditional issues that divide the Republican and Democratic Parties. According to this interpretation, alienation is mobilized when an issue is defined in terms of good and evil.

Two simple agree-disagree items are pertinent to this distinction between "pragmatic" and "moralistic" issues. The first asked respondents whether they thought the Federal government should help pay teachers' salaries. The second item asserted: "High taxes are largely a matter of government corruption." The relationship between alienation and responses to each of these items is presented in Table 4.

[6] Murray B. Levin and Murray Eden, "Political Strategy for the Alienated Voter," *Public Opinion Quarterly,* Vol. 26, 1962, pp. 47–63. See also Murray B. Levin, *The Alienated Voter,* New York, Holt, Rinehart and Winston.

TABLE 4 *Social Class, Alienation, and Attitudes toward the Federal Government (in per cent)*

	Nonmanual Alienation		Manual Alienation	
	Low (73)	High (33)	Low (16)	High (24)
Agree that the Federal government should help pay teachers' salaries	29	36	44	54
Disagree with item reading: "High taxes are largely a result of government corruption"	88	67	88	54

The first item, which is both a partisan issue and very much a matter of practical politics, is only slightly related to alienation. The second, a blanket attribution of corruption to the Federal government, is strongly related to alienation. While it would be unwarranted to make sweeping generalizations on the basis of responses to two questions, these responses do suggest that alienation is reflected in emotional hostility toward the agencies of government and is not significant in the formulation of policy judgments. To the extent that national political decisions are defined in terms of specific policies and programs, we should expect to find it a relatively unsatisfactory avenue for the expression of alienated moral indignation. Under normal conditions, presidential elections provide an occasion for voting for specific policies and programs. Both major parties present themselves as "responsible" national voices and both are in fact committed to the established political system.[7] As such, neither provides the citizen with the opportunity to validate his personal rejection of the political system.

One predictable consequence of these characteristics of the national political process is the withdrawal of alienated citizens from political participation. Such withdrawal was evidenced in the data in a number of ways. A measure of political consistency was devised by combining responses to questions of party identification and 1956 and 1960 voting behavior. Republicans who voted for both Eisenhower and Nixon, together with Democrats who voted for both Stevenson and Kennedy, were compared to other respondents whose party voting pattern was, in one way or another, inconsistent. Alienated citizens contributed disproportionately to the inconsistent response patterns. On items designed to test respondents' knowledge of propositions to be included on the ballot, alienated respondents were consistently less likely to give correct responses than were nonalienated respondents. When asked how interested they were in politics, alienated respondents expressed little interest relative to the responses of nonalienated respondents. These data are presented in Table 5.

Within the middle class and the working class, alienated individuals tend to withdraw from poli-

[7] Unfortunately, it is still too early to determine whether or not the 1964 election constituted a partial exception to this generalization.

TABLE 5 *Social Class, Alienation, and Participation in the National Political Process (in per cent)*

	Nonmanual Alienation		Manual Alienation	
	Low (73)	High (33)	Low (16)	High (24)
Are party constant voters	66	45	75	54
Are high on political interest index	52	39	44	29
Are high on political knowledge index	52	18	44	12

TABLE 6   *Social Class, Alienation, and Attitudes
toward Negroes (in per cent)*

	Nonmanual Alienation		Manual Alienation	
	Low	High	Low	High
Think Negroes have too little voice in community affairs	36	18	25	12
Feel that Berkeley Negroes get a poorer education than Berkeley whites	28	9	25	8
Would favor or wouldn't mind having a qualified Negro on the school board	94	85	100	79
Disapprove of Southern sit-ins	25	44	19	50
(Number of cases)	(73)	(33)	(16)	(24)
Classified as "high" on index of support for improvements in Negro status	69	40	67	40
(Number of cases)	(68)	(30)	(15)	(20)

tics, in terms of both their knowledge and their interest, and to vacillate between parties in their voting behavior. These features of alienated political participation serve, in turn, to insulate the national political process from the impact of alienation.

Local politics. Social status has long been recognized as one of the more important determinants of the way individuals are integrated in their local community. Our data indicate that the effects of the class system upon orientations toward and participation in the local community are in part a function of alienation. Furthermore, as the tables to be presented below show, alienation influences various forms of community participation independently of social status.

First of all, the data clearly indicate that alienation is closely related to the stance an individual takes toward other types of individuals in his community. Four questions concerning Negroes were asked in the questionnaire. These items covered a broad range of attitudes toward Negroes. But despite the substantive differences among the items, all were strongly related to one another[8] and

similarly related to alienation. On the one hand, alienated white respondents are, relative to non-alienated respondents of the same social class position, inclined to evaluate the current status of Negro citizens as favorable. On the other hand, they are disinclined to support proposals to improve the position of the Negro and are disapproving of attempts of Negroes to improve their status through nonviolent direct action. Furthermore, as the data in Table 6 indicate, the difference in the attitudes of white-collar and blue-collar workers toward Negroes is almost entirely a function of alienation. Finally, if the four items are combined into a simple index of support for the improvement of Negro status, the findings remain essentially the same.[9]

---

[8] The following items were asked: "(1) A community like Berkeley is made up of many kinds of people. When it comes to deciding how things should be done here in Berkeley, would you say that Negroes have too much voice in what is done, too little voice, or just about the right amount? (2) Some people have said that Negro children in Berkeley do not get as good an education as white children. Do you agree or disagree with this view? (3) Some people have said that there ought to be a Negro on the school board. Would you be in favor of having a qualified Negro on the school board? (4) The newspapers have carried accounts of 'sit-ins' by Negroes at lunch counters in the South. Do you approve of their actions, disapprove of them, or haven't you heard about them?" Using Guttman procedures and the same conventions used in constructing the anomia scale, these items yielded a coefficient of reproduceability of 0.91.

[9] This finding — which shows the relationship between social class and attitudes toward Negroes is almost entirely interpreted by alienation — holds irrespective of the choice of cutting points used for either the alienation index or the Negro support index. It holds whether oc-

TABLE 7 *Social Class, Alienation, and Acceptance of the Prevailing Community Power Structure*

| Group | % Saying Group Has about the Right Amount of Voice in How Things Are Done in Berkeley | | | |
| | Nonmanual Alienation | | Manual Alienation | |
	Low (73)	High (33)	Low (16)	High (24)
University Professors	53	24	63	21
People living on hill	58	36	69	38
Jews	58	46	63	33
Labor unions	45	27	56	29
Negroes	44	30	56	29
Rich people	59	39	63	46
Downtown businessmen	48	36	56	33
Working people	51	36	63	46
Catholics	55	49	63	50

The negativism that seems to be expressed by alienated respondents in their answers to questions concerning Negroes is paralleled by a dissatisfaction with the power and influence exercised by other groups in the community. Each respondent was asked to evaluate the role played by various types of people in determining how things were done in Berkeley.[10] The list of types included university professors, people living on the "hill," Jews, labor unions, Negroes, rich people, downtown businessmen, working people, and Catholics. Table 7 shows the proportion of respondents who felt that each of these "groups" had about the right amount of voice in community affairs.[11] Respond-

ents with low alienation scores were consistently more likely to be satisfied with the voice of other persons in the community than were those with high scores. This was true for every group compared and for manual and nonmanual workers alike.

If the items presented in Table 7 are combined into an index, it can be used to measure the extent to which respondents are generally satisfied with the distribution of power among the various groups about whom questions were asked. This procedure reduces the effects of idiosyncratic evaluations of the various groups stemming from the relationship between that group and the respondent. It provides us with a measure, albeit crude, of the respondent's level of acceptance of what he perceived to be the community power structure. This procedure reveals that alienated respondents are much more unlikely to accept the community power structure: 36 per cent of highly alienated nonmanual workers scored 7 or more on the power structure index, as compared with 64 per cent of those low in alienation; the comparable percentages for manual workers are 27 and 60. As was the case for attitudes toward Negroes, social-class differences in the acceptance of community power structure are almost entirely attributable to the intervening influence of alienation. Alienation, in either its middle-class or its working-class manifestation, is related to the rejection of the prevailing distribution of power and influence within the community.

In addition to markedly influencing the orientation of the individual toward others in his community and toward the structure of community power, alienation has a strong impact upon patterns of local voting. Respondents were questioned on their vote on three local political issues: (1) a proposal to add fluorides to the water supply, which had been defeated in June 1960, some five months before our study; (2) a proposal to authorize the school board to float bonds for local educational improvements, which had been narrowly defeated in June 1960; and (3) a measure

cupation or education is used as an indicator of social status. It is consistent with relationships previously reported between Srole's scale and negative attitudes toward Jews. Leo Srole, "Social Integration and Certain Corrolaries: An Exploratory Study," *American Sociological Review*, Vol. 22, No. 6, 1956, pp. 709–716; and Edward L. McDill, "Anomie, Authoritarianism, Prejudice, and Socio-economic Status: An Attempt at Clarification," *Social Forces*, Vol. 39, March 1961, pp. 239–245.

[10] The question was the first one quoted in note 23. It was asked separately for each of the groups mentioned in the text.

[11] A number of tables, not presented here, indicate that social-group affiliations determine whether one thinks specific others have too much voice (positive dissatisfac-

tion) or too little voice (negative dissatisfaction), but that both positive and negative dissatisfaction are in large measure a function of alienation. For this reason, we shall restrict our discussion to responses indicating satisfaction with the influence exercised by others.

TABLE 8 *Social Class, Alienation, and Local Political Behavior (in per cent)*

	Nonmanual Alienation		Manual Alienation	
	Low (73)	High (33)	Low (16)	High (24)
Favor the proposed tax measure	78	49	69	42
Voted for defeated school tax measure	55	27	25	21
Voted for defeated fluoridation measure	55	36	25	17

to increase the school tax rate, which had been narrowly passed in November 1960. Data on responses to these items are presented in Table 8.

Among white-collar workers, there is a strong relationship between alienation and voting on each of the three issues. Among blue-collar workers there is no appreciable relationship between alienation and reported past voting, but a very strong relationship between alienation and vote intentions. In distinct contrast to national voting, local voting is strongly — though not altogether consistently — affected by alienation.

DISCUSSION

The data presented above suggest that the stability of American politics is not merely a result of popular satisfaction with the American political system: while comparative data on alienation are not yet available, we can say with some assurance that there are sizable pockets of discontent within American society. The stability of the political system seems to rest more upon the absence of institutionalized channels through which discontent can be effectively expressed. When channels for effective and alienated participation do open, as in the rise of the late Senator McCarthy, or in the current activities of the John Birch Society, they typically open outside institutionalized avenues of political participation. This is almost necessarily true given the extent to which the American party system militates against the emergence of successful minor parties. Understandably, this absence of adequate and appropriate channels of participation is reflected in vacillation between the major parties and in withdrawal from the political process.

In this context, it is important to stress the difference between the role played by alienation in national and in local politics. Unlike national politics, local political systems maximize both the access and the potential impact of interested individual citizens. To the extent that local political systems are democratic in terms of the increased potential for individual participation, they provide their alienated constituents an avenue for expression. The Athenian model of political democracy de-emphasized the political importance of structurally based social inequality by assuming that the citizen accepts duly instituted rules of political procedure and uses political participation to pursue rationally political aims that the system deems legitimate. Our data suggest that the uses to which political participation is put are considerably more varied than would be expected on the basis of classical democratic theory. Indeed, there is reason to believe that a democratic system of participation increases the possibility for participation based upon the individual's hostility to and rejection of that system.

CHAPTER NINE

The Sociological Enterprise

We approach the end of our journey along some of sociology's pathways. Our objective has been to survey the terrain of the whole field rather than to focus on certain areas for a more detailed examination. For this reason we have traveled at fair speed along the main highways and, except for brief changes of scenery, have avoided numerous detours, dead ends, and rocky trails where much of the major road-building is in progress. Yet we hope the reader has gained more than a superficial conception of the giant freeways being constructed through the mountains, chasms, and dense jungles of man's social experience. The planning, building, and re-building of such freeways are the main tasks of sociology.

In charting the course of science, we have perhaps neglected many alternative pathways that have been forged by religion, morality, tradition, the humanities, and other systems of social engineering. Science must come to terms with these alternatives, and the attempt to link the systems involves problems as great as any we face.

Indeed, many observers have serious doubts about the competence and the relevance of science in the field of social engineering. However, such a harsh judgment is not warranted, we feel, because science has never been given a fair trial in this field. True, public agencies employ many scientists, but their chief assignment, for the most part, is to develop information pertaining to programs and policies that are formulated, implemented, and evaluated by criteria that have little connection with the framework of science. The collection and analysis of information is a necessary but not sufficient condition for scientific enterprise. Unless the information leads to the construction and corroboration of contestable theories, we have no science. And it is apparent that contestable theories are often regarded with suspicion by the officials responsible for managing public affairs.

Consider, for example, the way decisions are legitimated in the process of government. Many of our programs and policies had their origins in the industrial revolution. For generations their legitimacy was judged by their influence upon the private economy. Even today cost is often a primary consideration, and it is in fact economy, rather than any demonstrated superiority with respect to case outcome, that encourages the use of community services instead of institutional confinement in the treatment of deviant behavior, disability, and health problems in general.

The great depression proved that policies which are economically unwise may sometimes be politically advantageous. This encouraged separation of governmental and economic institutions and furthered the development of distinctly political criteria of legitimacy. Today government operates largely under a model of *consent* and *consensus.* Its programs and policies are called legitimate if they enjoy the support of the community's members, especially of those individuals and groups that are most immediately concerned. Accordingly, the ballot and the opinion poll threaten to displace the dollar as the chief determinants of political legitimacy.

Elections and polls may provide reliable indicators of the extent to which certain programs and policies receive public endorsement, but as guides to social engineering, they have some disadvantages. One problem is that opinion, even unanimous opinion, may be in error on questions of fact. This means that the long-range value of consensus depends upon the degree to which the community is informed on the relevant issues. Moreover, the attempt to inform runs the risk of creating dissent, and there is a question whether an informed disagreement has preference over an uninformed consensus, especially in the views of political leaders.

Another problem is the capricious character of opinion. On numerous issues, conflicting opinions may have approximately equal public support, many persons may be undecided or lacking a position, and rather drastic shifts of opinion may occur in response to changing conditions. Sometimes it may be easier for leaders to induce changes in people's opinions than it is to revise their policies or commitments.

When an attempt to regulate opinion is sensed by the community's members, the result may be a "credibility gap." Despite the complaint that government officials may "manage" the news, however, nurturing community opinion is a goal of numerous organizations. Among the purveyors of information in democratic societies, the mass media are perhaps the most powerful. But their diverse materials are often uncontested, because they tend to come from unchallenged "eyewitnesses," "authorities," and "confidential sources." Such unsubstantiated pronouncements may contribute little to the kind of valid and tested knowledge needed for a public to be well informed.

In addition, consent and consensus are not always achieved on a community-wide basis. More often the agreements are restricted to members of well-organized groups. And these special-interest groups can frequently circumvent or dominate public opinion in the determination of governmental policies. For the last thirty years, according to the opinion polls, more than 80 per cent of the adult population of the United States has favored a law requiring that the owners of firearms be registered by the government. Such legislation was nevertheless successfully resisted by an association of riflemen until 1968 when Congress, after the assassination of several national leaders, took some preliminary steps toward the control of shoulder weapons. There are many similar examples of the impotence of public opinion when it is confronted by well-organized special-interest groups.

The above discussion suggests that the consent model is in many ways inimical to science. In these respects it is similar to other models that have also been employed in government. Among the other authoritarian models is that of *divine rights,* in which the right to rule is uncontested, and the *power* model, which assumes that people act selfishly in their own interests to the limit of their capabilities. All these models tend to conceal rather than to reveal the assumptions involved in political programs. They seem to encourage a style of action in which goals are stated in nonspecific and ambiguous terms, controversies are minimized, and pro-

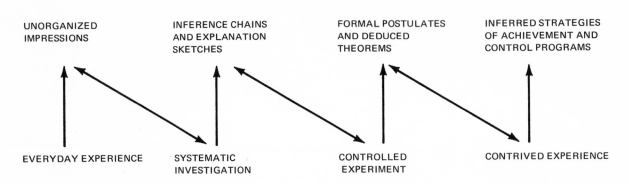

| CASUAL OBSERVATION | INFORMAL THEORY | FORMAL THEORY | APPLIED THEORY |

KINDS OF CONCEPTS

| COMMONSENSE TERMS | CONVENTIONAL DEFINITIONS AND OPERATIONALIZED VARIABLES | ABSTRACT THEORETICAL CONCEPTS | SOCIAL GOALS, OBJECTIVES, AND RELEVANT VALUES |

ASSUMPTIONS AND RELATIONSHIPS

| UNORGANIZED IMPRESSIONS | INFERENCE CHAINS AND EXPLANATION SKETCHES | FORMAL POSTULATES AND DEDUCED THEOREMS | INFERRED STRATEGIES OF ACHIEVEMENT AND CONTROL PROGRAMS |

| EVERYDAY EXPERIENCE | SYSTEMATIC INVESTIGATION | CONTROLLED EXPERIMENT | CONTRIVED EXPERIENCE |

Figure 1

Stages in the development and use of knowledge. Research and experimentation leads to the development of applied theory which enables man to control his environment and regulate his experience by rational means.

grams are compromised in order to nullify the potential opposition of various groups and organizations.

Science, by contrast, deals only with corrigible assumptions or theories that can be contested and corrected. It demands clearly defined problems, rational strategies, and an empirical basis for their assessment. It can answer few questions, but answer them well; while consensus provides a mechanism for answering nearly all questions, though perhaps with a lesser degree of certitude.

It follows that the recent marriage between science and government has not been a harmonious one. Many governmental officials feel that scientists are insensitive to public sentiment, that their methods are often impractical and likely to foster dissent among the voters, and that their demand for conclusive evidence tends to impede rather than stimulate, needed social action. Conversely, the scientists often feel that government's procedures are designed to protect the interests of the political establishment instead of speeding the development of needed knowledge, that they alleviate the symptoms of social problems instead of getting at basic causes, and that they restrict the scientist's role to that of a technician who is told which problems to investigate and which kinds of solutions to pursue. Neither side has enough understanding of the other's objectives and methods to produce an effective division of labor, and one result of inefficiency in their joint efforts is mutual disenchantment.

A better dialogue between science and government is essential for these systems to be linked more effectively. Their objectives are different, since science strives for an understanding of events that occur, and politics seeks the consensus and motivation that enable people to convert understanding into achievement. These differences encourage system linkages instead of discouraging them. For example, the science of politics is a distinct and rapidly growing field of inquiry, as is the politics of science. Future linkages will no doubt depend upon the growth of such mixed disciplines.

Moreover, these disciplines develop knowledge and understanding in a remarkably similar manner. They begin with casual observations and commonsense judgments, and proceed to the construction and corroboration of abstract theories. They search for technical advancements and social inventions which allow their theories to be used as guides to the conduct of everyday affairs, whether in the field of science or government. Application of theoretical knowledge produces significant changes in man's environment and his experiences. In this way the natural systems of the past are transformed into the contrived systems of the future (see Figure 1).

Each system must learn the boundaries of its own jurisdiction and the problems involved in coordinating activities at the points of intersection with other systems. Science must learn to do research within the context of a political system, to speak forcefully when the evidence justifies a certain conclusion, and to remain silent when such evidence is lacking. Government must learn that knowledge cannot be legislated into existence and that there are no substitutes for conceptual and empirical analysis in assessing rational strategies. Above all, it must learn how to operate under uncertain conditions, to make tentative decisions in the absence of adequate information, and to retain sufficient flexibility in implementing these decisions so that appropriate changes in policy can occur in response to new information and knowledge. Other systems, of course, have similar linkage problems which must be resolved if society is to learn how to utilize diversity for beneficial purposes.

SOCIOLOGICAL PERSPECTIVE

73   Sociology's Perspective*

Alan P. Bates

The discipline of sociology, as we have seen, is characterized by a set of concepts, certain assumptions concerning their relationships, and some distinctive methods for testing the assumptions so as to facilitate the explanation of social events. The following selection summarizes some of the concepts and assumed relationships in order to clarify the sociological viewpoint, in this way providing a synopsis of much of the material in this book.

In what main ways is the sociological perspective different from those found in psychology, anthropology, and political science? How do scientific and moralistic perspectives differ? What are the prospects for a rapprochement between science and ethics?

SOCIOLOGY'S PERSPECTIVE

Sociology overlaps its sister fields in many ways, but, like each of them, it has a distinctive orientation toward its subject matter. Most broadly and fundamentally, it is concerned with how human social behavior is organized and how this organization changes over time. Just now these words may convey little meaning, or may have a deceptive simplicity, but they state the case for what is unique in the point of view of sociology. The key words in this statement are "social behavior," "organization," and "change."

Social Behavior

As a specialist, the sociologist is not interested in all behavior which affects and is affected by other people, only in that which is interpersonally relevant. Social behavior, a very inclusive notion, refers to all behavior meeting this criterion. Quite a few specialists are interested in social behavior, so we must push further in order to grasp the sociologist's particular concern. We come close to the heart of the matter by stating that the sociologist is chiefly interested in being able to make *general* statements about social behavior — that under such-and-such circumstances a given kind of behavior is likely to occur. Inkeles puts it well in saying that the primary concern of the sociologist is "in the study of those aspects of social life which are present in all social forms." [1]

Such a statement means that the sociologist is interested in such things as the organization of American cities, the way in which power is distributed in groups, the relationship between masculine and feminine roles, the factors which produce conforming and deviating behavior, the ways in which change is induced or resisted (not to mention many other problems, of course). By the same token he is not, as a specialist, concerned with the Boston Tea Party, the Wagner Labor Relations Act, the family life of the American president, a quarrel between two young lovers of his acquaintance, or the personality of his mother-in-law.

We must be as clear as possible about this. In its purest form the sociological frame of reference does not take into account the idiosyncrasies of single persons or of separate historical occurrences. Or, looking at an individual case from this perspective, it will be seen as a single instance of a more general class of similar instances, deviating to a greater or lesser extent from the characteristics of the class. In other words, sociology is or aspires to be a generalizing science. In this it is like many other sciences. Human physiology is not the physiology of a single organism but of a

---

* Reprinted from Alan P. Bates, *The Sociological Enterprise*. Boston: Houghton Mifflin Co., 1966, pp. 4–13. Reproduced by permission.

[1] A. Inkeles, *What Is Sociology?* Foundations of Modern Sociology Series. Englewood Cliffs, N.J.: Prentice-Hall, 1964, p. 16.

class of organisms, and the characteristics of the class do not precisely describe all the attributes of a single case. As a science psychology is not concerned with the behavior of one particular human, but with that of classes of humans *seen as individuals*. The sociologist also is interested in the behavior of people, but only that behavior which links people together, at a level at which he can generalize about classes of such behavior.

Here is an example of a sociological generalization: "In American cities there is an inverse relation between the incidence of reported crime and distance from the center of the city." Note that there is no reference to any particular city, no mention of which persons actually commit crimes, or what kinds of personalities they have, only a statement of the relation between a condition and a class of social behavior. Here is another. "The higher the rank of a person within a group, the more nearly his activities conform to the norms of the group."[2] Again, no particular group is mentioned, the nature of the norms is not specified, and the many differences among group members are ignored.

When one first encounters the sociological perspective and begins to grasp its nature, an initial reaction may be that it omits one of the most important things about human behavior: that which is unique in each occurrence and in each person. Actually, the sociologist does not mean to belittle in any way such elements in human experience. In his personal life he is as sensitive to them as is anyone else. He does argue that there is a level of human behavioral organization, the social level, which is of enormous importance, and about which it is possible to develop a generalizing science which deliberately ignores the individual case in order to be able to discover how human behavior is socially organized.

Social Organization

The sociologist is interested in organized social behavior. Put very generally, this means that behavior which links together individuals or groups

[2] G. C. Homans, *The Human Group*. New York: Harcourt, Brace, 1950, p. 141. This is Homans' famous "rank-conformity" hypothesis, which stimulated much research and discussion subsequent to its publication.

of individuals is not random or haphazard. It has the properties of orderliness, pattern, repetitiveness, hence predictability. Here is a college classroom. During a particular semester at nine o'clock each morning, Monday through Friday, the room is filled with college students. Each goes without hesitation to a certain chair. A minute or two later a professor enters, stands at the front of the classroom, facing the students, and begins to talk. Most of the students write in notebooks. A few whisper covertly to one another. At the end of fifty minutes a bell rings, the professor ends his comments, the students close their notebooks, and all leave the room. We have here an identification and short description of an instance of *social* organization even though it does not use the technical language of sociology. It is clear that the behavior of these persons with respect to each other is patterned. This is true even though there are minor variations in the specific sequence of actions from one class meeting to the next. Our example includes no information about the psychological characteristics of students or teacher; it does not even mention the nature of the course, or whether it is advanced or elementary. We recognize a single specimen of a large class of social situations having a familiar kind of social organization which, by the way, significantly channels a good deal of human activity.

It is the *pattern of interdependent behavior* which interests the sociologist. This is the kind of unit he studies, not the individuals who participate in the pattern. He knows perfectly well that there are important differences between the class members and that from the viewpoint of another model, say, the psychological, these differences would be of first importance. But not for the sociologist. What is crucial for him is that all these persons, *despite their differences,* behave with respect to each other in an orderly, predictable fashion. Furthermore, he is not at all surprised to find that the patterned behavior of the people in this class closely resembles that of innumerable other classes, each with its own set of "unique" personalities and other special characteristics. Without knowing anything of the attributes of individuals in a given class he can know a good deal about how people will behave in this category of situations precisely because such settings are socially organized. True, he can't say a great deal about the psychological organization of individual students from knowledge of this kind of social organization. But by the same token, we cannot learn much about the social structure of college classrooms from the summated personality characteristics of college students. These are simply different levels of behavioral organization, interdependent to be sure, but not the same.

The order the sociologist sees in the social life of men is not perfect. Evidence of organization is sought in the pattern and predictability of actual behavior, but it is always true that some of the behavior in every situation does not fit the pattern and conform to the prediction. Similarly, if organization is described in cultural terms, it will be found that there is seldom, perhaps never complete agreement among all the actors on what behavior is called for in a particular real-life drama. There may even be radical disagreement on the cultural prescriptions. On the other hand, the fact that a group exists at all testifies that it is to some degree socially organized. Social organization is a "more or less" matter, and the sociologist is interested in differences in the degree of organization and the consequences for understanding behavior.

Social Change

The general statement about the sociological outlook made a few pages back indicated that this orientation is concerned not only with stability in social life but also with change. Consider the college classroom illustration again. It is possible to describe this situation as though there were no time dimension, and the sociologist often does this when he is primarily concerned with revealing the "structural" characteristics of a social situation. So we say that the classroom is organized so that the students sit in orderly rows facing the front of the room, each student occupying a particular spot in the arrangement. The instructor faces them, standing at the front. Interaction flows between the students and the instructor for the most part, with little student-student communication; students show more deference to the teacher than vice versa; and so on.

Such a description has a static quality. The fact is that what we see as social organization only

becomes manifest with the passage of time, as was better suggested in our first reference to the classroom. First event takes place, then that. We say there is organization and structure because the *sequence* of events is repetitive and predictable. The next session of the class will correspond closely to this one. Paradoxically, one form of change is a kind of absence of change. Since the pattern of events repeats itself over and over, we can observe change only as we watch the unfolding of a single manifestation of a pattern which itself does not alter.

A more familiar notion of change as applied to social organization involves some alteration in the patterned character of social behavior. The *pattern* is different, and presumably will not return to its former state. In a strict sense even very stable social organizations always undergo at least minor alterations through time. Our hypothetical college class will not have quite the same social organization ten weeks after its first session even though the main features of the structure appear to be the same. Similarly, on a larger scale, college classes in general are conducted somewhat differently today than their "sociological ancestors" were two or three generations ago.

Sociologists are interested in both cross-sectional, structural approaches to social phenomena and in time-dimensional, change approaches. Neither is inherently more important than the other. Both present fundamental problems to the discipline. The stability of social life and the inevitable accompanying change are taken for granted by laymen, but to sociologists they are a Janus-faced mystery that forever challenges.

THE SCOPE OF SOCIOLOGICAL INTEREST

The sociologist's interest in the general characteristics of all social behavior can take him into the study of any particular manifestation: economic, political, religious, educational, aesthetic, or any other. Also, for him the entire social world is subdivisible into innumerable progressively smaller units. For instance, the United States constitutes for him a single social structure, so incredibly complex that the social sciences cannot very adequately describe it at their present stage of development. Included within this single structure are a number of major social institutions, each a smaller social world within the larger. Below the institutional level are hundreds of thousands of organizations and associations of varying size and complexity. Still lower down the scale of size and complexity are millions upon millions of small, relatively informal, and transient face-to-face groups, each containing sub-groups. Finally, there are, in astronomically large numbers, single social acts, which can, if desired, be abstracted from context for analysis.

As a discipline sociology is interested in this whole range of social organization, as manifested in every sector of society and at every level of size and complexity. Furthermore, it is concerned with the interdependence of organization among different sectors and levels. In physical science man is interested in the features of the planet earth, but recognizes that part of his understanding of earth depends upon recognition that it is part of the solar system. Hence, the solar system is a level of organization of matter and energy worth studying too. But the solar system is part of a still larger organization known as a galaxy, and the galaxy of which our solar system is a part is only one among incredibly large numbers of other galaxies, all of which respond to some larger order of organization. In the social life of man, too, there are worlds within worlds, and while there is a rough inverse relation between size and complexity, the sociologist has learned to have a most healthy respect for the complexity of even the smallest and seemingly most simple unit of social organization.

It is worth stressing that sociology is concerned with all forms of organized social behavior. One sociologist, to be sure, may be interested only in the study of large, formal organizations, another in the structure of communities, a third in family disorganization. Specialization is as inevitable here as in other fields of knowledge. But the general viewpoint of sociology excludes no arena in which organized social behavior is found, and by the same token, the general viewpoint of the discipline will inform the specialized research of any true sociologist. This means that the importance or visibility of a phenomenon as a layman would see it is no criterion of its sociological interest. The discipline is interested in events where decisions of huge importance are weighed, but just as interested in homely, seemingly trivial, and commonplace events of everyday life. It is committed to the study of behavior that society judges deviant, bizarre, "bad," such as crime, alcoholism, and far-out religious cults, but no more so than to the analysis of conforming, normal, "good" behavior.

Culture

When the sociologist looks at his subject matter he makes a distinction between the social organization of people's actual conduct and the organization of people's ideas of what that behavior should be. This relationship is of utmost importance to him. A great deal of what social scientists call "culture" is made up of widely diffused ideas which either bear directly on social behavior or have indirect implications for actual behavior. While sometimes made a matter of written record, these ideas are crucially located in the minds of living people. It is not necessary to introduce the culture concept to readers of this book, but it is important in thinking about the sociological perspective to gain a general idea of how scholars in this discipline relate culture to actual conduct.

An analogy with helpful possibilities for our problem utilizes the drama. Culture is like the script of a play. Actors in a conventional play memorize the script before they go out onto the stage. Their performance each time the play is given may vary slightly from all previous performances. Nevertheless, what they *do* before their audience is always closely related to the script. In life, as we play out our parts in groups and organizations each of us performs according to a pre-existing script.

As analogies go this one isn't bad. It sets us thinking in the right direction, although like all analogies it is potentially misleading. For instance, there is the question of authorship. No single dramatist wrote the script of culture. It evolved through thousands of years, written by millions of persons, constantly undergoing modification and, in some respects, growth. Another difference lies in the attitude of the actor toward the play. Some actors, it is said, can temporarily immerse themselves completely in their parts, but by and large we may be sure that actors *know they are acting.* Most of the time in everyday life we are not aware of the degree to which social behavior is guided along the lines dictated by culture. Others besides sociologists and anthropologists, of course, sometimes achieve insights into this state of affairs, but such awareness is an essential part of the sociological perspective.

The analogy is imperfect in other respects too. Most plays (omitting some experimental variations in the contemporary theater) do not allow a great deal of latitude to the actor, at least insofar as speech is concerned. Variations in actual performance are likely to reflect the actor's skill in recreating the dramatist's intentions without departing from his written directions. But culture is not so restrictive on the ordinary actions of men. The script may occasionally be quite precise (the traditions for the inauguration of the American president), but more typically it gives only general instructions to the actors on the real life stage. Plenty of room is left for innovations, intended or inadvertent.

Finally, dramas in the conventional theater do not evolve out of the experience of the actors, whereas culture does. To the sociologist there is a complex interdependence between culture and social action. From one point of view, he seeks in culture some of the most important causes of human behavior. At the same time he also regards culture as a product or outcome of social behavior. In other words, even as the actors play out their parts according to the plan of the script they are by their very performance changing the script. In order to grasp the point it may be helpful to try to imagine a human group in which the social behavior of members is wholly unguided by any shared understandings of the situation and the kinds of action which are appropriate. It is extremely difficult to do so. Most groups which appear at first glance to be unstructured (such as many newly-formed groups) are only relatively so. Their members quickly discover that they agree enough on what behavior is called for to begin the development of a more explicit organization.

Culture both gives direction to on-going behavior and at the same time arises out of it. Speaking of norms (as a part of culture) Homans puts it this way:

If we can think of a norm as a goal that a group wishes to reach, we can see that the goal is not set up, like the finish line of a race, before the race starts, but rather that the group decides, after it starts running, what the finish line will be. Once the norm is established, it exerts a back effect on the group.[3]

Some degree of order and predictability in human behavior, both individually and collectively, is so critically important as to be a prerequisite for survival. We observe that in any situation in which individuals interact they will ordinarily do so in ways already organized for them by the culture they have collectively brought into the situation, and, where necessary, they will create new standardized ways of coping with one another and the environment. Culture as the arbiter of what is fitting and necessary in behavior and behavior itself are irrevocably intertwined, each a function of the other, each a source of both stability and change in the other. As it is sometimes put, the two are in a state of dynamic tension. Overt social behavior is never wholly determined by culture and its departures from the script may ultimately alter the script itself. Yet behavior cannot escape the modelling influence of culture.

[3] Homans, *op. cit.,* p. 126.

SCIENCE AND SOCIETY

74 The Transition to Science in Human Relations*

George A. Lundberg

In this selection George A. Lundberg, long an advocate of scientific sociology, makes a dramatic and provocative plea for social science by outlining some of its accomplishments and potentialities. He contends that the price we have to pay to further the cause of science includes the modification of provincial language usage and the destruction of moralistic interpretations of events. He suggests that accurate scientific knowledge is acquired through empirical demonstrations which are independent of the personal preferences of the research worker. If the results of an investigation are influenced by the social or political allegiances of the worker, then the methods employed are unreliable. The scientist develops research techniques that eliminate bias. A research project contributes to knowledge to the extent that its findings are consistently obtained whenever the study is repeated.

What have social scientists contributed to modern life that might increase public interest and confidence in research? How do these contributions compare with those of physical scientists? What are some of the prerequisites for a more effective social science in contemporary society?

Our technological developments and our methods of communication have resulted in a fundamental interdependence which dominates our

* Excerpt from George A. Lundberg, *Can Science Save Us?* New York, David McKay Company, Inc., 1961. Used by permission of the author and the publisher. (Copyright 1947, 1961, by George A. Lundberg.)

lives. This state of affairs requires, as we shall see, that we bring our social arrangements into line with this basic technological pattern, rather than vice versa. This basic technological pattern unquestionably rests upon natural science. On this ground, rather than on any assumption of absolute or intrinsic superiority of science as a philosophy of life, I think the following conclusion is inescapable: in our time and for some centuries to come, for better or for worse, the sciences, physical and social, will be to an increasing degree the accepted point of reference with respect to which the validity (Truth) of all knowledge is gauged.

If we accept this conclusion, then a number of questions arise. (1) What are some examples of what the social sciences have done or might do in furthering sound and orderly adjustments in human relations? (2) What are some of the requirements and the costs of a transition to a social order in which science is the final court of appeal? (3) What would be the effect of such a transition upon democratic institutions?

What are some examples of types of work by social scientists that are of vast importance in managing human relations?

When we speak of "types of work" by social scientists, we are obviously announcing an undertaking so large as to prevent even a summary within the confines of this book. There are at least five well-recognized social sciences, and if we use the larger category of "behavioral science," the number rises to twelve or more. The social sciences are well recognized, in the sense that they are firmly established as departments in nearly all leading universities and colleges as well as in professional, industrial, and governmental circles. Every year over a hundred journals publish hundreds of research reports of studies large and small, designed to yield new knowledge or to test and refine previous conclusions and to predict behavior under stipulated conditions. We shall confine ourselves to a few illustrations selected chiefly because they are individually of interest to more than one of the social sciences.

The work of such agencies as the Census Bureau is known to all and is more or less taken for granted. Without the data and the analyses which it provides, the administration of public affairs would certainly dissolve in chaos and perhaps in civil war. It is equally certain that no international organization can function without an elaborate organization of this kind to provide the essential facts regarding people and their characteristics and activities. Perhaps the most permanently valuable contribution of the ill-fated League of Nations was its establishment of an international statistical bureau which managed to survive until taken over by the larger information agencies of the United Nations. The Office of Population Research at Princeton University has engaged in detailed studies of local and international population trends in various parts of the world and has predicted the future areas of population pressure. This knowledge is of the utmost practical importance in the administration of national and international organization of any kind. The Scripps Foundation, the Milbank Memorial Fund, and many others are engaged in similar or related work of a character that measures up very well to the standards of the physical sciences.

Social scientists have also been prominent in pointing out one of the most serious of the world's problems, namely, overpopulation. As a result of the drastic decline in the death rate resulting from the application of medical science, world population is increasing at an unprecedented rate. For example, although it took thousands of years for the human species to reach the number of one billion of living people (about 1830), it required only one century to add the second billion. It is now taking less than thirty-five years for the world population to add a third billion — probably before 1965. The United Nations' population experts estimate that it will take only fifteen years to add a fourth billion, and another ten years to add the fifth billion if present rates continue. The idea that any expansion of the food supply could do more than temporarily alleviate the starvation of people under such rates of population increase is merely a confusion of wishful thinking with stern realities.

Reliable and objective knowledge of other peoples and cultures constitutes another field in which social scientists have made distinguished contributions. This knowledge has thrown a flood of light on our own civilization and permits the formulation and test of hypotheses regarding human behavior patterns in general. The Human Relations Area Files contain, systematically filed and indexed, virtually all present reliable knowledge regarding about two hundred cultures. If a researcher happens to be interested in some subject, as, for example, divorce, crime, education, law (and about a thousand other topics), in other cultures, he can go to one of the twenty or more libraries which subscribe to the File, and find all the known information on any or all of these subjects for each of about two hundred cultures. The information is neatly filed away, a separate drawer for each subject. Information scattered in hundreds of books in a library can be secured in a few hours from the File. The importance of this kind of knowledge and its ready availability in facilitating our contacts with people of other lands and cultures became very evident during and after World War II.

We mentioned the importance of instruments and methods of observation and measurement in the social as well as in the physical sciences. Social scientists have produced revolutionary developments in this field in the last thirty years. Thousands of such instruments have been invented by means of which vocational aptitudes, success in college and other undertakings, and social behavior of great variety can be accurately measured and predicted. Instruments and scales for the measurement of attitudes have opened vast new fields for investigation.

Perhaps the best known, but by no means the only one, of these devices is the public opinion poll. We have in this technique an illustration of how a development in the social sciences may be as significant for the future of social organizations as many physical inventions have been in our industrial development. The mechanisms by which the "public will" can make itself reliably felt in government and community action has always been in the foreground of political discussion. With the expansion of areas in which public opinion must operate, many students of the problem have despaired of the capacity of the town meeting technique adequately to make operative the "public will." In the face of this situation, the scientific public opinion poll constitutes an instrument which cheaply and accurately permits us to learn the beliefs, the attitudes, and the wishes of the rank and file of the population. Public opinion polls are at present frequently thought of as interesting devices mainly for predicting the outcome of elections. They do permit such prediction, but this is a very minor aspect of their full possible importance. Polls were extensively used in the armed forces in World War II as a guide to the administration of the invaded areas, the return of the armed forces after the war and in many other ways.

Public opinion polling may be a device through which can be resolved one of the principal impasses of our time, that is, the apparent irreconcilability of authoritarian control on the one hand and the "public will" on the other. It may be that through properly administered public opinion polls professionalized public officials can give us all the efficiency now claimed for authoritarian centralized administration, and yet have the administration at all times subject to the dictates of a more delicate barometer of the people's will than is provided by all the technologically obsolete paraphernalia of traditional democratic processes. In short, it is not impossible that as the advancing technology in the physical adjustments of our lives leads to a threatened breakdown of democracy, so an improved social research instrument may restore and even increase the dominance of the people's voice in the control of human society.

The time may come when the reliable polling of public opinion will be a science comparable to meteorology. Charts of all kinds of social weather, its movements and trends, whether it be anti-Semitism, anti-Negro sentiment, or mobmindedness, will be at the disposal of the administrators of the people's will in every land. A barometer of international tension has been designed to detect reliably and early the tensions that lead to war. It is true that mere knowledge of these tensions does not necessarily operate to alleviate them. But it is also true that a reliable diagnosis of the tension and an understanding of the feelings and sentiments that underlie it are essential for an effective approach to the problem.

We are not here interested primarily in the possible practical uses of these findings. I cite the case rather as an illustration of the possibility of arriving at scientific generalizations of social behavior essentially of the same sort as those that, in their full development, have proved so valuable in the physical sciences.

To those who constantly have their minds on quick and dramatic solutions to the world's troubles this type of research is likely to seem offensively trivial — a kind of fiddling while Rome burns. "Writers" are fond of referring contemptuously to basic scientific work as an "ivory tower" and as "lecturing on navigation while the ship sinks." Navigation today is what it is because some people were willing to study the *principles* of their subject while their individual ships went down, instead of rushing about with half-baked advice as to how to save ships that could not be saved, or were not worth saving anyway. As A. J. Carlson has recently said: "The failure of bacteria to survive in close proximity to certain moulds looked trivial at first, but few informed people would label the discovery of that initial fact *trivial* today."

So much, then, for a few illustrations, rather than a summary, of the type of work that is being done and that needs to be done in the social sciences. Is there enough of it being done? Clearly not, or we would not need to flounder as we are in national and international affairs, pursuing diametrically opposite courses within the same decade. Can the social sciences ever hope to catch up with the other sciences, the increasingly rapid advance of which constantly creates new social problems? Certainly we can, if we devote ourselves to the business with something like the seriousness, the money, and the equipment that we have devoted to physical research. Consider how the physical scientists are today given vast resources to concentrate on the invention of a new submarine detector or a new bomb, not to mention the peacetime occupation of these scientists with penicillin and sulpha drugs. Obviously, I am not criticizing this action. On the contrary, it is the way to proceed if you want results. Is there anything like that going on regarding the world organization and its numerous subsidiary problems, all of them important to peace and prosperity?

Comparatively speaking, there is almost nothing that could be called fundamental research into the basic nature of human relations. To be sure, there are endless petty projects, surveys, conferences, oratory, and arguments by representatives of pressure groups, as if argument ever settled any scientific question. On basic social research there is very little. Why isn't there more? Because it is not yet realized that scientific knowledge is relevant to a successful world organization. We still think that common sense, good will, eloquent leaders, and pious hopes are sufficient when it comes to management of social relations.

This brings us to our second question. What price must we probably pay for a social science of a comprehensiveness and reliability comparable to some of the better developed physical sciences? The costs are undoubtedly considerable, and it remains to be seen to what extent men are willing to pay them. What are some of the principal items both as regards material and psychological costs?

The mention of costs suggests that I am about to digress into the subject of research finance. The advancement of science undoubtedly does involve costs of this type. I shall not go into them here, because I am at present more concerned with other types of costs which have nothing to do with money or with budgets. Let me therefore dismiss the question of monetary costs with a brief estimate by Huxley: "Before humanity can obtain," he says, "on the collective level that degree of foresight, control and flexibility which on the biological level is at the disposal of human individuals, it must multiply at least ten-fold, perhaps fifty-fold, the proportion of individuals and organizations devoted to obtaining information, to planning, to correlation and the flexible control of execution." This may seem staggering to educators who are wondering how to maintain merely their present activities. But how does the entire expenditure for scientific research compare with what we have spent and are spending for war? Perhaps it will occur to some future generation to try a reallocation of public funds. If so, adequate research and training in social science can be readily financed.

But are we or is some future generation likely to change so radically our notions of what is worth spending money for? This brings us face to face with those costs of science which perhaps come higher, and touch us more deeply, than any of its financial costs.

First of all, the advancement of the social sciences would probably deprive us in a large measure of the luxury of indignation in which we now indulge ourselves as regards social events. The "cold" war is a case in point. Such indignation ministers to deep-seated, jungle-fed sentiments of justice, virtue, and a general feeling of the fitness of things, as compared with what a scientific diagnosis of the situation evokes. In short, one of the principal costs of the advancement of the social sciences would be the abandonment of the personalistic and moralistic interpretation of social events, just as we had to abandon this type of explanation of physical phenomena when we went over to the scientific orientation.

Closely related and indeed inseparably connected with the necessary abandonment, in science, of personalistic and moralistic types of explanation is the necessity of abandoning or redefining a large vocabulary to which we are deeply and emotionally attached. Concepts like freedom, democracy, liberty, independence, aggression, discrimination, free speech, self-determination, and a multitude of others have never been realistically analyzed by most people as to their actual content under changing conditions. Any such analyses, furthermore, are sure to seem like an attack upon these cherished symbols and the romantic state of affairs for which they stand. As every social scientist knows, these are subjects that had better be handled with care.

Social sciences worthy of the name will have to examine realistically all the pious shibboleths which are not only frequently the last refuge of scoundrels and bigots, but also serve as shelters behind which we today seek to hide the facts we are reluctant to face. The question is, how much pain in the way of disillusionment about fairy tales, disturbed habits of thought, and disrupted traditional ways of behavior will the patient be willing to put up with in order to be cured of his disease? He will probably have to become a lot sicker than he is before he will consent to take the medicine which alone can save him.

Finally, the advancement of the social sciences will cost the abandonment not only of *individual concepts* carried with us from prescientific times, it will require us also to abandon deeply cherished *ideologies,* resembling in form, if not in content, their theological predecessors. The notion of some final solution, preferably in our own generation, of the major social problems that agitate us is a mirage which even scientists have great difficulty in abandoning. Many of them still confuse the social sciences with various cults, religions, and political dogmas, from Marxism to astrology. Scientists must recognize that democracy, for all its virtues, is only one of the possible types of organization under which men have lived and achieved civilization.

It is a disservice to democracy as well as to science to make preposterous claims that science can prosper only under some particular form of government, that only under our particular form of political organization do minorities have rights, etc. The favorite cliché is that "science can flourish only in freedom." It is a beautiful phrase, but unfortunately it flagrantly begs the question. The question is, under what conditions will the kind of freedom science needs be provided? The historical fact is that science has gone forward under a great variety of forms of government, and conversely, at other times, has been suppressed and frustrated by each of the same types, including democracy. The first truly popular democratic government in Europe, namely, the French Revolution, declared itself to have "no use for scientists" and proceeded to behead Lavoisier, the father of modern chemistry. Only a few decades ago, several states, under the leadership of American "statesmen," passed laws against the teaching of evolution. American citizens of Japanese ancestry have even more recently discovered precisely what the Bill of Rights amounts to in a pinch, especially under an administration and a Supreme Court eloquent in their verbalizations about the rights of minorities. In short, the great democratic "gains" in this department appear to consist, in the opinion of qualified legal analysts, of creating a legal status for minorities in the United States somewhat comparable to that which they had in Nazi Germany.

In short, attacks both on science and on "freedom" *do occur* also in democracies. I would condemn them *wherever* they occur. The attempt to make science the tail of *any* political kite what-

soever must be vigorously opposed by all scientists as well as by all others who believe in uncorrupted science. Political systems have changed, and they will change. Science has survived them all as an instrument which man may use under any organization for whatever ends he seeks.

The mere fact that I, personally, happen to like the democratic way of life with all its absurdities, that I would find some current alternatives quite intolerable, and that I may even find it worth while to go to any length in defense of democracy of the type to which I am accustomed are matters of little or no importance as touching the scientific question at issue. My attachment to democracy may be, in fact, of *scientific* significance chiefly as indicating my unfitness to live in a changing world. To accept this simple notion is perhaps a cost of social science that few are prepared to pay.

We have reviewed above some of the costs that are involved in the transition to a scientific view of human relations. These costs affect scientists as well as other people. In addition, scientists have one special concern. What does the future promise for social scientists in the way of freedom to perform the tasks which I have outlined as their proper business?

Social scientists need not expect to escape the troubles which other scientists have encountered throughout history. Chemists and physicists from time to time have suffered persecutions because of the conflict of their findings with more generally accepted views. They have continued to hew to the line, however, until today they enjoy a certain immunity and freedom of investigation which social scientists do not share. Why do physical scientists enjoy this relative security in the face of changing political regimes, and how may social scientists attain a corresponding immunity?

The answer is popularly assumed to lie in the peculiar subject-matter with which social scientists deal. I doubt if this is the principal reason. I think a far more fundamental reason for the relative precariousness of the social sciences lies in their comparative incompetence.

Social scientists, unfortunately, have failed as yet to convince any considerable number of persons that they are engaged in a pursuit of knowledge of a kind which is demonstrably true, regardless of the private preferences, hopes, and likes of the scientist himself. *All* sciences have gone through this stage. Physical scientists are, as a class, less likely to be disturbed than social scientists when a political upheaval comes along, because the work of the former is recognized as of equal consequence under any regime. Social science should strive for a similar position. Individual physicists may suffer persecution, but their successors carry on their work in much the same way. If social scientists possessed an equally demonstrable relevant body of knowledge and technique of finding answers to questions, that knowledge would be equally above the reach of political upheaval. The services of *real* social scientists would be as indispensable to Fascists as to Communists and Democrats, just as are the services of physicists and physicians. The findings of physical scientists at times also have been ignored by political regimes, but when that *has* occurred, it has been the *regime* and not the *science* that yielded in the end.

The trivial effect of political interference upon the well-developed sciences should be noted. I recognize, of course, the frequently unfortunate effect of these movements upon individual careers and individual projects. But, if we plot the course of scientific advance during the past two hundred years, the impressive fact is how little its main course has been deflected by all the petty movements of so-called "social action," including the major political revolutions. The demonstrable superiority of science as a method of achieving *whatever* men want has caused even its persecutors to return to it, after only very temporary and superficial attacks and local crusades, chiefly against individual scientists. The recent history of Germany and Russia are cases in point.

I have emphasized that physical scientists are indispensable to any political regime. Social scientists might well work toward a corresponding status. Already some of them have achieved it to a degree. Qualified social statisticians have not been and will not be disturbed greatly in their function by any political party as long as they confine themselves to their specialty. Their skill consists in the ability to draw relatively valid, unbiased, and demonstrable conclusions

from observed data of social behavior. *That* technique is the same, regardless of social objectives. No regime can get along without this technology. It is the possession and exercise of such skills alone that justifies the claim of academic immunity. To claim it for those who insist on taking for granted that which needs to be demonstrated can only result in the repudiation for everybody of the whole principle of academic freedom. For the same reason, we had better not become so devoted to blatant crusaders for academic freedom that we forget to bolster the only foundation upon which academic freedom can ever be maintained in the long run, namely, the demonstrated capacity of its possessors to make valid and impersonal analyses and predictions of social events.

The temptation is admittedly considerable to bolster one's favorite "movement," by posing as a disinterested appraiser of the truth while actually engaging in special pleading. It is also tempting in this way to seek the right of sanctuary in the form of academic freedom to escape the ordinary consequences of pressure group activity as visited on less clever and less privileged people. Special pleading must be recognized for what it is whether it serves the C.I.O. or the N.A.M. I have no objection to universities maintaining forums for special pleading nor do I object to scientists taking part in such discussion as long as no attempt is made to pass the whole thing off as "science." Too frequently scientists forget this distinction and put forward absurd scientific claims for what they personally happen to prefer.

The form of social organization which will yield to men the satisfaction they desire obviously depends upon a great number and variety of factors, including traditions, resources, technology, scientific development, and education. Scientists would do better to make it perfectly clear that their personal preferences in these matters are merely their own current preferences and not scientific conclusions valid for all times and places or conditions of people.

My conclusion, then, is that the best hope for the social sciences lies in following broadly in the paths of the other sciences. I have not tried to minimize the difficulties that beset these paths. I have merely argued that they are not insurmountable, and that in any case we really have no choice but to pursue this one hope. For we are already so heavily committed to the thought-ways and the material results of science in so large a part of our lives that we are likely to go farther in the same direction. In short, the trends that have been strikingly evident in the social sciences in recent decades will, I believe, continue at an ever more rapid rate. Social scientists will talk less and say more. They will rely ever more heavily on a more economical type of discourse, namely, the statistical and mathematical. Much of what now passes for social science will be properly relegated to other equally honorable departments, such as journalism, drama, or general literature. As such, this material will have its uses as propaganda, news, art, and a legitimate outlet for the emotions of men. Indeed, nothing I have said regarding the possibilities of scientific study of human affairs should be interpreted as in any way contemplating an abandonment or a restriction upon the artistic, religious, literary, or recreational arts which also minister to the cravings of men. I have on the contrary rather advocated that the social sciences should not handicap themselves by aggrandizing to themselves roles which they cannot fulfill.

Social scientists, as scientists, had better confine themselves to three tasks: First and foremost, they should devote themselves to developing reliable knowledge of what alternatives of action exist under given conditions and the probable consequences of each. Secondly, social scientists should, as a legitimate part of their technology as well as for its practical uses, be able to gauge reliably what the masses of men want under given circumstances. Finally, they should, in the applied aspects of their science, develop the administrative or engineering techniques of satisfying most efficiently and economically these wants, regardless of what they may be at any given time, regardless of how they may change from time to time, and regardless of the scientists' own preferences.

75   Science, Learning and Culture*

Jerome S. Bruner

In the discussion below, a psychologist, Jerome S. Bruner, examines the relationship between education and cultural development, indicating some of the political and scientific problems encountered in the construction of pedagogical theory. One of the conclusions suggested is that scientific theories should not be assessed only on technical grounds but also as instruments of cultural, ideological, and political change. Consider especially the implications of this view for theories of government, religion, and technology.

Despite the books and articles that are beginning to appear on the subject, the process of education goes forward today without any clearly defined or widely accepted theory of instruction. We have had to make do and are still making do on clever maxims and moralistic resolutions about what instruction is and should be. The controversy that swirls around this tortured subject is a mirror of larger discontent with our culture and our morality. And so it should be — but not to the exclusion of dispassionate appraisal of the means whereby the sought-after ends might be achieved. And perhaps that, too, is overly much to expect, for if the past decade has taught us anything, it is that educational reform confined only to the schools and not to the society at large is doomed to eventual triviality.

There are a number of reasons why a theory of instruction may have little effect on educational practice. First, it could be that the theory is wrong — yet it is difficult to find a theory that is flat wrong and won't have some reasonable proposals to make. A second reason might be that it is inappropriate to the central problems of practice. For instance, a theory that is clearly excellent in respect to the instruction of children who are already motivated to learn may prove ineffective in dealing with the alienated Negro students of the inner-city school. A third reason might be its unmanageability — one aspect of which is obscurity in the path from the abstract to the concrete. No matter how deeply one is moved by the spirit of Froebel's theory, for example, it is difficult to know what one does to assure, in his metaphor, that a child be nurtured like a plant lest he be choked by the weeds of circumstance.

But even if a pedagogical theory is correct, relevant, and manageable, it may be practically ineffective when it fails to relate to the urgencies of a society.

While American society in the first decades of the twentieth century was deeply concerned with the problem of acculturating new waves of immigrants, the favored theory was once concerned with the teaching of content per se, with minimum emphasis upon formal discipline or the training of mental faculties. Those theories were perhaps too closely related to the education of special elites. Today they are popular again.

A theory fares well when it accords with a culture's conception of its function. Each culture has conceptions of the nature of a child, some conceptions of what constitutes good adults. It also has, at some implicit level, some conceptions of what it regards as the appropriate means of getting from the nature of a child to the nature of an adult. If a pedagogical theorist is to move that culture, he must forge a theory that relates to that range of acceptable means. The failure of a theory may be that it fails to accord with or overcome or relate to the "range of acceptable means" of a culture.

The net outcome of our probing is, I think, the realization that a pedagogical theory is perforce quite different from, and hardly as neutral as, the usual type of scientific theory. Indeed, it is even questionable whether it is principally a scientific theory in the explanatory sense. Nor is it a purely normative theory such as a grammatical theory, prescribing rules for reaching specified goals (such as "well formed sentences"). A theory of instruction is a political theory in the proper sense that it derives from consensus concerning the distribution of power within the society — who shall be educated and to fulfill what roles? In the very same sense, pedagogical theory must surely derive from a conception of economics, for where there is division of labor within the society and an exchange of goods and services for wealth and prestige, then *how* people are educated and in what number and with what constraints on the use of resources are all relevant issues. The psychologist or educator who formulates pedagogical theory without regard to the political, economic, and social setting of the educational process courts triviality and merits being ignored in the community and in the classroom.

It is neither surprising nor inappropriate, then, that critiques of pedagogical theories are as often as not in the form of social and political criticism and ideological debate. It has been instructive to me to see the manner in which some of these debates take shape. A book of mine, *The Process of Education* (1960), has been translated into several languages. In Italy, the book touched off a debate on the problem of revising Italian education to cope with the changing industrial society, and it has been used for clubbing Marxists and classicists alike. In the Soviet Union, one group of social critics has used the book's emphasis on discovery and intuition to castigate the dogmatism of remaining Stalinists who wish to set the dogma of socialism on the line in the classroom. That view has been seconded in Poland, Hungary, and Czechoslovakia.

In Japan, the social critics praise the book for indicating that school subjects that are technical and mathematical need not be without a proper intellectual structure and cultural grace. In Israel, a land surrounded by a ring of hostile nations, the book has been greeted as an invitation to avoid mediocrity in the preparation of new immigrants — a mediocrity that social critics fear will bring Israel to a state of dangerous vulnerability in her present isolated position. In the United States — and perhaps this is the only country affluent enough to harbor such thoughts — the principal social criticism has been a concern for the maintenance of spontaneity of the child. It has been a sobering experience to realize in what degree a book of this sort must perforce serve social and political ends and can never remain a technical book alone.

This brings me to a second conclusion, this time about the role of manageability in the impact of pedagogical theories. Manageability encompasses not only the so-called educational technology of films, books, computers, and the like, but also the scale of the enterprise in terms of people and funds. We have now entered an era in which the federal government, through the Office of Education, has established regional research and development centers to concern themselves with the betterment of our educational effort. They provide a fresh opportunity to explore deeply the feasibility of particular theories, comprehensive or segmental, concerning effective instruction.

I have had the intimate experience over the last five or six years of participating in and observing the attempt to translate a more general theory into one single course in the social sciences, "Man: A Course of Study" (1965), designed for the fifth grade. (It is being developed by what was originally Educational Services, Inc., and has now become the regional center, Educational Development Corporation.) The experience has taught us all not to be casual about means. For it soon turns out that what seems like a simple pedagogical premise would, if implemented, produce a minor revolution in teacher training or in filmmaking or in school budgeting. This is the engineering part of what is properly called the theory of instruction. It is something that we are only now beginning to understand. Innovation, by whatever theoretical derivation, involves vast development and engineering. By past standards of performance, we could not absorb many new innovative ideas. If we learn how to implement these matters in our generation, we shall lay the groundwork for a truly great impact of adequate theories of instruction in the next generation.

These observations on why theories of instruction are ineffective lead to a second question: What is it that is special or different about education in the sense of schooling in contrast to other ways in which we instruct? Consider the evolution of education as a cultural means of passing on skill, knowledge, and values. It is impossible,

of course, to reconstruct the evolution in techniques of instruction in the shadow zone between hominids and man. I have tried to compensate for this lack by observing contemporary analogues of earlier forms, knowing full well that the pursuit of analogy can be dangerously misleading. I have spent many hours observing uncut films of the behavior of free-ranging baboons, films shot in East Africa by my colleague Irven DeVore with a very generous footage devoted to infants and juveniles. I have also had access to the unedited film archives of a hunting-gathering people living under roughly analogous ecological conditions, the !Kung Bushmen of the Kalahari, recorded by Laurance and Lorna Marshall. I have also worked directly but informally with the Wolof of Senegal, observing children in the bush and in French-style schools.

Let me describe very briefly some salient differences in the free learning patterns of immature baboons and among !Kung children. Baboons have a highly developed social life in their troops, with well organized and stable dominance patterns. They live within a territory, protecting themselves from predators by joint action of the strongly built adult males. It is striking that the behavior of baboon juveniles is shaped principally by play with their peer group, play that provides opportunity for the spontaneous expression and practice of the component acts that, in maturity, will be orchestrated into either the behavior of the dominant male or of the infant-protective female. All this seems to be accomplished with little participation by any mature animals in the play of the juveniles. We know from the important experiments of H. F. Harlow and his colleagues how devastating a disruption in development can be produced in subhuman primates by interfering with their opportunity for peer-group play and social interaction.

Among hunting-gathering humans, on the other hand, there is constant interaction between adult and child, or adult and adolescent, or adolescent and child. !Kung adults and children play and dance together, sit together, participate in minor hunting together, join in song and storytelling together. At very frequent intervals, moreover, children are party to rituals presided over by adults — minor, as in the first hair-cutting, or major, as when a boy kills his first kudu buck and goes through the proud but painful process of scarification. Children, besides, are constantly playing imitatively with the rituals, implements, tools, and weapons of the adult world. Young juvenile baboons, on the other hand, virtually never play with things or imitate, directly, large and significant sequences of adult behavior.

Note, though, that in tens of thousands of feet of !Kung film, one virtually never sees an instance of "teaching" taking place outside the situation where the behavior to be learned is relevant. Nobody "teaches" in our prepared sense of the word. There is nothing like school, nothing like lessons. Indeed, among the !Kung children there is very little "telling." Most of what we would call instruction is through showing. And there is no "practice" or "drill" as such, save in the form of play modeled directly on adult models — play hunting, play bossing, play exchanging, play babytending, play house-making. In the end, every man in the culture knows nearly all there is to know about how to get on with life as a man, and every woman as a woman — the skills, the rituals and myths, the obligations and rights, the attitudes.

The change in the instruction of children in more complex societies is twofold. First of all, there is knowledge and skill in the culture far in excess of what any one individual knows. And so, increasingly, there develops an economical technique of instructing the young based heavily on *telling* out of context rather than *showing* in context. In literate societies, the practice becomes institutionalized in the school or the "teacher." Both promote this necessarily abstract way of instructing the young.

The result of "teaching the culture" can, at its worst, lead to the ritual, rote nonsense that has led a generation of critics to despair. For in the detached school, what is imparted often has little to do with life as lived in the society except insofar as the demands of school are of a kind that reflect *indirectly* the demands of life in a technical society. But these indirectly imposed demands may be the most important feature of the detached school. For school is a sharp departure from indigenous practice.

It takes learning, as we have noted, out of the

context of immediate action just by dint of putting it into a school. This very extirpation makes learning become an act in itself, freed from the immediate ends of action, preparing the learner for the chain of reckoning, remote from payoff that is needed for the formulation of complex ideas. At the same time, the school (if successful) frees the child from the pace-setting of the round of concrete daily activity. If the school succeeds in avoiding a pace-setting round of its own, it may be one of the great agents for promoting reflectiveness. Moreover, in school, one must "follow the lesson" which means one must learn to follow either the abstraction of written speech — abstract in the sense that it is divorced from the concrete situation to which the speech might originally have been related — or the abstraction of language delivered orally but out of the context of an ongoing action. Both of these are highly abstract uses of language. It is no wonder, then, that many recent studies report large differences between "primitive" children who are in schools and their brothers who are not: differences in perception, abstraction, time perspective, and so on.

As a society becomes yet more technical, there is a longer separation from actual doing, and education begins to take up a larger and larger portion of the life span; indeed, education becomes part of the way of life. More and more time is given over to telling (usually in print), to demonstrating out of the context of action.

We can already foresee a next step in technical progress that will impose further changes on our methods of educating. For one thing, the rate of change in the surface properties of knowledge will likely increase. That is, the theory of circuits will blossom, although likely as not it will do so on the basis of understanding more deeply some principles that are now known but not fully understood. In teaching, then, we shall be more likely to search out the deeper, underlying ideas to teach, rather than presenting the technical surface that is so likely to change. A metaphoric way of putting this is to say that technical things are more likely to appear changed to an engineer than to a physicist.

There will also be many more aids and prosthetic devices for processing information than ever before. Some of these seem certain already. For one thing, we are organizing our knowledge in a data bank accessible to a user by retrieval techniques inherent in modern computing. This makes knowledge more accessible and less subject to the ancient filing and recall gymnastics of the classical scholar. For another, there will be increasing pressure to reformulate problems in a well-formed fashion in order to make them accessible to the powerful devices of computing. Ill-formed problems do not lend themselves to computing. There are dangers and opportunities in such formalism. Whichever, the trend is already discernible. In general, I think it can be said that we shall in the next hundred years be using many more intelligent and automatic devices that we shall program in behalf of our problem-solving. We need not be Luddites about it, either.

I suspect that there are three forms of activity that no device is ever going to be able to do as well as our brain with its 5×10^9 cortical connections, and I would suggest that these three represent what will be special about education for the future.

The first is that we shall probably want to train individuals not for the performance of routine activities that can be done with great skill and precision by devices, but rather to train their individual talents for research and development, which is one of the kinds of activities for which you cannot easily program computers. Here I mean research and development in the sense of problem-finding rather than problem-solving. If we want to look ahead to what is special about a school, we should ask how to train generations of children to *find* problems, to look for them. I recall that wonderful prescription of the English Platonist, Weldon, to the effect that there are three kinds of things in the world: There are troubles which we do not know quite how to handle; then there are puzzles with their clear conditions and unique solutions, marvelously elegant; and then there are problems — and these we invent by finding an appropriate puzzle form to impose upon a trouble.

What this entails for education is necessarily somewhat obscure although its outlines may be plain. For one thing, it places a certain emphasis on the teaching of interesting puzzle forms: ways of thinking that are particularly useful for con-

verting troubles into problems. These are familiar enough in any given field of knowledge; they are the useful abstractions. What is needed is a sense of how to teach their use in converting chaotic messes into manageable problems. Much of the attraction of the use of discovery in teaching comes, I suspect, from the realization of the need to equip students in this way.

A second special requirement for education in the future is that it provide training in the performance of "unpredictable services." By unpredictable services, I mean performing acts that are contingent on a response made by somebody or something to your prior act. Again, this falls in the category of tasks that we shall do better than automata for many years to come. I include here the role of the teacher, the parent, the assistant, the stimulator, the rehabilitator, the physician in the great sense of that term, the friend, the range of things that increase the richness of individual response to other individuals. I propose this as a critical task, for as the society becomes more interdependent, more geared to technological requirements, it is crucial that it not become alienated internally, flat emotionally, and gray. Those who fret and argue that we are *bound* to go dead personally as we become proficient technically have no more basis for their assertion than traditional romanticism. Recall that the nineteenth century that witnessed the birth of the Industrial Revolution also produced that most intimate form, the modern novel.

Third, what human beings can produce and no device can is art — in every form: visual art, the art of cooking, the art of love, the art of walking, the art of address, going beyond adaptive necessity to find expression for human flair.

These three — research and development, unpredictable services, and the arts — represent what surely will be the challenge to a society which has our capacity to provide technical routine. I assume we shall teach the technical routines, for that is built into our evolving system. Will we be daring enough to go beyond to the cultivation of the uniquely human?

Another question we must ask, then, is: How can the power and substance of a culture be translated into an instructional form?

First we must look briefly at what we might

mean by the nature of knowledge as such, because this will prove crucial to our concern. Perhaps the most pervasive feature of human intellect is its limited capacity at any moment for dealing with information. We have about seven slots, plus or minus two, through which the external world can find translation into experience. We easily become overwhelmed by complexity or clutter. Cognitive mastery in a world that generates stimuli far faster than we can sort them depends upon strategies for reducing the complexity and the clutter. But reduction must be selective, attuned to the things that "matter." Some of the modes of reduction require, seemingly, no learning — as with our adaptation mechanisms. What does not change ceases to register: steady states in their very nature cease to stimulate. Stabilize the image on the retina by getting rid of fine tremor, and the visual world fades away.

There is another type of selectivity that reflects man's deepest intellectual trait and is heavily dependent on learning. Man constructs models of his world, templates that represent not only what he encounters and in what context, but ones that also permit him to go beyond them. He learns the world in a way that enables him to make predictions of what comes next by matching a few milliseconds of what is now experienced to a stored model and reading the rest from the model. We see a contour and a snatch of movement. "Ah yes, that's the night watchman checking the windows. . . ." It is in the nature of the selectivity governed by such models that we come increasingly to register easily on those things in the world that we expect; indeed, we assume that the expected is there on the basis of a minimum of information.

There is compelling evidence that so long as the environment conforms to the expected patterns within reasonable limits, alerting mechanisms in the brain are quieted. But once expectancy is violated — once the world ceases strikingly to correspond to our models of it (and it must be rather striking, for we ride roughshod over minor deviations) — then all the alarms go off and we are at full alertness. So man can deal not only with information that is before him, but go far beyond the information given, with all that this implies both for swiftness of intellect and for fallibility. Almost by definition, the exercise of intellect, involving as it must the use of short cuts and of leaps from partial evidence, always courts the possibility of error. It is the good fortune of our species that we are also highly adept not only at correction (given sufficient freedom from time pressure), but we have learned to institutionalize ways of keeping error within tolerable limits, science being the prime example.

The models or stored theories of the world that are so useful in inference are strikingly generic and reflect man's ubiquitous tendency to categorize. William James remarked that the life of the mind begins when the child is first able to proclaim, "Aha, thingumbob again." We organize experience to represent not only the particulars that have been experienced, but the classes of events of which the particulars are exemplars. We go not only from part to whole, but irresistibly from the particular to the general.

At least one distinguished linguist has argued in recent times that this generic tendency of human intellect must be innately human, for, without it, one could not master the complex web of categorical or substitution rules that constitutes the syntax of language — any language. Both in achieving the economy with which human thought represents the world and in effecting swift correction for error, the categorizing tendency of intelligence is central. For it yields a structure of thought that becomes hierarchically organized with growth, forming branching structures in which it is relatively easy to search for alternatives. The blunders occur, of course, where things that must be together for action or for understanding happen to be organized in different hierarchies. It is a form of error that is as familiar in science as in everyday life.

I do not mean to imply, of course, that man structures his knowledge of the world only by the categorical rules of inclusion, exclusion, and overlap, for clearly he traffics in far greater complexity, too. Witness the almost irresistible urge to see cause and effect. Rather, the categorical nature of thought underlines its rule-bound nature. The eighteenth-century assumption that knowledge grows by a gradual accretion of associations built up by contact with events that are contiguous in time, space, or quality does not fit the facts of mental life. There are spheres where such associative laws operate within limits — as, for example, with material that is strange and meaningless (the psychologist's nonsense syllables, for instance) — but in the main, organization is a far more active process of imposing order, as when we form a hypothesis and then check it not so much to be sure but to be clued in.

We do the greater part of our work by manipulating our representations or models of reality rather than by acting directly on the world itself. Thought is then vicarious action, in which the high cost of error is strikingly reduced. It is characteristic of human beings, and no other species, that we can carry out this vicarious action with the aid of a large number of intellectual prosthetic devices that are, so to speak, tools provided by the culture. Natural language is the prime example, but there are pictorial and diagrammatic conventions as well: theories, myths, modes of reckoning and ordering. We are even able to employ devices to fulfill functions not given man through evolution — devices that bring phenomena into the human range of registering and computing. Today, indeed, we develop devices to determine whether the events we watch conform to or deviate from expectancy in comprehensible ways.

A colleague, George A. Miller, put it well in speaking about computers: "Mechanical intelligence will not ultimately replace human intelligence, but rather, by complementing our human intelligence, will supplement and amplify it. We will learn to supply by mechanical organs those functions that natural evolution has failed to provide."

The range of man's intellect, given its power to be increased from the outside in, can never be estimated without considering the means a culture provides for empowering mind. Man's intellect, then, is not simply his own, but is communal in the sense that its unlocking or empowering depends upon the success of the culture in developing means to that end. The use of such amplifiers of mind requires, admittedly, a commonly shared human capacity, and each society fashions and perfects this capacity to its needs. But there is, I

believe, a respect in which a lack of means for understanding one matter places out of reach other matters that are crucial to man's condition whatever his culture.

Consider now the nature of codified knowledge. The past half century has surely been one of the richest, as well as the most baffling, in the history of our effort to understand the nature of knowledge. Advances in the foundation of mathematics and logic, in the philosophy of science, in the theory of information processing, in linguistics and in psychology — all of these have led to new formulations and new conjectures.

Perhaps the greatest change, stemming principally from the revolutions in physics, is in our conception of what a theory is. For Newton, inquiry was a voyage on the seas of ignorance to find the islands of truth. We know now that theory is more than a general description of what happens or a statement of probabilities of what might or might not happen — even when it claims to be nothing more than that, as in some of the newer behavioral sciences. It entails, explicitly or implicitly, a model of what it is that one is theorizing about, a set of propositions that, taken in ensemble, yield occasional predictions about things. Armed with a theory, one is guided toward what one will treat as data and is predisposed to treat some data as more relevant than others.

A theory is also a way of stating tersely what one already knows without the burden of detail. In this sense it is a canny and economical way of keeping in mind a vast amount while thinking about a very little. What is perhaps most important about this way of viewing theory is the attitude it creates toward the use of mind. We now see that the construction of theory is a way of using the mind, the imagination — of standing off from the activities of observation and inference and creating a shape of nature.

There are several conclusions to be drawn from this long excursion into the nature of intellect, into the nature of how one organizes knowledge to fit it. First of all, it becomes necessary to translate bodies of theory into a form that permits the child to get closer and closer approximations to the most powerful form of a theory, beginning with a highly intuitive and active form of a theory and moving on as the child grasps that to a more precise and powerful statement of it. I find no other way of bringing the child through the maze of particulars to the kind of power that would produce the combination of research and development, unpredictable services, and the arts. Second, this means that on a practical level the entire university community — indeed, the entire intellectual community — must have a role in education, that the separate education faculty is a misconception and probably one that requires rearrangement in the future. (Since this was written, Cornell has disbanded its faculty of education and reassigned its responsibilities to the entire faculty of arts and sciences.)

As my colleague, Philip Morrison, put it in respect to his field, there are degrees granted by departments of physics in theoretical physics, in experimental physics, and in applied physics. Why not one in pedagogical physics? Teaching is surely an extension of the general exercise whereby one clarifies ideas to oneself. All of us who have worked on curriculum have learned tremendous amounts about our subject matter simply by trying to convert it into a form that would be courteous and comprehensible to a young learner.

Now if this is the case, if we require that there be pedagogical physics and its counterparts, there is surely some need for a *special* coalition to devise means of teaching the symbolic activity involved in the kind of theory-making we have been discussing. I do not know what to call this coalition of fields; the symbol sciences might be appropriate, but it is an absurd name. Linguists, philosophers of science, philosophers of history, logicians, psychologists, teachers, substantive specialists who most understand the simple structures of their fields, mathematicians — such a coalition might show how a university might express its concern for the symbolic powers inherent in the use of a culture. We obviously do not understand what could be done by a group of this sort. They range all the way from teaching children to be brief and compact when that is needed to hold things in the range of attention, to devising the kind of mathematical program embodied in the report of the Cambridge Conference on School Mathematics (*Goals for School Mathematics*, Houghton Mifflin, 1963).

Finally, we may ask: How is intellectual development assisted by instruction?

Let me focus on the teacher in this process. One immediately invokes the phrase "teacher training." But before we do, consider a few points to be taken into account. We know that children do not readily or easily think in school. By school age, children expect arbitrary and meaningless (to them) demands to be made on them by adults — the result probably of the fact that adults often fail to recognize the task of conversion necessary to make their questions have some intrinsic significance for the child. Children, of course, will try to solve problems if they recognize them as such. But they are not often either predisposed to or skillful in problem-finding, in recognizing the hidden conjectural feature in tasks set them. We know that children in school can quite quickly be led to such problem-finding by encouragement and instruction.

The need for this encouragement and instruction and its relatively swift success relates, I suspect, to what psychoanalysts refer to as the guilt-ridden over-suppression of primary process and its public replacement by secondary process. Children, like adults, need reassurance that it is all right to entertain and *express* highly subjective ideas, to treat a task as a problem where you *invent* an answer rather than *finding* one out there in the book or on the blackboard. With children in elementary school, there is often a need to devise emotionally vivid special games, story-making episodes, or construction projects to re-establish in the child's mind his right not only to have his own private ideas but to express them in the public setting of a classroom.

But there is another, perhaps more serious difficulty: the interference of intrinsic problem-solving by extrinsic. Young children in school expend extraordinary time and effort figuring out what it is that the teacher wants — and usually coming to the conclusion that she or he wants tidiness or remembering or doing things at a certain time in a certain way. This I refer to as extrinsic problem-solving. There is a great deal of it in school.

There are several quite straightforward ways of stimulating problem-finding. One is to train teachers to want it, and that will come in time. But teachers can be encouraged to like it, interestingly enough, by providing them and their children with materials and lessons that *permit* legitimate problem-finding and permit the teacher to recognize it. For exercises with such materials create an atmosphere by treating things as instances of what *might* have occurred rather than simply as what did occur.

Let me illustrate by a concrete instance. A fifth-grade class was working on the organization of a baboon-troop — specifically, on how they might protect against predators. They saw a brief sequence of film in which six or seven adult males go forward to intimidate and hold off three cheetahs. The teacher asked what the baboons had done to keep the cheetahs off, and there ensued a lively discussion of how the dominant adult males, by showing their formidable mouthful of teeth and making threatening gestures, had turned the trick. A boy raised a tentative hand and asked whether cheetahs always attacked together. Yes, though a single cheetah sometimes followed behind a moving troop and picked off an older, weakened straggler or an unwary, straying juvenile. "Well, what if there were four cheetahs, and two of them attacked from behind and two from in front? What would the baboons do then?"

The question could have been answered empirically — and the inquiry ended. Cheetahs *do not* attack that way, and so we do not know what baboons *might* do. Fortunately, it was not. For the question opens up the deep issues of what might be and why it is not. Is there a necessary relation between predators and prey that share a common ecological niche? Must their encounters have a "sporting chance" outcome? It is such conjecture, in this case quite unanswerable, that produces rational, self-consciously problem-finding behavior so crucial to the growth of intellectual power. Given the materials, given some background and encouragement, teachers like it as much as the students. This is simply an example, and provided in that spirit only.

Let me now turn to dialogue. My colleague, Roman Jakobson, assures me that there is a Russian proverb to the effect that one understands only after one has discussed. There are doubtless many ways in which a human being can serve as a vicar of the culture, helping a child to understand its points of view and the nature of its knowledge. But I dare say that few are so potentially powerful as participating in dialogue. Professor Jan Smedslund, at Oslo, has recently remarked on our failure to recognize that even in the domains of formal reasoning, logic, and mathematics, the social context of discussion can be shown to be crucial.

It is a simple suggestion I am making. Entering the culture is perhaps most readily done by entering a dialogue with a more experienced member of it. Perhaps one way in which we might reconsider the issue of teacher training is to give the teacher training in the skills of dialogue — how to discuss a subject with a beginner.

Pedagogical theory, then, is not only technical, but cultural, ideological, and political. If it is to have its impact, it must be self-consciously all of these. The technical task, indeed, is more formidable than ever we suspected, and we may now be operating close to the scale where we can begin to do the appropriate engineering to realize the implications of even utopian theories.

Knowledge, to be useful, must be compact, accessible, and manipulable. Theory is the form that has these properties. It should be the aim of our teaching. But in the evolution of education, it is also the case that as we move to an ever more technical organization of our culture, and now to a period involving the use of information-processing automata, the pattern of education changes. Three uniquely human traits want especial cultivation to increase the human quality of human societies — problem-finding, the provision of unpredictable services, and art in its myriad forms from music to cuisine.

Finally, one of the most crucial ways in which a culture provides aid in intellectual growth is through a dialogue between the more experienced and the less experienced, providing a means for the internalization of dialogue in thought. The courtesy of conversation may be the major ingredient in the courtesy of teaching.

BIOGRAPHICAL NOTES

(The number in parenthesis refers to the numbered articles in this book.)

ASCH, SOLOMON E. (#28) is Professor of Psychology at Swarthmore College, and is an authority in the fields of perception, the psychology of learning, and social and experimental psychology.

BACK, KURT W. (#23) is Professor of Sociology and Medical Sociology at Duke University. He is the author of *Slums, Projects and People* and co-author of *The Family and Population Control* and *The June Bug: A Study in Hysterical Contagion.*

BATES, ALAN P. (#73) is Chairman of the Department of Sociology at the University of Nebraska. His major works are *The Sociological Enterprise* and *Parental Authority: The Community and the Law* (co-author.)

BATES, FREDERICK L. (#49) is Chairman of the Department of Sociology at the University of Georgia. He has taught at North Carolina State, Cornell University, and Louisiana State University, and is the author of numerous papers and monographs on methodology, status and prestige, role stress, disasters, and decision-making.

BECKER, HOWARD S. (#44) is Professor of Sociology at Northwestern University, and is editor of *Social Problems.* His special fields are social psychology, sociology of work, and deviant behavior. He is the author of *Boys in White, Outsiders,* and co-author of *The Other Side.*

BELLAH, ROBERT N. (#12) is Professor of Sociology and Comparative Studies at the University of California. His major fields are social evolution, comparative institutional structure, and the sociology of East Asia and Islam. His major works are *Apache Kinship Systems, Tokugwa Religion,* and *Religion and Progress in Modern Asia.*

BENDIX, REINHARD (#13) is Professor of Sociology at the University of California and vice-president of the International Sociological Association. He is the recipient of the American Sociological Association's MacIver Award and the "reflective year" fellowship of the Carnegie Corporation. His most recent books are *Work and Authority in Industry, Max Weber: An Intellectual Portrait,* and *Nation Building and Citizenship.*

BENEDICT, RUTH (#6, #54) was Professor of Anthropology at Columbia University before her death in 1948. Her major works include *Patterns of Culture, Zuni Mythology,* and *Tales of the Cochiti Indians.*

BERELSON, BERNARD (#27, #70) is Professor of Psychology at the State University of New York at Buffalo, and is an outstanding authority in the fields of communication, public opinion, and psychotherapy. In addition to his earlier writing on *Content Analysis in Communication Research, Voting, The Peoples' Choice,* and *Graduate Education in the United States,* he has co-authored *Seven Views of Psychotherapy* and *Beyond Counseling and Therapy.*

BERNARD, JESSIE (#10) is Professor of Sociology at Pennsylvania State University, and author of many articles and books in the fields of family, theory, and deviant behavior. Her most recent publications include *Academic Women, Marriage and Family Among Negroes,* and *The Sex Game.*

BERREMAN, GERALD D. (#9, #47) is Professor of Anthropology at the University of California. His major areas of interest are culture change, research methods, social stratification, and applied anthropology; his major articles, books, and monographs include studies from the United States, India, and the Aleutian Islands.

BLAU, PETER M. (#32) is Professor of Sociology at the University of Chicago and has done research in bureaucracy, occupational structure, and small groups. His most recent works are *Exchange and Power in Social Life, Dynamics of Bureaucracy,* and *American Occupational Structure.*

BRAUNGART, RICHARD G. (#42) is doing research and teaching at Pennsylvania State University in the areas of political sociology and social survey design.

BRUNER, JEROME S. (#75) is Professor of Psychology at Harvard University and is an authority in developmental psychology and the cognitive processes, especially perception, memory, and thinking. His recent major publications include *A Study in Thinking, Toward a Theory of Instruction,* and *Studies in Cognitive Growth.*

CLARK, BURTON R. (#69) is Professor of Sociology at Yale University. His fields of interest are formal organization and the sociology of education; his major books are *Educating in the Expert Society, Adult Education in Transition,* and the *Open-Door College.*

COLEMAN, JAMES S. (#68) is Professor of Sociology at Johns Hopkins University. His most recent books are *Community Conflict, Adolescent Society,* and *Introduction to Mathematical Sociology.*

COTTRELL, W. F. (#11) is Chairman of the Department of Sociology and Anthropology at Miami University at Oxford, Ohio. His recent publications include *The Railroader, Men Cry for Peace,* and *Energy and Society.*

DAY, LINCOLN H., and ALICE T. (#2) are co-authors of demographic reports in the United States and Australia. Lincoln Day is Professor of Sociology and Public Health and his wife is on the research staff at Yale University. Their major books are *Too Many Americans, Differential Fertility among the Catholics in Australia,* and *Disabled Workers in the Labor Market.*

DEFLEUR, MELVIN L. (#34) is Professor of Sociology at Washington State University. His areas of interest are social psychology, social theory, and methodology and statistics; his recent publications include *Theories of Mass Communication* and *Flow of Information.*

DINITZ, SIMON (#39) is Professor of Sociology and Research Associate in Psychiatry at Ohio State University. His contributions have been in the fields of sociology, social problems, and psychiatry. His most recent books are *Critical Issues in the Study of Crime,* and *Social Problems: Dissensus* and *Deviation in an Industrial Society.*

DOBRINER, WILLIAM M. (#19) is Chairman of the Department of Sociology at Hofstra College, and a leading authority in the field of social stratification and change and metropolitan sociology. Three of his major publications are *Class in Suburbia, The Suburban Community,* and *Natural History of a Reluctant Suburb.*

DORN, HAROLD F. (#1) was Chief, Biometrics Research Branch, National Heart Institute, until his death in 1963. He prepared the 1958 survey which

led the Public Health Service to search for links between lung cancer and smoking.

EDELSTEIN, ALEX (#35) is Professor of Communications at the University of Washington.

ELDER, GLEN H., JR. (#64) is engaged in research and teaching at the Institute for Human Development of the University of California. His areas of interest are culture and personality and the family.

ELLIS, ROBERT A. (#52) is Professor of Sociology at the University of Oregon. His writing and research are in the fields of social stratification, social mobility, and higher education.

EMERSON, RICHARD M. (#31) is Associate Professor of Sociology at the University of Washington. His research is in the areas of collective behavior, social movements, and stratification.

ERBE, WILLIAM W. (#30) is Associate Professor of Sociology and Associate Director of the Iowa Urban Community Research Center. He formerly taught at Washington State University and was Research Analyst at the National Opinion Research Center.

ERSKINE, HAZEL GAUDET (#27, #70) is a free-lance research analyst and is active in political organization in Nevada. She has done communications research at Princeton and Columbia Universities.

FEAGIN, JOE R. (#33) is Assistant Professor of Sociology at the University of California at Riverside, and has done research and writing in the fields of racial and ethnic relations, urban sociology, and the sociology of religion.

FERRY, W. H. (#48) is a writer and author and the vice-president of the Center for the Study of Democratic Institutions in Santa Barbara.

FINESTONE, HAROLD (#45) is Associate Professor of Sociology at the University of Minnesota, and author of a number of studies in the field of social deviance and criminology.

FIREY, WALTER (#16) is Professor of Sociology at the University of Texas. His interests include land use, conservation, and social theory. His writings include *Man, Mind, and Land, Land Use in Central Boston,* and *Law and Economy in Planning.*

FOSTER, ARNOLD (#24) is General Counsel and Director of the Civil Rights division of the Anti-Defamation League of B'nai B'rith.

GARBIN, A. P. (#49) is Associate Professor of Sociology at Ohio State University and Specialist in Occupational Sociology at the Center for Vocational and Technical Training. His fields of research include the correlates of occupational prestige, alcoholism, and an analysis of "contradictions of values" in the United States.

GAUDET, HAZEL (#27, #70), see ERSKINE, HAZEL GAUDET.

GESCHWENDER, JAMES A. (#60) is Associate Professor of Sociology at the University of Western Ontario. His areas of research and writing include race relations, industrial sociology, social movements, and collective behavior.

GLOCK, CHARLES Y. (#66) is Chairman of the Department of Sociology at the University of California and Director of the Research Survey Center. His most recent publications are *Christian Beliefs and Anti-Semitism, Survey of Research in the Social Sciences,* and *Religion and Society in Tension.*

GOFFMAN, ERVING (#43) is Professor of Sociology at the University of California and a specialist in the fields of social organization and interaction and the area of deviancy. His recent books include *Asylums, Behavior in Public Places,* and *Presentations of Self in Everyday Life.*

HALL, EDWARD T. (#7) is Professor of Anthropology at Northwestern University and specializes in intercultural communication and the selection and training of Americans for foreign service.

HOMANS, GEORGE C. (#41) is Professor of Sociology at Harvard University and past president of the American Sociological Association. He is the author of *The Human Group, Social Behavior,* and *Sentiment and Activities.*

HYMAN, HERBERT H. (#22) is Chairman of the Department of Sociology and Associate Director, Bureau of Applied Research at Columbia University. His major publications include *Survey Design and Analysis, Interviewing and Social Research,* and *Political Socialization.*

INKELES, ALEX (#50) is Director of Studies in Social Relations of the Russian Research Center at Harvard University and head of the Project on Sociocultural Aspects of Development. His recent books are *Public Opinion in the Soviet Union, What is Sociology?,* and *How the Soviet System Works.*

JOHNSON, BENTON (#67) is Professor of Sociology at the University of Oregon and is engaged in basic research and writing in stratification and the sociology of religion.

KERCKHOFF, ALAN (#23) is Professor of Sociology and Director of Graduate Studies at Duke University. His research is in the fields of collective behavior, family, and role behavior and he is the co-author of *The June Bug: A Study of Hysterical Contagion.*

KEYES, FENTON (#15) is President of Coker College. He is a sociologist specializing in the Far East and co-author of the three-volume history, *The China-Burma-India Theater of War.*

KIESLER, CHARLES A. (#57) is Chairman of the Graduate Area of Personality and Social Psychology at Yale University. His work is in the areas of attitude change, group influences on the individual, and theories of attitude change. He is co-author of the book, *Attitude Change.*

KOHN, MELVIN L. (#38) is Chief of the section on Community and Population Studies of the National Institute of Mental Health.

KOMAROVSKY, MIRRA (#8) is Chairman of the Sociology Department of Barnard College and author of several books, the most recent of which is *Blue-Collar Marriage.*

LANE, W. CLAYTON (#52) is Associate Professor of Sociology at San Jose State College, and does research and writing in the fields of social psychology, sociology of education, stratification, and social mobility.

LARSEN, OTTO (#35) is Professor and Director of the Institute of Sociological Research at the University of Washington. He is co-author of *Sociology, Flow of Information,* and editor of *Violence and Mass Media.*

LAZARSFELD, PAUL F. (#27, #70) is Professor of Sociology at Columbia University, and a former president of the American Sociological Association. His major publications include *The People's Choice, The Language of Social Research, Uses of Sociology,* and *Latent Structure Analysis.*

LEE, SHU-CHING (#63) is Professor of Sociology at the University of South Dakota. His research and publications are in the fields of the primary group, the family, the Hutterite community, and the Far East.

LINDESMITH, ALFRED R. (#37) is Professor of Sociology at the University of Indiana. His major writings are *Drug Addiction: Crime or Disease, Social Psychology,* and *The Addict and the Law.*

LIPSET, SEYMOUR MARTIN (#53, #71) is Professor of Government and Social Relations and Research Associate at the Center of International Affairs at Harvard University. He is the author of *Political Man, Agrarian Socialism, The First New Nation,* and *Revolution and Counter-Revolution.*

LOFLAND, JOHN (#56) is Associate Professor of Sociology at Sonoma State College. His interests lie in the fields of social organization, social control and deviant behavior; his major publications are *Doomsday Cult* and *Deviance and Authority*.

LUNDBERG, GEORGE A. (#74) was professor of Sociology at the University of Washington and a former president of the American Sociological Association before his death in 1966. Among his major publications are *Foundations of Sociology, Leisure, Social Research, Trends in American Sociology,* and *Can Science Save Us?*

MACK, RAYMOND W. (#3) is Professor of Sociology at Northwestern University with research and writing interests in stratification, occupational and industrial sociology, and race and ethnic relations. His most recent books are *Race, Class and Power, Our Childrens' Burden,* and *Transforming America*.

MARTIN, WALTER T. is Chairman of the Sociology Department at the University of Oregon and former president of the Pacific Sociological Association, currently on leave doing demographic research in Kenya. He is co-editor of *Readings in General Sociology,* co-author of *Suicide and Status Integration,* and author of *The Rural Urban Fringe*.

McELRATH, DENNIS C. (#3) is Chairman of the Department of Sociology at the University of California at Santa Cruz. His major fields of research include complex organization, medical sociology, and comparative urban analysis; his major book is *The New Urbanization*.

METZNER, ERIC L. (#58) is a member of the Psychology Department of the University of Arizona.

MILLER, NORMAN (#23) is Senior Study Director of the National Opinion Research Center at the University of Chicago.

MORRIS, RICHARD T. (#51) is Professor and Chairman of the Department of Sociology at the University of California at Los Angeles. His major publications are *A Typology of Norms* and *The Two-Way Mirror: National Status in Foreign Student Adjustment*.

MURDOCK, GEORGE PETER (#5) is Mellon Professor of Anthropology at the University of Pittsburgh. His major books are *Social Structure, Our Primitive Contemporaries,* and *Africa: Its People and Their Cultural History*.

MURPHY, RAYMOND J. (#51) is Professor of Sociology at the University of Rochester. He is the author or co-author of *The Structure of Discontent, Occupational Situs,* and *Problems and Prospects of the Negro Movement*.

O'BRIEN, ROBERT W. is Chairman of the Department of Sociology at Whittier College. He is co-editor of *Readings in General Sociology,* co-author of *Field Manual in Sociology,* and author of *The College Nisei* and *When Peoples Meet*.

O'CONNELL, JEFFREY (#36) is Professor of Law at the University of Illinois. He is the author of *After Cars Crash* and co-author of *Safety Last* and *Basic Protection for Traffic Victims*.

PEARLIN, LEONARD I. (#38) is Research Sociologist at the National Institute of Mental Health at Bethesda, Maryland. His writings include *Alienation from Work, Unintended Effects of Parental Aspirations,* and *Social Class, Occupation and Parental Values*.

RANSFORD, H. EDWARD (#25) is Assistant Professor of Sociology at California State College in Fullerton. His studies are of race riots and the reaction of whites to race riots.

RECKLESS, WALTER C. (#39) is Professor of Sociology and Criminology at Ohio State University. His major writings include *Juvenile Delinquency, Vice in Chicago,* and *Criminal Behavior*.

REINTJES, J. F. (#4) is Professor of Electrical Engineering and Director of the Electronics Systems Laboratory at Massachusetts Institute of Technology. He is the author of many papers on electronics, computers, automation, and engineering education.

RAMSOY, NATALIE ROGOFF (#53) teaches sociology at the Sociological Institute of the University of Oslo.

ROGOFF, NATALIE (#53) see RAMSOY, NATALIE ROGOFF.

ROSSI, PETER H. (#50) is Chairman of the Department of Social Relations at Johns Hopkins University. His recent publications include *New Media and Education, Education of Catholic Americans,* and *Impact of Party Organization in an Industrial Setting*.

SCHMID, CALVIN F. (#17) is Professor of Sociology at the University of Washington and a former president of the Pacific Sociological Association and the Sociological Research Association. He is the author of a number of books and monographs, including *Social Trends in Seattle, Social Sage of Two Cities, Handbook of Graphic Presentation,* and co-author of *Scientific Surveys and Research* and *A Primer of Social Statistics*.

SCHNORE, LEO F. (#18) is Professor of Sociology at the University of Wisconsin. His research and writing fields are population, urban sociology, human ecology, and methodology. His major publications are *The Urban Scene, Urban Research and Planning,* and *The Study of Urbanization*.

SCHRAG, CLARENCE C. is Professor of Sociology at the University of Washington and a former president of the Pacific Sociological Association. He is co-editor of *Readings in General Sociology,* co-author of *Sociology,* and a contributor to *The Prison* and *Manual of Correctional Standards.*

SEEMAN, MELVIN (#40) is Professor of Sociology at the University of California at Los Angeles. His major areas of research are attitudes, alienation, and race relations. His books include *On the Meaning of Alienation* and *Status and Leadership.*

SHARP, HARRY (#18) is Director of the Survey Research Laboratory and Associate Professor of Sociology at the University of Wisconsin. His publications are *Social Profile of Detroits, 1955, Correlates of Values About Ideal Family Size in Detroit,* and *Non-Residential Population of the Central Business District of Flint, Michigan.*

SHERIF, MUZAFER (#29, #62) is Professor of Social Psychology and Director of the Psycho-Social Studies Program at Pennsylvania State University. His recent works include *In Common Predicament: Social Psychology of Intergroup Conflict, Social Interaction,* and *Reference Groups.*

SNOEK, J. DIEDRICK (#59) is Associate Professor of Social Psychology at Smith College. He is co-author of *Organizational Stress* and has done research in role conflict, role stress, and social influence processes.

SHILS, EDWARD A. (#21) is Professor of Social Thought and Sociology at the University of Chicago and Fellow at Cambridge. He is the author or co-author of *Toward a General Theory of Action, The Primary Group in the Social Structure, The Indian Intellectual, The Torment of Secrecy,* and *The Present State of American Sociology.*

SONNENSCHEIN, DAVID A. (#58) is a member of the Psychology Department of the University of Arizona.

STARK, RODNEY (#56, #66) is a research writer and editor at the Survey Research Center of the University of California. His interests are the sociology of religion and research designs; he is co-author of *Religion and Society in Tension.*

STRAUSS, ANSELM L. (#37) is Professor of Sociology at the Medical Center of the University of

California in San Francisco. His works include *Images of the American City, Awareness of Dying,* and *Psychiatric Ideologies and Institutions.*

TEMPLETON, FREDERIC (#72) is a researcher and technical writer at the Survey Research Center of the University of California.

TERRY, ROBERT M. (#61) is Assistant Professor of Sociology at the University of Iowa, with his major work in the areas of deviant behavior, juvenile delinquency, and social psychology. His major publication is *Prevention of Delinquency: Problems and Programs.*

THEODORSON, GEORGE A. (#65) is Director of Graduate Studies in Sociology and Anthropology at Pennsylvania State University. His main areas of studies are human ecology and comparative family organization; his chief publication is *Studies in Human Ecology.*

VALLIER, IVAN (#55) is a Research Sociologist in International Studies at the University of California. Some of his books include *Religious Elites, Recent Theories of Development,* and *Social Change in the Kibbutz.*

WESTBY, DAVID (#42) is Associate Professor of Sociology at Pennsylvania State University, and is studying student political activism, community action programs, and other aspects of political sociology.

WHYTE, WILLIAM FOOTE (#14, #20) is Director of the New York State School in Industrial and Labor Relations at Cornell University. His major books are *Street Corner Society, Men at Work,* and *Money and Motivation.*

WHYTE, WILLIAM H. (#26) is an editor and writer, the author of *The Organization Man* and *Is Anybody Listening?*

WRIGHT, CHARLES R. (#22) is the Program Director of Sociology and Social Psychology at the National Science Foundation. He is author of *Mass Communication, Inducing Social Change in Developing Communities,* and *Public Leadership.*

ZURCHER, LOUIS A., JR. (#58) is Assistant Professor of Sociology at the University of Texas, and has published in the fields of culture and personality, group dynamics, adult role socialization, and role conflict.

Index

INDEX